Dutch Culture in a European Perspective, Volume 3
1900: The Age of Bourgeois Culture

The titles of the five volumes are:

1650: Hard-Won Unity
1800: Blueprints for a National Community
1900: The Age of Bourgeois Culture
1950: Prosperity and Welfare
Accounting for the Past: 1650-2000

Dutch Culture in a European Perspective

Volume 3

1900: The Age of Bourgeois Culture

Jan Bank and Maarten van Buuren

with the collaboration of Marianne Braun and Douwe Draaisma
translated from the Dutch by Lynne Richards and John Rudge

2004 ≫ ROYAL VAN GORCUM / palgrave macmillan

Published in the United Kingdom and throughout the World excluding continental Europe by Palgrave Macmillan Ltd, Houndmills, Basingstoke, Hampshire RG21 6XS, United Kingdom and 175 Fifth Avenue, New York NY 10010, USA.

Published in continental Europe by Royal Van Gorcum, P.O. Box 43, 9400 AA Assen, The Netherlands.

PALGRAVE MACMILLAN is the global academic imprint of the Palgrave Macmillan division of St. Martin's Press, LLC and of Palgrave Macmillan Ltd. Macmillan® is a registered trademark in the United States, United Kingdom and other countries. Palgrave is a registered trademark in the European Union and other countries.

The authors have asserted their rights to be identified as the authors of this work in accordance with the Copyright, Designs and Patents Act 1988.

Originally published in Dutch as *1900: Hoogtij van burgerlijke cultuur* by Sdu Publishers, The Hague. © 2000 the editors and authors.

The translation and publication of *Dutch Culture in a European Perspective* in five volumes has been generously supported by the Netherlands Organization for Scientific Research (NWO).

ISBN   90-232-3965-2 (Royal Van Gorcum)
         1-4039-3438-X (Palgrave Macmillan)

A catalogue record for this book is available from the British Library.

Library of Congress Cataloging-in-Publication Data

A catalog record for this book is available from the Library of Congress.

10	9	8	7	6	5	4	3	2	1
13	12	11	10	09	08	07	06	05	04

Layout and printing: Royal Van Gorcum, Assen, The Netherlands

Contents

Preface

The English edition of *1900: The Age of Bourgeois Culture* is the result of a collective effort. The authors wish to express their special thanks to the translators, Lynne Richards and John Rudge, for their enthusiasm and skill, and for the Anglo-Saxon phlegm with which they tackled and solved the problems that arose. This special gratitude also extends to Lilian Korteweg, the series editor, for her unceasing support, to Annemarie Marck, who assisted us in the editorial work, and to Douwe Fokkema, the solicitous chair of the Steering Committee of the NWO program *Dutch Culture in a European Context*.

The original Dutch manuscript was the basis of the English edition. We have edited and revised the text that was completed on February 1, 2000, and we have been able to consult a number of publications that appeared after that date, and incorporate the results in this edition. The manuscript for translation into English was completed on January 1, 2004.

In writing the original version, the authors were very fortunate in the support they received from numerous colleagues. We owe a debt of gratitude to Barbara Allart, Fons Alkemade, and Natascha Veldhorst, Ria Janssen and Monique Kienhuis for their contributions and preliminary studies for several chapters. At our invitation Boudewijn Bakker, Jan van den Berg, Piet Blaas, Sarah Blom, Carel Blotkamp, Pieter Boekhorst, Martin Bossenbroek, Jan de Bruijn, Thomas von der Dunk, Johan Giskes, Ria van Hemmen, Wim Koole, Tejo Medendorp, Josine Meurs, Pauline Micheels, Kees Peeters, Frans Ruiter, Piet de Rooij, Marlou Schrover, Ruud Stokvis, Edzard de Vrieze, and Emile Wennekes read parts of the manuscript and made invaluable critical comments. We are indebted to them for their contributions, which we have edited and revised in the light of our own insights, so that we are responsible for the final text.

We are likewise indebted to Els Jacobs and Belinda van der Gaag, to Marjan van Heteren and Sarabande van Bueren for their assistance, and to the members of the Steering Committee of the NWO program *Dutch Culture in a European Context*, particularly the chair, and Manfred Bock, Frans Grijzenhout, and Paul Post.

In the 1995-1996 academic year, Jan Bank benefited from the tranquility and inspiration of a fellowship at the *Netherlands Institute for Advanced Studies in the Humanities and Social Sciences* (NIAS) in Wassenaar. Truusje Middelhoff was a loyal companion in the search through exhibitions and the cultural heritage of 1900.

Leiden/Utrecht   Jan Bank
March 2004   Maarten van Buuren

Introduction

This is our good fortune: we who have become Europeans are pleased to feel Dutch again. We feel Dutch through land, air and way of life. We recognize ourselves as such through descent, tradition, and mentality. We reveal ourselves as such through feelings, memories, and beliefs. We realize that if we were not Dutch we would be worthless as Europeans.[1]

In 1907 the writer Albert Verwey provided a preface for the new edition of *Het Rijksmuseum te Amsterdam* by E.J. Potgieter, a merchant and man of letters. First published in 1844, Potgieter's essay sang the praises of the past and described the decline of his own times; he glorified the Dutch Golden Age in the seventeenth century on the basis of the Rijksmuseum's collection of paintings. The dominant theme in his essay was the idea of decline, but, as a leading member of the new literary generation of 1880, Verwey took the opposite view. "The time of doubt and vacillation is over. In the last quarter of the previous century we saw the Netherlands playing an ever more vigorous role in European life." Verwey's generation was entitled to measure itself against Potgieter's standard. For "We see ourselves as sons of the seventeenth century, which in trade, research, belief, art, poetry, and science, in strength and judgment, in freedom and self-restraint, set an example for the world, and even if we are not as strong or as great as our fathers, nonetheless we are resolved not to be unworthy of them."[2] The optimism in this preface is genuine. It is the "critical optimism" of a generation that believed that in 1900 art, the community and the future were on its side.[3]

Around 1900 Dutch culture was assessed by its exponents according to the norms of its European context. The results were positive. Consequently, one finds in the Netherlands expressions of collective self-confidence rather than of the decadence or nervousness normally associated with the fin de siècle. The latter two aspects were present, but they were overshadowed by a form of "constructivism" in which artistic creations also had a moral dimension as components of a better or grander society. They could then be the expression of a militant idealism, the positive answer in debate as contemporary as it was profound about the deprivation of the proletariat and the significance and implications of the new socialism.

Established nation

The Netherlands was an established nation around 1900. New states – Belgium (1830) and the German Empire (1871) – had come into being on its southern and eastern borders in the course of the nineteenth century, but their existence and location were no longer disputed and relations were friendly. As a result of German unification, however, the Netherlands was caught between Germany and Great Britain, two major European powers. This obliged the Dutch to opt for impartiality, interpreted as armed neutrality. The ability to mobilize rapidly would deter any possible enemy from invading. The imperialism of the European powers produced a specifically Dutch response: the Netherlands withdrew to its largest and oldest colonies and consolidated its rule there. This applied in the first place to the Dutch East Indies, but also to Surinam and several Caribbean islands, among them Curaçao. The former African possessions and various claims on Malacca were given up. The Boers in South Africa, who enjoyed considerable support in the Netherlands, were not in the end given any actual help in their war against the British.

The constitutional monarchy, the result of the democratic upheaval of 1848, was preserved. The main outlines of the form of government remained unchanged when the constitution was amended in 1888 and 1917. These amendments were milestones in the battle for universal suffrage and for state funding of private schools. The socialists and the left-wing liberals fought for the first cause, and the orthodox Protestant and Roman Catholic parties for the second. In 1888 the franchise was extended and subsidies for religious schools were made possible in principle. In 1917 both these changes were made general: universal male suffrage was introduced in return for general state funding of elementary schools. Both showed that the constitution of 1848 could allow for the emancipation of new groups in society without continuity being broken.

Population in the period 1889-1930

	Men	Women	Total
1889	2,228,487	2,292,928	4,521,415
1899	2,520,602	2,583,535	5,104,137
1909	2,899,125	2,959,050	5,858,175
1920	3,410,262	3,455,052	6,865,314
1930	4,791,443	4,834,056	9,625,499

Sources: Result of the seventh ten-yearly census in the Kingdom of the Netherlands on the thirty-first day of December 1889 (The Hague 1893), 1899-1959. Sixty years of statistics in timelines, compiled by the Central Bureau of Statistics (Zeist 1959).

This openness in the form of government was reflected in the appearance of numerous organizations in the area between the individual citizen and the state. Orthodox Protestants, Roman Catholics and later the socialist labor movement took advantage of the broader right of association introduced in the 1848 constitution to give concrete form to their emancipation. Consequently, citizens were more involved in developments in state and society, and the quality of political decision-making was improved. Between 1870 and 1914 new industrial relations gradually took shape, although this process was interrupted now and again by fierce conflicts, such as the railway strike of 1903. The strength and growth of these institutions is seen as the main reason why the Second Industrial Revolution was introduced in the Netherlands much more rapidly than the First had been at the beginning of the nineteenth century.[4]

The Dutch economy was flourishing around 1900. This was due chiefly to two developments: the opening up of the Dutch East Indies to commercial exploitation by private companies and the growth of the coal and steel industry in the Rhineland. Trade with both centers of growth was promoted by new waterways to Rotterdam and Amsterdam, and this had various side effects such as the expansion of the financial services industry, of the industrial processing of colonial products, and of shipbuilding. Almost all the major industries and multinational concerns date from the last decade of the nineteenth century and the beginning of the twentieth century. This expansion was reflected in the rise of new institutions such as the modern labor union movement and in government schemes in the field of social security.

These developments also brought to light the social deprivation of the proletariat. This had existed for much longer, but it became a subject of debate and a political issue after the Paris Commune of 1870. But this was not only because of the Commune. As a result of the rapid modernization of the Dutch economy in the eighteen-sixties, labor relations had become more businesslike, especially in the sectors dominated by large industrial companies. The working class expanded while agriculture declined because of new employment opportunities in industry and the service sector. This led to somewhat higher living standards and prepared the ground for the rise of socialism. It was not deprivation but rising expectations that turned the proletariat into a self-conscious political power.

Economic growth and the modernization of society can also be seen as factors underlying and even strengthening the bourgeois character of Dutch society. The sociological dimension of this was an increase in the old, but above all the new, middle class – self-employed businessmen and intellectuals, but especially officials and office workers. In terms of cultural history, this combination proved to be fertile ground for the flourishing of science and the arts, the practice of which was explicitly presented as a civic virtue. At the end of the nineteenth century essayists and artists made their own contribution to the prevailing notion that the bourgeois context was essential to the quality of Dutch culture. They found arguments and evidence for this in the generally recognized flowering of the seventeenth-century Republic, the Golden Age in the history of the Netherlands.[5] Around 1900 this awareness led to initiatives to again display seventeenth-century art now seen as classic and to combine it with contemporary work. "Amsterdam's celebrated Rijksmuseum and Concertgebouw were the creations of a few cultivated and enterprising merchants," wrote Peter Gay in his study of nineteenth-century bourgeois culture, *Schnitzler's Century*.[6] They are a Dutch example of how the turn of the century translated civic pride into grandiose creations in architecture, urban planning, and art.

Vantage point

In this volume in a series of five the historical research centers on the vantage point 1900. This means that the historian's field of vision is narrowed to a period in which 1900 is the focus, and the years before and after it make up the spectrum. We have decided to limit ourselves to a range of nearly four decades: from 1880 to 1900 on one side and from 1900 to World War I on the other.

The chosen vantage point is the turn of the century. Particular years have often been the subject of historical study, but the idea of the turn of the century is relatively new. It first became a factor of importance in the collective awareness of time in Europe in the eighteenth century. Two hundred years before, chronology had become detached from history. As Europe increasingly came into contact with other peoples and cultures, there was a need for a new method of counting time that would not derive its rhythm exclusively from the Bible or classical antiquity. A new chronology could tie in with the custom that arose in the Reformation of viewing history on the basis of historically "synchronous" units of one hundred years. Thus this unit was known as a "century" in English and "ein Jahrhundert" in German. Then the steps back to history, so to speak, were retraced, for a historical characteristic was attributed to the collection of one hundred years, or it was divided into historically nameable phases.[7] Subsequently 1800 was perceived for the first time as the turn of the century, a transitional point. In the collective consciousness the French Revolution, whatever view one took of it, had truly revolutionized the political and social structure.[8]

In French the turn of the century in 1900 was given a special name, "fin de siècle," to distinguish it from the more normal "fin du siècle." This name does not refer primarily or solely to a chronological fact but to a cultural-historical concept thought up by contemporaries. Through it they wished to express "what they regarded as the most essential quality of their age, namely that it was an end, a fall season or, to use another metaphor, a 'Dämmerung,' a twilight of civilization." [9] The term "fin de siècle" has been adopted in many European countries, yet one connotation – that of decadence – seems to prevail over all others. But in France the "fin de siècle" thought of as "decadent" was followed by a period known as "la belle époque" and seen as a change from the mood of doom towards vitalism and patriotism.

Synthesis

In the choice of the theme 1900 there is also often a desire for historical coherence. It is as if the ideals of the time, such as the *Gesamtkunstwerk* or *Gemeenschapskunst,* inspire the historian to seek an equivalent: the historical synthesis. The Dutch historian E.H. Kossmann, for example, gave the title "Synthesis" to the chapter on culture around 1900 in his study *The Low Countries 1780-1940.*[10] This was a reference to the desire at that time for a reconciliation of antitheses, a contemporary constructivism, through which writers and artists could free themselves from the crisis of individualism in the eighteen-eighties. In another context he made it clear that he had not chosen this title out of enthusiasm for it, and that it should be taken as a characterization and not as a concept of the crisis in

European civilization. In fact in the period around 1900 the Netherlands presented an animated and positive "time style": "lively, of a high standard, full of public spirit, constructive." Here decadence and "fin de siècle" had little or no appeal. According to Kossmann, this "time style" ended with World War I, when "national self-confidence" was sorely tested, and little optimism was left.[11]

The best known work about 1900 by a Dutch historian is Jan Romein's magnum opus *The Watershed of Two Eras: Europe in 1900* (1978; originally published in Dutch in 1967), and this too is a striking example of synthesis.[12] Published posthumously, it represents Romein's ideal of integral historiography in concrete form, although he was unable to write the theoretical part and the conclusion intended for the third volume, which never appeared. He had explored that ideal earlier, however, in an account of political, economic, social, and cultural phenomena in the Netherlands around 1870 that could be viewed as a complex. At that time he had complained that "history must always be written on the flat surface of the paper, when in fact it should be built up in space, so that the reader can consider all the interrelations at the same time."[13] This led to his geometrical metaphor of a three-dimensional reconstruction of historical reality, which the reader must visualize, however, through a projection onto a flat plane. On another occasion, in an address on "integral historiography," he found an example in Dutch history around 1900. He tried to relate the fight for universal suffrage to the dominance of ethics in science and modern theology, the rise of the labor movement, and the overcoming of "our eighteenth-century lethargy."[14]

Romein went further in his great work. He wrote a history on a European scale and chose a dialectical theme: the European bourgeoisie, who were preparing to gain hegemony over the whole world at a time when their confidence was being undermined by the workers' revolution and by the proliferation of arms among the major European powers. This dialectical moment formed "the watershed of two eras." With a nod to his teacher Huizinga, Romein also spoke of a "waning of European hegemony." In the end he did not have time to put this to the test. The two volumes published present a broad panorama of politics, religion, the arts and sciences in Europe in 1900, but they remain the chronicle-like pillars of an unfinished building.

Method

Taking a vantage point as the core of a history means that events are portrayed in depth, while more long-term developments must be dealt with in passing. To avoid the risk of a too kaleidoscopic approach, the authors have concentrated on a number of main themes. Encyclopedic comprehensiveness has not been our aim. So it is not only in relation to the length of time that there are illuminations and drawbacks; this also applies to the breadth of the culture around 1900.

The turn of the century in 1900 has been given the title "The age of bourgeois culture." This is a reference to the view discussed above that this period in the Netherlands was marked by a flourishing of science and the arts. Seeking a definition of the position of "culture" as the guiding principle of this study, we would like to adopt the one formulated by Willem Frijhoff and Marijke Spies in *1650: Hard-Won Unity*, volume one of this

The Netherlands and its eleven provinces in 1900

series. Accordingly, this is a study of cultural interactions and the cultural infrastructure around 1900 combined with an analysis of the views expressed by social and cultural groups about themselves and about society.[15] In our context the term "bourgeois" refers to a social rather than an artistic dimension; it does not refer to the romantic idea of the contrast between the "artist" and the "bourgeois."[16] Instead, it refers to the social standing of the bourgeoisie, which could make its dominance of society felt in various ways, in the use of the name "hogere burgerschool" for a modern type of education and in bourgeois patronage, in the prominent role of liberalism and in the promotion of science.

Albert Verwey was writing about his generation, which was again participating in European life in 1900, and about the Dutch, who had again become aware of their national origin and way of thinking, precisely as Europeans. For the Dutch cultural elite the European context was a frame of reference. It took in Western Europe, an area of large and small nation-states which had in common a past of Christianity, Enlightenment and Revolution, and which competed with one another in colonial expansion, especially after 1870. In the arts and sciences, Europe had become one cultural community with its own sense of identity. Major developments such as the rise of modern science or secularization not only took place on this European scale, but were perceived as European. It is fair to ask to what extent the eastern border of this cultural community had become the Urals in 1900, and whether the western border could be extended to take in North America, and in particular the United States, whose influence was felt in religion, art, and science, also before World War I.

Writing the history of Dutch culture in a European context means starting from our present state of knowledge of national history and then establishing the influence of or interaction with Europe in a number of areas. Again, we are in agreement with the observation made by Willem Frijhoff and Marijke Spies in Volume 1: a systematic comparison is perhaps the most appropriate method, but as yet a utopian one because not only the nature and accessibility of the sources but also the state of research vary so widely from country to country.[17] The tradition of research in a primarily national context is still strong. We try from time to time to broaden and Europeanize its scope.

The Herengracht in Amsterdam during the celebrations for Queen Wilhelmina's inauguration, decorated by the architect Willem Kromhout.

1

National celebrations, national images

The inauguration of Wilhelmina

The inauguration of the young Queen Wilhelmina (1880-1962) in September 1898 was above all a celebration of symbols. Half a century after royal rule had been confined within the bounds of a democratic constitution in 1848, the year of revolutions in Europe, the ceremony in fact marked the accession of a sovereign without personal power. It was now an opportunity to make the significance of the kingdom fully visible – an ideal image of the Netherlands as a bourgeois elite visualized it on the eve of a new century. This is why the inauguration of Queen Wilhelmina was lavishly celebrated, in the ceremony itself in the Nieuwe Kerk (New Church) in Amsterdam on September 6, 1898 and in the numerous events that surrounded it. This splendor should be seen as a festive manifestation of bourgeois self-confidence. It was a conscious attempt to make the idea of the unity of nation and dynasty triumph over religious divisions and political strife. The echoes resounded throughout the country.

Monarchy made its presence felt. In fin-de-siècle Europe both the old and the new dynasties had themselves fêted in expertly staged ceremonial entries and parades, particularly in the decades after the Commune (1871), the revolt in Paris, when assassins threatened their lives and the rise of socialism their royal status. Monarchy was a natural focus for the national parading of arms and drum beating so typical of the age. In autocratically ruled countries, pre-eminently imperial Russia, the court was the stage manager, but there was just as much pomp and circumstance in democratic Britain. David Cannadine has traced how the public image of the British monarchy changed between 1870 and 1914: its ceremonies, which had been imperfectly conducted and uninspiring, became impressive, public and popular. While in Kaiser Wilhelm II's Germany, in the Hapsburg dual monarchy of Austria-Hungary and in tsarist Russia the personal power of the monarch was enlarged through ritual, in Great Britain similar ceremonies expressed the power of the symbol of royalty without personal power.[1]

In the Netherlands too there was a loss of power. William III (1817-1890), the first sovereign to have to share power with a fully fledged Parliament immediately after acceding to the throne in 1849, had reconciled himself to the new constitution, although his preference was for an autocratic, patriarchal style of government. Despite this, the Orange dynasty's chances of surviving were reduced by other factors: the early deaths of the two crown princes William (1879) and Alexander (1884). A year and a half after the death of his first wife, Sophia von Württemberg, in 1877, William remarried. He was 61.

His bride was a 20-year-old German princess, Emma von Waldeck-Pyrmont (1858-1934). In 1880 she bore him a daughter, Wilhelmina, who became the sole heir to the throne after the death of Alexander. When the king died in 1890, his widow had to act as queen regent for eight years until her daughter came of age. Emma faced two challenges. As a foreigner, she had to demonstrate that she respected the Dutch constitutional system, and as a woman she had to show that she could establish her authority within it. Moreover, she wanted to strengthen the monarchy in the Netherlands by making it more of a national institution in accordance with a general trend in Europe towards anchoring the internationally oriented dynasties more firmly in the nation-state.

Queen Emma was conscientious above all else. A chamberlain who assisted her after 1900, Maarten Pauw van Wieldrecht, observed that the court in The Hague had become one of the most respectable in Europe, thanks to the proper and dignified example set by the queen regent. The other side to this was a certain dullness and rigid protocol.[2] In the political arena she held her own because of her remarkable sense of her constitutional duty. She resolved the greatest crisis in her reign, a conflict in Parliament in 1894 over extending the franchise, because she acquiesced in the political solution of dissolving Parliament, which was forced on her by the conservatives. This also had the effect of silencing any criticism about the fact that the head of state was a woman. The process of making the court more Dutch was reflected in the gradual replacement of French, the language of the court, by the vernacular. Queen Emma and her daughter were seen in every corner of the country. Together, they systematically visited the provincial capitals in the north, east and south and, now that the modern rail network had made it so much easier to move around, they seized the chance to make the monarchy visible on a national scale. Their visits were always largely symbolic in nature, but that accorded with the new notion of personal rule within constitutional limits.[3] "The image of a young queen with her hair hanging down, together with her mother, became a deeply cherished memory, etched, as it were, with a sharp needle in the national consciousness."[4]

The kingdom which they both toured was now administratively integrated. The Provinces Act (1850) and the Municipalities Act (1851), both arising from the Constitution of 1848, had put an end to centuries of regional particularism. This could also, finally, be said of Limburg, the most southerly province and the most marginal politically and culturally. Limburg was first unambiguously included in the kingdom after an international conference in London in 1867 had established that the Grand Duchy of Luxembourg, and by implication the Duchy of Limburg, no longer formed part of the (North) German Confederation. Some Limburgers had wanted to join the new state of Belgium in 1830, and in 1848 they had put out black, red and gold flags here and there in a gesture of solidarity with the champions of German unification. Limburg separatism continued to make its voice heard until 1918. At that point the Belgian government demanded the province (and Zeeland Flanders) as a prize for victory in the First World War. This demand was viewed with some sympathy by Henri van Groenendael, the member of Parliament for Weert in Limburg. As a result he lost his place in the Catholic group in Parliament. The Catholic elite of Limburg was prominently represented in Parliament in 1918, since Prime Minister Jonkheer C.J.M. Ruys de Beerenbrouck, and the leader of the largest parliamentary group, the priest W.H. Nolens, were both from

Limburg; the members of this elite wished to have no misunderstandings about the group's loyalty to the Dutch state.

Although monarchy had been eclipsed by constitutional democracy, there were still signs of a desire among the public for royal symbols. A passionate debate in the radical weekly *De Kroniek* in 1896 had shown that artists applauded the moral and even mystical significance of the monarchy at a time when art was dominated by symbolism. In May 1896 the young artist Marius Bauer attended the coronation of Tsar Nicholas II in Moscow while on his way to the Ottoman Empire, where he found the oriental inspiration for his paintings and drawings. He was excited by the spectacle and in a letter in *De Kroniek* he described the vision of the tsar when he appeared "high on the top step of the scarlet stairs, his gold brocade glittering, his crown giving off sparks in the fierce sunlight, and he held out wide the scepter and orb, and then the awesome cheering of thousands of people and the thunder of cannons, the blast of trumpets and the sound of the bells of all Moscow resounding over the golden domes." The tsar seemed to Bauer "truly majestic" and the "sole ruler of his vast nation." *De Kroniek* was edited by Pieter Lodewijk Tak, a radical and later a socialist, who was a lover of the good life but also had a sense of social justice. He wrote a leading article in which he observed that the fascination with the glittering of the all-powerful tsar was an expression of "Byzantinism" with the "aware" (such as Bauer) but an expression of the "childlike" in the case of the people. Here and there emancipation was beginning, but most nations were still in their infancy. According to Tak, the "display of splendor" in Moscow concealed the misery of a disregarded people.[5]

These remarks drew a response from the Catholic musician and essayist Alphons Diepenbrock. He saw in the coronation of the tsar a manifestation of "magnificence of life," sent by the setting sun of monarchy as a farewell to the ever more lackluster earth. Like Tak, he hoped for improved relations between the social classes, but he rejected the idolization of what was called "the people" and the materialistic denial of the spiritual. Diepenbrock's letter was followed by a debate in which the aesthetic significance of the monarchy was set against the moral need for social justice and against the new ideology of socialism. Writers such as Frederik van Eeden, Lodewijk van Deyssel, Frank van der Goes and Cornélie Huygens took part, as did the artist Jan Veth. The philosopher J.D. Bierens de Haan put forward an idealistic view of the monarch as representing the idea of justice. The debate ended inconclusively, but the monarchy had become an issue which divided those who had previously seen themselves as kindred spirits.[6] Artists who in *De Kroniek* each wanted to contribute from their own discipline to the coming together of the arts (*Gesamtkunstwerk*) were torn between the attraction of modern socialism and a liking for an archaic or archaistic monarchy.

Another example of the successful presentation of monarchy was to be found in two historical novels by Louis Couperus, *Majesteit* (1893; *Majesty*, 1894) and *Wereldvrede* (1895; World Peace). Couperus depicted the king as a model of moral responsibility. Both books were exceptionally well received, reprinted several times and translated. They were subsequently forgotten.[7] The flourishing of this genre was a passing phase: historical novels were especially popular in Republican France after the Commune. Couperus's portrait of the young crown prince Othomar in *Wereldvrede* is based on

Tolstoy's ideal of a monarch's love for the people. Othomar, who resembles the crown prince and later Tsar Nicholas II, tries to avert a crisis in the monarchy by distancing himself from his authoritarian father and taking up the cause of a utopian movement for international solidarity. His sensitive character enables him to feel understanding for the people and to become a "people's king." Here monarchy is seen as the ethical apex of a civilization.[8] It is even conceivable that Nicholas II himself read a (German) translation of *Wereldvrede*.

The Constitution of 1814 designated Amsterdam the site of the inauguration. It was a mercantile city like Venice and so lacked the palace and parade ground that were taken for granted when a city was a royal residence. The ceremony took place on the Dam, a square of bourgeois proportions, in a royal palace that had originally been an imposing town hall, and in the New Church, originally a Gothic parish church now used for Reformed worship, which "fulfilled the role of Westminster Abbey on a smaller scale as the repository of monumental tombs."[9] In 1898 the reshaping of the centre of Amsterdam, which resulted from the building of the North Sea Canal and the railway along the shore of the IJ estuary, was still in progress. Canals in the city were being filled to create modern traffic arteries and in the Damrak there was a modest attempt to create the kind of broad boulevard seen in Paris. Thus the new queen's entry into the city and subsequent drive was for the most part through narrow streets. Not surprisingly, the best known painting of this royal drive – by Otto Eerelman – was set on one of the few imposing squares in nineteenth-century Amsterdam, the Frederiksplein. It was dominated by the Paleis voor Volksvlijt, a building in glass and iron modeled on the Crystal Palace in London.

Wilhelmina's accession to the throne, to which contemporaries attached great symbolic importance, took the form of a solemn inauguration in the States General, the combined assembly of both Houses of Parliament. During this inauguration – not coronation – the sovereign and the members of Parliament swear loyalty to the constitution in each other's presence. The wording of the oath alludes to the feudal relationship in the Middle Ages in which the ruler offered protection in exchange for homage from his subjects. The inauguration had not had a religious dimension since the separation of church and state had been laid down in the new Constitution in 1848. What turned this inauguration into a glorious event that stayed in the collective memory of contemporaries? It was also captured in pictures, for the highlights were not only frequently photographed but also filmed. The film was shown throughout the country and attracted widespread attention as a new portrayal of the ceremonies.

The first answer lies in the youth of the new queen: a touching and, to the susceptible, even mystical factor in the ceremony. Wilhelmina's appearance and the clear tones of her speech, in which she explicitly identified with her father, had "electrified" her audience.[10] She was described as "the apple of the nation's eye."[11] The editor of the conservative *Algemeen Handelsblad*, Charles Boissevain, saw in Wilhelmina the personification of "the lyrical side of the Monarchy, which binds our nation together in harmony."[12] Her youth was praised in innumerable occasional verses. "The Royal Child ascends her Father's throne! Queen in Heaven's favor born," wrote the pastor and poet laureate of the time, Nicolaas Beets, who had often devoted his art to the service of the royal family.[13] "Thou, our Maid of Orange, now our most exalted Lady, you consecrate a new century" – with these words the priest and prominent politician Herman Schaepman opened his *Kroningslied* (Coronation Hymn). It evoked associations with the culture of hymns surrounding the Virgin Mary.[14] In a critical manifesto, the leaders of the Social Democratic Workers' Party in the Netherlands (SDAP) wrote that the same middle class, "who in 1848 made the monarchy in the Netherlands a sham, an ornament of the state, is now behaving as if it saw the monarchy as the sheet anchor of the entire fatherland."[15]

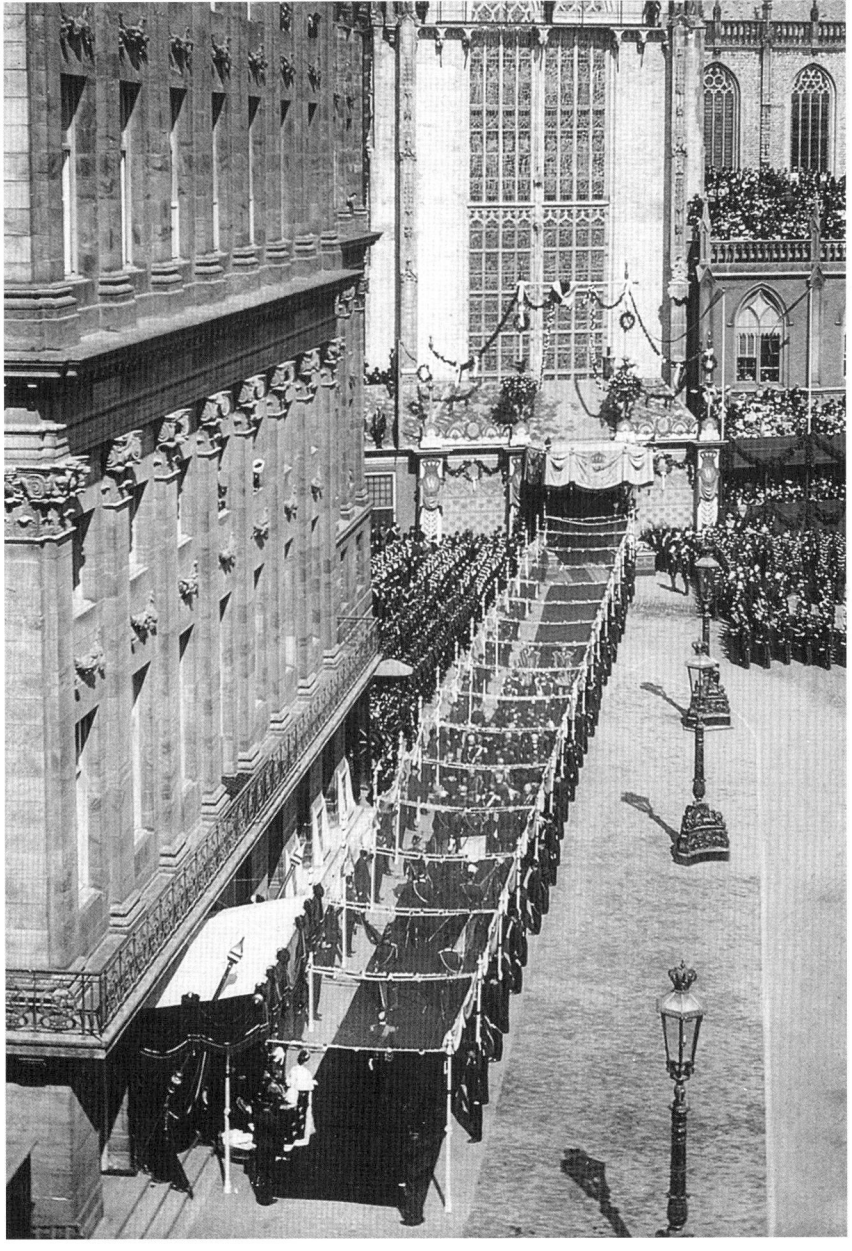

Queen Wilhelmina under an awning of fishing nets on her way to her inauguration in the New Church.

Citizens of Amsterdam form a mounted guard of honor during the inauguration.

The second answer can be found in the care and attention that was devoted to the splendor of the ceremony. Never before had the New Church been so lavishly decorated. High in the vaulted roof hung a gigantic canopy with trailing pennants. Behind the brass rood screen stood a forest of palm trees, a reference to the Dutch East Indies. The arms of Batavia, the capital of the East Indies, and of Paramaribo in the West Indies hung in the church alongside those of the Dutch provinces. This, and the presence of a delegation of Indonesian princes, was the physical expression of an image that the Netherlands had for some time been projecting on the international stage – the colonies were presented as an integral part of the kingdom. The baldachin, a sort of portable canopy and a traditional element in an inauguration, had become a pergola of fishing nets, beneath which the new queen was to walk from the Palace to the New Church.[16] This maritime flavor was part of an overall concept for decorating the city. The Amsterdam committee of residents had invited the architects Eduard Cuypers and Willem Kromhout to deck out the city for the celebrations. Kromhout, in particular, rejected the traditional repertoire of triumphal arches in imitation stone. He opted for a maritime theme, because it expressed a "specifically Dutch way of decorating." Contemporaries were especially taken with the illuminations in the evening as a manifestation of "Venetian nights in Amsterdam."[17]

The third answer has to do with the extraordinary significance that people attached to the occasion. While at the heart of the inauguration lay the solemn swearing of a political contract, the ritual surrounding it was motivated by a desire to bolster the nation's self-confidence. A celebratory spirit of enterprise is evident in the sheer number and variety of events that were mounted. They reflected the origins of the organizers, because the inauguration of 1898 was a middle class celebration. Three themes predominated: the flowering of a "new style" dynastic Orangism, the creation of cultural nationalism and a conscious effort to popularize folklore in the Netherlands.

An exhibition in the Rijksmuseum was devoted to the dynastic theme. The organizers, a committee of Amsterdam residents headed by the merchant Pieter van Eeghen, wanted to use an exhibition of paintings and objects belonging to the House of Orange to generate interest in the forebears of the newly inaugurated queen. There was a historical and allegorical procession, which wound its way across the square behind the Rijksmuseum. The procession was divided into three groups: William of Orange and his companions as the champions of the Revolt against the absolutism of the Hapsburg Empire, a cohort of naval heroes and explorers of the Golden Age of trade and expansion and, lastly, a representation of the court of Stadholder Frederik Hendrik. The members of the Orange dynasty were the only ones on horseback. Historical parades or masquerades like this were held in provincial towns and cities up and down the country. The prevalence of such themes reveals a deliberate attempt to anchor the Orange dynasty firmly in history by staging memorable spectacles.[18]

The most permanent feature in the creation of this dynastic image is the Golden Coach – a present from Amsterdam made from materials that came only from the Netherlands or its colonies, which has since become an indispensable element in the representation of the Dutch monarchy. Among European monarchies, a golden coach is the ultimate coronation vehicle. The fact that it could be added to the Oranges' mews after the inauguration can be explained as recognition, albeit belated, of the royal standing they had acquired, a modern variant of the royalist tradition. The initiative came from supporters of the House of Orange in the Jordaan, a working-class district of Amsterdam. The *Vereeniging van het Amsterdamsche Volk* (Association of the People of Amsterdam), which was responsible for raising the money by collecting innumerable small donations, included Orangist representatives from other working-class neighborhoods. The gift thus contributed another building block to the traditional image of Orange as "the people's monarchy." This myth had had a certain power of persuasion among the workers in Amsterdam in the earliest days of socialism, but in 1898 this homage to the monarch and the way the money was collected, in numerous small donations, was also perceived as an anti-socialist campaign.[19]

In the historical pageants, in newspaper leaders and in illustrations, people recalled the illustrious past of the United Provinces. The organized evocation of the seventeenth century – that legendary period regarded in the Netherlands as the Golden Age – reached its apogee in an exhibition of works by Rembrandt, which proved to be the most successful element of the inauguration celebrations. The exhibition was also of great importance to the public appreciation of Rembrandt. In 1898, more than ever before, the painter was seen as the national genius. This event, the first retrospective devoted to Rembrandt, was curated by the art historians Abraham Bredius and Cornelis Hofstede de Groot, who had selected and brought together 123 paintings and 350 drawings from

Queen Wilhelmina and her mother, Queen Emma, admire the Golden Coach, a gift from the
people of Amsterdam, in the Crystal Palace.

Dutch and foreign collections. It was staged in the Stedelijk Museum in Amsterdam, because the initiative for it came from the people of Amsterdam. This meant that the Rijksmuseum temporarily had to yield up the pride of its collection, the *Night Watch*, which hung in a gallery specifically designed for it by the architect, Pierre Cuypers. The moving of this painting sparked a new debate about its original position in the museum.[20] The Rembrandt exhibition was a huge success by the standards of the day. More than 50,000 people went to see it.

People could also revitalize their sense of national history by visiting the exhibition of *Nationale kleederdrachten van Harer Majesteits onderdanen* (National Dress of Her Majesty's Subjects), likewise in the Stedelijk Museum. This was a collection of historical costumes, some of which were actually still being worn in 1898. The committee in charge of the preparations was again headed by the businessman Pieter van Eeghen. There were some 225 costumes on display, grouped according to a historical classification of the Dutch people into three tribes – Franks, Frisians and Saxons.[21] A collection of dolls from the East Indies represented colonial society. The exhibition was so successful that it had to be extended, and it eventually attracted more than 25,000 visitors. This event introduced some 6,000 schoolchildren and their teachers to the contemporary views of folklore. It was a high point in organized public interest in Dutch folklore. It did, however, present a different, "more primitive" picture of the past than the art of the United Provinces in their Golden Age.

One important event was not on the official program for the celebrations. This was the *Nationale Tentoonstelling van Vrouwenarbeid* (National Exhibition of Women's Work), which opened in The Hague two months before the inauguration. It was designed along the lines of the Women's Building at the Chicago World's Fair of 1893 and was part of an international trend focusing on women's work. A number of active feminists had seized the chance presented by the inauguration of a woman as head of state to examine the circumstances of working women in the Netherlands and, more particularly, their opportunities. The new queen did put in an appearance at the exhibition in The Hague, but she avoided the slightest hint of any affiliation with political feminism. This notwithstanding, it was an important event in the history of Dutch feminism around the turn of the century, because the exhibition's wide-ranging displays and the twelve conferences organized in association with it provided effective information about a subject that was controversial in the Netherlands in 1898: women's work.[22] In 1899, a year after the exhibition, the government appointed the first female inspector of labor.

One event out of step with the rest was the symbolic absence from the ceremony of Pieter Jelles Troelstra and Henri van Kol, the two members of Parliament for the Social Democratic Workers' Party (the SDAP). The independent socialist member of Parliament, G.L. van der Zwaag, also stayed away. Another notable absentee was the leader of the Protestant *Anti-Revolutionaire Partij* (the Anti-Revolutionary Party, the ARP), Abraham Kuyper, who had gone to the United States in September 1898 to deliver the Stone Lectures on modern Calvinism at Princeton. In his case, his failure to attend should not be construed as a public demonstration of Republican leanings, although he did support Calvinist Republicanism. The absence of the socialist MPs was certainly politically motivated. They refused to swear the oath or pledge of allegiance to the monarchy, which they rejected. Their absence – without prior notice – underlined in a wider context the political divide of the time between conservative and religious parties who wanted to unite around the throne and the revolutionary socialist and social democrat members who wanted to distance themselves from it utterly. The committee in charge of organizing the public celebrations had made a specific effort to involve members of the general and denominational workers' associations in the official events. They were part of the historical and allegorical procession and they lined the route during the new queen's entry into Amsterdam. For its part, the SDAP had produced a manifesto calling on the modern workers' movement to distance itself from the inauguration, even though it understood that people were in a festive mood.

> We are well aware that in his joyless existence the worker feels a need to set aside his worries for once and to indulge in the excitement of the celebrations. This is why the great mass probably will be among those celebrating. But this unconscious expression of a thirst for some joy in life must not push the greatest task that working people have to fulfill into the background.[23]

The inauguration celebrations exceeded expectations. They overshadowed other festivities in 1898, such as the fiftieth anniversary of the democratic constitution of 1848 or the 250th anniversary of the Treaty of Münster (1648), when the Dutch Republic was

Queen Wilhelmina appears on the balcony of the Palace on the Dam to greet her subjects.

internationally recognized. Led by the conservatives and with the agreement of religious parties, the monarchy in the Netherlands was again embedded firmly in the national consciousness by celebratory plebiscite. From then on, Wilhelmina's birthday, August 31, ceased to be a princess's celebration and became the Queen's Day, a public holiday which let people forget their differences for twenty-four hours in the name of the Orange dynasty, even though committed socialists remained aloof.

Intermezzo: the heyday of liberalism

Shortly after the inauguration, Queen Wilhelmina delivered her first speech from the throne on the occasion of the opening of the parliamentary year. The prime minister, the liberal politician and banker N.G. Pierson, had sent her a draft in the usual way. This she had returned with a request that tribute should be paid to the colonial army, which was engaged in a war with the Muslim state in Aceh in the Dutch East Indies, and also that some words of appreciation should be addressed to the army and navy. The praise for the military achievements in Aceh was included. In response to the second request, however, Pierson replied that the government had wanted to rid the speech from the throne of "superfluous announcements" at the start of a new reign and that the "stereotypical sentence" about the armed forces was considered to be one such. The civilian public officials might, after all, think that they were being slighted. And this applied even more

Augmenting State Revenues. "Mr. Pierson: The blade's sharp; where are the customers?"
De Amsterdammer, October 3, 1897.

acutely in a year when the members of the armed forces "had confined themselves to their normal duties, whereas the introduction of new and important legislation had placed exceptionally heavy demands on numerous groups of civil servants."[24] There was no word of appreciation for the armed forces in the final version of the speech.

The increase in the size of the civil service and in the number of tasks it was called upon to do reflected the growth of government intervention and the increasing involvement of the state in society. This was driven by liberal politicians around the turn of the century. The eighteen-nineties were the electoral heyday of liberalism in the Netherlands. For ten years, from 1891 until the beginning of the new century, this political movement was able to leave its mark on government's influence over society and on the relations between citizen and state. Seldom was liberalism in the Netherlands more "etatistic" than in this period and never was it more productive in its legislation.[25] If we draw up the balance sheet for the new century, we see that the relationship between citizen and state has been modernized, and the government has been enabled to guarantee certain forms of social security and take the lead in the expansion of public housing.

The main achievement of the first liberal government, led by Gijsbert van Tienhoven (1891-1894), was the modernization of the tax system. Pierson, an economist of international standing, was given the credit for this change, at the heart of which was a shift away from indirect taxation towards tax on liquid assets and on earned income. We can

Johan Braakensiek, *N.G. Pierson, De Amsterdammer,* July 22, 1894.

identify three underlying reasons for this move – an economic motive, a social motive and an administrative motive. The first was that trade and industry throughout the country would benefit from a system of direct taxes on a national scale that put an end to the plethora of local tolls and duties. In social terms, abolishing these taxes would bring down the cost of living as far as food was concerned and thus help to improve public health. The administrative argument was that an overhaul of the state's income was essential, because the growth in state intervention would inevitably mean more civil servants and higher personnel costs. A start had been made on scrapping local authority and other levies as early as 1865. For two decades it was possible to offset the loss of income to the treasury against the revenues from the colonial rule of the Dutch East Indies, but from 1890 onwards it was not the state but private entrepreneurs who grew rich from this particular source. Pierson consequently proposed a new income tax, which was made up of two parts: a property tax (1892) and a business tax, including the income from an occupation (1893). The modernization of Dutch society was reflected in both forms since the industrial and service sectors gained much more from this than did traditional agriculture, while there was also an – admittedly restrained – progression whereby the better off were taxed more according to their ability to pay. This could be seen as proof of the state's social responsibility.[26]

The modernization of the citizen's rights – specifically the extension of the right to vote – ran into greater resistance, to the extent that it actually brought about the downfall of the Van Tienhoven government. Opposing views developed within the government majority: at one end of the scale the social liberals were calling for universal suffrage; at the other the conservative element was insisting that the sole qualification for voting had to remain the liability to pay tax (census). When the Constitution was amended in 1887 the proposition that other standards of suitability and social position, in addition to the payment of tax, could apply to men was included as an item for discussion. Women, in contrast, were explicitly denied the right to vote. The minister of home affairs, Joannes Tak van Poortvliet, saw an opposition majority build up against him. The conflict resulted in the dissolution of Parliament, and new elections. In the subsequent government – conservative-liberal in tone under the leadership of Jonkheer Joan Roëll (1894-1897) – the new minister, Sam van Houten, introduced a more moderate extension. His bill provided for the addition to the traditional taxpaying electors of new categories of "examination electors", "tenant electors", "saver electors," and electors in permanent employment – all, of course, male. The new act of 1896 gave forty-nine percent of the male population the vote. Increasing prosperity and better schooling pushed this up to sixty-five percent by 1913. General and active suffrage for men was introduced in 1918; votes for women followed in 1919.

The democratization of citizen's obligations also passed with the slimmest of majorities. In 1898, after years of debate, personal national service for men was introduced and the practice of paying someone to take your place was outlawed. It is typical of the development of the liberalism of the time that this act was presented as a form of social policy. Conscription, which made no distinction for rank or status, was regarded as an act of social justice and as contributing to the physical and mental health of the people.[27] In 1901, education was made compulsory between the ages of six and twelve. This was the culmination of liberal efforts to improve education as a way into society. This state intervention in the private domain of the family was then repeated in new child protection legislation introduced by the liberal minister of justice Pieter Cort van der Linden.

The predominant issue, however, was the political battle about how far the state should intervene in labor relations. "The social question" had been on the public agenda in the Netherlands since the defeat of the Paris Commune in 1871. The liberal Van Houten, at that time a member of Parliament, proposed legislation banning child labor, and in this climate it was accepted. 1886 saw the so-called eel riots – an uprising in response to the banning of the custom of eel-heading (a pastime that involved pulling the head off a live eel tied to a post) which got out of hand in the Jordaan, a working-class district of Amsterdam. In the same year, at the urging of the liberal member of Parliament, Hendrik Goeman Borgesius, there was a parliamentary enquiry into the working of Van Houten's Child Labor Act and into the conditions in factories and workshops in three Dutch cities: Amsterdam, Tilburg and Maastricht. The findings were shocking. The liberal social policy agenda was subsequently dictated by three priorities: state intervention to improve public health and housing, the promotion of regular consultations between employers and employees, and the introduction of insurance against industrial accidents. The Housing Act and the Health Act, both of which came into force in 1901, were the showpieces of the third liberal government (1897-1901) led by Pierson. The first of these proved to have a major impact on urban planning and housing quality. The latter created a system of inspectors, who were responsible for public health standards. The first form of systematic consultation between employers and employees was defined in the Chambers of Labor Act (1897). And lastly, the effort to combat workplace accidents gave rise to the first ever social insurance. A state inspectorate was set up for companies with more than ten workers. In 1901, an Act was passed making it compulsory for employers and workers to insure against the risks of accidents at work.

The parliamentary debate about the industrial accident legislation focused not, as had previously been the case, on the legitimacy of government action but on its limits.[28] In this, the eighteen-nineties generation of Dutch liberals differed from their predecessors in the seventies. That movement had been inspired by the assumption of a dynamic and productive capitalism, which was achieved and guided by an alliance of civilized citizens. Artisans would gradually be admitted to this alliance as increased prosperity and improvements in education turned them, too, into independent individuals. The way out of poverty thus lay in hard work, rationality, and morality. The parasitic "aristocracy" of landowners and people with private means would lose their power, while at the other end of the scale the proletariat would be marginalized. This was the view of the liberal vanguard of the eighteen-seventies, and it was shared by British liberals like William Gladstone and John Bright. They put their own interpretation on the doctrine of "productive labor" as the driving force of society that had been outlined in Saint-Simonism.[29]

While combating the "aristocracy" was a priority for the seventies generation, this aim had no practical significance for the next – for the British men and women of New Liberalism or the Dutch group of liberals associated with the *Sociaal Weekblad*. To them the question that had become urgent was that of the proletariat, because they saw this class getting larger, while the growth in mass production suggested that things would continue in this way for some time.[30] In the doctrine of productive virtue, the independence of the citizen had been defined in terms of economic and moral action. Anyone who could not get ahead by his own efforts was excluded from the political community because unemployment was seen as the consequence of the moral incompetence of the individual. This was now called into question by social liberals. They believed that positive intervention on the part of the state was called for when individuals got into difficulty through no fault of their own. Their view of the economic climate, industrial accidents and sickness implied that such circumstances were the rule rather than the exception in modern industrial society. Individual freedom no longer just took precedence over the state, it was also made possible by the protection of the government. In its relationship to the citizen, state power was no longer solely a limiting force – it was also a mechanism that created conditions and opportunities.[31]

Around the turn of the century, some social liberals – modeling themselves on the French example – started calling themselves *radicals*. The leading figure in this movement was the economist Marie Willem Frederik Treub, who was given the opportunity to pursue a new "etatistic" policy in local government when he was elected to the post of alderman in Amsterdam in 1893. Three years later, after a relatively short period in office, he became professor of political economy at the University of Amsterdam. Treub believed that while the French Revolution had indeed swept aside old ties of community and feudal institutions, the pendulum had since swung too far the other way in an unbounded expansion of individual freedom. In consequence, society had become a collection of isolated individuals who "were engaged in unbridled competition with one another." It was the state's responsibility to foster equality in the growth and development of individuals, to limit individual property rights, and to take economic monopolies out of the hands of private owners. Treub was a "utilitarian Darwinist"; he rejected the view that the improvement of society stemmed from a battle for survival of all against all, and argued the need for "equal living conditions," in which every citizen could develop according to his own capabilities.[32]

Liberalism was a broad church in 1900. As the political expression of a social elite, its sentiments could be heard wherever active and well-to-do citizens raised their voices.[33] As an early generation of liberals had used the literary journal *De Gids* (1837) as the platform for a broad discourse on social and artistic issues, so the new cohort of radicals presented themselves in *De Nieuwe Gids* (1885), the alternative polemic vehicle for artists and intellectuals who were all born between 1855 and 1865 and who were to bestow upon themselves the label of a generation: the Movement of the Eighties.[34] They were bound not so much by a common literary agenda as by the realization – in the words of the poet Willem Kloos – of being part of a younger breed, "whose various members differ greatly in opinions and work and consequence, but who nonetheless all stand against a single enemy, the older generation, one for this reason, another for that." The group used to meet in the bars in the center of Amsterdam and thus acquired the nickname of the "beer nomads." One of them, Frank van der Goes, a stockbroker but also a lecturer at the new Drama School, saw himself and his fellow group members, "Young Amsterdam," driven by "the unstoppable influence of the great, the historical evolution." He embarked on a political campaign against the liberal bourgeoisie as his fellow editors girded their loins in the battle against bourgeois literature. In the eighteen-nineties Van der Goes moved out of the bohemian life and stepped into the political arena, where he blazed a trail via radicalism to socialism.[35]

The patrician class had traditionally been at the heart of the Liberal Party. This class was made up partly of the families of the regents, who had a long tradition of holding office in the service of the public. In the second half of the nineteenth century they were joined by the new rich in trade, industry and banking, and officers in the armed forces.[36] The aristocracy in the Netherlands, in contrast, had had no significant power since the introduction of the Constitution in 1848. After the first direct elections for the new style Lower House in 1849, most of the aristocratic members of Parliament were to be found among the conservatives. After 1870, when the conservatives had lost power and substance, several politically active families allied themselves with the Anti-Revolutionary Party, a movement rooted in a political and social revival of Calvinism. The nobility and the patricians together accounted for some twenty percent of the male electorate, but in the period between 1848 and 1887 they held sixty to seventy percent of the seats in the

Left   Overview of cabinets 1879-1918   Right

Left	Year	Right
	1879	
		Conservative cabinet C. van Lynden van Sandenburg
	1883	
		Conservative cabinet Jan Heemskerk II
	1888	
		First Christian coalition Aeneas MacKay
	1891	
Liberal cabinet Gijsbert van Tienhoven		
	1894	
Liberal cabinet Joan Roëll		
	1897	
Liberal cabinet Nicolaas Pierson		
	1901	
		Second Christian coalition Abraham Kuyper
	1905	
Liberal cabinet Theo de Meester		
	1908	
		Christian coalition Theo Heemskerk
	1909	
		Christian coalition Theo Heemskerk (continued)
	1913	
Liberal cabinet Pieter Cort van der Linden		
	1918	
		Christian coalition Charles Ruys de Beerenbrouck

Lower House. A downturn set in shortly before the amendment to the Constitution in 1887. It was not until the elections to the Lower House in 1913 that a modern balance of power began to emerge and, for the first time, the aristocracy and the patrician class supplied fewer than fifty percent of the elected representatives.[37]

Notions of party discipline and the need for unity in adversity were not part of the psyche of the liberal elite. After 1848, when shaping public opinion could become more politicized, liberal citizens in several towns and cities set up debating societies, where not just the outcome of the debate but also the discussion itself, the argument, was elevated to an art, and polite parliamentary forms became the norm.[38] Throughout the nineteenth century, liberalism in the Netherlands was so strong and superior, and such little resistance as it met with in defending its interests was so weak, that it had no need to close ranks. It took the establishment of a confessional party on a national scale – the Anti-Revolutionary Party in 1878 – to jolt the liberals into uniting in a Liberal Union. The reason why, compared with Belgium and Germany, the Netherlands was late in creating modern political parties was that the structure of Dutch society, the legacy of a republican and bourgeois past, had for years made it possible for the liberals to dominate the political stage without encountering any opposition worth the name.[39]

Around the turn of the century, it was possible to identify a conservative and a radical variant of liberalism; a national liberal and a social liberal strand. The former manifested itself primarily in a militant form of nationalism, the origins of which went back to 1870, when officers impressed by the Prussian victory over the French set up the *Nederlandse Weerbaarheidsbond* (Dutch Defense League) and campaigned for discipline among the populace. A contrary view was expressed by the lawyer Bernardus Tellegen who, in an address as rector magnificus of the University of Groningen in 1870, spoke about "Germany and the Netherlands," contrasting the Dutch tradition of freedom with the culture of obedience in the country's huge neighbor. He said he was less afraid of annexation by a united Germany than of Dutch identification with its culture.[40] The desire for popular discipline reappeared around the turn of the century, but this time not in exclusively martial form. In the reverberations of the second Boer War, a popular defense league known as the *Vereeniging Volksweerbaarheid* was set up in the Netherlands. Among those behind this initiative were both liberal and confessional politicians; even Tak, who was later to become a socialist, initially pledged his support. Switzerland, which called every male citizen to arms at regular intervals in the name of national defense, was held up as an example.

In the Dutch situation, national defense did not mean importing Prussian-style discipline; it was concerned with raising the social responsibility of the individual citizen. Personal national service was the best proof of this. Democratic citizenship and patriotism were fostered in a culture of militancy.[41] In 1908 the league spawned the so-called *Tucht-Unie*, an umbrella organization which set itself the goal of "combating indiscipline among the Dutch populace, in order to improve its moral, mental and physical strength."[42] Its first chairman was Edo Bergsma, who was at that time also head of the *Algemene Nederlandse Wielrijders Bond* (ANWB), the body which looked after the interests of modern transport and tourism. The combination of discipline and defense, of social discipline and patriotism is one of the most striking tendencies in liberalism after the turn of the century.

The Christian section of the People on their way to government.
"The Maid of Holland to the coachman: 'My friend, my friend! Whatever will become of this!'"
De Amsterdammer, June 23, 1901.

In 1901 the liberals' defeat at the hands of the electorate put an end to their legislative productivity. The Pierson government made way for a Christian coalition headed by the leader of the Anti-Revolutionary Party, the clergyman Abraham Kuyper. The antithesis he advocated, the dividing line between religious and lay parties, meant that in 1913 the liberals had to seek the support of the social democrats in order to achieve a majority and form a government. It meant extending a hand to a party to which prominent social liberals like Tak and F.M. Wibaut had already defected. At its party conference the SDAP then ruled out the possibility of taking part in a coalition government. From then on, a liberal minority government ran the country. Like their counterparts in Britain, it was the liberals in the Netherlands who headed the government during World War I. It was they who had to coordinate the battle for neutrality and subject the country to far-reaching state intervention; and like their overseas counterparts they were not to be rewarded for it after the war, doomed as they were to being reduced to a permanent minority in the wave of European democratization. After the introduction of the universal franchise in the Netherlands in 1918, power shifted to the people's parties.

The picturesque Netherlands

In June 1873 Henry Havard, a Parisian merchant who had fled his city in 1871 after the defeat of the Commune, took a boat trip around the coast of the Zuiderzee in the company of the marine painter J.E. van Heemskerck van Beest. He wrote an account of this expedition in a book, which was published in Paris in 1874.[43] Havard set a new tone, for he was probably the first foreigner to describe the Zuiderzee towns in terms of a lost world. At the end of their trip, the companions had a farewell dinner in the Amstel Hotel on the river that flows through Amsterdam. Havard tells us how, leaning on a balustrade overlooking the Amstel, he became lost in thought about the haughtiness of the once so prosperous inhabitants of the Zuiderzee towns, who no longer took any notice of what was going on around them, but gave themselves up to keeping things as they were. Others would catch them up and eventually leave them behind without the power and the riches that they were no longer capable of generating.[44]

Havard's sketch of the lost towns on the Zuiderzee, which had echoes of Victor Hugo's literary work, had a reverse side: the discovery of the unspoiled and picturesque elements of a past that had been pronounced dead. The travelers expressed this themselves when they gave an account of their visit to Volendam, a village on the Zuiderzee that was not in fact one of the old towns. There Havard discovered fishermen who had been able to preserve their traditional dress and the customs of an earlier age, and family life that he regarded as a model of simple domesticity. Despite the short distance from the capital, Amsterdam, the villagers had remained foreigners in contemporary Europe. As they stood together in little groups of six or eight, unmoving and unmoved, with unfocused gaze, they looked more like "fatalistic Turks" than Dutch fishermen.[45] Their fur caps and baggy trousers also reminded him of the Ottoman Empire. It was not, incidentally, the first time that Havard and his traveling companion had been reminded of scenes of life on the Bosporus as they observed the people who lived on the coast of the Zuiderzee.

On his boat trip through the Netherlands, the Italian Edmondo de Amicis had visited Broek in Waterland, a village to the north of Amsterdam, where the houses on the water inspired in him fantasies about a toyshop in Nuremberg and a puppet theater in Japan. The village of Broek in Waterland was renowned for its cleanliness. It was said that the village women were even prepared to forego church on Sunday if something had to be cleaned. Nevertheless it seemed to him to be a survival of a more prosperous past. The wealthy merchants of the old days had abandoned Broek in Waterland, and this had made the village a place of interest. In the guest book he read the name of such illustrious visitors as Victor Hugo and Walter Scott.[46]

As early as June 1871 Havard was recorded in the Netherlands in the company of the painters Claude Monet and Henry Michel-Lévy, then budding impressionists. The police were interested in these foreigners, because the Paris Commune had fallen and they had to keep an eye on communards who had fled. The trio visited the collection of paintings in the Trippenhuis in Amsterdam. Monet also painted the landscape along the Zaan river, and city views in Amsterdam. In their artistic interest, they were no different from the travelers who came to look at the seventeenth-century art in the Dutch museums, and then tried to identify the painted Dutch landscape or the historic scenes in contemporary reality. The land of Rembrandt was, after all, also Ruysdael's landscape and, outside the growing towns and cities, could be rediscovered in a relatively unspoiled state. This rediscovery was then immortalized in a painting or drawing.[47]

What struck us was the artistic culture, wrote the German painter Max Liebermann, discussing his travels in the Netherlands in his autobiography.[48] In 1871, as a 24-year-old student at the art college in Weimar, he had visited the Netherlands for the first time. For several decades thereafter the Netherlands was his "Wahlheimat," his chosen homeland. He was to paint views of Amsterdam, of the Amsterdam municipal orphanage and the Jewish quarter in Amsterdam; he also immortalized the Dutch dune landscape in the villages on the North Sea coast – Katwijk (1889) and Noordwijk (1912 and 1913). He lived for a while in the artists' colony in the village of Laren to the southeast of Amsterdam. Liebermann became friends with Jozef Israëls (1824-1911), the central figure in the group of painters known as the Hague School and the grand old man of Dutch painting around the turn of the century.[49]

Domestic landscape art was also flourishing: at about this time the painters of the Hague School attracted the attention of connoisseurs and the art trade. They were inspired by an artistic practice that had grown up in France. French painters had gone out into the countryside, for example to the village of Barbizon in the Forest of Fontainebleau near Paris, to paint in the open air and free themselves of academic conventions. Their example had found followers in the Netherlands. The young Gerard Bilders, who had been commissioned through the Amsterdam artists' guild *Arti et Amicitiae* to paint Ruysdael for a Historic Gallery, recognized in the latter's depiction of the landscape not only his own intentions but also those of his admired contemporaries of the Barbizon School. He thought that the way the French painters had learned from Dutch painting of the seventeenth century was exemplary. Bilders once described his French inspiration thus, "So I am now thoroughly French, but precisely by being thoroughly French I am thoroughly Dutch."[50] The circle was closed; the French Barbizon School brought about a revival of traditional Dutch landscape art in its own country.

The painters of the Hague School portrayed nature in an unspoiled state. "They fixed their gaze on a slowly vanishing countryside and shut their eyes to the creeping urbanization of their surroundings." They increasingly concentrated on "atmospheric phenomena."[51] The life of fishing communities was another popular subject. This was not an unfamiliar theme in nineteenth-century painting; the Dutch had had their practitioners, who sought the picturesque in fishing villages like Scheveningen or Zandvoort or on the island of Marken. In 1855, when Jozef Israëls turned his back on history painting – the genre that predominated at the Academy – and devoted himself to scenes from the fishermen's life, this was a romantic discovery. In fact, of course, he was simply switching to another traditional genre. The fishing theme derived from "paysannerie," the depiction of scenes from peasant life. At first the choice of these subjects had been informed by an interest in the life of ordinary people and in the traditions they still preserved. Around the turn of the century the accent shifted to the precariousness and uncertainty of existence, to the drama and the wretchedness. The fisherman was also depicted as a rugged hero and as a child of nature, who lived in freedom, untainted by the moral decay of city

At Jozef Israëls's party.
"Rembrandt: 'I pay homage to you in the name of Dutch Art.'"
De Amsterdammer, January 27, 1895.

life.[52] Bourgeois ideals like piety and domesticity, loyalty and the work ethic were projected onto the fisherman. He was, for instance, praised and portrayed in an album on *De Kinderen der Zee* (The Children of the Sea) by the poet Nicolaas Beets and Jozef Israëls. This book, published in 1861, was reprinted five times, until well into the twentieth century.[53]

The boom in the genre was not an entirely self-motivated artistic development. The role that art dealers played is particularly important, since in the second half of the nineteenth century they increasingly made conscious efforts to influence public taste. They organized exhibitions themselves and assured certain artists of a regular income, in exchange for which they actively brought their work to the attention of potential buyers and collectors.[54] In 1861, for example, a branch of the French art dealers Goupil was opened in The Hague. It was run by Vincent van Gogh, the uncle of the painter. This firm and its international network became an important factor in the expansion of contemporary art in the Netherlands. It was above all the painters of the Hague School who profited from this. By the end of the century, the businessman Hendrik Mesdag, Jozef Israëls and Jacob Maris had all become wealthy artists.[55] In the Dutch pavilion at the Chicago World's Fair in 1893, the exhibition of living masters was devoted exclusively to the Hague School. This enabled Jozef Israëls to focus attention on himself in the United States, "the land of the speculative art trade."[56] Among the first collectors was George Eastman, the founder of the Eastman Kodak photographic company.[57]

Israëls's commercial enterprise in the United States also focused attention on the Old Country. Between 1880 and 1914, according to the art historian Annette Stott, more than three hundred American painters visited the Netherlands, and most of them stayed for some time, preferably in the summer. The Americans came to study the works of the seventeenth-century Dutch masters, and incorporated what they saw in new work. One of these visitors was James McNeill Whistler, but there were also numerous artists and students who remained in obscurity.[58] As a rule they had four motives for making the crossing – the desire or the need to see seventeenth-century Old Masters for themselves; a curiosity about subjects that were relevant in fin-de-siècle Europe or were a pattern of what was then regarded as picturesque; the discovery of a tradition of unspoiled innocence in the Netherlands; and lastly a certain sympathy with the Reformational ideas in Holland. In consequence, all-American artists' colonies were established in a predominantly Protestant environment – Rijsoord (near Dordrecht) and Egmond.

The encounter with the Netherlands led to new images of town, water and country. Havard had set the tone by comparing Amsterdam with Venice. The French impressionist Claude Monet was so fascinated by the city's waterside, by the reflection and the play of light, that he took an easel out on the Amstel to capture it. Whistler, who was a regular visitor in the eighteen-eighties, also viewed and painted Amsterdam and Dordrecht from a boat. He was interested not in the stately canal houses, but in the run-down dwellings in the working-class districts. In 1889 his work was shown at an exhibition mounted by the *Nederlandsche Etsclub* in The Hague and at the *Art of Living Masters* exhibition in Amsterdam. He wanted to inspire his fellow artists in the Netherlands to take a fresh look at Amsterdam. The painter Richard Roland Holst wrote that these etchings transformed Amsterdam into a "sunny, cheerful, Southern city." The art critic Jan Veth declared that Whistler had perceived old Amsterdam as a curious world of delightful slums and elegant docks and wharves; a decorative city "rising slender out of clear water, freed of Dutch grime." Whether Whistler ultimately succeeded in inspiring Dutch artists is debatable. In the creation of the image of the city, painters like Willem Witsen, George Hendrik Breitner and Isaac Israëls were to derive their ideas above all from the big city life of Paris, combined with the social criticism in the novels of Emile Zola.[59]

An important motive for the wanderlust of foreign artists was the quest for the unspoiled and harmonious rural life in an age of industrialization and utilitarianism. The German painter Liebermann concentrated on images of a simple society, free of conflict – hence he painted an orphanage in Amsterdam or a farmhouse in the countryside.

James McNeill Whistler, *The Embroidered Curtain*, Palmgracht 52 and 54, Amsterdam.

He sought the utopian ideal of a society of free and equal citizens, based on labor, in the Netherlands. To him, what he found there was an example of a liberal and tolerant society in which minorities, particularly the Jews, could have a place.[60] American painters discovered the Dutch farmer as the incarnation of a God-fearing pilgrim, who aroused the interest of the citizens of a New World deliberately conceived as classless.[61] The cleanliness and simplicity were seen as virtues, as were the national dress and the clogs. The traveler became an artist who had to record rural Holland with its farmers and country people and their traditional costumes before they were swept away by the rise of modern industrial society. They looked for an oasis, a place where, for the moment, time stood still. The village of Laren, to the southeast of Amsterdam, performed this function. William Henry Singer was the best-known American to visit Laren, and he settled there in 1911. Thanks to him and to fellow-countrymen like Joseph Raphael, the status of the village grew, while the value of their works of art rose in the United States.

The sea was a variant of the unspoiled theme. Painters from various countries came to coastal towns like Egmond, Katwijk or Domburg, particularly in the summer, to paint the water and the beach, fishermen and fishing boats. There they met Dutch artists like Jan Toorop, who were moved by the same subjects. The new stereotypes of the Netherlands, or more accurately those of Holland – the polder landscape and the fisherman – grew up amidst this reciprocity of influx and influence. They originated in art, but were soon being replicated as a trademark in contemporary forms of mass communications: the illustrated magazine, the poster and a modern form of customer relations, the picture card album.

Stereotypes

In 1865 the American author Mary Mapes Dodge published a children's book entitled *Hans Brinker, or the Silver Skates*. It was the story of two children – Hans and Greetje Brinker – who came from a poor family living in a village near Amsterdam. Through their own efforts and goodness they pull through and win a skating competition. The book also contained a reading exercise, telling the story of a boy from Haarlem, who stuck his finger in a hole in the dyke to prevent a flood. "That little boy represents the spirit of the whole country." The author had taken her inspiration from the American historian John Lothrop Motley, who had published his work on the Revolt of the Netherlands, *The Rise of the Dutch Republic*, in 1856. *Hans Brinker* sold 300,000 copies in the United States in 1865. As early as 1867, a critical adaptation by the schoolmaster P.J. Andriessen, a well-known author of historical books for children, appeared in the Netherlands. As a result of this edition, the anecdote of the finger in the dyke became popular in Holland too. In the new version, Brinker became the protagonist and the dyke was located in Spaarndam.[62] In 1894 William Elliot Griffis published *Brave Little Holland and What She Taught Us*. Holland's battle against the water was translated into American terms, by analogy with Frederick Jackson Turner's renowned treatise on the march of the American frontier to the inhospitable west, and the implications of this pioneering trek in forming the national character. Before long, comments were appearing in print to the effect that such heroism was a characteristic of the Dutch in the past in the struggle to preserve their land. The windmill as an instrument of water control became the symbol of a Dutch "frontier mentality."[63]

At home, too, Dutch stereotypes governed the way people looked at "the beauty of our country." They became an inevitable trademark on the posters aimed at promoting national and international tourism by rail. The Verkade albums proved particularly popular – they were a new form of engagement with the customers which really captured the imagination. Around 1900 this Zaandam-based confectionery manufacturer started to enclose picture cards with its candy and cookies. Albums were then issued so that collectors could keep the cards together. The initiative was so successful that in 1906 the teacher and biologist Jac. P. Thijsse was approached to write descriptions of the countryside. The pictures were derived from the art of the Hague School. The landscape was seen through the eyes of a modern city-dweller. The makers' vision "is dominated by the spring and summer. The fall appears less frequently, winter seldom. The grass is green, the blue sky, always with typical cotton wool clouds, is reflected in the water, the ducks enjoy life, and the cows are visibly contented." In some paintings, the lakes area between the provinces of Holland and Utrecht was transformed into a park landscape, inviting the viewer to sample the outdoor life.[64]

The effort to conserve natural values took on institutional form in 1905, with the establishment of the *Vereniging van Natuurmonumenten*. Four years later the organization representing drivers and cyclists, the ANWB, decided to mark its 25th anniversary by publishing a four-part series entitled *Ons eigen land* (Our Own Country), a real plea for domestic tourism. In contrast to the Verkade albums, this work used the modern medium of photography to illustrate the text. It was soon followed by a new series on places of interest, *Sprokkelingen door Nederland* (Gleanings in the Netherlands), edited by A. Loosjes. Publications like this were intended to reveal the beauty of the countryside and to promote the conservation of the national heritage, but were also part of a deliberate campaign to teach city-dwellers about nature. They were consequently not confined to Holland, in the center of the country – the ANWB books depicted the diversity of the Dutch landscape in the outlying provinces from the north of the country to the far south.

The other Dutch stereotype, the fisherman, found its home in Volendam – described by Havard and more or less discovered by tourists around the turn of the century. In 1880 and 1881 two American journalists, George Henry Boughton and Edwin Austin Abbey, traveled around the Zuiderzee for *Scribner's Magazine*. The accounts of their travels also appeared two years later in *Harper's New Monthly Magazine* and were eventually collected in a book, with illustrations, entitled *Sketching Rambles in Holland*. Volendam was described in glowing terms. They were welcomed as artists and asked if they would like to buy a traditional Volendam costume. This showed "that the Volendamers were already familiar with the traveling artist breed and its peculiar requirements."[65] In 1898 the British satirical magazine *Punch* ran an advertisement for cycling trips to Volendam. Back home, the painter and poster artist Willy Sluiter was particularly instrumental in popularizing the village and its way of life. The public perception was fixed by his depiction of high spirits during the annual fair in Volendam.[66]

By 1900 it was hard for anyone who came to the Netherlands to avoid Volendam. Artists and tourists liked to be received by Leendert Spaander, the owner of a hotel opened in 1881. The Hotel Spaander's visitors book contains the signatures of the Boer general Christiaan de Wet and the Norwegian composer Edvard Grieg, along with those of the Chief of the German General Staff Helmuth von Moltke, of the banker Pierpont Morgan, and of Lord Baden Powell, the founder of world scouting. At first, Volendam could be reached by sea or by barge through the Waterland. When a steam tram connection with Amsterdam was opened in 1906, the fishing village developed into a tourist model of traditional Dutch rural life and its cleanliness. Just how far-reaching this internationalization was is demonstrated by the fact that Volendam was chosen as the setting for *Lodoletta*, an opera by the Italian composer Pietro Mascagni, which premiered in Rome in 1917. The scene of the main action is a square in Volendam, where the heroine of the piece, Lodoletta, her foster father, the fisherman Antonio, and her Volendam admirer, Gianotto, sing their arias. The libretto was an adaptation of *Two Little Wooden*

A French Pathé film crew shot scenes from the film *Le Calvaire du Mousse, or The Agony of the Ship's Boy*, at Hotel Spaander in Volendam in 1912.

Shoes, a sketch by the British writer Ouida, which had been published in 1874. This story was set in Brabant; the librettist, Giovacchino Forzano, moved it to Volendam. Through the opera, the village acquired a place on the international list of typical fishing locations.[67]

The Golden Age in 1900

The retrospective of Rembrandt's works during Wilhelmina's inauguration in 1898 had been the first opportunity for Dutch and foreign visitors to see the reasonably complete oeuvre of a national artist. Another exhibition was mounted in 1906 to mark the tercentenary of Rembrandt's birth. Heavy illustrated volumes on his art were published during this period. They had to be updated constantly as paintings by Rembrandt were "rediscovered." The archive documents relating to the painter were also published in an index of sources. Among those responsible for such publications were Abraham Bredius and Cornelis Hofstede de Groot – both archetypal connoisseurs. The former was self-taught and became director of the Mauritshuis, the museum next to the Binnenhof in The Hague. The latter graduated in art history in Germany and founded the state agency for

Albert Hahn, *Rembrandt Experts.*

art historical documentation, the *Rijksbureau voor Kunsthistorische Documentatie* (RKD). They are the pioneers of art historical research in the Netherlands.[68]

A body known as the General Rembrandt Committee conceived and coordinated the festivities in 1906, the most notable being the dedication of the new gallery for the *Night Watch* in the Rijksmuseum and the granting of honorary doctorates by the University of Amsterdam to five Rembrandt specialists from the Netherlands and abroad. As well as Bredius and Hofstede de Groot, they were the painter and critic Jan Veth, the French art historian Emile Michel, and Wilhelm von Bode, director of the museums in Berlin's museum quarter. The awarding of these honors prompted the establishment of a chair of art history at a Dutch university; in 1907 Willem Vogelsang, a contemporary of Bredius and Hofstede de Groot, was appointed professor in Utrecht. A public collection was held to raise money for the purchase of Rembrandt's former house in Amsterdam. In the Stadsschouwburg, the capital's main theater, there was an "artistic gala," at which "Rembrandtesque" compositions by Bernard Zweers, Johan Wagenaar and Diepenbrock were performed. Twenty etchings were projected onto a white screen – a modern sensation – accompanied by the music specially arranged for the occasion and conducted by the renowned Willem Mengelberg. Elsewhere people organized an "edifying popular festival." Through local spin-offs and commercial exploitation the commemoration took on the proportions of a popular event.[69]

In the commemoration ceremony in the West Church in Amsterdam, when a memorial plaque was unveiled on one of the columns in the church to mark Rembrandt's lost grave, the Amsterdam professor Hendrik Quack gave the memorial address, in which he described Rembrandt and the seventeenth-century poet Vondel as the artists who had expressed "that which slumbered in the depths of the Dutch heart. Their blazing writing, their shining images have revealed the inner life, the intensity of being, of our people. They gave luster to the age. They created joy. And Rembrandt is the greater in that he is understood by the whole world."[70] This was Rembrandt's reputation in 1906. He was a genius, and he expressed the essence of the Dutch people, but the whole world could and did see that his work was among the most beautiful and most profound ever made by man. The speakers merged the cult of the genius with their nationalist rhetoric to such an extent "that in Rembrandt the fatherland could honor itself without petty-mindedness for what it had produced and had expressed through the medium of such art."[71] The nationalization of the artist had reached a peak around the turn of the century. In 1907 Victor de Stuers – at that time the representative of the district of Weert in the Lower House but previously the Netherlands' first official for the preservation of monuments and historic buildings – made a speech in which he drew a comparison between the Netherlands' lack of political and military power and the wealth of its artistic achievements.

> What makes us great and honored is our magnificent history and our importance in the fields of science and art – particularly in art because it has an immediate impact on the eye and makes the deepest impression. If we are now generally recognized and honored among nations, if we enjoy international popularity, it is above all because we are known as the land of Rembrandt, and people are aware that we, with Italy and Greece, have excelled in art as no other people have.[72]

As Rembrandt had become the key figure in the history of Dutch art and the yardstick against which the national significance was measured, so his work became the focal point of the new Rijksmuseum, which was opened in Amsterdam in 1885. Rembrandt's gallery was at the end of the Gallery of Honor, the central axis of the building, and exactly in line with this axis hung the *Night Watch*, "so that the triumphant citizens portrayed in the painting could march unimpeded." The décor of the room reflected the reverence for the genius, and also glorified him as a personality in accordance with the then current idea of the unity of work and life. The frieze depicted details of Rembrandt's life, including his marriage to the Leeuwarden burgomaster's daughter Saskia van Uylenburgh. This was a reference to the marital harmony in which a great artist should preferably live and through which the painter had gained access to the world of the great and the good.[73] Rembrandt, a free spirit in real life, was molded to accommodate the prevailing bourgeois morality. This moral edification had been in evidence as early as 1852, on the unveiling of his statue in Amsterdam.

The Rijksmuseum can be seen as an extreme endeavor to immortalize art as a chapter in a great historical synthesis. The trio responsible for the style and decoration of the building – the architect Pierre Cuypers, the government official Victor de Stuers and the

The Gallery of Honor in the Rijksmuseum with Rembrandt's *Night Watch* at the far end.

merchant and man of letters J.A. Alberdingk Thijm – wanted to achieve an apotheosis of Dutch art and history. On the tile tableaux on the building's exterior, artists were portrayed as self-assured citizens, free to practice their art. The design and decoration of the building incorporated not just the history of Dutch art with its great and lesser masters, but also the history of the Netherlands with the emphasis on towns and provinces. The whole thing was set against a background of the history of humanity, portrayed in the windows of the entrance hall.

However, after the *Night Watch*'s temporary sojourn in the Stedelijk Museum for the retrospective in 1898, there were increasingly insistent calls for a different approach. In 1906 the painting was removed from the Rijksmuseum's Gallery of Honor. There were essentially two reasons for this. The first was the result of the technical discussion about the significance of the north light when viewing the painting. The proponents of a different approach wanted it to be seen in the "warmer" south light in which the work had originally been painted. The other reason was a change in notions of how a work of art should be displayed in the museum. It was decided that the founders' efforts to achieve a total overview of Dutch art stood in the way of experiencing the individual masterpieces.[74] Influenced by impressionism, a change was occurring: a distinction had to be

The Stedelijk Museum and Paulus Potterstraat in Amsterdam under construction in 1895.
The new Rijksmuseum and the skating rink on Museum Square can be seen in the background.

made between artistic products that illustrated the past, and paintings that it had to be possible to see and enjoy in the moment itself – in the present.[75] In 1906 this led not just to the rehanging of the *Night Watch* but also to the scrapping of the historical trappings around it.

The contemporary trend in art history contrasted with the former attempts to achieve cohesion in a single cultural historical vision. It became a science based in the first instance on empirical research. Toward the end of the century it was practiced in the Netherlands primarily by Bredius and Hofstede de Groot. Unlike earlier researchers, who had concentrated mainly on great artists, they also brought to light information about forgotten painters. Hofstede de Groot's series in ten parts, *Holländische Maler*, appeared between 1907 and 1928, while Bredius published his seven-volume *Künstlerinventare* between 1915 and 1922.[76] It was only then that the sheer magnitude and diversity of seventeenth-century painting could really be appreciated to the full. At the same time, compilation works like these presented a problem for the historiography of art, because the specific character of Dutch painting and its role in the development of art in general was effectively impossible to define amidst the welter of data. Bredius and Hofstede de Groot stressed the picturesque at the expense of the profundity of the subjects. Dutch realism was thus linked to a contemporary vogue: the Hague School.[77] It was not without reason that around 1900 the aging Jozef Israëls (1824-1911) was hailed as a new Rembrandt.

In Germany, in contrast, a book entitled *Rembrandt als Erzieher* (Rembrandt the Teacher) was published in 1890. It portrayed the artist as the standard-bearer for a new culture. It was written "by a German," a rather grand pseudonym for Julius Langbehn, who after rootless wanderings as a student and soldier eventually studied art history in Munich. The book was a runaway success. It sold 60,000 copies in the first year; by 1891 it was in its fortieth impression, with two new chapters. It is neither a biography of Rembrandt nor a study of his oeuvre; the protagonist was the personification of an artistic ideal that was opposed to modern culture and science. Langbehn derived from German folklore the construction of a "Niederdeutscher"; a reference to the rural population in the North German plains, where the rural traditions were still relatively untouched and where extraordinary characters were cultivated. Rembrandt was not only a "Niederdeutscher" in general, but also a Hollander in particular. Hollanders, on the coast of "Niederdeutschland," were "seafaring peasants" like the ancient Greeks. Langbehn described Rembrandt's painting as "Schlammmalerei, aber im edelsten Sinne" – "mud painting, but in the noblest sense." The Hollanders were related to the continental "Niederdeutscher," but at the same time distinct from them.[78] Chaotically written as the book was, its intention was unmistakable; modern culture and science were condemned, the free man and the true Germanic nobleman were praised. Its tone reflected the author's intense suffering, which was in itself an extreme example of permanent criticism and dissatisfaction.[79] This is why the historian Fritz Stern regarded him as an exponent of the ideology of irrationalism in Germany and, by extension, as a trailblazer of National Socialism.

Rembrandt was honored at home and abroad – in fact, the way for the rediscovery of his genius had actually been paved in France and Germany in the nineteenth century. The study of seventeenth-century literature, in contrast, was very much a matter for Dutch (and Flemish) experts. Around 1900 it was not only older literary figures who found a theme in this history; it also attracted the new generation of poets and writers in the Movement of the Eighties – men like Frederik van Eeden, who drew the inspiration for his plays *Frans Hals* (1884) and *The Witch of Haarlem* (1914) from the seventeenth-century Haarlem painter. It was the literary evocations, far more than scholarly opinions, that shaped people's ideas about the seventeenth century. It happened directly, through the historical novel or the historical sketch, both flourishing genres in the nineteenth century, but the image was also disseminated in schools – in the children's books with a historical theme by an educational writer and in the school pictures by Johan Isings. The best-known example of a contemporary interpretation of Dutch literary history was the representation of the Muiden Circle, a legendary company of poets, writers, painters and musicians, who met regularly at the Amsterdam home of the patrician P.C. Hooft or at the castle near Muiden.[80] In the history painting of the nineteenth century, the Circle was portrayed no fewer than eight times as an evocation of the art of the Golden Age, and also of the cult of friendship and companionship, an image derived from the Enlightenment. Eventually this image foundered on the fact that it included artists who had not been or never could have been at Muiden Castle, for as knowledge of literary history increased so the demands of historical authenticity became more stringent. Nonetheless the Muiden Circle continued to be the educational subject that it had traditionally been. In the twentieth century, artists like Cornelis Jetses and Isings were still using it as a subject in their school pictures.[81]

The literary evocation of the Golden Age was linked to some extent to cultural commemorations which, like the celebrations of political history, were dictated by the calendar. In 1881, the tercentenary of the birth of the patrician and writer P.C. Hooft was celebrated with a performance of his play *Warenar*. A dispute broke out in the ranks of the festival committee as to whether this comedy should be expurgated to make it suitable for an audience of both sexes and all ages. An advocate of this censorship, the merchant J.A. Alberdingk Thijm, lost the argument and organized his own performance in the Stadsschouwburg, Amsterdam's principal theater, while a reading of the original *Warenar* was given by the Leiden professor Matthias de Vries in Felix Meritis, another theater in the capital. In 1885 the tercentenary of the birth of the poet and playwright Gerbrand Adriaensz Bredero was celebrated with a performance of his play *Moortje*, the first time it had been staged in two centuries. This proved to be the moment of truth for one scholar, Jan ten Brink, a professor at Leiden, who, after the German example of the "Romanprofessor," made fictitious contributions to the evocation of the Golden Age. He praised the dramatist for his natural voice; whereas in the seventeenth century "the glittering triumph of Latin humanism" had had a fatal impact on the development of an individual idiom, the lust for life evinced by Bredero and his counterpart in fine art, Frans Hals, proved to be the origin of a Dutch style, the "belly laugh of young Holland." After his death in 1901, Ten Brink vanished into scholarly oblivion. Predecessors, contemporaries and successors – literary scholars like Jan te Winkel and Gerrit Kalff – were not motivated in their history of the literature solely by a predilection for national art, and based their judgment on empirical research.[82] As in the case of art history, one can say that the history of literature acquired a positivist garb in a period when the poets and writers of the Golden Age were, more than ever, the cultural heroes of the nation.

The most spectacular happening in the literary evocation of the Golden Age was the resurrection of the poet Joost van den Vondel (1687-1779) on the Dutch stage; a resurrection that went further than the annual performance in the capital's Stadsschouwburg of *Gijsbreght van Aemstel*, Vondel's tragedy about the downfall of Amsterdam in the Middle Ages modeled on Virgil's *Aeneid*. It was one element of a major and enduring interest in the poet, expressed not only in new editions of his work – 23 of his plays were reissued between 1912 and 1914 – but also in the public domain. In 1867 a statue had been erected to Vondel in a new park in Amsterdam, which was subsequently named after him. Vondel, who converted to Catholicism in 1641, was so revered by his fellow Catholics that they even gave his name to the new neo-Gothic church in Amsterdam – officially consecrated as the Church of the Sacred Heart in 1880, it became universally known as the Vondelkerk. The commemorations of the bicentenary of his death in 1879 and the tercentenary of his birth in 1887 were echoed in Cologne (Vondel's birthplace) and Antwerp. In 1887 a plaque was mounted on the house in Cologne where he was born – at the combined instigation of J.A. Alberdingk Thijm and his Rhineland kindred spirit,

The statue of Vondel in Vondelpark, named for him, in Amsterdam. In the background, Vondelkerk, which also bears his name.

August Reichensperger, the champion of the neo-Gothic completion of Cologne Cathedral.[83]

The way for the return of Vondel's works to the theater was paved by writers of the eighteen-eighties and -nineties. In 1892 the poet Albert Verwey campaigned for Vondel's drama and was later to edit his complete works. In 1893 André Jolles, who worked on the radical journal *De Kroniek*, and the literary scholar Gerrit Kalff gathered around them a company of amateurs under the name *De jonge Joost* to perform the tragedies according to modern insights, in other words speaking Vondel's lines without the usual dramatic rhetoric. In 1898 two parts of Vondel's *Maeghden* were presented at a public rehearsal.[84] The same year also saw the publication of a monumental illustrated edition of *Gijsbreght van Aemstel*. The painter Antoon Derkinderen illuminated the text with medieval designs, Bernard Zweers composed the music, and the architect H.P. Berlage designed the stage sets. It was made clear in the introduction that the work had to be seen as an example of Dutch *Gesamtkunstwerk* – a synthesis of Dutch arts.

In January 1895 Vondel's play was staged in the Stadsschouwburg in Amsterdam – rebuilt after a fire – by the national theater company, the *Koninklijke Vereeniging "Het Nederlandsch Tooneel."* Adding force to the "opera style" that dominated performances of *Gijsbreght* at the end of the nineteenth century, characterized by the actors' sweeping theatrical gestures and the presence of a great many extras, was the performance of a large

Scene from Vondel's play *Adam in Exile,* with Willem Royaards in the center.

choir and the Concertgebouw orchestra. "All of them, without exception, broke the verses into pieces as if they were dry branches and not the supple green twigs of a living, flowering tree," wrote Gerrit Kalff, the advocate of the extraordinary power of Vondel's text.[85] The next generation of theater directors, men like Eduard Verkade and, above all, Willem Royaards, endeavored to put on versions sympathetic to contemporary thinking. They were the exponents of the ideal of a stylized theater, which took hold around the turn of the century and visibly tried to involve all the dimensions of the drama in a single, all-encompassing production – in the melding of sets, costumes and acting. Direction consequently became much more important. The theater director moved up to the level of the orchestra conductor.

Verkade's heart lay in the Middle Ages. His staging of Vondel's *Gijsbreght* in 1918 was consequently medieval in concept, and favored a non-illusionist set. Royaards concentrated primarily on giving readings from the literature of the seventeenth century. According to his biographer Top Naeff, his declamation of Vondel's epic poem *Geboortclock* (Natal Bell) in the Grote Schouwburg in Rotterdam on the occasion of Princess Juliana's birth in 1909 was "an event which, like a veritable bell, a warning bell, awakened in many people the awareness of a scandalous lack, and focused the public's attention on these national treasures lying hidden in closed books."[86] In 1908 Royaards directed a production of *Warenar* by P.C. Hooft, going on to perform several of Vondel's dramas with his own repertory company, often with music and sets by contemporary artists. The highlight of this series was the production of *Gijsbreght van Aemstel* he directed – most unusually performed in the summer – at the Dutch Music Festival in 1912. This time, Alphons Diepenbrock's music was played by the Concertgebouw orchestra conducted by Willem Mengelberg. It was this theatrical synthesis that Royaards wanted to achieve. In 1919 the director was honored by the University of Utrecht, where he was awarded an honorary doctorate by the art historian Willem Vogelsang. Royaards was praised for rediscovering the imagination, making the voices of the Dutch poets heard again, and achieving a unity of all dimensions of the drama. It was a hymn by and to "conservative grand-bourgeois thinking."[87]

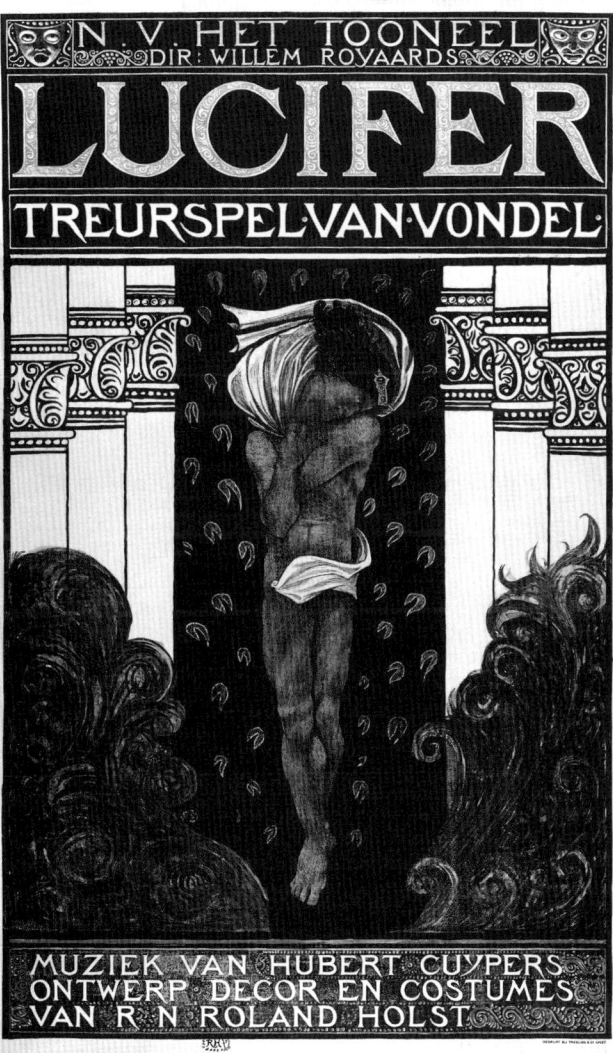

Poster for the performance of Vondel's tragedy *Lucifer* directed by Willem Royaards.

The statue of a dying Count Adolf van Nassau in Heiligerlee. The wording on the plaque reads: "May 23, 1563; the first victory in the eighty-year struggle for the freedom of the Netherlands."

Remembering the Revolt

In 1826 a monument, a small pyramid, was erected in Heiligerlee, a village near the town of Winschoten in the northern province of Groningen and the site of a battle between the troops of Count Louis of Nassau and the Spanish King Philip II in 1568 – the start of what came to be known as the Eighty Years' War. The monument had been built there on the initiative of a schoolteacher. The village had earned a place in the history of the nation and had consequently become a popular destination for excursions. Several times a year, the Winschoten militia would march to Heiligerlee, a procession that traditionally ended in one of the local hostelries, the Café Schrage. The militia were accompanied by boys from Winschoten who, equally traditionally, joined battle with their contemporaries from Heiligerlee. The annual Heiligerlee festival, held on or around the anniversary on May 21, was primarily an occasion for the gentlemen's club *De Harmonie* in Winschoten. The members tried to regulate the celebrations, although in 1870 there were complaints in the *Winschoter Courant* that the members were on the club terrace listening to music and speeches in comfort, whereas those who were less well endowed

The Admirals' victory float in the historical procession in Alkmaar in 1898.

In 1873 King William III lays the first stone for the Alcmaria Victrix monument to commemorate the Relief of Alkmaar.

with worldly goods had to seek their amusement in the heat and the dust outside in the street.[88]

Public concern about events like these grew markedly after 1848. There was pressure to make traditional festivities more respectable, and give them a meaning for the lower classes that reflected the values associated with the creation of the nation. This patriotic fervor initially came from the local branches of the *Maatschappij tot Nut van 't Algemeen* (Society for the Promotion of the Public Good), a national society dating from the Enlightenment. The calendar provided the dates, indicating the three hundredth anniversary of a number of memorable historical events. The most important dates of the Dutch Revolt were celebrated during the next few decades. In Heiligerlee, for example, the foundation stone for a new monument was laid in May 1868. A statue of Count Adolf of Nassau, who had fallen in the battle and was portrayed at the moment of his death, was built on the site of the pyramid. The new monument, the initiative for which came from the headmaster of the primary school, was not only larger than its predecessor, it was also more personal and dramatic. In 1873 King William III came to unveil the statue. A royal presence was standard procedure at such commemorations, so that the modern-day bond between the people, the country and the monarchy could be stressed.[89]

The celebrations were organized to boost the public's historical awareness. In the politically turbulent years after 1848 national history proved inimical to a single explanation, so these events also provided the opportunity for a national debate about the significance of the Revolt. Sometimes monuments were unveiled during the jubilee celebrations; where they replaced existing memorials, as in Heiligerlee, they were usually rather more melodramatic. If the events being commemorated were instructive, a committee of citizens would use this as an argument to make the festivities grander or more refined. There were organized historical parades rather than casual processions, didactic poems rather than popular ballads, and cantatas rather than drinking sprees. By European standards, the melodrama of the historical celebrations in the Netherlands was always fairly modest. On a tour through the Netherlands, the German urban architect Karl Scheffler observed that, while the revolt of a small nation against the vast Habsburg empire under Philip II had undoubtedly been a heroic drama of classic dimensions, the victory had not resulted in self-glorification: "Dutch heroism is anything but noisy." Scheffler was struck by the lack of excess in the official commemoration of the Revolt, the absence of grandiose and extravagant gestures like those with which other nations called attention to their glorious past. "The people are essentially not festive. So what their celebrations lack in appearance, they make up for in essentials. This is why in many ways Holland is so much more than the casual glance reveals."[90]

Alkmaar in North Holland is one of three Dutch towns – the others are Leiden and Groningen – to have the tradition of a local historical festival. In Alkmaar it was customary to commemorate the relief of the town on October 8: the date in 1573 when, for fear of the rising water and the risk of drowning, the mercenaries fighting for the Spanish Duke of Alva decided to abandon their siege. The festival was a rather disorganized affair, but in any event provided an annual excuse to let off fireworks, something that the people of Alkmaar regarded as the town's specialty. In 1860 the townspeople formed an

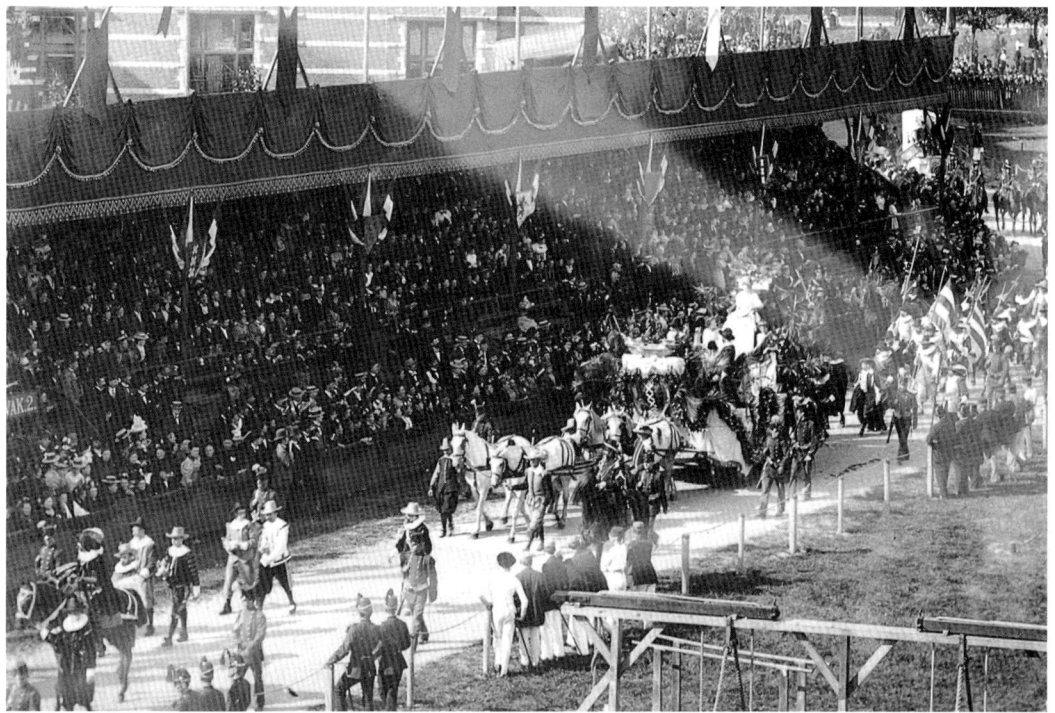

The historical and allegorical procession parades past the grandstand behind the Stedelijk Museum in Amsterdam, September 7, 1898.

association to celebrate the commemoration of the Relief of Alkmaar in a more orderly fashion. The annual festivals achieved a high point in 1873, during the tercentenary celebrations, when King William III came to lay the first stone for a monument to "Alcmaria Victrix" (Victorious Alkmaar). On this occasion, the festival committee also included Catholic townspeople, who had previously remained aloof from the whole business. In orthodox Protestant circles, in contrast, it was decided to hold a separate service of commemoration in the Grote Kerk. The statue of victorious Alkmaar, portrayed as Victoria, goddess of victory, was to be designed by a member of the panel of judges, who had rejected all the other entries before awarding the commission to one of its own. The new phenomenon of electric light was also seen in Alkmaar that evening. Members of the Physica society had stationed themselves in the attic window of a bookshop to generate electricity.[91]

Three years later, on October 8, 1876, the statue of "Alcmaria Victrix" was unveiled by J. Heemskerk, the minister of home affairs. He delivered an oration praising the spirit of freedom and the bonds between the Netherlands and the House of Orange. Unfortunately, the gale force wind rendered him inaudible and whipped away the covering from the statute before the official unveiling. After this, the organization of the celebration collapsed, although the annual fireworks, usually let off without any controls, continued to cause a commotion. After 1900 there was a change of mood and the celebrations of 1907 reflected a new spirit; they became a celebration of the House of Orange with nationalist undertones. The official speech was given by the chairman of the new

Algemeen Nederlandsch Verbond (General Dutch Alliance), who "drew on the past" and denounced national indifference – an attitude he condemned, referring to the Finns, the Poles, the Irish, the Boers in South Africa, the Frisians and the Flemings, who in their struggle for national recognition seemed to demonstrate on a daily basis the truth of the saying "a brave people will never perish."[92]

Parades

During the inauguration celebrations in 1898, there was a historical parade through the streets of Amsterdam, paying tribute to the foundation of the Dutch state and its colonies, and the glory of the arts and sciences in the Golden Age. Those who took part came from the non-socialist trade unions and Orange societies in Amsterdam. This procession was by no means unique; it was one expression of the passion for historical manifestations that was rife at the time.[93] In the Netherlands it was driven primarily by students, who organized masquerades during university anniversary celebrations in Leiden, Utrecht, Groningen and Delft. Sometimes these were allegorical parades, sometimes genuine historical pageants. The masquerade reflected a romantic view of history, because it could create for the spectators the impression of a past that was personalized through characters and brought to life through costumes and scenery.[94] By around 1900 the genre had developed into a veritable art form, requiring considerable organization and direction, and a significant contribution from the coffers of the local student body. In Delft and Leiden the organizers invited the artist Antoon Molkenboer to direct their events. In 1910 in Leiden he staged the "Entry of Stadholder William III into The Hague." He saw it as an opportunity to put his ideas of a *Gesamtkunstwerk* into practice, and asked the residents of Leiden who lived along the route to decorate their houses exclusively according to his directions. By then, the *cour* or "open court" had been an established finale to the parade for many years. It meant that the person portraying the stadholder not only had to be an accomplished horseman, he also had to be able to host a reception on a grand scale. Eventually this scaling up put an end to the student masquerade.[95]

Historical commemorations were customarily given a contemporary political spin. The unveiling of the new monument in Heiligerlee took place at a time when Bismarck's policy of forging German unification with blood and iron had awakened fears of an assault on the integrity of the Dutch state. According to the journal *De Nederlandsche Spectator*, the celebration was seen as a demonstration of the will to remain a free and independent people. "If our jubilant tones have penetrated to our powerful neighbor, as they probably have because we have held our celebrations close to the borders, he will have been convinced of this truth."[96] The official speaker in Alkmaar in 1873, the minister and national poet Nicolaas Beets, argued the thesis of "Christianity above religious differences" cherished by the liberal and Protestant elite. It had, he said, essentially been God's benison that had liberated Alkmaar – wind and weather had caused the weak to triumph over the Spanish besiegers. From this he drew the conclusion that it remained essential to "fear God, honor the King, put aside the pursuit of personal honor, sacrifice self-interest to the common good, suppress party bias, and rise above social problems through mutual consideration."[97]

"Christianity above religious differences" was an ideal that was coming under increasing threat in the last quarter of the nineteenth century. The historical celebrations caused an ongoing debate about the justification for the Dutch Revolt in a period when a liberal elite was setting the tone, but at the same time the orthodox tendency in Calvinism was becoming more militant, and Roman Catholicism was gaining in self-awareness. Around the turn of the century the socialists joined in. This debate was the historical and academic counterpart of the school funding controversy – a conflict about the fundamental principles and structure of education – and, in a wider context, the *Kulturkampf*, the battle over the influence of the church or the modern state on society, which was to assume more acute forms in the Netherlands' neighbor to the east, Prussia, and in France than it did in the Netherlands. Even the controversial commemoration of the Revolt had international repercussions.

On Sunday September 3, 1876, the Belgian city of Ghent celebrated the tercentenary of the Pacification of Ghent: the document of religious freedom in the provinces of the Netherlands. This celebration – the initiative of the uniformly liberal city council – subsequently became the subject of a quarrel between the liberal and Catholic press, both of which found in it historical ammunition for the "conflict of cultures" raging at the time between liberals and the pro-Rome Ultramontanes. The former saw the Pacification as the triumph of freedom of conscience over Habsburg absolutism. The latter interpreted the treaty as a form of deceit; the Calvinists and William of Orange misused the cessation of hostilities to fight the Catholic Church. The event was celebrated in Ghent with a historical parade, which acquired a degree of fame thanks to the participation of artists from the romantic school. The emphasis was on a contemporary, liberal interpretation of the Revolt. Portrayals of the Inquisition, complete with instruments of torture, and of the Spanish Duke of Alva's Council of Troubles, nicknamed the Tribunal of Blood, which condemned the Counts of Egmont and Hoorne to death, were calculated to focus criticism on Catholic absolutism.[98] Fourteen years later, in 1890, several statues were unveiled in Kleine Zavel Park in Brussels – they were of the leading figures in the sixteenth-century Revolt and were erected as part of the celebrations of the sixtieth anniversary of the Belgian struggle for independence. The city council organized a historical pageant, in which the natural desire for freedom was set against the tyranny of a foreign ruler. In the context of 1830 this was, of course, the Dutch king, William I.[99]

In the Netherlands, the leading exponent of the Calvinist vision was Guillaume Groen van Prinsterer, archivist to the Royal Household, who had published his guide to the history of the Netherlands, *Handboek der Geschiedenis van het Vaderland*, in 1846. Reprinted in 1862 and again in 1872, it was of significant influence because for a long while it remained the only work of its kind. Groen based his judgment on a theological concept: the Revolt against Hapsburg absolutism was fought on the principles and doctrine of the Gospels, and as a result the Netherlands prevailed and flourished. Its downfall followed on the abandonment of those same gospel truths in the nineteenth century. The book was laid out in textbook style in 1105 short paragraphs, comparable to verses in the Bible; the majority of them, almost 750, were devoted to the age of the Republic. Groen's argument ended on a depressed note; despite a moment of revival of faith after Napoleon was driven out in 1813, the Netherlands had again returned to the path of the

Revolution. His interpretation of Calvinism as the pre-eminent constructive factor in the history of the nation was picked up in the last quarter of the nineteenth century by the minister Abraham Kuyper, who derived from it the inspiration for his militancy. He wrote the political program for the first mass political party in the Netherlands, known as the Anti-Revolutionary Party (1879), a Calvinist rejection of the consequences of the French Revolution.

An overtly Catholic contribution to the commemorations and historiography of the Revolt was a relatively new phenomenon. Some people were inspired by Pope Pius IX's crusade against liberalism. The pastor of the village of Bovenkerk near Amsterdam, Jan Willem Brouwers, the prototype of the well-fed priest with a well-stocked wine cellar immortalized by the writer Lodewijk van Deyssel, wrote brochures attacking the historical celebrations. In one of them, he referred to the *Syllabus Errorum* by Pius IX, the document against liberalism in which the argument that "it is permissible to refuse allegiance to the legitimate rulers, indeed to foster revolution" was condemned as heresy. As it had been in 1568.[100] The longing for a share of their own in the history of the nation also inspired more gifted authors, among them the merchant and literary figure J.A. Alberdingk Thijm and, following in his footsteps, the physician from Westwoud, Willem Nuyens, who presented the Catholic view of the Revolt in a well-thought-out work. Thijm enlisted Nuyens to write a historical rebuttal to the Dutch translation of the influential book *The Rise of the Dutch Republic* by the American John Lothrop Motley. In their criticism of the "absolute dominance" of Calvinism in the motives for the Revolt, they rejected the idea that "Catholic" was synonymous with "Spanish" and argued for recognition of the Catholic role in the struggle against the absolutism of Philip II.[101] There was a change of emphasis in Catholic historiography. Thijm and Nuyens, both self-taught, shone the spotlight on the era before the Revolt, the Middle Ages, and looked critically at the history of the separation of the Northern and Southern Netherlands.[102] They could perhaps be seen as lone "Greater Netherlanders" long before the term acquired the meaning of a sympathizer with the ideals of the Flemish Movement around the turn of the century.

The liberal position in this historical conflict was the ideal of an impartial and positivist study of history. It was formulated by Robert Fruin who, in the 34 years he held the post of senior professor in the history of the Netherlands in Leiden – between 1860 and 1894 – was to acquire unparalleled authority. Fruin's philosophy of life was positivist by nature and, by extension, agnostic. This enabled him to combine thorough source research with an open, broad interest in various historical facets of the Revolt, and thus he was able to make a decisive contribution to the development of history into a discipline in its own right.[103]

After the Belgian revolution of 1830 and the disbanding of the union that had been brought about at the Congress of Vienna fifteen years earlier, Dutch historians were thrown back on the old fatherland: the Northern Netherlands. It was a reason for reconsidering an essential problem that had already cropped up in the revolutionary period at the end of the eighteenth century: how to establish a meaningful relationship between the glorious Republic of the sixteenth and seventeenth centuries and the new kingdom. Fruin tried to resolve this problem by means of a denial: because of the sovereignty of

250 years after the Peace of Munster.
The new peace between political, artistic and religious opponents,
De Amsterdammer, January 30, 1898.

the provincial institutions and because of its particularism, the Republic could no longer be a yardstick for the union that had come into being after 1795, under French rule. When he consequently described the Republic as "an interim period that is gone for ever," the description lived on until well into the twentieth century. "Do not the love of Orange and the republican convictions of our people, the components of our parliamentary monarchy, date from the Republic?" wondered the historian Gerhard Kernkamp in 1901. "Do we not owe to the Republic our colonies and our wealth, our self-esteem and our touchiness – the touchiness of a small nation with a great past?"[104]

In his empirical approach to the writing of history, which according to some contemporaries Fruin went about with "stoic composure," towards the end of the century he showed an increasing tendency to regard the Orange dynasty as a non-partisan beacon in the history of the nation. This embroiled him in several heated historical polemics about the character of William of Orange, whose violent death in 1584 was officially remembered in 1884. In a historical debate, fuelled by orthodox Protestant and Catholic emancipation, the images of "the Calvinist religious hero" or "the cunning Machiavellian strategist" persisted for some time. The polemic was ultimately resolved in favor of the image of "the moderate, tolerant and conciliatory Father of the Fatherland"; an old vision, but one brought up to date with a new force of conviction.[105] In Fruin's essays, the Orange dynasty was thus allocated a solid position in the history

The collection of national costume is brought out of the Rijksmuseum on its way to the
Open Air Museum in Arnhem in 1916.

De Amicis came across the cap brooches in a town, but the traditional dress was to be
seen mainly in the countryside. The exhibition of national costume in the Stedelijk
Museum in Amsterdam during Queen Wilhelmina's inauguration in 1898 attracted
25,000 visitors. It was a successful attempt to generate public interest in folklore. The
exhibits were displayed in groups based on three tribes. In the northern provinces and
in North Holland they were the Frisians; in the east of the Netherlands the Saxons; in the
southern provinces of Brabant and Limburg, including the area around Arnhem, the
Franks. The majority of the Dutch population actually belonged to the "Frisian tribe."[114]
The exhibition was governed by two notions. The first was that the traditional costumes
were originally linked to tribes and that one could tell the wearer's origins from his or
her dress. While great play was made of the "present unity of the Dutch people," the
traces of the former "differences between the tribes" nonetheless remained in evidence.
The second idea was that these original tribes continued to live in a relatively pure state,
particularly in rural areas. Town-dwellers were already displaying a certain homogeny
in their clothes. "In the prospect of dull uniformity, which, even in appearance, will probably one day be the fate of mankind," wrote Jan van Someren Brand, curator of the
Stedelijk Museum, "let us rejoice while we still can in the colorful garb, bearing witness
to the people's own taste and ingenuity" with which country folk contrasted so favorably with the conformity of the townspeople. Happily, he concluded, "as yet not all
Dutch men are imitation Londoners, not all Dutch women imitation Parisiennes."[115]

Was the rural community around 1900 still actually that bulwark of tradition the display in the Stedelijk Museum would suggest that it was? There were still local costumes; people sometimes even dressed in greater finery or bought larger cap brooches. On the other hand, people in the country increasingly started to wear town clothes. It was usually the men who first turned their backs on the local dress. Their work brought them into contact with the town and so they were more likely to dress according to the prevailing fashion, if only for fear of being pointed out as a peasant.[116] Both trends continued in women's dress; both fashion and the desire to retain a traditional costume. By the beginning of the twentieth century there were only a few districts where everyone wore the old costumes. The last bastions were in the province of Zeeland, along the southeastern coast of the Zuiderzee, roughly between Huizen and Staphorst, and on the islands of Marken and Urk. But even where people continued to dress traditionally, this fashion was itself subject to change. Caps became smaller or larger, garments fell into disuse or were actually introduced into the local costume. In other areas, as we have said, it was only the women who still wore the local costume (or parts of it), while men and children had effectively ceased to do so. There was also an evident trend everywhere for more subdued colors. In some cases this derived from a puritan sensibility among orthodox Protestants, but sometimes it was the result of the inescapable influence of city clothes.[117]

Local costume was sometimes deliberately chosen and disseminated as a national symbol. This was a European phenomenon. In Norway, for example, the Hardanger costume had played an important role as evidence of Norwegian identity in the struggle for national independence at the end of the nineteenth century.[118] In the Netherlands, the Volendam costume had become a factor in individual identity around the turn of the century. International interest threatened to make this tradition artificial. In the weekly journal *De Amsterdammer* of February 20, 1916, an advocate of folklore criticized this fashionable "Volendamery." Neither the government nor art historians had ever taken any steps to have the national costumes described or inventoried. The consequence was the inexpert exploitation of the Volendam fisherman. "Many people in other countries will find it impossible to imagine our country and its inhabitants other than as that image of rusticity, backwardness, lumbering gracelessness and stubbornness."[119]

In the Dutch variant, traditional costume was first and foremost an expression of regional differences. The northern province of Friesland was the first to endeavor to reconstruct a regional identity because people felt threatened by national integration, the consequence of the unitary state. The interest in the Frisian language and culture had led to the foundation of a society to promote the Frisian language and history, the *Friesch Genootschap voor Geschied-, Oudheid- en Taalkunde,* as early as 1827, followed in 1844 by a second, *It Selskip foar Fryske taal- en Skriftekennisse.* The former institution was more genteel and broader-based, numbered a high proportion of aristocrats and university graduates among its members, and was in essence an urban affair. The Selskip was also born in town, but eventually achieved its greatest success in the villages. It brought the modern idea of distinct and individual education and a distinct and individual culture from the town to the country, and then "dressed the villagers in old clothes."[120] The Selskip was dominated by the lower middle classes and focused on the "common people," tradesmen, laborers and farmers, who could already speak Frisian but now also had to learn to be Frisian. It was something that schoolmasters saw as being part of their job, and this was to persist in rural Friesland until well into the twentieth century, with the schoolmasters playing the main role in disseminating a regional culture.[121]

In their social structure, the two Frisian societies presented the same picture as nationalist movements elsewhere in Europe. It was the ministers, tradesmen and school-teachers who made up the nucleus of groups that devoted themselves to awakening a regional or national consciousness. What is remarkable is that the cultural identity of Friesland was reconstructed in a period when this same province was losing countless members of the aristocracy, the upper middle class and the farming classes to emigration. Here, too, the Frisian case is comparable to larger-scale examples of cultural nationalism elsewhere in Europe.[122] After the departure of the stadholder's court from Leeuwarden a century earlier, in 1747, and the closure of the provincial university in Franeker in 1843, wealthy Frisians followed the siren calls of The Hague as the seat of government or the Gelderland valley as a pleasant place to live. The less well-to-do were forced by the farming crisis in 1878 to try their luck elsewhere. Around the turn of the century there were remarkably high numbers of Frisian immigrants in Amsterdam and The Hague. They also featured in the books by Louis Couperus, who was himself of Frisian origin.[123]

Members of the Frisian Society also set about preserving antique objects with regional significance. As early as 1853, with their support, Joost Hiddes Halbertsma, a Mennonite pastor from Deventer, set up a collection of Frisian antiquities, the *Kabinet van Friesche Oudheden*. He had borrowed the format from the British example of regional folklore museums and had called upon the "Frisians" to realize that a Frisian collection would be a safe place to preserve the heritage which would no longer be cherished with such care in the "imminent assimilation of the nationalities of Europe." The collection was predominantly an assortment of clothing and household utensils from Hindeloopen, which had had an urban mercantile history and, unlike Volendam and Marken, was not involved with fishing. The town thus became the topos of Frisian folklore. The Hindeloopen living room was the greatest attraction at the *Historical Exhibition of Friesland*, held in 1877. The following year it was exported to the Paris Exhibition, where it became established as the image of the Netherlands.[124] Toward the end of the century this deliberate evocation of regional history also received royal approval. During their tour of the provincial capitals, Queen Emma and Queen Wilhelmina had seen the local dress. During her visit to Leeuwarden in 1892, Wilhelmina appeared in Frisian dress and was photographed in this maidenly costume.

In the second half of the nineteenth century, interest in the traditional elements of rural culture was also aroused outside Friesland. This was the start of what would lead, in the period between the wars, to mobilization for a regional culture and the formation of regional groupings, the best known of which was to be *Brabantia Nostra* in the Province of North Brabant.[125] One of the underlying motives for this regional awareness was a resistance – not necessarily overtly expressed – to the cultural ascendancy of Holland. We can surmise this from the lack of any such interest in Holland itself. In so far as either of the provinces of Holland – North or South – paid any heed at all to

The young Princess Wilhelmina in traditional Frisian costume during her visit to Leeuwarden in 1892.

popular culture, it was focused on the periphery, on Volendam, for instance, or the island of Marken. The reconstruction of "Old Holland" at the international hotel and travel exhibition staged in Amsterdam in 1895 was dominated by examples and buildings from "dead" towns. It is no coincidence that at the exhibition of costume in 1898 the traditional culture was divided into a Frisian (northwestern), Saxon (eastern) and Frankish (southern) sphere of influence, after the Germanic tribes that had supposedly originally settled in these areas. This breakdown meant that Holland could simply be divided up between the three tribes; a view that was to prevail in the literature of folklore and the associated philological literature until well into the twentieth century.[126]

The organized interest in popular culture was the product of a middle-class initiative, which also called on the Dutch not to be left behind in a European trend. The writer Marcellus Emants had noted in 1875 that the Netherlands had no museum of folklore in which the national costumes could be displayed, contrasting this with Sweden, which had two such institutions – the Nordiska Museet and Skansen, both in Stockholm. Following the Frisian success at the exhibition in 1877, the plea was at last heard and acted upon. In 1879 the Netherlands Museum of History and Art in The Hague opened a gallery of national costume, described as "the customs and traditions" of the people. In 1887 this institution moved to the new Rijksmuseum in Amsterdam, and the collection went with it.[127] Prompted by the successful exhibition during the inauguration celebrations, there was a groundswell of opinion about the need for a national ethnographic museum. Early in 1904 the philologist Johan Gallée argued in the *Nederlandse Spectator* that the study of ethnography should not focus exclusively on the colonies, but should also pursue Dutch folklore studies. Five years later his pupil, the philologist Henri Logeman, was pointing to the examples of the open-air museums in Sweden and Denmark. Thanks to the energetic soldier Frederic Hoefer, who went to Scandinavia to see for himself, *Het Nederlands Openluchtmuseum* – a society to promote the establishment of an open-air museum in the Netherlands – was founded in 1912. Six years later, in Arnhem, the museum of the same name opened to the public.

Shortly after the opening, the Nederlands Openluchtmuseum made a name for itself in what was regarded as a major folklore event: the *Vaderlands Historisch Volksfeest*. It was organized in Arnhem in September 1919 by the journalist and folklore enthusiast, D.J. van der Ven, and culminated in a folklore procession of 108 groups from regions all over the Netherlands. It was a combination of two initiatives: the desire to celebrate the peace in the year that saw the official end of World War I, and the endeavor to promote Arnhem and its new open-air museum in the emerging tourist trade.[128] The *Vaderlands Historisch Volksfeest* had very distinguished patrons and drew thousands of visitors.[129] The primary motive for the celebrations, the Paris peace treaties, meant that particular attention was paid to the areas on the Netherlands' southern border – the southern regions of Limburg and the Flemish part of the province of Zeeland – which had initially been claimed by Belgium during the Paris negotiations. It was an opportunity for the people of Zeeland-Flanders and South Limburg to demonstrate their national allegiance, and their popular customs and traditions were highlighted.[130] The magnitude of the celebrations also provoked criticism, aimed at two aspects. "It caused me deep sorrow," commented the philologist Joseph Schrijnen, "that these beautiful and intimate aspects of the life of the Dutch people should have been exploited as a public spectacle in Arnhem."[131] Other commentators focused their criticism on the excessive nationalism in this "celebration of reaction," which appeared to be a response to the socialist leader Troelstra's failed attempt at revolution in November 1918, almost a year before.[132]

There was a musical strand in this expansion of folklore, expressed in a deliberate attempt to trace old folk songs and get people to sing them. Around the turn of the century, a student in Utrecht, Frits Coers (1870-1937), became the most important propagandist for the Dutch song. Abandoning his medical studies, he devoted himself to collecting and publishing Dutch songs and getting them performed. In his view, these songs were both an expression of the language, "the most direct expression of the inner emotions in the minds of the people," and a form of musical expression, "one of the main factors of a national identity." Coers believed that the Dutch people would gain in self-confidence through the rediscovery of the treasury of national songs because it reflected a "fierce passion" and pointed the way out of "the still so lethargic, indolent, dull, apathetic masses."[133] He set up a society for the Dutch song, *Het Nederlandse Lied,* which was filled with cultural authorities. In 1914 it was granted the right to call itself "Royal." The prototype of the hotheaded fraternity student, Coers coupled an authoritarian nature with boundless romanticism. This alienated supporters, but in his excess he was the typical representative of cultural nationalism, student style, for it was at precisely this time – around the turn of the century – that the vogue for traditional culture took root in student circles and in the youth movement.

"As it was in other countries, saving, preserving, collecting before it is too late became the watchword of the intellectuals who flocked to the new science of folklore."[134] The Dutch variant of this scientific interest was always characterized by the existence of a dichotomy between a historically-focused elite culture – in which historians pointed to the Golden Age, to great painters like Rembrandt and great poets like Vondel – and a popular culture, which came from a town or a district and was tied to it.[135] The establishment of the journal *Volkskunde* in 1888 marked the birth of folklore as a science. It was characterized by a growing interest in rural culture as the refuge for age-old values and as protection for traditions in modern society. The earliest researchers in this field concentrated primarily on the subject of immutability, of continuity. They assumed the existence of a specific and authentic rural civilization, in which change had to be regarded as harmful and degenerate; loss was the key word in many publications.

This position was not abandoned until the twentieth century, when the philologist and classical scholar Joseph Schrijnen expressed a different point of view. Change and modernization were stripped of their negative connotations. Local costume and customs were no longer seen as the original expressions of an "individual popular identity" but as traditions that had to be able to survive in their own right and should not be kept alive artificially.[136] Between 1915 and 1917 he published the two volumes of his *Nederlandsche Volkskunde,* a compilation in which he threw light on the treasury of popular culture against the backdrop of the "cynically indifferent" spirit of the age. Schrijnen marked a transition from the quest for antiquities to a scholarly discipline which looked systematically at the social context. As a Limburger and as a Catholic, he was moreover the spokesman for the view that the Dutch nation should not be shored up by a monolithic

The *Vaderlands Historisch Volksfeest* in Arnhem, 1919.

cultural nationalism, but that there were religious and regional differences: it was possible to discover different strata in the "mother earth of popular culture."[137]

The source tapped for the past evoked in the presentation of popular culture around 1900 was a far cry from the Dutch Revolt or the Golden Age. Instead people harked back to a Germanic origin. This was derived from the *Germanenforschung*, which had developed in Germany under the scholarly direction of Johann Gottfried Herder before 1800 and Jacob Grimm after 1800. It did not catch on in the Netherlands until much later. The historian Willem Frijhoff sought an explanation for the delayed response to an attractive, romantic idea in the dominant focus on the past of the Republic. The bourgeois elite had studied popular culture and cherished it as the early history of the state less in the Netherlands than anywhere else in Europe. Unlike Germany, it identified not with a Germanic past but with the historical forms that Dutch culture had assumed since the late Middle Ages – and particularly in the seventeenth century. A "cultural nation" had been constructed in the religious, political and economic flowering of the Republic. This distinction between "cultural nation" and popular culture dictated the fate of Dutch folklore throughout the nineteenth century. The way the historian Johan Huizinga concluded his lecture for American students in 1924 – *How Holland became a Nation* – with a plea for the replacement of the adjective "Dutch" by "Hollandish" or "Netherlandish" is also relevant in this context. "Dutch," he believed, was too reminiscent of a Germanic entity. "If the vague and antiquated word Dutch got out of use, it would mean that the English speaking nations were beginning to see us as such as we are to-day and such as

Inhabitants of the island of Marken pose for tourists.

we ourselves wish to be known, no longer in the caricature of an old fisherman smoking a pipe."[138]

Against the image of the Golden Age, which despite all the differences between Protestantism and Catholicism nonetheless governed the collective memory, popular culture not only referred to a past prior to the seventeenth century but also introduced timeless elements. In the Netherlands, said Frijhoff, it specifically did not cover "the whole national culture, but was typical of local and regional individuality from the out-set." It was only in the second place that the regional culture acquired an added value on a national level, but then as a chamber of antiquities and not as the basic values of a national cultural community. At the end of the nineteenth century, ministers like Ottho Heldring and Jacobus Craandijk had discovered the charms of the local people's beliefs and the innocence of the local traditions during their walks through rural areas. "But they did not see them as an essential element of the national culture. On the contrary, progress would soon sweep away this local culture in favor of the national culture –

which was precisely why it was so industriously recorded." Folklore in the Netherlands became first and foremost a discovery of what was "different" in one's own country rather than a construction of what was "specific to the country" in comparison with surrounding countries. "People had the exotic at home, but the true national culture stood head and shoulders above it."[139] The fact that the exhibition of national dress in 1898 was surrounded by historical events to do with the Golden Age or in honor of Rembrandt actually seemed to be a confirmation of this hierarchy.

The Dutch centennial celebrations in 1913

In 1913 the Netherlands celebrated the centennial of her regained freedom – the overthrow of the Napoleonic regime in 1813 and the proclamation of independence by a triumvirate. But, above all, people were remembering that it was then that the Prince of Orange crossed the North Sea from England and landed on the beach at Scheveningen. This was the fact that caught the public imagination, not only because of the image it evoked, but also because it was in line with a political effort to identify the Netherlands with Orange. Nevertheless, the historical dimension of the centennial aroused ambivalent emotions. The landing of the Prince of Orange did not have the glamor of a heroic deed, while the promulgation of the proclamation by the triumvirate was similarly prosaic. From a historical perspective, moreover, French rule was not necessarily regarded as having been an oppressive occupation in all respects or by every citizen. It had also been the cradle of the modern state.

The independence celebrations officially started on June 18, (the day of the commemoration of the Battle of Waterloo) with jubilant peals rung on the church bells. The most appealing event in the celebrations of 1813, the landing of the Prince of Orange on the beach at Scheveningen, was re-enacted on various beaches in the Netherlands in 1913. The weekly journal *De Zondagsbode* stressed the commonplace nature of that moment. "One can scarcely look up without seeing the prince stepping ashore. So this is *the* great event that we have to remember and for which we ought to be thankful." The writer had "not been able to scrape up more than a paltry little pile of gratitude" because it irritated him "to see someone whose greatest act in his life was 'stepping ashore.'"[140] Festivities were organized in more than thirty towns in the second half of the year. The "1913 Plan," designed by the trade and industry association, the *Maatschappij voor Nijverheid en Handel,* for activities on a national scale, took shape in exhibitions and conferences, in special theatre performances and castle tours. Particularly striking were the *First National Shipping Exhibition* in Amsterdam-North and the exhibition *The Woman 1813-1913,* likewise in Amsterdam. This was a reprise of the successful exhibition on women at work staged during Wilhelmina's inauguration celebrations in 1898, as was the national costume event, a parade of traditionally clad citizens and country people in front of the royal family in Amsterdam. Against "the backdrop of sophisticated people and modern houses," Zeeland children danced a clog dance and a Frisian choir sang songs in Old Frisian.[141] In Eindhoven, the electrical goods company Philips sponsored a modern gymnastics display in which the children taking part performed exercises in time to Dutch folksongs.

Entrance to the exhibition *The Woman 1813-1913* in Amsterdam.

Historical reflection

In a special festival edition of *Het Nieuws van de Dag*, the historian Hajo Brugmans wrote that 1813 was much more significant than the event – the famous landing – that was the subject of most of the fuss. "We still stand on the soil shaped by the French era, brought to an end by 1813. We still live under the state institutions that we put in place during this period."[142] At the opening of the exhibition on *The Woman 1813-1913*, the historian Johanna Naber said that it would be foolish to try to deny "that Napoleonic rule was a great blessing to our country." During French rule, the Netherlands had acquired a civilian government that "created order and made each person's advancement dependent on merit and competence, and on that alone. The hard hand of the foreigner taught us to take seriously the application of the principles of a united people, of the equality of all before the law, about which people had been so passionately enthusiastic in theory, but which they had systematically backed away from in practice."[143] Amidst all the celebratory euphoria, the French oppressors could even count on sympathetic attention here and there. In *Propria Cures,* the weekly magazine for Amsterdam students, there was a complaint about contemporaries who seemed to forget the triumvirate "that gave us back our freedom," while honoring the man "who enslaved us: Napoleon. One may find a portrait of the brilliant tyrant above the desk in many rooms."[144]

"Why is it that, in this year of commemoration, we are finding it so hard to strike the right note of jubilation?" wondered the historian and Leiden professor Johan Huizinga, when on June 11, 1913 he delivered the memorial address to the society of Dutch literature, the *Maatschappij der Nederlandse Letterkunde,* on *The significance of 1813 to the Netherlands' spiritual civilization.* Looking back at the men of 1813 "there is inevitably mingled in our praise of them our impatience with the slowness and weakness of the others, and our epic voice always cracks. And even the bass has no force: the just cries of hatred of the tyrant no longer pass our lips: we have for so long learned to prize the benefactions of oppression."[145] Huizinga found no inspiration in 1813 – in the art it produced, in the aesthetic expression of the inner life and of the world, the seventeenth century soared far above the eighteenth. "By purely intellectual moral standards, the eighteenth century in the Netherlands, just as it did elsewhere, signified progress over the seventeenth. We should like to value it as progress, but our hearts ask for something different." For "the capacity for expression" had been "Holland's greatest treasure in Rembrandt's century." And Huizinga and his contemporaries had "again become supremely open" to this core value.[146]

Religious reflection

The political celebrations also had a religious dimension. The Protestants stressed the regaining of independence in 1813 as a sign of divine guidance. Or, as the minister of the Dutch Evangelical Church in Brussels, W. Hoek, put it, it was difficult to name a single event "that more strikingly brought to light and more clearly proclaimed the miraculous guidance of the Lord, with Country and People and Royal Family."[147] On Sunday November 16, 1913, one day before the official celebration of independence, the General Synod of the Dutch Reformed Church called on its members to "give praise and thanks to God for the blessings received from Him, and pray for His blessing on our Fatherland and our beloved Royal Family." In the context of the argument going on within Dutch Protestantism, this synodal letter provoked opposition. The minister Bart de Ligt described the letter as superficial and somber. "Complete lack of understanding of the great seriousness of the times. Complete lack of insight into this noisy and repeatedly failed celebration." He criticized the synod in a pamphlet. Surely, mused De Ligt, we are not supposed to give thanks because godlessness is on the increase among the masses, the church has lost its influence over the proletariat, and the great majority of workers are chronically overworked, while the people are robbed of their moral yardsticks by neo-Malthusianism, the cinema and salacious literature.[148] *De Blijde Wereld,* the organ of socialist ministers, reported that the figures for wine consumption in 1913 showed that a great deal of heavy drinking went on. "Our people have shown that they are liberated from the French, but not from alcohol."[149]

Catholics celebrated independence primarily through the coming of Willem, Cardinal Van Rossum, who was sent to the Netherlands as the papal envoy. This Redemptorist, the first Dutch cardinal since the Reformation, arrived in Amsterdam on July 4, 1913, went to Utrecht and his birthplace, Zwolle, and visited Queen Wilhelmina. He took his leave in a ceremony of homage in the Basilica of St. Servatius in Maastricht on August 17. This was typical of the group consciousness of the Catholic minority in the Netherlands. A cardinal from Rome was received and honored as a Prince of the Church. It was equally typical that a commemorative book was produced to mark the occasion, examining and extolling the ecclesiastical, social and cultural achievements of the Dutch Catholics in the century between 1813 and 1913, and confirming their loyalty to the Dutch state.[150] It was a way of gauging the progress of Catholic emancipation.

Peace Palace

Of all the celebratory events, it was the opening of the Peace Palace in The Hague on August 28, 1913, that attracted the greatest attention. It was the tangible result of two international peace conferences in The Hague. The home of a Permanent Court of Arbitration, it was to make The Hague a center of international law. In the presence of Queen Wilhelmina and the main sponsor of the building, the American businessman Andrew Carnegie, the chairman of the Carnegie Foundation presented the key to the front doors of the Palace to the president of the Board of Governors of the Court, Jonkheer R. de Marees van Swinderen, at that time still minister of foreign affairs in the Christian government headed by Heemskerk. A choir conducted by Anton Averkamp sang works by Palestrina and Valerius.

Andrew Carnegie (1835-1919), born in Scotland, made his fortune in the United States from his Pennsylvania Railroad Company and the Carnegie Steel Company. When he retired he devoted much of his fortune to founding libraries and universities. Later he extended his philanthropy to promoting international peace. He funded the construction of three "temples of peace," the Peace Palace in The Hague being the most striking. There was an international design competition, which was not without rancor, and eventually the design by the French architect Louis Marie Cordonnier was chosen. He had taken his inspiration from the *Nieuw-Vlaamse* movement, a school of architects who tried to replicate the historical buildings of a Flemish Renaissance in an eclectic style. The commended entries included one from the Austrian Otto Wagner, who broke new ground with his neo-classicist approach, but his design was ultimately rejected by the jury as being too modern. The Dutch architect H.P. Berlage also failed to win the commission. Cordonnier's design was eventually built, albeit with modifications by a Dutch architect, J.A.G. van der Steur. From the point of view of modern architecture, the fact that this prestigious building had been built in such a visibly historicistic style was perceived as a wasted opportunity.

The establishment of a Permanent Court of Arbitration had been the result of the first international peace conference, which had been held in The Hague in 1899 at the instigation of Tsar Nicholas II. At this meeting proposals were put forward for disarmament and for international rules of law governing war on land (the Hague Land War Rules), as well as for an international procedure of mediation and arbitration, and for a tribunal. The diplomats were able to agree to these if they were voluntary; an international obligation proved unacceptable. During the second peace conference in 1907, again held in The Hague, a Permanent Court of Justice was added, together with a Prize Court for the seafaring nations. Neither proposal was finalized at this meeting. The delegates parted, planning to meet for the third time in 1915. Meanwhile, in 1903, Carnegie had signed the charter for a foundation to finance the construction of the Permanent Court and a library of studies in international law.

The new Peace Palace in The Hague.

Queen Wilhelmina, Queen Emma, and Prince Hendrik return from the opening of the
Peace Palace in The Hague, August 28, 1913.

The Hague had become a preferred venue for international meetings, with a reputation comparable to those of Brussels and Geneva. The Interparliamentary Union had convened its annual meetings there in 1893 and 1894, and the first conference on international private law was also held in The Hague in 1893. The Dutch lawyer Tobias Asser had worked exceptionally hard to bring this about – eighteen years later, in 1911, he was to be awarded the Nobel Prize for Peace in recognition of his efforts. The Hague's image as the center of peacekeeping through international law had meanwhile set others thinking. While the city council and the government were deciding on the site for the Permanent Court of Arbitration (Zorgvliet), the *Stichting voor Internationalisme*, a foundation for internationalism headed by the physician and theosophist Pieter Eykman and the pacifist and adherent of spiritualism Paul Horrix, published a plan to found a city of world peace in the dunes near The Hague. In the spring of 1905, at their request, the architect K.P.C. de Bazel produced a design for a "world capital" with the "Peace Palace" at its heart. He had taken his inspiration from the "città ideale," the sketch for a model city named Sforzinda, by the Italian architect and sculptor Antonio Filarete (1410-1469) for the Sforza family in Milan. The foundation was never able to realize De Bazel's design, a circular city whose main roads lead to a single central square dominated by the Peace Palace, but Berlage adopted it when he designed an expansion plan for The Hague in 1908.[151]

National mission

This short-lived revival of a vision of The Hague as the capital of world peace inspired others. In February 1913 Cornelis van Vollenhoven published a pamphlet, *De eendracht van het land* (The Harmony of the Country), in which he undertook to bring about "a warm tide" in public opinion in the Netherlands, which would break the ice, so that "after two hundred years of decline, our country will have resumed its international role before the end of 1913." The jurist and liberal democrat Van Vollenhoven had been professor of colonial law and the customary law of the Dutch East Indies at the University of Leiden since 1901. In 1910, in the cultural journal *De Gids,* he had written about "Holland's vocation." The article was reissued in the jubilee year, and this time it provoked many more reactions. The key point of his argument was that the Netherlands should accept its vocation in bringing about a "militant Peace." The country should take the initiative in forming an international peacekeeping force, because the new Peace Palace in The Hague could only be a dynamic institution if there were sanctions against failures to call upon or comply with arbitration. The idea should be written into international law at the third international peace conference in 1915. "This task looms before us like Utrecht Cathedral."

According to Van Vollenhoven, the Netherlands was ready for this leading role, having pacified the whole of the Indonesian archipelago. At home, meanwhile, the people had successfully rid themselves of the status of "yokels." In his view, the Netherlands was now a country that wanted to seize the year 1913 with both hands to show that it was not made up of clog-wearing Volendamers, but was an energetic young nation which wanted to get back into the top rank.[152] This was not just an expression of contemporary zeal – it was also part of an ongoing debate on the question as to whether the Netherlands could ever resume the position it had once occupied during its Golden Age. It was a reaction to what the historian Gerhard Kernkamp had described a decade earlier as "the touchiness of a small nation with a great past." At the international historical congress in Rome in 1903, a colleague of Van Vollenhoven's, the Leiden professor Petrus Blok, had delivered a panegyric to the small nation whose great past actually gave it a right to a role of international importance. With the first peace conference and the establishment of the Court of Arbitration in mind, he had wanted to make it clear that The Hague had again become "a center of general diplomatic activity."[153] In 1913 Blok's successor, H.Th. Colenbrander, wrote that even if nothing were to come of it in 1913, the argument was in any event proof of "the new spirit" that possessed the best of the people.[154]

In the new century the Netherlands seemed to have transmuted the burden of its great past into a new national awareness based on an idealism founded in international law. This was put to the test sooner than expected: in World War I the country's large warring neighbors, Germany and Great Britain, respected the neutrality of the Netherlands. In a review of the war, Colenbrander counted himself and his nation fortunate in this idealism. "Situated on the borders, where French, English, German influence meet, subjected to all these influences, but dealing with them on its own, the Netherlands would best remain true to its vocation by not siding with Germany against England or vice versa." He added that this world war had also provided justification for two secessions: the international recognition of the secession from the Holy Roman Empire in 1648 and of the split with Belgium in 1839. "We have not been trampled underfoot, as must have been the case if there had been a kingdom of the seventeen provinces in 1914."[155] The ultimate reconciliation with a great past: in 1914 the Netherlands appeared to have been proved right by its national history.

Albert Hahn, *May 1, On The Wounded Earth, De Notenkraker*, March 28, 1917.

A Dutch maidservant pours jenever in the Dutch café with East Indies monuments in
Paris (1900), *l'Illustration*, June 2, 1900.

2

The Netherlands and the World

The tropical image of the Netherlands

The face that the Netherlands wanted to show the world towards the end of the nineteenth century had a tropical tint. The kingdom's entry for the 1900 world exhibition in Paris was an Indonesian pavilion featuring a Javanese village and a house with a curved roof from Minangkabau (Sumatra). Its exotic character attracted a good deal of interest. A Dutch flag had also flown over a Javanese village eleven years before at the 1889 world exhibition in Paris in the shadow of the Eiffel Tower. The presentation included gamelan players, dancers and a restaurant serving an Indonesian menu. It was here that the French composer Claude Debussy heard a gamelan orchestra. He said he was enchanted by the counterpoint in the Javanese music, which made the work of the rediscovered polyphonic composer Giovanni da Palestrina "child's play."

The efforts to depict a colonial dimension of the fatherland were to be seen abroad in Paris, in Chicago (1893) and also at home. In 1883 an international colonial and export exhibition was staged on the site behind the new Rijksmuseum in Amsterdam. Visitors were able to see colonial products and culture, and authentic inhabitants too. Delegations of people from Surinam and Java were assembled in communal houses under the supervision of a genuine official – an assistant resident. In 1898 the national exhibition of women's work featured the East and West Indies as a matter of course. Here, too, there was a mock Javanese village, a Kampong Insulinde, where visitors could experience the smells and colors of Indonesia and enjoy watching dancers and gamelan players from Solo. In the West Indian room there was Louise Yda, a Creole woman from Paramaribo, who had made the crossing especially for the occasion.[1] This exotic element was repeated at the exhibition *The Woman 1813-1913*, which was organized as part of the celebrations to mark the centenary of the end of French rule. The colonial section included an Indonesian house. It attracted considerable interest but was dominated by images of European women and their domestic circumstances.

This was a side effect of the growth in the European population in the Dutch East Indies. In 1860 there were 42,000 Europeans in the colonies, including some 11,000 women. By 1905 this number had more than doubled to 95,000. The percentage of women had increased from twenty-six to forty. The traditionally large proportion of military personnel among this colonial elite, on the other hand, had dropped.[2] These figures reveal that a European bourgeoisie was emerging in Indonesia and progressively giving

colonial life a more middle class image. However, compared with the thirty-seven million inhabitants designated as "natives," they remained a tiny minority.

Imperialism

The "treasure of Lombok" was exhibited in the Rijksmuseum in 1898. This was a collection of manuscripts and precious gold and silver objects that had been seized during a
punitive military expedition in 1894 to deal with the rebellious ruler in Cakranegara on
the island of Lombok. Public opinion in the Netherlands around the turn of the century
was fueled by tales of heroism during what was referred to at the time as the pacification of the whole Dutch East Indies – the subjection of regional rulers to colonial authority through conquest, starting in the center of Java and spreading to the Outer Islands.
The violent excesses of this action were glossed over, when they were reported at all. The
turn of the century was also the zenith of what, after a debate among historians, can be
described as the Dutch version of European imperialism. Imperialism can be defined as
an array of economic, political and ecclesiastical initiatives by European countries in the
deliberate colonization of overseas areas. The Dutch version was shaped by the policy of
a minor power above all to safeguard its own possessions in a period of great rivalry
between European nations in the acquisition of colonies in Asia and Africa.

In specific terms this meant consolidating earlier conquests and claims. The implication was that visible government had to be established in all relevant corners of the

Groete uit de Tentoonstelling Vrouwenarbeid 1898, 's Gravenhage.
JAVAANSCHE KAMPONG.

Greetings from *The Exhibition of Women's Work 1898,* The Hague. Javanese Village.

Indonesian archipelago, from the island of Sabang (Sumatra) in the north all the way to the town of Merauke in the western part of New Guinea. Under the dualistic system of government, the local ruler and the social elite were made to cooperate, be it willingly or unwillingly, with the colonial administration. They retained their positions, but a colonial official looked over their shoulders. The turn of the century was also the era of the "ethical policy." Alongside the establishment of authority, there was a civilization campaign that encompassed concern for public health, the beginning of Western education for the indigenous population, government regulation, administration of justice, and taxation. From an economic point of view, Dutch imperialism was shaped primarily by the expansion of companies trading in the products of tropical agriculture and extracting natural resources such as tin and oil – not solely on Java but above all in the Outer Islands, which were opened up to private investment in 1870. This expansion was backed by a circle of leading traders in Dutch cities. While the Dutch East Indies was not at that time an essential market for the products of manufacturing industry, which was getting into its stride for the first time in the Netherlands around the turn of the century, it certainly offered interesting opportunities for developing natural resources. It was during this period that the founding companies of multinationals like Shell and Unilever were set up.

During the last quarter of the nineteenth century, finally, the Christian churches started recruiting men and women for Protestant and Roman Catholic missions to Indonesia. The number of missionaries increased, and so too did the organization and the scale of their support base in the Netherlands.[3] Their arrival in Indonesia resulted in an increase in the Dutch share of missionary activity in addition to or displacing that of their German or Portuguese colleagues. This religious zeal came up against boundaries set by

The Surinam delegation at the *International Exhibition* in Amsterdam in 1883.

the colonial administration, in part as a result of the administrators' traditional misgivings about the appeal of Christian religious communities and in part so as not to provoke the largely Muslim Indonesian population.

The situation was similar in the West Indies colonies of Surinam and the Netherlands Antilles. For centuries the white elite in Surinam had resisted the conversion of slaves by ministers from the Dutch Reformed Church. In 1735 a German Lutheran group, the Community of the Moravian Brothers from Hernhut, was granted permission for a mission but this was limited to the Indians – the original inhabitants – and Maroons, who had freed themselves from slavery. From 1850 onwards this Community of the Moravian Brothers also reached the Creoles. In 1927 the Dutch branch of the movement, the Community of the Moravian Brothers in Zeist, took over the "Surinam Unity" completely and this "Creole church" became more or less Dutch. It was not until 1865 that priests (Redemptorist fathers) and nuns were sent from the Netherlands to a Catholic mission in Surinam on a systematic basis. On the Windward Islands of the Netherlands Antilles – Saba, St. Maarten and St. Eustatius – little or no effort was devoted to conversion. On the Leeward Islands of Curaçao, Bonaire and Aruba, slaves who wanted to convert to Christianity were baptized in the Catholic faith by priests of Spanish and Venezuelan origin. Here too Dutch missionaries first came to support and replace their colleagues in the second half of the nineteenth century.

Caribbean

When the group of twenty-eight people from Surinam – a mixture of Indians, Maroons, Creoles and one Hindu – had appeared at the international colonial exhibition in Amsterdam in 1883, the illustrated weekly *Eigen Haard* expressed the hope "that the increased awareness that the visitors from Surinam have created here about their birthplace will lead to greater interest."[4] This wish received little or no support around 1900. Public interest was focused primarily on the Dutch East Indies, which appealed to people's imagination because they were many times bigger in terms of size and population, and they also generated much greater economic rewards. The Caribbean, in contrast, was certainly not the jewel in the Dutch colonial crown.[5]

The reason was economic. During the nineteenth century the production and export of agricultural products such as cane sugar had declined throughout the whole of the Caribbean. The phenomenon of deserted plantations made this all too evident. In Surinam there were attempts to turn the tide by improving agricultural production and by recruiting new groups of workers after the emancipation of the slaves in 1863. Following the example of the surrounding Caribbean colonies, Chinese contract labor and workers from the British colony of India were taken on. The number of Chinese immigrants was modest, but this group was the advance guard of a substantial Chinese community. 34,000 people were brought from the Indian sub-continent to Surinam between 1873 and 1917. Only a third of these (34%) were to return to the country of their birth. The import of Javanese workers to the region was new. Between 1890 and 1938, 32,600 contract laborers came to Surinam from the Dutch East Indies. Only 22% of them returned to Java.[6]

This influx of contract workers from the Far East, the most important phenomenon during the period around 1900, increased the heterogeneity of what was already a mul-tiracial Surinam. The Indians imported the caste system. Most were followers of Hinduism, but there were also Muslims. They adapted as time passed. In addition to their mother tongue of Sarnami Hindi they learned to speak Sranantongo, the lingua franca of Surinam, formerly referred to as Negro English, and later on they spoke Dutch as well. This was because the elite of the ethnic melting pot that Surinam was and remained continued to adhere to Dutch culture. During the course of the nineteenth cen-tury the community of colonial officials and employees of Dutch firms, an ever-present group, was joined by a social elite made up of Sephardic Jews and educated half-castes parented by European colonists and native Surinam women during frequently tempo-rary relationships, known locally as Surinam marriages. To some extent they took the place of the "native whites" of European origin who had abandoned their estates in Surinam around 1800.[7] They conversed in Dutch and they often owed their social success to a Dutch education. As far as culture was concerned, they looked to the Netherlands rather than Latin America, to which geographically speaking Surinam belonged.

The slave population on the Netherlands Antilles had virtually no exposure to Dutch culture. They had a different language, a different culture and a different religion. Similarly, the elites on the Netherlands Antilles were not primarily interested in Dutch culture, as was the case in Surinam. English was spoken on the Windward Islands, whereas on the Leeward Islands the population spoke Spanish, Portuguese and Papiamentu (Curaçao) or Papiamento (Aruba). There were two groups of whites on Curaçao, Jews and Protestants, each of which had an elite and a stratum of humbler folk. In cultural and religious terms the Sephardic Jews had established their own prominent position on the island, but they had little or no interest in the Netherlands. The Protestant community, on the other hand, had more in common with the Netherlands through their background, and consequently they automatically had access to officials sent to the island from the homeland. Moreover, growing numbers of sons and daugh-ters went to the Netherlands for their secondary schooling and higher education. At the same time this group underwent a process of Latinization, as a result of which people increasingly became part of a Caribbean society and consequently were estranged from Dutch culture.[8]

Colonial Institute

The Dutch East Indies were the heart of Dutch colonialism. This was reflected in Dutch architecture. Historical figures and features recalling the Dutch East India Company were incorporated in the decorative schemes for the new stock exchange building, designed by Berlage, and the new Scheepvaarthuis shipping office. This colonial sym-bolism reached its zenith in the ornamentation of the Colonial Institute, now known as the Royal Tropical Institute, which was the biggest building in Amsterdam when it was completed in 1926. It was the result of an initiative in the Netherlands which dated from the turn of the century and was inspired by examples elsewhere in Europe – the Imperial Institute in London, the Deutsches Kolonialmuseum in Berlin and the Museum van de

Kongo in the Brussels suburb of Tervuren – to create an institution where the science, culture and knowledge of trade and industry in the East Indies could be concentrated. It was to be built on the site of an old cemetery on the eastern outskirts of Amsterdam. The project took a quarter of a century to complete, largely because of the problems associated with acquiring the graves. The huge scale of the building and the costly interior, which featured marble and a range of woods, were intended to contribute to the prestige of a center of imperialism. The architecture was based on the Imperial Institute. A "symbolism committee" chaired by the Director of the Rijksmuseum designed the interior and exterior decoration. "These days the naturalness with which the apparently incompatible was artistically combined is even more striking than was the case with the stock exchange building and the Scheepvaarthuis." The Roman goddess Minerva and the Hindu divinity Siva were depicted, as were the jurist Grotius and Cornelis de Houtman, the first Dutch trader and sea captain on Java. The religions of the Indonesian archipelago, senior Dutch officials and mythical elephants were symbolically linked together. National pride, humanitarian feelings and Oriental inspiration appear to be different facets of the same colonial diamond here. "Do not despair, for God is with us" is the inscription above the main entrance in remembrance of the pioneer of Dutch colonialism, Jan Pieterszoon Coen.[9]

The Colonial Institute was more than an imposing reflection in bricks and mortar of the imperialist doctrine. It was also a center for practitioners of sciences that were able to develop and even blossom through their connection with Dutch colonialism. Indonesia proved to be a challenge for a wider scope of activities than trade and shipping alone. In due course it also fostered a program of scientific research that was very firmly tied to the objectives of the colonial administration. The exploration of the archipelago and its multilingualism, the fight against tropical diseases, the development of a modern technical infrastructure and the confrontation with the indigenous population were among the themes of pragmatic study. The sociologist J.A.A. van Doorn formulated the concept of "instrumental rationality" in this context. He also typified Dutch colonialism as a project. "From the outset targeted decisions were taken using self-interest as a yardstick. Forts and factories were built at strategic locations, competitive manufacturers were eliminated and useless possessions were abandoned." The cultivation of agricultural products like coffee, tea, cinchona bark and rubber was tried out, encouraged on some occasions and limited on others. "For centuries price-fixing, control of production and monopolies were standard goals of colonial government; it was not until later that big business took over, supported by very intensive technical and scientific research."[10]

In cultural terms, the growth of Orientalism was the clear example of this "instrumental rationality." In the Netherlands the field attracted the Arabist Christiaan Snouck Hurgronje and the lawyer Cornelis van Vollenhoven – two extremely capable pioneers who perceived the colonial relationship with the Dutch East Indies as a stimulus to explore new, non-Western areas of observation and analysis. Snouck Hurgronje started his university career by reading theology, but switched to the study of Arabic culture, language and history. This equipped him to dig deeper into Islam. Using his knowledge

The Colonial Institute in Amsterdam; the present-day Royal Tropical Institute.

of Oriental languages and Islamic ethics, he joined the colonial government, which at the end of the century was entangled in a war about control over the Sultanate of Aceh, at the northern tip of Sumatra. He devised a policy that was intended on the one hand to crush native resistance and on the other, while recognizing the importance of Islam, to try to bind the indigenous elites to a Dutch administration through the idea of association. To push this through, he called on the services of Colonel Johannes van Heutsz, the commander who fought the guerillas in Aceh with fast-moving expeditions. In 1906 Snouck Hurgronje broke with Van Heutsz and returned to the Netherlands to take a chair in Arabic and the institutions of Islam at Leiden. In 1901 Van Vollenhoven held a chair at Leiden in the "customary law of the Dutch East Indies" and the constitutional and administrative law of the Dutch colonies. This distinction typifies his studies because he compiled and analyzed the original law in Indonesia so that it would be recognized by the colonial authorities as an independent system. He rejected the concept of legal unification on a European model.

Tropical hygiene

Scientific priority was given to combating tropical diseases. After all, they represented a risk to every colonial project in the East and West Indies. Around 1900 this type of task fell to the officers of the KNIL, the Royal Dutch East Indies Army. One of the first professors of tropical hygiene in the Netherlands was a "native" of Surinam, Paul Christiaan

Flu, who trained as a doctor before becoming a medical officer in Surinam and Indonesia, and ended his distinguished career at the University of Leiden. Another officer, Eugène Dubois, devoted his time to the theory of evolution published by Charles Darwin in 1859. In 1889 he discovered fossils near the river Solo in Central Java. Initially he thought they were from anthropoid apes (*anthropopithecus erectus*), but two years later he amended his conclusion to primitive man (Java man or *pithecanthropus erectus*). In 1893, after a further two years, he published his proof of the theory of evolution. As was normally the case after sensational palaeontological discoveries, it prompted a fierce debate between supporters and opponents.[11]

Another result of medical research conducted in military service was the discovery of a cure for beriberi, a dreaded disease leading to paralysis. It had been a scourge during the war in Aceh. Christiaan Eijkman and his assistant Gerrit Grijns investigated the causes in the Medical Research Laboratory in Jakarta, then known as Batavia. They came to the conclusion that beriberi was not an infectious disease but the result of a nutritional deficiency. This was later identified as a lack of vitamin B-1. "It was Grijns who actually discovered the principle. After a polemic lasting years, Eykman grudgingly accepted his former assistant's interpretation and in 1929 it was Eykman who was honored with the Nobel Prize for Medicine."[12]

There were no bounds to scientific adventurism. The missionary and linguist Hermanus Neubronner van der Tuuk became a legend, not just because of his systematic studies of such languages as Balinese, Old Javanese and Batak, but also through his identification with Indonesian society. He was the first European to reach Lake Toba and he spent his last years in a village in Bali where he owned nothing more than a sarong to wear around his loins and where he was known locally as tuan (lord) Dertik.

European exploration of unknown parts of the archipelago stimulated the imagination of the public back home. A geographical society was set up and in 1888 was granted permission to call itself the Royal Netherlands Geographical Society. Under the chairmanship of Pieter Veth, Professor of Geography and Ethnology in Leiden, the society saw to it that such expeditions were conducted scientifically and were also popularized. There were other organizations too, particularly in the field of biology. They were encouraged by the botanist Melchior Treub, who became Director of the Colonial Botanical Garden in Bogor in 1880, and by Lindor Serrurier, Director of the Anthropology Museum in Leiden. Among the best-known exploratory expeditions were the trans-Borneo quests led by the medical officer Anton Nieuwenhuis (1896-1900) and the Siboga expedition – named after the naval vessel that conducted oceanographic research in Indonesian waters – led by M. Weber (1899-1900). There were also a number of spectacular expeditions to New Guinea (1907-1913), an unknown and remote corner of Dutch colonialism. These voyages resulted in a literal and symbolic climax. The snow-capped mountains that were discovered in the interior were given Dutch names like Mount Nassau and Mount Wilhelmina. "In this way the Netherlands discovered its Mount Olympus in the tropics, complete with perpetual snow."[13]

Literature

The Dutch East Indies appealed to the literary imagination. Indonesian themes and authors have remained remarkably popular in Dutch literature. Conrad Busken Huet, who knew the East Indies of those days from personal experience, wrote in 1880 that the colony had also turned out to be "a literary milch cow." "Once our grandchildren start cataloguing, they will be surprised to see how many Dutch men and women of letters sucked on this teat in the second half of the nineteenth century." In his view, however, the milk they consumed had often been skimmed to such an extent that it was not always enjoyable.[14] The literary imagination was ignited when authors did not allow themselves to be dazzled by the magnitude of what the colonists had achieved and were sensitive to the social and racial contrasts that this regime created. This could be expressed in more positive terms. The encounter with a different culture and the exotic nature of this Asian country became a source of creativity. Two of the greatest Dutch writers were linked to the colonial administration in one way or another. The colonial officer Eduard Douwes Dekker, writing under the name Multatuli, demonstrated his literary talent in *Max Havelaar*, a satire about the Dutch spirit of enterprise and about oppression under native rulers in the East Indies. During his second visit to Indonesia in 1900 Louis Couperus, son of a justice of the supreme court of the Indies, captured the exotic nature of Java in his novel *De stille kracht* (1900; *The Hidden Force*, 1985), and also sounded the alarm that heralded the end of colonial power. In *De boeken der kleine zielen* (1901-1903; *The Books of the Small Souls*, 1914-1918) the inevitable decline is transposed to a circle of repatriated civil servants in The Hague. This novel in four parts was the Dutch version of the "degeneration epic" that reached its peak in Thomas Mann's *Buddenbrooks*, the story of a Lübeck merchant family. It is striking that Dutch Indonesian literature does not embrace the concept of imperialism as conjured up in English literature by Joseph Conrad or Rudyard Kipling, or in France by the soldier Ernest Psichari, who referred to "une affirmation de l'énergie morale" – an instrument for combating decadence.[15]

The Dutch East Indies were not discovered as a theme in the visual arts until after 1900, when the Orientalist Maurius Bauer traveled there, to be followed later by the architect Hendrik Berlage and the painter Isaac Israëls. In 1904 the artist Wijnand Nieuwenkamp discovered the beauty of an unspoiled Bali. He returned in 1906 and followed in the footsteps of the colonial army, which was fighting the rulers of Badung and Tabanan. He was able to see for himself how the Balinese aristocracy, when faced with a superior Dutch aggressor, surrendered to the ritual of disregard for death and self-destruction. His Balinese sketches provided the key to unlocking Balinese culture for pioneers like Walter Spies and Rudolf Bonnet and their efforts to adapt native conventions. Native music was discovered in an analogous fashion. Debussy was not the only composer who had evidently been bowled over by a Javanese gamelan orchestra. The violinist and lawyer Jaap Kunst, who collected Northern Netherlandish folk songs as a young man in Groningen, encountered it at the court of one of the rulers in Yogyakarta when he toured Indonesia with a Dutch trio. He heard an "amazing wall of sound" – a revelation that kept him awake all night. He then decided to remain in the Dutch East Indies and devote himself to studying native music. In 1930 he was even appointed the government musicologist. Over the course of fifteen years Jaap Kunst traveled the length and breadth of the archipelago, collected instruments and recorded the sounds on wax cylinders. He returned to the Netherlands in 1936 and became curator of the Colonial Institute, where he fostered ethno-musicology.

The scientific and artistic adventure in Indonesia should be seen against the backdrop of almost continuous war. Not all forms of colonial pacification were actually peaceful. The last quarter of the nineteenth century was defined militarily by a bloody war against Aceh. It started in 1873 and was deemed to have been won in 1904 after violent mopping-up operations by Van Heutsz's army units. There was a spectacular expedition against two rulers in the south of Bali in 1906, and the retaliatory action on the island of Lombok in 1894 received widespread approval. The Balinese in the court, including women and children, confronted the colonial forces and killed themselves with spears and krises rather than surrender to the barbarians. This fearless "puputan" (literally the end) made an impression on the Dutch press.[16] Public support for the victors in Lombok was orchestrated. The colonial army, which had initially suffered a defeat and did not conquer the palace of the rebellious ruler until it attacked a second time, was received with a great deal of respect at the beginning of 1895 because it had erased the indignity of the defeat. The two Queens headed the tribute. The excessive violence did not become public knowledge until a century later. The hero of Aceh, General Van Heutsz, was similarly able to enjoy his triumphal procession through the Netherlands in 1904.

The reverberations of such displays were comparable with the reaction of the public in neighboring European countries. The hunt for colonies was very much in the public forum. The rivalry in this thirst for possessions consequently also resulted in conflict between these European states, at least as far as public opinion was concerned. It happened in the Netherlands, for instance, when the Boers in South Africa took up arms against the imperialist aspirations of Great Britain.

The Boers and their kin

Around 1900 there was a great deal of sympathy in the Netherlands for the Boers in their fight against the British. Their leaders were seen as heroes because they were also defending the traditional culture of the fatherland. Expressions of solidarity primarily took the form of words and gestures. A community of colonists had become alienated from the British Cape Colony. They had set out on the Great Trek in 1835 and had founded three Boer Republics to the north – Transvaal, the Orange Free State and Natal. Most of them spoke Afrikaans, a language that evolved during the white colonization of South Africa under the control of the Dutch East India Company. Incidentally, the Dutch interest in South Africa was not entirely culturally motivated. It was also related to the discovery of diamonds on the border of the Cape Colony – a major cause of the Boer War – and to the operation of the mines which provided plenty of work and profit for the Amsterdam diamond houses between 1870 and 1876, a period referred to as the Cape Era.

The first act of British imperialism – the annexation of Transvaal in 1877 – resulted in immediate protests in the Netherlands. Forty-six professors in Dutch universities took up the cause, with the University of Utrecht in the vanguard under the leadership of the lawyer G.W. Vreede. In their – liberal – circle, the Boers were seen as the victims of brutal power politics. Among orthodox Protestants, on the other hand, the predominant image was of oppressed fellow believers. When the triumvirate of Paul Kruger, Petrus Joubert and Martinus Pretorius emerged in Transvaal as leaders of the resistance against British domination, the minister and political leader of orthodoxy, Abraham Kuyper, made an emotional statement that Dutch "Christian folk" would flee to Transvaal if they were to be oppressed in the Netherlands by a liberal elite. From the outset the bond with kinfolk in South Africa reflected the conflict between the need for communal support and the polemic between liberalism and orthodoxy.

During the First Boer War (1880 to 1881), on the initiative of another Utrecht professor, the pharmacologist, anatomist and geographer Pieter Harting, a petition to Queen Victoria was drawn up appealing to "the noble part of the British nation" to grant the Boers their independence. Some six thousand people signed it, including eighty-one of the 180 active professors in the Netherlands. When the Transvaal fighters defeated the British at the battle of Majuba in 1881, this was taken as evidence of their ability to cling to the traditional values of Dutch civilization. At the annual general meeting of the Society for Dutch Literature, its chairman Robert Fruin said that there was again hope for the position of the Netherlands in the world now that Dutch determination and Dutch valor on Majuba Hill had turned what was initially a defeat into a stunning victory. What had been lost forever with the abandonment of "New Netherland" in America could, perhaps, be regained in Africa.[17] The Boers were now seen as the freedom fighters of the nineteenth century. The president of Transvaal, Paul Kruger, was able to accept this honorary title personally when he visited the Netherlands in the spring of 1884. He made a tremendous impression as the prototype of a "South African Boer, powerfully built with strong features," although this idealized picture concealed a man who had "gigantically horrible" table manners and, when he wore morning dress and a top hat, looked more like a ringmaster in a circus than a head of state.[18] His delegation visited the towns and cities in the Northern and Central Netherlands, a predominantly Protestant area, and especially Den Briel – the town that was captured by the rebels, their first historical victory during the Dutch Revolt. The practical result of their tour was disappointing, but the political capital it generated was substantial.

The war prompted the establishment of a Netherlands South Africa Association in 1881. Its goal was to champion the "interests of our kinfolk" in South Africa by making agricultural and industrial resources available to them and by mobilizing public opinion behind them. The members of the committee were largely liberal and they included a merchant, a minister, a director and a professor. Abraham Kuyper was also on the committee. This combination was popular but it also contained a built-in fundamental difference of opinion. And indeed cooperation broke down in 1882. The brothers in Transvaal were informed by Kuyper that they had once again been delivered to "Jews and Heathens."[19] Under the guidance of the secretary, the philosopher Cornelis Spruyt, the Association was turning to nationalism. The Boer Republics should be strengthened and become Dutch settlements so that the "vigorous and active elements" of the Dutch

Former President Kruger takes the salute in the Hotel des Indes in The Hague.

people could find a new and at the same time familiar place in the event that "the old Netherlands succumbs in due course through historical factors that cause the small states to be absorbed by the large ones."[20] This was a reference to the fear that the Netherlands would be annexed by Bismarck's Germany. Emigration was not a priority of the "friends of the Boers," but by the end of 1898 some six and a half thousand Dutch people had gambled on a new life in South Africa. A number of them ended up in Transvaal, which thanks to the discovery of gold fields in the eighteen-eighties had become the powerhouse of the South African economy. The know-how that the Netherlands exported was practical in nature – civil engineering or business adminis-tration. In 1881, for example, the Amsterdam lawyer Willem Leyds was assigned as attorney general to the Republic of South Africa by way of Dutch legal assistance.

The Second Boer War, which broke out between Great Britain and the two Boer Republics of Transvaal and the Orange Free State in 1899, really roused Dutch public opinion. 140,000 people signed a protest petition "to the People of Great Britain." Sympathy was expressed by more than just the social elite and more than just orthodox

Protestants. The Northern Netherlands, parts of which were already under socialist control, and the Catholic South also expressed their concern.[21] The disillusionment was all the greater when it became clear that the Boers could not hold out against the British. The fatherland mourned one death in particular – Hermanus Coster, who had been president of the Leiden student body and had succeeded Leyds as attorney general of the Republic of South Africa. He was one of the few Dutch nationals in the Boer army. After two and a half years the Peace of Vereeniging in 1902 brought an end to what historians have subsequently deemed to be the biggest of all colonial wars as measured in terms of the loss of life and the cost. For this reason, and because guerrillas were involved in the fighting, it can be described as the first of the modern wars.[22] The big loser, Paul Kruger, had already arrived in the Netherlands. At the request of Queen Wilhelmina he had been collected in the port of Lourenço Marques by the Dutch warship *Gelderland*. The tens of thousands of spectators saw "a stooped old man, much fatter." It was a melancholy reunion that moved many. The young Willem Drees – who was to become prime minister after World War II – applauded Kruger warmly when he visited Amsterdam and drew from this sight inspiration for his burgeoning determination to devote his life to socialism and the fight against injustice.

Flanders

Sympathy with the Boers was an issue for the general public, whereas sympathy with the Flemish Movement was a matter for intellectuals. The Netherlands had viewed the rise of the Flemish Movement from behind a national and secure border, although it was encouraged by the language policy of the Dutch King William I during a period when the north and the south of the Low Countries were united in one kingdom. After the Belgian Revolution of 1830, however, the interest in it was determined by cultural factors – by the awareness of a common language. This interest was confirmed in a series of conferences on Dutch language and literature. Dutch-speaking men and women of letters from both banks of the Scheldt and the Maas, or Meuse, got to know one another. The first of these conferences was staged in the auditorium of Ghent University in 1849, and the second was held in Amsterdam in 1850. The first result was the joint publication of the *Woordenboek der Nederlandsche Taal* (Dictionary of the Dutch Language) and common spelling rules for the language as spoken in the North (the Netherlands) and the South (Belgium).

The regularity of the conferences reinforced the bonds between the North and the South and brought the Flemish Movement into a Dutch orbit after it had initially focused primarily on the German romanticists. However, it became clear that for the foreseeable future there would be no support in the North for a Greater Netherlands consciousness that would go beyond cultural collaboration. The national consciousness in the Netherlands after the Belgian Revolution was too steeped in the historical example of the seventeenth-century Republic of the United Provinces and in a Protestant culture. Catholic intellectuals found it easier to establish these ties, but they were few in number; moreover, Catholics in the North were convinced that their difficult quest for integration into Dutch society would be impeded by effective interest in the Flemish Movement.[23]

Incidentally the same Protestant culture restrained the desire on the Flemish side for close political cooperation.

Cultural contacts were intensified around the turn of the century. Practical and joint effort was devoted to unifying and improving language and pronunciation. This had not been possible for a considerable time because of opposition from a few linguistic particularists, mainly from West Flanders, and because generally speaking the participants from the Northern Netherlands did not mind the language that the Flemings spoke. "On the contrary, they found the naivety of Flemish pronunciation very pleasant and easy to listen to."[24] Flemish literature was moreover becoming better known and appreciated in the Netherlands. The editors of the Flemish literary magazine *Van Nu en Straks* made a substantial contribution to this. There was a related effort that arose out of the eleventh conference on Dutch language and literature in Louvain in 1869 in the form of an attempt to revive the theatre by founding a joint Dutch-language theatre company. In the end this company was not successful in uniting Dutch and Flemish theatre, but it was the origin of an improvement in the quality of drama productions in the North. An initiative that lasted longer was the setting up of an *Algemeen Nederlands Verbond* (General Netherlands Alliance) based on the examples of the *Alliance Française* in France and the *Alldeutscher Verband* in Germany. In fact there were two initiatives and they were both the brainchild of a teacher. Hippoliet Meert, who taught at the Koninklijk Atheneum in Brussels, founded the *Algemeen Nederlands Verbond* in 1895 in the "In den Vos" café in the Grand Place in Brussels. The second was founded in 1897 when Herman Kiewit de Jonge, a teacher at and later headmaster of the grammar school in Dordrecht, called for the founding of an *Algemeen Nederlands Taalverbond* (General Dutch Language Alliance) during the twenty-fourth conference on Dutch language and literature. The two initiatives were subsequently combined, with the Flemish name being linked to a secretariat in Dordrecht. The *Algemeen Nederlands Verbond* became dominated by Dutch. In 1908 the worldwide membership was 10,368, of whom 1,468 were in Belgium. It organized the conferences on language and literature from then on.[25]

In the end the most important impulse for a Greater Netherlands consciousness proved to come from contacts between Flemish and Dutch students. Such meetings were promoted around 1900 by the summer schools at the Universities of Leiden and Amsterdam and through participation by Northern students in Flemish student conferences. The student Pieter Geyl, who as a historian went on to open the debate about a Greater Netherlands historiography, attended one of these Flemish conferences for the first time in 1911 and was impressed by the power of the Flemish Movement. "People like this cannot be an appendage of the Netherlands. Precisely because of their diversity and their inner well-being, they will themselves create and communicate a spirit of their own."[26] This led another Utrecht student, Frits Coers, to publish a Greater Netherlands Student Songbook, thus giving Flemish songs a place in the repertoire of Dutch students. The meetings between students from the North and the South resulted in the setting up in 1910 of the *Algemeen Nederlandsch Studenten Verbond*, which proved remarkably popular. The estimated membership amounted to one in seven of the students in the Northern Netherlands.[27] However, when there was a split in the Flemish Movement during World War I between activists with German sympathies and supporters of Flemish independence

John Bull and the Dutch ambulance.
"The Maid of Holland to Minister de Beaufort: How can you allow this, without protest?"
De Amsterdammer, August 26, 1900.

within the Belgian state, Dutch adhesion to Flanders also split in two. The *Dietsche Bond* was founded in 1917. It was an organization that accommodated Dutch people who supported the approach by Flemish radicals to the German regime of occupation.[28]

During the liberating euphoria of the Boer War intellectuals tried "to escape from the paradoxical requirements that nineteenth century society had set – a critical frame of mind and strict self-control in regard to vigorous conviction."[29] They found or projected a community in Transvaal and the Orange Free State in which the unvarnished purity of the nation was expressed. "I felt as if I had been plucked from a very old, spiritualized, refined world and taken back to the natural state," wrote Geyl of the time he spent among Flemish students in Ghent. "The pleasant, good-natured dissipation, the simplicity of living and thinking, fulfillment with an important idea and a goal was rejuvenating. I can think of no better word for it."[30] For many of those who were involved personally, the experience of a cultural alliance was also a gateway to a more intense life and awareness, if not the beginning of a political awakening.

It is remarkable that in both cases of a nationalistic movement, the Dutch government was and remained on its guard against cross-border agitation. In regard to South Africa there was a reason of state, namely that the Netherlands had to maintain good relations with Great Britain because of the powerful position of the British in Southeast Asia.

There was no disputing the fact that the colonial administration in Indonesia had no room to maneuver without the consent of the British. The liberal politician Willem de Beaufort, a friend of the Boers from the outset, had become well aware of this in his position as minister for foreign affairs. In the cabinet he argued "that it was wrong to put ourselves in embarrassing situations for the sake of public opinion here at home. There was no reason whatsoever to do anything when the Republic of South Africa could gain nothing and we would make our relations with Great Britain even worse."[31] The same vigilance was applied to the Flemish Movement. The Dutch government did not want there to be any doubt about its respect for the integrity of the Belgian state. This is why the *Algemeen Nederlands Verbond* was closely monitored in its Greater Netherlands ambition. And it is why royal assent for its new regulations was initially withheld. As a result of this, the theme of solidarity with the Boers and with the Flemish acquired the character of a polemic and also a polemic power from a political point of view.

Immigration from the colonies

Immigration from colonized Indonesia to the European Netherlands remained a key ambition for one Javanese woman. Raden Adjeng Kartini had an aristocratic background. Tradition and opposition thwarted her quest for self-fulfillment. She was married off, and died in childbirth in 1904. She had seen the Netherlands as a country where she could become a schoolmistress, where she could broaden her horizons and enrich her mind. "The Netherlands should and will truly make me a free woman." Her letters to Dutch friends and acquaintances were published in book form in 1911. The Leiden historian H.T. Colenbrander wrote that Kartini had replaced Adinda, the heroine in Multatuli's *Max Havelaar*, "and see how much we have gained! Adinda suffers, whereas Kartini suffers and responds. She was the first to cast aside the anonymity of the native and show us that she was just as much as person as we are."[32]

Kartini's brother, Raden Mas Pandji Sosrokartono, did make the journey and enrolled at Delft Polytechnic School in 1896. He soon switched to reading Oriental languages at Leiden. In 1899 he gave a speech at the twenty-fifth conference on Dutch language and literature in Ghent. His audience was surprised to hear a Javanese prince talking about the Netherlands and Java in excellent Dutch. Sosrokartono urged the Dutch to abandon their condescending attitude to the Javanese and to speak to them in Dutch. "You are the rulers with the gospel of peace in one hand and the scepter of civilization in the other. Help foster brotherhood between yourselves and your subjects." For their part the Javanese would have to learn to master the Dutch language for the sake of cultural and social development.[33]

Sosrokartono showed through such comments that he was an advocate of the ethical policy in which Western education was a condition for emancipation. He was the first of a generation of aristocratic Indonesians sent to the Netherlands for secondary and higher education. They were officially introduced into the Netherlands during the inauguration of Queen Wilhelmina. The deputation from the Dutch East Indies consisted of the Sultan of Siak plus a delegation from the kraton (palace) in Solo, capital of one of the two principalities in Central Java, headed by the Pangeran Ario Mataram and two sons of the

Sultan of Kutei (Borneo). This delegation was certainly colorful but it was hardly representative of Indonesian rulers.[34] The Sultan of Borneo's sons were already in the Netherlands for their secondary education at a boarding school in The Hague, as were the three sons of the Pangeran Ario Mataram. More "Javanese princes" followed them to the Netherlands. The best known was Raden Mas Noto Suroto, son of one of the senior officials in the other principality in Central Java, Yogyakarta. He was a student in Leiden and in 1914, together with Raden Mas Surjo Suparto, crown prince of a principality in Solo, he joined up as a reserve officer when World War I broke out. However, his reputation was based on his performances as a Javanese dancer and as a poet. His first collection was published in 1915. Noto Suroto's poetry attracted attention more because of its exotic character than because of its literary quality. The writer Frederik van Eeden, who introduced him in an Amsterdam weekly, tried to see the Javanese poet as a pupil of the Bengal poet Rabindranath Tagore, who was awarded the 1913 Nobel Prize for Literature and whose work he had translated.[35]

Studying in the Netherlands was expensive and at that time was reserved for the sons of aristocratic families. They were the upper crust of a group of Indonesian immigrants who attracted attention around 1900 by virtue of their individual appearance rather than their numbers. They had greater visibility than the Indonesian servants who had traveled to the fatherland with colonial families. The 1909 census gives an indication of the scale of Indonesian immigration. At that time there were fifty-four Muslims in the Netherlands. Most of them were Indonesian students, and there were a few Persians and Turks as well as some Dutch believers.[36] Indonesian servants and nursemaids were not included in this census.

Abdul Rivai arrived in the Netherlands from the island of Sumatra in 1899. He had become a "dokter djawa" (Java doctor) because he had completed the course for native doctors. He wanted to continue his medical studies in the Netherlands, but he also wrote for newspapers and magazines. In his plea for good education in Indonesia he took "the liberty of suggesting that the powers that be should examine Japan, which owes its current progress to the fact that many young Japanese are being educated in Europe."[37] The Maharajah Sutan Casajangan Soripada from the Batak tribe in Sumatra also made an impact. He had completed an indigenous teacher's course to become a schoolmaster and endeavored to obtain his Dutch diploma at the state teacher training college in Haarlem, succeeding, after some ups and downs, in 1912. Casajangan was "a distinguished sight to which a gold lorgnette contributed." He was the designated representative of the Indonesian students on official occasions and he took the initiative of setting up the *Indische Vereniging* – the first association for Indonesian immigrants in the Netherlands to be given a Dutch name.[38]

In 1913 Ibrahim gelar Datuk Tan Malaka enrolled at the same state teacher training college in Haarlem. He had previously acquitted himself with distinction at the teacher training college in Fort de Kock, Sumatra. During World War I, Tan Malaka would develop into one of the radical Indonesian nationalists. He was the first of the Indonesian immigrants who became more aware of their Indonesian identity by virtue of their stay in the fatherland. This happened because in the Netherlands he was exposed to European concepts about rights to self-determination and also to socialism. Malaka was the pioneer of awakening Indonesian nationalism in the Netherlands and therefore became the Dutch example of a general development of nationalism among immigrants to Europe from the colonies. Other students from Sumatra, such as Mohammed Hatta and Sutan Sjahrir, were to follow him between the two World Wars.

The Protestant and Catholic missionary organizations in the Dutch colonies had their own educational links. These links enabled people who wanted to train to become ministers and teachers of religion to come to the Netherlands. From 1914 onwards, for instance, the Jesuit father superiors in the Dutch East Indies sent twelve Javanese to the Netherlands to complete their training as priests. Several of them died of tuberculosis while they were in the Netherlands, as a result of which the Jesuits decided to organize the training course themselves in Java. One of the first students was Albert Sugiapranata, who in 1940 became the first Indonesian bishop (of Semarang) and who in 1945 was elected to support Indonesian independence, which earned him the title of hero (pahlawan) of the Indonesian Revolution. One of the first black ministers from Surinam was Cornelis Winst Blijd, who was born into slavery in 1860. He traveled to Europe in 1913, on the occasion of the fiftieth anniversary of the abolition of slavery in the Netherlands (1863). During the emancipation celebrations he was promoted to Elder of the Evangelical Community of the Moravian Brothers. He was received twice by Queen Wilhelmina and he preached a sermon for the court. "He used the opportunity to commend his race to Her Majesty."[39]

The immigrant from Surinam was immortalized in literature in the character of William Kegge, the friend of the hero Hildebrand in the famous nineteenth-century novel *Camera Obscura* by the Leiden theology student Nicolaas Beets. Kegge was the colored boy from a good family who was sent to Leiden for a university education. "Unfortunately there is very little in the story about the black servants, but we get to know his sister, mother and grandmother very well. How many readers will have noticed that the boisterous, fortuitously successful father was the only Dutch person in the family?"[40] Kegge was the prototype of a migration of the elite. Around 1900 the students coming to the Netherlands for higher education were primarily the children of the colored bourgeoisie in Paramaribo. Others, such as Surinam jazz musicians or the hussar Anton de Kom, the first spokesman of Surinam nationalism, did not arrive in the Netherlands until the period between the two World Wars. The same was true of the Netherlands Antilles. However, the small number of young people from the elite of the Netherlands Antilles (white Protestants and Sephardic Jews) selected American or British educational institutions as well as Dutch ones. This was a particular advantage for students from the Windward Islands, where English was the primary language. In Surinam, on the other hand, the desire for social advancement was very much linked to focusing on Dutch values and standards. An education at a Dutch institution was a matter of course.

Immigration from Europe

The period around 1900 can be considered as a watershed in the history of immigration in the Netherlands. For centuries there had been a steady influx of Germans looking for work in the areas along the North Sea coast. Now, however, as a result of the spectacular

Ontwerp voor een toegangspoort voor een vluchtelingen-kamp (Systeem Muller)

"Abandon Hope, All Ye Who Enter Here."
Design for an entrance to a refugee camp (Muller System).
Albert Hahn, *Reception of Belgian Refugees.*

industrialization on the banks of the Rhine in Germany, the flow reversed. Dutch workers went to the Ruhr looking for employment in the mines and the steelworks. Meanwhile other immigrants had arrived in the Netherlands; these were forerunners of large influxes in the twentieth century, such as students and fortune hunters from the Dutch colonies. Hundreds of thousands of refugees drove, rode and walked across the border from Belgium in the summer and autumn of 1914. They came to the neutral Netherlands looking for a safe haven from German atrocities against the civilian population. They were the first people in the twentieth century to emigrate for political reasons. The Netherlands, which was a bystander in terms of the military dimension of World War I, was nevertheless confronted by the social reality of a major European conflict.

The flows of immigrants from continental Europe to the eastern border of the Netherlands were always greater than to the southern border. During the nineteenth century there was a constant influx of seasonal workers from Germany. Jews from the Russian Empire also arrived at the eastern border. For some of them the Netherlands, with its ports of Rotterdam and Amsterdam, was a transit country on the way to the New World, whereas for others it was a final destination. In the last two decades of the nineteenth century there was a trickle of people seeking refuge for religious reasons.

These were priests and monks from the Rhineland and Westphalia, who had to abandon their work as a result of the *Kulturkampf* – the political struggle between the German Chancellor Bismarck and the Catholic Church in Prussia. A few refugees also crossed the southern border at the beginning of the twentieth century. They came from France, where the Third Republic restricted the social and educational activities of monks and nuns.

Most German immigrants came from what had been referred to as "the missing pieces of the Netherlands where our language dominated until well into the nineteenth century" such as the German regions of East Friesland and Bentheim, Münsterland and Oldenburg, and also from the Rhineland.[41] Up to the middle of the nineteenth century these were seasonal workers who traveled and worked in groups, within which family relationships were very important. Many of these "Hollandgänger" ultimately settled in the Netherlands. The total number during the first half of the nineteenth century has been estimated at 140,000.[42] This migrant group continued to be significant after 1850, albeit at a lower level. Young men from Westphalia started arriving after 1865 because they wanted to avoid compulsory service in the Prussian army after the Prussian annexation of the Kingdom of Hanover and they looked for somewhere to stay with relatives and also for employment in the Netherlands.[43] There were no exact figures about the level of immigration for many years. The number of aliens was not recorded until the first national census in 1889. The result was 51,000 people – out of a total population of five million – of whom 31,000 were German nationals.[44] Another result was that of the residents who became naturalized between 1890 and 1919, nearly three-quarters were of German origin.[45]

Immigrants from the east and the south made their presence felt in the Netherlands primarily in the urban economy. New arrivals were a significant source of entrepreneurs who took the initiative and regenerated the retail business. General stores came to Dutch towns and cities from France and Belgium around the turn of the century. There was the Bazar de la Bourse in Amsterdam, the Bazar de la Paix in The Hague and the Bazar de Maestricht in the capital of Limburg. Most of them were founded by Belgian retailers and many of the staff came from France. Customers found a degree of charm in shopping in these establishments, where they could hear all sorts of French expressions and on occasion could buy typical Parisian knick-knacks. However, this very strong focus also had its drawbacks. The managers of the French stores were foreigners in the country where they were operating.[46] In 1921 the stores became part of one new company, the Galeries Modernes. This represented the transition from the general store to the department store, while retaining the image of somewhere for everyone to shop at low prices.

The retail business in the Netherlands was also regenerated by German immigrants and their descendants. Westphalian shopkeepers responded cleverly to the new trend in the garment industry for off-the-peg clothes based on standard sizes. They found sales opportunities in the expanding towns and cities in the west of the Netherlands, particularly in Amsterdam and Rotterdam. This business sector was dominated by former Catholic hawkers from Westphalia who had previously set up shop in the drapery business, starting in Friesland. The best-known individuals in this group were Clemens and

August Brenninkmeyer, originally from Mettingen in Westphalia, who opened their first drapery store in the Frisian town of Sneek in 1861. They opened their second store in Amsterdam over thirty years later, in 1893. This business developed into C&A, with stores all over Western Europe. A few years earlier Willem Vroom, in part of Westphalian origin, and Anton Dreesmann, from the German town of Tecklenburg, set up a drapery business that eventually grew to become the Vroom & Dreesman chain of large department stores.[47] And it was not only Catholic Westphalians who regenerated the retail trade. There were also Jewish merchants, among them the founders of the department store De Bijenkorf.

During the nineteenth century there were several distinct communes of German immigrants in the city of Utrecht. A poor district along the river Vecht was home to the Westerwalders, a group of men and women who made and sold Cologne pottery, earthenware from the Westerwald in the basin of the Lahn, a tributary of the Rhine. They were predominantly Roman Catholics. File makers from Ennepedal, south of Hagen in the Ruhr, formed a commune in another district. They were Lutherans. In the center of the city there were shopkeepers from Oldenburg, the Catholic owners of ready-to-wear clothes shops and department stores, who in many cases had recruited staff from the same area. Germans accounted for around one percent of the population of Utrecht.[48] German immigrants were tied by a common origin and also a specialization in certain occupations, or by a shared faith, either Lutheran or Roman Catholic. They often lived close together and most of them also married within their own community.[49]

The patrician class of Amsterdam presented a different picture. It was said to be easily accessible to the nouveau riches. These newcomers were divided into three categories; the Ashkenazi Jewish elite, the "Indonesian nabobs" and the German immigrants, in particular those from Oldenburg and Westphalia.[50] It was remarked in 1864 in regard to this last group of merchants and brokers that they displayed more initiative than their established Dutch counterparts. While this generated a degree of irritation in the relationship with the great and the good, it did not result in segregation and exclusion. An investigation into the ups and downs of twenty-two Amsterdam patrician families concluded that "the fact that the city has always been open to all attitudes and beliefs, and to talented and successful newcomers, and has made room for them in boardrooms, is one of the strengths of Amsterdam and has always contributed to its regeneration." Contrary to the traditions of the eighteenth century, marriages with members of the old powerful families were no longer necessary. The investigation into the origin of these new city dwellers – the twenty-two families – revealed that between 1700 and 1850 eleven families, in other words half of them, had emigrated from the west of Germany to Amsterdam and four had come from France. Only seven were of purely Dutch origin.[51]

For centuries the German seasonal workers had been met in the Netherlands with indifference or contempt. They were depicted as dimwitted country bumpkins in so-called "Hun farces." A traveler on the steamer from Purmerend to Alkmaar related how the deck was jam-packed with grass cutters from Hanover and there were continual shouts of "Huns" from women and children on the bank and the crews of passing boats. According to the traveler, who was also German, only rarely did the Hanoverians shout back "bastard."[52] In 1901 the widely-read writer Justus van Maurik described them as "these large, clumsy people with their snub noses, their wide, amiable laughing mouths and childlike eyes – they were models of innocent stupidity." He called women from Westerwald who traded in stoneware "china cows." "There you had great fat lumps of women with coarse yellow hair and brown faces covered in freckles."[53] The editors of the *Woordenboek der Nederlandse Taal*, the ninth volume of which was published in 1913, defined the word *mof* (Hun) as "a term of abuse for workers or servants, and also Germans in general, who were held in contempt by more prosperous Dutch people." However, the editors added that, "these days Germans are generally viewed differently and the expression *mof*, no matter how colloquially used, is often free of contempt."[54] This is consistent with an evident reversal in public opinion in which the emergence of the industrial might of Germany from 1870 demanded admiration.[55]

The German monks who had fled to the Netherlands as a consequence of the *Kulturkampf* in the eighteen-seventies were received with very few problems and absorbed into the community, even though as far as non-Catholics were concerned they were "just so many uninvited and only half-welcome guests."[56] In any event they made an impact in the form of the development of orders of monks and nuns in the Netherlands who devoted themselves to education and the care of the sick. It has been estimated that there were more than 1,300 clerical refugees and twenty-five orders and congregations from Prussia. According to these same estimates there were 840 nuns and 460 priests and friars.[57] The *Kulturkampf* was officially terminated in Germany in 1887. Some Prussian monks and nuns returned to their original establishments and others remained in the Netherlands. Some religious refugees from France crossed the southern border at the beginning of the twentieth century. The number is not known, but it was certainly smaller than the numbers of monks and nuns from Germany. They transferred their knowledge and culture by establishing a Benedictine abbey in Oosterhout and French-speaking boarding schools for girls in Vught and Ubbergen. Catholicism in the Netherlands received a fresh cultural impulse that extended beyond the mere presence of refugees.

It went without saying that immigrants had to integrate themselves in their new country because this was a period in which the creation of a nation state was being pursued with great conviction. Conducting religious services in Dutch, for example, was seen as one facet of a broader-based development in which a national pattern of language and knowledge had to be disseminated to the remotest parts of the country. This was also the case in the border region near the Limburg town of Heerlen, for instance, where sermons were still being preached in German and a German newspaper was still being published. At the end of World War I a Limburg priest complained that a stubborn colleague in a village in South Limburg continued to preach in German. However, the process of Dutchifying things in the previously very German-oriented province of Limburg had in the interim been stimulated by the development of tourism and the mining industry. "The influx of foreigners, combined with the mining industry, brought this process to completion in 'German' places, as Heerlen had been in the past, surprisingly quickly." This made it possible for people to assert that since August 1914 the preference for German in Limburg remained confined to "a few priests, traders and smugglers."[58] The strength of the drive towards Dutchification was also reflected in the desire to make High German or Ashkenazi Jews replace Yiddish, the language spoken in Jewish communities in Central and Eastern Europe, by Standard Dutch. However, this ran into resistance. In 1870 the Chief Rabbi in Rotterdam, Dr. Joseph Isaacsohn, resigned because he had been reproached for not preaching in Dutch. Yiddish was moreover maintained as the everyday language by an influx of immigrants from Eastern Europe after the first wave of pogroms in 1881, which were a consequence of an assassination attempt on Tsar Alexander II. In 1886 a number of older Jews left the synagogue in Leeuwarden when it was decided, after the death of the Chief Rabbi, that thenceforth sermons would be preached in Dutch instead of Yiddish.[59] It was typical that in the last quarter of the nineteenth century the Jewish community in the Netherlands decided to stop recruiting rabbis from Germany or Eastern Europe and to move largely to training rabbis in the Netherlands. The new Chief Rabbi of the Ashkenazic Synagogue, Joseph Dünner, moreover stated a preference for using Dutch as the language for teaching and for ceremonies in the seminary.

As we have already seen, a substantial number of German immigrants were Catholic. Their orthodoxy had an impact on Dutch Catholic culture. They used their increasing prosperity to contribute to the expansion of Catholicism. The part played by German immigration in the expansion of the Catholic community has been compared with the role played in the seventeenth century by Huguenots fleeing from Louis XIV in the growth of Calvinism in the Netherlands.[60] The upshot was that the immigrant character of Catholicism in the Netherlands was stressed now and again in anti-Catholic writing. The Catholic historian L.J. Rogier pointed out that this view touched a sensitive nerve. It is possible that there was a degree of false modesty involved. He felt that one of the reasons for this was the historical fact that "the children of German immigrants," unlike the French or the British in the Netherlands, have always tried to make people forget about their origins. After all, for centuries the Dutch have poked fun at the countless numbers "who had drifted down the Rhine on rafts. A Frenchman might be frivolous and affected, an Englishman might be supercilious and dry as dust, but Huns were needy and penniless, and in the eyes of a people whose respect for thrift was innate, there could be no greater offense."[61] Rogier concluded his rhetorical tirade by stating that time and again we are struck by the extraordinary ease with which this second generation could make people forget about its German origins and by "the naivety with which the Dutch public at large accepted this."[62]

3

Urban planning

Water and land

Without the Dutch, Holland would not exist, the Portuguese traveler Alphonse Esquiros wrote. "This fatherland is their work, their creation, and like the God of the Bible they have the right to decide that what they have done is good."[1] Travelers who recorded their impressions of the Netherlands consistently mentioned the planning and construction of the landscape, often with some emphasis. "In almost no other country does one learn to see so clearly," wrote the German architect Karl Scheffler, "how man has used and shaped the circumstances he encountered. In Holland the geological is experienced, indeed it is the fundamental experience."[2] One could add that the geometrical is also experienced. The shaping of the landscape according to geometrical patterns – a tradition dating from the Renaissance – is a demonstration of the fact that the Netherlands was constructed. In their ground plan, towns and villages present the appearance of a rectangle or square with a grid or that of a wheel with spokes.[3]

Planning is not a characteristic of one particular period in Dutch history. It is the fundamental characteristic at all times, the essential precondition for a civilization that had to settle and survive in the estuary area of three major rivers, the Rhine, the Maas and the Scheldt. In this delta the dividing line between water and land changed constantly. And from the early Middle Ages man also took the initiative in managing the water and creating land. Similarly, the division between water and land governed urban planning. Dutch towns were laid out as a mixture of canals and streets. Sometimes the houses were built immediately alongside the drainage ditches, sometimes the watercourse was altered as a result. The construction of Dutch society was in the first place an intervention to counter the excess of water and a pushing back of the border between water and land.

Around the turn of the century this age-old constructivism took on a new form in the so-called urban plan. From the national point of view, the need for planning arose from new hydraulic engineering works and from the modernization of public transport through the introduction of railroads. Big canals and modern railroads brought about visible changes to the structure of the major cities, particularly in the province of Holland. Similar effects were seen as a result of economic expansion, which was related to the new infrastructure, and of population growth. For such reasons the need for urban planning was put on the public agenda in the United States and several West European countries. It became the subject of "practical action, theoretical reflection and programmatic statements," a conscious transition from "pre-urbanism" to "urbanism." A planning movement arose which could call on the tradition of public works in Germany and of social housing in Britain.[4]

Until the second half of the nineteenth century the historical structure of almost all Dutch cities remained intact, a structure largely determined by town planning in the sixteenth century. It was dominated by the city walls, the ramparts, which were intended for defense against a siege and formed the indisputable outer edge of all planning policy.[5] In past centuries the fortifications builder had taken the lead in the design of extensions to the city. If, however, the need for defense became less pressing, until finally the walls were no longer required, then the town planner also lost his principal guideline.

The way in which the local councils smashed through the ancient town walls was savage, wrote the architect Willem Kromhout when looking back on what he called the first "encircling," the first belt of new construction around the historic towns. "Suddenly the splendid enclosed quality of the cities was gone." One saw the housing blocks going into the meadows like "gaping monsters," having proclaimed their arrival in advance through the kind of mess that only a big city can throw out. "Streets without end, which showed not the least inclination to curve, planless combinations hatched at the municipal offices of the day, without the slightest understanding of urban composition." Occasionally a waterway or watercourse could halt the "planless outpouring," but not for long. As soon as the obstacle was overcome, the housing blocks moved on, until like a serial they suddenly broke off somewhere with "to be continued."[6]

In 1900 the town planner is expected to counteract this building explosion because ideally he has become a "master builder," who combines academic knowledge of society with architectural imagination. "Instead of being a willing tool in the hands of the hosts who assist him," wrote one alderman in 1912, "he is their stringent critic and their general too." The master builder must have at his disposal statistics and calculations as well as a well-equipped library on the subject and "a collection of photographs, plates and situation drawings from other cities. If he has visited these places himself, he will of course have his notes." Lastly, "as the dominant leader," he must take the decisions; that is to say, produce "an efficient and beautiful whole from the chaos of data, recommendations and opinions."[7]

Waterways

The Netherlands has never lacked hydraulic engineering projects, but in the nineteenth century their economic importance and their scale were striking. The program of works was initially dominated by the building of canals and the draining of the large lake known as the Haarlemmermeer in the heart of the province of Holland. But after 1850 three spectacular projects in underwater hydraulic engineering were undertaken: the improvement of the navigability of the Rhine and the Maas, the construction of the New Waterway to provide a better connection between Rotterdam and the North Sea, and the digging of the North Sea Canal from Amsterdam through the dunes to the coast. The project for improving the navigability of the great rivers had been given a "firm push" in 1853 by Minister for Home Affairs Johan Rudolf Thorbecke, a liberal and the principal author of the Constitution of 1848. The two other projects were eventually carried out after the same Thorbecke, minister for home affairs for a second time from 1862, took the crucial decisions following a long-drawn-out debate and piloted the necessary bills through Parliament.[8]

Between 1875 and 1916 the depth of the Rhine was increased to three meters to meet the needs of modern steamships. The deepening of the main waterway to Germany followed from the government's decision to provide a quicker link between Rotterdam and the sea through the New Waterway. The construction of this link and of the North Sea Canal was a formidable challenge for the Dutch contractors because of the serious and complex problems of digging through the dunes region and of controlling the tides. The state took the initiative and formulated the commissions; the contractors were given the task of carrying out the plans.[9] The New Waterway was opened in 1871 and the North Sea Canal in 1876. But it was not until the eighteen-eighties that the depth of both was brought into line with the needs of modern shipping.

Historians of technology in the Netherlands emphasize that a traditional industry, namely the dredging companies, owed their technical advances and spectacularly increased scale of operations to these huge projects. The modernization and expansion of these family businesses was a consequence of these new public works. As the result of another phenomenon of the age, the expansion of the cities, they would soon be awarded new contracts to make the often swampy ground fit to build on. The town of Sliedrecht on the river Merwede, a continuation of the Rhine, was the home of most Dutch dredging firms. The specialism originated in the Middle Ages, when farmers and landowners were required to maintain their section of the river dyke, because the Merwede constantly flooded. This legal obligation gave rise to the dyke worker, who made it his profession to build and maintain dykes. For this purpose osiers were used; they were grown in the nearby Biesbosch (a small delta of rivers and land) and bought and sold in Sliedrecht. In the second half of the nineteenth century, because of the need to invest in expensive new dredging machines, the contractors merged to form a few large concerns: Bos, Kalis, Volker and Van Hattem. This was also the time when Sliedrecht, a model of industrial regeneration in a monoculture governed by Calvinist orthodoxy, began to accept immigrants who came to work for the dredging companies as technical staff. In the case of the North Sea Canal, the Volker company took over the digging through the dunes after an English contractor had suffered several failures. After 1880 the problem of the insufficient depth of the New Waterway was also solved. A so-called suction hopper dredger was used. "This was the finest hour of Dutch hydraulic engineering."[10] The result was that the Sliedrecht contractors became famous throughout Europe and were called on to assist with projects in France and Belgium. In 1886 Bos and Volker were among the founding members of the Zuiderzee Association, set up to gather support for the reclamation of the Zuiderzee. In its technical and organizational demands this project far exceeded the draining of the Haarlemmermeer, and it was not carried out until the twentieth century.

Railroads

The construction of the Dutch railroads in the nineteenth century may be roughly divided into three phases. Between 1838 and 1845 the private company *Nederlandsche Rhijn Spoorweg Maatschappij* (Dutch Rhine Railroad Company; NRSM) built a line from the ports of Amsterdam and Rotterdam partly along the Rhine to Arnhem; in 1856 it was linked to the German network via the border town of Emmerich. Another private company, the *Hollandsche IJzeren Spoorweg Maatschappij* (Dutch Iron Railroad Company; HSM), which started later but in 1839 became the first to offer a service between Amsterdam and Haarlem, extended this line to The Hague and Rotterdam in 1847. In these pioneering days the railroad followed the course of rivers or canals; the new train was a variant of the tow-barge or Rhine barge. The rail network in the Netherlands was a continuation of an older and by European standards remarkably dense system of transport by rivers and canals. "In effect, the adjustment to cheap mass transportation – in such matters as industrial location, urban systems development, and social customs – that most countries made suddenly after the introduction of the railroad, had been made two centuries earlier in the Netherlands."[11]

In a second phase, which had begun in 1860, the state played a leading role, as it had in the modernization of the waterways. This period saw the construction of the two main lines that gave this modern form of public transport a national range: the Zuider Staatsspoorweg and the Noorder Staatsspoorweg. The first ran between the seaport of Vlissingen in Zeeland and the southernmost city of Maastricht in Limburg. The second went from Arnhem on the Rhine to the northern cities of Leeuwarden and Groningen and ultimately Harlingen, the principal seaport for trade with England. An important

Railroad bridge over Hollands Diep (Moerdijk Bridge).

third phase in the building of railroads in the Netherlands – and in fact their completion – was heralded by the decision to bridge the great rivers. Up to then they had been left undisturbed; after all, rail traffic was oriented towards the seaports and the cities in the province of Holland. The choice eventually made was for a bridge over the Hollands Diep at Moerdijk and for three other bridges – over the Lek at the town of Culemborg, over the Waal at Zaltbommel and over the Maas at the village of Hedel. This system was completed in 1870. As a result, the position of the city of Utrecht as the central junction in the network was strengthened. Two years later the Moerdijk bridge was finished. The author and journalist Conrad Busken Huet, who returned to Amsterdam in 1877 after spending many years in the Dutch East Indies, admired the Netherlands for "its iron bridges," which stirred the imagination. "When crossing the Moerdijk bridge one has the impression of something fabulous. I heard more than one fellow traveler or person in my situation, having left the Indies shortly before or after me, express a lively satisfaction with the splendid bridges. It gave them a sense of reassurance, they said, to know that now they could reach the mother country directly from all points in Europe, at any time of the year. And at the same time a sense of security and relief that at any time they can leave again in any direction."[12]

Local railroads developed along with the national network, which was completed in 1890. The standards and rules applying to them were derived from the German "Secundär Bahnen." Indeed, the first to be built after the introduction of the Local Railroad Act in 1878 was a German initiative: in 1881 a local line was opened between

A locomotive crosses the bridge on the east side of Central Station in Amsterdam.

Dutch railroads in 1900

Dutch railroads in 1930

Since 1900 new railroads have been built only in the peat areas of the province of Groningen and in North and South Holland, and for the main route linking Eindhoven, Weert and Roermond.

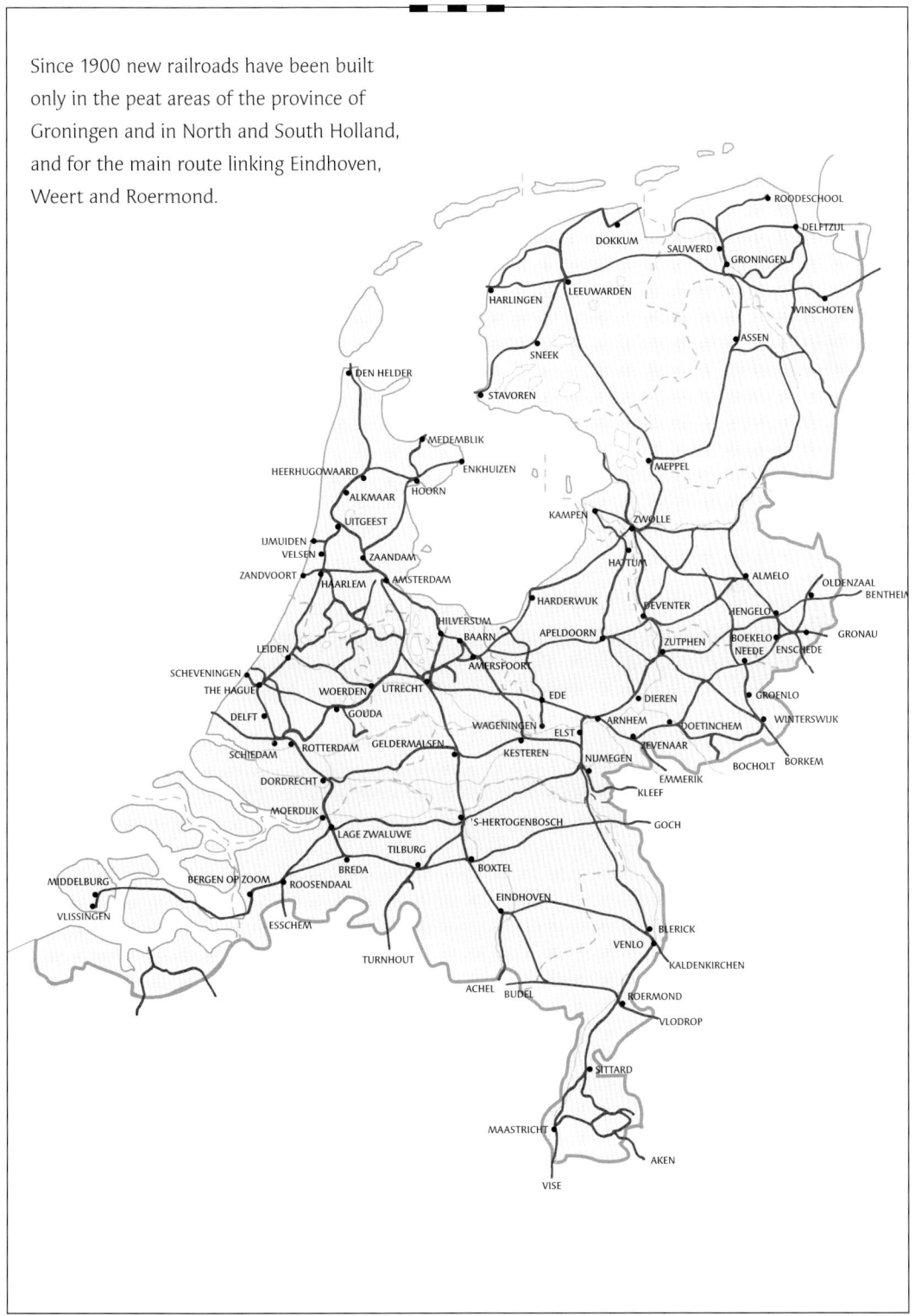

Dutch tramroads in 1930

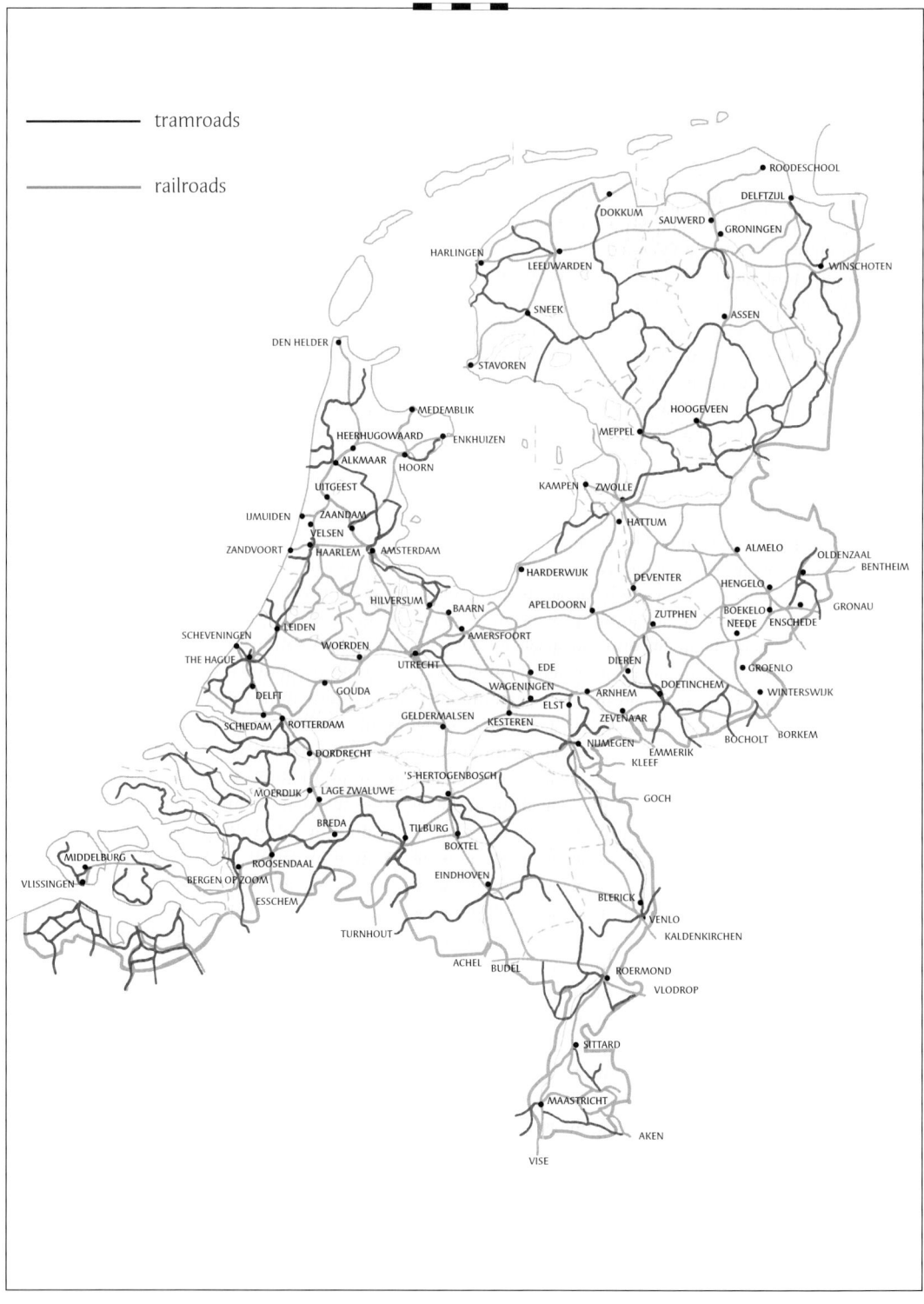

Den Dolder station on the Centraalspoorweg.

Haarlem and Zandvoort, the resort on the North Sea. The local railroads thus came to determine how the area developed, opening up as they did not just the seaside resorts, but also the scarce areas of heathland in the province of Holland. In 1874 the Oosterspoorweg line from Amsterdam through the Gooi heathland area to Utrecht came into use. This led to a noticeable trend among wealthy citizens to move from Amsterdam to the heathland villages of Hilversum and Bussum. When a decade later a steam tram began to run between Amsterdam and the Gooi region, Laren and the surrounding villages also attracted well-off commuters as well as artists.[13] The same applied on a still greater scale to the local lines around Utrecht. A country village like Zeist expanded as a result, while a commuter community like Bilthoven came into existence around the railroad stop. Bosch en Duin, a prosperous villa district, was developed on the initiative of the railroad company.[14]

In the first half of the nineteenth century the railroads were built up to the gates of the old cities of the province of Holland – in Rotterdam to the Delftse Poort, and in Amsterdam to the Haarlemmerpoort. When the city walls could be taken down, however, and the train was accepted as a modern means of transport for long distances – often indeed the only form of long-distance transport – people came to attach greater value to the grandeur of the station and the surrounding area, because they served as an introduction to the city. Grand stations were built in Groningen and 's-Hertogenbosch, complete with a boulevard in the latter case. In Nijmegen, which had been losing its importance as a fortress city since 1874 and was not connected to the national rail network until 1880, a prestigious district was successfully created. A large station was built, and at the same time the city walls were converted into boulevards with ring roads which incorporated the Keizer Karelplein; it became the earliest traffic circle in the Netherlands.[15]

The national range of the railroads led eventually to a uniform system of operation, rates and time. On January 1, 1911, a standard rate for travelers came into effect; it applied to the entire country and to all companies. A standard time had been introduced in 1909. "The statutory time in the Netherlands is the mean solar time of Amsterdam," so declared the law intended to abolish the regional differences in favor of a national standard with the capital as the measuring point. Earlier there had been a debate about adopting the same time as the neighboring countries, which had standardized local clocks at least a decade before. Should the Netherlands follow British time (the Greenwich meridian) or German (Central European) time? The choice was a compromise: Amsterdam time was 19 minutes and 32 seconds ahead of Greenwich time and 40 minutes and 28 seconds behind Central European time.[16]

Rotterdam

The new canals had a profound influence on the country they cleaved through. The building of the New Waterway meant the end of the economic pre-eminence of Dordrecht, the oldest city in Holland, and turned the Maas delta into one great industrial zone of shipyards, oil refineries and warehouses. A new settlement, IJmuiden, developed around the North Sea Canal sea lock. It became a fishing harbor which sucked people in from the traditional fishing ports on the coasts of the North Sea and of the Zuiderzee, long before the Zuiderzee had been dammed and partly reclaimed. New industry developed around the canal, and Nederlandse Hoogovens (1918) was to become an extensive conglomerate of steel factories.

No Dutch city was to grow as much as Rotterdam in the decades around the turn of the century. In the nearly fifty years between the first urbanization of the southern bank of the Maas (1869) and the annexation of the new town Hook of Holland at the mouth of the New Waterway (1913) the city's population almost quadrupled – increasing from 116,232 to 462,504. It was the city in which the nineteenth-century spirit of enterprise had been more evident than anywhere else in the Netherlands. The political support base was provided by a city council in which, until 1880, ninety percent of the members were merchants. For years the Rotterdam council was dominated by an elite drawn from trade and shipping, with the Mees, Stolk and Van Oordt families outdoing all others with between eight and ten scions in the representative body.[17]

Early on Rotterdam had a form of town planning which was primarily concerned with water management and the harbors. The city architects in the nineteenth century, Willem Nicolaas Rose and Gerrit Johannes de Jongh, had both been military engineers, the equivalent of the "polytechniciens" in France, servants of progress. Rose was a representative of the generation of engineers with a social conscience; De Jongh represented the positivists. Rose made his name with a project that supplied the city canals with fresh water from the Maas and provided a basic level of public health in a city that had been regularly struck by cholera epidemics. De Jongh was responsible for raising the level of expertise at the Municipal Department of Public Works; he preferred to recruit his staff

The elevated railroad through the centre of Rotterdam. In the foreground is the statue of Erasmus.

The construction of the bridge over the Koningshaven in Rotterdam.

from among the newly graduated engineers of the Polytechnic School in nearby Delft. He came from the world of business and he owed his reputation to a policy around the turn of the century that combined visionary harbor projects with crude housing policy.[18] In Rose's day the "polytechniciens" were steeped in utopian ethics, and in reaction to that De Jongh and his generation became hard-boiled realists. "Perhaps no generation in the entire history of man has been more self-assured in its healthy positivism or so blind to its limitations."[19]

This growth is explained by two developments. The most important was the economic resurgence of the Ruhr after the Franco-Prussian War of 1870. The rise of this center of mining and ironworking led to an increasing demand for transport. The resultant need for labor coincided with the crisis in agriculture in the last quarter of the nineteenth century, which turned numerous farmers and sons of farmers from the islands and polders of South Holland and North Brabant into fortune-hunters on the urban labor market. Rotterdam became the natural port for transshipping from Rhine barge to ocean-going vessel and vice versa. In the first half of the century the Netherlands had been positioned, economically speaking, on the edge of what was then the center of the world economy, Great Britain; in the second half, because of the spectacular growth of the German economy, it came to lie between two poles, Germany and Britain.

Rotterdam's wish to be accessible to modern steamships meant that the port facilities had to be substantially extended. To achieve this, the city jumped over the Maas: new harbors were built at Feijenoord on the left bank. Later came the Rijnhaven (1894), which took the place of the entire village of Katendrecht on the left bank, the Maashaven (1905) and finally the Waalhaven (1919). The elevated railroad, which extended the Rotterdam line to Dordrecht, also had significant effects on the old city. The question as to where this line should cross the Nieuwe Maas river was debated for twenty years. In the end nautical considerations and the international rules as regards free passage on the Rhine were the decisive factors in the decision to bridge the Maas at the (notional) dividing line between sea and river traffic. Consequently, the historical triangular heart of the city could not be spared. The line had to be built along the city river, the Rotte, which had to be drained for the purpose. The elevated railroad, the city viaduct, may not have been beautiful, but it was certainly up to date. "An unbroken series of engineering works over a distance of nearly forty-five minutes' walk has no precedent in Europe and is without doubt an eminently modern solution."[20]

As a result of the new railroad, the city center began to grow mainly towards the west. The Coolsingel was filled in and the neighborhood improved through slum clearance; the new boulevard was monumental in appearance. A new city hall was to be the culmination of this development and give proud expression to the civic spirit of enterprise. The liberal burgomaster Alfred Zimmerman took the initiative. In 1913 the old, picturesque quarter was demolished and construction to a design by the Delft professor and architect Henri Evers began. Seven years later the new city hall was complete, a building modeled on a French Renaissance castle and thus not dominated by modern forms of monumentality. The gold angel of peace on the clock tower reminds us that the building work coincided with World War I.

The (drained) Coolsingel in Rotterdam with new public buildings (including the town hall)
and the old mill.

The new town hall of Rotterdam with a remnant of the Coolsingel canal on the left.

The Delftsche Poort station in Rotterdam.

The leap across the Maas was spectacular: bridges followed by housing. In South Rotterdam the rail passenger had a view of rows of social housing apartment blocks with messy, narrow backyards and balconies facing the tracks. The south side of the Maas was rapidly turned into harbors or housing projects, but this was not based on any town planning. What might have served as the core of an urban design, a central square, was soon lost behind a maze of streets and railroads in drab working-class projects. Street layouts were approved piecemeal and were not coordinated. Because the individual owners of the houses had to be mollified, the city granted concessions which undermined the planning system. The expansion of Rotterdam resulted in "a city without joy, without green spaces, without highlight or resting point; hard and cold in its planning and without atmosphere."[21]

"In the first half of the century a faint echo of a glorious past can still be heard dying away slowly," thus the historian of urban expansion in the nineteenth century, the notary Van Ravesteyn, concludes his sketch; "but by the end there is little to value other than a certain honesty in the simple construction of workers' streets, whose layout and buildings have no other pretension than to provide dwellings such as the people desire." Each increase in the tonnage handled by the port brought more workers to the city, necessitated more clerks and attracted more tradesmen. "But the number of big employers who settled here permanently, the residents of the affluent neighborhoods in the new city, was negligible."[22]

Amsterdam

The new shipping route and the building of modern railroads also had far-reaching effects in the historic city of Amsterdam. The digging of the North Sea Canal in the eighteen-seventies gave rise to a westward movement in the port of Amsterdam. The shipping facilities had traditionally been on the "old side," that is the east side, of the city, which gave access to the Zuiderzee. However, the new locks, the Oranjesluizen, closed off this east side and so turned the IJ estuary into a final destination accessible to the bigger steamers and other vessels coming to Amsterdam from the west. They continued to sail past the center and chose to load and unload on the east side, where new quays and warehouses were built. The second factor in the reorientation of Amsterdam was the expansion of the rail network. The aim was to connect the lines from the north and west with those from the east. The existing termini were to be replaced by a single central station at the site of the open harbor front.[23]

There was a long and fierce debate about preserving the beauty of the city's waterside as against the benefits of a direct rail connection next to the port. It was eventually decided by the economic arguments. In 1889 a new Central Station was built in the IJ, right in front of the city's main artery, the Damrak, in fact the dammed river Amstel. The commission for the station was awarded in 1876 to two architects, Pierre Cuypers and Adolf van Gendt. Their design was monumental. It departed from the norms that had applied to railroad buildings since 1860. The engineers who advised the railroad companies had studied the Großstadtbanhöfe in Germany and Austria because "in layout and operation our railroads correspond most closely to the German railroads." Moreover, after so many heated debates it was felt necessary to make up for the picturesque quarters that had been lost. So the new station "must not be out of place, especially in the capital."[24]

The style chosen was Old Dutch. What exactly that meant was the subject of an ongoing debate. Cuypers had indeed looked at sixteenth-century Dutch houses, but he drew much more inspiration from the South Netherlands Renaissance style. The façade is probably derived from that of the chateau at Fontainebleau near Paris. The structure of the central section reveals "how Cuypers struggled to achieve a synthesis of his design principles, the requirements of a station and the palace model."[25] Historical examples were sought and cited in all manner of ways. The entrances to the royal hall – adorned with the arms of the ruling sovereign William III and Emma – are derived from the gates of the palace of Regentess Margaret of Parma in Mechelen and of Breda Castle, both dating from the first decades of the sixteenth century. The scheme of decoration for the interior and exterior was drawn up by the trio who had performed the same task for the new Rijksmuseum (1885): apart from Cuypers, they were Victor de Stuers, the official in charge of preserving historic buildings, and Jozef Alberdingk Thijm, merchant and man of letters. The latter composed a number of mottoes for the doors of the various waiting rooms. Through the reliefs in the tympanums of the arched windows, Cuypers wanted to create a link to two other prominent buildings in Amsterdam: Jacob van Campen's classicist town hall on the Dam, already a royal palace, and his own Rijksmuseum. In the station and on the rear of the town hall the peoples of the earth pay tribute to the

The Prins Hendrikkade in Amsterdam with the new Central Station on the left and in the middle the new St. Nicholas's Church. The telephone wires run along masts.

The monumental station at Nijmegen.

Amsterdam staple; in the Rijksmuseum it is the arts that do this. Most of the decorations in the station are, however, a (classicist) tribute to agriculture, trade and industry, which are fostered by this palace of modern transport.

The importance of a station in the heart of the city was demonstrated by the imposing façade, which closed off the Damrak, the old port with its warehouses in the center. The old inner city also changed its appearance rapidly. The trading premises made way for facilities for travelers, such as the Victoria Hotel. New shops were oriented towards the station and served to make the Nieuwendijk, in the west of the center, livelier. With the construction of the new department store De Bijenkorf, the Damrak acquired the allure of a boulevard. Berlage built his celebrated Exchange here. It was only in the Zeedijk, in the east of the center, that the atmosphere of the old port was preserved. The center of Amsterdam moved towards the west.

Urbanization and dismantling

Up to 1880 most towns in the Netherlands remained the same size they had been in the sixteenth and seventeenth centuries. Population growth, if it was discernible at all, was slow. This was to change in the second half of the nineteenth century. The town and urban space quickly took on a different appearance. In 1880 nearly forty percent of the Dutch population lived in towns. By 1930 the figure had risen to over sixty-five percent.[26] The eighteen-eighties were a turning point in another way as well. Expansion was accompanied by a measure of economic unification. Regional systems gave way to an economy on a national scale. Cities outside the province of Holland, which could previously be seen as serving a relatively closed area, were given and made use of the opportunity to develop economic functions for a larger market.[27] The balance between the city and its rural surroundings began to shift in favor of the former. The city was no longer dependent on the country, and the surrounding area came increasingly under urban influence.

City councils had to look for new building land. They found it outside the city walls; urbanization coincided with the pulling down of these walls, a consequence of new military technology. The same dynamic seen in the economic unification of the nation led to defense on a national scale. It was no longer conceivable that an enemy could be opposed city by city, so there was no longer any need to put the cities behind ramparts. According to a Ministry of War list, in 1854 the Netherlands still had twenty-three fortified towns and four municipalities in so-called organized positions. After the new Fortifications Act of 1874, which resulted from experience of the devastating effects of modern artillery during the Franco-Prussian War of 1870, this number was reduced to nine: these were towns along the Holland Water Line and smaller places in the ring of forts known as the Stelling van Amsterdam. There the ramparts had to be retained, and they thus formed a barrier to expansion.

In the context of Europe there was nothing unusual about urbanization in the Netherlands around 1900. Other West European countries showed relatively greater growth at this time; in fact the Netherlands lost its traditional lead. A comparison shows that the rate of urbanization was particularly striking in England and Wales.[28]

Percentage of inhabitants in towns with population between 20,000 and 100,000

	1801	1851	1900
England and Wales	7.2	12.4	22.8
France	3.9	4.5	10.4
Prussia/Germany	4.2	4.7	12.6
The Netherlands	13.0	14.4	16.6

Percentage of inhabitants in towns with population over 100,000

	1801	1851	1900
England and Wales	9.7	22.5	35.3
France	2.8	4.6	13.7
Prussia/Germany	1.8	3.1	16.3
The Netherlands	11.5	7.3	22.7

In the process of urbanization the decades between 1899 and 1930 tend to be referred to as the "industrial phase." During that period industrialization was largely an urban phenomenon.[29] People were drawn by the growing employment opportunities. Another important factor was the growth of the population due to an increase in the excess of births over deaths. Some Dutch cities may have been hard hit by the epidemics of cholera in 1866 and of smallpox in 1872, but in general they resulted in the introduction and collectivization of health care, a source of new life. A proper water supply had to be provided to slake the thirst of ever more people, and also to ensure that the drinking water was safe. The new system of sewers was a way of preventing a repetition of the cholera epidemic, but it was also made necessary by the increasing population density. In addition, the city was both a reason and an opportunity for innovations in communication. Its concentration of population made the operation of a telephone system profitable (at first it had been used mainly by "business people and tradesmen"). The same applied to building a streetcar network.[30]

The city became a challenge for young and enterprising people: "for the young who would not inherit their parents' farm, or who had studied longer than was required for a career in the provinces; unemployed farm laborers and the rural poor who could afford to make the journey; relatives of people who had gone to the city and been successful there, or so they claimed." These people fell under the spell of city life, of the conspicuous wealth and the excitement, and of liberation from the limits of small-minded village life and the ever-present supervision of parents, bosses and schoolmasters. "The metropolis meant adventure, affairs, erotic stimuli and cultural pleasures. Lack of economic opportunities may have driven the migrants to the city, but a yearning for cultural and

The Eusebiusstraat in Arnhem.

emotional experiences drew them there." The big city was and is "*the* place for adolescents; and adolescence as a phase of life is a modern and urban phenomenon."[31]
Some cities grew rapidly in the nineteenth century. Amsterdam and Rotterdam benefited from an influx of young people looking for work or liberty, while in typical residential cities such as Arnhem, Nijmegen and The Hague most of the immigrants were elderly.[32] The Hague also grew because it was the seat of government; the increase in the central government's responsibilities had consequences for the expansion of the city.

Arnhem

In the years after 1860 Arnhem was the fastest growing city in the Netherlands. It became an attractive place to live because it had been able to pull down its city walls unusually early in the century and develop on the wooded bank of the Rhine. From 1808 the walls and gates, with the exception of the Sabelspoort, were removed to make way for parks and villas on the boulevards encircling the center. It was above all "East Indian" families who had returned from the Dutch colonies having made their fortune who chose to live in Arnhem.[33] In the old center of the city, workers' housing was built, slotted in and added on. The occupants were in part the hundreds of migratory workers, principally from Prussia, who had come to Arnhem to do construction work.[34] The unhygienic conditions in these neighborhoods resulted in successive epidemics.[35] Because of its early expansion, Arnhem is also an example of a city where it was only at a late stage, and

The Velperplein in Arnhem.

even then rather tentatively, that urban development came to be dominated by municipal housing policy.

This striking growth was not underpinned by an urban plan. It was not until halfway through the century, in 1853, that the municipal architect set out the main lines of the expansion of the city in a design with the character of a street plan. The building code contained few planning rules, and the minimum requirements were not formulated precisely enough to prevent abuses. As a result, a working-class neighborhood like Klarendal could be built with a large number of one-room dwellings without light or air or sanitation. Arnhem's appearance was then dominated by houses in rows, with showy façades, with balconies and plaster decorations on the street side, while the backs were neglected. But "however barren and characterless such a façade may often seem in itself, however shabby and cheap the adornments, the terracotta heads and garlands, may be, together these houses and the trees and flowers have succeeded in giving Arnhem an atmosphere of wealth and prosperity, of summer, going out and pleasure."[36] In 1878 a property developer was active in Arnhem for the first time. It then became the rule to leave construction to private developers, while the city concentrated on imposing stricter regulations on the layout of streets and squares.[37] Towards the turn of the century there were developers in Arnhem who managed entire districts and neighborhoods. The city sometimes intervened to buy country houses, and in 1866 it acquired the Klarenbeek estate, in order to preserve its natural beauty, and in 1899 Sonsbeek. They were both turned into public parks.

The Hague

The growth of The Hague was favored by the fact that the ideal of a unitary state, which had been proclaimed while the country was under French domination, was preserved even after Napoleon had been driven out. Accordingly, in 1813 the central government was again established in the city, together with a central bureaucracy which would expand noticeably by the end of the nineteenth century as a result of all the state's new responsibilities. The Hague was also the residence of the sovereign. King William I (1772-1843) did not leave his mark on the city architecturally, but he took an interest in the enlarging of his palace, the Oude Hof on Noordeinde, which was to be of a size thought to be in keeping with the united kingdom of the Southern and Northern Netherlands. His successor did make his presence felt in the city. William II (1792-1849) made several building plans for The Hague. His preference was for neo-Gothic, with which he had become familiar while a student in Oxford. Buildings in the neo-Gothic style went up around the palace on Kneuterdijk, his residence, to a design by the "king-architect." After fifty years, however, they had to be demolished because of their ruinous state or the danger of collapse; the only exception was the Gothic Hall intended for his painting collection.

In the second half of the nineteenth century private enterprise made its presence felt. Initially, it was a case of several very wealthy citizens joining forces in a property development company. By the end of the century the field was dominated by limited liability companies working with the capital of affluent individuals, small investors and banks. They bought a quantity of land and designed a street layout. After this had been approved by the city council, the land was made ready for building, divided into lots and sold. The nineteenth-century belt around The Hague is largely the sum of these street layouts. A total of eighty of these plans were dealt with by the city council before World War I.[38]

Land also lay behind a social division in The Hague. Towards the coast the ground was sandy and was regarded as drier than the traditional peaty soil of Holland. Houses for the wealthy were built in the dunes and woods of Scheveningen and in the Haagse Hout, the woodland near the city. The attractions of these districts were increased by laying out water gardens and an unusual pattern of streets. To the east and southeast, around the railroad station of the Hollands Spoor, the *Hollandsche IJzeren Spoorweg Maatschappij* (HSM), lay peat ground. This is where the working-class districts were built. The harbor was also built there and there was room for industry. In the first decades the Hollands Spoor station was in fact hidden behind large industrial premises and was also just too far from the city center to have a decisive influence on town planning.

The sandy soil was building land for the wealthy; the peaty soil was for workers' housing. Such social segmentation was not unusual in nineteenth-century urbanization. But nowhere in the Netherlands was it as clearly visible as in The Hague. It became a classic example of spatial segregation, of the separation of the different classes in special districts. Whereas in the old city there had been a heterogeneous population within a homogeneous space, in the modern city the space was divided into "neighborhood communities" which were architecturally and socially homogeneous but also the heart of the separation.[39]

The neo-Gothic extension to Kneuterdijk Palace and the equestrian statue
of William of Orange in The Hague.

The neo-Gothic Willemskerk in The Hague.

The Hague in a peat area: the road and the waterway to Delft.

The Hague on sand: the expanding resort of Scheveningen.

Institutional factors

Urbanization is a process. Around the turn of the century, however, it could also be seen as the pursuit of urban planning. There were three institutional prerequisites: an increase in the scale of the city council's activities, greater powers to intervene in the field of private property and, as a consequence of that, the power to decide whether or not land would be built on in the interests of social housing.

The first prerequisite, an increase in scale, was put on the political agenda in the last decade of the nineteenth century, when the government submitted proposals to annex a number of suburbs around Rotterdam and Amsterdam. At the end of 1894 the minister for home affairs piloted a bill through Parliament that provided for Rotterdam to annex two municipalities, Charlois and Kralingen. This was the largest annexation since 1869, and it tripled the area covered by the city at a stroke. In 1896 the parliamentary debate on the proposal to incorporate large parts of the southern suburb of Nieuwer-Amstel into the capital Amsterdam led to sharp conflict. The minister defended this annexation as a deliberate step towards urbanization. "The national interest," he stated, "demands that thriving cities be created, equipped with everything that can promote the health and intellectual development of their inhabitants, the increase of their economic power, the safeguarding of their transport interests, and a reasonable sharing of the municipal costs of all this."[40] The opponents were motivated not only by local allegiances but also by the fear of encroachments on private ownership. They pointed to the example of Brussels, where urban expansion had not prompted the conclusion that the surrounding municipalities should be annexed. After the opponents lost this battle, annexation ceased to be controversial in subsequent cases of urban growth (such as The Hague). The Dutch answer to urbanization was the forming of large municipalities.

The chief obstacle to urban planning was the protection of private property. The right of the individual citizen to dispose freely of his property and interests had been laid down in the Dutch constitution since the French Revolution. Expropriation was only possible on the grounds of the "public interest" and "in the manner laid down by law and in return for proper compensation."[41] Gradually, a shift away from this view took place. *Salus publica*, the public interest, carried greater weight.[42] From 1887 the legislature could make as many exceptions to the right of property as deemed necessary.

It was thanks to the new Housing Act passed at the beginning of the new century that municipalities were finally given the power to make regulations in the interests of social housing and thus encroach on private property – the third prerequisite. Large cities were required to draw up a plan of expansion every ten years. The issue of housing had been raised at the same time that calls were made for a system of public health care. The resulting Acts, on housing (1901) and on public health (1901), represented the triumph of a new generation of liberal parliamentarians who believed the state had a role to play in the regulation of capitalism.

Expansion plan

The Housing Act was not the beginning of town planning in the Netherlands, but it did herald a new phase in planning based on social concerns. Previously, the expansion of the cities had been criticized primarily because of the unhygienic conditions, but now there was also criticism on aesthetic grounds. In the end it came down to the same: the so-called "engineers's housing" in the belts around historic city centers came under fire because of both health and aesthetic considerations. A pioneering study of the aesthetic norms applying to town planning was published by the Viennese architect Camillo Sitte in 1889.[43] Hendrik Petrus Berlage, who was to play a leading role in the modernization of town planning in the Netherlands both as a theorist and as an architect, read this study and wrote about it in 1892. He became one of the supporters of aesthetic norms in housing and planning. He called on his colleagues to create not a "street network" in expansion plans but a "townscape."

The first designs for urban expansion were essentially, and in accordance with a long tradition, street layouts. A telling example is the (second) expansion plan by the director of the Department of Municipal Works of The Hague, I.A. Lindo. He began designing it in 1902; in 1905 it was put on display. In the wave of criticism that it evidently inspired it was pointed out that the designer had confined himself to the highways and given no indications for the siting of monumental buildings. Moreover, he wanted to avoid compulsory purchase procedures as far as possible and so left the construction of housing to the private sector. There was no park, because in his view fresh air already flowed

Design by H.P. Berlage for the Gevers Deynootplein in Scheveningen.

through the city from all sides.[44] In 1907 a dissatisfied city council decided to pass over its Director of Municipal Works and to invite Berlage to design an expansion plan.

Berlage's design was published in 1908. It was a composition of townscapes, a combination of answers to "questions of utility," arising from requirements as to hygiene and traffic management, and artistic norms.[45] A key feature was the enclosed square: it formed the center of a district or quarter and it was here that public buildings were located. The highways were to have a monumental appearance. Berlage wanted to orient the center of The Hague according to two poles, one of which would be a new Central Station (on the site of the existing Hollands Spoor station) and the other a new city hall. This would create a monumental north-south axis from the station through the government quarter to the Scheveningse Bos, at that time the edge of the city. Berlage had to defend his plan with the help of Lindo. When he presented it, an old debate about municipal land policy turned out to be an obstacle. Should The Hague expropriate the area concerned in order to realize the aims of its plan or should it choose the method of a ban on construction? This administrative delay meant that the plan was not approved until 1911. In the end the only parts that were implemented unchanged were those which most closely corresponded to the streets in the earlier Lindo plan.

The failure of Berlage's plan in The Hague showed that all manner of institutional and political resistance stood in the way of modern town planning. Since 1901 there has been only one expansion plan that has been conceived on a grand scale and carried out on a grand scale. This was the so-called "South Plan" for expansion on the southern side of Amsterdam. It was presented in two versions. The first was designed by Berlage in 1900, positively received by the city council and approved in 1904, but never realized. A decade later, when according to the Housing Act a new plan was needed, Berlage came up with a second version which was largely implemented, thanks primarily to the

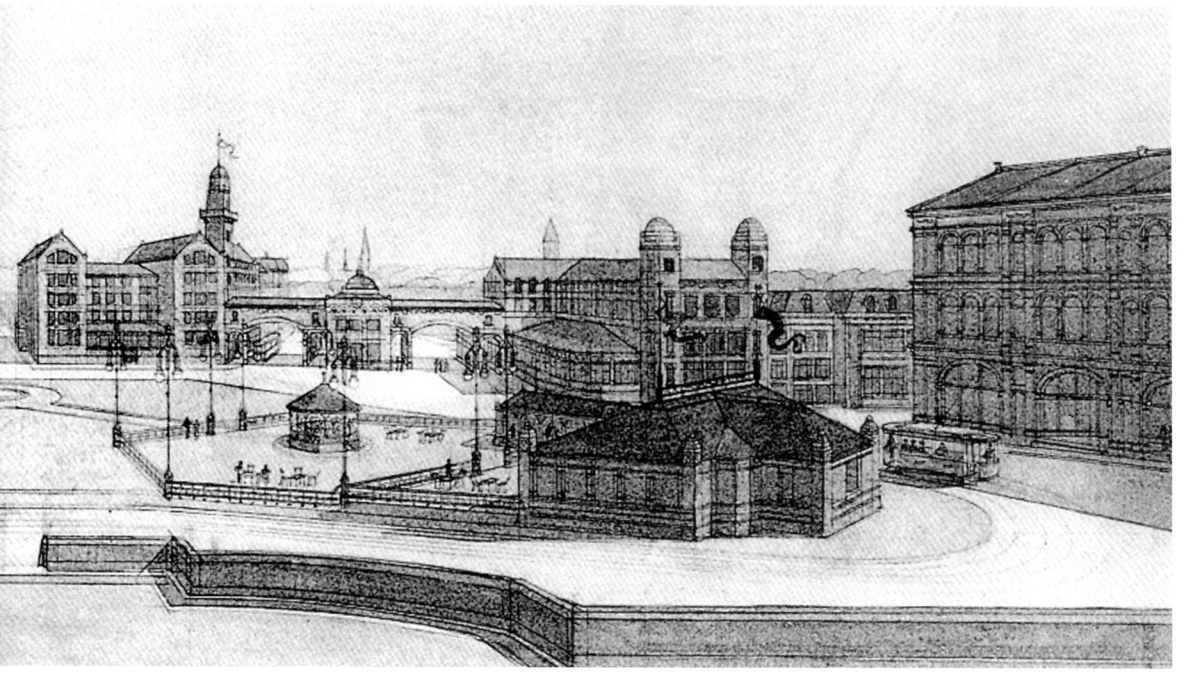

support and persistence of the Social Democratic alderman Floor Wibaut, who was responsible for housing. In this plan two developments came together: the innovations in architecture around 1900 and the creation of "mass-produced housing" – the task of building thousands of more or less similar dwellings and thus making an urban space.

Architects united in the *Architectura et Amicitia* society abandoned the copying of styles and eclectic approach that characterized the work of their masters, including Cuypers. A decorative application of the old vocabulary of forms no longer reflected the needs and characteristics of a changed society, they contended, but only the ideals of a bygone age. Their criticism focused on two aspects. They rejected the adoption of forms from earlier styles in neo-Gothic or neo-Renaissance buildings. The critics also argued that the primarily decorative use of old styles had led to the original concept of architecture being forgotten. The new generation was interested in rural architecture in north western Europe (Scandinavia, but above all Germany) or exotic dwellings and monumental religious buildings in Asia and Egypt. The attention paid to alternative forms was partly based on a fascination with the sources of architecture, with originality. At the same time they were open to a broad range of everything that was new and not seen before, which later led to a strong demand for up-to-date images of contemporary developments in other countries. During this period a great many concepts and ideas were exchanged between Europe and the United States.[46]

What Berlage had in common with other leading members of *Architectura et Amicitia* was commitment based on social idealism. With architects such as J.L.M. Lauweriks and Karel de Bazel this interest was more spiritual in nature, and sometimes derived from anthroposophy. Berlage was keenly interested in politics too. He was well acquainted with the lobby of hygienists and as a member of the Amsterdam health committee he had taken part in their "condemned dwellings tours." Another participant described how they visited the slums in the Jordaan district, going "up and down one staircase after another." "While one person was talking to the mistress of the house, Berlage's attention was often caught by the splendid colors or the atmosphere peculiar to the slum or neighborhood. The pace of the tour was somewhat reduced."[47] Berlage was inspired by socialism and believed that it represented the spiritual structure of future society. Social housing and buildings that served a community would dominate urban space. This political view of society and art was not shared by the main group in *Architectura et Amicitia*.

So it was Berlage who concentrated on new forms of mass housing in the Netherlands around the turn of the century. The modernization of Paris with its wide boulevards and beautifully situated public buildings was a perfect example; he wanted to refer to it when seeking new forms. He saw it as his task to build apartment blocks and street façades in the way it had been done in Haussmann's Paris. In 1893 he argued that a block with hundreds of identical rented apartments gave rise to striking architecture and must be an essential element in the modern cityscape. To some architects this sounded like a denial of their experience that rented apartments were a necessary evil belonging to the shady world of contractors and speculators. Furthermore, modern city traffic needed space, which was not available in the historic city center. Thus, unlike seventeenth-century Amsterdam, which was picturesque, the new city would have to be monumental.[48]

Berlage was supported in this view by publications about and concrete examples of housing in Germany. Paris may have been his historical model, but the blocks built in the new Berlin became his contemporary criterion. In 1910 a large exhibition on town planning was held in Berlin, and American designs were on view there. A year later Berlage was able to see them in the United States. The "barbarous beauty" of New York taught him that it was no longer possible to make a usable town plan with "old means." "One must free oneself of the sentimental predilection for the beauty of the old European cities and accept what modern life offers."[49]

The South Plan was Berlage's design, but it was carried out by various architects in the years between the two world wars. The second belt, which was now built around the first on the south side of Amsterdam, presented fine examples of unbroken street façades and contemporary block design. The urban space was shaped and traversed by three highways, the first of which began at the bridge (later named after Berlage) over the river Amstel. In the layout at that time this was the southeastern entrance to the city. The eastern part of the South Plan was realized almost completely according to Berlage's directions. The western part, however, was robbed of its symmetry when it was decided not to build the South station, the other entrance to South Amsterdam.

Block building and garden city

In the Netherlands the planning movement of 1900 left two legacies: imaginative social housing and the picturesque garden village in the city. The first became internationally known as the architecture of the Amsterdam School. The second was an import from England and Germany: the garden city movement.

The Amsterdam School is the name given to a generation of architects after Berlage who built specifically for the city and pursued, both in the individual residence and in the apartment block or public building, "space-architecture" and in particular a remarkable variety of forms. Through their original treatment of volumes and façades, they created a new architecture in the decade after 1911. The architect Hendrik Wijdeveld described the art of the Amsterdam School in 1918 as "the manifestation of the Imaginative, who play innocently with the treasures of rationalism."[50] The three architects who formed the core, Michel de Klerk, Piet Kramer and Johan Melchior van der Mey, had met at the office of Ed Cuypers, the nephew of Pierre Cuypers. Their architectural gifts were expressed mainly in the construction of apartment blocks. The first was built in Spaarndammerplantsoen on the west side of Amsterdam. They subsequently played an important part in the realization of the South Plan; they designed the area built by *De Dageraad*, a social democratic housing association, and they acquired an international reputation as "the Amsterdam School." Their concept of architecture in the service of the community was one they shared with Berlage, but they differed from him because of what they called new values: a preference for individuality and plasticity.[51] After 1915 this style would also strongly influence interior design, the decorative arts and graphics.

The garden city movement originated in Britain. Its founder was Ebenezer Howard, who in 1898 published a book calling for town planning reform rather than revolution

A housing block in the Spaarndammerplantsoen in the style of the Amsterdam School.

and in 1902, when it was reprinted, gave it the title *Garden Cities of Tomorrow*. Two factors were at work here: the international movement of the hygienists, and criticism of the disadvantages of the great cities, combined with a longing for simplicity. The first garden city, Letchworth, was located not far from London. The movement soon became known in Germany; in 1902 a *Gartenstadtgesellschaft* was founded. It was by way of Germany that the movement reached the Netherlands because German town planning was the model.[52] The first initiatives were taken after 1910: the Lansink district in Hengelo (1911) and Vreewijk in Rotterdam (1913). Lansink – probably the first example in the Netherlands – was a garden village built for the Hengelo Building Association, in which the Stork engineering company had a major interest.

Vreewijk, a garden village on the southern bank of the Maas, was designed by Berlage and completed by several architects, of whom Marinus Granpré Molière and Pieter Verhagen were to become the best known. The plan was strongly supported by Karel Paul van der Mandele, a banker and for many years president of the Chamber of Commerce. In 1916 the city council decided that it should go ahead and take the form of a limited liability company, the *Eerste Rotterdamsche Tuindorp* (First Rotterdam Garden Village).[53] In contrast to Berlage's picturesque preliminary design, Granpré Molière and Verhagen introduced more severity and straight lines in the treatment of the blocks and the street layout, especially when the area grew into an important district in South Rotterdam. In Vreewijk it was considered too expensive to drive piles under the housing

Vreewijk garden village in Rotterdam.

complexes, so the houses had to be constructed as lightly as possible, with low walls and a high roof. The architecture was characterized by "peace in itself." Each street was to have a character of its own in a detailed plan for the public greenery. In each case one variety of plant dominated: laburnum in one street, lilac in another, jasmine in a third. This detailing was also intended to encourage the inhabitants to take up gardening. Annual competitions for the most attractive backyard were held. In this way Vreewijk became a showpiece of Dutch town planning, "a midpoint between formalism and romanticism."[54]

Preservation of beautiful cities

While the city grew, the historical center was also modernized as a consequence of the building of railroads and of redevelopment to cope with the volume of traffic. The most striking redevelopment scheme was that for Raadhuisstraat in Amsterdam. In 1895 it was planned as a connecting link between the center and the western part of the city, which involved pulling down historic houses on Herengracht and Keizersgracht. The street was remarkable in two ways. It was laid out in a curve, and thus formed a counterpoint to the geometrical pattern of the canal belt around the inner city. In the way it broke through the canal ring, Raadhuisstraat resembled the Via Diagonale in the old center of Turin, and in its curved form it was like Regent Street in London. The second remarkable aspect was the type of buildings along the street. French ideas on the aesthetics of the city were adopted in an Old Dutch townscape.[55]

The redevelopment of the historic inner city aroused opposition. In 1883 an American journalist wrote "that the Dutchman of to-day will, whenever he gets a chance, pull down remorselessly his most lovely old ramparts and town walls or halls, or in fact, any relic of the past, to make way for a boulevard or a railway station." For "the demon of improvement seems to be let loose at the present moment all over the land."[56] Anyone wanting to get a picture of "a medieval town," according to a book on Dutch monuments, now had to do some traveling: "Here a church building preserved intact, somewhere else a town hall façade or chamber, a few hours away a fragment of a monastic house, or the front of a dwelling, or part of a hospital, and in other provinces a city gate, or a bridge or a section of the town wall or a forgotten old street or corner or alley." The hefty, three-volume work on *Oud-Nederlandsche steden in haar onstaan, groei en ontwikkeling* (The Origins, Growth and Development of Old Dutch Towns) showed that there was now a need to conserve historic buildings in the townscapes and skylines.[57]

Those who were concerned about this began to organize after 1900. *Amstelodamum*, a society for the promotion of historical knowledge of Amsterdam, was founded in 1900. The *Bond Heemschut* was established in 1909 by Adriaan Weissman, the architect of the Stedelijk Museum in Amsterdam. He "had been walking through Monnikendam when he was shocked to find a once beautiful corner building replaced by an architectural monstrosity."[58] He called architects and lawyers together to discuss setting up an organization for the preservation of historic towns. The name "heemschut" was taken from the German body *Heimatschütz* (1904), whose activities were known about in the Netherlands. The Bond Heemschut had a range of objectives: the preservation of historically important buildings and monuments, but also areas of natural beauty. Another aim was to help preserve folk art, traditional costume and folk festivities. One concern that also played a role in the founding of the organization was "disfiguring advertising" in the cities.

Urban planning in the Netherlands around 1900 presents a paradox: while aesthetic norms govern the new city, the South Plan, and its realization stirs the imagination, redevelopment schemes undermine the traditional geometrical forms of seventeenth-century Amsterdam.

St. John's Cathedral in Den Bosch.

4

Community art

In the last decade of the nineteenth century there was a sea change in the thinking about the relationship between art and society. The excessive individualism and impressionism of the Eighties Movement had brought about a need for more certainty, more style, more clear-cut direction and faith. The movement that grew up was driven by builders, artists, musicians, and social historians, in contrast to the predominantly poetic and belletristic forces of the previous era. "It was the constructive minds that had the floor," said Huizinga.[1]

The ideal image that the constructive minds envisaged was that of the cathedral. The cathedral shaped their ideas in three essential respects. Firstly, it defined the outlines of an ideal community. Secondly, it merged the separate fields of art (architecture, painting, sculpture, stained glass) into a *Gesamtkunstwerk* total work of art. And thirdly, it was the result of the efforts of craftsmen working together in harmony in a guild or brotherhood.

Ideals of community

In *De Kroniek* of February 17, 1895, Hendrik Petrus Berlage set out his idea of the art of the future. This would be "an art of and for the people, of and for the community." Berlage harked back to the Middle Ages as the period when the whole population had concerned itself with art: "was it not the whole urban community who built the great medieval cathedrals, those sublime artistic expressions, the result of the supreme endeavors of all the guild members, in other words of all working people?"[2]

Berlage used the cathedral as a model to paint a picture of a future in which art would give expression to a renewed sense of community. That model suggested an ideal society, whose contours were not clearly circumscribed. What did Berlage mean by community? It seems clear from his description that he primarily had the urban community in mind ("was it not the whole urban community who built..."), and particularly the city republics of Northern Italy (Siena, Florence). He saw the cathedral as the symbol and manifestation of an early democracy, a view he shared with the French architect Viollet-le-Duc, whom he greatly admired. It is quite possible that Berlage was inspired by the Frenchman in his choice of words. Berlage presented the cathedral (and this is a second striking characteristic) as the "result of the supreme endeavors of all the guild members, in other words of all working people." It was a monument to the workers – the people – who had made this supreme effort. It appears from this that the word "people" should not be conceived of in the ethnic sense, but in the sense of a social class, in the very precise meaning that the progressive liberals gave to it at the end of the previous century, that is "the working population."[3] The "guild members" refer, in Berlage's view, to a sort of trade union.

A striking aspect of Berlage's later publications – from 1910 onward – is the conviction that the art of the future would arise out of a belief. Berlage was inspired in this by the theosophist Matthieu Schoenmaekers, whose credo "our religion is a worldly religion" he repeatedly used as a motto for his articles.[4] That belief was a belief in the community. In the place of the traditional notion of God and the new political ideology, Berlage put the community, which thus acquired a metaphysical dimension.[5]

It was the painter Antoon Derkinderen who gave the *gemeenschapskunst* – community art – of the eighteen-nineties its impetus. His first mural in the antechamber of the city hall in 's-Hertogenbosch, which was completed at the end of 1891, sparked a debate about the relation between art and society. Or perhaps more accurately, this mural caused the sudden crystallization of a development that had been latent for some time in the minds of a number of artists of the period – Jan Veth, Alphons Diepenbrock, Richard Roland Holst, Berlage and others. In March 1893 Derkinderen signed a contract for a second mural in the same city hall. The contract stipulated that the subject of the painting would be the building of the city's Cathedral of St. John. The initial designs of 1894 and Derkinderen's explanation of them confirm this. But in the course of the preparations Derkinderen changed the design. The finished painting, unveiled in July 1896, depicted not the process of construction, but the completed building. This shift from the dynamism of a work in progress (on which Berlage placed the emphasis) to the stasis of a building in which the movement of history itself is solidified and cast out in favor of a timeless social order is revealing. The figures – stiff, Byzantinesque depictions of Duke John, flanked by the Pope and the Emperor – reinforce the idea of a rigid feudal power structure. The cathedral in the painting is the symbol of fossilized authority. Revealing, too, is the fact that "the people" are entirely absent from the scene.

The composer and essayist Alphons Diepenbrock believed in the same ideal of community as his friend Derkinderen. In 1895, in an article in *De Nieuwe Gids*, he wrote of Beethoven's *Missa Solemnis*: "It is as if one saw all humanity prostrate in adoration, when, as the solo voices bring to an end the mystical canticle with the words 'ex Maria Virgine,' the choir almost soundlessly murmurs the repeated 'Et incarnatus est de Spiritu sancto ex Maria Virgine.'"[6] Diepenbrock saw it as the task of the priest / artist to evoke an image for adoration that would be silently worshipped by the people.

The views of Berlage on the one hand, and Derkinderen and Diepenbrock on the other, typify the rift that began to make itself felt during the eighteen-nineties in terms of the community ideal. On the one hand a vague socialist ideal, a prospective ideal that projects the hope of a better society into the future. Among the adherents of this ideal, as well as Berlage, were Richard Roland Holst, Henriëtte Roland Holst and Herman Gorter. On the other hand there was the retrospective community ideal, strongly influenced by Catholicism, to which – alongside well-known champions like J.A. Alberdingk Thijm, Pierre Cuypers, Alphons Diepenbrock and Antoon Derkinderen – the group of architects who surrounded Lauweriks, De Bazel and Walenkamp subscribed. The irreconcilability of these two ideals did not come to light until after the turn of the century. In the eighteen-nineties, Berlage and Derkinderen still thought that they were talking about the same thing when they referred to the cathedral.[7]

The new concept of art marked a break between the Eighties Movement and the Nineties Movement, between impressionism-individualism and *gemeenschapskunst*, between the leading journals *De Nieuwe Gids* and *De Kroniek*. Dissatisfaction with the subjectivist aesthetics of the Eighties Movement (take, for instance, the dictum of the poet Willem Kloos, who advocated the "most individual expression of the most individual emotion") was already being felt and expressed by the contributors to *De Nieuwe Gids* themselves. Looking back, the poet Albert Verwey put these doubts into words:

> Perception, sensitivistically individuated, lost its link with the mind. The elevation of the ideal, intensified to self-glorification, lost its link with society. Unrestrained surrender, partly to sensory perception, partly to individual emotion, increasingly provoked the antagonism of those who craved a mental synthesis in which emotion and perception were subordinated to an idea that had suprapersonal value.[8]

Opposition to this was expressed in *De Nieuwe Gids* itself. In the very first piece he wrote for *De Nieuwe Gids*, "Melodie en Gedachte" (Melody and Idea), in December 1891, Diepenbrock trumpeted his criticism of the journal's principles. The community, he said, was going under in a welter of the "lyrical art of the Ego." And, "The epic art of the past, which is the revering, immortalizing, monumental-contemplative, the oldest primitive art of the Seer-of-God in the visible and invisible, of the God of the community ... is now foreign and far from this century of the low horizon of the many."[9] The following year, in a detailed response to Derkinderen's town hall wall, Jan Veth formulated the principle of the "isolation art" of the Eighties Movement as against the "community art" of the Nineties artists. Whereas the former was "flowing and lyrical," the latter was "static and epic." Whereas the aesthetics of the former were based on the expression of personal feelings that led to nothing but loneliness and isolation, the latter was rooted in a form of community thinking that was fueled by resurgent piety and "social movement." Veth regarded them as two impulses toward the same *gemeenschapskunst*, and did not touch on the differences in conception that would only later become manifest. In a later article on Derkinderen, Veth added to this analysis that the Eighties preferred the form, the Nineties the substance, leaving it in no doubt that this latter was the only important factor: "All greatness and beauty must lie in the intellectual substance, expression can achieve nothing higher than to be subsumed in the substance. The more modestly language retires in the face of this substance, the more effect it will have."[10]

By 1891-1892 the resistance to the principles of *De Nieuwe Gids* had already caused so much internal dissent within the magazine itself that a single spark was all it took to set off the explosion. This spark was struck in 1891, when Frederik van Eeden criticized Edward Bellamy's *Looking Backward* which had just been translated by Frank van der Goes as *In het Jaar 2000* in 1890. Lodewijk van Deyssel responded to this socialist view of the future with an article in which he defended an art based on aesthetics. Art, to his mind, was inextricably associated with affluence. When the finite quantity of prosperity was shared out in the way the socialists wanted, there would be nothing left of art. Van der Goes and Van Eeden took offense and wrote a rebuttal. Willem Kloos piled into the debate, sided with Van Deyssel and attacked both Van der Goes and Van Eeden. Van Eeden and Van Deyssel each replied in turn, with the result that the editorial board was now irrevocably split. Van Eeden defended his religious humanism, Van der Goes his Marxist socialism, in which he was supported by the journalist Pieter Tak. Kloos, with his anti-Christian and asocial individualism, backed Van Deyssel. The relation between art and society was the divisive element that led to the collapse of the magazine when Kloos took over the running of it, and first ignored and then fired the other members of the editorial team (1892-1894).

Some of the contributors to *De Kroniek* were recruited from among malcontents from *De Nieuwe Gids*: Veth, Berlage and Diepenbrock. The journal's credo was community art – *gemeenschapskunst*, which was also described as public art, monumental art, the art of ideas, decorative art, life art, applied art or social art, art of the people, democratic art, and even proletarian art.[11] This credo was expressed in the subjects that were covered. In the column on painting, Veth advocated monumental, decorative art. André Jolles wrote an influential series of articles about the "Primitives," that is to say the old masters of medieval Florence – Cimabue, Giotto, Fra Angelico, Lippo Lippi and Botticelli – and the gradual degeneration of their social art into individualism in the early Renaissance. Berlage dominated *De Kroniek*'s architecture pages. From the start of his career until the early eighteen-nineties, Berlage had conformed to the prevailing neo-Renaissance style. But in his first article for *De Kroniek*, he converted to *gemeenschapskunst*. The extract quoted above is taken from this article.

The arts and crafts column was particularly typical of *De Kroniek*. Book printing, book binding, sculpture and carving, wrought iron work, stained glass: all the important contributors – Huizinga, Coenen, Derkinderen, Jolles, Kalff, Lauweriks and Roland Holst – wrote for it. In music it was Diepenbrock who revealed himself as the foremost apostle of the new art. His first articles were devoted to Wagner. Over the years his enthusiasm for the composer waned, but he remained engaged with the "monumental expression of the idea" in music.

This swift overview reveals the extent to which the social involvement of art was the focus of interest. Just how much ideas were governed by the desire to give art back its social role can also be seen from the titles of some of the major contributions: "Art and Socialism" (Jan Veth, July 5, 1896), "The Purpose of Art" (William Morris, October 18, November 1, November 8, 1896), "Theater and Community" (Jan Kalff, July 21, October 13, November 17, 1895), "Art for the People?" (Abraham van Collum, December 3, 1904), "Art and Science, and Socialism" (August 20, September 6, September 20, 1902), "Literature and Life" (J.H. Labberton, March 6, March 23, 1901).

The polemic in *De Kroniek* described earlier, which arose out of reports by Bauer about the coronation of the Tsar, brought to light a divergence of opinion between the "artist-socialists" (Tak, Veth and Van der Goes) and the "artist-aristocrats" (Bauer, Diepenbrock and Van Deyssel), as they were described at the time. This polemic was a pendant to the one that had raged in *De Nieuwe Gids* a few years before. The social position of art was the key issue in both cases, but there was an essential difference. The debate in *De Nieuwe*

Gids was concerned with the question of whether art should or should not be socially engaged. For the contributors to *De Kroniek*, this question had already been answered in the affirmative. This time the polemic was about the question of the form this engagement should take: socialist or Catholic-aristocratic.

Community of the arts

The term *gemeenschapskunst*, or community art, which Jan Veth coined in 1892,[12] referred not only to an "art for the community," but also to the cooperation and collaboration between the arts in an encompassing, usually architectural whole, a *Gesamtkunstwerk* – a total art work or synthesis of the arts. According to J. A. Alberdingk Thijm, the medieval church was also a model for this community of the arts: "the highest calling of Fine Art is not to be piled up as collected trade goods in a storehouse, often without any sort of order – but to be part of life." The "Christian church" was the "highest expression of the unison of the arts."[13] It was architecture that set the tone in this choir of the arts. Painting, sculpture and stained glass worked together in a communal endeavor led by the master builder. The revival of this collaboration was celebrated in the decoration of the Rijksmuseum. The three large stained glass windows in the entrance hall are dedicated to sculpture (east window), painting (west window) and architecture (central window). The extent of the emphasis on medieval techniques and models in this central window is striking. Of the four buildings that are presented as exemplars, the two medieval edifices – the Mariakerk in Utrecht and the Ridderzaal – are given pride of place.[14] The Rijksmuseum was the first important building in which, as we shall see later, there was a response to Thijm's call for a revival of *gemeenschapskunst*. At the start of his article, Thijm outlined the situation that had arisen after the disintegration of the medieval ideal. According to Thijm, in the course of the Renaissance the arts had detached themselves from the collaborative context and become isolated. The painters and the sculptors had developed into free artists. They no longer worked on the construction site; instead they moved into studios where they produced works of art that were movable and marketable. In consequence, the work of art became alienated from the community context, in the specific sense of the building of which the work of art formed part, and in the abstract sense of a community of faith from which both building and work of art derived their meaning. The museums, in Thijm's eyes, were therefore degenerate institutions that were a cross between "charnel-houses" and "warehouses" (terms used in the same article). Thijm sketched a situation of fragmentation, alienation and commercialization in the arts, and this formed the basis for his call to reintegrate art into an architecturally and socially meaningful whole.[15]

Thijm's complaint was directed not just at the lack of cooperation between the arts, but also at the management of the artistic heritage, in other words at the museums. Both his first and his second plea received a response. Pierre Cuypers and Victor de Stuers put the first (reintegration of the work of art in an architecturally and socially meaningful whole) into practice in the construction of the Rijksmuseum. The building was a fusion of collaborating arts. What is more, the museum had been designed such that the works on display worked together in a meaningful (architectural) whole; they were, one might say, incorporated as elements in a *Gesamtkunstwerk* – a synthesis of the arts. We shall return to this twofold achievement later.

Jan Veth referred to Thijm in his controversial article on *gemeenschapskunst*. He, too, was thinking of the "community of the arts" when he thought about *gemeenschapskunst*, but of course he never lost sight of the fact that these collaborating arts were the concrete manifestation of community awareness. The cohesion of the arts was, after all, directly related to and dependent on the cohesion of the community. This was the tenor of Veth's contention, and here he recalled Wagner, who had argued in "Die Kunst der Zukunft" that when the community fragments, the *Gesamtkunstwerk* also disintegrates.[16]

Berlage adopted the idea of the *Gesamtkunstwerk* expressed by Thijm, Cuypers and Veth. In 1894 he aligned himself with the community of the arts:

> After the Middle Ages, architecture gradually lost her status among her sister arts; no longer did she compel sculpture and painting to do her bidding; no longer did she lead; later yet, each of the three sister arts went her own separate way, and architecture, reduced in rank, was thought of as the least of the three. In antiquity and the Middle Ages she, the high, beautiful, proud sister, who commanded respect, was, as we have said, not even considered to be an art. It has proved possible, in the second half of the nineteenth century, through the efforts of a great many skilled architectural artists, to reverse this opinion entirely in architecture's favor; in the view, too, of painters and sculptors who, biased as they too had been for a long time, likewise had their doubts about architecture as an art. The great rapprochement of all the arts that should lead to cooperation, the artistic ideal of *all* ages, is becoming discernible again.[17]

Art and industry

The reflections on the social function of art brought about a significant boost for the applied and decorative arts. In England, at the end of the eighteen-thirties, the architect and architectural historian Augustus Pugin had said that the industrial revolution had led to degeneration. In *Contrasts* (1836) he drew a comparison between the city during the late Middle Ages and that of his own time, with the intention of demonstrating just how seriously the quality of life had deteriorated. The core of his criticism was that the medieval community ideal had been lost as a result of the growth of modern capitalism. But the degeneration was also manifest in mass-produced goods for everyday use. Pugin argued that the quality of these articles could be improved if artists were to be involved in their design and manufacture. The idea was taken up by the very energetic Henry Cole, who in 1857 founded the South Kensington School and the South Kensington Museum (later the Victoria and Albert Museum), a museum for the applied and decorative arts. Cole was also the driving force behind the organization of the Great Exhibition "of arts and manufactures" from all over the world, which was staged in London in 1851. The exhibition in turn stimulated a debate about the quality of applied art and how to improve it,[18] and prompted Gottfried Semper, a pupil of Cole's, to write a standard work, *Wissenschaft, Industrie und Kunst* (1852), which was to have a very great influence, not

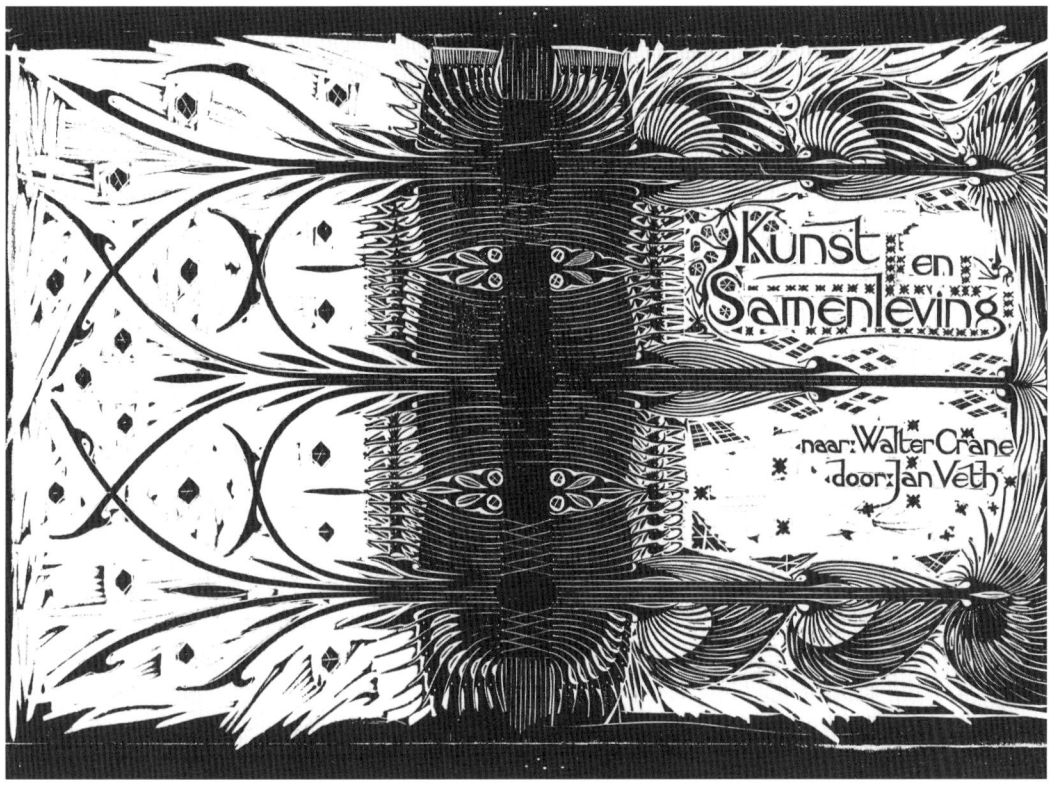

Gerrit Dijsselhof, cover of Jan Veth's *Kunst en Samenleving,* woodcut.

least on Berlage. Semper's proposals for improving arts and crafts education included establishing collections of decorative arts products, giving lectures, setting up workshops and awarding prizes. Arts and crafts education in England was reorganized at his instigation. 1854 saw the establishment of the Working Man's Guild, in which artists and craftsmen worked together for the first time – among them the essayist and social reformer John Ruskin, the poet and painter Dante Gabriel Rossetti and the artists Ford Madox Brown and Edward Burne-Jones. It was followed by many other well-known guilds, most of them grouped under the heading of "Arts and Crafts."

Pugin, Cole and Semper took a very pragmatic view of the use of machinery. Their aim was to reunite industry and art in industrial art. This approach was radically revised by the actions of John Ruskin. Ruskin had a lively dislike of the practically-minded Cole. He accused Cole of a half-hearted attitude, particularly where the use of machines was concerned. To Ruskin, the machine was the source of all the problems. Everyday objects were ugly because they had the soulless perfection for which machines alone were responsible: "Our modern glass is exquisitely clear in its substance, true to its form, accurate in its cutting. We are proud of this. We ought to be ashamed of it. The old Venice glass was muddy, inaccurate in all its forms, and clumsily cut, if at all, and the old Venetian was justly proud of it" (*The Nature of Gothic,* 1853). The quality of these products was, in his view, dependent on the amount of manual work that was invested in them: "For it is not the material, but the absence of human labor, which makes the thing worthless" (*The Seven Lamps of Architecture*, 1849). Ruskin condemned all forms of mechanical production and banned the use of machines in the St. George Guild that he founded. In 1888 W. Benson organized a famous exhibition under the title *The Combined Arts* (the result of collaboration between Walter Crane, Lewis Day and many others). The title of the exhibition was later changed to the *Arts and Crafts Exhibition*, and this name was adopted to signify the whole movement. Ruskin had immense influence on the Working Man's Guild and on other famous guilds (including William Morris's "Firm"). He dominated the whole of the Arts and Crafts movement, which meant that in the second half of the nineteenth century all sorts of crafts were revived in enterprises modeled on medieval guilds which, almost without exception, therefore called themselves "guilds." But this approach led to an inevitable dead end. The hand-made, often lavishly decorated furniture, the forged ironwork, the rolls of hand-printed wallpaper were of superb quality, but completely out of the reach of the ordinary working man. William Morris, one of the mainsprings of the Arts and Crafts movement, a member of the Social Democratic Federation and one of the founders of the Socialist League, became discouraged by the realization that only the rich could afford to buy his products. At the end of the century Charles Robert Ashbee, who had founded the Guild of Handicraft in 1888, concluded: "We have made of a great social movement a narrow and tiresome little aristocracy, working with great skill for the very rich."[19] The sociologist Thorstein Veblen denounced the prestige that technically imperfect, hand-made and prohibitively expensive articles had acquired. In his view, this prestige acted as a brake on the development of modern design. Frank L. Wright mocked the movement by producing objects to which imperfections were deliberately added – by machine – to create the impression of manual work.

The turning point in the Dutch attitude to art and industry was the exhibition *Kunst toegepast op nijverheid*, or art applied to industry, which was mounted in 1877 in the Paleis voor Volksvlijt on the initiative of the *Vereniging ter bevordering van Fabrieks- and Handwerksnijverheid*. This organization, an association that aimed to promote manufacturing industry and applied art, and a predecessor of today's employers' organization, was founded in 1851, inspired by the Great Exhibition held in that year. Victor de Stuers was a member of the branch in The Hague and, from 1873, Holland at its narrowest onward, a member of the main organization. He played an important role in the organization of the exhibition, both directly as a member of the main board and indirectly as the author of a number of influential publications in which he argued the importance of the decorative arts: "Holland op zijn smalst" (1873, Holland at its narrowest), "Iteretur decoctum" (1874) and "Unitis Viribus" (1875), in which he stressed the government's role in the artistic education of the nation.[20] In 1875 De Stuers was appointed to head up the newly established Arts and Sciences Department at the Ministry of Internal Affairs. In this post, he was extraordinarily active on behalf of applied arts education. He organized the 1877 exhibition and, also in 1877, wrote (without attaching his name to it) the report of the government committee set up to examine the status of Dutch art education. He ensured, by means of a focused grant policy and a specific inspectorate for art education, that the reforms advocated in the report were put into effect. He saw to it that schools, societies and museums were founded, among them a museum for applied art education in Haarlem in 1877, with an associated school (1880), the Rijksschool Quellinus in Amsterdam (1879, based on the team of craftsmen and builders that Pierre Cuypers had put together in 1877 for the construction of the Rijksmuseum) and a school in Utrecht in 1886. He added applied arts departments to existing institutions; and he encouraged the establishment of the Arti et Industriae society in The Hague in 1884 as well as two other similar societies that organized exhibitions. The results of all these educational stimuli became apparent after 1890. Several ceramics factories were set up (no fewer than six in 1894-1898) and various interior design studios, including the famous studios of Lauweriks and De Bazel (1895), Van Wisselingh and Co.'s "De Amstelhoek" (1900), where Gerrit Dijsselhoff, Carel Lion Cachet, Theodoor Nieuwenhuis and others all worked, and the "Binnenhuis" studio established by Berlage and a number of entrepreneurs in 1900. Others included "De Woning" (1902, Willem Penaat), "Die Haghe" and "Arts and Crafts" in The Hague (established in 1898 by the architect Chris Wegerif and his wife), and there were also studios in Breda and Zaltbommel. Decorative arts magazines appeared – the *Maandschrift voor vercieringskunst* (1896) and *Bouw - Sierkunst* (1898) edited by Lauweriks and De Bazel. Architectural and general journals carried regular columns on the applied arts; *De Kroniek* started to focus specifically on the decorative arts, and many mainstream artists like Jan Toorop and Johan Thorn Prikker also started working in the decorative arts. The result of these efforts could be seen at three foreign exhibitions: in Paris in 1900, in Turin in 1902 (the *First International Exhibition of Modern Decorative Art*) and in Krefeld in 1903, the *Holländische Kunstausstellung*. The strength of the rejuvenated sector was also reflected in the foundation of an association for craftsmen and artists in the decorative arts, the *Nederlandsche Vereniging voor Ambachts- en Nijverheidskunstenaars* (VANK), in 1904.

In a most remarkable way, the educational structure was the work of a single man, Victor de Stuers. Circumventing the existing legislation, he set up a whole branch of specialist education: training in applied arts. He saw to it that the responsibility for the applied arts lay with the Department of Arts and Sciences at the Ministry of Internal Affairs. When De Stuers appointed Wilhelmus Molkenboer as inspector of art education in 1886, the applied arts colleges were even exempted from regular schools inspections. This was possible because they were private schools, set up by school associations of which old societies were a part, societies like the *Maatschappij ter Bevordering van de Nijverheid* (Society for the Promotion of Industry) in Haarlem. At the level of establishment and management, they were run by private individuals who played a role similar to De Stuers's role in the department. Bervoets (1985) described De Stuers's policy thus:

> In his post, he turned himself into a statesman with almost dictatorial powers. The personal nature of his administration is typical of him. His immediate superior, the secretary-general, supervised the introduction of an immense body of laws and regulations, but had to put up with the way that, by formal and informal means, De Stuers's department developed a policy that was not enshrined in a single law on the statute book. Everything that De Stuers brought into being as a senior government official he made concrete in organizational structures which, by the time he left the department, had formed the basis of a sort of unwritten law.[21]

In 1900 the minister, Hendrik Goeman Borgesius, put an end to De Stuers's power. Fifty-nine colleges subsidized by the government were removed from his control and his authority to award grants was withdrawn. Applied arts education as it had come into being under his guidance was not regulated by law until an act was passed in 1919.[22]

The English Arts and Crafts movement had a major impact on the Dutch applied arts field. In 1884 the poet and art critic Carel Vosmaer translated *Some Principles of Everyday Art* by Lewis Foreman Day as *De kunst van de Daaglijksch leven*. Other booklets by Day were also popular, witness Berlage's enthusiastic reaction in *De Kroniek* in 1896. Jan Veth translated Walter Crane's *The Claims of Decorative Art* (1893) under the title *Kunst en samenleving* (Art and society) with magnificent woodcuts by Gerrit Dijsselhof. This book stresses the social function of the crafts: applied art is *gemeenschapskunst*. Richard Roland Holst spent 1893-1894 in London, where he encountered the work of William Morris, Walter Crane, Charles Ricketts and Charles Shannon. In 1893 he wrote in a letter that the future of art would lie with decorative (community) art: "the constant production of paintings and drawings as illogical wall decorations is surely failing, it cannot be other-wise, and the new way of applied art is leading to immense fields in which anything can yet be done." In 1886 Toorop examined Morris's ideas, but he was more strongly influenced by the Belgian Art Nouveau movement. The English magazine *The Studio*, which commenced publication in 1893, was one of the channels through which the Arts and Crafts movement exerted an influence in the Netherlands and elsewhere. In 1893 there were exhibitions of work by Crane, Kate Greenaway and others. During this period, from the launch of *The Studio* onward, the Arts and Crafts movement started to display characteristics of Art Nouveau. Despite fierce resistance from various quarters, including Walter Crane, who described Art Nouveau as a "strange decorative disease," the "whiplash line," which was later to be regarded as characteristic of Art Nouveau, can be recognized in many designs. It is also significant that the Arts and Crafts movement exhibited embroidery by Hermann Obrist, the maker of the embroidery known as "Peitschenhieb," (whiplash) whose name and decorative principle were extended to became the trademark of Art Nouveau: the "whiplash style."

Art Nouveau, for which the Arts and Crafts movement paved the way, flourished on the continent. The name was derived from the shop opened by Siegfried Bing in Paris in 1895 – the Galérie de l'Art Nouveau – where work by Henry van de Velde and others was exhibited. But the real cradle of the movement was Brussels, the city of Victor Horta and Van de Velde. It was there, through the *Société des Vingt*, that Jan Toorop saw the new trends, with which he started to experiment himself, incorporating in his own work the undulating line that is so characteristic of Art Nouveau. Art Nouveau's influence spread via the link between Brussels and Toorop, via Johan Thorn Prikker who was a friend of Henry van de Velde's, and through the Wegerifs' interior design shop Arts and Crafts in The Hague, where work by Van de Velde was exhibited at the opening in 1898.[23] Around 1900, The Hague and Scheveningen became a center of Art Nouveau, and this was encouraged by Scheveningen's rapidly rising popularity as a seaside resort. Restaurants and hotels were constructed in the new style. The elevations were mockingly described as "built book pages." The pier, built by the architect W.B. van Liefland in 1899-1900 and destroyed in World War II, was a true monument of Art Nouveau.

The reactions to Art Nouveau expressed by many established Amsterdam architects – Cuypers, Berlage and the group involved in the society of architects known as *Architectura et Amicitia* – were devastating. In a speech in 1901 Cuypers talked about "an infectious disease," a "parasitic plant, introduced by architects, furniture-makers, paper-hangers, decorators, painters and metalworkers." He called the style a "fin-de-siècle" phenomenon, "the diseased state of mind of the unhappy doubt that displays all its misery at the end of the nineteenth century" and bears the unmistakable signs of sickness and decadence. "L'Art Nouveau displays all the symptoms of the consumptive, who with a deceptive glow in his cheeks, feverish and excited, wants to enjoy life for a few short years."[24]

The flamboyant lines of Van de Velde and his followers stood in stark contrast to the rationalist tradition in which Cuypers and Berlage, following in Viollet-le-Duc's footsteps, had grown up. The overriding principle in the "Amsterdam" conception of community art was the collaboration of all the arts within an architectural context that was dominated by proportion. The applied arts had to be in harmony with the logical – architectural – proportions of the whole. On this Cuypers and Berlage, despite their differences, were of one mind. "Every decorative excess [is] a weakness in architectural power," wrote Berlage. The new art, on the other hand, confined itself to "pinning on loose, stylized ornaments." The clash between the Art Nouveau of The Hague and Amsterdam rationalism touched on the essence of an aesthetic and philosophical view. The view held by Cuypers and Berlage was governed by a norm that can best be summarized as "structural." According to Cuypers and Berlage, applied art should serve the overall lines of the architectural structure; the structure, in turn, should serve a social goal. The Rijksmuseum is exemplary in this regard. The design served a social and an educational goal; the painting and sculpture likewise served this goal and the architectural manifestation of it. The Amsterdam architects' rage was fueled by the fact that the adherents of Art Nouveau seemed to be mocking the structural principle that formed the foundation of Dutch *gemeenschapskunst*.[25]

At the end of the century, the arts and industry movement had resulted in a social revaluation of the decorative arts. Various sources reveal that "fine" art had lost status relative to applied art.[26] But, as it did in England, the exclusive focus on craft work led to a dead end. Only a small, well-to-do upper class could afford to buy arts and crafts products. Applied art was therefore not *gemeenschapskunst* – community art – in the sense of the people's art, to the great frustration of its practitioners, who were often motivated by social idealism. The erroneous identification – applied art equals handicraft – remained current until as late as the nineteen-twenties, when it was challenged by Piet Zwart.[27] Zwart saw applied art as a historical mistake, spawned by a misplaced protest against the machine. He deplored the nostalgic yearning for hand-made craftwork, and advocated the development of design that made use of modern technology: photography, typography, film. "Industry" essentially meant products made by machines in factories; "applied art," on the other hand, meant workshops where craftsmen produced goods by hand. The chasm was made even wider by the fact that applied artists, responding to the social upgrading of their occupation, started to associate themselves with "higher art" and

Pierre Cuypers (in black) in his studio in Roermond.

distance themselves from the simple artisan. On balance, in consequence, the praiseworthy ambition to reunite industry and art in "industrial art" had the opposite effect. At the turn of the century, art and industry were further apart than ever.

But there were also positive results. The endeavors in the field of the applied arts had contributed to the revaluation of crafts and applied monumental art. The prevailing view of art and artists had been fundamentally altered in favor of a socially engaged art. The significance of "art" had been moved in the direction of art that was important to the community and bound up in collaborative projects in which it was harmonized with other arts.[28]

The rise in the status of applied art was largely due to the reappraisal of monumental art, "structural painting," as Derkinderen, echoing Alberdingk Thijm, described his mural, and "structural sculpture," a term likewise coined by Thijm,[29] as well as stained glass, tile panels and ornamental metalwork. The rehabilitation of structural sculpture can be traced back to an article by Thijm ("On the new sculpture," Rotterdam 1886) and to the way Cuypers put this idea into practice. Both men followed Viollet-le-Duc's Gothic-inspired "architectural rationalism." The academic tradition was at odds with structural sculpture. In this tradition, sculptors were "statuaires" (makers of statues), who had nothing to do with the work of the "imagiers" (applied or ornamental sculptors). Viollet changed all this. He wanted the sculptor to go back to the construction site and brought the concept of "technicien de la taille directe" back into fashion – in other words working directly in stone, without making models or using a mechanical device. Cuypers (the "Dutch Viollet-le-Duc") used the principle in his studio in Roermond,

H.P. Berlage, tile panel for the offices of the Algemeene Maatschappij van Levensverzekering en Lijfrente insurance company, Amsterdam.

which he founded in 1853, and again in the site workshop he set up in Amsterdam in 1877 for the construction of the Rijksmuseum. Well-known sculptors, among them Pier Pander, Bart van Hove and Joseph Mendes da Costa, received their training there.

The actual application of that principle in Cuypers's workshop should, however, be taken with a large pinch of salt. In a fascinating article,[30] Aart Oxenaar points out that Cuypers did try to have the structural painting and sculpture for the building done in his workshops by craft methods, but did not in fact succeed. Cuypers was unable to stem the tide of mechanically produced, assembly line construction materials. The structural sculpture was first drawn in his workshop, fashioned by "modelers," and only then given to the sculptors to execute. The wrought ironwork for the Rijksmuseum was ordered from a Belgian factory, which produced it in accordance with precise instructions that had been worked out in drawings and three-dimensional models. Cuypers's workshops were in reality drafting offices. One of the aims of the later Arts and Crafts movement – the indivisibility of head and hand, the condemnation of drawn and modeled objects and the insistence on simultaneous design and execution – proved unattainable in practice.

Structural sculpture rapidly flourished, but in the early eighteen-nineties Berlage put a brake on its growth when he renounced the Renaissance as a building style and started to hark back to the Middle Ages. One of the consequences of this was that the main lines of the structure were not to become overgrown with ornamentation. Mass and line should dominate. Berlage called this the "reduction to the simple, large beauty" (*Architectura* 2, 1894) and used the somewhat misleading term "impressionism" to describe it.[31] Berlage illustrated the principle with his building for the De Algemeene insurance company on Amsterdam's Damrak (1893). The building had "large-scale forms with simplified enclosed outlines." The stone ornamentations were executed in the skin of the building itself. Lambertus Zijl made a likeness of Johan de Witt, standing in a niche built into a corner of the building. This decoration was part of an overall scheme to engender public confidence in life insurance – a new phenomenon. The public's distrust of speculating with borrowed money had to be overcome by – quite literally – creating an image. The purpose of the sculpture of the statesman Johan de Witt – the guardian of national values – was to give the insurance business national prestige. Other works by Zijl, depicting a cockerel (vigilance), an owl (wisdom) and a pelican (mutual care) confirmed the nature of this imagery. Berlage himself designed a tile panel on which life insurance was portrayed as a guardian angel. In 1896 Antoon Derkinderen embarked on a series of murals (completed in 1900) on the themes of "Affluence - Want", "Health - Sickness," the "Staircase of Life" and "The Principle of Life Insurance." Commissioned by the insurance company, Jan Veth wrote a pamphlet about the paintings, in which he praised the wisdom that "allows life insurance an elevated view of human existence." Veth's pamphlet completed the *Gesamtkunstwerk*, in which architecture, sculpture, tile panel and text worked harmoniously together. But to what end? The answer has to be to create an image that concealed the capitalist character of the insurance business behind a lofty façade. Berlage's dignified and medieval building style was part of this false representation. That the company was indeed, in Manfred Bock's words, a common "profiteer" became clear in 1907, when it ran into serious difficulties as a result of mismanagement.

And here we put our finger on one of the most sensitive problems that impeded the revival of *gemeenschapskunst* and ultimately made it impossible. The institutions that had the financial resources to commission the making of a *Gesamtkunstwerk* were for the most part enterprises that worked for profit, not for the community.

The "community of the arts" also proved more difficult in practice than in theory. Derkinderen's murals in 's-Hertogenbosch city hall are a good illustration. There is a glaring contrast between the murals and the overall architecture. After a fire in 1669, the city hall was rebuilt in classical style. The elevation and the chamber bear all the familiar classical style characteristics. In this context, the medieval-looking wall painting strikes a discordant note. Added to this, the imagery and subjects on the two walls – Duke John, flanked by the Pope and the Emperor on the first wall, the Cathedral of St. John on the other – and the glorification of the feudal world view are entirely out of step with the nature of the city hall, which is, after all, the center of civic community spirit.

The role of the artist

As well as the meanings referred to above (the art of the community and the community of the arts), *gemeenschapskunst* had a third meaning – the corporative context in which the artists worked together. The model envisaged at the end of the century was the medieval guild. J.L.M. Lauweriks put this desire into words in his series of articles "The Cathedral Builders" (*Architectura* 1904). In them he stressed the idea that the members of the medieval guilds were "builders" in the broad sense that they were masters of more than one trade: architecture, sculpture, joinery, metalworking, fresco painting. They worked in a collaborative context with international ramifications. The construction of hundreds of churches in Europe required a "large, general brotherhood of architects and sculptors," with different branches in every country. Senior churchmen were part of this brotherhood. There were international "grand masters" and national "magisters," and below them builders ("murarii") and stonemasons ("operarii"). There were "scolas" for apprentices, "laboratoria" for tradesmen, and "operas" or "fabricia" for the masters. These last were called freemasons, because they were exempt from tax and duties, and could travel wherever they wanted. This system collapsed when the painters broke away after the invention of the technique of oil painting. The Siena Guild of St. Luke was the first to break away, in 1355, followed by the Florentine Confraternità dei Pittori. The next phase of disintegration was the commission awarded to Brunelleschi in 1420 for the dome of the cathedral in Florence. Brunelleschi refused to become a member of the guild. He was not a master, nor did he want to be. The conflict with the guild was decided in his favor in 1434. The conclusion that Lauweriks drew was this.

> It goes without saying that not only must architects work together, but all the trades must jointly strive for a single goal in order once again to achieve the healthy conditions that we find in every great period when the arts blossomed. The great error made by painters and other craftsmen when they left the great guild of the master builders led to a failure to understand the relationship between the arts, as a result of which they increasingly

became alienated from one another and eventually denied any idea of a mutual link.

Lauweriks believed that this broad community ideal deserved to be reintroduced.

> It would of course be very difficult in our age to put in place something that corresponded with the guild of the medieval master builders. Yet it would not be impossible if only more cohesion could be achieved between the existing organizations, a sort of trust of the arts, a general association founded on good, clear principles.[32]

He referred to encouraging initiatives in that direction. He was doubtless thinking of the influential society of architects Architectura et Amicitia, of which he was a long-time member and whose journal *Architectura* he edited from 1902 to 1904. And indeed, many applied artists did join this architects' association. Others became members of the painters' association, the Guild of St. Luke, but because they were not given the right to vote, they founded their own organization, the VANK, in 1904. The architects also established an organization to represent their interests – in 1908 they set up the *Bond van Nederlandse Architecten* (BNA). The emancipation of the applied arts sector, which had arisen fifty years earlier out of the desire to bring all artists together on an equal footing as craftsmen, thus produced the opposite result, in other words applied art's emancipation and independence from architecture. Lauweriks's guild ideal had to make way for a modern-style form of organization in trade unions.

Nevertheless the ideal of the brotherhood of artists continued to reverberate for a long time, not least because people found examples in other countries by which they could be guided. In his article "Gemeinschaftsideale unter den bildenden Künstlern des 19. Jahrhunderts,"[33] Nikolaus Pevsner traced the different steps by which the brotherhood ideal developed in Europe. The groups he names are important, because they were also cited as examples by Cuypers, Derkinderen, Veth, Holst and Lauweriks. They were, at the beginning of the nineteenth century, the *Nazarenes*, some young Viennese painters who founded the *Lukasbund* in 1809 (Overbeck, Wintergerst and Sutter) and who later moved to Rome, where – their numbers swelled by the addition of Cornelius, Veit and Schadow – they called themselves the *Fratelli di S. Isodora*. In England this idea of the guild was picked up in the mid-nineteenth century by the Pre-Raphaelites: Ford Madox Brown, Holman Hunt, Dante Gabriel Rossetti and John Millais. Their philosophy was closely allied to that of the Roman Fratelli: a harking back to the Middle Ages as "more true and less artificial," and a preference for early Italian and early Christian art. The Pre-Raphaelites believed that poems and paintings should have a message; the emphasis was on a picture that should kindle the viewer's interest. Following the example of the Nazarenes, the Pre-Raphaelites called themselves a "Brotherhood" and, like the Nazarenes, signed their work with a guild mark, PRB.

The establishment of the Brotherhood was occasioned by the publication in 1843 of John Ruskin's *Modern Painters*, a book in which early Italian art was presented as the pattern of honesty and piety. In the Netherlands the brotherhood ideal was shared by all the leading representatives of *gemeenschapskunst*: Cuypers, Thijm, Berlage, Veth, Derkinderen, Holst and Lauweriks.[34] The best example of imitation in the Netherlands was Cuypers's studio in Roermond (1853) and his construction site workshop at the Rijksmuseum, from which the Quellinusschool later emerged (1879). Alberdingk Thijm wrote an enthusiastic piece on the occasion of the establishment of this workshop (Thijm 1855), in which he welcomed the revival of the medieval guild ideal. From 1903 to 1906 Derkinderen ran *De Zonnebloem* in Laren, a workshop for glass painters and stained glass makers. It was one of the attempts to breathe new life into the guild ideal. To the best of our knowledge, no study has been undertaken into the extent to which the guild ideal in the Netherlands, derived from the English example, played a role in the establishment of decorative arts studios around the turn of the century. It is also unclear how far Veth, Derkinderen and Holst embodied this guild ideal in the educational innovations that they put in place at the Rijksacademie at the beginning of the century. What is clear is that the guild ideal did not have such a strong influence as it did in England, with its numerous Arts and Crafts workshops, many of which literally referred to themselves as "Guilds."

The idea of a guild community contained an ambiguity. The artist was attracted by the idea of collaboration, of solidarity, and of subordination to the great Idea, but he expected this humility chiefly from his colleagues. For himself, he saw the role of seer, priest, or master. This perception was particularly marked among the architects. Berlage, open as he may have been to the idea of a structural work of art that would be made in collaboration with others, had an image of himself as the Renaissance master builder of genius. In this he took his lead from Burckhardt, who had cited architects like Brunelleschi as examples in his *Cicerone*. He believed that the architect was the master of the work of *gemeenschapskunst* (see for example "Bouwkunst en impressionisme," 1894). His great predecessor Pierre Cuypers not only laid down the architectural line, he also checked (and, if necessary, designed) every curlicue and rosette used in the decoration. He was, in Richard Roland Holst's words, "a master of ceremonies of the highest order, who leads, goes forward and celebrates." Cuypers, said Roland Holst, put *gemeenschapskunst* on "a higher spiritual plane," which reflected "principles of divine origin."[35] At the end of the century this conceit of the priest-architect was adopted and elaborated upon by the Architectura et Amicitia society, particularly by Lauweriks and De Bazel. According to De Bazel, the master builder's task was to "reflect, purely, in his own earthly work the transcendental order inherent in the realm of creation, as natural forms embody the separate forces according to their nature."[36]

The other people involved in the *Gesamtkunstwerk* certainly did not regard themselves as subordinate to the priest-architect. They – the poets, writers, composers, painters and sculptors – also demanded the role of independent creative artist, and sometimes that of priest-seer too. After the architect, the poet was the main candidate for the priest's role. Wagner declared that the poet is the high priest of the divinity that reveals itself in the work of art, and Richard Roland Holst endorsed this. Albert Verwey was the most self-assured defender of this view. He regarded poetry as the highest of all the arts, because poets expressed ideas. According to Verwey, history was a succession of "ideas," embodied in great men: "An era is great because of the greatness of one or more of its individuals."[37] This put him in a singular position with regard to the *gemeenschapskunst* that he otherwise passionately supported. In contrast to the medieval community idealized by

Derkinderen, he envisaged a community "that is led by individuals who, through their elevated consciousness, are capable of giving substance to the idea." The philosopher J.D. Bierens de Haan followed the same Hegelian track as Verwey. He, too, reconciled the irreconcilable when he stated that the most profound sense of community is to be found in the individual. The individual, said Bierens, was not an atom, released from the organism of which it formed part, but a complete universe in miniature. Artists were those who "recognize the infinite in themselves." Their individuality was their "transcendental foundation."[38] Bierens de Haan and Verwey were thus, in fact, returning to the individualism of the Eighties Movement.

Diepenbrock, Derkinderen, Vermeylen, Cuypers and Berlage also combined their openly confessed ideal of brotherhood with an individualistic view of being an artist that was in conflict with it and that was, moreover, strongly reminiscent of the movement they so fiercely opposed: the Eighties Movement. The brotherhood ideal came to grief on this fact. The people working on the common project regarded themselves as monarchs of their own little kingdoms. The result was friction and conflict. Derkinderen is the prime example of this internal contradiction. He was essentially an individualist. His *gemeenschapskunst* was based on "I pleasure with a We veneer," as the artist and author Willem Arondeus so succinctly put it. Almost all the collective projects on which he worked ended in conflict.

The altered conception of the relation between art and society brought in its train a radical change in the historical perspective. According to the orthodox view, founded on nationalist convictions, history was a process of nation-forming whose outlines had gradually taken shape since the Middle Ages and which reached its temporary apogee during the Republic of the United Provinces. The seventeenth century was a self-evident high point in this development. After the disappointing eighteenth century, the nineteenth century was a second peak – regained economic and political power went hand in hand with a regained sense of nationhood. This image was radically attacked and even overturned by the new insight into the relation between art and society. The associated historical perspective attributed to the Middle Ages the status of a form of community of an unequalled standard. The trend since the Renaissance had been one of progressive decay, with the end of the nineteenth century and the Eighties Movement as its nadir.

This view of history was constructed around one central theme: social cohesion. Medieval society was characterized by cohesion, the society of later periods by ever worsening disintegration. Disintegration first and foremost because of the collapse of the Holy Roman Empire into numerous small states. Lauweriks pointed to this in his article, and in his essay on art and society, "Kunst en samenleving." Berlage also refers to nationalism as a "particularization," a dissolution of the great medieval society.

Disintegration, next, of the community of faith of the Catholic Church. Alberdingk Thijm laid the emphasis on the disruptive effect of the Reformation. Since Protestants were forbidden to express the divinity in material substance, there had been, he said, a breach between religion and art, between "mind and matter," that had never been healed. Art had been driven out of the church and had fled to secular regions. This, said Thijm, had led to art's becoming materialistic, sensualized and degenerate. Several artists, Berlage and Holst among them, echoed his sentiments.[39]

Disintegration, furthermore, of the community of the arts. The guild, in which all artists worked together until the Renaissance, broke up into special interest groups. But most objectionable of all was that, since the Renaissance, the arts had extracted themselves from the *Gesamtkunstwerk* and developed into independent arts.[40] This "particularization" chiefly hit the arts that were tied to buildings: sculpture, painting, music. Architecture itself, according to Holst, remained untouched, because buildings are so bound to material restrictions (client, financing, social purpose) that to a greater or lesser degree they always express the idea of the age. The independence of the sister arts led to their alienation from their social purpose. In painting, this was most clearly manifested in the rise and flourishing of the practice of making paintings, as opposed to the art of painting – by which he meant the painting of murals. Paintings had become art products, because they had been detached from the great artistic and philosophical whole from which they derived their meaning, because they were made in studios, because they were portable, transportable and hence marketable. Holst fulminated constantly against this making of paintings. He pointed to the connection between the birth of the practice of making paintings and the emergence of the art trade and market in the first city republics. The most typical type of painting (and thus the one most in conflict with mural art) was the portrait. It was in the portrait that the relation with the powerful citizenry was most clearly expressed. Walter Crane had already argued that the movability of works of art was a bad omen, contending that the fall of art coincided with its absorption into the portable forms of private property, or into material or commercial speculation. [41]

Disintegration, lastly, of the artist who, divorced from the community of faith and from the brotherhood, lapses into subjectivity – subjectivity, that is, as a characteristic of disintegration and decay. "All eras in a state of decline and dissolution are subjective; on the other hand, all progressive eras have an objective tendency. Our present time is retrograde, for it is subjective: we see this not merely in poetry, but also in painting, and much besides. Every healthy effort, on the contrary, is directed from the inward to the outward world; as you see in all great eras, which were really in a state of progression and all of an objective nature."[42] Berlage quoted this passage by Goethe, and, with a clear reference to the Eighties Movement, added that in eras without culture artists become subjective. According to Holst, individualism had descended step by step since the Renaissance to the low point that was impressionism. The artist who is thrown back on himself, said Holst, works from two different but wholly erroneous aesthetics. One is focused on the expression of individual emotions (romanticism), the other on the depiction of observable reality (realism, naturalism). These two pernicious principles came together in the Eighties Movement.

The Eighties Movement – this much will by now be abundantly clear – was seen as the nadir of decay, or "decadence," as it was called in the debates at the time. Recent studies have devoted a great deal of attention to this concept. What exactly did the doom-mongers of the nineteenth century actually mean by it? And was it current in the Netherlands?

The fear of decadence certainly existed in the Netherlands. We have seen that the members of the Nineties Movement projected the concept of decadence onto the Eighties

Movement. What fell into decline among the members of the Eighties Movement was the medieval ideal of community.[43] The ideas associated with "décadence" in France were applied by the members of the Nineties Movement to the Eighties Movement.

The generation of the Nineties set themselves the goal of putting together what had fallen apart, of integrating what had disintegrated, of giving a home to that which was homeless. The image (the caricature) presented of the writers of *De Nieuwe Gids* was simplified to that of mere "wordcraft." This meant words that had acquired an independent status, isolated from the syntactical context. The sensitivist sketches by Lodewijk van Deyssel (written at the end of the eighteen-eighties and in the early nineties, like *Snow*) and Gorter's sensitivist verses are striking examples of this. Afterwards the members of the Nineties Movement recognized in this sensitivism the characteristics that had been described as "decadentism" by Bourget in his famous article (Bourget 1899). From 1892 onward, Albert Verwey opposed this threatening and all-encompassing decadence. He acknowledged that in his own Eighties period he too had experimented with poetry that was "actually not verses, just words, just syllables," but now he fiercely opposed "the sensational single word" and mounted a campaign for the sentence. Henceforth he wanted "poems to join together into series, series into books, books into inseparable complexes. The cohesion seemed to me to be at least as important as the single poem."[44] His collaboration with Van Deyssel – co-founder of the *Tweemaandelijksch Tijdschrift* in 1894 and co-editor from its inception – became increasingly difficult ("his mind does not recognize the structure, only the sequence," said Verwey). Their disagreements ultimately led to a breach. Verwey was very well aware that his campaign for the sentence was closely related to the campaign for the community ideal. Diepenbrock, Veth, Crane and Henriëtte Roland Holst all expressed the same concern in similar words.

"Integrating what had disintegrated" applied equally as a slogan for painting. The members of the Nineties Movement saw the essential characteristics of impressionism as decadent, particularly the subjective and momentary impressions and the technique of using separate touches of color no longer bounded by lines. Where painting was concerned, the battle against disintegration was fought by means of a strong plea for *line*. In his *Claims of Decorative Art*, Crane said that nothing so much revealed the significance and depth of a master as his understanding and treatment of line, nothing spoke louder and clearer of the vigorous or enervated state of any period in art than its line drawings. Lines, he continued, were the nerve fibers of art, connecting and controlling the whole body, but weakened and powerless in its days of decline. Here again, there is a striking biological metaphor which, as in Bourget, describes decadence as a degenerate organism and community spirit as a healthy one.

The intention was, by reintroducing the line, to create the awareness that painting was not about subjective, momentary impressions, but the expression of collective and eternal concepts. Richard Roland Holst set himself up as the champion of the art of the "Sign," by which he meant images that were reduced to simple linear patterns (for example, the Cross) so that they could serve as a symbol to refer to community values.[45]

The Rijksmuseum and the style question

The enthusiasm for Gothic in the second half of the nineteenth century was the work of two powerful thinkers, Eugène Viollet-le-Duc (1814-1879) and John Ruskin (1819-1900).[46] In 1840 Viollet-le-Duc was commissioned by Prosper Mérimée to restore the Madeleine Cathedral of Vézelay. It was the start of a series of impressive restorations of medieval monuments, including Notre Dame in Paris, the walls of Carcassonne and the Château de Pierrefonds to the east of Compiègne. Through this work he developed into an unrivaled expert in Romanesque and Gothic architecture, and set out his ideas in a ten-volume *Dictionnaire Raisonnée d'Architecture* (1854-1859). Unlike Viollet, John Ruskin was a writer and essayist, not an architect. Like Viollet, however, he had a liking for the High Gothic of the thirteenth century, for the cathedrals of Reims and Amiens, and for Westminster Abbey. But there were striking differences. Ruskin was a deeply religious man; Viollet was an agnostic who left instructions that there should be no priest at his funeral and bequeathed his body to the *Société d'Autopsie*. Ruskin was authoritarian. He believed that architecture could only flourish under the iron hand of a central authority, as in early Venice. Viollet's politics, in contrast, made him a revolutionary. He rejected every "monastery and all imposed authority" and believed that art belonged to the people. In his view the Gothic was the product of waning royal power and growing secularization, of the downfall of feudalism in favor of a "communal organization." The cathedral must therefore have chiefly served a "municipal function." Ruskin regarded architecture as a trade – a decorative trade. He believed that architecture was that which was applied to a building. "Thus, I suppose, no one would call the laws architectural which determine the height of a breastwork or the position of a bastion. But if to the stone facing of that bastion be added an unnecessary feature, as a cable molding, *that* is architecture" (*Seven Lamps*, 1849). It followed from this, according to Ruskin, that sculpture and painting were superior to building. Viollet's view was diametrically opposed. To him, architecture was based on the concept of construction or structure. This had to be "rational." Gothic, in his opinion, was the ultimate rational architecture, by which he meant that the structure of a building had to be governed by the purpose of the building and by the nature of the material: "If you want to make a box, you do well to think first about what you wish to keep in it." He consequently found it absurd to make all the windows in a wall identical if the rooms behind them had different functions – just as absurd as using the same façade for a town hall and for a church. To Viollet, rational building was more important than building in a historical style. "One must," he said, "study the past thoroughly and carefully, and not make an effort to revive it, but become familiar with it in order to make use of it." He therefore used ostentatiously modern technologies and materials, such as iron structures. Ruskin abhorred modern technology in general and iron structures in particular.[47]

In the light of the above, it is remarkable that Pierre Cuypers was influenced not at all by Ruskin and wholly by Viollet when he introduced neo-Gothic into the Netherlands around the middle of the nineteenth century. We may assume that this was because Viollet was a professional, Ruskin was not.[48] Cuypers was led by the Frenchman to such an extent that he was nicknamed "the Dutch Viollet." Viollet went to Roermond, where he commented favorably on Cuypers's restoration of the Munsterkerk. The far-reaching consequences of this influence manifested themselves in the second half of the nineteenth century, when a great many Catholic churches had to be built or enlarged. A considerable number of the commissions were awarded to Cuypers. Thijm devoted himself to the promotion of a revival of Gothic in church-building. *De heilige linie* (1858; The Holy Line), which Thijm himself reckoned to be his masterpiece, was a fervent plea for neo-Gothic. Cuypers greatly admired *De heilige linie*: "This work is a monument, I cannot get my fill of it," he wrote Thijm.[49] He first came into contact with Thijm in 1854, and that contact developed into a lifelong friendship. In 1895 Cuypers, a widower, married Thijm's sister.

The connection between neo-Gothic and Catholic emancipation throws light on the specific context in which Viollet's ideas were received (and adapted) by Cuypers. Cuypers, unlike Viollet, was a deeply religious Catholic and, politically speaking, conservative. To him, neo-Gothic was the concrete manifestation of the revival of Catholicism and of the key role faith played in society and the arts. Philosophically, politically and artistically, he was the opposite of Viollet. Cuypers interpreted as the standard, what to Viollet was an example. Viollet believed that construction should be contemporary, according to principles whose main outlines were found in Gothic, but he was opposed to the imitation of Gothic as a *style*: "It is not good enough for artists to admire the arts of the past; copying them is an admission of powerlessness." This, the use of neo-Gothic as a style, was exactly what Cuypers did.[50] Successors accused him of constricting and distorting Viollet. Lauweriks, much as he was influenced by Cuypers, later criticized his "clerical historicism."[51]

The style question played a significant role in the culture of the second half of the nineteenth century. The influence of the Catholics grew rapidly. Alberdingk Thijm's voice rang out in contributions to *Dietsche Warande*, the magazine he founded in 1855. Cuypers's influence likewise grew rapidly, in part because in 1865 he allowed himself to be persuaded by Thijm to settle in Amsterdam. There he made the acquaintance of the ministry official Victor de Stuers, who had become extremely powerful in a very short space of time: he became the first secretary of the *College van Rijksadviseurs voor de Monumenten van Geschiedenis en Kunst*, a body advising the government on historic and artistic monuments, in 1874, and a year later director of the Department of Arts and Sciences at the Ministry of Internal Affairs. De Stuers used his influence to get Thijm, with whom he had become friends, appointed professor at the national art academy – the Rijksacademie – in 1876. De Stuers also had an important say in awarding commissions for the construction or restoration of public buildings. He brought the question of the national museum to the forefront and saw to it, with Thijm's support, that the commission went to Cuypers. To many people this was a triumph for Catholic emancipation. The liberals watched this development with deepening suspicion. They accused the triumvirate of Thijm, Cuypers and Stuers of anti-national and even ultramontane intentions. In reaction they announced that Dutch Renaissance was the typical national building style. Neo-Gothic thus became the issue in a debate that ranged far beyond architecture and into political and ideological realms. Most architects followed the liberal line. They came out in favor of the Renaissance style and against Gothic, because they believed that the Catholic trio was beginning to exert a disproportionate influence on government policy and because they were worried that tying architecture to purpose and material, as advocated by Viollet, would curb their artistic freedom.

Monument to the restoration of independence, 1813, The Hague.

This polarization spawned a whole series of incidents. There was the conflict surrounding the national monument to commemorate the country's independence in 1813. In 1863 there was a competition to design a monument to mark the fiftieth anniversary of the event. The entries had mottos and were anonymous. The design called "Ebenezer" won; the runner-up was "Netherlands, Orange." The latter was by Cuypers. The secretary of the jury formulated his report such that the committee of recommendation reversed the order. The painter Johannes Bosboom protested in *De Nederlandsche Spectator*. In 1864 Carel Vosmaer published a brochure entitled *Het nationaal gedenkteeken*. In an article written in the same year, he said explicitly that "medieval architecture, both Romanesque and Gothic, came about *outside our soil*. It is not indigenous to the Netherlands." At the end of 1864, probably because of the pressure exerted by this campaign, it was decided to construct Ebenezer after all. Vosmaer was jubilant. In a response in *De Nederlandsche Spectator* he said: "Since 1500 classical culture has lived in us; the literature and art of the seventeenth century was inspired by it; and to this day it is still what it always has been: a source of truly human civilization, and a powerful antidote to the old Christian suppression of nature, senses and reason."[52]

We can recognize in Vosmaer's words the political and ideological differences of opinion about the Gothic versus Classical question that began to emerge. Gothic, in Vosmaer's view, equated to Catholicism, Ultramontanism, anti-nationalism and lack of freedom; classical, in contrast, meant Protestantism, nationalism and freedom. This debate was the prelude to the great conflict that raged around the Rijksmuseum.

In 1862 a committee was appointed to oversee the preparations for the establishment of a museum of art. The aim was to replace the Trippenhuis (Trip House), which had serious deficiencies as the home to the most important national collection of paintings. Thijm was appointed secretary to the committee – an odd post, one might think, for a man who was against museums on principle. He must have seen it as an opportunity to put his ideas about integrated art into practice in the new building for what would be the largest museum in the Netherlands. It was Thijm who inserted the section about which there was subsequently such a furor: "building style and materials must be in keeping, both with the monumental intention, and at the same time with the purpose of the building: the preservation and exhibition of Dutch art treasures, particularly of the XVI and the XVII century." In the competition for what was now being called the "Muzeum Koning Willem I" Cuypers came second. The first place went to the classicist design by L. and E. Lange. Thijm resigned from the committee and distanced himself from a building that in his view had nothing to do with its contents (sixteenth- and seventeenth-century art). A debate ensued as to whether classicism really was in keeping with the seventeenth century and whether it was "national" or "foreign," a question that was all the more pertinent since the new museum, like the national memorial to commemorate 1813, was to be a symbol of national unity. Thijm's decision was without doubt also prompted by pique because Cuypers had lost out. The initiative ran aground for a number of reasons. In 1874 Victor de Stuers, in his capacity as secretary to the national advisory committee, resurrected the matter. He invited four architects, among them Cuypers, to submit a design for a national "Rijksmuseum." The terms of reference quoted above remained in effect. Cuypers submitted two entries – a Renaissance design and a Gothic design, of which he preferred the latter. The panel of judges chose Cuypers's first design by fifteen votes to one. The lone dissenting voice was Vosmaer's. Cuypers won the competition and was immediately appointed as the architect of the Rijksmuseum buildings by Minister of Internal Affairs Dr. Jan Heemskerk. Cuypers worked closely with Thijm and De Stuers on the design and internal arrangement of the museum. *De Nederlandsche Spectator* created a tremendous stir. Vosmaer, who until that moment had got on very well with Thijm (he defended Thijm in 1876 when the latter's appointment to a professorial chair was contested), had complained about Cuypers and Thijm's restoration of St. Willibrord's Well in Heiloo and about their proposal for a university building in Leiden. Thijm's acid reaction ("Een bouwkundig spook" – an architectural phantom – in *De Gids* 1877) provoked something in the nature of a declaration of war on Vosmaer's part.

> The situation seems to me to be simply this, that what the Ultramontane tendency is doing in every field is now also being done in that of art. What we are seeing is the subjection of the people to the principles of a party that does not tolerate freedom; it is the battle against all that is classical, that is science in the independent sense that the Protestant world honors; it is the imposition of medieval art forms.[53]

The new Rijksmuseum.

Vosmaer drew attention to the change that Cuypers had meanwhile made to the design for the Rijksmuseum. In 1876 Cuypers had indeed sent the minister an amended design based on his rejected design of 1875. The king got wind of Cuypers's intentions and wrote the minister a letter in which he said that he did not like the new design. Despite this, the minister (ostensibly, but in fact the head of the Arts and Sciences Department, or in other words De Stuers) approved the design.[54] Vosmaer cited the high roofs, the arches, the columns and capitals, the lancet windows and the checkerboard brickwork that are so typical of Cuypers's church designs. He resigned from the advisory committee (as did Professor Leemans and the committee chairman, Cornelis Fock), stating that he had lost all confidence in Thijm, and denounced De Stuers's bureaucratic tyranny. He now turned savagely on the construction of the Rijksmuseum, castigating the large budget overruns and the changes that made the building more Gothic. He pointed to the connection between "Catholic" policy on the state, education, science and art, and in 1882 wrote furiously: "Now the country is overrun with parasitic plants from the old stock; everywhere medieval forms, ecclesiastical building styles, cruciform windows, bricks endwise, crosswise, slantwise, higgledy-piggledy; the ornamentation consisting of ugly masks and insipid reliefs, and above all beaten black and blue with tiles; and everywhere steeples, steeples and steeples, a veritable steeple mania" (*De Amsterdammer* 1882).

The Rijksmuseum was officially opened on July 13, 1885. The cantata written for the occasion by J.J.L. ten Kate with music by Daniël de Lange was performed by a choir and orchestra under a glass roof that had been erected over the east courtyard. The king did not put in an appearance. "I shall never set foot in that monastery," he is supposed to have said.

There were more conflicts of this kind: the row about the Justice Ministry in 1881 (architect Cornelis Peters), the clashes involving the university building in Utrecht (1891) and particularly the battle that raged around Amsterdam Central Station (1881-1889).

The style question provides a picture of the typically Dutch context in which neo-Gothic was received and elaborated upon. The style question also colored the ideal of *gemeenschapskunst* that had been imported along with neo-Gothic and had its first great monument in the Rijksmuseum. The Rijksmuseum was a work of *gemeenschapskunst* in all the above aspects. It was a *Gesamtkunstwerk*. Wall paintings, tile panels, stained glass – everything worked together under Cuypers's direction in a plan he had drawn up (with Thijm and De Stuers). One exceptional aspect of this *Gesamtkunstwerk* is that its purpose was to provide an ideal exhibition space for the country's most prestigious art collection. Thijm, in particular, worked on incorporating the collection as part of and integrating it into the *Gesamtkunstwerk*.

The Rijksmuseum was also a product of *gemeenschapskunst* in the sense of a brotherhood – a guild – of artists whom Cuypers brought together in the construction site workshop. This workshop marked the start of the emancipation of the decorative arts in the Netherlands and was hence a turning point of historic significance. Thijm rightly drew attention to it. It was, after all, *gemeenschapskunst* in the sense that the building and the works of art integrated in it had directed and shaped a national community spirit. The Rijksmuseum was to make the Dutch people aware of the close ties between history, art and the Dutch State. The collection of seventeenth-century masters (including Rembrandt) did this very well. It could at least be demonstrated that the seventeenth century was a high point in national, historical and artistic terms. We have seen in this section that Cuypers's pseudo-Gothic was not "in keeping" with this aim, and that his Gothicism cast doubt on the nature of the community spirit that should be reawakened in the Netherlands.

Monuments and museums

In 1873 Victor de Stuers published a lengthy article "Holland op zijn smalst" in *De Gids*. It was an attack on the disgraceful carelessness with which the Dutch treated their artistic treasures, from historic buildings to art collections in museums. The article brought about a revolution. It gave rise to a policy that resulted in the concern for and preservation of the national heritage that exists in the Netherlands today. It also impelled the energetic management of the national art collections. The concern for the national heritage and museums was a consequence of the same desire for *gemeenschapskunst* that also gave rise to the revival of the decorative arts and the rise of structural painting and structural sculpture. The aim of all these initiatives was the same: to give art back the social function it had once had.

We have already seen that *gemeenschapskunst* developed out of a neo-Gothic-inspired renewal movement driven by three leading figures in Catholic emancipation: Cuypers, Thijm and De Stuers. The same triumvirate also laid the foundations for a reappraisal of historic buildings and museums, which resulted in De Stuers's attack in 1873. Ever since the first issue of the *Spectator* and later in his own *Dietsche Warande*, Thijm had published articles in which he condemned the "vandalism" of the nation's heritage. In 1848 Thijm wrote an open letter to the Dutch Royal Academy of Sciences, the *Koninklijk Instituut van Wetenschappen*, about "the preservation of our monuments." He proposed setting up a committee to list historic buildings – a committee that would have to be consulted whenever one of these monuments was threatened with demolition. (De Stuers repeated this call in 1869 as part of his thesis.) The academy's response was that it would do no such thing. In 1855 Thijm denounced this laxness in a long article on the country's art and archeology, "De kunst en archaeologie in Holland," which in tenor and intent is the direct forerunner of De Stuers's "Holland op zijn smalst."[55]

Cultural nationalism was an important driving force behind the renewed concern for historic buildings and art, as it was in the case of various scientific and art historical initiatives in the mid-nineteenth century: the research into early Dutch texts by philologists, the start of Vondel studies, and the beginning of the great dictionaries, the *Middelnederlandsch Woordenboek* and the *Groot Woordenboek der Nederlandsche Taal*. Historians, notably Robert Fruin, focused on national life. In literature the historical novel was all the rage, with authors like Jacob van Lennep and Trui Bosboom-Toussaint. It is against this background that we must see Thijm's battle against "vandalism." Thijm inveighed against neo-classical and hence "foreign" architecture – because it was borrowed from the Greeks, it was by definition "heathen." The *de facto* prime minister Johan Thorbecke came off worst in this debate. His controversial pronouncement, "art is not a matter for the government in so far as the government has no opinion nor any authority in the field of art," uttered in a debate on the king's speech at the opening of Parliament in 1862, provoked numerous reactions and later gave De Stuers the handle he needed to clarify his position.[56]

In the mid-nineteenth century, "monument" meant a reminder of an illustrious past. A modest sum in the government's budget was earmarked for the "preservation of historic monuments" (Muiden Castle, the Gevangenpoort in The Hague, the tombs of naval heroes in Middelburg, etc.). In France, preservation of the national heritage had begun after the revolution, and the post of Inspecteur général des Monuments Historiques had been created in 1830. Prosper Mérimée, one of the first to hold the post, said that "repairers may well be just as dangerous as destroyers," which is why he instructed the architect Viollet-le-Duc to inspect Vézelay Cathedral. Viollet drew a link between the preservation of national heritage and national memory: "monuments of stone or wood decay and it would be foolish to keep them all, but what cannot and must not decay is the spirit that caused the monuments to be built, for that spirit is ours, it is the soul of the nation." In 1887 France passed the Historic Monuments Act, on which she had been working since 1833. In 1913 there was a new act, which extended the protection to the immediate vicinity of a historic building (a radius of five hundred meters).

In Germany it was nationalism in the post-Napoleonic era that was the chief spur to the preservation of heritage. In 1835 a start was made on the restoration of Cologne

Cathedral – which is to say that the ninth-century nave was demolished and replaced with a new nave in the style of the thirteenth century. Germany was in the vanguard with the listing of historic buildings in the then still independent Länder. Baden-Württemberg had a register of this kind as early as 1841, Prussia in 1844 and so on. British late nineteenth-century practice was little short of brutal. Between 1870 and 1880 a Gothic section of Oxford Cathedral was demolished and rebuilt in Romanesque style. Belgium, lastly, earmarked fifteen to twenty times as much money for the purpose as the Netherlands at the end of the nineteenth century, but this was not reflected in the results. The organization of the conservation work was poor. Restoration usually meant knocking down, and rebuilding a corrected and enhanced copy.

In the Netherlands there was effectively no question of public concern for historic buildings before 1873. After a brief, relatively encouraging period at the beginning of the nineteenth century, shortage of funds as a result of the Dutch policy of war against the Belgians meant that work on looking after historic buildings was halted. In 1850, restoration meant patching up and adding on. The restorers used a romantically tinged style of their own, paying no attention to the local styles. For instance, the reconstruction of the west door of Utrecht Cathedral in 1831 – demolished again in 1939 – totally ignored the medieval Gothic style in which the cathedral was built.

Cuypers had made a name not only as an architect but also as a restorer of churches. In the mid-nineteenth century there were two conflicting views about what to do with historic monuments. To Viollet, caring for these structures meant more even than restoring them to their original condition. "Restoring a building not only means preserving, repairing and remodeling it, it means putting it back in a more complete state than it may ever have known at any time in its history." He had put his words into practice in spectacular fashion in various restoration projects, the best known of which are the Château de Pierrefonds and the city walls of Carcassonne.[57] John Ruskin, in contrast, advocated preservation rather than restoration. He saw his endeavors crowned in the still active Society for the Protection of Ancient Buildings, founded in 1877 by his most eminent student, William Morris. Ruskin did not want to intervene any more than was strictly necessary. He believed that old buildings should be allowed to die with dignity. Morris followed his lead. The ideas of Ruskin and Morris governed the policy of English conservation: "renewal should be avoided" (in the *General Advice* of the Royal Institute of British Architects, 1865, revised 1888, renewed 1926).

Cuypers took no account of the precautions Viollet urged, particularly with regard to respecting changes that had been made over time. The rood loft of St. John's in 's-Hertogenbosch is a case in point. In 1862 it was decided to demolish the rood loft, but the work was delayed. In 1866 Cuypers wrote, "the removal of the rood loft must be regarded as a boon for the beautiful cathedral." Because of this letter it was decided that the rood loft should indeed go, and Cuypers was commissioned to build a neo-Gothic partition. The rood loft was sold to the South Kensington Museum in 1871. For reasons that remain unclear, the building of the new choir screen did not go ahead. The design, which has survived, conforms to the orthodox standards that Thijm set for a rood loft, namely that the line of sight through from the (divine) choir to the (human) nave had to be guaranteed (this was not true of the old screen and loft) and that it had to embody medieval

Munsterkerk in Roermond before restoration.

Munsterkerk in Roermond after restoration.

design. Cuypers also restored the Munsterkerk in Roermond. It was a complex building. The east end was late Romanesque (thirteenth century), the west end early Gothic. The base of the east towers was thirteenth century, the upper section late seventeenth, early eighteenth century. Lastly there was the baroque central tower dating from the early part of the eighteenth century. In 1863 Cuypers, who was at that time the city architect, submitted a plan for restoration, based on the principle of restore and complete. Everything dating from around 1700 was demolished. Both the (originally baroque) east tower and the (planned but not built) west tower were built from scratch – all in the style of thirteenth-century Rhineland Gothic. There was considerable protest, but Cuypers won the argument, thanks, among other things, to Viollet's personal intervention. "On the old drawing the Munster has a charm that the newly created hard doctrinairism lacks," says heritage conservation expert Jan Tillema cautiously.[58]

The turning point in the policy on museums and historic buildings was "Holland op zijn smalst." The article was a passionate argument, larded with numerous anecdotes, from which it is clear that over many years De Stuers had built up very extensive knowledge about the state of the national heritage, citing cases that Thijm had exposed in his "Vandalism" column and in his "Kunst en archaeologie in Holland." He quoted many examples of demolition and mismanagement of historic buildings, and then went on to describe the neglected condition of the state collections. There had been no additions, said De Stuers, the collections were scattered far and wide and often untraceable, and much had been sold abroad. The article had been occasioned by De Stuers's visit to the South Kensington Museum where, to his great indignation and distress, he had seen the rood screen from St. John's on display. De Stuers dealt with this case exhaustively. This detail is fascinating, given the close involvement in the removal of the screen of the man who was later to become a friend of De Stuers, Pierre Cuypers. De Stuers's criticism focused on the lack of government policy that had made it possible. De Stuers stressed the interest that he believed would be served if such a policy were to be established – the proper self-interest of industry and state: "the material benefit that derives from it for those manifold branches of industry which must wither away without the practice of fine arts is tangible." He insisted that "art education" was indispensable if the Netherlands did not want to be driven even further out of the industrial art market by neighboring countries. He was talking about the manufacture of china, carpets, embossing, painted glass and furniture. In order to recapture these areas of industry, "the feeling for art" had to be awakened "in all the people." The second argument, after the furtherance of industry, was national pride. "If, therefore, with a view to the advancement of Industry, the preservation of our historic buildings and our collections is a national issue, it is no less so in regard to the interest that these historic buildings, which are directly linked to the history of our people, deserve. The dissemination of knowledge of our national history is also in the interest of the state. For as much as – if not more than – language, religion or mores, history is the tie that binds populations into nationalities and keeps them bound." These words make plain just how much De Stuers's initiative was driven by the desire to give art a social function, or in other words to transform it into community art – *gemeenschapskunst*. The maintenance of art collections and historic buildings had a social function in the dual sense of awakening national – community – consciousness and promoting industrial decorative arts.

The publication of "Holland op zijn smalst" had immediate consequences. A national advisory committee on historic and cultural monuments – the *College van Rijksadviseurs voor de Monumenten van Geschiedenis en Cultuur* – was appointed in 1874. Its tasks were firstly to advise on listing and preserving historic buildings, secondly to advise on national collections, and thirdly to advise on the construction or restoration of public buildings. This was followed in 1875 by the creation of the Department for Arts and Sciences in the Ministry of Internal Affairs, with De Stuers as the senior official. The budget for arts and sciences shot up – by 20,000 guilders in 1874, and by 70,000 guilders in 1875. After De Stuers's appointment its increase can only be described as spectacular. In 1876 the budget was more than doubled from 265,000 to 546,000 guilders, after which it rose steadily to 837,000 guilders in 1882 – and this despite the lack of enthusiasm shown by the responsible minister.[59] After 1882, the budgets dropped again and continued to fluctuate around 500-600,000 guilders, in part because the Rijksmuseum was completed in 1885.

All the progress notwithstanding, De Stuers's policy was one of stopgap measures. He did not tackle the problem at its roots. Everything changed after 1900. Three circumstances conspired to bring the change about: the foundation of a society for antiquities – the *Oudheidkundige Bond*, which drew up a schedule of principles – in 1899, the appointment of a committee for national conservation – the *Rijksmonumentencommissie* – in 1903, and the end of De Stuers's reign as the senior department official in 1901. From the outset the *Oudheidkundige Bond* advocated legislation for the preservation of the nation's heritage. In 1907 a committee was appointed to draft legal provisions for the protection of national monuments and historic buildings. The committee submitted its report in 1910; the act did not reach the statute book until 1961. This act defined "monuments" as follows: "monuments are items of real property or groups thereof, which were made at least fifty years ago and which are of general importance because of their beauty, their significance to scholarship or their value to cultural anthropology." Strikingly little is made of their historic, national and educational value, the consequence of a change of perspective that took place in the nineteen-twenties.

Museum policy also underwent a radical change. In the second half of the nineteenth century museums were regarded as temples of history and art, in which one pondered on the greatness of one's people, and found inspiration for the future. De Stuers extended this goal, specifically to include education and industry: "one of the most indispensable and powerful driving forces in the development of the people, in the furtherance of art and industry, and lastly in the increase of general prosperity" ("Holland op zijn smalst"). Museums were learning resources for artists and craftsmen. The revival of the decorative arts and the change in the policy on monuments and museums sprung from the same endeavor.

Berlage's Exchange

Three phases of development can be seen in the three monuments of community art that were built at roughly fifteen-year intervals: the Rijksmuseum (1885), Berlage's Exchange (1903) and the Scheepvaarthuis (1916).

Berlage's reputation essentially rests on the Amsterdam Exchange. This is hardly surprising, since Berlage made history with the building, but it also means that his reputation is distorted in so far as earlier and later work is completely overshadowed by it. Above all, it conceals the arduous development of which the Exchange was, for the time being, the culmination. Manfred Bock refers to this in his exhaustive study of Berlage's early work. He points out that around 1890 Berlage was still designing entirely in the Renaissance style. At that time, Berlage was working according to the approach outlined by the society of architects.[60] A prime example is the design for Zutphen town hall (1889-1890). Berlage began – cautiously – to depart from this line in his design for the Reformed church in Apeldoorn (1890) and for a church in Enge, near Zürich (1890-1891),

Berlage's design for the town hall in Zutphen.

H.P. Berlage, the offices of the Algemeene Maatschappij van Levensverzekering en Lijfrente insurance company, Amsterdam.

for which occasion he explored the Gothic style. In 1888 he had given a lecture on his thoughts after a trip through Normandy, but at that time his opinion of Gothic churches was governed by W. Lübke (*Geschichte der Renaissance in Frankreich*, 1885). Only the Renaissance, he thought then, had developed a national design language; Gothic was international. The question of the national character was particularly sensitive in Apeldoorn, because the church there had to serve as the royal church when the royal family (who were members of the Dutch Reformed faith) were in residence at Het Loo Palace.

In his essay of 1890, Berlage again defended the Renaissance as the wellspring of modern architecture. Gothic, he said, was a naked man who had been clothed by the Renaissance. The building of the Algemeene in 1891-1894 was his last attempt to reconcile medieval and Renaissance principles, as Cuypers did. Around 1895, however, he started to turn toward medieval construction and Viollet-le-Duc, although the change took place slowly because Viollet's reputation in the Netherlands had been filtered through Cuypers's view of him as a champion of the neo-Gothic style and was thus associated with Catholic emancipation with all its ideological and political connotations. It took Berlage a long time to break through this image and to discover, behind Cuypers's Viollet, a very different Viollet who was to help him complete the move to modern architecture. He was aided in this by the encouragement of a group of young architects, of whom K.P.C. de Bazel and Matthieu Lauweriks were the most important. In 1896 these

Berlage's Exchange, Amsterdam.

two brilliant young men founded the Vâhâna lodge, a branch of the Belgian-Dutch Theosophical Society.[61] From 1897 to 1902 the lodge organized a famous drawing course, which was taken by a large group of architects and applied artists. They were also very active in the society of architects, *Architectura et Amicitia*. In 1891 W.C. Bauer gave a lecture for the society in which he unequivocally stated that Viollet "never dreamed of a renaissance of Gothic design," but with his modern ideas showed architects the way to the future.[62] On September 21, 1892, Willem Kromhout delivered a lecture on rationalism in France, in which he, too, argued against the image of Viollet as the champion of a style. The same issue of the journal in which this was printed also includes extracts from Viollet's *Entretiens*, in the translation by Lauweriks.[63]

Berlage adopted the principle of rationalism through this "de-Cuypersed" Viollet. He declared that he agreed with Viollet's idea that the structure had to serve the purpose of the building and the potential of the material, and he used these structural principles to detach himself from every sort of "neo" style and develop a contemporary, modern style. In the article on architecture he wrote in 1898 ("Over architectuur") he consequently distanced himself from Cuypers, whom he accused of "remaining too much in the Middle Ages in his notions and his deeds." He asserted that Cuypers's buildings suffered from an excess of details and that, in terms of "simple distribution of volume," they were "certainly not the best." His conclusion was that architects should no longer build in a "style." The architect had to disengage himself from earlier architectural styles and build *constructively*. This was the only respect in which the Middle Ages could serve as an example.[64]

Lambertus Zijl, decoration above the entrance to Berlage's Exchange in Amsterdam.

At the same time as his conversion to Viollet, Berlage also turned toward *gemeen-schapskunst*. His first explicit utterance on the subject came at the end of "Bouwkunst en impressionisme" (1894), from which the quote at the beginning of this chapter was taken. From subsequent publications it emerges that he saw the community ideal as a secular religion. He envisaged a "religion of the people,"[65] taking his inspiration from the then very popular theosophist Matthieu Schoenmaekers, whose slogan "Our religion is a worldly religion" he repeatedly quoted. Following the lead of Van der Pek (whose 1894 article in *De Amsterdammer* he quotes in its entirety in "Over Architectuur"), he stated that "this love, inspiring all, (shall) therefore not be a love of the divine; a jubilant optimism can also be born out of the love of person for person." This is the community ideal he had in mind when he designed the Exchange, and he afterwards continued to profess his belief in the "religion of the people." Berlage's faith is characterized by his endeavor

H.P. Berlage, the offices of the Algemeene Nederlandsche Diamantbewerkers Bond (ANDB),
Amsterdam.

The execution of the scheme ran into problems. From the outset, Antoon Derkinderen was not happy with the set-up and concerned about his personal contribution. He expressed his rancor in his correspondence with Berlage and Verwey. This resulted in a discussion between Verwey, Derkinderen, Berlage and Zijl in 1899 at which Derkinderen let it be known that he was not minded to go along with Verwey's suggestions. He did, it is true, sign a contract on May 7, 1900, but the designs he delivered in May 1901 departed very significantly from the theme set by Verwey. Verwey, for example, had used the idea of the four winds and their importance to Amsterdam as a mercantile city. Derkinderen abandoned this idea altogether and arranged his walls "by story" such that they lead from the abstract ("peace and conflict," "spring and summer," "fall and winter") to the concrete (the microcosm of humanity and then the significance of Amsterdam). There is absolutely no sign that Derkinderen took any notice of the iconographic scheme for the Exchange decorations. Verwey reproached Derkinderen for failing to devote any attention to the historical development of Amsterdam: "Thus, finally, all the development was excluded." The seasons, asserted Verwey, had nothing to do with the building, and nor did the north wall, for which Derkinderen had conceived a sort of emblem dedicated to "pride chastised." Verwey saw it as "an evasion of history." This controversy led to a court case in December 1901. Derkinderen compiled his grievances in a booklet, *Aan de verzoeningsraad* (To the Reconciliation Board), which appeared in the same year. The case was settled amicably; Derkinderen only had to change a few of the elements, and the window was ready in time for the official opening in 1903. The execution of the murals (which were to be completed by 1906) did not go ahead because of problems with the acoustics.[71] The conflict brought to light the irreconcilability that had until then been hidden – that between the static, regressive community ideal based on a medieval world view espoused by Derkinderen, and the vaguely socialist, utopian community ideal promoted by Verwey and Berlage.

But there was an even more fundamental conflict that calls into question the very principles on which the Exchange, as a work of *gemeenschapskunst*, was based, and that is the contradiction between the purpose of the building (a money and commodity exchange) and the symbolic (or ideological) function that Berlage and his associates attributed to it. The symbolic function embodied a criticism of contemporary, unjust society and a looking ahead to a classless society. It is paradoxical and almost grotesque that this function was expressed in a building that housed the quintessence of capitalism. This inconsistency did not escape Berlage's contemporaries. In 1903 *De Opmerker* gave a caustic reaction to the new exchange in "De nieuwe Beurs te Amsterdam en de Proletariërs (Toorop, Derkinderen, Berlage)":

Yet, if our proletarians are right, is the whole Exchange not a misplaced thing? Misplaced not only in terms of the field, but also in the realm of art? Would the three proletarians not have done better to refuse to work on the Temple of the Golden Calf, which they so despise, instead of accepting the commission and writing their professions of faith on walls that were not intended for them?[72]

One practical consequence was that the Chamber of Commerce felt uncomfortable in its new quarters. At the request of the Stock Exchange Association, ornaments were removed from the gate that gave access to the stock exchange. They represented a hand swearing an oath above a bag of money. Berlage defended himself with the argument that he had meant to express the sentiment "I swear to be honest in monetary affairs," but his explanation did not convince his critics. A member of Amsterdam city council also suggested that Toorop's tile panels depicting the past, present and future should be painted black.[73] In 1909 the stockbrokers got around the problems by commissioning Jos Cuypers (Pierre Cuypers's son) to build a new stock exchange. The same absurdity (that is to say the clash between the principle of a socialist community ideal and its manifestation in a capitalist building) was repeated in the many banks and insurance corporation offices that Berlage built. Far from being incidental, the absurdity of the concept that underpinned the Exchange was evidence of the unbridgeable chasm between utopianism and social reality.

Both these paradoxes reflect the internal contradictions that started to make themselves felt around 1900. The first was the conflict between a retrospective endeavor, aimed at reviving a medieval Gothic society and practice of art (Derkinderen), and a prospective endeavor, focused on the creation of a utopian socialist society (Berlage and Verwey). The second was the conflict between the utopian *gemeenschapskunst* and the reality of capitalism. These internal contradictions meant that the community art ideal began to crumble, and ultimately it disappeared.

Van der Mey's Scheepvaarthuis

The construction of the Scheepvaarthuis marked the growing importance of the larger shipping companies in Amsterdam. They wanted to seal their loyalty to the city by establishing the limited company Het Scheepvaarthuis (1912).[74] The architect awarded the commission was Johan Melchior van der Mey. He had virtually no experience, but the fact that he was the illegitimate child of one of the principals may well have had something to do with his appointment. Be this as it may, Van der Mey envisaged a modern building "built with modern resources and modern in essence, yet not denying our old art of the golden age … in which is echoed the voice that resounded across the Ocean in the days of national greatness." There are other statements that stress this combination. Van der Mey attracted a choice selection of architects and artists. The architects were Michel de Klerk and Pieter L. Kramer, whom he knew from his days working in Eduard Cuypers's office. For the structural sculpture he brought in Hendrikus van den Eijnde, Hildo Krop and W.C. Brouwers, for stained glass windows Willem Bogtman and for the interior Theodoor Nieuwenhuis (who worked closely with Wisselingh and Lion Cachet). The foundation stone was laid in 1913. World War I meant a delay, so that the building was not opened until 1916.

Precisely what Kramer and De Klerk contributed is not clear. De Klerk probably influenced the design of the façade. He designed the boardroom on the fourth floor and, with Kramer, the boardroom on the third floor, and he was also responsible for the

J. van der Mey, Scheepvaarthuis, Amsterdam.

design of wall paneling, clocks and lamps. The metalwork is probably by Kramer, but his input is much less easy to identify than De Klerk's. There were the inevitable wrangles and rows between Van der Mey and the artists and architects. Van der Mey allegedly went so far as to bar Kramer and De Klerk from the construction site.

The crucial feature of the Scheepvaarthuis is that the very specific and consistent decoration has nothing to do with the function of the building. The building consists of a concrete skeleton, designed by the Van Gendt brothers, who later made the concrete structures for the building of the Handelsmaatschappij on Vijzelstraat (De Bazel 1920-1926) and for De Nederlanden van 1845 in The Hague (Berlage 1924-1927). This concrete structure relieved the walls of their load-bearing function. "The façade stands like a petrified curtain, draped in folds around the skeleton, has to bear nothing but its own weight, is in fact supported by the core structure," explained Van der Mey. The contractors were thus completing a building that was actually already there. Their job was to dress a skeleton. This gave them great freedom in the use of materials, which could now be employed "unnaturally": bricks were cemented to the ceilings of porticos, roof tiles were affixed to the elevation. It was mockingly described as "pinafore architecture."[75] The building was a decorative object and structural considerations were very much secondary. It is most telling that in an article on the Scheepvaarthuis Van der Mey devoted four pages to structural aspects and twenty-eight to decoration. The character of the materials ("material authenticity") and "technical authenticity" were, however, respected.

The elements of the decoration scheme formed a cohesive whole. This interaction can be described as a *Gesamtkunstwerk*, but only in as much as the collaboration between the arts had a purely aesthetic function. It was not underpinned by any social ideas. In this respect there is consequently an essential difference between this building and "monuments" like the Rijksmuseum and the Exchange. Van der Mey was an outspoken opponent of the application of socialism to art. He thought that socialism was too materialistic and too collectivist. He envisioned an image of society in which people would come into their own as individuals. His building is consequently sometimes described as an example of expressionism.

Van der Mey stressed the distinction between architecture (engineering) and expression (art). The integration of the two was one of the principles of rationalism (Viollet, Cuypers and Berlage). Van der Mey was therefore also opposed to his predecessors' views and described his own opinion as "reverse rationalism" (in *De Ingenieur* 1915). In essence, Van der Mey returned to the concealing style of construction of the early nineteenth century that Thijm, Cuypers and others had so vociferously condemned.[76]

The Scheepvaarthuis represented a denial of Berlage's innovative ideas. The difference is evident, among other things, in the use of brick. To Berlage, brick was a structural material. He believed that the pointing should be clearly visible to emphasize the structure. To Van der Mey, brick was "dressing." The contrast can be summed up in that between Berlage's impressionism as against Van der Mey's expressionism. Berlage placed the emphasis on a powerful silhouette – strong lines, sobriety of detail, and decoration only in relevant places. Beauty should emanate from the structure. Van der Mey's notions were the precise opposite: he believed that beauty lay in the ornamentation that could be freely developed as soon as it was liberated from structural constraints. Berlage could not have disagreed more. He took the view that individual expression led to the degeneration of the general idea.[77]

It should not be inferred from this that the whole Amsterdam School abhorred Berlage's methods. In an article written in 1916 and published in the *Bouwkundig Weekblad*, Michel de Klerk commented with surprise and admiration on the fact that Berlage hid "the brand new product" of "cement and iron construction" behind a curtain of non-functional bricks. De Klerk found this example appealing and worked it up into the fundamental principle of the Amsterdam School. Although this put him in a position that was diametrically opposed to Berlage's impressionism, he himself believed (and in a sense he was right) that he was following Berlage.[78]

In the 1900-1912 period major commissions like the Peace Palace in The Hague (1906) and Rotterdam City Hall (1912) were awarded to architects who put up a mishmash of old tried and trusted styles. The building of these prestigious monsters depressed modern architects like Berlage and his colleagues in the architectural society *Architectura et Amicitia*. It was obvious that modern building was not catching on – worse yet, it seemed clear that modern building had ended in failure. But when the important commission for the construction of the Scheepvaarthuis in 1912 was awarded to a number of young modern architects, there was once more a gleam of hope. The Scheepvaarthuis became a shining example for new architecture and in this respect was unique.[79]

Aftereffects

World War I put an end to idealism about the utopian society and the role of art in bringing it closer. Nevertheless, *gemeenschapskunst* continued after this, albeit under the name "monumental art." Champions of monumental art – Derkinderen, Veth and Holst – acquired influential positions in art education. In 1907, on the recommendation of Veth and Diepenbrock, Derkinderen took up the post of director of the state art college, the Rijksacademie, where he implemented reorganizations in the direction he wanted.[80] In 1918, during his tenure, three extraordinary professors were appointed, among them one for "monumental art" (Roland Holst) and one for "portrait art" (Veth). After Derkinderen's death in 1925 Roland Holst took over as director. He, too, made changes in the syllabus to promote crafts and monumental art. Holst created two distinct subjects – "fine" art and "decorative monumental" art. He remained in the post until 1933. Immediately after his departure "fine" art regained the position it had lost, and monumental art as a defining element disappeared from the Rijksacademie.

The *gemeenschapskunst* concept lived on in the Amsterdam School. The School's heyday was 1917-1925, the period of the "South Plan." Berlage had produced an overall plan for the expansion of the city; the design of the actual buildings was left entirely to architects of the Amsterdam School. The great success of these architects was due, in no small measure, to Amsterdam City Council, which insisted that only architects could be involved in construction and supervised this by means of a planning committee manned by adherents of the Amsterdam School. The power of the Amsterdam School spread through firms of architects, architecture courses, and the Department of Public Works, which awarded important projects to the Amsterdam School: the municipal transport company's building, the extension to City Hall, several high schools and, of course, the bridges. And the influence of the School was not confined to Amsterdam. Elsewhere (in Groningen and Utrecht) major projects were built in the style of the Amsterdam School. The impact was felt not only on the architecture and the ornamentation incorporated in it, but on the interior too. "Interior design," a relatively new concept, became the province of eminent architects like Kramer and Krop, who designed and made extraordinarily beautiful furniture, wall coverings, floor coverings and lamps.

Pieter L. Kramer's building for De Bijenkorf, a department store in The Hague (1924-26), was the last great tour de force, but by then the Amsterdam School was already so conformist and used its position of power so overtly to quash any initiatives from the New Realism movement (Dudok, Duintjer and their associates) that this building was described as a "large-scale example of commercial conservatism." The Amsterdam School's extensive use of stained glass (from the Scheepvaarthuis to De Bijenkorf) sparked a veritable craze. "No school celebration or office party can pass without some generous benefactor or committee putting the glazier to work."[81] It can justifiably be said that the *gemeenschapskunst* ideal really was achieved in a number of the Amsterdam School's projects. The community ideal no longer, it is true, set its sights on commissions for monumental buildings in which architecture, fine art and the decorative arts worked together, but on public housing, where the unity of architecture, urban planning and society was achieved in aesthetically well designed and government-supported house building.

A second important offshoot of *gemeenschapskunst* can be found in *De Stijl* (1917-1931), a movement which introduced a new generation of artists under the guidance of Theo van Doesburg, Piet Mondrian, Jacobus J.P. Oud and Bart van der Leck. At the beginning of his career, Van der Leck modeled himself on Derkinderen. He wrote admiringly about Derkinderen's stained glass window for the University of Utrecht (1894). Van der Leck tried to make *gemeenschapskunst*, but for the ordinary man and not, as Derkinderen did, for Catholic intellectuals. In 1907 he moved to Laren, where Derkinderen also had his studio, and bombarded Derkinderen with reproductions of his work. At first Derkinderen responded with the occasional non-committal note; later he did not bother to reply at all. *De Stijl* pursued a community idea in the sense that they wanted to express universal harmony, the laws that govern man and the universe, in their work. Their chosen means of expression was abstract and this triggered a polemic between *De Stijl* and Roland Holst. Holst was against abstract painting and against the new building style, as exemplified by the Van Nelle factory by Brinkman outside Rotterdam. He was attacked by Van Doesburg and by Huszar, who declared that monumentality was only found in the *Nieuwe Beelding* – Neo-Plasticism – not in the work of Roland Holst.[82] The position taken by *De Stijl* can be characterized by Mondrian's criticism of the *gemeenschapskunst* idea. In Mondrian's view, it was painting, not architecture, that predominated. He experimented with this notion in his own workshops. Mondrian wrote two articles for the journal *De Stijl* in 1917, in which he asserted that architecture had to be subordinate to neo-plasticism, because it offered the viewer the illusion of a flat surface that would generate a meditational impulse in him. In Carel Blotkamp's words, Mondrian's workshops were "model dwellings for the spiritualized man."[83]

Some observations in conclusion

Gemeenschapskunst – community art – did not survive the confrontation with social reality. In retrospect it proved to be precariously based on a naive form of idealism. Nevertheless it had something fundamental to say. It identified a problem that is still current: what social function does art fulfill?

The term *gemeenschapskunst* has been used in this chapter to describe a broad movement around the turn of the century. This movement gave rise both to a re-examination of the relation of art to society and the relation of the arts to one another, and to a renewal of the decorative arts and a systematic policy on museums and the preservation of the national heritage. The latter two aspects are not generally associated with *gemeenschapskunst*. In our view, however, they must be seen as part of it. We say this with some emphasis because it is in precisely these areas that we see the lasting results of an endeavor that has otherwise disappeared. We consequently also believe that the concept of *gemeenschapskunst* is a much broader one than has hitherto been acknowledged.

There is a singular correspondence between *gemeenschapskunst* and totalitarian art (that is to say, art under totalitarian regimes). The collaboration of all the arts as a means to achieve a social objective, the emphasis on the art of the symbol rather than that of the image, the subservience to a centrally run social system – all this makes *gemeenschapskunst* very akin to the art that developed under totalitarian regimes. Holst's writings are larded with passages which reveal just how fervently he was seeking an ideology that could fill the void in which *gemeenschapskunst* was wandering in confusion. In such passages we can see the gaping hole around which totalitarian regimes clustered at the time.[84] Is there a historical relationship between *gemeenschapskunst* and totalitarian – communist or fascist – art in the between-war years? What is this relationship? Did the work of leading practitioners of *gemeenschapskunst* like Derkinderen and Holst become more and more unworldly and utopian because they distanced themselves from the emerging great ideologies and nonetheless clung on to a *gemeenschapskunst* – a community art – for which the social basis was increasingly missing? Was the decorative superficiality into which *gemeenschapskunst* declined in the years between the two world wars likewise a consequence of the fact that its practitioners were unable to identify with the totalitarian ideologies, but outside those ideologies could find no social basis of support for their work?

After World War I the cathedral lost its power as a source of inspiration. Holst, Derkinderen and Berlage did still refer to it, but without much conviction. This change is typified by the publication in 1919 of Huizinga's *Herfsttij der Middeleeuwen* (*The Waning of the Middle Ages*, 1924), which paints a much less rosy picture of the late Middle Ages. Derkinderen and several other hardliners of *gemeenschapskunst*, including Lauweriks, reacted bitterly to this book because it did not suit their idealized image of the Middle Ages, but the spell was broken.

5

"In this manner one approaches Spirit" – From symbolist to early abstract painting

Between 1912 and 1917 Piet Mondrian developed from a figurative into an abstract artist. The writings in which he set out his ideas and the works in which those ideas took shape made him the leading figure associated with *De Stijl*, the journal founded in 1917.

Mondrian said that the cubists were his immediate predecessors. Picasso and Braque had formulated the principles from which he had drawn the ultimate conclusions. Symbolism, on the other hand, had been an obstacle on the road to "Nieuwe beelding" or neo-plasticism. This account by Mondrian is not entirely accurate. Recent research has shown that he was able to take the step to complete abstraction because he attributed symbolic value to the elementary visual components (horizontal and vertical lines, three primary colors) to which he had limited himself. Mondrian's aesthetic rested on symbolist foundations. Without that basis, he would not have been able to make the move to abstraction.

But which symbolism are we talking about? The Dutch symbolism of Jan Toorop, Johan Thorn Prikker, Richard Roland Holst and Antoon Derkinderen? Or the French symbolism of Paul Gauguin, Maurice Denis and Albert Aurier? We shall look first at the broad outlines of French symbolist aesthetics, before examining the differences between French and Dutch symbolism through contrastive aesthetics. Finally, we shall show that Mondrian's aesthetic is closely connected to French symbolism and opposed to Dutch symbolism.

Symbolism in France

Art historians avoid the term "symbolism." They prefer more limited and local descriptions such as "neo-impressionism," "the Pont-Aven group," "Nabi" and "Rose + Croix." Yet all these movements were expressions of an approach to art that was beginning in the eighteen-eighties to free itself from the dominance of impressionism. The essence of this new view lay in its opposition to realism and positivism. Symbolism offered the representation of ideas in place of the depiction of contemporary social reality. It offered carefully considered construction in place of the "snapshot" of the sensory impression. In retrospect, this development looks like a clash between irreconcilable views of art, but in reality it was a gradual transition. The symbolists built on advances made by the impressionists. The dissection of mixed colors into their component parts by Renoir, Monet, Manet and others was radicalized by

Seurat and Signac into pointillism and divisionism. But the principle was the same. The transition may have appeared to be a break because for so long impressionism was thought of as the pictorial equivalent of naturalism, which put exclusive emphasis on the photographic depiction of social reality and cared little about the means by which this depiction was achieved. Emile Zola was among the chief exponents of this view. He defended the early impressionists because he believed they were pursuing the same kind of naturalism as he was. The consequence was a profound misunderstanding. Zola had absolutely no sympathy for Manet's innovations, let alone Monet's experiments. He regarded their work as a betrayal of the "true" aim of impressionism, namely the depiction of social reality.[1] Opposition to this misunderstanding first became organized when Redon, Seurat, Dubois-Pillet and Cross joined forces in 1884 in the *Salon des Artistes Indépendants*. The forming of this new movement coincided with the break up of the impressionists. Pierre Renoir refused to take part in any more joint exhibitions. He did not want to be associated with Gauguin and Pissarro, and least of all with the wild young men of the *Indépendants*.[2] The divisions became apparent at the 1886 exhibition in which some of the impressionists and Seurat took part. Seurat's *Une dimanche à la grande Jatte* had a tremendous impact. The next year it was shown by the group *Les XX* in Brussels. Félix Fénéon's important essay "Le néo-impressionisme" (May 1887) was inspired by this exhibition (among others). The Dutch artist Jan Toorop, who was a member of *Les XX* and had shown work in Brussels since 1885, probably first saw the work there. 1886 was also the year in which Jean Moréas wrote his "Manifeste du symbolisme" and the year in which Gauguin went to the village of Pont-Aven in Brittany to join Emile Bernard, Louis Anquetin and Charles Laval in working on a new kind of painting. His efforts resulted in 1888 in *Jacob Wrestling with the Angel* (also known as *Vision of the Sermon*), which was shown the next year by *Les XX* in Brussels. Gauguin gave the name "synthèse" to his new approach (in a letter to his friend Schuffenecker in 1888), and that term was applied to the art of Pont-Aven in the general form of "synthetism."[3]

In the summer of 1888 Paul Sérusier visited Pont-Aven. Under Gauguin's guidance he painted a landscape, *Paysage du bois d'amour*. He returned to Paris with the painting and, like Moses with the tablets, presented it to his friends at the Académie Julian (Maurice Denis, Paul Ranson, Pierre Bonnard) and the Ecole des Beaux-Arts, including Edouard Vuillard.[4] Sérusier gave the name "Nabi" (the plural of "nebiim," Hebrew for "prophet") to the group working according to the new ideas. It is important to note that they expressed their ideas not only on canvas but in the decorative arts too: fabric designs, glass painting, wallpaper design, and book illustrations. The principle of decorative art was an important element, as we shall see, of the new approach.

The painters were in close touch with the poets who were trying to form a symbolist movement at this time. Of the many journals taking a symbolist line that were published in France in the mid-eighteen-eighties, there were two that carried real weight: the *Revue indépendante*, founded by Félix Fénéon (1884, the contributors included Mallarmé, Verlaine, Huysmans, Moréas and Morice) and the *Revue Wagnérienne* edited by Edouard Dujardin (1885). Fénéon was the chief intermediary between the new painters (Seurat,

Gauguin, Degas) and the poets. He wrote important pieces about the new art, pointing out the great significance of Seurat and rejecting Renoir.

Two articles signaled the prominence of symbolism in painting: "Définition du néo-traditionnisme" by Maurice Denis (1890) and "Le symbolisme en peinture" by Albert Aurier (1891). These two brilliant artist-critics demonstrated how painters and poets were working from a fundamentally new point of view, and they defined the principles behind what had developed in the preceding years into a real movement. Somewhat apart within or beside this movement was the highly curious figure of Joséphin Péladan with his *Rose + Croix*. In 1892 Péladan, who called himself "sar," opened a Salon where he showed work by painters who, like him, opposed impressionism and took their lead from the Pre-Raphaelites. They were not taken seriously by other artists. Their work was too innocent, too anecdotal and not "modern" enough.[5]

Vincent van Gogh likewise stood apart, but for different reasons. He went to Paris in 1886, that is at the point at which divisions were emerging. There he borrowed ideas both from the impressionists and from Gauguin and Seurat. From 1886 his work certainly has symbolic elements, but it is so irreducibly idiosyncratic that it cannot be categorized as symbolist. Aurier calls him a symbolist in the only article about Van Gogh published in his lifetime, but he himself responded by remarking that as far as he was concerned there was no reason to drag symbolism into it. Moreover, he felt no affinity with symbolist literature. Van Gogh was extremely well read, but he did not at all care for the poets who directly influenced the symbolist painters (Baudelaire, Verlaine, Mallarmé). He preferred Zola and Goncourt. To what extent can he be called a symbolist? Objects in Van Gogh's paintings often have a symbolic meaning, for example Gauguin's chair, or the cord in the hands of Madame Roulin (*La Berçeuse*). They are actually metonymies standing emblematically for a thing or person of which they show part. But Van Gogh also tried through color contrasts and synthetism to express feelings and in doing so to leave aside representation. He was "exaspéré par la perfection photographique" and tried to transcend depiction by using "intensely felt" forms and colors.[6] Van Gogh blazed new trails, but they led in the end to expressionism.

The painters sought support from the poets in developing a new approach. Pissarro wrote in a letter to his son that he was developing a new style under the influence of reading Baudelaire and Verlaine. Aurier's articles are permeated by implicit and explicit references to Baudelaire. Gauguin and Denis knew the work of Baudelaire, Verlaine and Mallarmé.

In *Le Symbolisme en peinture* Aurier quotes the first quatrain of Baudelaire's "Correspondances," which is generally regarded as the beginning of symbolism in literature.

CORRESPONDANCES

La Nature est un temple où de vivants pilliers
Laissent parfois sortir de confuses paroles;
L'homme y passe à travers des forêts de symboles
Qui l'observent avec des regards familiers.

Comme de longs échos qui de loin se confondent
Dans une ténébreuse et profonde unité,
Vaste comme la nuit et comme la clarté,
Les parfums, les couleurs et les sons se répondent.

Il est des parfums frais comme des chairs d'enfants,
Doux comme les hautbois, verts comme les prairies,
- Et d'autres, corrompus, riches et triomphants,

Ayant l'expansion des choses infinies,
Comme l'ambre, le musc, le benjoin et l'encens,
Qui chantent les transports de l'esprit et des sens.

CORRESPONDENCES

The pillars of Nature's temple are alive
And sometimes yield perplexing messages;
Forests of symbols between us and the shrine
Remark our passage with accustomed eyes.

Like long-held echoes, blending somewhere else
Into one deep and shadowy unison
As limitless as darkness and as day,
The sounds, the scents, the colors correspond.

There are odors succulent as young flesh,
Sweet as flutes, and green as any grass,
While others – rich, corrupt and masterful –

Possess the power of such infinite things
As incense, amber, benjamin and musk
To praise the senses' raptures and the mind's. [7]

Baudelaire presents nature as a forest of symbols. They bring about a "vertical" relation which connects human reality to a higher, metaphysical reality. Here Baudelaire is drawing on the ideas of the Swedish mystic Emanuel Swedenborg (1688-1772), but he voices his doubts as to the nature of universal harmony. Not only does he leave us in the dark as to the reality referred to by the symbols (nowhere in the sonnet is there any mention of a transcendent, let alone divine, reality), but he also makes it clear that the symbolic correspondence functions imperfectly: nature only whispers a few words "sometimes" and they are perplexing to boot. In the second quatrain he gives another, horizontal twist to the correspondence. It now refers to similarities between fields of sensory perception, synesthesias, whereby "les parfums, les couleurs et les sons se répondent." In the sextet, finally, he explains that some of these synesthesias give access to a world of purity and innocence, while others, more numerous and stronger, evoke a world of sin and corruption.

An important point is that Baudelaire invokes romantic commonplaces (Swedenborg's ideas had been absorbed by writers like Schelling, Sainte-Beuve, Victor Hugo and above all Balzac, whose mystical novels were also very popular with the symbolist painters of the fin de siècle), but he casts doubt on them. In Baudelaire there remains only a defective metaphysical dimension.

Many of Baudelaire's poems (and this is a second important aspect) suggest that "symbol" should be understood not so much as the translation of an individual feeling into an image but as the harmony between corresponding sensory experiences. Baudelaire comes back to this idea in his art criticism. In "Exposition Universelle 1855" he asks himself where Delacroix's secret lies. He answers in the form of the following quatrain:

> Delacroix, blood lake, malign angels' haunt,
> Shadowed by firs, a forest always green, where
> Under a dismal sky, strange fanfares
> Blow like stifled sighs, Weberian.[8]

The red of the blood contrasts with the green of the foliage, red's complementary color. This "color chord" corresponds with the musical chords of Carl Maria von Weber. The symbolic value of the work lies in the double harmony that becomes apparent: that of the colors on the canvas and that of the colors and the sounds. For Baudelaire the scene portrayed was not the most important thing (he objected fiercely to the realist tradition of his age–Courbet–in which this was considered the principal task of art). For him what mattered was to use painterly means (particularly color) to give an added value and thus confer on the work a supernatural dimension.[9]

Baudelaire formulated an approach to art that was only put into practice later by his followers Verlaine and Mallarmé. The latter went furthest along the road indicated by Baudelaire. In a relatively simple poem like "Mrs. Mallarmé's fan" (1891), the disruption of the syntactic structure is such that it can no longer be read "linearly."

EVENTAIL	FAN
de Madame Mallarmé	of Mrs. Mallarmé
Avec comme pour langage	With nothing that speaks
Rien qu'un battement aux cieux	But strokes in the air
Le futur vers se dégage	The verse to be breaks
Du logis très précieux	From its most choice lair
Aile tout bas la courrière	Carrier wing restrained
Cet éventail si c'est lui	If it is this fan
Le même par qui derrière	This through which behind
Toi quelque miroir a lui	You a mirror shone
Limpide (où va redescendre	Clear (where only some
Pourchassée en chaque grain	Unseen ash hounded
Un peu d'invisible cendre	In each grain will come
Seule à me rendre chagrin)	Down and make me sad)
Toujours tel il apparaisse	Long may it look thus
Entre tes mains sans paresse	In your hands tireless.[10]

The reader is forced to arrange fragments of sentences in a way different from the normal word order. Three word fields emerge in the poem: 1 (fan), a woman before a mirror takes a fan from a case and waves cool air at herself; 2 (wing), a flapping wing takes to the air and shoots past in the mirror; 3 (pen), a pen that frees itself from the penholder writes the poem.

The great step that Mallarmé takes is that he views the relations between the word fields as symbols. The field "fan" stands symbolically for the field "wing;" both stand symbolically for the field "pen." The theme of the poem (but what is the theme?) is secondary. The anecdote recedes and is syntactically deformed for the sake of the harmonic correspondence between word fields. The poem breaks completely with any representative function (the fan, the wing and the pen are not symbols of things that exist in reality) or with any expressive function (these objects are not symbols of the poet's feelings). For the moment the painters did not go as far as this. But the example of Baudelaire and Mallarmé shows what they had in mind with their new art. What were the main features of their approach?

Harmony and idea

The painters' thoughts about ideas and symbols (with or without a capital letter) were not carefully thought out. But it was clear that they wanted to put an end to the prevailing aesthetic of realism, which was well defined. The following statement by Courbet is like a reverse image of what the symbolists aspired to:

> I regard painting as a fundamentally concrete art which can exist only as a represen-
> tation of things that are real; it is a completely natural language which in my view
> consists of all visible objects. An abstract, invisible, nonexistent object has no place in
> the field of painting.

In their rejection of realists, naturalists, positivists and materialists, they turned for support to various idealists: Swedenborg, Schelling, Schopenhauer, Hegel, Bergson and
Schuré. The crisis in naturalism led to "an idealistic and even mystical reaction" said the
young writer Albert Aurier. Opinions differ as to the nature of these "ideas." Aurier
pointed explicitly toward Plato and Plotinus, and he described symbols as the "representative depiction of the highest and most truly divine things in the world, Ideas." The
painter Paul Sérusier at first interpreted "ideas" in a theosophical and later in an increasingly Christian sense. According to him, the symbolist painter sought the divine behind
phenomena. He stressed that God became manifest in harmonies of color and line:
"Harmony is the only means, together with prayer, of putting us in contact with
God."[11] The concept of "harmony" so much invoked in symbolist circles has associations
with the musical concept of harmony and, through music, with the "harmony of the
spheres." We know of no study of the significance of "harmony" around the turn of the
century. A lexicographic / semantic description of the word fields "harmony" and
"rhythm" as used around 1900 would provide detailed information about one of the
most characteristic aspects of the mentality of the period.

Maurice Denis was very definite in declaring that Gauguin, Cézanne and Bernard did
not believe in a supernatural world: they were "without metaphysics" and "wanted to
subject themselves to the laws of harmony that ruled the relationships between colors,
forms and lines."[12]

One of the ways in which symbolism (both in painting and poetry) differed from
romanticism was in the high value it placed on reason. During the fin de siècle the making
of art was very much an intellectual activity, and probably what was special about symbolism was that the artist believed that through a quasi-scientific method and mathematical precision he could find the key to the world of ideas that he presumed lay behind
natural phenomena: "A kind of scientific mysticism seems to be developing," wrote
Frédéric Paulhan in 1891 in *Le nouveau mysticisme*, "the joining of the spirit of science and
the spirit of faith, the widely felt need for harmony taken to the point of mysticism,
seems to be the characteristic feature of the new spirit."[13] The coming together of science
and mysticism was evident on a broad cultural front. Many of the leading figures of positivism – Hippolyte Taine, Claude Bernard and Louis Pasteur – veered towards mysticism. A scientific approach was taken to the study of consciousness: positivist / experimental methods were deployed to define such phenomena as "mind" and "soul." The
effect of colors and shapes on the human mind was scientifically examined. Charles
Henry, the brilliant polymath, investigated the scientific foundations of harmonies and
correspondences.[14] Gauguin drew his ideas from scientists like Eugène Chevreul (*De la
loi du contraste simultané des couleurs*, 1839) and David Humbert de Superville (*Essai sur
les signes inconditionnels dans l'art*, 1827). Henry was a major and direct influence on the
symbolist painters, particularly Seurat and Signac, who were friends of his. The same

applied to the *Grammaire des arts du dessin* by Charles Blanc (1867). The new painting liked to react against impressionism in this respect. Gauguin described impressionism as brainless art ("un art acéphale"). Maurice Denis observed, "A work of art is only of value to the extent that it is the outcome of a carefully considered intention. What determines its value, and I would go so far as to say its beauty, is the part of his intellectual life that the artist gives us, the part of his conscious, dynamic and serious life."[15] Aurier referred to the artist as an "algébriste des Idées."[16] Perhaps Sérusier expressed this mystic formalism most clearly. "The Egyptians," he wrote to his friend Jan Verkade, "have given me the key to the Sacred Proportions and I do not work without a proportions compass." "I had the feeling that I was the tool of a higher intelligence." "Sacred Proportions" is also the tenor of his posthumously published *ABC de la peinture*. There he says that painting is a matter of finding the "universal language," a language based on the "science of numbers, especially the simple numbers, the mathematics which, when applied to art, is geometry."[17] The treatise has a kind of table that gives the symbolic value of colors, forms and numbers. Thus there is a list of the numbers 1 to 9 with the value of each explained: "2 is the expression of the conflict between two principles. The conflict remains sterile if it does not lead to a result which, added to these two principles, forms the number 3." "The number 3 means God or the Creator"; the equilateral triangle is the clearest manifestation of this. 4 is 2 squared and "the square means balance in matter." "The straight line is a spiritual line, because it is never found in matter."[18] It is clear from the treatise that by symbols Sérusier meant relationships between forms, numbers and colors, and that the idea manifested itself in these relationships. Sérusier leaves open the question whether that is the Idea, God, or a self-enclosed harmony tending towards autonomy.

Composition, autonomy, abstraction

The belief that "painters give expression to God's harmonious logic"[19] has far-reaching consequences. If the symbolic effect of the painting rests on the harmonious combination of color and form on the canvas, then this implies the autonomy of the image at the expense of representation, leading ultimately to abstract art, that is, painting that relies only on the non-figurative harmony of color and form. All this arises from the persuasion that the symbolic effect of such a non-objective harmony makes visible something of the supernatural interrelationship of things. Maurice Denis begins his celebrated article on neo-traditionalism with the following proposition: "Consider that a painting – before it becomes a warhorse, a naked woman or any other anecdote – is in essence a flat surface that is covered with colors applied in a certain arrangement."[20] In this statement a form of symbolism is evident that is fundamentally different from the figurative symbolism with which the term is generally identified. Denis points to this difference. "There is," he says, "a type of art that makes use of cultural clichés and manipulates the viewer's feelings in a cheap way: images of hands folded in prayer, a figure with bowed head, a scene from the first communion." Denis contrasts this kitsch variant of symbolism with the true symbolists:

They draw less of their inspiration from life, and in order to realize the absolute they study the intimate secrets of nature and numbers. A supernatural beauty emerges from the mathematical relationships between lines and colors. It consists of the charm of the perfect chord, the glory of the immobile. Instead of depicting objects to stir up our tired old feelings, the work itself is meant to move us. The invincible spiritual beauty corresponds with the perfection of the décor; wonderful relationships stand as a sign for the truth from above; proportions give expression to concepts; there is equivalence between the harmony of forms and the logic of dogma. Think of the Egyptians, the Byzantines (mosaics in Italy), Cimabue.[21]

The difference is crucial: on the one hand cheap symbolism based on depicting clichéd images; on the other, the abstract, "decorative" and authentic symbolism that tries to make God visible in the "harmonious logic" of the visual elements. Notice that Denis is very firm about the symbolic function of lines and colors: they are a "sign" of the "truth from above." He clearly indicates that the value of this symbolism lies in the movement that turns its back on representative art and searches for an object-less, if you will abstract, art. We should add that the concept "abstraction" merits separate study. It does not always mean the same for the four painters discussed here. The term "non-objective art" does not mean the same now as it did at the turn of the century, when in turn its meaning was different from at the beginning of the nineteenth century, the time when it was first used in relation to painting. To Gauguin "abstract" meant a decorative representation, not something without a subject. For Mondrian it indicated a process of spiritualization (as we shall see). As with the terms "harmony" and "rhythm," a lexicological / semantic study of the word would bring to light much of value.

Synthesis, deformation, decoration

Based on what has been said above, two key concepts in symbolism –"synthesis" and "deformation" – can be placed in the right relationship. The artist believes that the truth behind phenomena can be evoked only through deforming them. The painting is meant to be a "synthesis" and synthetization is not just a matter of simplifying the image by leaving out details; it involves *transforming* and simplifying it in order to make it understandable. Imposing hierarchy is essential: the images must be subject to an underlying rhythm.

The artists were aware that the art they were aiming for was decorative in nature. They related the gradual denial of perspective to this. This denial was not total: Gauguin, Denis and others simplified the imaginary space down to two levels, a background and a motif in the foreground. They no longer used color to suggest depth; instead they set colors opposite each other for the sake of their internal relationship within the painting. Denis points to earlier forms of art thought to be purer: "In the beginning there was the pure arabesque, as little 'trompe-l'oeil' as possible; the wall is blank, it must be filled with marks that are symmetrical in form and harmonious in color (stained-glass windows, Egyptian paintings, Byzantine mosaics, kakemonos)."[22] The importance of ornament was emphasized by research undertaken at the time into the effect of color. The influential Von Helmholtz pointed out the effect of color in, for example, tapestries, and

French theorists such as Séailles (*Essai sur le génie dans l'art*, 1883), Théodore de Wyzéwa and Charles Henry followed his lead.[23]

Visual elements

The greater autonomy of the visual elements applied to both color and line. Only a few fragments of Seurat's writings have been preserved. In them words like "harmony" and "rhythm" are crucial to a system of laws on color and line with both scientific and meta-physical ambitions.[24] These fragments also show that Seurat closely studied the work of Eugène Delacroix, and in particular the way in which he created color harmonies through the sophisticated use of complementary colors. After studying *Les convulsion-naires de Tanger* (1878), Seurat noted: "In the foreground a red, or rather an orange, man, beside him on the right a boy dressed in dark blue. The blue and the orange harmonize again in the man to the right of the convulsive falling backwards. He wears an orange garment with a great deal of vermilion in it. This color is surrounded by the bluish gray fabrics worn by the figures in the center."[25] The symbolists and in particular the neo-impressionists built on the discoveries of Delacroix and thus continued the tradition of the colorists or Rubénistes.[26] But the symbolists also attached great importance to line. They continued not only the legacy of the Rubénistes but also that of the "Davidiens," the draftsmen. Through Blanc and Henry, the symbolists rediscovered the work of the Dutchman David Humbert de Superville. In *Essai sur les signes inconditionnels* (1827) he had contended that lines have symbolic value according to a basic system in which the straight line stands for balance, order, dignity and stability; the obliquely rising (or expansive) line for fierce passions, movement, agitation, instability and change; and the obliquely descending (or converging) line for reflection, deep thought, edification of the soul, solemnity and the sublime. Humbert found these types of line, with their symbolic values, in depictions of nature, in facial expressions and in the compositions of paintings. His theory was adopted complete with illustrations by Charles Blanc (*Grammaire des arts du dessin*, 1867) and Charles Henry ("Introduction à une esthétique scientifique," 1884). Seurat studied these theorists and copied Humbert's diagrams ($\downarrow$, $\uparrow$) in his "credo," the letter he sent to Maurice Beaubourg in 1890. Humbert's theory also encompassed color. As with the symbolism of lines, he distinguished between balanced (white), expansive (red) and contracting (black) colors. Seurat explicitly mentions this system too in his let-ter.[27]

There was another way in which the fin-de-siècle painters attributed symbolic value to lines (not just on the basis of their direction), and that was the simplification of images to signs. Around 1888 Gauguin, Bernard and Anquetin began to simplify forms and sur-round them with broad black lines. Edouard Dujardin called this "cloisonisme," a term derived from an enameling technique. The effect was rather like that of stained glass.[28] The aim was to make the image abstract until it became a sign pointing above and beyond the image (now reduced to a mere first step) to a universal syntax. This image reduced to an ideogram reveals the second way in which symbolism laid the ground for abstract art (the first was through color harmonies). Aurier talks about paintings that express an abstract idea symbolically like a "page of ideographic writing that recalls the hieroglyphic texts on the obelisks of ancient Egypt." Natural objects, he says, are "letters from a vast alphabet that can be read only by a genius." Objects are important only to the extent that they are "signs of Ideas."[29]

It was Sérusier above all who developed the theoretical basis of symbolism in this ideographic direction. He emphasizes the fact that this "art of the sign" rejects representative art: "In order to make the work of art expressive a system of signs is required, a script."[30]

Subject and memory

The subject played a crucial role in the aesthetics of symbolism; it also gave rise to many misunderstandings. Aurier calls subjectivity one of the chief features of symbolist painting and he defines the role of the subject as follows: "subjective, because the object is never regarded as an object, but as a sign of an idea that is perceived by the subject." The discussion is muddied by a number of unclear points: are the objects Aurier is talking about symbols of a subjective thought (idea) or of a transcendent Idea? Is he referring to an object as it occurs in nature or as it is depicted in a painting? Here various matters are mixed up which need to be distinguished to avoid disastrous confusion. They are: (a) the natural objects; (b) the Idea assumed to be behind them; (c) the mind of the artist; (d) the objects as depicted by him in the painting; (e) the effect of the objects depicted on the viewer.

The premise from which Aurier (and Gauguin and Denis and the other symbolists) starts is that the natural phenomena are symbols of an interrelationship that holds the cosmos together in a mysterious manner. This interrelationship is only apparent to artists of genius. They witness the deep connections in their mind and translate the sense of interrelationship into a pictorial expression through artistic means. In so doing, they transform the natural phenomena (the famous "deformation") with the aim of making the mysterious harmony visible for those who lack the inner eye (the public). The emphasis that almost all symbolist painters place on the importance of the subject has led to the misunderstanding that their aim was to express their "états d'âme," and that symbolism was an expressive aesthetic rooted in the subject of the artist. Nothing could be further from the truth. The spirit of the artist has an intermediary role. "The spirituality of the artist," mirrors the "fundamental spirituality of the divine objective beings," says Aurier elsewhere. The artist's "spiritual receptivity" is a "transcendental receptivity"; his mind is put in turmoil by the "turbulent drama of abstractions."[31]

This starting point, anti-subjectivist in fact, is in agreement with the views of Mallarmé. He eliminated his "I" for the sake of an absolutely "transcendental receptivity," to put it in Aurier's terms. He wanted to be the crystal receiver of secrets whispered to him from language. Subjective feelings had no place in this. They would only have disturbed the lucid analysis of the cosmic connections and their manifestation in language.

The cosmic interrelationship puts the mind of the artist in turmoil and, if all goes well, his work of art conveys this turmoil to the mind of the viewer. Images derived from music, such as "chord", "harmony," and "mood," are constantly used to make this clear.

We may add that the word "mood" was very much in vogue in the Netherlands and that it encompassed this three-fold link (the mysterious correspondence between the "universal spirit," the spirit of the artist and the spirit of the viewer / reader).

Finally, memory is important. The great value that the symbolists placed on it may be explained by the intermediary role discussed above. Gauguin always insisted that the artist should work not from nature, but from the images that his memory had distilled from it. He taught Vincent van Gogh this lesson after he joined him in Arles in 1888. Vincent painted too realistically for Gauguin's taste: he needed to "abstract" more, to work more from memory. Vincent took this advice and painted *The walk (souvenir of the garden at Etten)* (1888). Denis also says that the artist can only penetrate to the hidden interrelatedness of nature if he is guided by the "mental image" that he reconstructs in memory. And Sérusier warns the artist not to paint faithfully from nature, for "copying" weakens the capability on which his art is based, namely the "mémoire des formes," a phrase whose Platonic connotations give extra weight to the intermediary role of memory.[32]

In 1895 Gauguin was criticized because of the "red dogs" and "pink skies" in his paintings. "They are absolutely meant to be like that," he responded,

> they are essential and everything in my work is calculated and carefully considered. It is music, if you like. I take a random object from life or nature as a start and I transform it, through arrangements of colors and lines, into symphonies, harmonies that depict absolutely nothing real in the banal sense of the word, that do not express a particular idea, but that provoke thought, the way that music does, without the aid of ideas or images, simply through the mysterious affinities that exist between our brains and such arrangements of colors and lines.[33]

This quotation summarizes almost everything said above: the rational, calculated manner of painting, in contrast to the impressionists' spontaneous methods; the evocation of feelings in the viewer, instead of giving expression to the artist's feelings; the deformation of the realistic image (the red dog) with the aim of eliminating representation in favor of an objectless harmony occurring on the canvas itself; the symbolic value, which reveals itself in the mysterious correspondence between this harmony on canvas on the one hand and the minds of the artist and the viewer on the other.

Perhaps the most important point about Gauguin's remarks is that they invite us, a century later, to look at his work and that of his colleagues in a different way. The questions we ask about their paintings usually have to do with the people and objects depicted in them: who or what are they; what do they "mean"? Gauguin makes it clear that the depiction is no more than a starting point for what the painting is really about, its meaningful harmony.

Dutch symbolism

Dutch symbolist painting flourished between 1890 and 1900. The leading figures, Jan Toorop, Richard Roland Holst, Johan Thorn Prikker and Antoon Derkinderen, were in close touch with developments in France. As a member of the Brussels group *Les XX,*

Toorop was aware of the exhibitions in which Seurat and later Signac took part. In her standard work on Dutch symbolism, Bettina Polak defines the symbol as a "visible sign for an invisible Idea." She explores the nature of that sign through an overview of symbols: the femme fatale (Salome, Cleopatra, Medusa), Pan, the innocent young woman (the bride), the lily, the lotus, etc. According to Polak, these symbols give "expression to the deepest impulses of the soul." She also believes that their expressive function is weakened at the point when symbolism has passed its peak (around 1894). "The personal difficulties have been thrashed out, the passion has ebbed away, the feelings have been vented, the symbols have served their purpose."[34] Finally, Polak points out the paramount importance of the stylized line.

In defining Dutch symbolism, Polak and other art historians[35] refer to French theories. They cite Aurier, Denis and Gauguin, they mention Henry and Blanc. The effect of this is to suggest that Dutch symbolism was a logical extension of French symbolism. This is misleading. The Dutch symbolists differed from their French models in one essential respect. They took their lead in part from them, but they particularized (or, perhaps better, narrowed) the French symbolist aesthetic and made it basically figurative. In 1892 Jan Toorop (1858-1928) designed a poster for the recently founded artists' society, the *Haagsche Kunstkring*: *The Knight at the Gate*. In it he made use of archetypal images. The castle stands for The Hague; it has the city's coat of arms with a stork above the gate. The scene as a whole – a hedge of thorns around a castle, a knight fighting his way to the gate – alludes to the Sleeping Beauty motif. Through these images Toorop is also referring to the battle between the art of the past and modern art. Using its rigidifying powers (the hedge of thorns and the castle), the art of the past tries to imprison the coming flowering of the modern (the princess in the tower) in deadly slumber, while the avant-garde artists (the *Haagsche Kunstkring*) stand ready to break the spell and free her from captivity. This self-referential twist (that is, the work of art alluding to itself) is, we believe, characteristic of Toorop's symbolism and probably of Dutch (and perhaps European) symbolist art in general. In nearly all his works Toorop presents a picture of the battle waged by the powers of darkness against the powers of light. In *Les Rôdeurs* (1890) a young girl is asleep on a burial mound. She is the symbol of innocence and pure love. A nun watches over her. Four men reach out towards her in lust; a goat symbolizes their lechery. Two gravediggers stand to one side. Their attention is fixed on apples that suggest temptation and fall. The somber expectations as to the outcome are belied by the ivy which, as the sign of eternal life, provides the only gleam of hope. Through these symbols Toorop gives expression to his personal mythology, his fear of sin and death and his yearning for purification. He declares, in striking contrast to the rational working methods of Gauguin, Denis, Aurier, Sérusier and others, that the images are suggested by his unconscious. It is worth noting that here too the battle between good and evil, however much it is also the visualization of personal hope and fear, has a self-referential implication, in which evil stands for the art of the past and good for symbolism itself.[36]

Toorop thought that symbols could best be expressed through lines, thus in drawings. Interestingly, drawing these emblems, most of them personifications, led to a considerable degree of abstraction. Toorop often furnished the objects and figures with a décor of parallel lines which were purely decorative: stylized hair, twisting branches (as in his famous *Poster for Delftsche Slaolie*, 1894). He also used lines to depict sound or smell (for instance, the bells and the sound lines streaming from them in various drawings), and thus gave an unusual (linear) interpretation to Baudelaire's idea of the correspondences between the senses (smell, sound and form).[37] The meaning Toorop attributed to these lines is not entirely clear. As far as we can judge from correspondence and interviews (Toorop's use of language is somewhat incoherent), the lines had both a decorative and a "symbolic" function: "lines of this kind often change shape, according to whether they serve as décor or as ornamental filling, but their movement never changes, namely the lines expressing sadness, affliction, sorrow, etc. etc."[38] Toorop did not have a consistent view of the symbolic significance of lines. "The line is the expression of the idea, the color of the sensory," he said in an unpublished interview.[39] But this may be taken with a grain of salt. According to Albert Plasschaert the lines do not represent a world of ideas, but "*moods*, springing from more or less general *thoughts*, but never work from a single center, from an Idea fully controlled."[40]

The almost stereotypical use of the same visual elements all the time – branches with thorns, open graves, young girls and hollow-eyed women – has an abstracting effect. The stylization of the lines removes individual characteristics for the sake of simplification into a sign. Toorop simplifies objects and persons into ideograms that are added to the work in changing arrangements like words in a sentence that is articulated slightly differently each time it is spoken. By working in this way he certainly takes a step towards "abstraction," in the sense in which we use that term today (object-less), but with the important reservation that he retains representation.

Richard Roland Holst was another champion of Dutch symbolism. He declared his conversion to the movement in 1891-1892. One of his first works, the poster for the exhibition *Keuzetentoonstelling* (1891) is typical. It combines several traditional symbols: the rising sun, a freshly plowed field fertilized by rain and an apparently pregnant woman. These are all allusions to the burgeoning of the new art. The well-known poster for the Vincent van Gogh exhibition (1892) is similarly constructed from stereotyped symbols that repeat and reinforce each other. The sunflower, a traditional emblem of vitality, stands more particularly for Vincent and his contribution to the renewal of painting. His death is symbolized by the broken flower, the setting (or rising?) sun and the aureole. Around the turn of the century Holst changed his approach. He began to incorporate ideas developed in the society of architects and applied artists *Architectura et Amicitia*. Under the influence of theosophy, a system of geometrical symbols closely related to that of the French symbolists was propagated within this society. Holst's later work shows a clear evolution in comparison with his ideas and paintings of the eighteen-nineties. In a 1918 article about Frank Brangwyn he refers to the "geometrical mystery" as "the sole source from which rhythm can evolve." Wall paintings must "come into existence according to number and size ... before they develop their naturalness, to otherwise prove and celebrate the naturalness and divinity of number and size in more flourishing and recognizable harmonies." On the subject of a (twenty-five-year-old) woodcut by De Bazel and Lauweriks he says, "first the rhythm must be set and then the depiction of nature must develop to that rhythm."[41] That is exactly what abstract symbolism intended. In this later work Holst points to the importance of a rational approach, geometry and systematic design. To the artist the visible world is simply a sign of the "invisible Godhead."

Jan Toorop, *Les Rôdeurs*, 1890.

Antoon Derkinderen, "First Bosch Wall," 's-Hertogenbosch, 1891.

Antoon Derkinderen, "Second Bosch Wall," 's-Hertogenbosch, 1896.

Antoon Derkinderen, *The Joyous Entry of Wenceslas II and Johanna of Brabant in 's-Hertogenbosch, 1356.*
One of the panels from a design for the "First Bosch Wall," 's-Hertogenbosch, 1884.

Johan Thorn Prikker, *The Bride,* 1892-1893.

Piet Mondrian, *Passionflower*, 1908-1909.

Piet Mondrian, *Mill by Sunlight,* 1908.

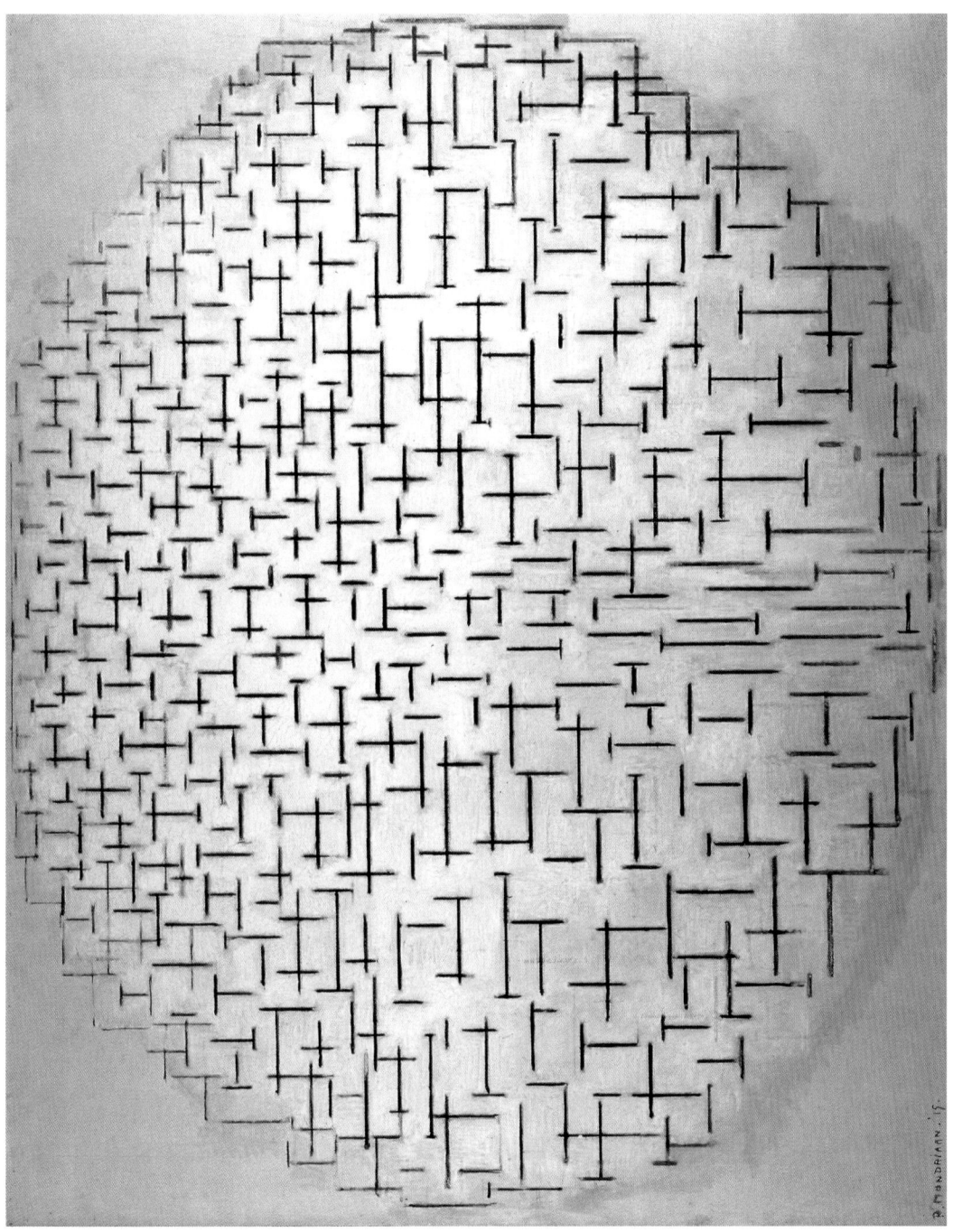

Piet Mondrian, *Composition No. 10, Pier and Ocean*, 1915.

Piet Mondrian, *Composition with Red, Yellow and Blue*, 1921.

He (the artist) follows in the footsteps of earlier artists, of whom Holst says that they "did not start from observation of nature, but built up their design from a general, abstract recognition of life." These abstract concepts "developed from geometry" and the geometry then determines "the rhythm" of the art. "The work of art with true style is inconceivable without the compelling, but at the same time concealed, power of geometry." Music is the model because silence gives it meaning and confers a "rhythmic tension." The Egyptian and Roman artists "could devote themselves entirely to high spiritual expression ... through what we could term ecstatic mathematicality."[42] But even in his later work Holst did not abandon the figurative principle. After 1900 his work was more harmonious and rational in composition, but the subjects remained clearly recognizable and were stylized into signs or stereotypes, mainly of class struggle.[43] Holst's refusal to take the last step towards abstract art is most clearly evident from an article of July 1917, in which he reacts to the abstract artists who had come together that year in *De Stijl*. Holst fiercely rejects their "aformism": "life is eliminated, the life forms lie withered and unrecognizable."[44] Ironically, Piet Mondrian and Theo van Doesburg were able to make the move to abstract art on the basis of exactly the symbolist principles that Holst had formulated so tellingly.

Antoon Derkinderen was no doubt acquainted with the work of the French symbolists, but his broad orientation also took in Desiderius Lenz, who was much concerned with the importance of fundamental forms and geometry, as well as the Pre-Raphaelites, and Morris and Crane. He referred to his first wall painting for the town hall in 's-Hertogenbosch as a "spiritualization into lines and color composition." He also deliberately worked at "flattening" the image by eliminating perspective effects, citing "the art of the catacombs." But his main concern was to breathe new life into the traditional (religious) symbols. He studied and admired Gourmont's *Le Latin mystique* (1892) and derived motifs from such studies as *Eléments d'iconographie chrétienne* by Louis Cloquet (Lille, 1890).[45] He examined medieval emblems meticulously before designing his wall paintings and stained-glass works. In all his art Derkinderen had one didactic aim: it must serve to instruct the many members of the public who came to the buildings where his wall paintings and stained-glass windows could be seen. To this end he employed traditional symbols, and he simplified his depictions into signs, in the same way that Toorop and (later) Holst did. His windows and walls are didactic texts in pictures. The individual elements must be understood as "words" in a didactic "sentence" that he put in the window or on the wall. The orthodox iconography to which Derkinderen conformed (Hammacher described his work as "liturgical") prevented him from attributing any autonomous value to the visual components. There was certainly a process of "abstraction" in Derkinderen's work, but it was aimed at the removal of any form of ornament in favor of, as Hammacher puts it, the "purely figural." This explains why (just like Holst) in 1918 he fiercely opposed "non-representational themes."

Of the four artists discussed here, Johan Thorn Prikker (1869-1932) was the least often in the spotlight. Nonetheless, his paintings and drawings from the early eighteen-nineties represent perhaps the most interesting attempt to go beyond a particular symbolist approach in the direction of abstract art. In the Netherlands the first reference to symbolism in painting was in connection with Thorn's work.[46] His letters show that for him symbolism meant emblematic symbolism. He made abundant use of such symbols and wrote about them approvingly, especially in the period (around 1892) when he was following the work of Toorop. But in the course of 1893 he came to doubt their value: "Symbolism, oh yes – a woman drawn a little differently with a flower added. But that's nonsense, it should *not* be like that. The wretched thing is that I don't know how it should be." Six months later he said flatly that all symbolism was nonsense.[47] This switch from enthusiasm to doubt and dislike was directly related to a change in his view of Toorop. Up to the beginning of 1893 he was full of admiration for him. His drawings and sketches reveal how closely he followed the admired master. But in the middle of that year he dissociated himself from him: "That is not a renaissance of the old art that has always existed," he said of Toorop, "but throwing together different bits of art that were done much better by others long before our time."[48]

Toorop's influence on Thorn is interesting because Thorn saw a way of freeing himself from symbolism (which for him was emblematic symbolism) in Toorop's characteristic, decorative lines. At the end of 1892 he gave a description of "A Love" (now lost), in which a Madonna, a shepherd and animals were to be seen. Thorn wrote that he wanted to surround these figures with repeating lines (in the style of Toorop). What did these lines represent? Thorn's ideas on this point can perhaps best be summarized by the term "mystic élan." They are lines of force that make visible a spiritual dynamic. In his later drawings Thorn put ever more emphasis on this metaphorical value (we would prefer to say "symbolic value," but Thorn did not use that term here): "From the flower come a great many very thin lines that indicate the great motion, that go through and past everything." They express "becoming aware, or rather, the conscious arising, going upwards straight through all opposition."[49] In the course of 1893 he came to distinguish between symbolic figures that he dismissed as passé nonsense and the lines that freed themselves from those figures. He now attributed a much more autonomous function to these lines. At a stroke he rejected symbolism and the work of Toorop, which he associated with it. He conveniently forgot that it had been Toorop who gave him the idea of the autonomous lines. In this phase of his development Thorn produced two superb and highly characteristic drawings, *Moine Epique* (1894) and above all *Le Forgeron* (1895). They are also characteristic in the sense that they mark the limit of where Thorn succeeded in freeing himself from "dolls." The figures dissolve into intriguing arrangements of lines that resemble the grain of a piece of burr wood, the veins of a rock formation (Thorn was actually studying these examples at the time) or the contour lines on a relief map. And just as the contour lines are the symbolic representation of a certain height, so the lines surrounding the monk and the smith stand for forces emanating from them ("it is now pure line, each line is force in itself and means something within the whole").[50]

Yet Thorn's point of departure continued to be a recognizable subject (human or thing). True, the lines free themselves from it in repeating patterns, but they can only do that to a limited extent; they can still be traced back to a face, a hand, a silhouette. Thorn did not dare let go of them. The work always had to have a recognizable form; from it "a great movement of lines" could start, "with repeating forms around the forms." The final point that Thorn reached in his development towards a kind of abstract symbolism (though he didn't call it that) was figures disappearing in a "course of lines."[51]

Geometrical symbolism did become established in the Netherlands, but this was in the circle of architects and applied artists who founded *Architectura et Amicitia* (1893-1918). From the beginning their ideas were influenced by theosophy. In 1894 two leading members, K.P.C. de Bazel and J.L.M. Lauweriks, joined the Theosophical Society (founded in 1892). In 1896 De Bazel and Lauweriks set up the Vahâna lodge, and from there they, together with Herman Walenkamp and Jan de Groot, organized the Vahâna drawing course on theosophical principles. The aesthetic of these artists was based on the essential features of what we have called abstract symbolism. There was a deeply rooted conviction that the cosmos was organized on geometrical principles. The Flemish writer August Vermeylen put it like this:

> God has become the immanent necessity, the inspiring power that destroys and creates in eternal movements, eternal growth, the greatest mystery: Life which, both in the cell as in the universe of turning worlds, is an arrangement of elements, a form of organization; and the principle of that organization, which we do not know, is the Rhythm of Life, God. We and everything else are a function of that Rhythm. It is exactly because I believe in God, in the Harmony of things, that I recognize only the inward natural law.

The lecture in which Vermeylen made these remarks was printed in its entirety by Lauweriks in *Architectura* (December 1894), the journal of *Architectura et Amicitia*. Various attempts were made from within the Vahâna lodge to define the fundamental cosmic formulas, that is to state them in geometrical figures and numbers. The best known was *Driehoeken bij het ontwerpen van ornament; voor zelfstudie en voor scholen* (Triangles for the Design of Ornaments) by Jan and Jacoba de Groot (1895). The authors offered a mathematical interpretation of the rhythm idea. Jan de Groot also wrote articles in *Architectura*, which he collected in *Beginselen bij het ontwerpen in architectuur* (Amsterdam, 1900; Principles of Architectural Design). In 1898 Lauweriks introduced the "module" as the unit of measure for the interrelationships in a design. It could be a geometrical form, or a number or a mathematical series. Lauweriks first discussed the design system of squares and circles in *Architectura* in 1899 in connection with the book *Zur Aesthetik der Beuroner Schule* by the Benedictine father Desiderius Lenz.

Starting from the proportions of the great royal chamber of the Egyptian pyramids (width: height: length = 10: 12: 20), Lauweriks says, "these three numbers, 10, 12, 20, have their basis in a figure consisting of a square with a circumscribed and an inscribed circle." According to Lauweriks, Lenz also shows that these "unshakeable" intervals recur in colors, music and basic forms.[52] Jacques van den Bosch, the director of the decorative arts studio 't Binnenhuis around 1900, defined the cosmic interrelationship as a system of number relations, forms and colors which corresponded to music. He contended that the system of squares and circles was a reflection of mathematically definable laws that applied in nature, and he explained this through series of numbers that he drew up according to the methods of occult numerology. These relations between numbers were in turn linked to the six-pointed star: Bosch argued that the triangle pointing upwards (male) represented the three primary colors red, yellow and blue, and the downward-pointing triangle (female) the secondary colors green, indigo and orange. Herman Walenkamp expounded similar ideas in a series of articles in *Architectura* in 1904-1905. He said that the essence of design lay in the relationships or proportions of the parts to the whole. Everything turned on the question of which "law governed this harmony of the parts." The simplest law was that of the square, but the Ancients had a clear understanding of the natural system of consecutive number sequence: 1 ell = 2 feet = 3 handbreadths = 4 fingerbreadths, and so on.[53] De Bazel remarked: "The structure that governs the first form expressed in proportion is thus the vehicle for the idea, and that spirit will produce the rhythm permeating the whole work in every part ruled by its structure."[54] De Bazel refers to "structure" in this context and that term is enlightening because the attitude to symbols of *Architectura et Amicitia* and especially of the French symbolist painters can be described as structural in the sense later given to the term in philosophy, namely as a pattern of relations that can be transferred from one system (that of the cosmos) to another (a painting or building). Key words such as "rhythm," "laws," and "harmony" may be read as "structure" in the sense now current. This association with the present term is all the more appropriate since, according to the artists of the turn of the century, the artistic structure was intended to allude symbolically to the original cosmic structure. It is evident that the *Architectura et Amicitia* architects / artists were seeking this fundamental view of the symbol. To cite Lauweriks one last time, he remarked in *Architectura* in 1895: "Keeping strictly to a universe-philosophy must result in an art in harmony with these laws."[55]

It was the *Architectura et Amicitia* artists who paved the way for Mondrian and the other early Dutch abstract painters. We can distinguish between the two approaches to symbolism as follows.

1 Emblematic (or figurative) symbolism:
    – The artist depicts existing objects, animals and figures in the awareness that they refer to an abstract reality beyond their concrete form. He derives his motifs from an old, established tradition.
    – The emblems have an expressive function. They are an expression of the artist's intense emotional life.
    – The line is the predominant means of expression. Subjects are greatly simplified through line stylization. This technique means that the painting comes closer to decoration. The stylized lines lead towards the abstract because they reduce the forms to ideograms applied to the canvas in a particular syntax. The similarity to hieroglyphs is mentioned here and there. In the Netherlands this line stylization has a special connotation because the line is used as a weapon against what was viewed as the decadence of impressionism. This anti-decadence aspect is typically Dutch.
    – An appeal is made to the viewer's knowledge of cultural symbols.

2 Abstract or structural symbolism:
    – Visible reality refers to an invisible reality, but this does not manifest itself in figurative emblems. Its nature is that of a cosmic interrelationship hidden below or

behind natural phenomena. The artist has to abstract from natural scenes, and break through and deform the superficial phenomena to track down the occult interrelationship. He avoids mimesis. The cosmic interrelationship is manifest in "rhythm" and "harmony," which can be reduced to mathematical formulas and geometrical models.

- The artist is an intermediary agent. His soul is an instrument made to vibrate by the cosmic rhythm. He tries to translate the cosmic structure he intuitively senses into an artistic structure using visual means. He works rationally.
- Rhythm and harmony are translated on the canvas into compositions of line and color. Line has a symbolic function, but it is composition and the division into planes above all that match the fundamental rhythm of the cosmos through their proportional relationships. Two paths to abstraction are becoming evident: color harmony and line or plane composition.
- The non-figurative harmony appeals to basic forms present in the viewer's memory as Platonic recollections.

Mondrian

Contemporary influences were certainly important in the development of Piet Mondrian (1872-1944), but they were incorporated in a personal evolution each phase of which was a slow and hard-won move towards an ever more fundamental form of expression. This development was based on a symbolist theory of art, more precisely, the transition from emblematic to structural symbolism. Mondrian's early work does not stand out. His paintings and drawings from the middle of the eighteen-nineties to 1908 are exercises in the prevailing styles of the day – the Hague School and the Amsterdam School. Mondrian was less interested in the symbolists (Richard Roland Holst, Antoon Derkinderen, Johan Thorn Prikker). It was not until 1907-1908 that he encountered the avant-garde movements that came from Paris via Jan Sluyters, Jan Toorop, Kees van Dongen and Otto van Rees. These painters had absorbed the influence of Fauvism (Sluyters / Van Dongen) and neo-impressionism (mainly Toorop). Their work was exhibited in the Netherlands and, under the influence chiefly of Sluyters and Toorop, Mondrian was tempted into painting experimental works in which he applied division-ist principles to his colors and greatly simplified the forms. These canvases were a first step towards non-figurative art. Mondrian took the next step while in Paris, which he probably visited for the first time in 1911 and where he lived from 1912 to 1914. He tried to join forces with Picasso and Braque, whom he greatly admired, but did not succeed. He began painting in the cubist manner (see for example *Woman*, 1913), and abandoned the Dutch spelling of his name, Mondriaan with two a's, in favor of the more interna-tional Mondrian when signing his canvases.[56] But apart from a favorable review of the above painting by Apollinaire, he remained unnoticed.[57] In Paris he also began writing the sketchbooks that contain the beginnings of his theory of art. During a short visit to the Netherlands in 1914, he was caught out by the German invasion of Belgium. He could not return to Paris, so he had to stay in his native country. He settled in Laren near

Amsterdam, which at that time, together with Blaricum, was the home of many artists and artists' colonies.[58] There he continued to work at simplifying his paintings, first by reducing the form to ensembles of (mostly oval-shaped) vertical and horizontal lines, while also restricting the colors to black and white (the so-called plus-minus period).[59] Later (1917) he applied areas of color that were separate from each other, a technique that he borrowed from Bart van der Leck and then further developed in order to distance himself from Van der Leck (see for example the two *Compositions with color planes*, 1917). In 1913 Mondrian painted his first entirely abstract works (*Oval composition with bright colors, Composition no. 7* and *Composition in blue, gray and pink*). But he alternated these with works with recognizable motifs (façades and trees), which he alluded to in the titles. His work may not have been entirely abstract until after the 1917 compositions with color planes. The uncertainty on this point is because, as we shall see, abstraction in Mondrian's work was a continuous process that began well before then and continued long afterward, and because to him "abstract" meant something different from what we now understand by the term.

Theosophy was a crucial factor in this development. Mondrian was interested in this movement probably from as early as 1899, and at all events from 1903. His friendship with Cornelis Spoor, who was also a believer, made him decide in 1909 to become a member of the Theosophical Society. Works such as *Passionflower* (around 1908) and *Devotion* (1908) provide clear evidence that he was deeply involved with theosophy.[60] When he went to Paris in 1911, he found accommodation in the building of the French Theosophical Society. In the winter of 1913-14, at the request of *Theosophia*, the journal of the Dutch Theosophical Society, he wrote his first major theoretical essay. *Theosophia* refused to publish the article and the text has been lost, but it is likely that drafts of it are contained in *Sketchbook II*. On his return to the Netherlands Mondrian became acquainted with Mathieu Schoenmaekers, who had gathered a small circle of artists around himself (among them the painter Bart van der Leck and the composer Jakob van Domselaer). With them Mondrian frequently discussed "positive mysticism," a curious offshoot of theosophy that Schoenmaekers had developed.[61] Mondrian's admiration for Schoenmaekers seems to have been largely based on a sense of recognizing a kindred spirit. He said later that he was in agreement with Schoenmaekers, but that he had already got his own ideas earlier from Blavatsky's secret teachings.[62] His borrowings from Schoenmaekers (for instance, the concept "neo-plasticism") indeed seem to have been mainly terminological. But Schoenmaekers' ideas must have left deeper traces than Mondrian was prepared to admit in 1917, when he dissociated himself from the mystic / philosopher. This was the case with the two opposing and absolute principles, the horizontal and the vertical line, brought together in the cross or Tao, to which, according to Schoenmaekers, the "cosmic motion" could be reduced. Another example is the color doctrine. Schoenmaekers stressed the importance of the three primary colors, to which he attributed not only directions (yellow = vertical; blue = horizontal) but also expansive and contracting properties (yellow "radiates"; blue "shrinks"). These ideas appear to be derived from the color theories of Humbert de Superville and Kandinsky,[63] and it is interesting to see that in reducing his palette to the three primary colors Mondrian took Schoenmaekers' theory into account and even mentioned him explicitly in the relevant passage on primary colors in his major text on "neo-plasticism."[64] We mention these details to emphasize that Mondrian could take and dared to take the step to abstraction because of an aesthetic based on theosophy, and that this aesthetic was in turn based on what we have called structural symbolism. What are the main elements of this aesthetic and how did they affect Mondrian's views on art and his way of painting?

Mondrian's aesthetic was at the same time an ethic. The laws he imposed on his art were also the laws that laid down how he should live. The fundamental principle of this aesthetic/ethic was the duality between spirit and matter. Mondrian continually linked this fundamental antithesis to others: man–woman, vertical–horizontal, abstract–concrete, evolution–degeneration. In his thinking matter was equated with suffering and tragedy, and the spirit with uplift and evolution. He was guided by the teachings of theosophy, according to which the cosmos develops from matter to spirit through successive levels. For Mondrian art was an important, if not the most important, means in this evolution. The foundation of art (and of human actions and the evolution of the cosmos in general) was to struggle free of matter in the direction of spirit: "If one conceives these intermediate forms as increasingly simple and pure, commencing with the physical visible forms of appearance, then one passes through a world of forms ascending from reality to abstraction. In this manner one approaches Spirit, or purity itself."[65] In this comment (from the first sketchbook) Mondrian succinctly formulated the essence of his artistic convictions and philosophy of life. It is evident from the letter he wrote to Israël Querido in 1909 that he had arrived at these beliefs early on. He writes: "Art is the path to being spiritual." It is "the upward road, away from matter."[66] As the capital letter in the above quotation indicates, "Spirit" refers not to the individual spirit, but to the world spirit. Mondrian is indebted to Hegel, whom he mentions explicitly several times.[67] When Mondrian talks about the "expression of the Spirit,"[68] he does not mean his own spirit, but the world spirit as far as it can be deduced from the matter surrounding us. Every form of expression (in the sense of expressing personal drives) is alien to this.

Mondrian saw and described the matter–spirit duality in terms of surface–depth, outward–inward: "By turning from the surface one comes closer to the inner laws of matter, which are also the laws of the Spirit."[69] The famous "beelding" is the making evident, that is making visible through concrete means, of universal and fundamental principles underlying the interrelationship of the cosmos. To this end the artist must penetrate deep below the surface of things, revealing the laws underneath and transforming them into a plastic-artistic equivalent. This equivalent should be as far removed as possible from the superficial-natural appearance of things; this is why Mondrian opts for such non-natural elements as the straight (horizontal and vertical) line and the three primary colors. In fact these "abstract" (in the sense of wresting themselves free from natural phenomena) colors and lines cannot be a perfect representation of the pure spirit. It would be paradoxical to represent it by material means. The primary colors are no more than "symbols" of the spiritual light and thus in essence an intermediate step on the road leading away from nature towards pure spirit.

In nature the spiritual principles are "veiled." Mondrian uses this word often: "These laws were veiled by the surfaces of objects. Now they emerge in all their purity."[70] In nature the universal "is expressed only hidden or veiled in natural color and form."[71] The aim of "beelding" is to unveil the universal-divine, the true reality. Artist and viewer come into contact with true reality only when "the content and appearance of things are unveiled."[72] Here Mondrian is almost certainly alluding to *Isis Unveiled* by Helena Blavatsky, the work from which he specifically said he had drawn his own philosophy of life.[73]

Mondrian's vision of the cosmos is dualistic. He regards the antithesis between matter and spirit as the tragic division of an original unity: "The state of being positive or negative is the cause of the rupture of unity, cause of all unhappiness. The *oneness* of positive and negative is happiness."[74] Under the influence of Mondrian, Theo van Doesburg put forward similar views: "The conflict that is rooted in the structure of life is a conflict between two polar forces. We may call them nature and spirit, or the female and male principle, negative and positive, static and dynamic, horizontal and vertical – these are the *unchanging elements* on which the contradiction of our life rests and which are made manifest in *changeability*. Ending this conflict, neutralizing these extremes, eliminating this polarity is the essence of life and the elementary subject of art."[75] Jaffé takes the view that Mondrian and other members of *De Stijl* resolved the polarity in a dialectical process: "the balance is dialectical."[76] But this term seems less applicable to Mondrian, because dialectic suggests a continuing process in time, whereby thesis and antithesis merge in syntheses that in turn form new theses and antitheses. Mondrian, however, seeks the stable equilibrium between both principles. With him the universal is at rest. Neo-plasticism is concerned with the "manifestation of the unchanging," the "depiction of pure balance."[77] The metaphors Mondrian uses ("equilibrium" and "balance") are not without significance. They evoke the image of the scales (balance) that come to rest when an equal weight is placed on each side. This "equi-librium" brings about the healing of the antagonisms raging in nature. For his part, Theo van Doesburg strives to express "polarity," an image suggesting tension and energy through the reference to opposite electrical poles. So the harmony that both men say they are aiming for is different in each case.

In point of fact Mondrian and Van Doesburg's concept of harmony differs in turn from that of the symbolists insofar as it is dualistic and antagonistic. When Baudelaire, Gauguin and Mallarmé speak of harmony, they have in mind a pleasing harmony of notes or chords, or a special moment at which all sensory experiences begin to correspond with each other through synesthesia to form a delicate moment of "harmony." Mondrian and Van Doesburg think of harmony as a balance between two opposed principles. Their harmony is not necessarily pleasing or symmetrical: "I believe that *balanced relations can exist* with dissonants, don't you?" (letter to Van Doesburg, 1920).[78] Their concept of harmony brings to mind that of Kandinsky ("Gegensätze und Widersprüche – das ist unsere Harmonie") and could have been borrowed from him. Kandinsky specifies that "present-day" harmony is concerned "zu spalten, in Widersprüche zu tauchen."[79] In this way he gives a modern, not to say modernistic, twist to the romantic/symbolist concept of harmony which, differently interpreted, can also be found in Mondrian and Van Doesburg. This asymmetrical twist to the harmony concept explains why in the course of 1917 Mondrian suddenly dropped the centripetal style, often governed by ovals, in favor of eccentrically arranged, colored blocks, and why a few years later, in 1920, he broke with centripetal compositions and opted for asymmetric, "peripheral" paintings in which he often left the center strikingly open. Mondrian wanted to avoid "balance" being associated with symmetry or centering.

Differences as to the nature of the cosmic harmony were at the heart of the conflict and the eventual break between Mondrian and Van Doesburg. From the start Mondrian had no doubt that time and change meant suffering. He noted in his sketchbook: "The positive and negative states of being bring about *action*. They cause the loss of balance and of happiness. They cause the eternal revolutions – the *changes that follow one upon the other*. They explain why happiness cannot be achieved in time."[80] Mondrian believed that harmony was timeless and static and that only contemplation of static figures could lead to higher consciousness.[81] Ultimately his conflict with Van Doesburg was a conflict between space and time. At the beginning of the nineteen-twenties Van Doesburg became increasingly persuaded that reality was movement, dynamics. Mondrian resisted this view: "I am not at all in favor of this *position in time* …, because the new concept eliminates time"; "I want to abolish time, especially in the contemplation of architecture" (letter to Van Doesburg, May 1922).[82] In 1922-1923 this difference of view led to a breach. Van Doesburg went his own way and introduced the diagonal line intended to express tension and dynamics; Mondrian persisted with the static balance of horizontal and vertical lines.

The link between Mondrian's theosophical beliefs and his work is direct and complete, but in our view its nature is not such as is usually attributed to it. Much of the literature points out the symbols that Mondrian borrowed from theosophy (and Christianity). These are emblematic symbols seen in particular in the paintings from his figurative period (up to 1914). Attention has rightly been drawn to the metaphorical meaning (female, passive, material) of the horizontal lines in the many landscapes and seascapes and to the opposing meaning (male, active, spiritual) of the trees, windmills and towers. The windmills especially have attracted attention because in several paintings the vertical and horizontal lines join to form a cross. To our knowledge, Mondrian painted and drew twenty-two mills between 1904 and 1907.[83] With two exceptions, the sails always stand in the position of a cross (+). The suggestion of a cross is strengthened because Mondrian always shows the mills from the back, so that the sail pointing downwards is out of sight and the sails, together with the silhouette of the tower, form less a + than a cross. Mondrian thus used every opportunity to underline the Christian symbolic meaning of the mill. But in 1907 he abruptly stopped doing this. With all the mills he painted and drew between 1907 and 1917,[84] he avoided associations with a cross. He did this in the same systematic way in which he had earlier created this association. He now positioned the sails in an X, and depicted them from the front, so that all four could be seen, or from a sharp angle so that the sails were foreshortened, and in one case almost reduced to a nearly vertical line. Finally, in ten cases he cut them off at the top, so that the upper sails disappeared from view. This marked change in the manner of depiction appears to have been prompted by Mondrian's decision (at some point in 1907) to avoid Christian symbolism in future. The reasons for this may have lain in his growing interest in theosophy, which coincided with his alienation from and break with Calvinism, but perhaps above all in his decision to avoid too obvious symbolism henceforth (we discuss his remarks on this point below).

The symbolic significance (in the theosophical sense) of the flowers in works such as *Devotion* (1908), *Passionflower* (c. 1908) and *Dying Chrysanthemum* (1908) has been pointed out,[85] as has the symbolic meaning of the color red, which according to Mondrian alludes to matter and nature,[86] although this reading is hard to reconcile with the opposite meaning of "spiritualization" that Mondrian attributes to red elsewhere (in his letter to Querido of 1909 about the red in *Devotion*, 1908). Attention has been drawn to the triangles and hexagons in the *Evolution* triptych (1911). These are all true, unambiguous indications as to the ideas that Mondrian was incorporating into his neo-plastic aesthetic at this time.

But in retrospect Mondrian was unhappy about what he regarded as the too obvious symbolism. When the speakers in the "Trialogue" pause by a windmill, Z. (Mondrian's alter ego) says that what appealed to him about windmills was "the cross formed by the sails." With hindsight he no longer finds this form attractive, he says. Moreover, the upright cross is too easily associated with "a particular, more *literary* idea."[87] Elsewhere he says of the cross that such a traditional "symbol" is at once too limited and too perfect.[88] He is against the use of such symbols because they are emblematic, and as such too closely associated with coded meanings, with an iconography. Something else is evident from these passages directed against symbols and symbolism. Mondrian opposes the symbolist movement because he identifies it with the group around Holst and Thorn Prikker, who were by now referred to as "symbolists." We know that Mondrian preferred to have little to do with them. Thus what he was opposed to was symbolism in the narrow, emblematic sense in which it manifested itself in the Netherlands.

If we look, however, at the artists of the Vahâna lodge, with whom Mondrian had an affinity, and at the French symbolists, we see artists who were able to move on to abstract art because they were pursuing a symbolic representation of reality in the way theosophy had taught them to understand it. Mondrian's writings and work correspond remarkably closely to this form of symbolism, which we have called "abstract" or "structural." Seen in this light, it is also understandable that Mondrian placed great emphasis on the composition and on the relationship of line and color. He wanted them to reveal the interrelationship of the cosmos. "Through exact depiction of the cosmic relationship it directly expresses the universal."[89] The strongly structuralist (before the term existed) nature of Mondrian's view of symbolism is also apparent from such statements as: "We can now define the emphasis of the art of painting as *the most consistent expression of pure relationships*."[90] His neo-plasticism was intended to depict a deeper reality in a symbolic way, as is shown by such terms as "mirroring:" "We must see *abstractly* and above all *universally. Then we shall see the natural as pure relationship*. Then the outward will be for us what it is indeed: *a mirroring of the truth*."[91]

At the beginning of the "Trialogue" the speakers stop and look at the starry sky. The stars offer the best image, says Z., of neo-plasticism as "relationship expression." The relationships "pronounce themselves" in the starry sky and provide an image (a symbol) of world harmony, without being a representation of it.[92] Mondrian's great affinity to Mallarmé is nowhere more clearly evident than here. In his *Un coup de dés* Mallarmé evokes a similar constellation with the same intention: to create in words an autonomous model that summons up the ordering of the world. Mondrian does in art what Mallarmé had done thirty years earlier in poetry.[93]

6

The dawn of mass education

Teachers

The avant-garde among the students training to become teachers in 1900 were inspired by social ideals and so felt hampered by norms of middle-class respectability. They wanted to let people know this, all the more so because under the regime of the teachers college they were made thoroughly aware of the bounds of obedience. The slouch hat, the soft collar and the elegant, loosely knotted black tie formed the visible signs of their break with a "life of routine." They let their hair grow, and wore a velvet collar and cuffs on a no longer impeccable ready-made jacket. The girls showed a preference for square-necked dresses in velvet fabric.[1]

This desire for simplicity and beauty was coupled with a puritanical opposition to social abuses. In 1906 a number of students at the State Teachers College in Haarlem, among them Wim Banning, the later sociologist and social democrat, founded a teetotal organization, the *Kwekelingen Geheelonthouders Bond*, with the aim of combating drunkenness among the workers. "We are giving something, something of the best in us, to others," wrote one of them in the first manifesto. "We want to raise a smile about many sad things, we want to make zest for living and energy rise up in poor, misguided folk. We have heard the call of the suffering people; united we advance, confident of bringing support and blessing."[2]

Two social trends came together in this youthful idealism: the higher status of the teaching profession and the phenomenon of the autonomous youth movement. The first was the result of the expansion of education and of the need to achieve statutory standards of professionalism in new and better training courses. The number of students rose and so did the number of courses for teachers. At the new teachers colleges the students could satisfy their thirst for knowledge and develop their abilities. For many it was the first chance to receive higher education. The other trend, the free youth movement, arose from commitment which "stemming from dissatisfaction with social conditions and the power structure, ultimately implied a desire for a new man and a new community." These young people elected to have an organization of their own without adult leaders.[3] They wanted to be different from the older generation and in 1900 they were inspired by the spirit of the age with its emphasis on sensory consciousness.

The student teachers lived under the fairly authoritarian regime and the paternalism of the principal. They were often accommodated in lodgings from a young age, so that they outgrew their family background both in knowledge and socially. This isolation

Meeting of the Dutch Teachers Association, Rotterdam, 1912.

brought them together and provided fertile ground for a "Bunderlebnis," a sense of a bond between youthful companions. In 1897 the first issue of a journal that reflected the growing self-awareness of young student teachers was published in Haarlem. The initiative for it came from Theo Thijssen, later a well-known teacher and social democrat. Many pages pointed out the edifying nature of the teaching profession, so that students could feel called on to perform a mission in society. There was also a great deal of interest in pedagogical issues, for the same spirit that had led to the rise of the youth movement caused more attention to be paid to education, and to the theoretical basis of their future profession.

Around the turn of the century teachers colleges were an important factor in the professionalization of education. This was brought about by the liberals' School Act of 1878. To raise standards, six state teachers colleges were founded by central government. In 1884 there were 4,108 students, and six years later 5,293. Town councils also took action: in 1876 the first municipal teachers college was founded in Amsterdam. There were also Protestant and Catholic teachers colleges. There had been a Protestant normal school, Klokkenberg, in Nijmegen since 1846. It was based on German and French models and was imbued with the pietism of the Protestant Réveil. Four Protestant teachers colleges were added to this one up to 1900; by 1914 there were seventeen.[4] In the Catholic sector the liberals' School Act, which had been fiercely resisted for political reasons, actually had the effect of improving the quality of Catholic education. Many Catholic schools were run by nuns. During the parliamentary debate on the Act in 1878, some convents organized a "prayer tornado" in protest. But to no avail. The Act made necessary exactly what the praying nuns wanted to avoid: more individual study. Instead of halting the activities of the nuns, the Act encouraged them to study. Otherwise they would have gone on regarding their spirit of sacrifice and devotion to their task as compensating for their limited knowledge.[5]

In 1850 on average an elementary school had 1.7 qualified teachers, but by 1900 this figure had risen to 4.5.[6] The higher status of the teacher and the regularization of training courses made the profession attractive to those seeking to climb the social ladder. A study of six grades at the teachers college in Haarlem between 1899 and 1912 showed that a quarter of the students were from teaching families and that the rest came from the class of small businessmen or small farmers.[7] The rise in the percentage of women teachers was spectacular, climbing after 1850 from 10 to 33. In denominational schools this increase was considerably larger, but in the course of this period this difference was reduced.[8] After 1860 municipal and private institutes for the training of girls were established. This expansion resulted in the founding of the first state teachers college for women at Apeldoorn in 1894. Research has shown that around the turn of the century the social background of these women teachers was still higher on average than that of their male colleagues, but two decades later these differences had vanished. It was no longer mainly the daughters of clergymen and physicians who became teachers, but now the daughters of teachers, farmers and storekeepers too.[9]

Compulsory education

The act making education compulsory came into effect on January 1, 1901, the first day of the new century. It was a landmark in a hundred years of education policy aimed at ensuring that Dutch children systematically attended schools of a reasonable standard. Henceforth school was compulsory for children aged between six and twelve. By the time the act was brought in, the fight against illiteracy had in fact been more or less won. Around 1900 the rate of illiteracy in the Netherlands had fallen to below ten percent. Incidentally, this drop was also apparent in neighboring countries. The Netherlands belonged in the same group as Scandinavia, Prussia and Scotland, countries where illiteracy had declined from under thirty percent to under ten percent in the course of the nineteenth century. In England and France the starting percentage was over thirty, while in Italy, Spain and Austria-Hungary the rate was still higher than this in 1900.[10]

The introduction of compulsory education did indeed lead to higher attendance at elementary school. This applied particularly to older children (aged between nine and twelve). The increase in their rate of participation was 5 percent; the increase for all pupils was 1.4 in 1902 and nearly 2 in 1905. The legislation had a greater effect on girls' participation than on boys'. As a result, there was even a shortage of places at some schools. In general one has to conclude that the introduction of compulsory education was above all the final stage of a long-term increase in the number of pupils. So here too the immediate effect of the act was limited.[11]

The elementary school had been the principal institution for passing on and spread-

Amsterdam schoolchildren in the Veluwe region on a school trip, 1912.

ing literacy and a national culture since as early as 1800. Compulsory education and the higher status of the teacher ensured that around 1900 teaching emerged as a profession in which most of the members no longer had to combine their work with other functions, for example in the church. Teachers were inspired by free ideals of communicating knowledge and educating. They could even take their idealism beyond the limits of their now clearly defined profession. As described in chapter 1, the growth of interest in nature around the turn of the century was promoted by two Amsterdam teachers, Eli Heimans and Jac. P. Thijsse. Heimans taught at a school for the poor in the city center and used the Sarphati Park for his first field trips with pupils; this was also where he first worked on the descriptions of flora and fauna published in *De levende natuur* (Living Nature), the journal he and Thijsse founded.

Teachers were responsible for maintaining the standard of penmanship and instilling the "received pronunciation" of Dutch. Wim Banning was born in a village in Friesland and recalled how he had to unlearn his dialect and expand his vocabulary at the Haarlem teachers college to correct what was seen as a disadvantage in relation to other students.[12] It was teachers who wrote accounts of national history through books about heroes and heroic deeds during the Dutch Revolt or, as it was then portrayed, the Eighty Years War.[13] In these accounts of the rise of the Dutch state there is an echo of the remarkable role played by teachers in nationalist movements elsewhere in Europe as transmitters of and activists in a national culture.[14]

combining the first and second grades of the Secondary School for Girls with the same grades of the new six-year HBS for girls. The name "girls lyceum" had not yet been invented.

The new secondary school resulted from the arguments of modern pedagogy, but the idea had a long history. At the beginning of the nineteenth century, in 1809, a state commission had drawn up the blueprint for a combined classical and modern course, but it was not implemented. At the end of the century, in 1898, the pedagogue Johannes Hermanus Gunning, then principal of the gymnasium in Zwolle, took up the cause in an article in the journal *De Gids* in which he called for more general education in secondary schools. Pupils should not have to choose at the age of twelve between gymnasium or HBS, between classics or science. Gunning took his arguments from psychology. He identified three benchmarks in the development of the human individual, of which the second, puberty, had to be seen as a crisis. The "scandalous denial" of this by legislators and teachers caused "untold harm." He advocated a longer phase of general education: three years, at the end of which secondary school could be completed at the HBS or at the gymnasium.[31] In the new lyceum it became two years.

In the same year in which Gunning published his article, the teacher and banker Dirk Bos, later a member of Parliament for the *Vrijzinnig-Democratische Bond* (Liberal Democratic League), drew up the outline of a new school system. He was also in favor of general education in the period between elementary school and HBS or gymnasium. It might take the form of a single preparatory year or three years of "general development education."[32] In 1906 an experiment was carried out. Under the auspices of the *Haagsche Schoolvereniging*, which managed an elementary school, a secondary school was set up to enable pupils to receive general education for a few years. Rommert Casimir became its principal.

Politically speaking, these pioneers in The Hague had the times on their side. By 1900 a general need was felt for comprehensive regulations to govern secondary education, which was divided between so many institutions and curricula. In 1903 Minister for Home Affairs Abraham Kuyper, appointed a state commission to make recommendations for a new system. It quickly became known as the "mergers commission" because it sought to achieve useful combinations, for example between the general first and second grades of HBS and gymnasium. The name "lyceum" was devised within its ranks. It was an instant coinage that provided a name for the experiment in The Hague. The final results of the commission's work took rather longer.

From the experiment in The Hague came the Netherlands Lyceum, intended to be a test school for the whole country. Those behind this initiative were a mixture of right-minded citizens and pedagogues: Casimir and Gunning were joined by the progressive schoolmaster Jan Ligthart, and by leading liberal politicians such as Dirk Bos, and by the Nobel Prize winner H.A. Lorentz. The school opened in September 1909 with 51 pupils and two lower grades. There was a lengthy discussion over whether in this construction the HBS should be as long (six years) as the gymnasium. But in the end the HBS was kept at five years on the grounds (put forward by Lorentz and Bos) that the Technical College in Delft and industry preferred to have young engineers and thus a shorter secondary school.[33] The Hague model was followed at the Amsterdam Lyceum, which was founded

The class of 1913 at the Netherlands Lyceum.

in 1917. The first principal was Christiaan Gunning, the son of the pedagogue Gunning. The Amsterdam Lyceum opted for a six-year HBS.

Johannes Hermanus Gunning was also in favor of introducing handwork into the curriculum of the lyceum. He had two arguments. The first was the value of maintaining a certain level of craft skills in a time of growing mechanization. The second was that class conflict, which he saw as the real danger to democracy, was based on a false distinction between manual workers and intellectuals. Making handwork a school subject would stop people looking down on it. Another new feature was the school council at both lyceums. According to Gunning, this form of "self-regulation" would help to give the pupils a sense of responsibility and build character, while also promoting discipline and self-control.[34]

The experiment caught on. In the commuter localities Baarn and Bloemendaal lyceums were set up on non-denominational principles by private initiatives. In towns like Enschede and Zaandam the municipal council took the lead. For secondary education on Protestant or Catholic principles, which was just beginning to expand in the years before and after World War I, this type of school turned out to be an obvious choice. The first Catholic lyceum (for girls) was founded in The Hague in 1915, and the first Protestant lyceum in Haarlem in 1918. In the education of girls the new type of school was a model in another way, not because of the contribution of general education but because of the sequel at a gymnasium or HBS. The first experiment was the combination of the existing Secondary School for Girls in The Hague with a new HBS in two joint lower grades in 1905. Following the general development provided by the Secondary School for Girls, an opportunity was created for girls to pursue the intellectual or scientific education offered by the HBS.[35]

Around 1870 girls had begun to gain access to secondary education. This took place in two ways: the founding of separate schools for girls, or the admission of girls to schools that had previously been solely for boys. The first strategy was exemplified by the foundation in Haarlem in 1867 of a school that was intended only for girls and so was named the Secondary School for Girls. The emphasis was on general education. The teaching content, including the natural sciences, was to be dealt with in less depth than at the HBS, because the "practical intelligence" attributed to women was to be taken into account, together with the likelihood of female work associates. The example set by Haarlem was followed in 1872 in Amsterdam and Rotterdam – in the former after prolonged debate, in the latter after near unanimous agreement in the city council.

The second strategy consisted of gaining access to existing schools reserved for boys. The gate to the gymnasium had never formally been closed, but that to the HBS was in practice. In the 1870-1871 school year Aletta Jacobs, later to become the first woman graduate, took some lessons at the state HBS in Sappermeer in the province of Groningen, which offered a three-year course. She was preparing for the admission examination for university. The first woman to be officially allowed into the HBS in the following school year, 1871-1872, was her sister Frederika. Her father, the physician A. Jacobs, had sought the help of the minister for home affairs to make this possible. Until 1907 the parents of girls who wanted to go to the HBS had to ask the minister for permission. It was only after this rule was dropped that the number of girl pupils rose into the hundreds.[36]

The Secondary School for Girls was a subject of discussion at the *National Exhibition of Women's Work* held in 1898. The lack of a recognized school-leaving examination conferring the same rights as that of the HBS was particularly criticized. A solution was sought in a higher form of secondary education, whose curriculum would still be suited to what were then seen as specifically female characteristics. The result was the HBS for girls. The example of The Hague was followed in Rotterdam and Groningen. After World War I these initiatives evolved into the girls lyceum. This type of school was also adopted in Catholic circles, but for a different reason. There was opposition on more or less religious grounds to co-education, with girls and boys in the same class. The first Catholic HBS for girls was founded in Amsterdam in 1914; it later became the "Fons Vitae" girls lyceum. The more direct route to a Catholic girls lyceum was taken in The Hague in 1915.[37]

The Hogere Burger School (HBS)

The HBS was the successful product of an earlier modernization of secondary education in the eighteen-sixties. At that time the minister for home affairs, Thorbecke, said, "We are going to do the country a great and permanent service. We are going to create forces and organizations that will increase the intellectual and the practical productive capability of the core of the people."[38] He had opted to reserve the existing Latin School in future for the traditional "educated class" and to use the modern burgher school for the merchants and manufacturers, who were after all to be the bringers of a new industrial era. In the same Act the state was offered the possibility of itself founding and running such modern institutions.

There were two variants of the HBS: a three-year or a five-year course. The first five-year state HBS opened in Groningen in September 1864. The second followed in October in Roermond. The first three-year HBS was founded in Gouda. This type was established in smaller provincial towns as a state HBS. Ten years after the passing of the Act there were forty-eight HBS institutions, seventeen of which were managed by the state. In the years after 1900 the figure grew to 167.

The Protestant and Catholic churches thought the founding of a state HBS brought closer the threat of modern education with a liberal bias. The school was identified with the rise of the natural sciences and of Darwin's theory of evolution. It was not until around 1900 that this distrust of the HBS diminished, and that Protestants and Catholics began to establish such schools of their own. The new type of school attracted talented teachers, thanks in part to the first generation of school inspectors, who had a decisive influence on how the law was applied. In 1867 eighty-eight of the teaching staff at twenty of these schools had a doctorate. One of them was the chemist Jakob Maarten van Bemmelen. He had begun as a teacher at a technical school before moving to the HBS and subsequently becoming principal of the HBS in Arnhem and then in Groningen. In 1874, after teaching for sixteen years, he became professor of inorganic chemistry at Leiden. In Groningen he had taught the later Nobel Prize winner Heike Kamerlingh Onnes, and in Arnhem Hendrik Antoon Lorentz, another Nobel Prize winner; in Leiden he discovered the talent of the physicist Hendrik Willem Bakhuis Roozeboom. Lorentz remembered how his teacher Van Bemmelen had made him run round a concert hall at different speeds while holding a wind gauge tied to a piece of wood. Then he had to define in mathematical terms the relation between the readings on the gauge and the running speed.[39] The laboratories in the new type of school were equal in quality, relatively speaking, to those at the universities.[40]

Classic versus modern

The success of the modern HBS was bound to have consequences for the traditional institution, the old Latin School. It was run by municipal authorities and gave access to Dutch universities because there the language of instruction was Latin, but in the course of the nineteenth century its standards and importance had declined. Since 1853, when there was no longer a generally accepted leaving examination or specialist inspectors, the school had been "brought to the edge of the abyss." There were institutions where one could be sure of obtaining a diploma by paying a thousand guilders for a last year at school. "No gymnasium gave more beautiful certificates, nowhere else was the successful pupil honored with finer epithets."[41]

The Latin School came under the law governing higher and pre-university education. When in 1876 it became necessary to reform the universities, the traditional institution of classic education was also modernized. The Latin School was abolished and replaced by the gymnasium. This too offered pre-university education, but now had its own school-leaving examination and inspectors. Science had a special place in its program: in the fifth and sixth year a division was introduced between preparation for a university course in theology, literature or law (the alpha stream) and that for a course in medicine or mathematics and physics (the beta stream). The 1876 Act also brought about a change in the development of this traditional type of school. The package of new requirements proved too much for the smaller Latin Schools, and they had to close their doors. This marked the end of institutions where in extreme cases a single teacher might face a single pupil in some years. The Act laid down that only municipalities with over 20,000 inhabitants were obliged to found and maintain a municipal gymnasium. Though the number of schools consequently declined, the number of pupils rose sharply after 1876.[42]

The modernization of the Latin School but above all the founding of the HBS and the expansion of vocational education were in line with European developments. In the decades between 1860 and 1920 new types of school came into being all over Western Europe, and they were soon competing with the traditional institutions. The old distinction between elementary and secondary education gave way to that between classical and modern. It was true that, because of their orientation towards trade and industry, the new schools had less prestige, but they attracted the largest number of pupils, especially from the commercial and industrial middle class. After comparing the secondary school system in the Netherlands with those in the three great states of Europe, France, Prussia and England, the historian Kees Mandemakers reached the conclusion that the development of new school types had taken a somewhat different form in the Netherlands: a systematic expansion and improvement of more practically oriented education.

Another comparison led him to the conclusion that there were two systems in the Netherlands. In the north a type of education had evolved which was based on a middle-class tradition with a utilitarian slant and which attached less value to the classic curriculum. In the southern provinces of North Brabant and Limburg a different pattern was evident, one showing some resemblance to French education. There, under the influence of a dominant Catholic Church, a parallel system had been created of preparatory seminaries (including several old Latin Schools run by priests), boarding schools with modern and classical streams and colleges under episcopal authority (Limburg) or the Jesuit Order. It was notable that boarding schools flourished in the south, whereas elsewhere they were gradually disappearing because of the spread of HBS education and improved transport by tram and train. To the extent that more practical education was given in the commercial departments of these institutions, it was primarily concerned with modern languages and mental arithmetic. Apart from at the renowned boarding school at Rolduc in Limburg, no great attention was paid to the new natural sciences, which in fact were initially treated with suspicion in church circles.[43]

Recruitment: social factors

On a skilled worker's wage, families could not afford the annual tuition fees at the state HBS. To lower this barrier, in the eighteen-eighties in some towns places were reserved for

Priests and pupils at Rolduc boarding school.

gifted children whose parents or guardians could not meet the costs of tuition and course materials. In The Hague, for example, from 1883 two places were reserved at the five-year HBS and four at the three-year school. In Amsterdam the number was five per HBS; for the trade school and the gymnasium there were three. The first step in the democratization of secondary education was taken in 1892, when gifted children were exempted from paying for tuition and course materials. In 1916 the proportional tuition levy was introduced; it was proportional to the income of the parents. The effect was to make free admission of pupils a right rather than a favor. The Netherlands differed from its European neighbors as regards these measures: steps were taken earlier than in France or England, but they were more limited in scope by the standards of the later democratization in those countries. The Dutch system of the proportional tuition levy was and has remained unique of its kind.[44]

Did secondary education in the Netherlands become more accessible in the last quarter of the nineteenth century? The answer is not clear-cut. For the "humble citizens" the opportunities for individual mobility doubled between 1880 and 1920. This was chiefly due to a decrease in the size of families, because the number of those in employment also grew. Within the group of the self-employed, it was mainly children whose fathers were in industry and trade who were relatively disadvantaged up to 1920. But because of the expansion of the secondary school system, the chances of getting an education eventually increased for children in these categories too. The children of teachers and of the "not self-employed," the wage earners at all levels of society, were particularly mobile. It is also noticeable that among the "educated class" the rise in the number of children in high school was less than the average increase. This indicates that this group was no longer able to supply enough pupils to keep up with the pace of expansion in secondary education. This did not apply to the gymnasium. A child from the "educated class" actually had a greater chance of going to the gymnasium in 1920 than it had in 1880, for, although there had been a relative decline in the number of pupils, it was the "educated class" who kept this type of school going, even more so in 1920 than in 1880.[45]

A European comparison of the social background of pupils leads to the conclusion that in general the situation in the Netherlands corresponded closely to that in Prussia. One difference of some significance was the greater proportion of pupils from university-educated families in the Netherlands – in particular the children of lawyers and high-ranking civil servants – as against a higher percentage in Prussia of pupils from an industrial background. There were proportionally more pupils from the trade and services sector in the Netherlands, and so the total number of pupils from "industry and services" was about the same in both countries. In the case of France the most striking feature was the relatively low percentage of high school graduates who came from university-educated families. The explanation for this must be sought in the type of clergy: the celibate priests of the Catholic Church had no children, unlike Calvinist ministers in the Netherlands and Lutheran pastors in Prussia. Another difference was the relative importance of agriculture. In France the "propriétaires" and "cultivateurs/agriculteurs" produced more than a quarter of the graduates from the "lycées" and "collèges."[46]

All the statistics make it clear that around the turn of the century secondary education had reached an unprecedented level, quantitatively and qualitatively. This expansion was promoted by the government and can be seen against the background of the modernization of Dutch industry at this time. Initially it was central government that took the lead, by making free places available and lowering tuition fees. In addition, entrance examinations were declared unnecessary. Around 1920 the Netherlands was ahead of the rest of Europe in the rate of participation in education and the results of school-leaving exams. It lost this lead later as the result of cutbacks during the Depression.

A study of the success rate at Dutch high schools also produced favorable results. Over the fifty years from 1875 to 1926 the pass rates of examinations at the HBS remained fairly stable: between eighty-five and ninety-one percent of the pupils passed. Similar stability was evident in the pass rates at the gymnasia: between eighty-six and ninety-three percent. After 1900 Dutch pass rates actually exceeded those in France and Germany. In 1910 the Netherlands had more high school graduates proportionally than Germany or France, fifty percent more in 1920.[47]

Sport and gymnastics

In his great narrative poem *Mei* (May) – a standard work in Dutch literature – Herman Gorter has the protagonist awake at a moment when she can see two young gods approaching over the sea. He uses a comparison from the new sport of cycling to describe their movement.

The circles turn and the white path
Slips away: their eyes on each other's wheel,
They pedal grimly, in their souls
Envy and hate, one is ahead,
The other catches up and passes
In blind despair. The last surge to the line
Unleashes shouts and cheers.[48]

Herman Gorter was a passionately keen sportsman. He enjoyed cricket and tennis and was an enthusiastic footballer. He played cricket on a field behind the Rijksmuseum in Amsterdam with the artist Richard Roland Holst, and soccer at the Haarlem Football Club ground on the outskirts of that city. If there was an important match coming up, Gorter had to steady his nerves with Hoffmann's drops or valerian. He hoped to increase his stamina through exercise and to keep up his resistance to disease. Moreover, ambitious as he was, through sport he could obtain the acclaim that he had not yet secured for his poetry.[49]

The club that would soon be known as the Haarlem Football Club was founded in 1879; it was the first for footballers who wanted to play according to clearly defined rules and standards of conduct. The members were high school pupils and students. Their leader was Willem Johan Herman Mulier, who called himself "Pim" and liked to pronounce his surname as "Mool-yea" as a reminder of his French ancestry. "Strenuous game of soccer in Haarlem on Sunday," reported the writer Frederik van Eeden, then a medical student, in his diary on November 20, 1894. Sometimes young fellows such as Van Eeden, Gorter and Roland Holst lay on the pitch "with other men in the new movement, leaders in fields other than football and cricket, discussing literature and sociology." Looking back, Pim Mulier placed his sporting initiatives in the context of a larger movement of economic and cultural progress in the Netherlands. "Between 1880 and 1890 our country underwent a true revolution. We woke up, became more up to date."[50]

The fact that he wrote the words "up to date" in English was not coincidental. Sport in the form in which it was introduced to the Netherlands toward the end of the nineteenth century was British in origin. The clubs in the new field of leisure activities tended to have an English word or a classical hero in their name, so their origins, British and scholastic, were perpetuated. Such names reflected the popularity of sport among high school pupils, students and graduates from middle-class backgrounds. The pioneers were sufficiently literate to be able to record their initiatives in commemorative volumes. But the sport described and pictured in them is only the tip of the iceberg at the turn of the century. Beneath it lies an undocumented and often narrowly local range of sports and physical exercise. In streets and neighborhoods, remembered one president of the Haarlem Club, the classical scholar and principal of the municipal gymnasium, Cornelis Spoelder,

where the boys from the area, who knew nothing about sport as yet, the sons of tradesmen, shopkeepers, even the odd tramp in clogs, came to play their old-fashioned games after school, on free afternoons, on summer evenings before bedtime.

Skating race at Joure (Friesland), 1914.

Their jargon was pure Haarlem dialect, their language more colorful, their vocabulary richer than that of the well brought-up lads; without doubt they had more of the stamp of the real Haarlem kid.[51]

Around 1900 in the Netherlands as elsewhere sport had come to mean a regulated game with a particular code of behavior ("sportsmanship") as its ideal. Other forms of organized physical exercise were known before. Harness racing was one of the three great national diversions in the provinces of Holland and Friesland. This also applied to skating: the art of skating was practiced mainly for speed in Friesland and for its beauty in Holland. Ice games were "a general feature of Dutch society; even our art and our literature are rich in ice pieces."[52]

By the nineteenth century sailing, the third great diversion, was organized in sailing and rowing clubs, the regulated form of the age-old yacht racing and rowing matches. There were also gondola parties, sometimes graced by water illuminations. Among ball games, *kaatsen*, a type of handball, *kolfspel* and pall-mall were popular. At the end of the century the alleys where they were played were still visible, for example the Maliebaan in Utrecht.[53]

Matches were organized on the occasion of the annual fair or traditional holidays. Many were made possible by innkeepers and taverners. Such events were popular entertainments; well-off citizens tended to stay aloof from them, because they led to excesses and drinking sprees.[54]

This is why they attracted the attention of the middle-class elite, as represented by the Society for the Promotion of the Public Good, who wanted to civilize and refine such amusements.

English influence

In 1883 the French baron Pierre de Coubertin visited the English public school Rugby. He saw the neo-Gothic monument to Thomas Arnold, the former principal, in the chapel. While contemplating it, De Coubertin heard a fair-haired pupil "with the face of an angel" singing a psalm, and was rapt in ecstasy, for before him lay the embodiment of a national educational system that had produced the "gentleman." A link was made between stamina and courage in games and the pioneer spirit in the expansion and continuance of the British Empire. The Duke of Wellington's remark that the battle of Waterloo was won on the playing fields of Eton resounded for a long time. Admiration of English sport in the public schools inspired De Courbertin in his attempts to revive the Olympic Games.[55] The International Olympic Committee was established in a blaze of publicity in 1894. Two years later the first modern Olympics were held in Athens.

Sports like cricket, soccer and tennis were introduced to the Netherlands or promoted by English immigrants or Dutchmen with experience of English schools. Pim Mulier had attended a college in Ramsgate. The founder of the *Utile Dulci* cricket club in Deventer was J.R. Dickson Romijn, who had been brought up in England. His father had previously founded the Hague Cricket Club in 1878. Englishmen had also played an

Ajax (Amsterdam) vs. Sparta (Rotterdam) in a title game in Rotterdam, 1912.

The Dutch soccer team in 1894.

important part in creating an organization for cyclists, the *Nederlandse Vélocipèdisten Bond*, in 1883. The first chairman, Charles Bingham, was English, as was another member of the executive, D. Webster. Englishmen were prominent in the organization of soccer. The first known match between two clubs was between HFC and the Amsterdamse Cricket- en Football Club "Sport." With one exception, the players were English. One of the earliest tennis clubs in the Netherlands was the Anglo-Dutch Tennis Club in Rotterdam (1855). In the early days of tennis the English were in the majority in tournaments.[56]

The English word "sport" was probably first used in Dutch by Simon Gorter, clergyman, journalist and father of the poet Herman. While taking the waters on the French Riviera in 1866, he observed the British tourists and admired "the sturdy, long-legged chaps, developed through sport." The first sports paper, *Nederlandsche Sport*, appeared in 1882. It determined that in the past a true "patriot" could only respectably indulge in physical exercise in the form of hunting or riding. The first sportsmen came from middle-class backgrounds. They perceived sport as a form of behavior through which they could distance themselves from the more lowly placed. The code of behavior was epitomized by the notion of sportsmanship. It required "the will to win and a competitive attitude, with dignity in defeat and courtesy in victory."[57] Another important factor was the international transmission of these norms. The British system of sporting rules could evidently be adopted without problems in other countries and in all regions. Consequently, people from different areas or countries could easily take part in matches with or against each other. Diversions that varied from place to place did not have this advantage. This was seen as a hindrance now that, because of greater mobility, sportsmen were increasingly organizing their matches on a national or international level.[58]

English expressions such as "fair play" and "this is not cricket," which referred to norms of behavior, became fashionable. It was not only that the rules of sport were formulated in Britain; the spirit was too. English words like "fair" and "unfair" were regularly used in Dutch around 1900. The actual matches did not always take place in accordance with these loudly proclaimed ideals. One aspect of "fair play" was respect for and loyal cooperation with the referee, but in 1890 there were public complaints about the players not having any respect for the officials. "Not only did every player consider himself entitled to loudly air his opinion of the referee, but after the game the unfortunate fellow was held up to ridicule in letters to the editor in a way that none of our modern officials has ever undergone."[59] So conflicts over the interpretation of the rules were not unusual. One report of a boat race shows that there too the rules were not obeyed unquestioningly. In 1882 a crew from the Fortuna club continued the race after their opponents' boat had capsized. The other crew turned out not to be able to swim. The incident caused indignation: the Fortuna crew were told that they ought to have rescued their opponents rather than concentrating on their certain victory.[60]

Cyclists

The cycle, a new means of transport and diversion, developed from sport around 1900 in the Netherlands. The oldest known cyclists' club dated from 1871 and was established by high school pupils in Deventer and given the German name "Immer Weiter." At first wooden cycles were used, but gradually steel machines were introduced. They were easier to ride in the cart tracks on gravel roads. With the introduction of the "safety," a low cycle with two wheels, it was possible to travel faster. Soon some of the HBS pupils in Zutphen were able to cycle to school. The principal called them "cycle gents," as opposed to the "peasants" or "boors," boys from the surrounding villages. In 1891 a study was made of the use of the bicycle for work. Though not based on a representative sample, it showed that a large number of traders and artisans made use of the bicycle. Teachers, manufacturers, physicians and office workers also used it fairly often. The number of workers who cycled was low at that time. This did not change until cheap models came on the market around 1900. On the other hand, it was possible that some people felt they were too high up the social scale to go on cycling.[61] During World War I a survey was carried out among the mobilized troops which showed that ninety percent of them could ride a bicycle.

In the spring of 1883 the members of the Vélocipède clubs of Haarlem and The Hague encountered each other on their Sunday ride half way between the two cities. After getting acquainted, they decided to ride together to the village of Bennebroek. The captain of *De Ooievaar* (The Stork) club of The Hague was the Charles Bingham mentioned above, and that of the Haarlem club was D. Webster, both of whom had been members of the Cyclists Touring Club in England for some time. They agreed to set up a Dutch

The gentlemen of the Hague Cycling Club during the inauguration festivities, 1898.

organization, the *Nederlandse Vélocipèdisten Bond*.[62] Two years later the name was changed to *Algemeen Nederlandse Wielrijders Bond* (ANWB). In 1891 there were over 10,000 cyclists, of whom a third were members of the Bond. Three decades later there were 100,000 cyclists, of whom 40,000 were members. This first mass organization in the Netherlands put on cycle races but also felt it had a duty to promote the use of the bicycle in general. It campaigned for the abolition of tolls and put up signposts (from 1884). In addition, it developed standards for proper behavior on the roads.

In its early years the ANWB took the initiative in encouraging cycling as a sport. It organized track and road races, from which Jaap Eden emerged as the victor. He was the first modern sports hero in the Netherlands. Between 1893 and 1896 he won first prizes in skating as well as in the modern sport of cycling: he was world champion on ice in 1893, 1895 and 1896, and world champion on the bicycle in 1894 and 1895. At receptions in Arnhem and Haarlem he was presented as proof of the nation's fitness. In his tribute in 1895 the president of the Arnhem ice club said: "Steel your muscles, strengthen your legs, young Holland! Honor Jaap Eden, who is the supporter of our youth and will be the champion if our independence is endangered."[63] In 1898 the ANWB decided to give up its sporting activities because it wanted to go on supporting amateurism and disap-

The ladies of the Hague Cycling Club during the inauguration festivities, 1898.

proved of the growing professionalization of cycling.

Thereafter, under its youthful chairman Edo J. Bergsma (1862-1948), who was 21 when he succeeded Bingham in 1884, the ANWB concerned itself with promoting well-regulated traffic and national tourism. In 1888 there were 176 hotels approved by the ANWB throughout the country. The cycle became an acceptable means of transport – acceptable in this context meaning that even in remote areas the cyclist was no longer regarded as an oddity. In its call for traffic rules the ANWB was in tune with a desire in society for order and discipline, which found expression in the founding of the *Tucht-Unie* in 1908. The bond between executive and members had to be close. If the rules were infringed, members were individually called to account by the officials.[64] The driving force behind all this was Edo Bergsma himself, who combined his chairmanship of the ANWB with that of the *Tucht-Unie*. He embodied the combined pursuit of a disciplined society and physical exercise. This was not only an educational ideal of contemporary liberalism but also a precondition for the contemporary desire for "an able-bodied nation."[65]

Gymnastics

In the Netherlands gymnastics was older than sport. Under pressure from Parliament, it had been included in elementary education as a non-compulsory subject in 1857. The concept of school gymnastics had been imported from Germany, from among others the "turn-verein" movement of the nationalistic Friedrich Jahn, which had a substantial influence. Around the turn of the century there was the added attraction of a Swedish method developed by the Royal Institute of Gymnastics in Stockholm. This was introduced to the Netherlands by a naval officer, W.H. Hubert van Blijenburgh (1881-1936). The Swedish example resulted in new exercises in posture and new equipment such as wall bars. Van Blijenburgh was head of the Navy Sport and Gymnastics School and had great influence on the teaching of gymnastics in the armed forces. Through his efforts a substantial number of military personnel secured jobs as gymnastics teachers. The swift rise of the subject was linked to the ideas about the total education of the whole person that prevailed at that time.[66]

In high schools gymnastics was made compulsory by the 1863 Act. But here too it was some time before the subject was taught in an orderly fashion in orderly settings. In the gymnasia, where physical exercise might have offered a demonstrable counterweight to intellectual education, there was no question of its being compulsory. It was found in 1913 that thirteen of the thirty-one municipal gymnasia in the Netherlands did not teach physical education, nor did fourteen of the fifteen denominational gymnasia. In 1914 a National Congress on Physical Education was organized at which the view was expressed that a "reaction against the hyperintellectualism of our age is needed."[67] Gymnastics did not become a compulsory subject at the gymnasia until 1921.

The German influence of gymnastics and handball was noticeable in every province when the rise of British sport began. The early national organization of gymnastics teachers, the *Nederlandsch Gymnastiek Verbond* (1868) must have been the cause of this. Around the turn of the century there were about 12,000 gymnasts in the Netherlands. Gymnastics was probably the second most popular sport after skating. The gymnastics associations had nearly 30,000 members in 1914 and were not overtaken by the football association until the inter-war period. Handball, which also came from Germany, was not as popular in the Netherlands, but this did not apply to the Dutch variant, *korfbal*.[68]

Sports and gymnastics did not immediately go together. Teachers objected to sports fixtures in school time. In 1900 there was some rivalry between those who did gymnastics in school and those who participated in sport outside school. Sport seemed to be an activity in which high school students, often from affluent backgrounds, could find their own space and free themselves from the norms of "good behavior" that were constantly held up to them.[69] The existence of sports clubs and sports culture can even be seen as an expression of resistance by the young to the prevailing code of politeness. The expansion of secondary education around the turn of the century brought large groups of young people together. In the same way as in the Industrial Revolution, when large numbers of workers were brought together in bigger factories, thus creating the conditions for the rise of militant labor unions, school children aged between twelve and eighteen could put up a common front. When they set up sports clubs, especially a soccer club, there was an element of deviating from the standards of order and good behavior upheld by their

Gymnastics display by the Netherlands Gymnastics League on the Malieveld in The Hague, 1898.

teachers and parents. In a survey of sport around 1900 it was asserted that the first generation had to fight a "hard battle" to secure recognition for soccer and "to move the implacable hearts of rigid schoolmasters and timidly stubborn fathers." The principal of the municipal gymnasium in Haarlem who was quoted above, Cornelis Spoelder, wrote in a memoir in 1929 that "our old guard" could still vividly remember when school and soccer got on "like cat and dog." "School and sport, teacher and soccer player, faced each other like sworn enemies."[70]

Meanwhile bridges were being built. In 1905, the first soccer tournament for schoolboys was held during the Easter vacation. Moreover, on the initiative of the military, the *Nederlandse Bond voor Lichamelijke Opvoeding* (Netherlands Union for Physical Exercise) was established in 1908. It opted for cooperation in the interests of promoting sports. The increased concern with the physical development of (male) youth was not unconnected to the introduction of the draft in 1901, which meant that there was an even greater emphasis in the armed forces on having an able-bodied nation.

Democratization

Sports continued to develop outside schools, but relations between the two improved. In fact the growth of sports was linked to the expansion of secondary education. There was agreement between them on values, because sports culture stressed standards of behavior that were the same as the norms of high school: striving to achieve, diligence and perseverance, good manners and restraint. Moreover, the school became the place to meet for more and more boys and girls, who became acquainted through taking part in sports and through sports clubs.[71]

Gymnastics display by the Netherlands Gymnastics League in Purmerend, 1911.

Children's party given by the Amsterdam Union for Physical Education, 1919.

In 1900 the number of people taking part in sports was estimated at 30,000, that is, registered members of clubs. Ten years later the number had more than doubled. This growth was reflected in the founding of national associations. They were proof that local initiatives were coordinated and that the new branch of sport was well established in the Netherlands. The first national organization of sailing and rowing clubs dated from 1847. The first gymnastics league was set up in 1868. The sports imported from England, such as cricket, soccer, hockey and tennis, were organized nationally from the eighteen-eighties and -nineties. Sporting encounters at the national level were made easier by the increasing travel possibilities, a result of the extension of the train and streetcar networks. In the early years of the soccer league whether and when matches took place was decided by the existence of railroad stations and journey times. The growth of sports was also reflected in the sporting press. The magazine *Nederlandsche Sport* was published from 1882. It was owned by the Nimrod Hunt and the national harness-racing association, and was probably the first publication to be devoted to sports. In the first volume rowing and skating were the main sports covered. Later the editors turned their attention to swimming, cycling, cricket and tennis. Between 1889 and 1905 three new sports magazines were launched, followed in 1913 by an illustrated periodical, *De Revue der Sporten*. It is also worth noting that in the same period the leading daily papers found room for a full-time sports reporter: *De Telegraaf* in 1902, the *Nieuwe Rotterdamse Courant* in 1905 and the *Algemeen Handelsblad* in 1911.[72]

This expansion must also be seen as a sign of the democratization of sport. In the decades leading up to 1900 the initiatives had come mainly from the sons, and to a lesser extent the daughters, of the well-off, but around the turn of the century this exclusivity no longer applied. In Haarlem pupils at the technical school established the soccer club *Eendracht Doet Overwinnen* (Unity Conquers All) in 1897. It is regarded as the first working-class club in the history of sports in the Netherlands. After 1900 soccer and cycling were open to working men. But most associations were still closed to them. The Dutch Rowing Association even had an article in its statutes which said that membership was forbidden for manual workers.[73] Even in the popular branches of sport, workers played a small part up to World War I. Research has been carried out into the social background of the players in the national soccer team between 1894 and 1951. In the early period (1894-1905) ninety-five percent of the one hundred and four players came from "good backgrounds" and four percent from the "respectable middle class." Between 1906 and 1918 the first percentage fell to eighty-two, while the second rose to fourteen. In the first period there was only one player from the working class, but in the second period there were three.[74]

The real democratization took place after World War I. From 1919 more than half of the players in the national team came from the working class. This change may be seen as evidence of the general popularization of sports. The mobilization of draftees during World War I had undermined club life, but it had also led a growing number of young men to become acquainted with new and previously rather exclusive forms of physical exercise. That and the introduction of the free Saturday afternoon – the result of a reduction of working hours by law in 1918 – were the factors favoring a spectacular development of sport as a leisure activity.

7

Higher education and the sciences

Higher education

In 1849 the Ewijck government commission made some notable recommendations about the system of higher education, which the commission believed should be regarded as pre-vocational education. The university was to "prepare students through thorough instruction for positions in society, and in every discipline equip them to study independently, and to continue practicing and applying their knowledge."[1] These recommendations were diametrically opposed to the prevailing view, as set out in a decree, the *Organiek Besluit* of 1815. It stated that the task of the universities was to prepare young noblemen for a life in the highest circles. "The term higher education," said the decree, "is defined as education intended to prepare the student, after elementary and secondary education, for a learned rank in society."[2]

"A learned rank" did not mean a "class of learned men" but a class which was distinguished from the middle classes and the common people by being "learned."[3] The decree confirmed the difference in rank between the aristocracy and the working class and widened the gap between university education and everyday professional practice. This point of view was endorsed by the Roël commission in 1828. It stated emphatically that pre-vocational education did not belong at the university: "This eliminates from university education the idea that its aim is to train young persons for certain professions, and most importantly this rules out technical education, where the main concern is practicing and applying in particular cases and not the pursuit of knowledge, a popular treatment taking the place of fundamental theory."[4]

Against this background, the revolutionary nature of the position taken by the Ewijck commission is clear enough. Its view that higher education should serve the needs of professional practice and thus of the middle classes effectively broke down the class system that had previously kept the levels of education separate. Johan Rudolf Thorbecke, the minister for home affairs, was the only man with the nerve, power and revolutionary sympathies to push through such far-reaching proposals. In a drastic change of policy, he incorporated the recommendations of the Ewijck commission in the Secondary Education Act and piloted it through parliament in 1863. This Act included radical measures benefiting vocational education. The most important, as mentioned in chapter 6, was the creation of the *Hogere Burger School* (HBS) for practically oriented education. In addition, Thorbecke provided greater opportunities for vocational colleges, such as the School of Veterinary Medicine in Utrecht and the Polytechnic School in Delft.

After the resounding success of the Secondary Education Act, much was expected of the bill regulating higher education. It was naturally assumed that in this bill Thorbecke would continue to pursue the revolutionary line he had taken in the 1863 Act. But the bill finally submitted and passed in 1876 was an anti-climax. Its intentions were unclear, and it was half-hearted and a source of potential conflict. On the one hand it created some scope for pre-vocational university education, but on the other it made it clear that this was a secondary and not strictly proper aim for a university, whose first and foremost task was to civilize the youth of the elite.

Mention of the word "civilization" or "Bildung" brings us to the influence of the German system on higher education in the Netherlands. Here too Thorbecke played a crucial role. He had gone to university in Germany and had been influenced by German ideas about education, in which Bildung was central. Bildung meant "education" or "civilization" in the sense of inculcating "a knowledge of the classics."[5] According to the educational reformer Wilhelm von Humboldt, the university ought to instill this civilization by means of "Wissenschaft" (knowledge). Humboldt believed that conveying this knowledge was the university's chief educational task, and what he meant by knowledge encompassed both knowledge of the classics (in that sense it was synonymous with the "learning" referred to in the *Organiek Besluit*) and the "independent research" to which the Ewijck commission referred. Thorbecke was guided by this ambiguous notion of "Bildung durch Wissenschaft" when, after returning to the Netherlands and going into politics, he developed plans for reforming the educational system. The question is not whether the German model influenced the legislation he introduced in 1863 and 1876; all the historians are agreed that it did. The question is: in which direction were the Dutch laws propelled by the German example? On this point opinion is sharply divided. Marita Matthijssen believes that the German model had a regressive effect on Dutch education. Von Humboldt had defined Bildung as a new kind of humanism, with the intention of keeping pre-vocational education out of the universities. Applying this ideal to the Dutch system meant a return to the principles of the *Organiek Besluit* and an endorsement of class-based education.[6] Arnold Labrie disagrees. His view is that the German Bildung meant that brilliant students could qualify for higher education on the grounds of their individual talent, regardless of the class in which they were born. The introduction of this ideal to the Netherlands was an important stimulus towards democratization of education: the middle classes were eager to seize this chance to send their talented children to gymnasium and university, and to gain access to a level of higher education from which they had previously been excluded. According to Labrie, the Bildung ideal thus had a democratizing effect on Dutch education.[7] Who is right? Just to make matters complicated, both are. The Higher Education Act of 1876 left scope for contradictory interpretations of Bildung: on the one hand, the progressive interpretation, whereby students could qualify on the basis of individual talent, and on the other the reactionary interpretation that endorsed a class-based system.

These contradictions underlay the stormy times around the turn of the century. It was stipulated in law that university and pre-vocational education were separate paths. The status of the HBS and the polytechnics was regulated in the Secondary Education Act of 1863, that of the gymnasium and the universities in the Higher Education Act of 1876.

The equipment in an HBS classroom around 1900.

One of the consequences of this legal difference was that HBS pupils could not gain access to university. In practice, however, the law proved weak. Under the pressure of a number of developments, higher education was forced to take account of what was happening in society; for their part, secondary schools developed into pre-research institutions. The main reason for this trend was the demand from trade and industry for highly trained workers.[8] Up to then businessmen and industrialists had received their training on the job: academic education was not considered necessary. Indeed, there were hardly any graduates in business. This began to change after 1890. In that year over sixty percent of students were studying law or theology, but by the turn of the century the majority chose a technical science, commerce, math or physics.[9] Higher education adapted to these social changes. It was increasingly recognized that the universities had a role to play in the training of highly qualified technical personnel, that science and technology should go hand in hand, and that vocationally oriented subjects needed a scientific basis in order to safeguard prosperity and progress.[10]

The HBS developed in a direction that the 1863 Act had neither intended nor foreseen. After passing the school-leaving examination, the HBS student was expected to go off to a factory or office. But the great success of the new type of school ensured that this did not happen. The educational program at the HBS was so excellent and provided such a thorough grounding in the sciences (it should be remembered that, until the division into HBS-A and HBS-B in 1921, the HBS was especially strong in the exact sciences; in 1867 science accounted for nearly half the timetable of the examination classes),[11] the teachers were so outstanding, and the schools, particularly the laboratories, were so well equipped that in practice the HBS far transcended its original aim and quickly developed into a pre-research, if not semi-university, institution. One gets a fair idea of the academic level of HBS education by browsing through Johannes Bosscha's physics textbook *Leerboek der Natuurkunde en van hare voornaamste toepassingen* (1875). The topics it covers, the experiments described and the tasks set are undoubtedly of university level. Carrying out these experiments did not prepare the student for life as a bookkeeper or bank clerk, but for life as a researcher. And that is exactly what happened. Many of those who had been to the HBS passed the demanding state examination (with its Greek and Latin) that stood as an obstacle between them and higher education, and thus gained access to the university. There they achieved such overwhelming success that around the turn of the century the academic elite at Dutch universities was made up of brilliant scientists who did not strictly belong there and had slipped in through a back door. The discrepancy between the *intention* behind the Acts of 1863 and 1876 and their effect in practice was pointed out by Jacob van 't Hoff, who was awarded the first Nobel Prize for Chemistry in 1901. In an address given to a national congress on physics and medicine in 1891 he observed that university courses in physics and chemistry were thriving as never before: "Is this not the fruit of our HBS courses, which are so outstanding in many respects, and wouldn't they flourish even more if the path from HBS to university was made easier?"[12] We are concerned mainly with the last remark, in which Van 't Hoff called for the law to recognize what was already taking place in practice, namely the rising status of the HBS as a first-year university course. Van 't Hoff's argument was in fact irrefutable: six of the seven Nobel Prize winners in physics and chemistry prior to 1914 had attended an HBS. The seventh, Johannes Diderik van de Waals, had been educated at a gymnasium, but he had begun his career as a teacher at an HBS. The emancipation of the HBS and the polytechnics, and the concomitant blurring of the distinction between pre-vocational and higher education, could not be stopped, despite the obstacles raised by the university establishment. The Faculty of Medicine grieved to see its auxiliary disciplines of chemistry and biology[13] gradually developing into autonomous sciences. Its response was to obstruct the admission of physics and chemistry to the university on the grounds that these newcomers lacked the civilizing preliminary training in the classics. This resistance inhibited the development of the science departments. The humanities also strongly resisted the emancipation of the exact sciences.[14] Showing their insecurity and sense of inferiority when faced by these sciences, they reminded the minister that the university's first duty was "character building" (Bildung) and not (or much less so) practicing a science or preparing students for a profession.

But the evolution of higher education towards "scientific research" and "vocational preparation" continued. An ardent plea for higher education to be oriented towards scholarship was made by the philosopher Jan P.N. Land in his address at the opening of the 1885-1886 academic year. Land's view was that universities ought to be research centers, not institutes for general education. The old universities had been mediocre according to Land, because they produced civil servants and men of letters rather than statesmen, poets and thinkers. The old university set out to reproduce the canon of classical knowledge; the new university was concerned with research into sources, critical observation of nature and the autonomous development of new ideas (Land thus interprets Bildung in the progressive sense of "independent research," not in the regressive sense favored by the medical and humanities faculties of reproducing the canon).

These trends were reflected in some twenty changes to the Higher Education Act between 1905 and 1940. The Polytechnic School in Delft was given the status of a college in 1905 and then came under the Higher instead of the Secondary Education Act. In 1918 several vocational courses were accorded the status of higher education: a change to the law in that year meant that the "Higher School of Agriculture, Horticulture and Forestry" at Wageningen became the "Agricultural College," and that the "School of Veterinary Science" was also made a college. In 1937 the private commercial schools and the Roman-Catholic College of Commerce in Tilburg were recognized as colleges and accordingly came under the Higher Education Act.[15] But the most important change was the Limburg Act of 1917, which stipulated that in future pupils who had graduated from an HBS would be admitted to university.[16]

All in all, the situation in higher education at the turn of the century was marked by opposing tendencies. The universities had taken increasing account of social change in the years 1876 to 1910, and they had narrowed the gap between higher education and professional practice, but it was not until well into the twentieth century that this rapprochement was reflected in legislation. The end of the century was a period in which the tide was turning: the "ancien régime," with its ranks and classes, was still legally in power but it was beginning to lose ground to the democratized university.

"Second Golden Age"

The brilliant scientists who appeared in the last quarter of the nineteenth century were the leading figures in what has become known as the "Second Golden Age" of Dutch science. Thanks to them, research in physics reached a level not achieved since the latter half of the seventeenth century and the beginning of the eighteenth century (Huygens, Van Leeuwenhoek).[17] The new period of great achievements was heralded by the publication of Johannes van der Waals's thesis in 1873.[18] This study of the relation between the pressure, volume and temperature of substances in the gaseous and liquid states made a great impression abroad. The renowned British physicist James Clerk Maxwell once told Van der Waals that he had wanted to learn Dutch simply to be able to read his thesis.

The second golden age was also the era of the biologist Hugo de Vries (active 1878-1918), the chemist Jacobus van 't Hoff (1877-1896; Nobel Prize for Chemistry in 1901), the astronomer Jacobus Kapteijn (1877-1921), the physicists Hendrik Lorentz (1877-1910; Nobel Prize for Physics in 1902), Pieter Zeeman (1894-1935; Nobel Prize for Physics in 1902) and Heike Kamerlingh Onnes (1882-1924; Nobel Prize for Physics in 1913). There were other scientists who made significant contributions, such as the Groningen physicist H. Haga, the Leiden chemist Hendrik Bakhuis Roozeboom and the Delft bacteriologist Martinus Beijerinck. They were often overshadowed by their more prominent colleagues, but their importance should not be underestimated.

The appearance of Van der Waals's thesis virtually coincided with two other major events. In 1874 Van 't Hoff published a pamphlet which laid the basis for stereochemistry, and in 1875 Lorentz gained his doctorate for an electromagnetic study of the reflection and refraction of light. Together with thermodynamics (Van der Waals's research field), these were the three themes that dominated Dutch scientific research for many years.[19]

The "Second Golden Age" followed a period of decline that had begun during the eighteenth century and reached its nadir at the start of the nineteenth century. Science, which up to then had been the preserve of the "learned societies," was moved to the universities, or more correctly the faculties of philosophy. There hardly any research was carried out. The chief concern was to educate teachers.

The great success of the sciences at the turn of the century was due to two developments already described: the introduction of the HBS in 1863 and the Higher Education Act of 1876.[20]

At the universities – at that time only Amsterdam, Leiden, Groningen and Utrecht – the fields of learning, and certainly the sciences, were "formed into disciplines," that is grouped around particular areas and the questions they raised. This led to the professionalization of research (the professors and their assistants were no longer teachers who also did some research) and to an increase in scale. Science was like a business.[21]

The number of professors (and thus the number of specialties) was increased; the facilities were expanded (number of assistants, construction of laboratories).[22] Student numbers also grew. In 1850 the total number of students was 1,000, and in 1900 around 2,800. The number of math and physics students was 31 in 1850, 144 in 1880, 285 in 1890 and 439 in 1900.[23] In 1900 thirty-six percent of students were studying a science, the highest percentage of all disciplines.[24] The number of doctorates in math and physics rose towards the end of the nineteenth century: there were six in 1880-1881, four in 1885-1886, five in 1890-1891, ten in 1895-1896, and twenty-three in 1900-1901.[25] In Leiden the number of math and physics students grew faster after 1885 than the total number of students.[26]

The introduction of the HBS and university reform were not the only reasons for this golden age. Wachelder[27] points out that the development of research coincided with changing attitudes to the content, status and organization of higher education. Willink[28] cites four factors that encouraged the flowering of science or at least typically accompanied it: educational reform, rapid growth of employment just before the golden age, low student/teacher ratios (in the sense that each lecturer only had to teach a limited number of students) and an increase in material investment.

Willink points to three more factors indirectly linked to this phenomenon. Firstly, the prestige of learning added to the motivation to choose a career at the university. Secondly, professionalization meant that the universities' research tasks were more demanding and were increasingly carried out by professional researchers. Thirdly, there was the growth of specialization. Lastly, Willink[29] says that the success of Dutch science was to some extent only relative. It contrasted favorably with the position in other countries, where science was in something of a decline after flourishing earlier.

At the end of the nineteenth century there was as yet no question of a structural government policy in this field, but the government did give some encouragement indirectly. For example, as a result of the agricultural crisis of 1878, it decided to promote the application of scientific research to industry. A commission was set up and it recommended that experimental stations should be established. Moreover, in the course of the nineteenth century several research institutes were founded by the state: the Royal Dutch Meteorological Institute (1854), the State Institute for Fisheries Research (1882) and the Chemical Laboratory of the Artillery Institutes (1896).

It is difficult to determine how great the public's interest in science was around 1900. Brookman[30] observes that the nineteenth century was fairly indifferent to the arts and sciences. But there was a lively interest in the discoveries being made in the physical sciences at the end of the century. This is reflected in the rise of popular science magazines like *De Natuur, Album der Natuur, Wetenschappelijke Bladen* and *Isis*. To give some idea of the range of topics covered, in 1900 the *Album der Natuur* had articles on weather forecasting, hydrogen, the dragon tree, eating earth, sugar beet, Robert Bunsen, advances in agricultural chemistry, narcosis in plants, light-emitting animals, digestion, the life of fish and the scientific explanation for the origin of species.

In "family magazines" scientists were often portrayed as heroes. In 1900 *Mannen en vrouwen van beteekenis in onze dagen* (Important Men and Women of Our Time) published three portraits of leading scientists: Van 't Hoff, Van der Waals and De Vries. Of the first the magazine said that he had been bought by the Germans for cash, just as Huygens had been enticed to France by Colbert in the seventeenth century: "France and Germany, bent on capturing our stars in the sciences, deprived us of Huygens and Van 't Hoff."

The award of the Nobel Prizes naturally did wonders for the image of science. In 1903, after Lorentz won his Nobel Prize, *De Prins* said, "This hero of science, who has upheld the honor of our country, and whose great services to the welfare of humanity were recently recognized abroad by the award of the Nobel Prize..."

Physics

Physics developed throughout the nineteenth century. Around the beginning of the century the classic – mathematically oriented – sciences were gradually combined with the experimental – Baconian – sciences.[31] The result was what has come to be known as modern physics. As knowledge increased, it became increasingly difficult to cover the whole field and so in the course of the century a distinction developed between experimental and theoretical physics. Looking at the Dutch Nobel Prize winners and their colleagues, we see that Kamerlingh Onnes and Zeeman were primarily experimental physicists, while Van der Waals and Lorentz were theorists. The two groups cooperated to good effect and they influenced and stimulated each other. Kamerlingh Onnes did experiments derived from Van der Waals's theorys. Zeeman did his experimental research for his doctorate – under Lorentz – in Kamerlingh Onnes's laboratory. De Vries and Van 't Hoff, Lorentz and Zeeman and Van der Waals and Kamerlingh Onnes were in touch and influenced each other's work. The mathematician Korteweg, one of Van der Waals's doctoral students, played an important part in mediating between the theoretical and experimental physicists.[32] Within this scientific community the Royal Netherlands Academy of

Arts and Sciences (KNAW) served as a forum where new knowledge could be presented orally and in writing, and disseminated.

The man with whom the flowering of Dutch science began, Johannes Diderik van der Waals (1837-1923),[33] is the exception to the success story linking the HBS and the Second Golden Age. He came from a humble family and it was quite an achievement that after finishing grade school around 1850 he was allowed to go on to advanced elementary education. He then gained every teacher's qualification he could in German, French, math and sciences and in 1864 became a math and physics teacher at an HBS. In 1866, while still teaching, he began studying math and physics at Leiden University, but he was unable to take any exams until an exemption was made for him in 1871. He gained his doctorate in 1873 with a thesis that attracted international attention. In it he formulated a general law for the relation between the pressure, volume and temperature of a substance in the gaseous and liquid states. In contrast to the law of Boyle-Gay Lussac, Van der Waals's law of corresponding states took account of the size of the molecules and the attraction between them. Moreover, his law made it possible to predict the critical temperature of a gas. At that time thinking about atoms and molecules as real entities was still controversial. It is striking that none of the Dutch scientists were skeptical about this, which enabled them to build up a lead over their colleagues abroad. Van der Waals made an important contribution to thermodynamics in this way. Resistance to this mode of thinking came above all from the "energeticists" Wilhelm Ostwald and Pierre Duhem. They tried to reduce all natural phenomena to energy transformations.

In 1877 Van der Waals was appointed professor of physics at the new University of Amsterdam. Despite his affinity with experimentation during his time as an HBS teacher, at the university he was primarily a theorist. The laboratory that was specially equipped for him in 1881 was used mainly by his assistants and students, though under his supervision. Van der Waals kept in close touch with colleagues elsewhere in the county, including Heike Kamerlingh Onnes in Leiden. From 1896 to 1912 Van der Waals was secretary of the Royal Netherlands Academy of Arts and Sciences, and in this position he ensured that Dutch publications appeared in English-language *Proceedings*.

Heike Kamerlingh Onnes (1853-1926)[34] attended an HBS and took the state examinations in Greek and Latin so that he could study at Groningen University. He was an excellent student and spent three semesters at the University of Heidelberg, where he studied under Robert Bunsen and Gustav Kirchhoff. Here he had the idea of looking again at Foucault's mechanical proof of the earth's rotation. In his thesis on this subject (1879) Kamerlingh Onnes defended the proposition that Foucault's pendulum needed to be only 1.2 meters long to prove his theory, not 16 meters. From 1878 to 1882 he worked at the Polytechnic School in Delft as assistant to the physicist Johannes Bosscha, who had just been appointed director there. At this time he came into contact with Van der Waals in Amsterdam and thus with the issues surrounding the molecular theory of matter. Van der Waals's approach had been purely theoretical, whereas Kamerlingh Onnes wanted to test the theoretical findings experimentally and broaden them.

In 1882 he became professor of experimental physics at Leiden. In this position he was responsible for creating the renowned and extremely well-equipped physics laboratory that has become known chiefly for low temperature research. He also ensured that

A doctoral degree ceremony at the new University of Amsterdam around the turn of the century.

he had a supply of highly trained technical personnel by setting up the instrument-maker's school.[35] He was awarded the Nobel Prize in 1913 for his method of making helium liquid (1908). The challenge here lay in the fact that the critical temperature of helium was extremely low, 268°C. The helium gas thus had to be cooled to that temperature first before it could be made liquid under pressure. Until 1923 his laboratory was the only one that could produce liquid helium. During his research into the properties of substances at extremely low temperatures, Kamerlingh Onnes also came across the phenomenon of "superconductivity." Because the electrical resistance of a metal disappeared – became zero – at a certain temperature, it proved possible to maintain an electrical current without adding new current. Quantum physics was later much occupied with this phenomenon. Kamerlingh Onnes was very internationally minded and closely involved in developments in science and technology.

Hendrik Antoon Lorentz (1853-1928)[36] was reputed to be a true genius. At the HBS he went straight into the third year, where he was taught physics by Van der Stadt and chemistry by Jacob van Bemmelen. In 1869 he began studying math and physics at

Leiden and two years later he was awarded his bachelor's degree summa cum laude. He became a teacher while also working for his master's degree and later a PhD. He gained his doctorate in 1875 at the age of 22 with a thesis on the theory of the reflection and refraction of light, and at the age of 24 he had a choice of two professorships: mathematical physics at Leiden or math and physics at Utrecht. He chose Leiden. There he worked on his "electron theory," a refinement of Maxwell's theory of electromagnetism, which explained such phenomena as light and electrical current more satisfactorily. Up to 1892 Lorentz had little contact with foreign colleagues and he published little. Then he presented his electron theory and became a central figure in international research into electromagnetism. The work for which Lorentz and his colleague Pieter Zeeman won the Nobel Prize in 1902 concerned the explanation for the broadening of spectrum lines in a strong magnetic field (the Zeeman effect) with the aid of Lorentz's electron theory. Using the same theory, Lorentz was also able to predict these phenomena. At the beginning of the twentieth century Lorentz's electron theory had to compete with Einstein's theory of relativity (1905) and the atomic theory of Niels Bohr. Zeeman's experiments in the nineteen-twenties showed that Bohr's atomic model (1921) could explain certain phenomena better than Lorentz's electron theory.

By 1900 Lorentz's reputation was internationally established. When the University of Munich offered him a chair in 1905, Leiden recruited J.P. Kuenen to ease Lorentz's teaching load and he decided to stay where he was. In 1912 he became curator of the physics department at Teylers Museum and secretary of the *Hollandsche Maatschappij voor Wetenschappen* (Holland Society for Sciences), both in Haarlem, and his chair in Leiden was made part time. But this was far from being retirement in disguise: he continued to give popular lectures on science and seminars on current research for advanced students, and was involved in various organizations, including an advisory committee on the damming of the Zuiderzee, a scientific committee on national prosperity and defense, and the Advisory Council for Education.

After attending an HBS, Pieter Zeeman (1865-1943)[37] studied classical languages at a gymnasium for a further two years so that he could go to the University of Leiden in 1885. He studied under Lorentz and Kamerlingh Onnes, and in 1887 he was made an assistant in Kamerlingh Onnes's laboratory. He investigated the effect of magnetism on the reflection of polarized light (the so-called Kerr effect), and received a gold medal from the Holland Society for Sciences for this work. He gained his doctorate for a thesis on this subject in 1893. He spent a year in Strasbourg and was then offered an appointment as an unsalaried lecturer at Leiden. There, in 1896, while repeating an 1862 experiment by Faraday, he "discovered" the effect later named after him: the magnetic splitting of spectrum lines. Through this he proved that magnetic force can directly affect light particles. With the aid of the discovery of the electron by J.J. Thomson in 1895 and Lorentz's knowledge of the electron theory, Lorentz and Zeeman were able to explain the phenomenon. The theorist and the experimenter continued their collaboration. A year later in Amsterdam Zeeman succeeded in bringing about other predictions in practice. Their cooperation led to the discovery that spectroscopy could play a leading role in research into the structure of atoms. Zeeman and Lorentz were jointly awarded the Nobel Prize for this work in 1902.

Pieter Zeeman is feted at the University of Amsterdam on the occasion of his
seventieth birthday, 1935.

Zeeman became a lecturer at the University of Amsterdam in 1896. Unfortunately, he
could not carry out his experiments with sufficient accuracy because of the shortcomings
of his laboratory. He had to wait until 1923 before a new laboratory became available. In
the meantime he researched the speed of light in moving media. From 1912 to 1920 he
was secretary of the physics department of the Royal Netherlands Academy of Arts and
Sciences. He then became rector magnificus of the University of Amsterdam.

Chemistry

In the eighteen-eighties chemistry underwent a major transformation, in which the
Netherlands played a significant part. Up to then organic and inorganic chemistry had
been mainly concerned with analyzing and synthesizing substances. Now there was a
greater interest in understanding general chemical phenomena and chemical systems.
One new feature was that formulas from physics, and particularly thermodynamics,
were applied to chemical phenomena, so that this new branch came to be known as
physical chemistry.[38] The traditional experiment – associated with bubbling test tubes –
gave way in this branch to a new type of research characterized by measurements,
mathematical calculations and quantitative precision.

Besides Wilhelm Ostwald in Latvia and Svante Arrhenius in Sweden, the founders of physical chemistry included the Amsterdam professor Jacobus Henricus van 't Hoff (1852-1911).[39] After the HBS, Van 't Hoff followed a course in chemical technology at the Polytechnic School and then went to Leiden – with an exemption for classical languages – to study math and physics. After gaining his bachelor's degree in 1872, he left for Bonn, where he studied organic chemistry with August Kekulé. He then took his master's degree and at the beginning of 1874 went to Paris, where he studied with Adolphe Wurtz. His thesis of 1874 made little impression, but a small publication a few months earlier certainly did. It consisted of only twelve pages and was entitled "Proposal for the extension of current chemical structural formulas into space, together with a related observation on the connection between optically active power and the chemical constitution of organic compounds." What he did in this work was to replace the normal two-dimensional formulas for the structure of carbon compounds by three-dimensional, spatial figures. This solved the problem that one formula could refer to different structures. By adding a third dimension to the formulas, asymmetry became visible. It turned out that molecules could have a left- and a right-rotating variant. In this way he laid the foundations of stereochemistry.

This did not mean that Van 't Hoff immediately "had it made." At first he gave private lessons and in 1876 he accepted a job teaching physics and chemistry at the School of Veterinary Medicine in Utrecht, where he stayed for two years. The Act of 1876 made it possible for him to be appointed a lecturer in theoretical and physical chemistry at the new University of Amsterdam, and in 1878 he became professor of chemistry, mineralogy and geology there. While holding this post, in 1884 he published *Études de dynamique chimique* (Studies in Chemical Dynamics), which is regarded as his most important review.[40] Later he worked on a study of osmotic pressure. He published the results – the theory of osmotic pressure – in 1885 in the Dutch journal *Archives néerlandaises des sciences exactes et naturelles*. In 1901 he was awarded the Nobel Prize for Chemistry for this study. He was offered a chair at Leipzig in 1887, but the University of Amsterdam managed to hold on to him by promising him a new laboratory. It was to be 1892, however, before this laboratory was completed. In 1894 Van 't Hoff again rejected an offer from abroad – Berlin this time – but he could not refuse the third offer from Germany, a position at the Prussian Academy of Sciences in Berlin. There he would be able to concentrate entirely on his research.

When Van 't Hoff left for Berlin in 1896, he was succeeded by Hendrik Willem Bakhuis Roozeboom (1854-1907),[41] who had developed his own variant of physical chemistry, the phase rule, with an empirical and a mathematical-theoretical component. Bakhuis Roozeboom had also reached the University of Leiden via the HBS and lessons in Greek and Latin. He passed the entrance examination, but could not afford to pay for his studies, so he became a chemical analyst in The Hague. The Leiden professor of chemistry Jacob van Bemmelen had known Bakhuis since they had done research together into the soil in the new IJ polders near Amsterdam, and he appointed him his research assistant in 1878, so that he was able to study chemistry after all. Bakhuis gained his doctorate in 1884 with a thesis (twenty pages long) on the relations between three states of matter at different temperatures and pressures. From 1881 to 1896 he made a living by teaching at the Leiden HBS for girls. He also continued to do research in chemistry.

In 1882 he began to experiment with heterogeneous equilibria, through which he came into contact with Josiah Willard Gibbs's work on thermodynamics. From 1889 he was successively an unsalaried lecturer, and lecturer in physical chemistry at Leiden. This made it possible for him to carry out extensive experiments. As a professor in Amsterdam, he continued with his own research into heterogeneous equilibria. Besides his theoretical work, Bakhuis also did socially useful, practical research such as analyzing drinking water. His phase rule overlapped with the work of the physicist Van der Waals and that of the mathematician Korteweg, all of whom were at the University of Amsterdam. From Amsterdam the phase rule began to dominate physical chemistry in the rest of the country, and around 1920 it had captured every chair in the field.

Biology

Biology, too, developed dramatically at the end of the nineteenth century. The theory of evolution had already focused attention on such phenomena as variation and selection soon after the middle of the century. From the eighteen-seventies this discipline was no longer concerned primarily with systematizing and defining – it spawned an experimental branch that wanted to understand and explain the phenomena of life. Experimental embryology and plant physiology were among the areas that developed as independent sub-disciplines.

Hugo Marie de Vries (1848-1935)[42] had an interest in plants from an early age. After the gymnasium he went to Leiden to study natural sciences, with the emphasis on botany. Leiden provided little scope for his areas of special interest – evolutionary theory and experimental research – so after taking his PhD under Willem Suringar in 1870, he found more opportunities in his field in Germany. He worked in Wilhelm Hofmeister's laboratory in Heidelberg and attended lectures by Robert Bunsen and Herman von Helmholtz. In 1871 he went to Würzburg, where he conducted experiments in plant physiology in Julius Sachs's laboratory. In September of the same year he started work as a teacher at the HBS in Amsterdam, but without fail spent all his vacations in the Würzburg laboratory. After four years De Vries got the chance to work full time in Würzburg on experimental botanical research for a series of monographs on agricultural crops. In the same period he also wrote a qualification dissertation to make himself eligible for the post of unsalaried university lecturer in physiology in Halle. He was not a success in this post; there was little interest in his lectures. In 1878 he was offered a part-time professorship in plant physiology at the University of Amsterdam – an offer he gratefully accepted. He was the first plant physiologist to hold a chair in botany. At around this time De Vries visited Darwin, and in the years that followed he concentrated on research into speciation and variability. In 1881 his post was made into a full professorship.

De Vries's most important contribution to plant physiology was the law of isotonic coefficients, which could be used to calculate the concentration of saline solution at which the protoplasm of the cell wall of a plant cell permits transfer. In this work De Vries made use of Van 't Hoff's physical-chemical research into osmosis. Van 't Hoff subsequently became a formidable rival to De Vries. De Vries's findings were also used in research into isotony in animal cells.

Around 1890 De Vries devoted himself to his second love: research into evolution and heredity. As early as 1880 he had already started to carry out experiments in heredity in his physiological research. The selective breeding of plants was a subject that had been occupying him since 1875, and he was particularly fascinated by the variation within a species. In his research at a theoretical level, he took his lead from Darwin's pangenesis theory. "Pangenes" were supposedly germs of the various elements of which an organism consists. A complete set of these hereditary particles was present in the nucleus of every cell and thus determined all the hereditary factors of the organism. In order to explain changes in a species on the basis of these constant pangenes, De Vries introduced the concept of mutation. Mutation had taken place if new forms that were very different from the parent plant developed from the seed of a purebred species and behaved like a purebred species when they were crossed with one another. A new species could arise in a single generation as a result of the emergence of a single new pangene. In his book *Die Mutationstheorie* (1901-1903) he put forward, among other things, the theory that new species did not develop over very long periods of time, as Darwin postulated, but by abrupt changes – saltatory mutations – which it ought to be possible to prove experimentally. His mutation theory was ultimately to make him world famous. To prevent De Vries from being lured away by Columbia University in New York with the promise of more money, the University of Amsterdam gave him the use of a new building – the present-day Hugo de Vries Laboratory – and appointed Th.J. Stomps as part-time professor to relieve him of some of his teaching load.

Dutch microbiology is inextricably linked with the name of Beijerinck. Martinus Willem Beijerinck (1851-1931)[43] came from a wealthy family in which his father had failed to maintain the tradition of success. Beijerinck was nonetheless able to get a good education thanks to a legacy from an aunt: he was among the first cohort to attend an HBS. During his schooldays he got to know Frederik van Eeden Sr. and Hugo de Vries. In 1868 Beijerinck went to study chemical engineering at Delft, where he made friends with Van 't Hoff. This friendship continued when in 1872, thanks to an exemption for classical languages, the two young men went to the University of Leiden – Van 't Hoff to study chemistry and Beijerinck biology. While he was studying, Beijerinck also worked as a teacher for a while, and in 1876 he got a job as a botany lecturer at the Higher School of Agriculture, Horticulture and Forestry in Wageningen. Here he also had time to work on his research into plant galls, with which he gained his doctorate cum laude in 1877. In 1884 he was elected to the Royal Netherlands Academy of Arts and Sciences (KNAW) and, through the kind offices of Hugo de Vries, secured a good research post as a microbiologist with the "Delftse Gist- and Spiritusfabriek." He did a great deal of research in the laboratory that he had available to him there – research that proved to be of great benefit both to his employers and to science in general. In 1895, again thanks in part to De Vries, he was appointed professor of bacteriology at the Polytechnic School, where – a researcher first and foremost – he struggled under the burden of his teaching duties. A microbiology laboratory built especially for Beijerinck and his students was opened in 1897. In this laboratory he succeeded in isolating the first free-living aerobic bacterium, he discovered a non-bacterial pathogen "contagium vivum fluidum" – which was later to be dubbed a "virus" – and he succeeded in producing pure bacteria cultures for scientific research. One of Beijerinck's greatest contributions to the development of microbiology was his application of the methods used in chemistry to research into micro-organisms. He was also largely instrumental in introducing the experiment into biology.

Medicine

Many of the advances in medicine at the end of the nineteenth century can be traced back to the developments in physiology. New knowledge about the human body led to new diagnostic techniques and methods of treatment, and there was a recognition of the importance of nutrition in the proper functioning of the body. Microbiology also had a major impact on research into pathogens.

Willem Einthoven (1860-1927)[44] took lessons in Greek and Latin while studying at an HBS, and then went to Utrecht to study medicine. His professors included Franciscus Cornelis Donders, Theodor Wilhelm Engelmann and Christoforus H.D. Buys Ballot, and he gained his doctorate in 1885 under Donders's supervision. Immediately afterward he was offered a professorship in physiology and histology at Leiden. He had a keen interest in the electrical activity of the human heart. Einthoven was in the audience at the First International Congress of Physiologists in Basel in 1889, when Augustus D. Waller used a capillary electrometer to demonstrate current in the hearts of frogs and humans. Einthoven was fascinated by this technique and, with his university friend (later to be his brother-in-law) Willem Henri Julius, he immersed himself in his books in a search for a means of improving the sensitivity of the capillary electrometer. When this did not work, he turned his attention to the reflecting galvanometer. In 1901 his modifications resulted in the string galvanometer. The highly-conductive silvered quartz "string" moved in response to rapid changes in electrical current. The movements of the string were magnified with the aid of a microscope, and recorded photographically. Two years later, in the *Proceedings* of the KNAW, he published the first electrocardiograms obtained with this instrument.[45] As well as making technical improvements, Einthoven also laid the foundations for a mathematical theory of the ECG and introduced a systematic nomenclature for electrocardiograph charts. In 1924 Einthoven was awarded the Nobel Prize for medicine in recognition of his work. Einthoven encountered great difficulty in getting his instrument onto the market because manufacturers had no confidence in the product. For a long time it remained unclear as to what the galvanometer actually measured. Initially the electrocardiograph was primarily a physiological instrument; the technique was not introduced into medicine until after 1908.[46] The use of the electrocardiogram did not become routine until it was standardized in 1938.

Christiaan Eijkman (1858-1930)[47] was educated at the boarding school run by his father. He then went to an HBS, and also took lessons in Greek and Latin. This meant that in 1875 he was able to go straight to the University of Leiden to study medicine. Later he moved to Amsterdam, where he gained his doctorate in 1883 under the supervision of Thomas Place. His thesis was on a physiological subject: polarization in the nerves. He went to the Dutch East Indies as a medical officer, contracted malaria and returned to Europe, where he studied bacteriology – first with Joseph Forster in Amsterdam and then with Robert Koch in Berlin. It was probably in Berlin that he met the pathologists Cornelis Winkler and Cornelis Adrianus Pekelharing, and in consequence he was asked in 1886 to join a commission charged with studying the disease beriberi in the Dutch East Indies as a researcher. Initially the commission believed that it had found the cause of beriberi in a microorganism that caused nerve cell degeneration, similar to the bacterium that caused diphtheria. The findings were not entirely satisfactory, however, and the research was continued in the military laboratory in Weltevreden in Batavia (present-day Jakarta), of which Eijkman was appointed director. The experiments that Eijkman conducted with his colleague Gerrit Grijns demonstrated that chickens with the symptoms of beriberi were cured when they were fed uncooked rice, whereas those that were fed cooked rice did not recover. Because the researchers were thinking in terms of a pathogen, they started by studying the cooked rice. When they failed to find an obvious pathogen, they shifted the focus of their attention to uncooked rice and they found that the coat on the rice grains that was polished away before cooking contained a substance which they initially took to be an antibody against infection. Eijkman's colleague Gerrit Grijns and the Inspector of Public Health on Java, Adolph Vorderman, were in fact the first people to make the connection with nutritional deficiency. Even so, it was not until 1926 that the first components of the vitamin B complex were isolated by B.C.P. Jansen and Willem Frederik Donath. In the end it was Eijkman who received the Nobel Prize in 1929, while the important contributions made by Grijns and Vorderman were not even mentioned.[48] Eijkman returned to the Netherlands for good in 1896, and two years later was appointed to the chair of public health and forensic medicine at the University of Utrecht. In this post he concentrated on tropical medicine, tropical physiology and bacteriology.

Mathematics

At the international level, mathematics in the nineteenth century had gradually come to focus on applied mathematics. The Netherlands, however, did not follow this trend. The revival in Dutch mathematics around 1895 was to a significant degree thanks to David Bierens de Haan (1822-1895), who brought cohesion back to the math fraternity in the Netherlands. It was at his instigation that the *Wiskundig Genootschap*, a mathematical society, founded a journal providing a bibliography of the mathematical literature. Under the guidance of the editor, Pieter Schoute, the whole Dutch mathematical community was involved in compiling and reviewing mathematical literature for the journal.[49]

Thanks to L.E.J. Brouwer's topology and intuitionism, and Bartel L. van der Waerden's modern algebra, Dutch mathematics made an important contribution to international science in the early years of the twentieth century.[50] Internationally, applied mathematics had become a self-contained discipline in the nineteenth century, setting itself apart from physics, but in the Netherlands the relationship with physics was still much closer. Thus the book on differential and integral calculus published in 1882 by the physicist Hendrik Antoon Lorentz was the textbook for applied mathematics.

Diederik Johannes Korteweg (1848-1941) was another important Dutch mathematician.[51] In 1863 he was already too old to benefit from the establishment of the HBS, but he was able to take advantage of the improvements to the Polytechnic School in Delft, where he trained as an engineer and later studied math. His first job was as a teacher at an HBS, and in 1877 he became mathematics assistant to Johannes van der Waals in Amsterdam. He gained his doctorate a year later, defending his thesis on the propagation speed of waves in elastic tubes. He assisted various scientists (Van der Waals, Van 't Hoff and others) with mathematical research until in 1881 he himself became professor of mathematics, mechanics and astronomy. Korteweg was very interested in the applications of mathematics. His fame rests on the Korteweg-de Vries Equation, which was defended in his PhD student Gustav de Vries's dissertation in 1894. This is a formula that describes self-sustaining nonlinear periodic oscillations. This was an important discovery for mathematics (chaos theory), but no less for technology and industry. Korteweg had a very international view of the world and was part of the "universalistic movement" of scientists that existed around 1900.

Luitzen Egbertus Jan – Bertus – Brouwer (1881-1966)[52] went to an HBS when he was just nine years old, completing his studies there by the time he was fourteen. Two years later he also had his humanities and sciences gymnasium diplomas in his pocket, and he went to Amsterdam to study math and physics. Brouwer became Korteweg's assistant. Brouwer was a mathematician, but he was also a nature-lover, mystic and philosopher, and he tried to unite these factors whenever he could. His publication *Leven, kunst en mystiek* (Life, Art and Mysticism) (1905) and his thesis *Over de grondslagen van de wiskunde* (On the Principles of Mathematics) (1907) are early examples of this. It was from these ideas that he later developed his intuitionist mathematics.[53] By using the term intuitionism, Brouwer wanted to express the idea that mathematics was a free activity of the mind, independent of any language and independent of experience. Mathematics was a form of "philosophy of the mind." An importance consequence of this was the abandonment of significant areas of classical mathematics. Brouwer's intuitionism unleashed a revolution in mathematics, which was based at that time either on the logicism of Bertrand Russell or on the formalism of David Hilbert. In 1912 Brouwer succeeded Korteweg as professor and his influence grew.

Astronomy

In the nineteenth century Dutch astronomy, practiced at the universities in Leiden and Utrecht, was primarily observational. In Leiden, Hendricus Gerardus van de Sande Bakhuyzen (1838-1923) had become director of the Leiden Observatory on the death of Frederik Kaiser in 1872. Van de Sande Bakhuyzen was not an innovator; he contented himself with the traditional work of measuring the positions of stars by means of a meridian arc. In 1898 the Observatory acquired a photographic telescope, but the results obtained with it in Leiden were disappointing. The young astronomer Antonie

Pannekoek noted the atmosphere of traditionalism and lack of enthusiasm in Leiden and this led him to take his leave in 1906. Willem de Sitter (1872-1934) was appointed professor while the director was Ernst Frederik van de Sande Bakhuyzen, his predecessor's younger brother. After Ernst Frederik's death in 1918, De Sitter drastically restructured the whole organization of the Leiden Observatory.

In Utrecht, Martinus Hoek had established a tradition of optical research, including work on the speed of light. His successor J.A.C. Oudemans (1827-1906) was professor of astronomy at the Sonneborgh Observatory in Utrecht from 1875 to 1898. He was an inspired and inspirational lecturer, but his lectures did not necessarily deal with astronomy. Meanwhile the observatory had not kept pace with the needs of the times, which meant that his successor Albert Antonie Nijland (1868-1936) had to improvise with the available space until 1907. Nijland was first and foremost an astronomer. He carried out research into the orientation of asteroids, position and brightness determinations of comets, and Jupiter and its moons. All the same, astronomical research was not entirely dormant in Utrecht in Oudemans's time. The credit for this must go to Willem Henri Julius (1860-1925), professor of physics and director of the physical laboratory from 1896 to 1925. He had a particular interest in solar research, studied the solar spectrum, took part in eclipse expeditions, and established a "solar watch."

The revival of Dutch astronomy can be found around 1900 in Groningen. In about 1850, researchers in Germany had embarked on the "Durchmunsterung" – the systematic mapping – of the night sky above the northern hemisphere. In about 1885, in Cape Town, the British astronomer David Gill had started to photograph the night sky over the southern hemisphere, with a view to using the photographs to calculate the positions of the stars. In Groningen it was Ko Kapteyn who brought this form of astronomy to the Netherlands. Jacobus Cornelius Kapteyn (1851-1922)[54] came from a family of teachers, was educated at the boarding school run by his father, and went to the University of Utrecht to study math and physics when he was seventeen. He was taught by Buys Ballot and C.H.C. Grinwis, and gained his doctorate in 1875 with a thesis on vibrating membranes. He became an astronomer at the Leiden Observatory, where he met Hendricus G. van de Sande Bakhuyzen. In 1877 he was appointed professor of astronomy and theoretical mechanics at Groningen. This university had neither an observatory nor a telescope, however, so that the prospects for the professorial post were distinctly limited. Kapteyn made great efforts to establish an observatory in Groningen, but his colleagues in Utrecht and Leiden did everything in their power to thwart his endeavors because they feared the competition.

Given the idea by an article by David Gill, between 1885 and 1900 Kapteyn worked in the physiological laboratory of his colleague Dirk Huizinga on determining the position of half a million stars in the southern hemisphere on the basis of the photographs Gill had taken at the Cape Town Observatory – this became known as the "Carte du Ciel." To do this, Kapteyn used a statistical method rather than the traditional empirical method. This work brought Kapteyn an international reputation and also restored Dutch astronomy to a prominent place in the scientific world. In 1906 he presented his "Plan of Selected Areas," an international collaboration between thirty observatories all over the world that would make it possible to catalogue the stars in 206 areas. It was not until

1913 that he got his own "astronomical laboratory." Using the huge volume of data at his disposal, Kapteyn also succeeded in identifying a structure in the Milky Way galaxy – which at that time was described as "the universe." Stars appeared to move in two main directions in relation to the sun: the theory of two star streams. This confirmed Kapteyn in his view that the galaxy had a spiral structure and that the sun was in one of the arms of the spiral. In 1922, shortly before his death, he published his definitive "theory of the universe" – a theory that is known to this day as the Kapteyn Universe. In addition to his work at the university, Kapteyn was also a very active popularizer. He was much in demand as a speaker at public lectures, and was always happy to enter into discussions with his audiences.[55]

Colonial science

"Colonial science" has already been mentioned in chapter 2. From the mid nineteenth century onward, a scientific career in the tropics was an attractive – because it was lucrative – alternative or addition to an academic career in the Netherlands. The tropical regions in the southern hemisphere offered interesting areas for research in many respects: tropical flora and fauna, geology and mineralogy, tropical medicine, tropical agriculture, anthropology, and astronomy. In the East Indies a botanical garden was established in Buitenzorg – present-day Bogor – in 1817 for the study of tropical plants and research into agricultural techniques and crops. In 1820 a special scientific committee for the Dutch East Indies, the *Natuurkundige Commissie voor Nederlands-Indië,* was set up to promote scientific – particularly botanical – research. Thirty years later, this committee was wound up and replaced by the *Natuurkundige Vereeniging in Nederlandsch-Indië,* which in 1858 was granted the right to use the title "royal" and became the *Koninklijke Natuurkundige Vereeniging.* The scientific climate was improved by the abolition in 1870 of the so-called Culture System, which dictated what crops were to be grown, etc., so that for the first time there was an independent middle class. This set the scene for the blossoming of the colonial sciences.[56]

Colonial science staged a revival in the eighteen-forties with the return of scientific expeditions to the colonies. First and foremost there was a need for geographical maps of the region, but there was also considerable interest in the presence of lucrative natural resources. The Utrecht astronomer J.A.C. Oudemans was one of the first in his field to go to the East Indies to map the region and establish the latitude and longitude of various places. The job kept him busy for twenty years. After his return to Utrecht in 1875 there was still so much work to be done that the modernization of astronomical research in Utrecht suffered as a consequence. His successor as professor of astronomy in Utrecht, Albert Antonie Nijland, concentrated on research in the tropics. The Dutch expedition that studied the solar eclipse of 1901 from West Sumatra was organized in part at his instigation, in association with the Utrecht physicist Willem Henri Julius, who was working on solar physics. After Oudemans' departure from the East Indies, astronomical research came to a standstill for a while. It was not until 1920 that, thanks to the efforts of the Dutch East Indies astronomical society, the *Nederlandsch-Indische Sterrekundige Vereeniging,* a permanent astronomical observatory was established in Lembang, a site that is virtually on the equator.[57]

Geomagnetic research of the Indonesian archipelago officially began in 1874, when Elie van Rijckevorsel, who was undertaking a scientific expedition in the region, was given permission to carry out measurements. This type of research was later organized under the umbrella of a research institute in Weltevreden, which in 1898 acquired the name *Koninklijk Meteorologisch en Magnetisch Observatorium* (KMMO). The KMMO only really started to flourish during Willem van Bemmelen's time as director (1908-1920). In 1898 the KMMO had been equipped with seismographic instruments which, in the nineteen-thirties, provided a new understanding of the source of earthquakes in the archipelago.[58]

The biologist Melchior Treub (1851-1910) was an influential figure in the development of colonial botany. In 1880 he took over as director of the botanical gardens, 's Lands Plantstuin in Buitenzorg, which flourished as never before under his leadership. He added an agricultural college, he founded a journal – *Mededeelingen* – which published the results of research, and he established a laboratory. Treub acquired an international reputation by persuading foreign researchers to work in Buitenzorg. He never missed an opportunity to lobby for scientific research in the Dutch East Indies and his efforts were successful: the *Maatschappij ter Bevordering van het Natuurkundig Onderzoek der Nederlandsche Koloniën,* a society to promote scientific research in the Dutch colonies, was set up in 1890. He also encouraged the planters and plantation owners to invest in research that might benefit their yields or the quality of their products. In the eighteen-nineties the botanical gardens were extended again. Several new laboratories– phyto-chemistry, pharmacology, agriculture, and field research – and a zoological museum were built, and a Buitenzorg Fund was established for pure scientific research by promising Dutch scientists.

Physical anthropology and paleontology also made great progress in the colonies, and foremost among the researchers in this field was, as mentioned earlier, Eugène Dubois (1858-1940). He had been interested in plants and fossils since childhood. He attended an HBS and in 1877 went to Amsterdam to study medicine. During his time at university he was assistant to Max Fürbringer, a pupil of Haeckel and Gegenbaur, and he taught comparative anatomy at the state training college for art teachers. In 1884 he qualified as a doctor of medicine, and two years later he became a lecturer in anatomy in Amsterdam. Through his comparative anatomical research he became increasingly interested in the phylogenesis of man and the animals. He pursued his interest and embarked on a quest to find the "missing link" between man and the apes. In 1887 he went to the East Indies as a medical officer second class in the KNIL, the Royal Dutch East Indies Army, and was soon stationed in the Sumatran interior. Here he found large numbers of fossils, but none of them human. In 1890, at his own request, he was transferred to Java, where he had more luck. In 1891 his workers found a molar, the top of a skull, and a femur, which Dubois claimed belonged to a humanoid – a creature that he called *pithecanthropus erectus* in the description he published in 1894. His scientific colleagues were not convinced that Dubois really had found a missing link, and he was widely criticized. Nevertheless, when he returned to the Netherlands in 1897 Dubois was made a part-time professor and in 1907 a full professor of crystallography, mineralogy, geology, and paleontology at the University of Amsterdam. He also became curator of the geological collection at Teylers Museum in Haarlem and director of the collection of East Indies fossils in Leiden.[59]

The end of an era

The second golden age of natural sciences in the Netherlands came to an end around 1914. Little is known about the reasons for this decline. What is clear is that World War I had an adverse impact on science, and can be regarded as the end of the period of growth. This is not to say that the Netherlands did not have any productive and famous scientists in the years between the wars. Great men like Paul Ehrenfest and Hendrik Anthony Kramers were certainly on a par with their predecessors, but their work did not come in for such lavish public praise. Between 1913 and 1953, in any event, no Dutchman won a Nobel Prize for Physics.

We shall look now at a number of factors that contributed to the end of the golden age. Further research will be required to establish what their relative significance may have been.

Was there a brain drain of academics? This does not seem to have been the case. Van 't Hoff's departure for Germany had been a blow,[60] but it was a more or less isolated instance. Van 't Hoff was the only major scientist to leave the Netherlands.

Were Dutch scientists overburdened with teaching duties so that they did not have enough time to devote to research? According to Van 't Hoff, this was certainly true in comparison with the situation in other countries. In 1895 (the year he left the Netherlands) he advocated the introduction of two different posts – that of researcher and that of teacher. Van 't Hoff was offered just such a dream position in Berlin, as a researcher with no teaching duties. He believed that the clause in the Constitution which stated, "Education is an object of national concern" should be amended to read "Education and research are objects of national concern." "May not there be, side by side with our men whose duty it is to teach and who may, if they have the time and the inclination, also do a little research, others whose duty it is to carry out research and who may, if they have the time and the inclination, also do a little teaching?"

Was there a lack of government policy? It was perhaps rather unsystematic by our standards; nevertheless there were plenty of sound initiatives. The government set up special commissions. The KNAW yearbook for 1900 reports on a commission appointed by the Dutch government to observe the total eclipse of the sun in the Dutch East Indies. In the same year, the minister also provided funding to set up a regional office to create a scientific catalogue. It is likely that cuts in the universities' research budgets played a significant role.

Was the end of the golden age related to the growing specialization and fragmentation in science? We have already seen that these phenomena were becoming apparent at the beginning of the glory days. It is striking that Dutch scientists, going against the general trend toward self-contained disciplines, tried to safeguard the unity of science.[61] The desire for interdisciplinary cooperation was evident – not least from the fact that all the prominent scientists enrolled as members of the Dutch Physics and Medicine Congress, which was founded in 1887. The result was that real cooperation was established between different disciplines, such as biology and chemistry, medicine and biology, and chemistry and physics.

Nonetheless, this desire for unity could not prevent a schism from forming between experimental and theoretical research. Scientists did one or the other. It is possible that this split contributed to the decline. In 1901 the mathematician J.C. Kluyver warned that the ties between mathematicians and physicists – once so close – had been lost. The physicists sometimes failed to understand mathematical language, while the mathematicians for their part had lost interest in physics problems, said Kluyver.

Did the relative decline in research have something to do with a change in the attitude of the general public? There is no doubt that there was a backlash against scientific research at the end of the nineteenth century. "Throughout the last two decades of the nineteenth century, the natural sciences were subjected to unprecedentedly fierce criticism. The attack was mounted by a broad alliance, drawn from artistic, philosophical and religious circles. The criticism struck both at the ambitions and at the values and implications of these sciences."[62] The offensive was a reaction to the positivist belief in progress that had characterized the eighteen-sixties and seventies. The critics accused science of having been unable to solve social and philosophical problems.

The physicists responded cautiously. "On the one hand they acknowledged that physics did not lay bare any unique, profound truths; on the other, however, they strongly denied that searching for truths and deeper meanings had anything to do with physics."

Around 1900 many physicists recovered their self-confidence as a result of a rapid succession of spectacular discoveries. Despite this, the outside world's attitude toward scientists was no longer what it had once been. The initiative to erect a statue to Huygens came to grief when the Hague City Council rejected the proposed design in 1908. K. van Berkel describes this event as symptomatic of the lack of recognition of and interest in the natural sciences at this time, and a harbinger of the subsequent gulf between the sciences and the humanities.[63]

Did Dutch researchers do too little to promote themselves abroad? Dutch scientists' contacts with colleagues in other countries do seem to have been built up painfully slowly. For many years Lorentz had virtually no contact with foreign researchers. It was not until 1897, at a German physics convention, the *Naturforscherversammlung* in Düsseldorf, that he ever met any German scientists. The frequency of his foreign appearances picked up after this (the International Physics Congress in Paris in 1900, as a speaker at the *Elektrotechnischen Verein* in Berlin in 1904, and at the *Société Française de Physique* in Paris in 1905, and a trip to the United States in 1906), but Dutch science would have been a much more obvious presence on the international stage if Lorentz had established contacts like these earlier on.

It seems that other European countries picked up on the new developments in quantum mechanics and the theory of relativity more quickly than the Netherlands. Lorentz continued to cling doggedly to the concept of the existence of the ether, even after the Americans Albert A. Michelson and Edward W. Morley had demonstrated in 1887 that this mysterious ether would have to move with the earth, which made its existence highly questionable. Einstein simply omitted the ether from his 1905 theory of relativity. Lorentz never opposed Einstein's theory, but at the same time he simply could not conceive of a world without ether. The Amsterdam research group probably also fell into decline because Professor Van der Waals Jr. was not interested in quantum mechanics.

And, lastly, might it perhaps have been the character traits of "the Dutch scientist" that stood in the way of continued development? According to the general view,[64] Dutch scholars had inquiring minds, but were individualists, not willing to accept the guidance of a teacher nor inclined to form schools. Vermij observes in this regard: "The Dutch style in the practice of science could perhaps be described as the style of merchants rather than producers. The high-flying idea, the development of bold new theories have never been highly regarded here. On the other hand, Dutch scientists always took care to be fully aware of the important developments that were taking place elsewhere, and they often played a significant role in the dissemination of these theories."[65]

Nationalism and science

There is an interesting relationship between nationalism and science. Crawford points out that while the institution of the Nobel Prize in 1901 undoubtedly increased the international nature of science and scientists' universal sense of solidarity, World War I rekindled the flames of nationalism.[66]

Dutch scientists around 1900 saw their research as part of a national tradition. They referred back to the national scientific heroes of the past and linked their renowned achievements with the present state of national science. In hindsight, it is clear that science was part of a more general movement toward "cultural nationalism." In other fields, too, there was an appeal for a new national élan around the turn of the century based on recalling the glories of an illustrious, usually seventeenth-century, past.

Professor Barend Stokvis, who chaired the first Physics and Medicine Congress in 1887, spoke in his opening address of the existence of a specifically Dutch approach to the practice of science. Its characteristics – independence, tenacity, keen powers of observation, technical skill, honesty, simplicity, and an eye for detail – were, said Stokvis, perfectly embodied in great scientists like Stevin and Van Leeuwenhoek. Stokvis admitted that those glory days were in the past, but they could return if the Dutch were to restore science to its rightful place: "We must educate our young people, not to look humbly to other countries, but in the firm conviction that a scientific education is also possible in their own land."[67]

Self-confident voices were also heard in other quarters. A certain J. Le Roy wrote in the *Album der Natuur* in 1898: "It is salutary for the national mood that the land of Simon Stevin and of Christiaan Huygens is still referred to with respect by the practitioners of science. The contribution made by Dutch scholars to the great scientific movement of the second half of this century is larger than many people know. The shades of Stevin and Huygens may be reassured, their spiritual descendants are upholding the old standard."

Some people even believed that they could discern unique preconditions for success in the Netherlands. Speaking of Van der Waals at the Physics and Medicine Congress in

1895, the chemist Johannes J. van Laar said, "And the chemists in Holland ... may think themselves fortunate to have had a demanding taskmaster like Van der Waals (and like Lorentz in Leiden), because as a consequence the standard of *Dutch* chemists stands out above that of most foreigners, who generally have an inferior education in mathematics and physics."

Was there such a thing as a "Dutch style" of research? John T. Merz, who examined the "scientific spirit" in France, Germany and England at the beginning of the century, believed that the differences in approach that had undoubtedly existed in earlier days had largely disappeared in the second half of the nineteenth century: "The great problems of science and life are now everywhere attacked by similar methods."[68] Even so, according to Merz, there were still differences in approach between Great Britain and the continent. Merz does not say whether the Netherlands displayed any special characteristics within this continental approach. Nor does he broach the question as to whether national research styles had an influence on a country's scientific rise or decline. France, for example, had acquired a prominent scientific position at the beginning of the previous century thanks to a style of scientific research that was strongly math oriented. Was it as a result of this approach that France lost her leading position in an age (at the end of the nineteenth century) when the mathematical approach was no longer in line with the nature of the subjects of research?

The "national" character of the way that science is practiced has been a widely discussed theme for centuries. According to Brookman, nationality can manifest itself in three "styles" – verbal, intellectual (a way of thinking), and socio-cultural (a way of life).[69]

As far as the first of these is concerned, for a long time French was the language of science. German, and to some extent English, came to the fore at the end of the nineteenth century. As regards the second point: in physics the "English school" had had many supporters in the last half of the century. This approach can be briefly summed up in the term "mechanistic": physical phenomena were reduced to classical mechanics. The French physicist Pierre Duhem poured scorn on English working methods in every imaginable way, enthusiastically aided and abetted by his German colleagues. Brookman has little to say on the third point.

Around the turn of the century there was a conviction in the Netherlands that Dutch scientific research differed in clearly definable respects from research elsewhere. The winner of a competition about the European reception of Lavoisier's theory wrote in 1893: "The Dutch chemists distinguished themselves from the Germans by their greater self-reliance, independence, and freedom; from the English and the Germans by their broader knowledge of foreign languages, by their more all-round development, and by their greater interest in everything that happened elsewhere in the realm of science. They were like the French, on the other hand, in their acumen, their objectivity, their correct appreciation of the phenomena that were observed, their aversion to derived [= abstract] reflections, and in their extensive interaction with other peoples of Europe. And since they, lastly, more than the English and Germans, shared in the general intellectual development of the eighteenth century, they were at the same time better prepared and equipped than they to play a fruitful part in the solution of the numerous questions that thrust themselves upon the human mind at that time."[70]

8

The future century of psychology

In 1909 Gerard Heymans (1857-1930), at that time vice-chancellor of the University of Groningen, revealed a vision of "The future century of psychology." A few generations hence, he said, the science of the mind would have assumed the prominent position that had been occupied in his day by the natural sciences. Heymans was at the threshold of a development in which psychology was to acquire a permanent and well-defined place in academia and society. Typical aspects of the culture in 1900 came together in his pioneering work – a fascination with the theory of personality and the study of heredity, initial steps in empirical research, the topicality of feminism and of a utopian humanism. The rise of the new science in the Netherlands is closely related to Heymans's explorations.

Psychology has since become an established science, but the memory of its founder in the Netherlands as a person has been erased. What we do know about him relates to his books and articles, his scholarly correspondence and a less than exciting career as a professor of philosophy and psychology spent entirely at Groningen University. Virtually no letters of a personal nature from Heymans have survived, the only time he ever kept a diary, as far as can be established, was during his years as a student, and even the traces he left in the lives of other people seem to have been primarily in the intellectual sphere. In 1922, when he was asked to write a chapter in the series *Philosophie der Gegenwart in Selbstdarstellungen,* whose formula expressly invited contributors to take an autobiographical approach, Heymans provided a list of what he had contributed to the theory of knowledge, ethics, aesthetics and metaphysics.[1] On the last page of this list, after the final entry, there is a line, followed by a paragraph on "persönliches, was den Leser interessieren könnte."[2] In it Heymans revealed that he was born in 1857 in Ferwerd, Friesland, that he studied political science and philosophy in Leiden and Freiburg, had been a professor at the University of Groningen since 1890, and owed a great deal to his teachers, Land and Windelband. Having shared these intimate details with his readers, he went on to say that he had been inspired by the young Kant and Fechner, and also by English philosophers like Hume and Sidgwick. Then, with the sudden haste of a man who wonders why he ever embarked on this in the first place, he concluded with a short list of titles of articles on psychology. Heymans lived his life without any consideration for biographers.

Reticent as Heymans was about his personal circumstances, however, he was completely candid about his scholarly motives and aspirations. This self-reflection is most evident in the lecture he delivered in 1927 on his retirement from his university post.[3] In it, Heymans looked back on what had essentially been a scholarly life. His audience knew that this life, measured against external yardsticks, could only be described as productive and well spent. Heymans's principal works on the theory of knowledge, ethics and metaphysics had been published by the prominent Leipzig publisher Ambrosius Barth and each of them had to be reprinted three or four times.[4] His articles on psychology had been published in the leading journals of the day, the German *Zeitschrift für Psychologie* and the French *l'Année psychologique*. Heymans' monograph on the psychology of woman was originally published in German (1910), but rapidly appeared in a Dutch translation (1911), followed in 1925 by one in French published by Félix Alcan.[5] Even an occasional address like the one on "The future century of psychology" (1909) was published in German and French, while the Dutch version was already into its third reprint by the following year.[6] The wide-ranging esteem in which Heymans was held at home and abroad was reflected in more than reprints and translations – he was also showered with honorary memberships and awards. From 1900 Heymans was a member of the Netherlands Acadamy of Arts and Sciences, the *Akademie van Wetenschappen*, assigned, after some hesitation between the science and the literature sections, to the latter; he was an honorary member of the German *Kant-Gesellschaft* and the British Psychological Association; the French government awarded him the *Légion d'Honneur* (a decoration he later returned in protest at the treatment of Dreyfus); and he had received invitations to take the philosophy chair at Leiden, Halle, Bonn and Berlin – all of which he turned down. It was thanks to him that the first Psychological Laboratory in the Netherlands was founded at the University of Groningen. His authority as a university administrator was undisputed. As vice-chancellor he had overseen the reconstruction of the academy building, which had been destroyed by fire in 1906. And, lastly, he was a celebrated teacher: his lectures attracted so many students – in some years a quarter of all the students at Groningen – that they had to be given in duplicate until the building of a special auditorium solved the problem. At no time in his academic career had Heymans lacked recognition, sympathy or a willing audience, and he could have looked back on all this with satisfaction and fulfillment in his valedictory lecture. In fact the tone of his address was depressed, bordering on the disillusioned.

"Two principal ideas"

All his work, began Heymans, had been based on two "principal ideas."[7] These could be found in the very first thing he had ever published on philosophy, an article about the methods of ethics that had appeared in 1881, in other words almost half a century before.[8] The first idea related to the indispensability of the empirical method in the philosophical sciences. As science and psychology had arrived, step by step, at laws and theories through empirical research, so metaphysics, as the science of the most general laws and theories, should make use of empirical methods. The same was true of normative disciplines like logic, aesthetics and ethics. The objects of these sciences, judgments about the true, the beautiful and the good, are only given to us in "introspection." It is the job of these sciences to investigate the cases and circumstances in which we *actually* arrive at logical, aesthetic or moral judgments.

Heymans described the second principal idea as the "belief in the reality of con-sciousness and of all conscious experiences."[9] He had always considered it an absurd idea that the consciousness was not consciousness but the movement of physical parti-cles. His life's work was directed toward testing an instinctive mistrust of materialism and theories derived from it. In psychology he had consequently sought the explanation for the phenomena of the consciousness in *psychological* laws, without invoking physiol-ogy or neurology.

Heymans told his audience that he could not relinquish either – empirical method, or authenticity of the consciousness – without losing all meaning from his oeuvre. So it was all the more remarkable, he went on, to note that the two principal ideas had been expressed in separate traditions in the philosophy of the last few centuries. Heymans began by describing this schism in terms that he derived from William James. There had traditionally been an opposition in philosophy between the "tough-minded" and the "tender-minded."[10] The former are rational and realistic, they seek the last elements of experience in the hope of explaining the changing of phenomena from their connections. The "tender-minded," in contrast, are sentimentalists and idealists. They need a fixed basis, independent of opinions and phenomena, for their thought and action, and they do not believe that it can be discovered in constantly changing experience. Heymans projected a *geographical* scheme over this *psychological* interpretation. In history the "tough-minded" were represented predominantly by English philosophers, the "tender-minded" by Germans. Heymans's elaboration of this division merits a lengthy quotation.

> It was, after all, the English philosophers who, starting with Locke, introduced the empirical method into the theory of knowledge, ethics and aesthetics; but in apply-ing this method they were always led by the preconceived view that in the final analysis all consciousness contents must be explainable as connections of observa-tions and observation residues, and thus arrived at the theories of empiricism, utili-tarianism and association psychology. The Germans always felt that this did not do justice to the specific character of the higher cognitive and will phenomena; but they were at the same time sufficiently impressed by the work being done on the other side that they regarded its findings as inherent in the application of the empirical method, and thus they believed that they had to seek other routes by which to approach these higher cognitive and will phenomena. This is why they usually completely accepted association psychology for the explanation of the *facts* of the consciousness, and totally segregated research into its *norms*; without stopping to think that these norms also manifest themselves in *actual* opinions and judgments, and influence *actual* acts.[11]

Heymans's argument then proceeded to take the turn that some of his more well-informed listeners must have dreaded. In a diagnostic analysis that can have taken no more than fifteen minutes to deliver, Heymans drew up the balance sheet of his life's work. This had consisted of an attempt to integrate the English and German traditions. He now had to concede that no one had followed him in this endeavor – worse yet, in his early work he had had to make a stand against one side, materialism and utilitarian-ism, and in his later work against the other side, idealism. This war on two fronts was unwinnable. One side took offence at the method, the other at the results. The upshot was that he had ended up in an "isolated position" in the academic community.[12] Ignoring awards, translations, reprints and other outward signs to the contrary, Heymans decided that his life's work had ended in failure.

It can do little to diminish the personal tragedy inherent in this conclusion, but ironically enough it is precisely because of his unhappy position between two philosophical and academic cultures that Heymans is such an excellent choice as the protagonist in a study of Dutch culture in a European context. Heymans represents the intellectual who, in the decades before and after the turn of the century, drew his inspiration to a significant degree from Anglo-Saxon and German (and to a slightly lesser extent French) culture. The fact that he tried so determinedly to persuade the scientific community to follow him in the integration of two cultures – and failed – provides a sharp focus on the outlines of these cultures.

There is a second argument for choosing Heymans. He wrote his works in German – the scholarly language of his day – and French. As we have seen, his articles and books were very well received outside the Netherlands. The fact that Husserl described Heymans in a letter to Heidegger as "eigentlich der einzige sehr ernste holländische Philosoph"[13] is a measure of Dutch influence in the opposite direction. The many reviews of his work in German, French and English journals, by such diverse philosophers as Bertrand Russell and Eduard von Hartmann, point the same way. The argument is one of symmetry. Of the Dutch philosophers who were active during this period, Heymans is the only one whose work provoked reactions that give an impression of the perception that people elsewhere had of Dutch culture.

The third argument, lastly, is the simplest. Heymans lived in interesting times. He was the first psychologist in the Netherlands, but at the same time the last to practice this profession in a personal union of psychologist and philosopher. The emancipation of psychology took place during his lifetime and he was consequently also the first person to be confronted with the question as to how psychology ought to be demarcated from disciplines like philosophy, neurology and physiology. Heymans saw how science was gaining an ever greater share in social management and government. In an age when many people believed that physics was "finished," Heymans tried to form a picture of the importance of a science of the mind and its value in such social issues as the position of women or the treatment of delinquents, and even in questions in the personal realm such as choosing a spouse or a philosophy of life. Much of what was at issue in the Netherlands had its origins in developments that had started earlier in England, Germany or France, but Heymans was among the intellectuals who had to determine their position as to what the reaction to these developments should be.

In what follows, the accent will lie primarily on the period between roughly 1890 and 1910. It was in these years that Heymans wrote his most important works. In 1890 experimental psychology hardly existed; by 1910 it was developing into a discipline with well-equipped laboratories, its own curriculum and a specific academic style. 1905 saw the publication of Heymans's philosophical magnum opus, the *Einführung in die Metaphysik*, a book that contained the formulation of his theory of panpsychism and contributed greatly to his international reputation. In 1909 he gave his lecture on the "future century

Gerard Heymans, portrait dating from *c.* 1895.

of psychology," which unleashed a storm of reactions in the Netherlands and beyond. What we can learn from Heymans about the position of a Dutch intellectual who took part in the most important European scientific and philosophical debates can be located in the two decades that span the year 1900.

Scientific psychology

The teaching post that Heymans accepted in 1890 covered education in "the history of philosophy, logic, metaphysics and psychology." The majority of Heymans's publications in the decade prior to his appointment related to the first three elements of the job description. True, he had studied political science at Leiden, but his chief interest had always been philosophy. He graduated in the fall of 1879, and took his doctorate in political science in the summer of 1880 on a methodologically oriented thesis.[14] The summer after that he acquired a second doctorate, this time in philosophy, having studied with the neo-Kantian Windelband. His second thesis was a critical treatise on utilitarianism.[15]

The articles that he wrote in the years that followed were also primarily philosophical, such as the one on the question of responsibility and reward[16] and a series on Kant's theory of knowledge.[17] His first two books after the theses, both published in the year he was appointed, dealt with the laws of scientific thought and the concept of causality.[18] All these writings qualified Heymans for a chair in philosophy – but on what grounds would the powers that be entrust the psychology course to him? The answer can be found in the view that in Heymans's conception psychology and philosophy had in common both their method – empirical research – and their object – phenomena of consciousness – so that to a certain extent they coincide. To be a philosopher one has to be a philosopher *and* a psychologist.

At the beginning of the 1890-1891 academic year, Heymans elaborated on this idea in his inaugural lecture "The experiment in philosophy."[19] By philosophy, he was referring here to the "newer philosophy," a science that was convinced of the relativity of knowledge and investigated the problems that arose out of this notion. Philosophy should try not to overcome this relativity, but to understand it from the inside out. Thus, argued Heymans, the newer philosophy dissolved "into the psychology of thought."[20] Like any empirical science, philosophy could also avail itself of the experiment. It has to be said that Heymans chose a broad definition of experimentation. Every observation of phenomena that have come about under selectively introduced conditions is an experiment. These phenomena could be sensory perceptions, aesthetic judgments, feelings of evidentness with a valid syllogism, but also conclusions of thought experiments or intuitions about causal relationships. The decisive factor is always that these perceptions, judgments, feelings and intuitions are given in the consciousness and thus, in the final analysis, belong to the domain of psychology.

The idea of psychology as the center of traditional philosophical disciplines recurs in the grant request, a two-and-a-half page handwritten letter, which Heymans submitted to the *College van Curatoren*, the university governing body, in 1891.[21] He starts by declaring that until recently scientific psychology could scarcely hope "to claim the status of an exact science." But the work of German researchers like Weber and Fechner had changed all that: the experiment had made its entrance, sensations could now be measured, the laws of the memory had been investigated, reaction times recorded. Moreover, experimental psychology now had two journals of its own. Psychology was a serious and exact discipline – the natural core, argued Heymans, of the different subjects he had to teach.[22] This new status should also be reflected in education. A second-hand report of experiments was just as unsatisfactory in a psychology course as it would be in natural science: lectures would have to be enlivened with demonstrations. And then follows the strategic twist that one still frequently comes across in grant applications to this day.

The instruments and other equipment needed for experiments during lectures are made available in abundance for the various empirical sciences; only psychology is an exception in the Netherlands. I specifically say: in the Netherlands. For several foreign universities are allocated larger or smaller government grants annually to set up and maintain psychological laboratories.[23]

The tenor is clear. If the University of Groningen wants to be a force to be reckoned with in the development of this new, advanced science, money will have to be forthcoming. And Heymans gets straight down to cases: he needs a Hipp chronoscope (280 Marks), a pendulum apparatus for complication experiments (150 Marks), a time sense apparatus (130 Marks), plus a stereoscope, tuning forks, tone meters, scales, etc. On the basis of "information I have obtained from German professors whom I know," Heymans could say that the University of Göttingen spent 800 Marks and the University of Leipzig spent 1500 Marks a year on their psychological laboratories. After these sums, Heymans's own proposal in his concluding sentence must have come as something of a relief to the Groningen governors. "The undersigned assumes, on the grounds of this and other information, that an annual grant of 200 guilders, added to an initial grant of 400 to 500 guilders, would enable him to set up and maintain a psychological laboratory that meets the most stringent standards."[24]

The letter had the desired effect. Heymans received a lump sum of 500 guilders for 1892, and an annual grant of 200 guilders in subsequent years. There was as yet nothing resembling a laboratory in the modern sense – an institution where knowledge is generated by experimental means. Heymans kept his instruments at home and took them to lectures when he wanted to give a demonstration. At home, however, he did fit out a room in which he could experiment in peace and quiet. In 1905 he got the renowned Dutch architect Hendrik Berlage to design a villa on Ubbo Emmiussingel (now number 108). At the rear of the second floor, next to the study, was a spacious room for experiments. It was not until 1909 that the "laboratory" moved to the university.

Bills from instrument makers allow us to reconstruct Heymans's buying policy fairly accurately. He rapidly acquired a Hipp chronoscope – a precision timing device that was the beating heart of every psychological laboratory.[25] It was followed by tuning forks, rotation apparatus, a Bunsen photometer, electromagnets, a camera obscura, kymographs with recording drums, episcotisters and olfactometers. Within a few years Heymans had put together a standard set of experimental equipment. The great majority of the instruments were ordered from German firms like Zimmermann – supplier to Wundt – and Spindler & Hoyer,[26] but apparatus was not all that came from Germany.

Inhibition

Heymans's first series of experiments was in the realm of psychophysics, a discipline that had its origins in German physiology. In the mid nineteenth century the physiologist Ernst Weber (1795-1878) had determined experimentally how large the minimum difference between two weights had to be in order for a person to detect a difference. This "just noticeable difference" proved to be in a fixed ratio of 1:30 to the standard weight. If 1 gram had to be added to a 30-gram weight for the difference to be noticeable, 2 grams would have to be added to a 60-gram weight. The ratio, which is now known as the Weber fraction, differs for each of the senses: the eye, for instance, perceives relatively smaller differences than the organs of taste. In 1860 Gustav Fechner (1801-1887) refined this ratio to produce the law that bears his name: it states that the strength of a sensation increases as the logarithm of stimulus intensity. Fechner thus formulated not only a formal

Sketch of Heymans's house by H.P. Berlage, built in 1905.
Now number 108 Ubbo Emmiussingel, Groningen.

relationship between stimulus and sensation, he also proved that psychological phenomena could be measured. The first generation of psychologists revered him as the researcher who had opened up the human mind to measurement and number.

In his experiments, Heymans investigated the phenomenon that a sensation loses intensity or even disappears in the event of the simultaneous occurrence of a second sensation. This "inhibition" is the reason why a weak pain stimulus in one hand can no longer be felt as soon as the test subject feels a slightly stronger pain stimulus in the other hand. Inhibition effects of this kind occur both within and between sensory domains, and Heymans tried to quantify the properties of psychological inhibition.

It was not only the subject of his research but the style of his experimentation that was German through and through. The historian of psychology Danziger defined three "experimental cultures" in early psychology, each with a specific geographical source.[27] In the clinical model, developed in French psychiatry, the roles of the investigator and the test subject were fixed. The investigator, usually a male doctor, had a hierarchical relationship with the test subject, typically a female patient. Their relationship was characterized by a difference in status and knowledge: the test subject demonstrated the theoretical hypothesis formulated by the investigator. The same difference in status between investigator and test subject also existed in the experimental model that Francis Galton (1822-1911) introduced into English psychology, but there was no question here of experimenting duos. In order to measure differences in intelligence, memory and other psychological characteristics, large numbers of test subjects were subjected to psychological tests. Their individual performances were only of interest to the investigator as results in a statistical series.

Heymans's early experimental work was inspired by what Danziger called the "Leipzig model" and which was, indeed, found in its purest form in Wundt's laboratory. As in the clinical model, the investigator and test subject acted as a duo but, in contrast to the medical-psychiatric experiment, they could switch roles. Sometimes one researcher would act as the test subject and his colleague would administer the stimuli, then the former would become the investigator. Both researchers were familiar with the theory being tested. Within the constraints of the experiment, their relationship was free of any form of hierarchy: professional, theoretical, social. They often appeared jointly as the authors of the article in which the findings were published.

Heymans conducted his inhibition experiments with regular test subjects, and for a long time with just a single test subject – his wife Antonia Barkey, whom he had married in 1881. She did not appear as co-author, but she did embody Wundt's ideal of the dedicated, disciplined test subject. The first series of experiments in which she took part involved color perceptions. Heymans and his by degrees "extremely well-trained observer" then experimented with sensations of taste, hearing and touch. They worked through hundreds of tests for each of the senses. The experiments with sensations of pressure on the skin alone involved no fewer than 6,680 tests. Adding up all the tests carried out in this period – the couple set to work immediately after breakfast – produces a total of 11,008 experiments. Mrs. Heymans must have loved her husband very much.

In the tradition of German psychology, the individual test subject was conceived as the access to what was later called the "generalized mind."[28] In an article about his new

Heymans and his wife Antonia Barkey (1857-1910).

A psychological laboratory was set up in the college building after the rebuilding in 1909.
The photograph above, taken in 1914, shows "Room C." The hatch above the table on the right
gave onto a lightproof and soundproof room. The researchers and equipment were in Room C;
the test subject sat in the other room. Communications during the test were by telephone.
The photograph below, taken ten years later, is of the same wall. The rapid increase in the
experimental instruments available gave the room an appearance familiar from German
laboratories of the time – a cross between a telegraph office and an engine room.

laboratory, Heymans explained that the characteristics of the test subject as an individual have no significance, the unit of study is the systematic relations in human consciousness and these laws are the same for everyone.[29] With his German theoretical background, German equipment and German experimental conventions, it comes as no surprise to learn that Heymans chose a German journal – the *Zeitschrift für Psychologie* – in which to publish his findings. Between 1899 and 1909 it carried seven long articles about psychological inhibition.[30]

The heredity questionnaire

Heymans's experiments on inhibition came under the heading of general psychology, focusing on the processes and characteristics that are the same for everyone, and so too did his experiments on visual illusions. The German physicist Müller-Lyer had published his illusion with the inward- and outward-pointing arrows in 1889, and Heymans tried by experimental means to identify the factors that inhibit or enhance the illusory effect.[31] A second series of experiments extended the research to include the German astrophysicist Zöllner's "herringbone illusion."[32] These experiments, again using Mrs. Heymans, but this time fellow professors and a few students as well, required thousands of trials, 3,334 to be precise. But even when added to the experiments on psychological inhibition, Heymans's work in general psychology pales into insignificance, in terms of scope, against his efforts in differential psychology.

This domain of psychology is concerned with the study of individual differences, such as intelligence, personality, temperament, etc. The origins of this branch of psychology most definitely do not lie in Germany – Wundt always kept well away from it and the majority of his colleagues followed his lead – but in England. Danziger's description of the English experimental culture as the "Galton model" is entirely accurate, because it was Francis Galton who asked the first questions in this direction, developed a methodology for it and designed the statistical tools for processing and analyzing the findings. Each of these elements can be found in Heymans' study of individual differences.

In 1905 Heymans and his Groningen colleague in psychiatry Enno Dirk Wiersma (1858-1940) sent a questionnaire to all the family doctors in the Netherlands – around three thousand of them. In the accompanying letter they wrote that psychology had no reliable data about the hereditary aspects of psychological characteristics. They asked the doctors to select a family they knew well and answer a series of ninety questions about the father, the mother and each of their children. They chose doctors, wrote Heymans and Wiersma, because it could be assumed that their scientific training and the nature of their work would have given them a knowledge of human nature.[33] It is evidence of the prestige that psychology as a science had meanwhile acquired – and perhaps also of the importance that doctors attached to questions of heredity – that 458 completed questionnaires were returned. Their heredity questionnaire gave Heymans and Wiersma access to no fewer than 2,523 personal assessments. This material was to be the source of essentially all of Heymans's work on differential psychology: his personality theory, his psychology of woman, even his ideas about eugenics.

Galton was the first to ask whether and to what extent psychological characteristics are hereditary. The theory of evolution had focused attention on biological differences and their value in the process of variation and selection. Galton – who was Charles Darwin's cousin – set himself the task of linking evolutionary theory to psychological characteristics. In *Hereditary Genius* (1869) he published an analysis of the family trees of 269 English high court judges between 1660 and 1865. It revealed that one in nine judges was the son, father or brother of someone who was himself a judge. This analysis was supported by research into the family connections of other "persons of eminence" – the description is Galton's – such as statesmen, artists and writers. The general conclusion was that talent "runs in the family" according to a distribution that corresponds with the laws of heredity. Responding to the accusation that he had failed to give due weight to the contribution of nurture and environment in the development of talent, Galton decided to submit a questionnaire to the members of the Royal Society, asking for information about their family backgrounds, education, character, talents outside the field of science, etc. The hundred or so reactions he received formed the basis of *English Men of Science* (1874).

With these two books Galton had established a new discipline, the psychology of individual differences, given the agenda of the subject a Darwinist flavor, and provided its practitioners with a tool, the questionnaire. Heymans and Wiersma's heredity questionnaire was the first large-scale use of that tool in the Netherlands. The questions were grouped around traditional psychological categories like emotions, reason and propensities. The characteristics were always illustrated with examples. "Suspicious" was followed between brackets with "e.g. of servants; believes he/she has secret enemies"; the example for "credulous" was "gives credence to advertisements." By not underlining, underlining or double underlining characteristics, the doctors could give their opinion about such bipolar characteristics as quickly appeased/holds a grudge, attached to old memories/taken up with new impressions, broad outlook/narrow-minded, avaricious/altruistic, compassionate/selfish, reformist/conservative, and so on. Some of the questions, with at most a little updating of the jargon and the addition of a seven-point scale, still appear in present-day personality questionnaires. Others immediately reveal the yawning gulf of almost a century, for example where Heymans and Wiersma ask whether the subject treats the servants well ("makes them feel their inferior position as little as possible") or want to know whether he or she is an "anarchist, socialist, spiritualist, theosophist, vegetarian, teetotaler, adherent of natural cures, adherent of spelling reform." A "yes" on two or more elements characterized the subject as someone who tended toward modernism.

The heredity questionnaire generated an overwhelming amount of material. The initial rough processing alone – converting several thousand responses to ninety questions into percentages – must have taken months of calculations. In their first article on the questionnaire, Heymans and Wiersma published ninety tables with the raw scores of fathers, mothers, daughters and sons for each characteristic studied, and a summary of them in percentages.[34] Their conclusion about the hereditary component of each characteristic was always based on simultaneous variation: if the presence of a given characteristic decreased in the children uniformly in line with whether this characteristic was found in both parents, one of the parents or neither of the parents, it was decided that there was a hereditary component. In the case of musical talent, for instance, the percentages in the children under these three conditions fell from 85 percent through 40 percent to 9 percent. The relative contribution of father or mother was also examined. The father was primarily responsible for some characteristics – including rapidly appeased, ambitious, literary talent – for other characteristics – such as musical, tolerant, sporting – it was the mother. But most characteristics, concluded Heymans and Wiersma, were passed on equally by both parents.

It is typical of the positivist slant of science at the time – first facts, then hypotheses, lastly laws and theories – that in a second article Heymans and Wiersma reported on the elaborate further mathematical processing of the questionnaire material.[35] They expressed the contributions of the two parents – again for each characteristic individually – in heredity coefficients, calculated, as a control, according to two different methods. It was only after this statistical refinement that a third article dealt with methodological and theoretical questions.[36]

One of the questions that Heymans and Wiersma asked themselves was whether the relations that they had found "really are based on heredity and not, wholly or in part, simply on upbringing."[37] The question is an obvious one, since in their approach the contribution of heredity could not be separated from that of nurture, as they themselves conceded. The percentages found for musical ability, for instance, could equally well be consistent with the effect of upbringing. However, they were not willing to take this possibility really seriously. If one compared characteristics in their questionnaire that are strongly influenced by upbringing – diligence, patriotism, political views – with characteristics on which upbringing has little effect – comprehension, memory – the heredity coefficients were of the same order of magnitude. Considerably higher coefficients were found for most characteristics. There are no references to twin studies like those that Galton had already conducted in the United Kingdom; the cursory treatment of the question of nature and nurture is yet another indication that, as far as Heymans and Wiersma were concerned, the dominant influence of genetic factors was both their conclusion and their starting point.

Heymans's Cube

Psychology was only an examination subject for philosophy students. When Heymans took up his post in 1890 there was no more than a handful of them and this situation did not change in the first decade of the new century. The rapid rise in the popularity of Heymans's lectures in the same period had to do with factors outside the university curriculum. In the first place, there had long been considerable interest in psychology among educationalists and teachers. Derksen qualified the description of Heymans as the founder of psychology in the Netherlands by pointing to the literature on psychology that already existed.[38] It was written by and for teachers, inspired by German educationalists. Heymans' rise to fame has obscured this early psychological work; the notion that scientific psychology in the Netherlands began in 1892 – as commemorated by the society of Dutch psychologists, the *Nederlands Instituut voor Psychologen*, in 1992 – is in part the

The phlegmatic citizen

Heymans himself must have had the feeling that his typology brought order to ideas and suspicions that he had long cherished. The opposition between people with primary and secondary reactions is already evident in the heredity questionnaire. Ten questions asked whether the subject was quickly comforted or remained upset for a long time, liked or disliked change, was guided in his actions by the thought of the distant future or the immediate result and so on. There is little doubt that Heymans's sympathies lay with the secondary reaction phlegmatics. Theirs were sober, industrious and persevering natures, prudent, even-tempered and sensible. In politics they adopted a moderate or conservative stance, leaving the more radical positions to primary functioning people. Fortunately for Heymans, the secondaries and the actives were significantly over represented in the heredity questionnaire – the result, he believed, of a beneficial Darwinist mechanism: evolution gradually eliminated their opposites. One might also say that the phlegmatics combined in their persons the bourgeois virtues that were also those of Heymans himself and which – viewed more broadly – characterized the social stratum from which he came.[46]

But the moral dimension of the secondary function was expressed much more clearly in an article dating from 1901, in other words before Heymans could quote the results of his heredity questionnaire or biographies study.[47] This article, officially a review of two essays on criminology by the Amsterdam police surgeon and novelist Arnold Aletrino (1858-1916),[48] was in fact a frontal attack on what criminology in the style of Lombroso had produced in terms of theories, methods and findings. Aletrino was no more than a trigger, albeit as "the most complete embodiment of the methodological errors of which, in my view, many practitioners of criminal anthropology are guilty to a greater or lesser degree" a very suitable one.[49] Heymans began by commenting on the physical abnormalities that Aletrino held to be characteristic of madmen and criminals. They were anything but characteristic, believed Heymans, because they also occurred in people "with impeccable ways of life" and were absent in some criminals. The statistical relations between the mentally handicapped and criminals could not be equated, but suggested a third variable. This variable, proposed Heymans, was degeneration. The degenerate was less capable than other people of concentrating his attention. He was at the mercy of the impressions of the moment and did not think about consequences. Degenerates were "children of the moment." They reacted impulsively to insults, acceded to requests without thinking and, with their low threshold of tolerance for monotonous work, rapidly descended into "vagabondage and begging."[50]

Heymans thus characterized the degenerate as someone with a serious lack of secondary function and in passing dragged the study of the criminal within the boundaries of his own subject. The criminal, after all, was someone with a *psychological* defect: his powers of judgment and concentration were impaired. If we take a step or two back, we can also see a strategic interest in this maneuver.[51] Where criminal anthropology was dominated by forensic medicine around the turn of the century, Heymans was demanding a role for psychology in the study of criminal behavior. His disparaging remarks about the scientific content of criminal anthropology are also of a piece with this atmosphere of implicit rivalry. He portrayed the subject as an immature science in which "the precise definition and the strict proof" – second nature to the established sciences – were all too often lacking.[52] Heymans drew a contrast between criminal anthropology and "orderly science," with the suggestion that psychology was better equipped for the study of the criminal than the theoretically and methodologically erratic criminal anthropology.

Heymans got his doctoral students to explore the domain thus claimed for psychology. In 1905, several years after Heymans's fierce attack – unusual for him – on Aletrino, Van Dijck obtained his doctorate with a thesis in which the personalities of different categories of criminals were described in the terms used in Heymans's typology.[53] Other doctoral candidates focused on the psychology of the arsonist[54] and the vagrant.[55] The psychological-criminological program of Heymans and his students was distinctive enough for it to be described as the "Groningen school."

Shortly before his death, Heymans completed an introduction to differential psychology entitled *Inleiding in de speciale psychologie*, aimed at a broad readership.[56] Heymans's typology had already acquired great popularity among the general public. Part of its attraction, suggested Van Strien and Feij, lay in what has to be described as a "literary achievement": Heymans portrayed his types convincingly and recognizably, with an eye for detail.[57] A second factor was the scientific prestige associated with this typology. The large-scale questionnaire that had supplied the material, the sophisticated statistics with which the factors were identified, the experimental machinery that established the scope of the secondary function – all this contributed to the idea that literary speculation about character and personality had now made way for exact measurement. This was also the sense that was put across in textbooks for the teachers colleges. In dealing with Heymans's typology ("shrewd in structure and scientifically verified") the experiments to determine secondary function were described at length, as was the "study of respectable magnitude" that was associated with the questionnaire and the biographies.[58] Quantification of psychological characteristics, one could say, had acquired an authority of its own outside academic psychology. From being a methodological procedure, "scientific verification" had become a quality mark. It was precisely this seal of approval, this quantification conceived as sanction, that was also to give Heymans's psychology of woman social authority.

"The amazing complexity of the female mind"

In 1878, as a student in his early twenties, Heymans confided a number of thoughts about women to his diary. Woman, he noted, must remain aloof from social functions, not because she is not suited to them, but because they will sully her purity. If she wishes to develop, then it should rather be in areas where she will not get her hands dirty. "This is why woman (not women!) is so divine, because she gives the purest picture of the ideal, who rules without mixing with brute strength."[59] Some thirty years later "woman" would again be the subject of reflection for Heymans when he was working on his monograph *Psychologie der Frauen* (1910). Woman is no longer pure and divine, she is now the bearer of a pattern of psychological characteristics. She has transformed from ideal into a scientific problem, more specifically a problem that belongs in the realm of differential psychology and has to be studied with the methods of that discipline – the questionnaire and the experiment.

But all the differences aside, there is one detail that still connects the 1878 note with the 1910 monograph. The distinction implicit in the formulation "woman (not women!)" recurs in the introductory pages of the *Psychologie der Frauen*. Just as in 1878 what applied to "woman" did not apply to all individual women, so the "woman" who is the subject of the psychology of women does not correspond with all individual women. In the psychology of gender differences, woman is not an idealization or abstraction, but a statistical construct. She is the summary of averages. The correct formulation is not "woman has or women have characteristic A; not even most women have characteristic A; but only women on average have characteristic A to a greater degree than men."[60]

Heymans wrote his psychology of the *femme moyenne* at the invitation of two German psychologists, Ebbinghaus and Meumann, who assumed that Heymans would be able to use the material from his heredity questionnaire for a study of the psychological differences between man and woman. A series of books on the subject had already appeared around the turn of the century. An extremely active women's movement had opened the debate about the position of women in public life, in academic study, in science and politics. The Dutch contribution to this international debate must, in Heymans's perception, have been limited: only two Dutch publications figure in his bibliography, an insignificant number compared with the three Italian, eight Anglo-Saxon, twelve French and twenty-six German books on the list. The book that Heymans himself added in 1910 was to dominate the debate about the position of women in the Netherlands until the beginning of World War II.[61]

The introduction to *Psychologie der Frauen* contains three caveats. The first is that unequal characteristics do not necessarily imply any difference in value; the second that the differences between man and woman are not qualitative but gradual; the third that these differences are statistical in nature. Then begins a disciplined march through the findings of the heredity questionnaire. Heymans's favorite secondary function soon puts in an appearance in the first chapter. Current views ascribed a lack of secondary function to woman, that fickle creature, but there were nonetheless strong indications that her thoughts and actions were no less affected than men's by her past experiences. How else can one explain female tact, "that wonderful sensitivity that enables her, with infallible assurance, to find precisely that nuance in word, tone of voice, look, which is appropriate to comfort a crying child, calm an angry man or fatally wound a hated enemy?"[62] It is to this same secondary function that woman owed her capacity for "always seeing that which she has once loved in the flattering light of that old love, despite great disillusionment, so that in general the love of the wife and mother can withstand much greater shocks than that of the husband or father."[63] What is taken to be a shortage of secondary function, suggested Heymans, is actually an excess of sensibility. The female pattern of characteristics corresponds with that of the male artist. In her sympathies she is hot or cold rather than lukewarm; compared with woman, the average man is, in the words of Laura Marholm, "ein meditativ rauchender Organismus" – which Heymans considered "drastic" but tellingly put.[64]

At ninety pages long, the chapter on the female intellect is almost a book within a book. It touched on such topical social issues as women's emancipation and the admission of women to university study and public office. Votes for women – of which Heymans, as a member of the Dutch women's emancipation union, the *Bond voor Vrouwenkiesrecht*, was a supporter – were not to be introduced for another ten years or so, in 1919, but female students were already far from the exception. Around 1910 female students accounted for some fifteen percent of the total student body; in Heymans's own Faculty of Humanities and Philosophy the figure was close to thirty percent.[65] Several of Heymans's fellow professors had daughters who were studying.[66] This meant that woman's suitability for study could be discussed in the light of actual results and that lecturers had already had their first experience of female students. For Heymans, the use of a tried and trusted tool was self-evident.

In February 1909 the 214 professors and lecturers at the Universities of Amsterdam, Utrecht, Groningen and Leiden were sent a questionnaire asking "which of the following characteristics (37 in number) do you have the distinct impression you have encountered more in male students, more in female students, or in equal measure in both?"[67] The questions enquired about memory, general knowledge, critical faculties, diligence, love of the subject, receptiveness, dexterity, abstraction ability, etcetera. The responses were an extension of the results of surveys previously conducted in Germany (1897)[68] and France (1903)[69]. In the judgment of the (male) professors, the studying *homme moyen* can apply what he has learned through his own thinking or research, he reads material around and outside the examination requirements, studies sensibly ("not slavishly"), is highly observant, has good logical reasoning powers and can identify the essentials, if necessary he can think up something new and continues to read and publish after he graduates. The female student is persistent and industrious, studies conscientiously, has a good memory, attends all the lectures and is highly obedient and receptive to good advice. She excels in subjects that assume factual knowledge, such as anatomy, but performs less well in clinical research, where it is necessary to apply knowledge independently. Heymans completed the picture with a few anecdotes, like that from the German physiologist Vogt, who "found in his female listeners an excessive tendency to take notes, to the extent that they actually ignored the preparations that were passed around."[70]

Heymans had a great deal of confidence in the findings of his questionnaire. There would undoubtedly have been individual prejudices about women among the professors, he felt, but they did not all tend in a particular direction and the law of large numbers meant that they would cancel one another out. The differences indicated by the findings were also much too large to be attributed to coincidental errors; they either had to have a basis in reality or reflect a systematic error – such as a common prejudice. But this last was effectively impossible, said Heymans, for the respondents were, after all, "all scientifically trained men, who were accustomed to test their views against the facts every day; it is almost inconceivable that the often many years of experience that such men have would not enable them to correct an unfounded traditional opinion."[71] Moreover, had the professors not – contrary to the received wisdom – indicated that in practical scientific work female students actually displayed *less* dexterity than male students?

The response to the professorial survey was not great. Just over seventy forms were returned, some of them with only a few of the questions answered. Not all of the professors who filled out a form had personal experience of female students. Furthermore, the questionnaire did not ask for judgments about specific individuals, as the family doctors had had to give, but for general impressions, which made the answers susceptible to distortion by prejudices. This was a criticism leveled at Heymans from close to home. His own student Anna Wisse wondered "whether a large number of these 74 professorial respondents had not enhanced their scanty impressions with their own preconceptions, which were not entirely free of prejudice."[72] Heymans promptly gave Wisse the financial resources for a questionnaire among the students themselves.[73] Her findings corresponded almost exactly with those from the survey of professors: professors and students were evidently touchingly at one about how male and female students differed from each other. Heymans incorporated Wisse's results in later editions of his book.

The statistics on course results were another source of information. Heymans asked for the results of university examinations for the 1903-1908 period, arranged them in tables and found that a significantly greater percentage of women passed in all the faculties and in all types of exam.[74] They also tended to graduate *cum laude* slightly more often. Nevertheless women were no match for men when it came to what he called "real scientific achievements."[75] History showed that great discoveries and inventions were the work of men. There was no female Newton, no Gauss, no Helmholtz; mathematics did have a Sophie Germain and a Sophia Kovalevsky, but even they were inferior to the most gifted male mathematicians. Heymans sought the explanation for this in the emotional tendency of the female mind. Women focus on the concrete and specific, they perceive abstraction and analysis as bloodless. Woman has a "non-juridical nature." Even if a science is in tune with her interests – Heymans mentioned botany – she will be disappointed because "the rigorous scientific work" does not satisfy her love of flowers.[76] The biographies study provided corroborating evidence. Scientific work thrives best "in the soil of moderate sensibility."[77] In terms of his own typology: nervous and sentimental individuals tend to be artists; it is only when sensibility is weakened, such as in sanguine and phlegmatic people, that a Bacon, Gauss or Darwin emerges.

Women are more likely to have the type of mind that is generally described as "intuitive." Heymans gave a few examples from everyday life:

We are talking to a woman we do not know very well about a somewhat delicate subject. We feel ill at ease and awkward, have difficulty finding the right words, interrupt ourselves and become confused. She, in contrast, speaks simply and naturally, is not lost for words and yet does not say a single word that ought not to have been said. … Or lastly: a woman's opinion of some acquaintance or other differs considerably from ours; we adduce grounds, she never or almost never does; yet subsequent experience often proves her right. Such and similar achievements are the pride of women; they rightly regard them not as individual, but as gender-linked privileges, and like to make gentle mock of the dumb men, who cannot see anything that they have not laboriously worked out first.[78]

Here Heymans was formulating a traditional opposition – that between the logical man and the intuitive woman – but his evaluation of this difference was anything but traditional. There is not a trace of condescension in his treatment of female intuition. On the contrary, almost, the lack of intuition in men is a regrettable defect that is only partly compensated for by logic. The intuitive judgment derives its quality from the secondary function. Women's conclusions are based not only on the conscious grounds of the moment, but also on collected previous experiences. As a result, a certain "inference may apparently suddenly surface in the consciousness, without its even being possible later to account for they way it came about."[79] Women involve more reasons in their considerations than the premises that fit into a simple syllogism. The fact that not all of these reasons are accessible to the consciousness means that women feel disoriented when asked for their arguments.

Heymans attributed the majority of the psychological differences between man and woman to women's greater sensibility. They may be able to remember things better than men, but their sensibility makes their memory more selective: they only retain what interests them. The consequences are anyone's guess: "there are women who assert that they cannot possibly find their way around a railroad timetable; others who never learn to use a compass when out on a walk; yet others who are incapable of imprinting on their memory even the most rudimentary outlines of historical chronology, and are always uncertain as to whether Napoleon lived before or after the Crusades, and so on *ad infinitum*."[80] But the same sensibility also confers positive characteristics on woman. She has a livelier imagination and a "generally acknowledged greater eloquence." Girls learn to talk earlier than boys and continue for longer in old age. Women find the right words more easily than men, so that "doctors and lawyers always prefer to turn to women to get clear and accurate explanations."[81]

In the last chapter, Heymans discussed the explanations for the psychological differences between man and woman. The psychological difference is too constant in different eras and varying social circumstances to be regarded as a "cultural addition." We are dealing here with a "very old inheritance." This inheritance may be a product of natural selection, so that the psychological differences are a reflection of the "character traits that each of the sexes values most highly in the other." Above all, however, we have to be aware that we are on the border of speculation. It is not until we have "very much more numerous, but above all much more accurate and much more surely supported data" that we can allow ourselves a substantiated standpoint.

On the crest of the first feminist wave, *Psychologie der Frauen* went through four Dutch and two German impressions. In 1925 it was translated into French. The second feminist wave brought renewed interest in it. The divided reception accorded Heymans's work among feminist authors, both then and now, is striking. For every fierce critic[82] there is a corresponding sympathizer.[83] Even now it would not be easy to get agreement as to whether Heymans was a misogynistic scholar. If he was a misogynist, his misogyny was certainly not of the traditional kind. Nowhere in Heymans's work, unlike in the works of German authors like Möbius and Runge, does one find any treatises about smaller skulls and lighter brains, no warnings about the deleterious effects of "men's work" on femininity, the danger to fertility or the irreconcilability of scholarship and motherhood. He opposed Lombroso's assertion that woman's intuitive nature puts her closer to the animals, which live by instinct. His high regard for intuition's contribution in forming an opinion appears to be sincere. He was evidently well read in international feminist literature and, where possible, derived his own views from empirical research. On the other hand, it is not difficult to quote passages from his book that prove just how much he was enmeshed in the prejudices and established opinions about women that prevailed in his day. His refusal, in the discussion of his survey of professors, even to entertain the idea that "scientifically trained men" could be mistaken ("it is almost inconceivable..."), so that he automatically excluded any possibility of a collective prejudice, is just one example of what now appears as a rather naïve confidence in the detachment of male judgment. And on the last page of the chapter on the female mind, the long expedition through the statistical material of the surveys and experiments proves to have led to a familiar destination – the family as a woman's natural place. "Here we find, fully active, what we have sought for so long and with so little result in science and art: *the female genius*."[84] The question as to whether Heymans shared in the misogyny of his age is perhaps impossible to answer. Even the historian Bosch, who reaches firm conclusions on the question of the misogyny of other scholars in her book on the gender of science, has to remain non-committal in Heymans's case. She says that it is "in some sense a question of style" and takes the view that the ambiguity of Heymans's monograph is responsible for its divided reception.[85] Heymans promised an objective, scientific treatment of the differences between men and women, but nonetheless frequently took refuge in anecdote and generally accepted opinions, prefaced with such formulations as "certainly no one will dispute the fact that...." Whereas many women expected objective scientific research to have an emancipating effect, the reception of *Psychologie der Frauen* was primarily governed by what people appreciated in it – either the attempt or the results. Bosch points out that in the Netherlands Heymans's book had a great influence on debates about professional work for women – she refers among other things to the training of nurses, the suitability for office work and the opening up of the judiciary – but says that it achieved authority primarily with "opponents of a redefinition of the relationship between the sexes."[86] This selectivity is a consequence of the ambiguity in *Psychologie der Frauen* and can also be identified in the international reception of the work. In her discussion of foreign reviews, De Wilde is able to quote numerous compliments.[87] The sexual psychologist Havelock Ellis found it "one of the most skillful and penetrating books which we have on this subject," the psychiatrist Claparède called it "un ouvrage très remarquable," others praised Heymans's "exact wissenschaftlichen Arbeit." The psychologist Fürth commended the book as "vorurteilsfrei" and "so gut begründet"; her American colleague Thompson Woolley found it "exceedingly readable, but not altogether convincing." Several female reviewers were in agreement that Heymans's theory of women's greater sensibility and its adverse effect on their scholarly achievements was due for an overhaul. It was also remarked that it was still too early to base overly definite theories on the current research.

This last was Heymans's own opinion, too. With the still immature and rudimentary research that the present tools permitted, his monograph could not be more than a "rough framework."[88] The beginning and end of *Psychologie der Frauen* were reserved in tone. In the introduction Heymans wrote that many male authors – he mentioned Lombroso and Mantegazza by name – showed an insufficient understanding of "the amazing complexity of the female mind."[89] His own book had equally failed to solve the riddle. In the concluding paragraph he stated that current psychology could only enclose the image of woman in straight lines, not draw it. As psychological methods became more refined, so the scientific lines would soften into flowing curves which would be more in line with the actual image of woman.[90] The metaphor borders on the sensual and makes it very clear that Heymans was well aware of the limitations of his knowledge.

Meanwhile it remains touching to see how, with that exhaustive, anecdotal and often contradictory material like women's diaries and correspondence, biographies, personal observations, adages, and above all with his endless calculations of percentages – he barely takes his eyes off the thirty-one tables in his book – Heymans nevertheless tries to get a grip on that "amazing complexity of the female mind," as if he had found himself in a huge labyrinth with a faulty compass. His method is entirely that of a man – but the man sketched in his own book, an analyzing and abstracting being that quantifies its thoughts wherever possible. At the end of *Psychologie der Frauen* one cannot help recalling the lament of one of Heymans's female acquaintances, "how stupid you men must be, to have to study so much."[91]

Panpsychism

Aesthetics, wrote Fechner in his *Vorschule der Aesthetik* (1876), has a *Weg von oben* and a *Weg von unten* – an approach from above and an approach from below.[92] In the former case, people philosophize about aesthetic judgment in terms of general ideas about the essence of beauty; in the latter they investigate the laws that govern the actual judgment of beauty. Fechner himself had made a start on the *Weg von unten*. He asked test subjects to choose the most beautiful rectangle from a series of rectangles with different ratios of length to width. The results of hundreds of tests, supplemented with measurements of visiting cards, cabinets, windows and memorial crosses, supported the aesthetic content of the golden section: the ratio of the short side to the long side equals the ratio of the long side to the sum of the short and long sides. What Pythagoras had called the ideal ratio on mathematical grounds was anchored, according to Fechner, in a psychological law.

Heymans chose the same bottom-up approach in his study of aesthetics. He began his aesthetics lectures – reconstructed by Hubbeling from lecture notes[93] – with Fechner's distinction, and then firmly gave the subject a psychological focus. Aesthetics is the science of the perception of beauty and seeks the laws that govern our judgment of what is beautiful or sublime. English aestheticians like Hogarth and Burke had preceded him in this, said Heymans, and in Germany, too, Fechner and Lipps had already done pioneering work. Aesthetics should be practiced as an inductive and, where possible, experimental science.

Heymans subjected ethics to a similar psychologizing process. It is a psychological fact that we make moral judgments, and it is the job of ethics to identify the laws governing the way we make these judgments.[94] Heymans' major work on ethics shared its subtitle – "on empirical principles" – with his work on metaphysics, a subject which, in Heymans's view, had like aesthetics and ethics to be approached from below, inductively, empirically, proceeding from facts to theories. To Heymans, metaphysics was "the science that endeavors to bring about a knowledge of the world that is as complete and as little relative as possible."[95] The term that is expressly avoided here is *absolute* knowledge – science provides provisional, hypothetical knowledge, and in metaphysics this knowledge is directed toward reality as a whole. Individual subjects explore areas of reality, but the sum of this knowledge is still not knowledge of reality as a whole. A neurologist investigates the phenomena of the brain and a psychologist the phenomena of the consciousness, but the nature of the connection between the two cannot be explained by either of these two sciences and this is where metaphysics comes into its own. The results of the specialized sciences are the point of departure for metaphysics. Metaphysical theories have to satisfy the same criteria as theories in individual disciplines: consistency, explanatory power, economy. In his *Einführung in die Metaphysik*, Heymans postulates panpsychism as the theory that best meets these standards. His inspiration came from Gustav Fechner, the philosopher-psychologist who was also behind his psychological inhibition tests in the eighteen-nineties.

In *Die Tagesansicht gegenüber der Nachtansicht* (1879) Fechner had contrasted materialism (the night view) and panpsychism (the day view). To a materialist, he wrote, there are only atoms that move blindly and silently through space. It is an illusion that matter produces color, taste and odor: all these properties are added to it by the mind and the senses. Without a consciousness that perceives everything that exists as light, heat and life, everything would become darkness – this is the perspective of the night view. Someone who looks at things from the day view, in contrast, believes that the material world consists of consciousness. It is not only people and animals that are alive – plants, minerals and even heavenly bodies are too. In *Nanna* (1848) Fechner looked at the soul life of plants, in *Zend-Avesta* (1851) that of stars and planets. To him all of reality was consciousness, in varying degrees of intensity.

Heymans came to an identical conclusion, but by a different route. He deduced panpsychism from an analysis of the mind-body problem. For a physiologist, every physical phenomenon is determined by the sum of the phenomena that precede it. Everything that can be observed in people and animals, including what goes on in their brains, can be reduced to an uninterrupted series of material processes. A physiologist need not take account of psychological explanations. "Just as paper money only has value because it can be exchanged for precious metal, so psychological explanations only have value for the physiologist in so far as he is convinced that they can in due course be replaced with purely physical ones." The reverse applies to a psychologist. He is supposed to explain all consciousness content from previous consciousness content and may not make use of physiological explanations to do so. Both physiology and psychology investigate closed causal chains.

Brain processes and consciousness processes continually keep pace. The question is then how this accurate parallelism can be explained if the two causal chains have no open links that leave room for an interaction. A possible solution is to assume that both series of phenomena relate to one and the same reality, which then presents itself to our observation in two ways, "such as a vibrating string that can be observed both by the eye and by the ear." This is the assumption of monistic theories. Materialism says that this single reality is material in nature and regards the phenomena of consciousness as illusion, panpsychism conceives reality as one whole of consciousness phenomena and denies the "real" existence of matter. To Heymans, the latter theory had a decisive advantage: a link to our direct experience. Material things are given to us only as *observations*. I can only infer that the pen I am using to write this really exists from the fact that I observe the pen, and this observation is a psychological condition. Other means of recording material processes, for example with scientific instruments, ultimately result in human observations and hence in consciousness processes. There is only one substance, mind, which we perceive from the outside in as matter and from the inside out as consciousness. The reality as a whole forms a world consciousness. We can only find out about the nature of the world consciousness if we conceive of it by analogy with the human consciousness. It is an empirical fact that consciousness can intensify, for instance when the attention is concentrated. In an analogous manner, the human consciousness is a temporary intensification of the world consciousness. Thus panpsychism, in Heymans's words, meets "an important emotional need": the desire to live on after death. After the body dies, our consciousness will be absorbed into ever higher units of consciousness. The analogy – also borrowed from Fechner – implied that there was no longer any question of a strictly individual existence. Heymans did not regard this as a loss.

> Is this way of looking at it comfortless? Is it actually less satisfying or less elevating than the religious view that promises every individual soul eternal life? I firmly believe it is not! For it does not seem to me that being bricked up in the narrow cell of one's own individuality for all eternity is ideal; nor do I see it as a specter to first fuse with one's nearest and dearest to complete unity, and then see the ever receding boundaries ever collapsing, and thus, in continual, although perhaps asymptotic development, one's thinking, feeling and endeavors widening to that of the universe.[96]

In the first edition of his introduction to metaphysics, the German version published in 1905, Heymans wrote that it is here that the point is reached where logic and probability transform into a "purely subjective credibility, informed in part by wishes and inclinations' and that it is wise to go no further. He ended with the resigned conclusion that we will have to make do with the suspicions he has formulated. But in the third edition, published in 1921, there follows at this same point an animated reflection on death and eternity. "By basing all (consciousness) individuations on a single I, panpsychism characterizes our deepest being as eternal and capable of eternal development, and it is precisely in this that its actual message of salvation lies."[97]

Einführung in die Metaphysik was widely read. It was reprinted twice in both German and Dutch. In the very year it was published, William James wrote to Flournoy, "The book that has interested me most this summer has been Heymans's *Einleitung in die Metaphysik* (I think that is the title). I dare say you've read it and will agree with me in considering it a masterpiece of clear composition."[98] James saw a relationship between his own theory of neutral monism and the panpsychism of "two Germans, Petzoldt & Heymans."[99] In his in-depth discussion of Heymans's philosophical work, Verwey locates the reception of panpsychism in the broader pattern of *fin de siècle* movements, directed at restoring harmony and balance in a world that was losing cohesion through industrialization, urbanization and secularization. Heymans's "central intuition" is the reconcilability of antitheses and oppositions, and it is here, too, that the desire to trade dualistic theories for a monistic theory fits in.[100] In his view, Heymans's panpsychism is a secular redemption doctrine, derived from science, the rational counterpart of the many "petites religiones" around the turn of the century. To this can be added the fact that panpsychism always remained a "petite philosophie." In psychology itself, philosophy faded into the background. The great metaphysical systems like dualism, materialism and panpsychism disappeared from the debate in this branch of science. In philosophy, one of the forerunners of the Vienna Circle, the physicist-philosopher Ernst Mach, praised Heymans's *Einführung in die Metaphysik*.[101] The irony of the situation was that – like Heymans – the Vienna Circle took its inspiration from scientific research, but its members declared metaphysical statements to be scientifically meaningless and on a par with poetry. Heymans appears to have anticipated this turn of events when he wrote that as far as he was concerned people might say that most metaphysical hypotheses "are ill founded, in short are failed hypotheses; however, there are such hypotheses in the other sciences too, without their having been called poetry for that reason. Bad science is bad science and not poetry; one should not rechristen it, but try to improve it."[103] For Heymans, the choice was not between metaphysics or no metaphysics, but between good and bad metaphysics. The Vienna Circle, the philosophical school that had the greatest affinity to Heymans's scientific outlook, took a different view.

"The future century of psychology"

In 1909 Heymans stepped down as vice-chancellor with the address on "the future century of psychology."[103] This speech received a great deal of attention in the Dutch press and was generally seen as a remarkable cultural historical dissertation. The delivery of the address was an event in itself.[104] The auditorium was crammed to bursting half an hour before the start, and hundreds more people had to return home disappointed. Those who had managed to obtain a seat heard what a psychology that had reached maturity would mean to individuals and society. The perspective was one of centuries, the tone elevated, the prospects utopian.

The last century, began Heymans, had been the century of the natural sciences. We admire the precision of their predictions, the stringency of their proofs, the wealth of applications. The technology derived from science had brought us fertilizer, anesthesia and electricity. The control of the forces of nature had changed our world beyond recognition. Alongside the natural sciences, the last decades of the previous century had seen the development of the science of human nature. Scientific methodology and tools had been a source of inspiration for psychology. This new science had now progressed as far as the natural sciences had reached several centuries ago, it had discovered various empirical regularities and drawn up a few exact laws, but could not yet serve as a basis for technical applications.

With an adroit alternation of the stylistic devices of analogy and contrast, Heymans explained that psychology would have to mature to the level of the current natural sciences. This development would be measured in centuries rather than generations; there was no possibility that the twentieth century would be the century of psychology. But once it had reached maturity, psychology would be able to answer more essential needs in a social and philosophical sense than could science. For had the past century of science not also been the century of pessimism and disorientation? Of suicide, divorce, neurasthenia? Despite the ever faster gratification of our material needs, we stand empty and unsatisfied in life, triply alienated, from "ourselves, our fellow human beings and the essence of things."[105]

The fact that we are alienated from ourselves was the fault of the rapid increase in the complexity of modern life. We are exposed to more impulses and influences than our parents' generation. We read newspapers and novels, go to the theater, attend lectures, and all these impulses are no longer tempered by traditions as they were in the past. Thus we become our own labyrinth. People are increasingly losing their way in the important decisions in life. The number of divorces is rising alarmingly. The questionnaire he had conducted with Wiersma had revealed that in the parents' generation three percent of men had repeatedly changed their occupation; by the children's generation, with a career that had only just started, this had already risen to twelve percent. So much happiness wiped out, so much harmony lost!

The same individualization also alienates us from our fellow human beings. We each live as if we are in a cell, only parts of our personality touch parts of that of other people. The intimacy of coinciding wishes, feelings and ideals has become rare. Do we not have the impression that "our fathers and grandfathers expressed much more of their whole personalities in their circle of friends and acquaintances than would be possible for us now?"[106] Even in our closest relationships, those between parents and children, between husband and wife, between friends, misunderstandings arise that can lead to estrangement or even an open breach. Again: what a loss of happiness.

And finally we are alienated from the essence of things. Religion is starting to lose its value as a philosophical context. Non-believers or semi-believers drift between agnosticism and materialism and are beginning to lose the ability to see the beauty of life. The characteristics associated with a religious attitude to life – and according to the questionnaire they include a readiness to help, perseverance, honesty, a sense of duty, each and every one of them values that sustain society – are in danger of receding still further into the background.

Exactly halfway through his address, Heymans concluded the diagnosis and invited his audience to ask themselves, with him, whether in developing psychology our culture was not perhaps concocting a remedy. Psychology at its present stage would not be able to achieve much, although we knew more about children, criminals and the mentally ill than we did a quarter of a century ago because of "technical sciences" like pedagogics, criminology and psychiatry. The psychology of the future, in contrast, would allow a far-reaching control of human nature. The present crude typologies would be refined into networks of accurate psychological correlations. Reliable empirical measures would be found for character traits, like the ones already available for secondary function. The classification of characters would approach the ideal of a "character formula, in which different values only have to be substituted for a number of constants to make them fit all the different individuals, and make possible exact predictions of their expressions of life in every area."[107]

If the model of an accurate predictive science is already evident here, Heymans's sketch of the salutary consequences of an exact personality classification evokes associations with the periodic table of the elements. We would not acquire knowledge of ourselves and others only in later life, with the associated disappointment and failure, but at a time when we could use that knowledge in ordering our personal lives, such as when choosing a marriage partner or a profession. Overestimating oneself would be inconceivable for someone who "knows himself as an example of such and such a group in such and such a class in such and such a main division of a psychological classification, and who also carries a little list in his head about the restrictions, weaknesses and shortcomings to which membership of this group predisposes him."[108] Once psychology had found its Mendeleyev, was the suggestion, parents and teachers would understand their children and pupils better, while doctors of the mind would be on hand for the difficult cases.

The position in a specific pigeonhole in the character classification meant that personal limits were also fixed. Each individual could only "revise" himself or herself, as Heymans formulated it, within narrow boundaries. Improvement and edification would only be possible for humanity as a whole. Psychological characteristics were hereditary – something that Heymans considered too obvious even to discuss – and this should be used by successive generations. It would be foolish to leave the improvement of the human race to a blind struggle for existence. The improvement of breeds among our pets was not the result of a struggle for existence, was it? And a cattle farmer did not let his animals overwinter on a barren heath as a means of selecting the strongest, did he? In the future, humanity would take control of its own development by means of active selection. A marriage arranged by the state, as Plato had proposed, would not be necessary in order to achieve this; one could make use of the mechanism, already working, "that all individuals, including the wicked ones, were attracted by good; *ceteris paribus* the choice of a marriage partner will be more likely to be directed toward people who are morally superior rather than morally inferior; *ceteris paribus* the former will have a greater chance of participating in the procreation of the race than the latter."[109] Psychology was at the same time the prerequisite for and the instrument of moral edification. A deeper knowledge of psychological characteristics would guard us against the blunders of the instinct. As character and personality gained in transparency, for ourselves and others, so our choice of spouse would be a happier one. Future generations would be aware of the obligation, in decisions about procreation, to keep in mind the intellectual and moral standard of the next generation. If the sense of personal responsibility were to fall short, strong public opinion would correct it. This ideal state, Heymans told his audience, was still far off. "But what does that matter? Humanity has time enough; and the brief duration of the individual life, which prevents us from observing its progress, is itself the indispensable condition for this progress. I know of no idea so suitable as this to comfort ourselves, even to make us rejoice in our mortality. We die to make way for our betters."[110] Heymans was affected more than fleetingly by the eugenetic views which Galton had started to formulate in the eighteen-eighties and which had floated into the general social consciousness on the thermals of right-wing concerns and left-wing ideals around the turn of the century. The right was afraid of the growing numbers in the "lower" classes.[111] In *An Essay on the Principle of Population* Malthus had endeavored to avert the danger of overpopulation by recommending that people should marry later in life, and many people feared, with Galton, that it would be the intelligentsia who would follow this advice, thus setting in train a fatal decline in the average standard. The left saw in eugenics the possibility of a direct and efficient intervention in the biological mechanisms behind the major social differences. And there was generally a fear that improvements in hygiene and care for the insane, coupled with ever increasing philanthropy, would cancel out natural selection mechanisms. These ideas were also current in the Netherlands. The insanity in the Netherlands is increasing, warned the Utrecht professor of pathology Koster in 1893: people had to realize that the improved life expectancy that resulted from medical treatment primarily benefited the weak.[112] Eugenic views met with relatively little response in the Netherlands.[113] Heymans was one of the most prominent adherents, but he never advocated an active eugenic policy – not positive eugenics and certainly not negative eugenics. His students took it a good deal further. In 1913, a year after he gained his doctorate on the psychology of the arsonist, Pannenborg wrote that rehabilitation and re-education would ultimately result in increased fertility in criminals and that an effective policy would do better to make use of such measures as prohibiting marriage, incarceration for life or even sterilization and castration.[114] Another student, Luning Prak, suggested that politicians might like to consider reserving one of the West Frisian islands for a permanent population of retards.[115] Heymans himself preferred to leave the edification of mankind to personal responsibility, invoking arguments that were in line with his doctrine of panpsychism.

Heymans reserved the end of his address for what he called "our relationship to the essence of things."[116] As psychology developed further, so scientifically oriented philosophies like materialism would fade into the background and panpsychism would take their place. A consequence of this doctrine is that individuals are not isolated beings, but part of a higher, in the final analysis all-embracing consciousness. Once we realize that a psychological organism is developing in mankind and the world, "we no longer see ourselves as individuals but as organs; we understand that our ultimate objectives must lie not in us, but far beyond us; we see the sharp demarcating line blurring, the line that divides the single from the all, the finite from the infinite."[117]

While at the start of his address the natural sciences had been the teacher of and inspiration for a young science, in the closing lines Heymans explained that "the wonderful strength of scientific technology" was not able to satisfy essential human needs. "It provides playthings and sweetmeats, with which the crying child can be distracted from his pain and kept quiet for a moment, but it cannot heal the malady itself. What we crave and need in the depths of our soul is not amusement, diversion or comfort, but peace with the world and with ourselves."[118] Only psychology could provide this peace.

facts of hypotheses, theories and finally even a philosophy with a decidedly *non*-Anglo-Saxon character gave his work the singular tension that so hampered its reception. Method and results were at right angles to each other – exactly like gimbals.

In psychology the gimbals were formed by the experimental traditions that Galton and Wundt had established. The lines of influence are relatively easy to follow. Heymans's research in general psychology related to the intensity of sensations and visual illusions. Both subjects had their origins in German psychology, and Heymans set up his experiments along the lines laid out for this type of research in Germany. The whole pathway – the formulation of the problem, the instruments, the methodology, the hypotheses and theories, the publication of the results – proceeded according to German conventions. His articles on psychological inhibition and the illusions of Müller-Lyer and Zöllner in the *Zeitschrift für Psychologie* could have been written by a German, as some historians of psychology thought they actually had been.

The relationships were different in differential psychology. The large-scale question-naires that provided the basis of Heymans's research into individual differences were inspired by Galton, who had introduced the questionnaire as a tool in psychology. The background that gave meaning to all the research – the ideas about heredity applied to psychological characteristics – was English in origin, but Heymans and Wiersma reported their findings in German, not English. In consequence their publications contributed to the distribution of differential psychology in German-speaking countries. One could view this, to use a commercial metaphor, as a chain of import, processing and onward transport. In the traffic of ideas, Heymans took a position that accorded with the geographical position of the Netherlands. That his efforts were appreciated is evident from the fact that Heymans's psychology of woman, a major element of differential psychology, was written at German instigation.

Gimbals can also be seen in the research itself. Heymans's attempt to capture sensations and perceptual phenomena in measurements and numbers – the research of the eighteen-nineties – was an innovation in the Netherlands, but from a more international perspective was part of what was already almost an established tradition. The same applied to his later research into the heredity of psychological characteristics and personality. Psychologists in Germany and England had developed their own experimental culture with specific standards, styles and conventions. This culture was characterized by quantification and precision measurement, and Heymans was its first and for a long time its only exponent in the Netherlands. His innovations were derived from traditions.

Perhaps Heymans's psychology of woman is the clearest illustration of the paradox that it is precisely the endeavor to escape the prevailing views and prejudices that most tellingly demonstrates the impossibility of doing so. Unlike almost all his contemporaries, Heymans tried to tackle the issue of "the amazing complexity of the female mind" and its implications for the social position of women by means of a consistent empirical approach. To this end he compiled several questionnaires. But the "professorial questionnaire" asked for the views and experiences of respondents who were almost without exception men, and Heymans waved aside any possibility that their judgment might be the reflection of a common prejudice as being beyond the bounds of probability. His frequent references to what is "generally known" or "disputed by no one" illustrate just

Heymans on the occasion of his retirement in 1927.

how much the researcher who is trying to be an innovator actually moves with his times.

While in psychology Heymans undertook research in both general and differential psychology, two elements which – even then – were usually practiced as specializations, so that he made, as it were, a double contribution, it appears that in philosophy one contribution canceled out the other. His ethics, aesthetics and metaphysics were intended to reconcile the "tough-minded" with the idealistic "tender-minded," but the result was that neither school accepted his work. The same fate awaited his grand design for a philosophy. Panpsychism was developed from scientific premises, along lines of logic and observation, but at the same time had an idealistic and synthesizing intent. The culture around 1900, wrote Aerts, needed the restoration of unity. "The modern multiplicity of schools of thought, styles, movements and aspirations was more often perceived as a problem than as a boon."[124] Heymans hoped that his panpsychism would provide a rational humanist alternative to religion, which he saw losing its influence. He pursued his cause with a zeal bordering on the religious. There was so much at stake: confidence in oneself and one's fellow man, peace with the world, the prospect of immortality. To win minds for these ideals, panpsychism had to be widely disseminated and accepted. Even in his lifetime, Heymans could see that this had not happened.

Heymans's last two public appearances revealed his isolation. When he chaired the Eighth International Congress for Psychology in 1926, it appeared that there had already been a changing of the guard. The psychology in the style of Wundt that Heymans had made his own had vanished from the center of the discipline. In his presidential address he had to take a position against the three movements that were preparing to fill the vacuum: behaviorism, Gestalt psychology and "verstehende" psychology.[125] For Heymans, psychology remained the science of the consciousness, with the task of deriving elementary causal laws from consciousness experiences. In his view, in these new movements psychology was going in no fewer than three different directions, each of them wrong. Heymans must have felt himself to be the last of a generation. As we have seen, the subject of his valedictory lecture a year later was different but the tone of isolation was the same.

A quarter of a century earlier, in his book on religious experience, William James had written that even the most successful people sometimes live with a sense of tragedy and failure. "But take the happiest man, the one most envied by the world, and in nine cases out of ten his inmost consciousness is one of failure. Either his ideals in the line of his achievements are pitched far higher than the achievements themselves, or else he has secret ideals of which the world knows nothing, and in regard to which he inwardly knows himself to be wanting."[126] Heymans never made any secret of the ideals that drove him, but he must have felt the same disillusion. His last years were clouded by the sense of having failed and no form of outward success could eradicate that feeling.

Nicolaas Beets at the time of the tribute, 1884.

9

Religion: Protestantism

Pastors and poets

Introduction

On September 13, 1884 the poet and minister of religion Nicolaas Beets celebrated his seventieth birthday in Utrecht, an event that also marked his retirement as professor of theology at the university there. He could not complain of lack of interest, quite the contrary. In the Tivoli banquet room he was given several honors, among them the highest imaginable in such circumstances – the Grand Cross in the Order of the Dutch Lion – but also that of Officer in the Order of Leopold, a sign of Belgian esteem for the Dutch-speaking poet. Beets, who was the very picture of bourgeois well-being with his portly figure, rosy cheeks and gray side-whiskers, was immortalized in a bust in Italian marble. A festive cantata with words by his friend, fellow poet and minister Johannes Petrus Hasebroek, and music by Richard Hol, a specialist in choirs and male choral societies, was sung for him. The highlight, however, was the presentation of an *Album amicorum*, in the form of a chest full of original manuscripts. The 338 contributions were packed in a case with brass fittings lined with blue velvet. On top were five contributions by the whole royal family. Prominent figures from the church, the arts and politics had added their thoughts or poems to the album.

The celebrations for Beets had a national impact, for the entire Dutch press covered them. The *Nieuws van den Dag* compared them to the national tributes paid to Hendrik Conscience (1881) in Belgium and to Victor Hugo (1882) in France, which had been viewed with some envy in the Netherlands. Such international comparisons might put Beets's stature at risk, wrote Jozef Alberdingk Thijm in the liberal *De Amsterdammer*. He himself would rather have given a Dutch laurel wreath to the poets Willem Bilderdijk and Isaac da Costa from the first half of the nineteenth century, but on the other hand he wanted to take advantage of these favorable circumstances "for eloquently expressing the thanks of the nation to a genius who appeared later and did not attain the same heights as his predecessors."[1]

The liberal *Algemeen Handelsblad* called Beets a benefactor and a champion of Dutch culture. The editor drew an idyllic picture of "his happy zest for life, accompanied by a simple, genial, truly religious sense; his dignified language and serious tone accompanied by impish humor and cheerful jesting; his love of domesticity, of his wife and children; the whole development of the talents and gifts of a pastor who first addressed his countrymen from a world full of love, poetry and birdsong, from the sunny, friendly village parsonage amid the gardens and dunes of Holland."[2] *De Amsterdammer* agreed that Beets revealed a pre-eminently Dutch character. "It is not perhaps easy to say in a word, and so that general agreement may be assumed, in what this specifically Dutch quality consists. Yet there will be agreement on this point, that truth, honesty and sincerity are qualities nowhere more practiced and honored than in the Netherlands."[3]

Despite all the sentiment, Beets was also weighed and judged. As a writer, he was praised above all for *Camera Obscura*, a satire on the Dutch bourgeoisie in the early nineteenth century, written with elegantly masked mercilessness (according to the critic Potgieter). The Catholic priest and poet Herman Schaepman recalled in the *Album* that the youthful Beets had had a Byronic period in which he had "drifted into sultry black" depths before rising to become a "sovereign genius," one of "Vondel's sons."[4] As a minister, Beets was honored for his irenic position in the conflict between the churches that was raging at the time and for his *Stichtelijke Uren*, a pastoral expression of bourgeois Pietism and domestic devoutness. His professorship of theology, a late addition to Beets's career, seemed to go largely unhonored.

"I consider Nicolaas Beets to be the last eminent poet that the Dutch language was destined to bring forth," wrote Conrad Busken Huet in the *Album*. He had once been a clergyman but had resigned in 1862. Allard Pierson, another former minister, viewed the celebrations as the ultimate expression of the "friendly picture" of undogmatic "above all aesthetically agreeable, biblical and national religion." The reader should, however, realize "that our nation apparently does not intend to view life as idyllically in the future." According to Pierson, on Beets's seventieth birthday the Netherlands could gather for one more time around the image represented "by the venerable, jovial graybeard." "They wanted to clasp in their arms once more the Netherlands of the poet, before the flow of history engulfs it and a democratic Calvinism takes the floor."[5]

"Poésie du foyer"

Beets was a pastor and a poet. He and other clergymen with literary tastes chose art to express piety or domestic virtue, moods or love, usually married love. But poetry was also a tried and tested instrument for articulating memorable moments in national history or a conciliatory approach to church disputes. Readers of Beets could recognize "the soul of our people in his scenes inside our houses and rooms."[6] Busken Huet coined the term "poésie du foyer," poetry of the domestic hearth, for this literature.[7] Devotion to the House of Orange was also one of Beets's hallmarks. He was in fact the court poet, who followed the royal occasions and the childhood of the future Queen Wilhelmina in verse. The presence of five royal manuscripts in his *Album* is evidence that the fondness was mutual. When he was buried on March 17, 1903, on his instructions only one wreath was permitted in the mortuary, that of Queen Emma, the Queen Mother, and on his coffin there was only Wilhelmina's palm wreath.

Beets was not alone among clergymen in his devotion to the House of Orange. There was a tradition in the Reformed Church of openly stated patriotism, which was equated with and expressed through devotion to the Orange cause. This tradition was even institutionalized. In the document that first set out the statutes of the national Reformed Church, the *Algemeen Reglement* of 1816, King William I had had an article included stating that "fostering a love of King and Country" should be a principal aim of those "responsible for governing the church in various offices." The Constitution of 1848, which again stated the principle of the separation of church and state, had not changed this. The new *Algemeen Reglement* of the Dutch Reformed Church of 1852 incorporated the old text. It was not a dead letter, as is shown by the frequency of national sermons on royal occasions or during commemorations.

Because of their university education, ministers were assured of a place in the intellectual elite; they were the "modern version of the medieval 'clerk,' the professional in the field of culture."[8] Given the priority of the sermon in their pastoral task, they had to make time for reflecting on and writing it. Eloquence underlined the differences between the pastor and his congregation, but could also bridge this gap. For he had been taught not only to stand out from them but also to seek to approach them and instruct them in knowledge of the Bible and moral understanding. Moreover, he owed it to his intellectual status to cultivate and strengthen Dutch as the language of everyday speech. As professional practitioners of public speaking, ministers had to maintain high linguistic standards.[9] Rhetoric in the Netherlands was largely shaped by these "Servants of the Word," who had to make themselves heard unaided in large, echoing churches.

The minister Johannes Jacob van Oosterzee prided himself on his knowledge of literature. "My head and heart were like a house with several rooms, in which a small salon remained open for literature," he wrote in his memoirs. But the "second floor" was still devoted to the church and theology.[10] Van Oosterzee was a great preacher and thus represented another dimension of Dutch literature, rhetoric. "Blessed pulpit, what hours, lived for eternity, do I already have to thank you for!" And after a successful sermon he wrote, "I had angels singing for an incredible host."[11]

On the other side sat the listeners, the congregation. A best-selling novel about the church in the nineteenth century, *Het Leesgezelschap te Diepenbeek* (The Reading Circle of Diepenbeek), gives this description:

> The Diepenbekers, like most of our countrymen, had their own way of sitting in church, which might make the uninitiated suspect them of indifference or idleness, most unfairly indeed. The great distinction was whether they were awake or asleep. If the eyes were open, then the sermon was being favorably received (one could count on it), even though there was not the slightest sign of interest or approval. If it was not well received, people sat a little more at their ease than they had been, and soon it could be seen, and sometimes heard, that the seed was not falling on fertile ground.[12]

A professional body

Around 1900 the Dutch Reformed Church, the main Calvinist church, had over 1,600 positions for ministers. According to a rough estimate, another 400 positions could be added from the dissenting churches – in the first place the Lutherans and Mennonites, but also the Remonstrants and the so-called *Christelijk Gereformeerde Kerk*. The last two

Collectors and deacons of the North Church in Amsterdam, *c.* 1880.

were the result of schisms in the seventeenth century and in 1834 respectively. Despite all the differences in character, tradition and belief, these 2,000 clergy shared an awareness of the community of ministers. This awareness was also fostered by their common social background. Among the ministers there were a fair number of sons who had followed their fathers into the profession. Most came from the middle class. Busken Huet saw them as the representatives of the third class. His explanation was "that we are a bourgeois people and by the nature of things any good clergy bears the stamp of its nation. In order for them to be entitled to the respect and trust of the masses, as ministers are, a measure of learning is required of them. Now the talents acquired through work and study are most plentiful among the in-between class in society, where birth counts for nothing and everyone must try to build his future by his own efforts."[13]

Reformed, Remonstrant, Lutheran and Mennonite ministers had come to resemble each other more, not only because since 1800, under the influence of the Enlightenment, they had put aside their differences over dogma, but also because to a large extent they had followed the same university education and now earned about the same income. It was true that the theological faculties at the state universities were reserved for the education of Reformed ministers, but the student at a Remonstrant, Mennonite or Lutheran seminary followed much the same curriculum. In the nineteenth century, moreover, the

Mennonite ministers were almost always professionals (as opposed to the amateur preachers), and Lutheran ministers only rarely came from Germany.[14]

In or outside the churches a *clerus minor* was also active; it consisted of catechists, lay readers and evangelists. The catechist was now known as a teacher of religion and with the permission of the church council he could lead devotional gatherings. The lay reader was a central figure among those who had left the Reformed Church in 1834 in the cause of orthodoxy. He was active in circles where the Bible was read intensively, and did this work without church training or a formal appointment, although he might also be a teacher of religion. The third group consisted of the evangelists. They were qualified as teachers of religion, certainly in the Dutch Reformed Church, but not actually working as such. They were usually employed by a Christian society to do missionary work among the members, among other religions or in the colonies.

In the nineteenth century it went without saying that the minister was a man. The first woman minister in the Netherlands, Annie Zernike, began work in 1911. She was called to the Mennonite Brotherhood, who traditionally considered "everyone, including women, entitled in principle" to lead the service and to administer the sacraments, "although in practice this is almost always done by the minister." The dissenting churches were the first to admit "female servants of the Word" to the ranks of their clergy after the turn of the century. In the Remonstrant Brotherhood the first sister was called as a minister in 1920.[15] A group somewhat neglected in the historiography of Protestantism in the Netherlands is the deaconesses – women inspired by religion to live a life of celibacy and to devote themselves to caring for the sick and teaching. The oldest organization was founded in Utrecht in 1844. It had its origins in the Protestant Réveil and was led by an aristocratic lady, A.H. Swellengrebel. Around the turn of the century deaconesses' hospitals were established in the main cities, not only Reformed but Lutheran too, for the roots of what may after all be called a religious movement of deaconesses lay in Kaiserswert near Düsseldorf.[16]

In the village community the minister was *primus inter pares*; his peers were the notary, the doctor and possibly the burgomaster. "In our village we are in a sense equal to the king, who is also unique in his kind," wrote Cornelis Eliza van Koetsveld in his widely read novel about life as seen from the parsonage in Mastland.[17] The nineteenth-century parsonage tended indeed to be a substantial residence. The minister of the church was a pastor and conducted the services for marriages and funerals, but beyond this he was also a welcome guest at civil ceremonies or social gatherings. In the larger cities the minister had a place among the intellectual elite. There he was expected to be dignified and to live the life of a solid citizen. In the villages he would pay house calls without making any distinctions, but that was exceptional in the cities. The minister derived his authority, moreover, from the fact that he had some influence on poor relief. In an age in which charity was still largely a matter for the church and in which material support was linked to religious observance, the minister was expected to pronounce judgment on the religious behavior of applicants for help.

The position and status of the Reformed minister in the Netherlands and of the Anglican vicar in England were to some extent similar. Just as the medieval church or cathedral held its own in the midst of the modern city full of factories, new housing districts and public buildings, so the Anglican clergy retained its primacy. "In most villages the vicar was the most powerful individual, or the most powerful individual next to the squire; in the town the vicar was part of a much larger and more variegated elite, but he still enjoyed a great deal of prestige and influence."[18]

The rhetoric of disputes

The national tribute to the poet Nicolaas Beets took place in September 1884. A year later the first issue of *De Nieuwe Gids* appeared. It was the journal of the Eighties Movement, which was started by poets and writers who absolutely rejected the bourgeois piety and domesticity of the pastor-poets. Three months later, in January 1886, the minister Abraham Kuyper and a few like-minded supporters sawed open the door to the vestry of the Nieuwe Kerk (New Church) in Amsterdam. He did this to express his intention to break the power of modern theology in the Dutch Reformed Church. The subsequent conflict in the Church put an end to the image of an irenic, if not idyllic, culture of the parsonage. In the same year the former Lutheran minister Ferdinand Domela Nieuwenhuis, who had meanwhile become a socialist, had to face charges arising from the publication of an article criticizing the monarchy in a journal he ran called *Recht voor Allen* (Justice for all). This was regarded as lese-majesty. The prison sentence he received was the consequence of a revolutionary movement dedicated to opposing the alliance of God, Fatherland and Orange so lauded at Beets's birthday celebrations. Allard Pierson and Busken Huet were proved right sooner than even they may have expected.

The numbers leaving the clergy increased. Some went into journalism. Not only Busken Huet but other theologians too secured prominent positions in the liberal press. Around the turn of the century there was a notable rise in the number of members of Parliament who had studied theology. Most of them were ministers of religion and though they formed a smaller group after 1888, they rivaled the lawyers (the largest group among the college-educated parliamentarians) "not only in a figurative but in a real sense."[19] As elsewhere in Europe, the eighteen-eighties saw the advent of the free intellectual and he was often a former clergyman.

The poetry of the pastors foundered because there was no longer a demand for domestic poetry based on a bourgeois sense of well-being and faith. Religious rhetoric, on the other hand, and especially the age-old preaching on disputed points of doctrine, flourished once more. This is clearly evident in a sharp change in the political culture of the eighteen-eighties. The leaders of new political movements such as the Anti-Revolutionary Party (ARP), a party formed by the orthodox Protestant middle class, and the socialists tried to mobilize their supporters through major religious or social themes that stirred the feelings and allegiances of the people who made up the electorate. The preservation of an orthodox faith was on the agenda, and social deprivation too, but the "nation" also took on a new emotional value and a new political significance.[20] These leaders were former clergymen – Ferdinand Domela Nieuwenhuis and Abraham Kuyper, each a superb orator in his own way. The new political culture had its origin in the pulpit.

Modern theology

In the second half of the nineteenth century Protestantism in the Netherlands (and else-where in Europe) was marked by a confrontation between so-called modern theology and orthodoxy. The significance and impact of this conflict were far-reaching. The sig-nificance may be judged by the fact that in the censuses between 1879 and 1920 a major-ity of the population said they belonged to one of the Protestant churches, with the Dutch Reformed Church in the lead. Up to 1900 about sixty percent were Protestant; this was the case from the 1879 to the 1899 census. Afterwards this figure gradually declined until at the 1930 census it fell below fifty. Moreover, in that census the proportion of those with no religion rose above ten percent for the first time.

The impact may be regarded as far-reaching because it was not just a question of a confrontation between academic theologians; the arguments and counter-arguments reached the various congregations from the pulpits. In the Netherlands, Protestant the-ology was academic theology. The ministers of the Dutch Reformed Church were uni-versity-educated and saw for themselves in the lecture rooms how Protestant doctrine was being tested against new insights gained in philosophy and science. The result was so-called modernism, which created a new standard of scholarship in theology but also caused a crisis of faith among the clergy and deep divisions in congregations.

The privileged status given to the Dutch Reformed Church at universities was not really compatible with the separation of church and state. It could be explained as a relic of the public position of Calvinism at the time of the Republic in the seventeenth and eighteenth centuries. It was also a result of the constitutional control of the Church by King William I, who in this way oversaw the quality and content of the education of the clergy. Other religions in the Netherlands, on the other hand, such as the Protestant dis-senting churches, the Roman Catholic Church and the Israelite Synagogue, had their own seminaries, where their theological training was concentrated. Only the schools of the dissenters were increasingly linked to universities; the Catholic and Jewish institu-tions were completely private. An attempt to impose state control on the training of Catholic priests led to a serious conflict between the king and the Catholic Church and was a portent of the secession of Belgium.

The argument about the privileged position of the Reformed Church flared up in the eighteen-seventies when a new higher education act was debated. A compromise was reached in Parliament. Theology was retained in the university system on the under-standing that teaching posts in Reformed dogma and practical theology would be entrusted to lecturers with a church affiliation. In future there would be a *duplex ordo*: professors, who would be appointed by the state, and chairs, which would be held by candidates in the name of one of the churches.[21]

This *duplex ordo* in the theological department was welcomed by the modernists because it implicitly recognized the scientific nature of theology – scientific, that is, in the new, contemporary sense. The principal spokesman for this movement, Jan Hendrik Scholten, rector magnificus at Leiden in 1877, expressed satisfaction that theology had not been reduced to a "luxury."[22] The Lutheran professor Abraham Dirk Loman believed the Act heralded a new age of secularized religious studies. For the first time, without any direct connection to the church, theology would have to legitimize itself as a true science for the children of the age.[23] The university guaranteed an academic study of theology based not on church dogma but on the laws of empirical testing and the free pursuit of truth.

Theology is central to Protestantism, not only as a discipline in the education of the clergy, but also in the experience of faith. In the words of the German historian Thomas Nipperdey, the churches of the Reformation were "Theologenkirchen," and their piety was "Reflexionsfrömmigkeit," piety in reflection. The relation of the individual to the world was theologically colored, as was the tension between tradition and contemporary form.[24] By 1900 modernism in Protestant theology was half a century old. The confrontation between traditions and contemporary scientific insights had matured. Three main themes may be discerned in this development: the tension between faith and natural sciences, especially after Darwin's theory of evolution; the tension between scripture and historical study of the Bible; and lastly the tension between the Christian doctrine of original sin and redemption and the contemporary emphasis on the autonomy of man.

There was a history behind this development: the flame had been lit in Utrecht in 1800 (as a result of the Enlightenment), fanned in Groningen in 1830 and turned into a blaze in Leiden around 1860. Looking back from 1900, the encouragement of new theology at the university in Groningen was still a landmark. It was raised by Petrus Hofstede de Groot (1802-1886), who in 1829, at the age of 27, became professor of theology and with some sympathizers started a new movement. In their circle belief was not a collection of doctrines and prescriptions: *religio habitat in sensu* (religion resides in the heart). The accent was on the moral ideals of a civic Christianity and on its importance for upbringing and education.

Even after the Groningen movement began to lose its importance, one aspect of it continued to be influential. In their desire to play down the dividing lines drawn by Calvin and to get back to a general Christian church, Hofstede de Groot and his sympathizers turned to the history of the church in the Netherlands, where they discovered other sources of piety and religious inspiration in the medieval movement of the *devotio moderna*. They also found kindred spirits in Thomas à Kempis and Geert Groote and his Brethren of the Common Life. They rediscovered humanists like Erasmus and Grotius, known for their dislike of strict divisions in the Christian religion. According to the Groningen theologians, this original religious culture was stunted in its growth by the foreign influences of Luther and Calvin, who replaced biblical, practical principle by a speculative, legalistic mentality and suppressed and smothered the indigenous seeds.[25] This "theological Netherlandism" laid the foundation for new studies in ecclesiastical history dealing with the late Middle Ages and the early Reformation in the Low Countries. What Hofstede de Groot put forward largely intuitively – a picture of one original reformation in the Low Countries, without different movements – would be confirmed by research in the next century.

System building and system criticism

In Leiden the flame was lit by the minister Jan Hendrik Scholten (1811-1885), who taught natural theology and the history of religion and philosophy there from 1843. In 1848 he published the first volume of his *De Leer der Hervormde Kerk, in hare grondbeginselen uit de bronnen voorgesteld* (The Teachings of the Reformed Church, Presented in Their Basic Principles from the Sources). The second volume followed two years later. It made him nationally famous because of its historical and systematic organization.[26] "There was something in Scholten," wrote a student of his fifty years later, "which meant, it seems to me, that he met a deeply felt need of his time, a desire to *understand*, to fathom the reasonableness of things, to know how everything is and must be; he provided a *system* in which there was no longer any room for reasonable doubt."[27]

In the terminology of the day Scholten was a "monist" and an "anti-supernaturalist." He earned the first qualification because he did not think in terms of material versus spirit or world versus God. Nature was the revelation of "a harmonious universal life"; natural laws were the expression of God's thoughts. In this scheme there was no place for a double order, for intervention by God in worldly events, thus no supernaturalism, no miracles. Scholten's religion was also a testimony to liberal optimism about the autonomous individual, as opposed to the old Protestant pessimism about sinful man. The language he used was derived from modern scientific thought and not from the Bible.

Historians have analyzed Scholten's theological system by comparing and contrasting it with the theses of Cornelis Willem Opzoomer (1821-1892), a jurist and philosopher at the University of Utrecht who believed in a radical intellectualism in knowledge of religious truth. Opzoomer became professor of philosophy at Utrecht in 1846, at the age of 25. He was also a jurist and wrote about liberal doctrine and theology. In the Netherlands he has come to be seen as the proponent of empirical philosophy. He and his pupils, such as Allard Pierson mentioned above, were guided by the "passion of reality," the reality that was being dissected with increasing success by the physical sciences and ordered by laws. Opzoomer rejected large parts of the Bible as contradicting this empirical science.

He defined belief in a way that deviated from what he saw as the superseded ideas of speculative philosophy. Belief in God could only come from the second source of knowledge, inward perception or feeling. "The religious feeling bears witness to the existence of God as immediately as sensory perception bears witness to the existence of the world."[28] The value placed on the religious feeling went back to German Pietism, whose principal interpreters were Herder and Schleiermacher. The critical commentaries on Opzoomer's thesis presented him with two counter-arguments: to some his religious feeling created the possibility of bottomless subjectivity, and to others it was mainly an error whereby he "mistook an echo of instilled beliefs for something original."[29]

The historian of modernism, the theologian Karel Hendrik Roessingh, accorded praise and criticism in his conclusions. "It was Opzoomer above all who, through unsparing criticism, put our theology in medias res, and who, even if at first it was in a

man's sinful nature. The notion that there was no salvation outside the Christian doctrine of grace was no longer valid. In the last quarter of the nineteenth century the autonomy of man and a correspondingly humanist morality gained in importance within theology. By then Protestant modernism in the Netherlands was also guided by an alliance with liberalism and with a moral idealism that was expressed in the new sciences of psychology and education.[36]

Ethical theology

Around 1900 "ethical theology" became a collective term for the views of a new generation of modernists. They shared with their predecessors a respect for empiricism and a distaste for supernaturalism, but they were no longer preoccupied by developments in the natural sciences and no longer aspired to the kind of fixed and solidly founded theology that Scholten and his colleagues had formulated. In the terms of the Lutheran theologian Conrad Willem Mönnich, "What good is a belief in Providence, interpreted as a religious translation of the unbreakable laws of nature, if ethics, the human decision, freedom of moral action and responsibility to our fellow man are at issue? Firm ground is to be found in ethics, not in nature; that is where faith is to be understood."[37]

This development in theology should be seen less as a break than as a change of emphasis. Now that age-old dogma had been undermined by new science and traditional biblical exegesis had been replaced by literary and historical criticism, attention turned to ethics as an opportunity for theological reflection on freedom and human consciousness. Here again there was a legacy from the Enlightenment. This matter had come up before, when in a dispute with Conrad Busken Huet, who by then was no longer a minister, Abraham Kuenen had called the church "a seedbed for religion and morality." The essence of the Reformation was not in his view subordination to the Bible but "firm upholding of conscience, with the support of the authority of the holy Mother Church."[38] Around 1900 this received further emphasis as a result of the rise of humane disciplines such as psychology and education.

The Walloon minister Daniel Chantepie de la Saussaye (1818-1874), whose family had come to the Netherlands as refugees in the eighteenth century, is regarded as the pioneer of this movement. He first became a professor in Groningen in 1872, succeeding Hofstede de Groot. He was inspired by the German theologian Schleiermacher, who interpreted religion in his *Glaubenslehre* in terms of consciousness of God and not conception of God, and believed its core lay in ethics. Chantepie de la Saussaye attempted to free the "ethical Calvin" from the folds of "metaphysical scholastic" Calvinism.[39] Towards the turn of the century ethical theology took on an orthodox but above all social dimension through the work of Johannes Hermanus Gunning (1829-1905). He became a church-appointed professor at Amsterdam in 1882 and an ordinary professor at Leiden seven years later. His appointment took place against the recommendations of the faculty and board of governors. The minister of home affairs, Aeneas Baron Mackay, leader of the first coalition of Protestant and Catholic parties, wanted to bring about a "change of course" in fifty years of modernism in Leiden by giving the post to Gunning.

Gunning acquired a reputation for being a "Protestant father of the church" who bore witness rather than argued. His position was that religious truth was essentially ethics; belief in God was not a philosophical notion or a logical conclusion but a moral deed. Viewed from the standpoint of psychology and anthropology, religion was not a function within the whole of the human character but a prerequisite for and constitutive factor in it.[40] Under the influence of his teacher Opzoomer, Gunning had studied Spinoza, who pointed him in the direction of modernism. But Gunning took the opportunity offered by the erection of a statue of Spinoza in The Hague to openly distance himself from him. He described Spinozism as naturalistic (regarding nature as an organic whole above and beyond which nothing exists) and pantheistic (regarding all finite things as revelations of the one Universe, the impersonal Absolute). Gunning rejected this naturalism in the name of ethics, because it made absolute laws found by way of experience and conferred on them a normative character.[41] In this way he also implicitly distanced himself from the direction in which modernism in Leiden was moving.

The theologian A. Bruining (1846-1919) was, however, a model of ethical modernism. Through the intervention of Mackay, he had not been appointed to the chair in Leiden, but from 1900 he was a professor in the theology department of the University of Amsterdam. He too contended that theology should leave the path of monism and concentrate on the theme of ethics. "And by putting only the moral-religious life in the foreground and by reducing all points of doctrine to moral values, the ethical movement fulfils the requirement to make religion in all its dimensions a matter for the heart and the heart alone. Consequently, one need no longer refuse to describe someone as a religious person simply because he has rational objections to a metaphysical theory."[42]

Ethical theology was also advocated by Gunning's successor in Leiden, Pierre Daniel Chantepie de la Saussaye (1848-1920). In his inaugural address he referred to the radical Danish philosopher Sören Kierkegaard, who had understood better than anyone else in his time "that God's thoughts are not 'after man.'" He turned against the "religion of science" but also against the prevailing spirit of skepticism. Knowledge of God must be found in a personal encounter and this is why Chantepie de la Saussaye emphasized individual ethics. In the minds of his students, his successor Roessingh said of him, he "aroused new feeling and new openness for old, pious experiences of the soul."[43]

The ethical theologians of the first decade of the new century were diverse in their insights and concepts, but what they shared was an interest in psychological debate and an emphasis on individual religious experience. This is hardly surprising at a time that Heymans called a "future age of psychology." In the new decade there were two influential figures in the Netherlands. One was Heymans himself, who attracted the attention of theologians because of the metaphysical dimension of his "psychological monism."[44] The other was the Leiden philosopher G.J.P.J. Bolland, who, partly because of his rhetorical talents, was a renowned advocate of a new Hegelian idealism and because of that influenced students of theology. An "apostle of disbelief," he was concerned about a decline of Christianity among humble believers. "If the Christian faith is gone, in the enlightened minds of the future masses it will first be true night." So he encouraged the theologians in his audience to make use again of old dogmatic formulas and to explain the Bible in terms of allegory.[45]

During the First World War the generation of Bruining and Chantepie de la Saussaye retired. New theologians with their own special concerns appeared. Before long they were led by two professors, Roessingh and Gerrit Jan Heering. Both were Remonstrants and belonged to a group of thirty ministers formed at the beginning of the century under the name "Malcontents." Several were to become influential theologians: in addition to Roessingh and Heering there was Hendrik Tjakko de Graaf. They were given the label "malcontent" by outsiders. They interpreted it as meaning not "discontented" but "unsatisfied," because they did not share the humanistic optimism of modern theology and wanted to return to the doctrine of pessimism about sinful man and redemption. According to Roessingh, this change meant saying goodbye to the scholasticism of modernism and greater concentration on human self-knowledge under the influence of the rise of psychology. They wanted to elevate the debate about the historicity of Jesus Christ by no longer concentrating on historical criticism but instead seeking the meaning of his appearance "supra historiam," above history. "Anyone not completely unfamiliar with the history of Christianity sees here the long line of strong, robust minds who set the tremendous, joyful power of their belief in God against this black background and found in that the driving force for a life in this world in the service of God."[46]

The consequences for the Church

Academic modernism reached the pulpits of the Reformed Church through newly trained ministers. There was a perceptible distance between this theory and religious practice in local churches and sometimes it was considerable. Centers of traditional piety resisted; the young minister could not always count on the support of his audience for the ideas with which he had become familiar. "One was humbly content with few listeners for one weighed them and did not count them," wrote the minister Hendrik Pierson. The modernist felt he was part of the spirit of the age. "The awareness of strength, of having influence, of having the learned and cultivated among one's ranks, the fact that half the teachers and the younger generation were, if not on one's side, not opposed either was indeed sufficient reward."[47]

The confrontation between the young modernist and his orthodox congregation was intensified by the fact that in the Dutch Reformed Church the minister did not have a probationary period in which to get used to the job as an assistant. In this he was different from his colleagues in Britain, Germany and Scandinavia. Young ministers did not begin their career in a position of dependence in relation to the previous generation. This is crucially important for understanding the development of the Dutch Reformed Church around 1900. "It may for instance explain why 'modern', historical and critical theology in the Netherlands, although it arrived much later here, was able to grow into a much broader church 'movement' than in Germany."[48]

The opposition to modernism came indeed from below. An important point of contention was the election of elders and deacons. In 1852, influenced by the liberal Constitution of 1848, the Synod had ruled that the right to appoint elders and deacons and to call ministers belonged to the congregation. The old co-option rights of the nobility were abolished. It was not until 1866 that agreement was reached on how this was to be implemented. From March 1, 1867 men aged 23 and over could elect the church council. This right was exercised in slightly over half the Reformed congregations; in most of them orthodox elders secured a majority. The banner of orthodoxy waved from the towers of St. Martin's in Groningen, the Dom in Utrecht, St. Peter's in Leiden, the Westerkerk (West Church) in Amsterdam and along the railroad from Amsterdam to Rotterdam, exulted the ultra-orthodox minister Andries Willem Bronsveld. Modernist ministers found themselves faced by orthodox elders who raised objections about the validity of the professions of faith made and the baptismal formula, or frustrated the acceptance of new members.[49]

Those who regarded themselves as liberals then left the Reformed Church and joined the Calvinist dissenters in the Remonstrant Brotherhood. Its resulting growth was reflected in the founding of new congregations and in a sometimes spectacular program of church building. In the three northern provinces the number of Remonstrants rose from just 72 in 1849 to nearly 3,000 at the end of the nineteenth century and 3254 in 1920.[50] But in reaction to the orthodox backlash there was a measure of solidarity among the modernist members who wanted to remain in the age-old national Church. They were encouraged by favorable results in 1890 in a second wave of church council elections in several towns, among them Haarlem, Dordrecht, Nijmegen and Sneek. In 1906 the liberals in the Reformed Church joined forces in a Central Committee and later in an association. This gave the modern left wing of the Reformed Church a centre for solidarity and campaigning.[51]

Opzoomer drew a different conclusion. He was the driving force behind the founding of the *Nederlandse Protestanten Bond* (NPB) in 1870. It was modeled on the Protestantenverein in Germany, which had been established in the eighteen-sixties to bring together Protestants across the dividing lines of state and denomination. Opzoomer presented the Bond for "baptism" on Reformation Day (October 31, 1871). It was to unite kindred spirits inside and outside the existing congregations. He certainly succeeded in this to some extent, as shown by the striking number of Bond churches built in the years after World War I. Yet the fact is that within the overall Reformed system in the Netherlands such specific organizations remained more or less marginal. Many within modernism stayed in the traditional Church, where they tried to form a liberal tendency.[52]

The culture of liberalism

While forming a group was not a typical ambition of the liberals, they did display recognizable group behavior. Moreover, in 1915, partly as a result of Heymans's influence, there was a psychologist in these circles who studied liberal culture. This was Michiel C. van Mourik Broekman. He characterized the modern movement as a combination of personal religious experience and subjective piety. "Whereas orthodoxy, by its nature, is primarily intellectual, modernism, by its nature, is primarily emotional." Modernism could not offer a system, but it could provide elements of a world-view. Modern preaching

Building of the Vrije Gemeente (Free Church) in Amsterdam, *c.* 1920.

of the faith was elastic: not irrevocably tied to a time, person or attitude, it could absorb contemporary ideas and aspirations "without this fermentation process leading to the bursting of its essential nature." Modernism led to a greater emphasis on moral idealism.[53] But in practice ethical theology could sometimes be reduced to a more or less woolly religiosity and moralizing that was not always inspiring. Both were side effects of the culture of liberal Protestantism. "Intangible things such as *the* divine, *the* holy, *the* religious still haunt us – adjectives elevated to substantives, because substantial substantives are missing," wrote the Lutheran theologian Mönnich.[54]

The freedom of thought in modernism, the absence of a doctrinaire climate, led to new forms of religiosity. Ethical idealism could result in unusual manifestations of a social conscience, possibly in socialism. An example of the first is the so-called Vrije Gemeente (Free Church). The second is exemplified by the "red pastors."

The initiative for the Free Church, which was based on an American model, even went beyond the bounds of the Christian religion. On Reformation Day 1877 the minister Petrus Hermanus Hugenholtz announced from the pulpit of the New Church in Amsterdam that in protest "against any prescribed dogmatic creed" he would resign from his post with the Dutch Reformed Church. His brother Philip Reinhard followed suit. The two of them and 131 like-minded men and women formed a new community, the Free Church. Reformed canon law and administering the sacraments were abandoned in favor of freedom of creed and open examination of what other religions had produced. Six months later the church had 353 members and 314 supporters. This liberal elite did not lack funds and in May 1880 they were able to move into a new building of their own on Weteringschans in Amsterdam. In its organization and membership the Free Church remained largely limited to Amsterdam.[55]

The later teacher Theo Thijssen and his brother Henk attended the Sunday school of the Free Church. "This greatly pleased Grandma Fieggen, who was now reassured that we would not be brought up as complete savages; and Granddad Thijssen said, when he heard of it, that in any event a person had to be something. The memories of that Sunday school are all faded and vague. We sang hymns that we learned by numbers, to do-re-mi, just like at ordinary school. The master told one story from the Bible and one ordinary story. But there was one unusual thing that I do remember: if you liked a story, you were 'allowed' to write an essay about it at home; you didn't have to. And when you had a certain number of essays in your exercise book, ten or twenty, I don't remember, you were entitled to a book, at Christmas. Sometimes a well-written essay was read out. Now and again I wonder whether there was ever any praying at that Sunday school, for I can't remember."[56]

Social conscience

Moral idealism led to a social conscience at a time when the social question was high on the political agenda. In the context of the alliance between religious and social liberalism, ethical theology influenced the latter. On the so-called Protestants Day in 1887 the *Nederlandse Protestanten Bond* held a conference in Nijmegen on the social question. The social-liberal member of Parliament Hendrik Goeman Borgesius urged on the liberal Protestants the need for an active, practical Christianity. "With the social question, too, the main thing is the moral moment." He rejected both classic liberalism and the new socialism from a Christian standpoint. "From a religious, moral point of view it is hard to say which is the greater evil: the old economic system with its worship of self-interest or socialism with its worship of a despotic state regulating everything."[57]

Another outcome of practical Christianity might be opting for socialism. This was the choice made by those who had welcomed the freedom of thought in modern theology but found a lack of social concern in the rationality of the new theses. Some among the generation who studied theology around the turn of the century took this path. As students they became aware of the social question and they did not find their concerns shared by university teachers. The later "red pastor" Jan Anthonie Bruins said that the Leiden professors had taught them all kinds of things, but not what went on in the souls of people in a poor village in Friesland. A minister was to be a theologian and nothing but a theologian; he was not to become involved in social issues.[58] One exception by all accounts was Johannes Hermanus Gunning, who has already been mentioned. "Preaching in the least respected and least popular churches in Leiden," he acquired a loyal following among the students and gained the admiration of his colleagues. This support was "symptomatic of the emotional deficit" of agnosticism or even reasonable religion.[59] A former student wrote that "the spirit of the modern age seemed to come closer when we heard [Gunning] speak of Tolstoy and Nietzsche, names that were never mentioned ex cathedra at that time except in rancor or mockery."[60]

Around the turn of the century the red pastors emerged from the ranks of these students with a social conscience. They were found mainly in the northern provinces, the cradle of agrarian socialism in the Netherlands. At this time socialism was identified with active atheism or at the least agnosticism. This was also true of the Social Democratic Workers' Party (SDAP). Despite this, ministers who wanted to give their support without leaving the clergy sought each other out in an attempt to reconcile ideology and the Christian religion. The first issue of a Christian-socialist weekly, *De Blijde Wereld* (The Joyful World), appeared on November 1, 1902. The founders stated that they would "work enthusiastically for the realization of a better society" and "the coming of a joyful world" under the banner of Christianity and socialism. The founding of their journal was in itself an expression of joy. The initiators had each contributed an article, "which they read to each other on a beautiful September day, floating in a rowboat on the lovely waters" in Oranjewoud, a village near Heerenveen in Friesland.[61]

One example was the red pastor Frederik Willem Nicolaas Hugenholtz (1868-1924), who was called as a minister for the Nederlandse Protestanten Bond in Schiedam in 1895. He had been educated in Grand Rapids (Michigan), where his father was a minister and he himself had briefly headed the congregation of emigrants from Friesland and Groningen. "He was an impressive figure with his full beard and well cared-for clothes, extremely eloquent and sharp in debate, feared especially for his excellent documentation." When he arrived in Schiedam he felt an affinity with the manufacturer Jacob Cornelis van Marken, who was well known as a pioneer in the reform of working conditions in his Delft factory. In 1898 Hugenholtz wanted to found a workers' church in Schiedam. During the celebrations for the inauguration of Queen Wilhelmina he got into trouble with the middle-class citizens. Hugenholtz resigned in 1899; out of "love for religion" he ceased to be a "minister of religion." But he had become pessimistic about the power of preaching the faith and so left the church when in 1899 he moved to Voorburg and there became a propagandist for the SDAP. In 1901 he became member of Parliament for the West-Stellingerwerf district in Friesland.[62]

The rapprochement between the clergy and social democracy was a European trend. In Germany a group of young Lutheran pastors caused a stir at an "evangelical-social congress" in Berlin in 1890 by opting unequivocally for socialism. Five years later the Berlin Obenkirchenrat condemned this kind of "Pastorensozialismus." The founders of *De Blijde Wereld* had been chiefly inspired by English examples such as the minister John Trevor and his Labor Church (1892). They first joined the SDAP in 1905, when the party leadership stated that, while it was the task of social democrats to break the political and economic power of the Church, they did not want to offend against the religion of individual citizens inside or outside it. In 1907 a minister, the "red pastor" Bruins, was included in the commission charged with revising the party manifesto. His most important contribution was the stipulation that the party congress would "morally condemn" capitalism. This approach marked a break with the scientific foundations of Marxism and indeed was not approved without a fight at the party congress of 1912.[63] When, however, these "moral principles" had been incorporated in the party program, the way was clear for actual involvement by the red pastors. One of them, Willem Banning, would play a decisive role in the nineteen-thirties in the SDAP's change of course towards reformism.

Neo-Calvinism

Soon after the end of the century the University of Geneva came up with a plan to honor John Calvin with a monument to mark the 400th anniversary of his birth in 1909. Its inauguration was to be the highlight of the 350th anniversary of the founding of the university, originally an academy established by Calvin. The historian Charles Borgeaud was invited to give the plans concrete form. He had no doubt that Calvin should not be honored with a statue for he had not even wanted a gravestone. It would have to be a monument to Calvinism, not to Calvin; to the reformers and statesmen and pioneers who had propagated Calvinist thought. The result was a design in which sculpture had the leading role and allegory was avoided.[64] The monument, completed in 1917 and placed against the wall of the old bastion, consisted of statues of four reformers: Calvin, flanked by his countrymen Guillaume Farel and Théodore de Bèze and by the Scottish Presbyterian John Knox. To the left and right of them were the statesmen and pioneers and the great political events inspired by Calvinism such as the Edict of Nantes of 1598, the Glorious Revolution of 1688 in England, the Huguenots driven from France being welcomed in Potsdam by Friedrich Wilhelm, Elector of Brandenburg, and the Pilgrim Fathers founding their colony in New England in 1620. Naturally, a place in this gallery of honor was found for the House of Orange.

The Reformation Monument, as it has come to be known officially, depicts not only the King-Stadholder William III, but also his great-grandfather William of Orange, the leader of the Dutch Revolt, who is always referred to as William the Silent in Geneva. There is also a relief of the meeting of the States General which on July 26, 1581 approved the Act of Abjuration, the decision to end the sovereignty of Philip II of Spain over the Netherlands. Quotations from this Act are carved into the wall; they state that the ruler must not govern his subjects arbitrarily but with justice and fairness. The right to rise up against tyranny is derived from Calvinism. The choice of the theme of the Dutch section had not been easy. Borgeaud had suggested to Paul Frédéricq, his colleague in Ghent, that the subject should be the Pacification of Ghent (1578), but Frédéricq did not think this religious peace was typical of the heritage of the Reformation. Subsequently the Act of Abjuration was chosen, as proof of the Calvinist right to resist tyranny and because of its international influence, on the English Bill of Rights of 1688 and the American Declaration of Independence of 1776. It proved more difficult to make a historically accurate depiction of the meeting of the States General on July 26, 1581 because there was absolutely nothing unusual about it and there was no special record of it in the archives. The scene had to be reconstructed with the aid of the historian Nicolas Japikse.[65]

The importance of Calvinism in the founding and shaping of the Dutch state had also become a topical concern in the Netherlands. In November 1873, on the twenty-fifth anniversary of the Constitution of 1848, the minister Abraham Kuyper referred to it as the "origin and safeguard of our constitutional liberties." In the same breath he linked liberal principles and Calvinism in its "power for development." Dutch Calvinists, claimed Kuyper, did not want a return to the old privileging of the Reformed Church. They based themselves on the foundation of the new Constitution and wanted equal rights for all; their preference was for a constitutional monarchy but also for separating schools from churches. In the contemporary move towards a separation of church and state Kuyper saw an opportunity for religion to develop on its own. He compared the political program of Calvinism with the Lutheran Reformation, "which rebuilt but did not build new." After all, its churches bowed to the national ruler. In Germany and the Scandinavian countries the constitutional system of the Middle Ages had been continued "by transferring spiritual authority from the Roman Curia to the ruler's cabinet." In his eyes Calvinism in particular had the strength to derive its own political system from its own principles, "that are always recognizable by their republican character even under a monarchical system. Calvin did what Luther could not: he founded nationalities. Our Union, the England of the Glorious Revolution, the Scotland of the Covenant and the United States of America are foundations in his spirit."[66]

Belief in the importance of Calvinism had to be formulated in modern terms; orthodoxy had to be shrouded in contemporary clothes. Kuyper saw himself as a man of the nineteenth century, not the sixteenth. The "honor beckoning us" was "to make God's truth, which is of *all* centuries, the foundation of the development of the nineteenth century." Calvin provided the foundations on which it was possible to modernize the building of faith "in strictly logical style."[67]

With his creative intellect and rhetorical powers, Abraham Kuyper (1837-1920) dominated the orthodox Protestant movement in the Netherlands from 1872 to World War I, both theologically and politically. He studied in Leiden and it was there that he became familiar with modern theology and learned to value it. But in the first phase of his career as a minister of the Church his allegiance was to orthodoxy. We can get some idea of the impression he made on his audience from the notes of a student from Kampen who traveled to Amsterdam in October 1899 to hear Kuyper speak as vice chancellor of the Free University. He saw Kuyper stride in like "a powerful prince of the church." The culmination of his address was "immensely impressive and sent cold shivers down your spine." When he saw Kuyper in the street the next day the spell was broken. "On the street Kuyper made no impression at all; he just trudged along."[68] He combined his dramatic talents with a virtuoso mastery of the Dutch language. In speeches to a large audience he used all his powers of persuasion, to such a degree that the listener "goes home not just encouraged but ready to make any sacrifice, and communicates his enthusiasm to those who stayed at home."[69] At such moments his rhetoric was capable of influencing the nation, and he revealed a talent for the political leadership of a mass audience. Kuyper was a nervous character: on several occasions in his life he was forced to leave the stage because of stress. His passionate curiosity made it possible for him to constantly adopt new roles and views.

Mainly because of his deliberate pursuit of a schism, Kuyper's combative personality casts a long shadow over the history of Protestant orthodoxy in the Netherlands, but

Abraham Kuyper as an honorary doctor of Princeton University in the United States, 1898.

there was more to it than the conflict of 1886 in which he and his followers turned their backs on the Dutch Reformed Church. Two contrasts are apparent. The first is between the activism of Kuyper's followers and the Pietist attitude of other orthodox believers. The second is between internal criticism and separation, between the orthodox who wished to strive for improvement, because they wanted to be able to go on seeing the Dutch Reformed Church as the national Church, and those who pursued a strategy of conflict because they wanted their fellow believers to face up to what they regarded as an inevitable choice.

Pietist experience of God

In traditional Calvinism, once the Church had become established as a public institution in the Republic, there was fertile ground for a Pietist strain. Ministers called for a "Further Reformation," a movement against decline and for a truly personal conversion. This Pietism was also characterized by strict rules about behavior on Sunday and during the week. It insisted on zeal in religious obligations, encouraged activities such as repeating the Sunday sermon and catechization at home, and emphasized the sinfulness of misusing language, lewdness, vanity and worldliness. But pseudo-piety was thought as reprehensible as half-heartedness and godlessness.[70] A special place was reserved for the book – first of all the Bible and in it the Psalms, but also collections of hymns and edifying tracts. In the nineteenth century this tradition was reborn, after hibernating during the Enlightenment, as it were. This was loudly proclaimed by the exodus of the orthodox from the Dutch Reformed Church in 1834, known as the orthodox Schism.[71]

Criticism by the orthodox of what they saw as the elimination of the Reformation heritage in the Dutch Reformed Church did not necessarily lead to the founding of a new church, as happened in the Schism. In the provinces of Gelderland and Utrecht the orthodox adopted a passive attitude to the institution of the Church. In the region on either side of the Merwede river there were communities who could be seen as continuing an age-old Reformation consciousness: they acknowledged their own guilt for the split in the national Church and their powerlessness to do anything to change the situation. They regarded their regular "gatherings" as temporary "accommodation" until "it pleased the Lord to put matters right in the Church of the Reformation Himself."[72] The right wing of Calvinism indeed presented a wide range of individualism, from idiosyncratic ministers and evangelists to deliberately separate congregations.

The most extreme consequence of repentance and aversion was "keeping company" or "staying at home." This form of collective or individual piety had a long tradition in Dutch Protestantism. These were ways in which believers who preferred the company of only the like-minded, and "stay-at-homes," who read a sermon in their own circle, showed their rejection of church organization. This attitude was often the result of testing the existing churches – usually those in the surrounding district – by the standards of Pietist writings of the seventeenth and eighteenth centuries. Such communities were to be found in the polders beside the Rhine and the Maas but also in Rotterdam, which had expanded to take in part of the surrounding countryside. The influx of immigrants from the islands in the province of South Holland and in Zeeland led to there being an unusual number of splinter groups and companies in the city. Where they felt abandoned by religion, immigrants formed groups themselves, often inspired by evangelists and united in an emotional solidarity.[73]

An unusual type of company arose from the view "that church life in the Netherlands was so deeply corrupt that God refused to have anything more to do with it and so there were no longer any ministers called by God." Not even evangelists were recognized. Only "keeping company" had any value. Those who thought like this were unchurched on principle.[74] The stay-at-homes included those who did not attend church services because they did not want to make use of any means of transport on the day of rest. The area around the Merwede river was the heartland of these companies and of this deliberate non-attendance at church.

First Schism: 1834

The Schism of 1834 actually resulted from a synodal disciplinary procedure against Hendrick de Cock, the minister in the village of Ulrum in the province of Groningen. On the grounds of "old Reformed truth" he had turned against the new hymns of the Enlightenment and against the power of the state in the Dutch Reformed Church, which had been given a central organization in 1816. He and his congregation refused to accept the authority of the Synod and other ministers followed suit. But the individual nature of the protest was characteristic. The Schism, also called secession (*Afscheiding*) did not take place at a stroke, but spread like an oil slick; it was an accumulation of local schisms for which the ground was laid by a tradition of conventicles and lay readers. By the end of the century they had a national church, the *Christelijk-Gereformeerde Kerk* (1869), with its own theological school in Kampen (1854), which was crucially important in combining forces at the national level.

From the social point of view the supporters of the Schism were humble folk: bargemen, farm workers and petty bourgeois. In their religion they opted for a return to the "old Reformed truth" and for personal experience of God, Pietism, which was directed inwards and was not an invitation to activism (social or otherwise).[75] In the census of 1849 the "Christian dissenters" of 1834 were mentioned separately for the first time. They numbered over 40,000 and fifty years later they had grown to nearly 190,000. As a percentage of the population they rose from 1.3 to 4.2. In 1889 they were most often found where the Schism began, in the far north of the country. It was precisely in these areas that opposition to the enlightened ministers of the Groningen movement had been strong.

In the provinces of North and South Holland the dissenters were concentrated in Den Helder, where a large naval base was built, or in areas like the island of Texel and the Haarlemmermeer, which had been reclaimed for new settlers. Fairly large numbers of Christian Reformed farmers from South Holland, from Goeree-Overflakkee and other areas, moved to Texel. Many dissenters turn out to have moved to the Haarlemmermeer polder; they made up nearly eleven percent of the settlers there. The leading Dutch politician in the first half of the twentieth century, Hendrikus Colijn, came from one such family. The new land was called "little America"[76] for this reason.

What was left of the companies in the shadow of the Reformed Church was severely diminished by the next schism, the secession known as the "Doleantie" of 1886. Abraham Kuyper had great respect for the power of these private groups and he attempted to bring their vitality into his church when he offered the lay readers an opportunity to switch over.[77]

Second schism: the "Doleantie"

The schism at the turn of the year in 1885/1886 was a deliberate break, the culmination of a lengthy strategy of conflict. Kuyper's militancy was at its height; his campaign for orthodoxy was deliberately aimed at separating the "whole-hearted" from the "half-hearted." The fact that the Anti-Revolutionary Party, the party of orthodox

Protestantism, and the new orthodox Protestant Free University were involved in the tumult was typical of the creative power of this new Calvinism. They wanted to make their presence felt in various spheres and this ambition was cast in a modern form. It was also characteristic that the split in 1886 took place in Amsterdam, the country's cultural center, and not, as in the Schism of 1834, in small communities on the periphery. It was in the city that Kuyper and his supporters encountered the tradesmen and workers who found a source of individual identity and social militancy in active Calvinism.

The first major point of contention lay where church and society had traditionally come up against each other, in the field of education. During the nineteenth century the state took on more and more responsibility for extending and improving education. This meant that it increasingly encroached on an area that the orthodox Protestant elite thought of as their own. In 1857 Parliament passed an act stipulating that state schools must offer education in the general Christian and social virtues. The political leader of Protestant orthodoxy, Guillaume Groen van Prinsterer, concluded that the aim should be private Christian schools free of state influence. With this in mind, in 1861 a society for the promotion of Christian national education was set up. It had an extensive network of agents, Bible salesmen and correspondents and in this way it was the first organization in which the "people behind the electorate" were actively and, through a system of contributions, financially involved.[78] The slogan through which in 1869 Groen announced a break with the liberal wing of Protestantism – "our strength lies in isolation" – led to the formation of his own power center in the "anti-revolutionary" movement, which was opposed to several principles of the French Revolution. In this conflict Groen described himself as both an "enfant du Réveil" (i.e. a child of Pietism) and "issu de Calvin" (i.e. a militant reformer).[79]

The followers of Groen, with Abraham Kuyper in the lead, continued to draw similar conclusions. The earlier society gave rise in 1872 to a new organization, the Anti-School Law League, which was modeled on the Anti-Corn Law League in Britain. Its aim was to make private schools the rule in the Netherlands and state education supplementary. In the elections for the Lower House of Parliament in 1874 the League was the instrument of a party political campaign, the first example of the mobilization of large numbers of voters. In 1877 it opposed the new education act backed by the liberal minister Johannes Kappeyne van de Coppello, who raised the standards of state education and thus extended their lead over private Christian schools. A petition was drawn up and over 300,000 signatures were collected. Support was mobilized by Kuyper, who had started his own newspaper in 1872. Through *De Standaard* his religious and political messages from the pulpit would reach a national audience. In 1877 it was also the vehicle for giving national publicity to the positions taken in *Ons Program*, the political charter of the Anti-Revolutionary Party.

Free University

The next object of orthodox mobilization was in a sense the culmination of the conflict over schools: a Protestant university free of state influence. The success of modern theology had led to a desire for a new and determinedly orthodox university course for ministers. The founding of a Christian university became an aim in Kuyper's program after the constitutional provision on freedom of education had acquired the force of law for universities too in 1876. At that point he was in the Swiss Alps recovering from a long period of stress. When it also became clear that a proposal made by the Reformed Congregation in Amsterdam for an orthodox professor in the new theological faculty of the city's university (i.e. the appointment of Kuyper) would not be approved, the question of a separate university was decided. In December 1878 the Association for Higher Education on Reformed Principles was founded in Amsterdam. In an academic session at the New Church in Amsterdam on October 20, 1880 the Free University was inaugurated. At that stage theology was the only department. As the first rector, Kuyper delivered an opening address on "Sovereignty in one's own sphere." On this slogan of Groen van Prinsterer's he based not only a new philippic against the absolutism of the state but also his plea for independent research and the free pursuit of knowledge. He referred to the historical example of Spinoza, whose studies were "flawed" in the eyes of Calvinists, so that his conclusion must be a "lie," but who must be admired and praised because "seeing what he saw as he saw it, he resolutely refused to lend himself to a violation of the sovereignty of science in his sphere." This freedom had to be defended tooth and nail. "At the very real risk of being damaged by science, the Church must itself insist that science, without ever becoming a slave, upholds the sovereignty to which it is entitled in its own field and flourishes by the grace of God."[80]

With the independent pursuit of knowledge included in the foundation address, the Free University could become a platform for the encounter between modern science and neo-Calvinism. In the early years, when a standpoint had still to be established, this confrontation was sometimes polemical or defensive. In 1899, for example, Kuyper again delivered the rector's address, this time on the modern theme of evolution. His opening remark became famous: "Our nineteenth century is wasting away under the hypnosis of the evolution dogma." Up to then in his view only the Christian religion had an all-encompassing system, but now its opponents "had acquired an all-encompassing system, a world-view and philosophy derived from a single principle." Kuyper called for resistance to these ideas, not to the biological theory as such but to the newly conceived system in which the strong must destroy the weak and in which not the individual but the species was all-important.[81]

The new university offered an opportunity to provide Protestant orthodoxy with a systematic theology. Between 1893 and 1894 Kuyper wrote his *Encyclopaedie der Heilige Godgeleerdheid* (Encyclopedia of Holy Theology) in three volumes. It was his magnum opus, giving the reader not only a theological structure but also an epistemology, for he wanted to bring the whole of Calvinist knowledge "into rapport with the human consciousness" of his age. The theological college founded in Kampen after the 1834 Schism had a similar influence. In the spring of 1895 Professor Herman Bavinck published the first volume of his *Gereformeerde Dogmatiek* (Reformed Dogma). He had been inspired by the renewed interest in the Catholic Church in the teachings of Thomas Aquinas and wanted to formulate a new system for orthodox Reformed theology. The fourth and last volume appeared in 1901.[82] Both Kuyper and Bavinck gave the orthodox campaign an intellectual foundation, and thus secured the same position as the Leiden theologian Scholten with his systematic theology of modernism.

in 1886, but now there were also urban ministers of authority who had left their mark on numerous places and often stayed in touch with their former congregations. In 1834 it was a matter of a group of men who still had to find their way theologically and only years later understood how a church organization founded on the orthodox Reformed creed should be set up. In 1886 the leaders were sure of their cause and the models were ready, for the local community and for regional and national organization. In 1834 the activists had to communicate with kindred spirits by means of pamphlets sent by barge or stagecoach. In 1886 there was a daily press, and telegraphy and trains served to disseminate new ideas. In 1834 no prominent theologian had become involved with the Schism, and only the odd student had joined the cause. In 1886 there was a Free University, which through its existence alone forced the theological departments of the state universities to define their standpoint.[85]

Both orthodox groups came to terms in 1892: 400 dissenting congregations joined up with 300 *Nederduitse Gereformeerde* churches. Henceforth they were known as the *Gereformeerde Kerken* in Nederland. They had roughly equal numbers of members: 190,000 *Christelijk Gereformeerd* (dissenters) and 180,000 from the *Doleantie*. There was a greater difference in the number of ministers: 120 from the *Doleantie* and 305 dissenters. As a matter of fact, in the end only three-quarters of the 190,000 dissenters proved ready to reunite. The others numbered nearly 55,000 in 1899, more than one percent of the population.

Neo-Calvinism and other countries

Neo-Calvinism, which in the Netherlands under Kuyper's leadership became a form of mass mobilization, was modeled on foreign examples. In the eighteen-seventies Kuyper studied Lutheran Germany, and in particular the court chaplain in Berlin, Christian Adolf Stöcker (1835-1909), who had a social conscience and called for internal missions to the workers. In 1878 he founded the *Christlich-Soziale Arbeiterpartei*, and the next year he won a seat in parliament. Stöcker was an inspiring speaker and combined his social conscience with Lutheran piety and German nationalism. He did more than anyone else to put social issues on the church agenda. In his attacks on liberalism, however, he increasingly struck an openly anti-Semitic note. In September 1878 Kuyper and the Amsterdam brewer Willem Hovy paid him a visit in Berlin. The question has since been raised whether in certain anti-Jewish remarks Kuyper made he was inspired by Stöcker, whom he admired for his social views. Kuyper had been writing about the Jews since as early as 1875 and in 1879 he sent the party charter *Ons Program*, including articles on "Liberalists and Jews," to Stöcker. As part of his campaign against state schools and liberalism, he opposed the social and secularizing influence of the Jews. Kuyper was anti-Jewish but not anti-Semitic. In any case his views date from 1875 and were not first inspired by Stöcker. The latter was not in the end included in the list of foreign models in Kuyper's *Ons Program*.[86] The *Christlich-Soziale Arbeiterpartei* was not as successful in Germany as the Anti-Revolutionary Party in the Netherlands. The German historian Thomas Nipperdey attributes this failure to three causes, one of which can be related to the fact that in Germany Protestantism was not at bay as it was in the Netherlands and

Switzerland – or could be portrayed as such. Another reason had to do with the Lutheran tradition in Germany, where there was no place for such interweaving of politics and religion.[87]

Kuyper later turned more and more to the Anglo-American world, first to Britain until around the turn of the century he developed an aversion to British politics because of the Boer War. The liberal Gladstone was his great example. In 1898 he crossed the Atlantic to deliver the Stone Lectures at Princeton. He found like-minded Dutch communities in the New World. America was a new world for emigrants who had chosen to leave the Netherlands for other than economic reasons. Between 1844 and 1857 about ten percent of the dissenters left the Netherlands; they made up thirty-five percent of all the Dutch Protestant emigrants. In addition to the agricultural depression, the religious factor, the repression of the Schism, was a strong motive for leaving. Fellow believers in America formed a network which could embrace newcomers. It was the promised land in two senses: they could practice their religion freely and they could find work. In this way a Reformed Church of America came into existence and later, after a dispute over policy on Freemasonry, a breakaway Christian Reformed Church. The Kuyperian variant of neo-Calvinism also reached the United States.

The characteristic features of the Dutch Schism, a measure of personal faith and individual repentance, were accordingly typical of these emigrants in the beginning. "Dutch-American piety focused on God's mercy, endless and abounding; on Christ's self-humiliation and suffering; and on the utter dependence of the redeemed. Life viewed from the Dutch pulpit and pew was not, then, the energetic, optimistic, progressive thing so familiar to American Protestantism. The Dutch pastoral ethic was not one of perfectionism but of penitence, of tribulation." At the end of the century, when the dissenters in the Netherlands united with Kuyper's orthodox Reformed group, the emphasis changed. "An occasional Neo-Calvinistic voice declared that under the Lordship of Christ 'all the earth' belonged to the faithful, but just as soon warned the faithful not to become earthly." The integration of the Dutch emigrants was perhaps a stronger stimulus encouraging a certain activism. For in the growing number of sermons in English in the Reformed Church of America there was ever more evidence of moderation, mildness and joy. "But the pulpit achieved its harmony only by skirting the most nagging issue: 'Americanization.' Agreeing to become 'American Reformed' had been easy; defining exactly what 'Reformed' and 'American' meant was far more difficult. In sum, the intellectual history of Dutch America between 1900 and 1916 is the story of debate over these concepts."[88]

Reformed orthodoxy

The *Doleantie* of 1886 was not only a conflict with modernism but also a split within orthodoxy. For many of the orthodox wanted to remain loyal for various reasons to the Dutch Reformed Church, the national Church of the people. To a large extent the dividing line was socially determined. Many of the ordinary people followed Kuyper's lead and left, but the majority of the Protestant nobility, the patricians, the well-off middle class and the ministers, if they were orthodox, continued to identify with the Reformed

Church. This was also true of the head of state. Queen Wilhelmina, who had no official func-tion in the Dutch Reformed Church, never forgave Kuyper for damaging the national Church of her forebears. In 1886 the core orthodox group split in two. The majority remained loyal to the national Church for ideological and tactical reasons. Only a minority of the ministers and politicians, no more than a hundred, put themselves at the head of the *Doleantie*.[89] Insofar as the orthodox wanted to be a distinct group within the Dutch Reformed Church, they formed a wing. In 1906, twenty years after the split, they set up an identifiable association, an orthodox league which in 1919 became the *Gereformeerde Bond tot verbreiding en verdediging van de Waarheid in de Nederlandsche Hervormde (Gereformeerde) Kerk* (Orthodox Reformed League for the dissemination and defense of the Truth in the Dutch Reformed [orthodox Reformed] Church).

The so-called middle orthodox movement found an eloquent champion around the turn of the century in the minister Philippus Jacobus Hoedemaker, the only professor at the Free University who did not join the *Doleantie*. He was an example of an orthodox believer who aligned himself with the strictly Calvinist wing up to 1886 but in the end shrank from the consequences of a split. Hoedemaker was seen as a theologian who could give a new meaning to the so-called "confessional movement," which wanted to uphold orthodox doctrine and restore the creeds of the Synod of Dordrecht without undermining the rules currently in place. He now emphasized the (Protestant) nation, the organic whole of individuals with a common character and a vocation of their own, united in a complex of memories and vicissitudes. The Netherlands was "a Christian, Protestant, Orthodox Reformed nation," which he did not want to divide according to norms of Calvinist purity. From this arose the slogan "All the Church and all the People." Hoedemaker wanted to uphold the whole confession but it had to be able to be given new interpretations as long as this was done by a statutory body assembled for the pur-pose. He rejected the use of disciplinary measures to expel modernists from the Church.

Following naturally from this was the attempt to offer an alternative to the Protestant Anti-Revolutionaries who refused to follow Kuyper after the split in 1886 and thus appeared to be at a dead end politically. This was why in 1896 two ministers founded the *Christelijk-Historische Kiezersbond*. From this in 1903 came the *Christelijk-Historische Unie*, which was supplemented with a group of former supporters of Kuyper led by the jurist Alexander Frederik de Savornin Lohman. In 1896 he had resigned from his post as a pro-fessor at the Free University. Despite cooperating in the "Doleantie," he had continued to have good relations with ethical ministers and theologians such as Gunning and Hendrik Pierson, and had rejected Kuyper's polemical distinction between the "whole-hearted" and the "half-hearted" in the orthodox world. A commission of enquiry at the Free University headed by the theologian Herman Bavinck concluded by a large major-ity that orthodox principles were not sufficiently expressed in Lohman's lectures. Lohman resigned. He became the most important politician in the new Christelijk-Historische Unie, the rallying point for orthodox Reformed believers.

To this picture of the Dutch Reformed Church as a complex institution with several shades of opinion must be added Methodism. It had its own past in the Netherlands in the Protestant Réveil, the product of a romantic revival of religion during the Restoration (1814-1830). In the eighteen-forties it had become a society for church recovery, the term for an orthodox counteroffensive against the rationalist influence of the Enlightenment. The "Christian Friends," as they called themselves, were characterized by Pietism and by a certain elegance derived from the aristocratic or middle-class backgrounds of the members. Thanks above all to the minister Otto Gerhard Heldring (1804-1876), the Christian Friends took an interest in the problems associated with poverty and social degeneracy. Indeed, in the last quarter of the nineteenth century, the "Indian summer" of the Réveil, this was their most prominent activity. Since 1845 the six-monthly meetings of the Christian Friends had become a sort of exchange where existing and new projects were traded. Thus out of the Réveil came missionary societies in the Dutch East Indies, but also institutions for "fallen women," difficult youths and the disabled, as well as diverse organizations such as the mental homes in Zetten and the Klokkenberg teachers' college in Nijmegen. Ladies also took part in this work; the Deaconesses Foundation in Utrecht was one result.[90]

In the eighteen-eighties the significance of the Réveil became a subject of debate in Kuyper's offensive for orthodoxy. He drew a distinction in Dutch orthodoxy between an indigenous and national movement – neo-Calvinism – and a foreign and international movement, the Réveil imported from England and Switzerland, which had gained ground among the upper classes especially. In his view it suffered from the one-sidedness of Methodism, which indeed delivered souls from the world but otherwise left the world unchanged. This was a variation on the theme of "politicophobia," of which he also accused the Reformed descendants of the Réveil like Beets and Chantepie de la Saussaye. In Kuyper's polemical presentation the Réveil appeared as a movement that had surrendered state, society and scholarship in order to be able to withdraw into the spiritual. Moreover, the aristocratic supporters of the Réveil had contributed to the petit bourgeois and the lower classes being made inarticulate and held back. Aristocratic and patrician families were after all represented on the boards of a series of philanthropic foundations. Nonetheless, this patronage of "our Christian people" had been ended by the introduction of the right to vote in the Reformed Church.[91]

This vision was inspired more by militancy than by detached observation. Reformed orthodoxy was present at the Christian Social Congress held in 1891, the first large event organized by Anti-Revolutionaries at which poor working conditions and poverty were discussed. At this congress there were thirteen dissenting ministers, nineteen from the *Doleantie* and ten Reformed. Of the twelve members of Parliament present, five were Reformed. The 500 delegates tried to preserve Reformed unity through a demand for workers to have influence in the national government and for improved working conditions and housing. Five years later a Church Congress for an Inner Mission was held; it can be seen as the new Réveil of Reformed orthodoxy. It was organized by ministers who characterized the gathering as a "medical congress of our church family." The "church of mercy," so closely associated with the Réveil, was the old and at the same time the new answer to the militancy of the socialist labor movement. With its emphasis on inner missions and its system of charitable institutions, and its so-called midnight missionaries who visited the brothels to protest against prostitution, after 1895 the Réveil was a symbol of the movement for the restoration of the national Church that had flowered in the face of Kuyper's conflict strategy.[92]

Another notable initiative, which arose from Reformed orthodoxy, was the founding in January 1896 of the *Nederlandse Christen-Studenten Vereniging* (NCSV). The founders drew their evangelical inspiration from the Anglo-American awakening movement led by John Mott, which resulted in 1895 in the setting up of a World Federation of Christian Student Societies. Initially this Methodist inspiration was dominant within the NCSV. It was a form of piety that was closely related to that of the Réveil: mildly orthodox with an emphasis on personal experience and practical implementation of belief. The society was open to all Protestant students but attracted mainly orthodox Reformed members. More strictly Calvinist students also joined; most of them came from circles that had been influenced by the Réveil. There was also an occasional Lutheran or Mennonite member.

In the local branches the accent was on Bible study and prayer. In contrast to the American and English models, the NCSV paid hardly any attention to missionary work in the European colonies. The pre-eminent and most popular activity was the annual summer conference. The summer camp for secondary schoolboys, which began in 1896 and was based on an English model, also came to be an important part of the work done by the NCSV. In 1899 there prevailed "an unnatural exaltation of subjective pious feeling" and a "surge of sentiment." The conferences were increasingly marked by Pietism.[93] In 1918 the NCSV changed character. As a result of the efforts of Hendrik Kraemer, the later missionary theologian, the society transformed itself from a "Pietist circle" of kindred spirits into a "testifying vanguard" in the student world. In the nineteen-thirties the society became a source of renewal under the influence of the Swiss theologian Karl Barth. Members of that generation played a leading role in the church resistance to the German occupation of the Netherlands in World War II.

Church building and worship

At the end of the nineteenth century churches and church towers dominated the skyline of Dutch towns and villages. They were the expression of a history of Christian confession and of the church's prominence in local relations. The church had to disseminate piety, and the tower was a call to worship. The local authorities accepted the church's prominence because the building and the tower were characteristic features of the town or village. In most cases the oldest church was Reformed, although it might have medieval (and Catholic) origins. There was no attempt to conceal this. In numerous medieval town churches the Catholic past in the form of choir screens, pulpits, wall paintings and baptismal fonts was respected. In the interior brass chandeliers, pews for prominent citizens, memorials to leading townspeople and tombs of naval heroes pointed to the centrality of the Reformed Church in urban life. In contrast to the famous interiors painted by Pieter Saenredam, the inside was often so colorful that the ruling Protestant Church could be seen as "High Church," in the sense of a pleasant and emphatically liturgical space.[94] In more recent times the church had also been provided with a parsonage, which was the size of a gentleman's residence with a large garden, so that a call would be attractive to ministers. Church and parsonage were not only typically located in the historic centre of the town or village; they were proof of gentility.

The Dutch Reformed Church made use of the medieval churches that stood in the old heart of the towns. The towers, however, were usually owned by the municipality because of their "worldly" functions, such as publicly indicating the time. The historic buildings gave the Reformed churchwardens an advantage but were also a burden. They set the standard for what the Protestant dissenters and Roman Catholics had in mind for their new churches. But the need for maintenance made them a burden on the church finances, especially at a time when greater attention was being paid to the preservation of historic buildings. This is what prevented the Reformed Congregation in Amsterdam, which had to maintain ten ancient churches including the expensive New Church and the West Church, from developing a major building program.

Next to the medieval Reformed churches arose the new houses of worship of the dissenters. Now that the separation of church and state had ended the privileged position of the Reformed Church, the Remonstrants could come out of their clandestine churches and erect buildings that might now be seen. For the Lutherans and the Mennonites the transition to the new situation was not that spectacular because they already had visible churches or because they went on building in a tradition of austerity. Dissenters of more recent origin, those of the 1834 Schism, had built humble houses of worship with a standard Gothic front in their pioneering days, a sign of repentance and of the rejection of artistic architecture.

The program for the interior of the church was laid down in the age-old practice of Reformation worship. The church was a place to sit and listen. The central point was the raised pulpit, which was sometimes hung from the wall, fitted with a sounding board. A prominent position for the proclamation of the Word was the only distinctive feature they could or would permit themselves. At the foot of the pulpit a space was reserved that was marked off by a railing and sometimes called the baptismal enclosure. Inside or before it the Communion table was set out. Pews and chairs always faced the pulpit and the baptismal enclosure. "The term 'cramming' is appropriate here because no free space is left next to the pews, chairs and aisles, to the detriment of the church's spatial effect."[95] There was no impressive liturgy, noted the German architect Scheffler in his travel notes on Holland, so that apart from the singing of the congregation there was only the predominantly moralistic sermon by the minister. "Which is all the more surprising, since the Hollanders are a visually oriented people. The distaste for a ceremony that is empty, without content, is stronger than the desire for forms and colors." The Dutchman experienced the eternal no less deeply than others, but he expressed his respect for it in another way. "In his religious experience he is occupied with himself and not receptive to decorative mysticism. Inwardly he is Protestant to a high degree."[96]

Dutch Renaissance

When new churches for Reformed worship were built in the second half of the nineteenth century, a historical style was chosen: neo-Gothic or more often Dutch Renaissance. For, more than Gothic, so-called Dutch Renaissance had determined the style of Protestant church building in the Netherlands. It was understandably chosen

Reformed church in Katwijk aan Zee.

when old churches had burnt down and had to be replaced, but it also dominated in the churches built around 1900 in the new districts laid out in the major cities. This had to do with a reassessment of this style, which was associated with the seventeenth-century architects Jacob van Campen and Hendrik de Keyser. The latter was particularly honored as the architect of the West Church in Amsterdam (1631). In this way Dutch Renaissance became not only a national style and a source of what was seen as picturesque; it was also a reference to the great age of the Reformation.

It was not only in the Netherlands that this style flourished. The building programs in a number of European cities such as Berlin, Vienna and Antwerp demonstrated the international support for exploring the Renaissance to meet the needs of a contemporary bourgeois culture. Inevitably, this international movement, which was spread through the media and commerce in various forms, had a major influence in the Netherlands. This was furthered by the publication of illustrated books, which were also a source of inspiration for architects. In 1882 the Society for the Promotion of Architecture organized an exhibition of designs in "a sort of old Dutch style," that is, sketches in the style of the Italian, German or Flemish and French Renaissance or of Berlin Gothic and Berlin classicism.[97]

The new Reformed church at Katwijk, a fishing village on the North Sea coast, was the result of a competition in 1884, shortly after this exhibition. It produced designs in the Romanesque, neo-Gothic and neo-Renaissance styles. The winning entry was by H.J. Jesse.[98] On January 12, 1887 the church was ceremonially inaugurated. Jesse had submitted a design in the style of the Dutch Renaissance which the jury found to be as simple as it was effective. The foundation stone was laid by Baroness Van Wassenaer van Catwijk, whose husband held the right to appoint the clergyman at Katwijk and was head churchwarden too. He also had a share in the financial disasters of the construction process and had to help out from time to time. The architect combined the practical advantages of a large basilican plan with the architecturally interesting shape of the cruciform church. The result was a clearly ordered space which, because of the few supports, offered an unobstructed view of the pulpit from almost everywhere. The careful detailing and decorative use of materials give the church a picturesque appearance.

The Muiderkerk, built in a new district in east Amsterdam and completed in 1892, was also in a neo-Renaissance style. In design and furnishing it was a typical "preaching church."[99] At Apeldoorn a competition was held in 1890 for the rebuilding of the old town church, which had burned down. Because of its proximity to Het Loo Palace, the royal family's country house, it was also used as a court church. The winning design was for a large, prestigious cruciform church in Dutch Renaissance style with a high tower. The best known architect at the turn of the century, Hendrik Petrus Berlage, had taken part by invitation, although he had no connection with the Reformed Church. He produced a design based on the Zuiderkerk (South Church) in Amsterdam (De Keyser, 1600): a cruciform plan with a dominant nave and two aisles on the sides. The jury thought Berlage's design insufficiently national; it was rationally and simply developed. Afterwards a debate ensued in the architectural press about the significance of the historical style. One of Berlage's colleagues argued that he had designed a characteristically Protestant church interior that brought to mind the dignified and in a sense severe churches of Hendrik de Keyser. The celebrated architect Pierre Cuypers sprang to Berlage's defense and said that with his neo-Renaissance design he had developed a national style, because he took the view that the Renaissance had favored the development of a national architecture, whereas neo-Gothic was an international style.[100]

Contemporary church design: sketch of the Reformed church in Apeldoorn by Hendrik Petrus Berlage.

Contemporary church design: Remonstrant Church in Rotterdam by Henri Evers.

After the turn of the century the dominance of the Dutch Renaissance style was broken. This can be seen in the work of the architect Henri Evers, who built the neo-Renaissance city hall[101] and a new Remonstrant church (1896) in Rotterdam. In 1886 Evers was still defending the profession against the charge that they were no longer designers but copyists of historical architecture, no longer artists but archeologists. Five years later he dissociated himself from the rationalism of neo-Gothic, which he found too doctrinaire for modern architecture. Evers sought inspiration in "Oriental monuments," not for archeological reasons but because in contemporary architecture he wanted to get away from traditional solutions. In this eclectic quest for Oriental or Byzantine figuration or an "American-Romanesque" experiment in church design, Evers's aim was to rejuvenate the "dying movement of style architecture."[102]

Reformed church building

At first church building was not an urgent matter for the Reformed Church. It was urgent, however, for those who had left the established church and needed new accommodation. There was a wave of new building after the *Doleantie* of 1886 when the new *Nederduitse Gereformeerde Kerk* needed churches of its own. For their principal church, on Keizersgracht in Amsterdam, they even held a competition. It was won by Gerlof and Alexander Salm, father and son, whose entry bore the motto *Soli Deo Gloria*. They designed a building with a striking and exuberant exterior. It was intended to be imposing as the first church of orthodoxy in Amsterdam, the centre of the *Doleantie*. The broad façade consists of a central section flanked by two towers. The decorative effect of the whole is strengthened by the alternating use of various types of stone. A notable feature of the design was the Gothic forms, which were actually "regarded as suitable for Roman Catholic churches."[103]

Tower and façade increasingly came to be the expression of an ambitious presentation of new orthodox Reformed building. The Nieuwe Westerkerk in Rotterdam was given two towers, one more than the Reformed Westerkerk, although that did not really fit with the Dutch Renaissance style and as a result the church, which was in a narrow street, acquired the silhouette of a cathedral. As long as they were tied to a site in a street frontage in the inner city, the desired effect was not always achieved or achievable. When new districts were laid out, however, it was possible to harmonize the church with the urban design. "Sometimes the church serves to close off an urban situation; often a site is sought near an intersection, ideally on a square. The church tower comes to play a more prominent role in the composition. At a later stage the high roof comes into vogue as well as the tower to let the church speak its language in the wider surroundings."[104]

The most productive architect in orthodox Reformed church building was Tjeerd Kuipers (1857-1942), who marks the transition from the historical to the "Berlagian" style. Kuipers learned his trade from his father, a carpenter and contractor, and in architectural offices, including Berlage's. In 1900 he opted for austerity and for design inspired by Berlage, and gave up quoting historical styles.[105] The first church in the new style was the Wilhelmina-kerk in Dordrecht, founded in the year of Wilhelmina's inauguration (1898) and completed a year later. The plan is round; the congregation sit in an

Reformed church on Keizersgracht in Amsterdam.

amphitheater around the pulpit. The Zuidkerk in Groningen (1901) has a related design. Subsequently Kuipers built numerous churches, the most monumental being the Bergsingelkerk in Rotterdam (1914). His architectural breakthrough is all the more impressive in the light of the fact that around 1900 many churches were still being built in the neo-Gothic style.

Hymns

In Calvinist worship the proclamation of the Word alternated with the singing of psalms or hymns. They had a function in the passing on, memorizing and experiencing of religious truths. This purpose was more important than cultural edification. An artistic interpretation might even be rejected on the grounds that it might weaken the hymn's religious significance. Hymns were sung in the church and at home. In the decades around 1900 there was a culture of domestic hymn singing. The instrument most often used for the accompaniment was the harmonium; its volume could not cope with large spaces but that made it ideal for the living room. The verses of psalms or hymns learned or sung each week from the hymn book in church could be repeated at home round the harmonium and made part of the individual's life in memorized form. "Many gained something through this that stayed with them for the rest of their life. Some reaped the benefits during the war in prison or concentration camp, others experienced the power during illness or on their deathbed."[106]

Dutch Protestantism traditionally imported the words and melodies of German hymns. In the latter half of the nineteenth century, however, the influence of Anglo-American religious music began to grow.[107] At this time gospel hymns became known in the Netherlands, initially through the efforts of the minister Carel Adama van Scheltema. In London he had heard the American soloist Philip Phillips, known as "the Singing Pilgrim," and he included a selection of his songs in one of his hymnals. The most important figure in the spreading of gospel hymns in Europe was the American singer Ira D. Sankey, who made a revivalist tour of the United Kingdom in 1873. Sankey had no musical training but did have perfect delivery and great charisma. These "witness hymns," with simple melodies but infectious rhythms, were introduced to the Netherlands by the minister Meyer Salomon Bromet. He had been born in Paramaribo in Surinam to Jewish parents but at an early age he converted to Christianity. He and other Dutch ministers, among them Abraham Kuyper, went to a revival in 1875 in Brighton, England, where Sankey performed. The impression these meetings made on him led to similar events being organized in the Netherlands.

The principal exponent of the Anglo-American revivalist worship in the Netherlands was Johannes de Heer (1866-1961). He was a self-taught organist. After the death of his small daughter he had joined the Seventh Day Adventists. Later he became a member of the Jeruël city mission in Rotterdam. De Heer had encountered revivalist meetings in Wales. They were religious gatherings with the emphasis on testimonies and spontaneous singing. In 1905 and 1906 such meetings were held in the Netherlands. De Heer collected the hymns from these meetings in his *Zangbundel* and preserved this form of religious experience in the Maranatha movement, which organized meetings in the expectation of Christ's imminent return. He was not guided by aesthetic criteria because "concert singing" and "evangelist singing" were two mutually exclusive categories in his eyes; the expression was more important than the quality of the singing. De Heer managed to fascinate both the evangelical and the orthodox Reformed tendencies in Dutch Protestantism. After World War I he became familiar with the new mass medium of radio, for which he presented hymns from his *Zangbundel*. As a result his popularity was unrivaled.[108]

Johannes de Heer plays from his hymnal.

The Jonas Daniel Meijerplein in Amsterdam with the Great and the New Synagogue on the left and on the right the towers of the Catholic Church of St. Antony, better known as the Moses and Aaron Church, and in the distance the tower of the Reformed South Church, 1900.

10

Religion and emancipation: Judaism and Catholicism

The Jewish community

In 1900 the Jewish community found itself half way between the isolation of the ghetto and complete assimilation. The granting of civil rights – in 1796 under the Batavian Republic – can be seen as the start in law of a process of liberation from institutionalized separation, although in individual cases it had already proved possible to cross the barriers. Now larger numbers could gradually free themselves from the ghetto, which should be thought of as both a closed district and a collective mentality. The first step in this process was to climb out of poverty. A powerful means of achieving this was the battle for improved conditions waged by the socialist labor movement, whose vanguard was made up of Amsterdam diamond workers, many of whom were Jewish. Another means was education, which had always been held in esteem by the Jewish community and now pointed the way up the social ladder. Emancipation also often meant leaving behind religious doctrines and traditions. At the end of the nineteenth century life and thought in the Jewish community were dominated by the conflict between religion as the foundation of Jewish solidarity and secularization resulting from deliberate assimilation.

The two elements in the Jewish diaspora – the Portuguese (Sephardim) and the High German (Ashkenazim) – were both represented in the Netherlands. In the sixteenth century Portuguese and Spanish Jews were able to enter the Dutch Republic. From the seventeenth century this "nation" was outnumbered by Jewish immigrants from Central and Eastern Europe. So by 1900 the Portuguese Jews could look back on centuries of residence in the Netherlands and on forefathers who were among the most prominent merchants in the Republic, although a number of families had finally declined into poverty. The High German immigrants, on the other hand, had usually entered the country at a later date and they generally suffered greater poverty. Moreover, a new stream of immigrants arrived in the eighteen-eighties and eighteen-nineties as a result of pogroms in Eastern Europe after the assassination of Alexander II in 1881. By the turn of the century the distinction between the two "nations" had become less sharp. This was due in part to their varying economic fortunes. Some Portuguese families lost their wealth and some High German ones soon moved up the social scale, and this removed the barriers to marriage between them. After 1900 mixed marriages (to Ashkenazi Jews) made up half of all marriages among Portuguese Jews.

According to the census of 1879 there were over 80,000 Jews in the Netherlands. By about 1900 that figure had risen to over 100,000, and by 1920 to 115,000. For a while, even, the Jewish share in the growth of the Dutch population was greater than that of other groups, but from 1909 it decreased again.[1] The number of Jews grew because of a positive migration balance. The wave of pogroms in the Russian Empire after 1881 made many emigrate to the West, to Western Europe and the United States. On the other hand, the birth rate among the indigenous Jewish population steadily declined. After 1900 some Jews abandoned their faith, so that in the official statistics their numbers fell, since in the Dutch registers Jews were entered under their religion.[2] One striking aspect is the concentration of Jews in the three main cities, The Hague, Rotterdam, and in particular Amsterdam. Around 1900 more than half the Jews lived in Amsterdam.

The old Amsterdam ghetto was a source of literary inspiration precisely at the time that it was being abandoned. The writer Siegfried Emanuel van Praag considered it the characteristic, if not the only, western European ghetto. "Here the Eastern Jew in his black kaftan, with side earlocks (payess) and full beard, is often seen but not welcomed by genteel folk. But he is only a guest." Van Praag believed one of the characteristics of the inhabitants was a lack of thrift.

> If the ghetto has money, if need be from charity, it is perfectly ready to buy a chicken on the Sabbath, even though God created the chicken for the rich. It eats its plentiful sweets in the too numerous patisseries, its countless cold meats in the 'bread rolls with meat shops' opening up at an alarming rate; its fruit shops and basements cannot be fruitful enough for the fertile families of the ghetto inhabitants. The ghetto decks itself out in colorful clothes and has little feeling for harmony between wearer, hat and boots, between leg and stockings, blouses and bosom. The ghetto goes loyally to the movie theaters in its streets and the city center; it is pleasure-seeking and cheerful, and if it gives 'offense' this is not to be blamed on its bad intentions but rather on the intolerance of genteel Jews and non-Jews.[3]

Outside Amsterdam there was no real ghetto except for the area around the Wagenstraat in The Hague. Elsewhere in the country the highest proportions of Jews were found in the northern towns of Coevorden and Winschoten. In relative terms Coevorden actually had the largest Jewish community in the Netherlands. In such towns they lived in fairly close-knit "communities, often with a taste for bickering because of their smallness," where there was still a sharp distinction between rich and poor so that they were visibly divided into two halves. "These provincial Jewish communities, whose core is made up of tradesmen such as drapers, butchers and bakers," according to Van Praag, "are often ruled by a small town mentality, in this case the spirit of the forecourt of a small synagogue. The provincial chief rabbi and the news from Amsterdam, brought to them by the weekly Jewish periodical, are stars of considerable allure in these hot-tempered communities." The writer Carry van Bruggen described such communities "in their helplessness when confronted by the anti-Semitism of the majority of the population."[4]

In the center the classicist grave of Chief Rabbi Joseph Hirsch Dünner
in the Jewish cemetery in Muiderberg.

Acculturation and assimilation

Around 1900 the religious life of Dutch Jews was marked by two tendencies: accultura-
tion and secularization. Jewish worship was made more Dutch; the immigrants' religious institutions took part in the process of assimilation being undergone by the members of the congregation and were thus more firmly rooted in Dutch society. But secularization also had an impact: Jews began to move away from religious belief and from
religious rules. This did not necessarily mean that they gave up all aspects of a Jewish
way of life. The road to complete rejection often proved to be very long. Both tendencies
came together in the leaders of the congregations, the parnassim. They were often prominent figures and in the process of going up the social scale they had in a sense lost touch
with their religious origins. But they continued to lead the congregation because of their
management skills and often because of their financial resources too.

As an institution, the Jewish religion in the Netherlands had gone through the same
development as the Christian churches. Under King William I the two "nations" had
been united in one religious community, provided with a central authority, and linked to
the state in return for official recognition. After 1848 this link was broken. In 1870 the
statutory basis of the religion was laid down when the local congregation was given

chief rabbi in North Holland, a post that had been vacant for thirty-five years. In effect this made him the spiritual leader of Dutch Jewry. He continued the civilizing campaign that he had begun in the seminary. He tried to rid the Jewish congregation of the aspects attributed to it by the deprecatory term "Jews' church," meaning a place where people all talk at once. In the ritual he scrapped certain cabbalistic traditions. "Religious life took on an increasingly ordered and solemn character. This emphasis on decorum was in line with the wishes of the Jewish middle class and bore the hallmarks of further adjustments to Dutch bourgeois society."[10] Having studied in Germany, Dünner was the classic example of a "Bildungsbürger," a member of the intellectual bourgeoisie. He supported the Jewish community in Palestine and was one of the few rabbis in Western Europe to give his endorsement to the Zionist movement.[11] In politics he was a liberal. He kept his distance from the social conflicts in the diamond industry during the Boer War and dismissed the campaign by Jewish social democrats as "misleading." In turn, the red proletarians perceived the liberal leadership of the congregation as hostile to the workers. "The great Rav (rabbi) was confronted by colossal problems, which he simply could not handle."[12]

The Jewish proletariat let itself be guided, insofar as it was still interested in religion, by rabbis and teachers who were concerned about social problems, for example because they themselves lived in impoverished conditions. The best known of them was Meyer de Hond, at whose initiative a nursing home for the chronically ill, De Joodsche Invalide, had been founded in Amsterdam. Around the turn of the century, in the shadow of the intellectual synagogue a series of religious societies flourished in which the tradition of "lernen" and mysticism was cherished.

The question has been raised of why the reform movement, which found such a response among German and American Jews around 1900, had hardly any influence in the Netherlands. This movement had its origins in the Enlightenment and aimed at assimilation because its proponents believed it was possible to renew the ancient religious traditions through the expansion of education and the process of becoming middle class socially and culturally. The historian Dan Michman gives three reasons for the absence of a Dutch version. The first is that the secularization process in the Netherlands was not accompanied by a public debate on belief and the character of Judaism, which might have made a deep impression in the minds of many. In Germany there had been just such a profound and fundamental debate between Jews and those around them on the religious and national "essence of Judaism."

The second reason given by Michman is that in Germany, Britain and the United States the reform movement was a class phenomenon. Only the well-off middle class and intellectuals responded to the reform movement's abstract and universal ideas and its concern with the aesthetics of worship. In the Netherlands, and particularly in Amsterdam, the great majority of the Jewish population belonged to the proletariat. By the end of the nineteenth century most of the poor Jews no longer went to the synagogue. They represented a "popular Judaism" in which their identity lay mainly in social and cultural customs and occasional ceremonies such as circumcision, weddings and funerals. Despite this move away from traditionally perceived Judaism, this group did

Interior of the new synagogue in Folkingestraat in Groningen, 1916.

not produce a single attempt to create an alternative form of the Jewish religion. For its part the bourgeoisie found an alternative in assimilation, indifference or the Zionist movement.

The third reason is the increasing use of Dutch in worship and the combination of a fairly orthodox rabbinate and a liberal to atheist governing body. With increasing secularization, the larger part of the congregation had in fact become liberals. "Although many Jews found their way to the left-wing and liberal parties and associations, there were still strong ties to the Jewish group. As a result, belonging to the Jewish congregation was a matter of social rather than religious significance. Thus there was little sign here of a different religious orientation."[13]

The success of emancipation

The most tangible evidence of integration was the building of new synagogues in the expanding cities. They reflected the fact that the Jewish middle class was spreading into new districts; this was the exodus from the ghetto for those who could afford it. The most telling example was not in Amsterdam, however, but in the Jewish quarter of the northern city of Groningen, where around 1900 a synagogue that was monumental by Dutch standards was built. The commission for it had been awarded to an orthodox Calvinist architect, Tjeerd Kuipers, who opted for an oriental style in line with the tendency at that time to incorporate historical elements in architecture.

Jewish manufacturers played an important part in the industrial initiatives that transformed the landscape and society of the Twente region in the east of the country and the area around Eindhoven in the south. In towns like Enschede and Almelo textile merchants could work their way up to become entrepreneurs as textile production was mechanized. In 1924 sixteen of the nineteen clothing manufacturers in Enschede were Jewish. Entrepreneurs from the Philips family settled in Eindhoven, and the largest cigar factory there was owned by the Van Abbe family. Both were originally Jewish but had converted to become Protestant and Catholic respectively. Other important Jewish industrialists were two inhabitants of Oss, Daniel van den Bergh (of the Bergoss carpet factory) and Samuel van den Bergh, the founder of the margarine company that would become the multinational Unilever. Another pioneer was Dr. J.C. Hartogs, the founder of the *Eerste Nederlandse Kunstzijdefabriek* (ENKA) in Arnhem, which would grow into another multinational, Akzo Nobel.

In the words of his biographer, the banker Abraham Wertheim might "appear at synagogue extremely rarely, he might transgress against the code in public, he might even achieve the unheard-of by presiding over a meeting of a Christian religious society (the Salvation Army in 1895), for the Dutch Jews he remained not only the model of a successful Jew par excellence, but also their protector, their friend and their counselor, to whom they could turn with all their problems. And not only them: he also helped foreign Jews who came here."[14] For the Jewish proletariat this role was played by Henri Polak, the founder and first chairman of the diamond workers' union, the ANDB, one of the first Dutch labor unions to have a large number of Jewish members. "In Jewish families there were of course no saints," the historian Jacob Presser recalled, "but you might say we had a kind of household saint, like all those families in fact, and he was Henri Polak. One has to realize that Henri Polak – he has been called 'the diamond workers' rebbe' – was someone to whom a whole development could be ascribed. Something happened to those people, the wretched of the earth who still sang the Internationale with enthusiasm. I must have heard that from childhood. Those people awoke, those people started to read."[15]

Polak began a campaign to civilize the diamond workers. At first the emphasis was on order and respectability, a certain code of behavior. But he saw this as merely preparation for entering the realm of beauty. Polak expected an ideal community from the new art. As a social democrat, he wanted to give the workers access to the culture which had so far benefited only the social elite. Among the diamond workers there was a strong tradition of choral singing. The socialist choir "The Voice of the People" was recruited from their ranks. It performed new socialist songs that made a deep impression at the social democrats' congresses.[16] Their love of opera and operetta was legendary. Opera companies could always count on a large contingent of diamond workers, who had often already seen the Italian and French operas several times. "The works of Wagner were appreciated only later. In factories the best-known arias resounded, often with homemade comic words."[17] The diamond workers did not all immediately turn into art lovers, but they worshiped Polak, because he had emancipated them not only as workers but as Jews. "Thanks to Polak, they felt, they had evolved from a group of despised, primitive ghetto-Jews to the universally respected elite of the Dutch working class."[18]

Jewish bourgeoisie: Family portrait of Carel Daniel Asser and his wife
Wilhelmina Asser-Torbecke and their children, 1923.

The Jewish contribution to the arts in the Netherlands around the turn of the century ranged from the paintings of Jozef Israëls to the novels of Carry van Bruggen. The first Dutch winner of the Nobel Prize for Peace (in 1911) was Tobias Asser, acclaimed for his services to the development of private international law, which he helped to shape in a series of international conferences. He came from a Jewish family which had played a prominent role in jurisprudence and the administration of justice for generation after generation since 1798. The extent and quality of Jewish emancipation did not go unnoticed at the time. The social sciences turned their attention to the position of the Jews early on: the Jewish physician Julius Leydesdorff obtained his doctorate in Groningen in 1919 with a thesis on this subject. It was based on a questionnaire about psychological characteristics that had been sent to over 3,000 Dutch physicians by the psychologists Gerard Heymans and Enno Wiersma in 1905. Some 202 completed questionnaires were made available to Leydesdorff and he was able to study forty families. He found that "the radical element among the Jews is not so strongly represented in the Netherlands as in the countries where they are subject to oppression." His sample was, however, one-sided because "the great majority of the people described in this survey are not members of the working class." Leydesdorff had also observed "quite clearly in my practice that on average the Jewish child is more intelligent than the non-Jewish child, although it certainly does not follow from this that the best pupils in school are Jewish. It is a pity that, to the best of my knowledge, no statistics on this subject are available in this country."[19]

Others have since taken an interest in this issue. In a recent study of the flourishing of the arts in Vienna and Budapest around 1900, an important role is attributed to the Jewish communities in these cities. It is also clear that a greater proportion of Jewish children received secondary and higher education compared with their Christian contemporaries. One possible explanation for this is the emphasis placed on learning and knowledge in the Jewish tradition. But the author of the study, Peter Hanák, also looks for the causes in alienation from that tradition. Following the lead of the sociologist Thorstein Veblen, he argues that Jewish intellectuals played a disproportionate role in the cultural vanguard because they had "a skeptical frame of mind." And this skepticism is a result of the alienation from tradition caused by secularization. "It is by loss of allegiance to the people of his origin that he finds himself in the vanguard of modern inquiry." Hanák cites the psychologist Kurt Lewin, who acknowledged from another vantage point that the assimilation of Jewish intellectuals into "gentile society" pushes them to the margins and causes psychological conflicts. He summarizes Lewin's case as follows: "These are socially and psychologically harmful, he argues, but may be beneficial for creative work."[20]

The Jewish community in the Netherlands did not establish a political power bloc. The political scientist H. Daalder considered the question of why, compared with the orthodox Calvinists and the Catholics, Dutch Jews made very limited use of the system of "pillarization" and the opportunities it offered for setting up their own organizations and adapting them to the existing order, not only to increase awareness of emancipation but to direct it as well. They went no further than establishing Jewish schools and welfare organizations. Daalder sets out one of the reasons for this: "Many Jews were always apprehensive about making specifically Jewish demands, even in the relatively open society of the Netherlands. The importance of this motive is confirmed by the fact that Catholics showed the same reluctance for a century or longer. But in their case the Catholics could in the end fall back on larger numbers and on strong regional concentrations with their own culture and institutions."[22]

Catholic church architecture

A new cathedral was built on the west side of Haarlem around the turn of the century. Everything about it was meant to impress: its size – it is a five-aisled cruciform basilica – its ribbed vaulting, its elegantly tapering dome, and the two towers in its façade. The scale of the building was to be lasting proof of a Catholic revival in the Netherlands. The cathedral is basically neo-Gothic. This applies to the ground plan, the choir with seven chapels and the façade with towers. But the architect, Jos Cuypers, added Romanesque and even Oriental elements to this basic type, thus displaying his "architectural erudition." His style might be described as eclectic; nonetheless, one architect has consciously tried to realize a total vision of the contemporary cathedral. In its design and decoration it reveals a blend of tradition and modernity that is typical of the period.

This blend was Cuypers's trademark and it put him at odds with colleagues in his generation, although earlier they had accepted that very same view from his father, Pierre Cuypers. In the series of seven lectures on architecture organized by the *Architectura et Amicitia* society in 1907, Jos Cuypers expressed his belief that "a true flowering of architecture [is] possible only through a historical connection."[22] An architecturally pure revival of a historical style would in his opinion take the life out of the design. But an absolutely new "formal vocabulary, free of all archeological memories" was equally unacceptable in the "European society" of his time.[23]

The new building was intended to provide the Bishop of Haarlem, who had been restored to his office in 1853, with his cathedral. It had been commissioned by the bishops, Caspar Bottemanne and his successor Augustinus Callier, both eminent and stylish prelates. Construction was actually overseen by Augustinus Callier, who came from a family of Belgian pilots in Vlissingen and was an authority on the poet Vondel. In the twenty-five years of his term of office he saw the church almost completed. It was dedicated to St. Bavo, a relic of whom had been brought to Haarlem from St. Peter's Abbey in Ghent by Dirk II, Count of Holland, and his wife Hildegard, daughter of the Count of Flanders. Bavo had become the patron saint of the great medieval church in Haarlem. The new cathedral was inaugurated on Sunday, February 25, 1906 with a procession of the Blessed Sacrament. This was a deliberate historical choice, for through this liturgical act the link with the past before the Reformation was emphasized. On May 29, 1578, Corpus Christi, Protestants had forced their way into St. Bavo's during nones, afternoon prayers, to disrupt the service. According to the president of the diocesan seminary in Warmond, the new church had been built, among other things, in atonement for the offences against the Sacrament committed during this Haarlem nones.[24]

When the cathedral was built the Sacred Line was taken into account; this was a key term in the plea by Josephus Albertus Alberdingk Thijm for the Christian tradition to be followed and for churches to be oriented, that is built with the altar facing east, pointing towards Jerusalem. In the case of Haarlem the result was that the choir of the church faced the public highway and the city center, a distinct disadvantage from the point of view of town planning. Another tradition gave rise to the view that chapels around the choir must be dedicated to Dutch saints. Some were reserved for this purpose, but the church was also a perfect example of the general devotions prevalent around 1900. The romantic experience of faith included the devotions to the Sacred Heart and to Joseph, proclaimed the patron saint of the Catholic Church by Pope Pius IX, to Antony of Padua, and to the Holy Family, whereby a religious emphasis could be given to the ideal of the family. Other chapels were made available for Dutch saints such as the Martyrs of Gorcum, who were canonized in 1867 because they had been killed as martyrs by the Sea Beggars during the Revolt, Liduïna van Schiedam (1380-1413), a woman whose devotion was approved by the Vatican in 1890, and Jeroen, a priest at Noordwijk in the ninth century who was martyred under the Normans and whose devotion was promoted by the Haarlem diocese. Incidentally, Jeroen has since been removed from his chapel and replaced by Francis of Assisi.[25]

The cathedral towers over the neighborhood and dominates Haarlem's skyline on the western side. It forms a counterpoint to the medieval St. Bavo's in the heart of the city, which is a Reformed church. The new building was to be the apotheosis of a liturgical

St. Bavo's Cathedral on Leidsevaart in Haarlem. The towers on the front have not yet been added.

Official portrait of Bishop Augustinus Callier.

and aesthetic revival in Dutch Catholicism. It was a revival because tradition was the criterion and its historical content was passionately debated out of a need for antiquarian purity. Much of what in those days could be called an expression of Catholic culture stemmed from a desire to claim a distinct share in the Dutch heritage and to add it to the collective memory.

In the nineteenth century Catholics came out of the clandestine churches, where they had been forced to practice their religion in secret. They chose to build new places of worship in public spaces with a recognizable exterior and high towers. The first new buildings were modest in size or even what might be called upgraded clandestine churches, but in the last quarter of the century the new churches became large and high. The size of the churches and the towers was intended to bear witness to the renewed self-confidence of a formerly oppressed minority. "Today we shall never experience the delight," wrote the Catholic art historian Gerard Brom in a review of church architecture, "with which a Catholic saw his church actually rising above the highest houses in the neighborhood. What a relief after such long oppression!"[26] In the fifty years between the restoration of episcopal authority in 1853 and 1903, 506 new churches were consecrated in the Netherlands. Half were in the north and half in the south. The funds required were generally raised through the commitment, sometimes passion even, of private individuals.

The church in the town of Sneek in Friesland is an example. In the first half of the nineteenth century the clandestine church was replaced by a new building – on the same site, modest in its dimensions, and overseen (and subsidized) by central government. The Catholic community of Sneek numbered 1300 (nearly twenty percent of the town's population) and could not have raised the money for a larger church at that point. That had to wait until Henricus Kamp became the priest in 1855. He campaigned for a new building on the lines of the churches in the Frisian towns of Bolsward and Leeuwarden. There Catholics had built neo-Gothic churches with three aisles that evoked medieval Friesland. In 1868 Father Kamp proposed to his churchwardens that the commission for a new church should be given to the young architect Pierre Cuypers, who had already made a name for himself. One of the wardens, Edon Jans Hollander of Goënga, who had private means, came from the agrarian sector. The others were merchants, and some came from Westphalia in Germany: Karl Lampe, Clemens Brenninkmeyer and Frank Terwischa van Scheltinga. They were taken aback by the amount Cuypers asked for, which was 100,000 guilders. Nonetheless, work started in 1869, for the priest went ahead with the support of the Archbishop of Utrecht and despite the objections of Brenninkmeyer in particular. Because of his travels on business, he took no part in the final decision and resigned as a churchwarden. The great church envisaged was built; the funds were topped up to the amount required by money from a legacy from the unmarried Edon Jans Hollander, who died in 1888. But even that capital was not enough to pay for the large tower that Cuypers had designed. It was never to be built, for Father Kamp, the driving force behind the project, was struck by falling scaffolding during construction and died before the church was consecrated in 1872.[27]

For half a century, from 1853, Cuypers was to dominate Catholic church architecture in the Netherlands, not as the holder of a monopoly but as the first among equals. Where necessary, he himself made sure of this. When he first appeared on the scene, he had a

Interior of St. Martin's Church in Sneek.

beard and long hair, and wore a floppy hat and an "artist's suit."[28] Even at an advanced age – Cuypers lived to be ninety-three – he was an imposing and romantic figure, a successful architect who had lost some hair but not his beard and who had to submit to a public tribute every five years from his seventieth birthday. "In Cuypers I always admired the honesty, the single-mindedness, the unfailing youthfulness," wrote his nephew, the author Lodewijk van Deyssel in a memoir. With these qualities he had turned the tide in the "unpoped and unmonked" Netherlands.[29] Another family member, the composer Alphons Diepenbrock, drew attention at one of the birthday celebrations to Cuypers's background: "not a Dutch-Protestant but a Gallo-Germanic-Catholic current in historical Romanticism."[30]

Cuypers studied at the Academy of Fine Arts in Antwerp in Belgium. He then made a study tour of the Rhine, during which he was able to observe the work going on to complete the Gothic cathedral in Cologne. Back in his native town of Roermond, he founded a studio for religious decorative arts. He built his first church in the village of

St. Lambert's Church in Veghel.

Oeffelt in North Brabant (1853), but his big chance came with the commission to design St. Lambert's Church in Veghel. It had to be both monumental and cheap. "Quiet thrift had to be combined with public swaggering," wrote Gerard Brom. "Apart from the fact that such a vainly overdone and niggardly executed structure, in which everything was made as sharp and thin as possible, would require expensive maintenance in due course, this cathedral with statues on the front and a ring of chapels round the choir was utterly out of place in a country village."[31] This monumental commission was followed by another in a city: St. Catherine's (1859) in Eindhoven. Next came St. Barbara's Cathedral (1866) in Breda, the first new church with five aisles in the Netherlands since the Reformation.

Cuypers was not the kind of architect who "simply followed ancient monuments when erecting new buildings." He belonged to the group within the neo-Gothic movement who believed that this style could be further developed and perfected.[32] He was pre-eminently a builder, and he knew how to deal with the most diverse sites and

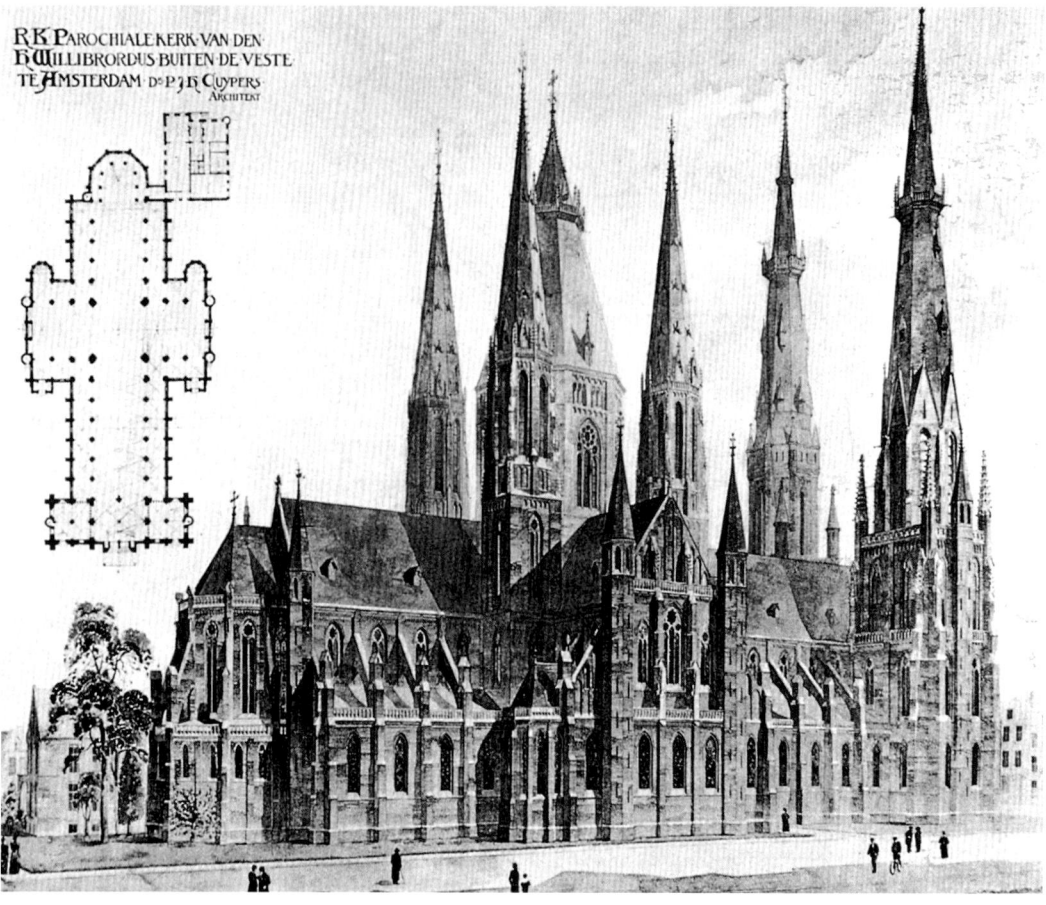

Pierre Cuypers, drawing of the Church of St. Willibrord outside the walls in Amsterdam.

dimensions. For the new churches often had to be built in existing urban districts. In 1865 Cuypers moved to Amsterdam. His designs for churches changed as a result of the commissions he received for public buildings in the city like the Rijksmuseum and Central Station. He also created neo-Renaissance forms, which he regarded as an old, typically Dutch style. But first he built two neo-Gothic churches in Amsterdam which stand at the two extremes of his architecture, the monumental and the intimate. Outside the walls of Amsterdam in an area full of market gardens stood St. Willibrord's Church. At the initiative of the priest, it was to be transformed from a wooden peat barn into a monumental edifice on the Amstel river, built according to the ground plan of the Gothic style in northern France. On the model of the cathedrals in Chartres and Reims, seven towers were planned. Admittedly, this monumental church would stand in a working-class district of Amsterdam, but "from the banks of the Amstel" it would openly proclaim that the Catholics were no longer celebrating their holy secrets "in ramshackle shed-churches far from the highway, with low walls and roofs and no tower." The church was built of Dutch brick, so that its exterior was somber in character. Moreover, only one of the seven towers was built in the end; its octagonal form suggested space but not a dizzy height.[33]

The intimate church was the result of Cuypers's activities as a real estate developer. Together with another architect, N. Redeker Bisdom, he submitted a proposal to the Amsterdam council for a street lined with imposing residences between the Leidse Poort and the Vondelpark. The street divided to go round a square and this was to be the site of a church with a central plan. But Cuypers remained loyal to the rules laid down by his friend Alberdingk Thijm, who specified a cruciform porch, and a broader nave and sanctuary. Thus the original central plan became an oval. The tower had to rise over the octagonal center; the new one built after a fire in 1904 did this even better. "One need not wait for the morning half light to experience the devoutness of this shrine," wrote Gerard Brom.[34] The church was dedicated to the Sacred Heart in 1873; this was a nineteenth-century devotion. But it was to become best known as the Vondelkerk after the great seventeenth-century poet Joost van den Vondel, and the street was also named after him.

The choice of neo-Gothic in church-building was not determined by a single architect, not even the enterprising Cuypers. An important role in assessing quality and establishing standard forms in Catholic architecture was played by the Guild of St. Bernold. Its foundation was closely connected to the fact that in 1868 state supervision of church-building was abolished and both the assessment of quality and the organization were left to the clergy. In reaction, an attempt was made to tie priests with building plans to an architectural norm. One priest, Gerardus Wilhelmus van Heukelum, set up a "guild" and took as his model the Belgian Guild of St. Thomas and St. Luke, which was in turn based on the British Ecclesiological Society, an Anglican initiative in a neo-Gothic movement on a European scale. St. Bernold became the patron of the Dutch Guild; he had been Bishop of Utrecht in the eleventh century and was believed to have built the medieval city churches in Utrecht and Deventer.

As a result of Van Heukelum's efforts, craftsmen skilled in religious art, such as the sculptor Friedrich Wilhelm Mengelberg and the stained-glass painter Heinrich Geuer came from Cologne to the Netherlands. They were joined by the goldsmith Gerard Bartel Brom, but his place was soon taken by his son Jan Hendrik. The choice of an architect for what was to be called the "Utrecht Quartet" took a little longer. In the end Alfred Tepe became the preferred architect for new churches in the archbishopric of Utrecht. In 1873 Tepe and Mengelberg together designed St. Nicholas's in Jutphaas, where Van Heukelum was then the priest. The iconographic program for the interior decoration was to be a model of the guild's art historical ideals. Tepe also built the monumental churches in the villages Schalkwijk (1877) and IJsselstein (1885), which tower over the surrounding countryside. He had been trained in Germany and was principally inspired by the styles of the Rhineland. But he tried to add a Dutch slant by committing himself to Late Gothic, medieval examples of which are also to be found in the Netherlands. From an international point of view, the Utrecht Quartet were among the first to promote the revival of a regional style so emphatically and systematically. There are two other Dutch characteristics in Tepe's architecture. The first is the consistent use of brick, which he applied in striking variations and in a wealth of decorations. The second is his talent for integrating new buildings in the existing architectural setting. This was a challenge he often faced when having to transform a clandestine church into a building whose

The Church of the Sacred Heart at Wyck, Maastricht.

façade must now bear witness to worship and whose size was determined by the street layout. The new church, known as the Krijtberg, on Singel in Amsterdam was a remarkable example of this talent.[35]

From the outset the Guild of St. Bernold was criticized for its "overly archaistic approach," its "mere repetition of conventional forms, particularly those of German origin." The seminary lecturer T. Borret warned against the danger of "canonizing defects and sanctifying monstrosities" because of an exclusive preference for the neo-Gothic style in church architecture and religious art.[36] Van Heukelum was rewarded for his services by being appointed a canon of the Utrecht chapter in 1900. This marked the beginning of his swan song as a source of artistic inspiration in church-building in the archbishopric. In 1906 Tepe left for Germany. The monopoly of the neo-Gothic style sanctioned by the Catholic Church had led eventually to creative paralysis.[37]

The breakthrough came from Cuypers's pupils, among them his son. In the eighteen-eighties one pupil, A.C. Bleijs, built a church in Hoorn and one in Amsterdam in a mixture of the Renaissance and baroque styles. The Amsterdam church, St. Nicholas's, has a cruciform plan with a remarkable dome and a façade with small towers facing Central Station. It was intended to strike travelers when they first saw the city, just as the church of Santa Maria della Salute does in Venice.[38] Traditionalism, with its emphasis on Roman unity, drew attention to the early Christian basilica. It was in that style that Jos Cuypers and Jan Stuyt designed the Rosary Church (1908) in Amsterdam with a wooden roof and a semi-circular apse. Jan Stuyt did this with even more purism with St. Agnes's (1920) in

Amsterdam, locating the choir next to the high altar as a sign of receptiveness to new liturgical ideas.[39] From 1920 another kind of traditionalism is seen in the churches of Alexander Jacobus Kropholler: a version of elementary Gothic in robust blocks in brick, but with a clearly laid-out, highly concentrated interior under a wooden roof. Here the memory of the humble old village church is combined with the traditional methods, the visible brick volumes and the concept of space from the work of Berlage.

After 1900 the influence of a new liturgical movement became increasingly evident. The demands for a so-called people's church, in which the faithful would have an unobstructed view as far as possible of the altar and the pulpit, led to the adoption of a central plan on the lines of the Byzantine Hagia Sophia in Istanbul. The culmination of this development is the domed church in Wijck-Maastricht designed in 1920 by A.J.N. Boosten, a pupil of Jos Cuypers. This was the first use of a central plan in a Catholic church and the first use of concrete as a building material.

In 1953, on the centenary of the re-establishment of the Catholic hierarchy, the art historian Frits van der Meer asked himself what an intelligent foreigner would make of a century of church-building in the Netherlands:

> Sound, dignified churches, he would say. The faith is solidly housed here; nothing is skipped. It is a sort of carefully considered domestic luxury, and this applies equally to the older, full neo-Gothic and the newer, bare functionalism. For whatever may have changed in a hundred years, the strips of thick carpet, the flower arrangements, the small-sized candles, the shining copper and silver, the profusion of cushions and prie-dieux, the spotless and constantly changed linen and the blocks of pews that dominate everything and destroy the architecture, plus the box-like confessionals – all that has remained; it has just been slightly modernized. To date, despite all scholae cantorum, the singing gallery, the choir stalls, has proved to be indestructible, and that feature – we hasten to add – does not derive from the Italian cantoria, no, it derives from our house churches with their galleries dating from before 1895. It is part of the domesticity of our churches. Whether we like it or not, the foreigner will immediately name the principal characteristic of our church interiors: domesticity with a touch of modest luxury (just like in our homes).[40]

At one bound, at least with our principal churches, we were at the high point of the era, and at an international level. They were not to know at the time that today, at a distance of nearly 100 years, the style of that era would not seem particularly impressive. Nor did they see that they had gone from academicism to antiquarianism; and in fact they were at least as occupied with rediscovering elementary building logic and the preparations for the present functionalism as with medieval archeology, which incidentally was as much a learning experience for them as a ready-made pattern book. It was much less clear then than now that with their pseudo-medieval shrines they would in the end artificially separate the Church from contemporary life, for in the beginning their intention was indeed to restore the sole truly Christian art, that is the Gothic style (from prior to the Italianate Academy), in complete opposition to the spirit of the age, and thus to change the spirit of the age. And they had to cling to the illusion that they were more or less successful in this, for towards the end of their great generation parts of the Rijksmuseum and Central Station looked like parts of Cuypers's churches, just as the silhouette of Parliament Buildings looked like some Perpendicular cathedrals, and not the other way round.[41]

Worship

Believers (and former believers) among writers remember the theater of the liturgy, the rituals, more than any other aspect of Catholicism. The nineteenth-century church "wanted to put on a show on high days and holidays, when our forefathers were allowed to splash out for once," wrote Gerard Brom.

> Then round the tabernacle gleam silver candlesticks in every size up to the most awkward, just as long as the foot leaves room for chasing; real silver, all brightly polished and anxiously saved for a few days each year, sumptuously placed amid flowers and candles like princely tableware. Then the rare High Mass makes a more solemn impression as it becomes more difficult for the assistants, chased by a hunting party of acolytes, to budge inside the tight frame. Then the sanctuary, where the chairs knock against the communion rail, is full of worshipers, full of listeners, full of spectators. Anyone who has ever heard a Mass by Johannes Verhulst or Henri Viotta or J. van Bree resounding through the packed space acquires a warm memory for life and feels within those first churches the blessed devotion from which our full freedom and ripeness bloomed. The rhetoric of that plastered stage simply had to be accompanied by the pathos of theatrical music, brimful of solos, unisons, sequences, endless repetitions in incessant fortissimo: after the Amen of a Gloria, Gloria again; after the Amen of a Credo, Credo again, as in romantic opera.[42]

This image of elaborate rituals in intimate spaces is often found in the literature. It was counterbalanced by the liturgical movement, with its preference for the austere and aristocratic. This was a phenomenon of the years around 1900 and involved both priests and laity. Its general aim was a renewal of the rituals and of the verbal and musical expressions of devotion. It was a complex movement which manifested itself in two distinct phases, first in a reborn uniform and aristocratic Roman liturgy in monasteries, and subsequently in the democratic ideal of active participation by the faithful. The movement was international; the Dutch branch drew inspiration from centers in France, Belgium and Germany, and was led from Rome. The changes, which were often difficult to introduce, caused breaches in a liturgy that had been laid down by the Council of Trent in the sixteenth century and had proved more or less immutable since then as a part of the Counter-Reformation.

In the historically-oriented culture of the nineteenth century the liturgical movement influenced the development of research into the roots of early Christian worship. Step by step the foundations of worship were laid bare and its evolution charted. The Roman liturgy turned out to be not an unchanging pattern but a complex of rites and devotions that grew over time. "Eyes were opened," according to the liturgist H. Wegman, "when the other liturgical traditions were discovered and the Jewish roots of Christian worship became known." The most important and ultimately most successful study was undertaken by the French Benedictine Prosper Guéranger (1805-1875), who as a young monk had bought a derelict priory in Solesmes (between Le Mans and Angers) after the Revolution. He and a number of kindred spirits moved into it with the aim of breathing new life into the Benedictine tradition in France. From there later monks went to Germany (Beuron, Maria Laach), Belgium (Maredsous) and England (Farnborough), and in this way spread a reborn monastic culture. In his own abbey Guéranger created a workplace where the liturgy of Rome was cherished, but in addition scholarly research was carried out to trace and restore the purest forms of that liturgy and of song. In his view the Benedictines had represented a specific church tradition in the past and they must do that again after the Revolution. This tradition could be traced back to the age of the church fathers and the Middle Ages.

Guéranger began a crusade against the rituals in French Catholicism that were based on fashionable devotions and what he regarded as "hyperindividualism." In contrast, the Roman liturgy offered an unrivalled balance between reason and emotion. Moreover, its rituals confirmed unity with Rome. Guéranger combined his historical insights with the ultramontane belief that uniformity was the expression of an essential alliance with the Pope.[43] Inspired by the work of the anthropologist Clifford Geertz, the medievalist Peter Raedts views Guéranger as

> the first to appreciate the social nature of ritual, the first to see that groups are formed and held together by symbolic gestures. Long before anthropologists began to study religion systematically, he saw almost intuitively that religion is a cultural system that is maintained not primarily by organization or words, but by rituals, by symbolic acts that influence people profoundly because they order and represent the cosmos.[44]

The rediscovered Roman liturgy was marked by monastic austerity and exaltedness. The "officium divinum," divine service, was strictly ordered and ceremonial in style. Church Latin was also part of this. After 1901 it had to be pronounced with a Roman diction on the orders of Pius X. Despite this attempt to impose uniformity, the language was no longer immediately intelligible, thus adding to the mystery and holiness of the rite. The liturgical revival was accompanied by a rediscovery of ancient hymns and antiphons, and of Gregorian chant as the pre-eminent style of church singing. And because it was recreated in an abbey, it was given an aristocratic touch. The non-ordained faithful were kept at a distance behind the communion rail. The liturgy was there to be looked at and listened to and possibly smelt, when incense was burned in solemn ceremonies.

Around the turn of the century the monks at Solesmes were forced by anti-clerical laws to leave their abbey and move to the Isle of Wight in England. Monks from the abbey of Wisques, a monastery belonging to the order of Solesmes, came to the Netherlands in 1907 after various travels. They founded St. Paul's Abbey in Oosterhout. Thus the Benedictines came back to the area from which they had been driven during the Reformation. This French foundation attracted Dutch novices and became a center for

St. Paulus-Abdij. Oosterhout.

The abbey of the French Benedictines in Oosterhout.

the communication of ideas and developments in French Catholicism. One of these was the Roman liturgy rediscovered at Solesmes, particularly performance in the Gregorian style. Priests and church musicians were taught how to do this at liturgical congresses in Amsterdam (1910) and Breda (1911).[45]

The choice of Gregorian chant as *the* church music above all was the result of a romantic rediscovery of this ancient form with its unusual tonality and mysterious notation. Once its priority was established, a dispute arose as to how it should be performed. The Vatican Congregation of Rites committed itself to the practice set out in a publication of 1614 called *Medicaea,* and granted the right to print the Gregorian songbooks to the Catholic publisher Pustet in Regensburg, Germany. This city had a church music school and in the eighteen-seventies it had become the center of a movement for renewal, the Allgemeine Cäcilien-Verein für katholische Kirchenmusik. Its ideal was in fact a return to historical styles such as Gregorian chant and the polyphonic music of the Renaissance, preferably by or in the manner of Palestrina (1525-1594). The followers of this Cecilian movement idealized the musical practice of sixteenth-century Rome and wanted it to be continued in both performances and contemporary compositions. A scholarly dispute arose over the authenticity of the Vatican's interpretation of Gregorian chant. This often happened when church authorities decided to canonize one particular historical style. Pope Leo XIII put an end to debate in 1901. The outcome was that from 1904 Gregorian chant was to be written and sung according to the method of the Abbey of Solesmes.[46] A year before, in 1903, Pope Pius X had issued a *Motu proprio* in which the subservience of music to the liturgy was made a principle.

This Vatican monopoly was respected in the Netherlands, albeit with growing doubts as to its scholarly validity. The driving force behind this loyalty to Rome was the St. Gregory Society, founded in 1878 by the priest Michael J.A. Lans, then a music teacher at the preparatory seminary in Haarlem. At its core was a group of clergy who wanted to reform the practice of church music on the model of the Cecilian movement in Germany. In open letters following a congress on church music in Arezzo in 1882, Lans put the case for the Regensburg movement, and criticized the views of the French Benedictines. The St. Gregory Society was established thirteen years after the council of the Dutch arch-diocese had put a limit on musical embellishment in the national churches. It decided that special permission would be required for the use of instruments, other than the organ, in church, while women singing in choirs was categorically forbidden ("strictis-sime prohibetur"). This meant the end in due course of a musical culture that was some-times centuries old, as in the case of St. Anthony's (Moses and Aaron) Church on the Waterlooplein in Amsterdam, which was renowned for its choir *Zelus pro domo dei* and its orchestral Masses. The second ruling struck a blow at the heart of the choir. The women could not be immediately replaced by a properly trained boys' choir, and the normal repertoire for mixed choirs was also affected. The turning point came with the founding of the St. Gregory Society. This led to a preference for Gregorian chant and sub-sequently to a desire to return to the polyphony of Palestrina. Contemporary composers were required to take this style as their guide.

The Cecilian movement was remarkably in tune with the new interest in the polyphony of the fifteenth and sixteenth centuries. The part played in this by composers from the Low Countries such as Jacob Obrecht and Josquin des Prez was now discovered, as it were.

Around 1900 Dutch choirs took to performing a capella works from the Renaissance, which were made available partly through the publications of the Society for Dutch Music History. The works of Jan Pietersz Sweelinck, for example, were published between 1894 and 1902. On the initiative of the musician Daniël de Lange, small vocal ensembles were formed which made a wide audience aware of the beauty of polyphony. In 1892 an occasional ensemble of eighteen leading soloists toured Vienna, Berlin, Liège and London, where they received ovations for their programing and sublime choral singing. The resurrection of this Renaissance music created links between church choirs and ensembles; church conductors gave remarkable performances of a capella choral works in concert halls.[47]

At the same time, however, both the Cecilian movement and the papal guidelines were limiting the room for maneuver of those wishing to compose contemporary church music and have it performed. Polyphony or Gregorian chant were norms in worship, with the inevitable risk of inferior imitations and rigidity. The composer Alphons Diepenbrock discovered this when in 1890, while living close to St. John's Cathedral in 's-Hertogenbosch, he started work on a Mass for a male choir. It reflected his admiration for medieval culture but also incorporated contemporary musical forms. Between 1892 and 1894 he revised the first version, turning it into a Mass for two choirs, on the lines of the antiphonal style of singing of two choirs facing each other in St. Mark's in Venice. He saw his composition as "radiant with memories and raptures" from his childhood. "The emotions of my highly religious early youth, which now lie so far behind me, are strong and beautiful enough to turn into sound even now." The *Missa in die festo*, as it came to be known later, was written in accordance with the liturgical rules of the day – for a male choir with organ accompaniment. Diepenbrock knew about the Cecilian movement, but believed his work showed "an independent development of the Palestrina style through Bach and Wagner, with all the intoxicating richness of modern musical methods." This was a problem that earlier composers like Anton Bruckner and Franz Liszt had struggled hard to resolve. He dreamed of expressing in music the religious community life that he believed the Middle Ages had known.[48]

The composer had expressly intended his Mass for Catholic worship; the denial of this amounted to an "absolute negation of my artistic credo." For the time being the work remained unperformed in the Catholic Church, in the first place because it proved too difficult for the church choirs of the day, but also because it had not been submitted to the church censors for approval. It was not until October 2, 1916 that it was first performed in the cathedral in Utrecht at the intercession of J.A.S. van Schaik, the head of the preparatory seminary in Culemborg. The music caused a sensation among the listeners. The composer Matthijs Vermeulen wrote that Diepenbrock's Mass would remain a monument of the age.

> When I see how the many voices sing together in one universe, each detail of which is organic and inspired like Gothic architecture, those voices praying back and forth, which the organ joins with an entirely separate wealth of sound, when I see those multiplicities of rhythm, and the endlessly alternating harmony, la nuance et encore la nuance, then I feel an immense respect for the craftsman in Diepenbrock, who here piles up a magnificence of technique over a magnificence of musical imagination.[49]

The fate of Diepenbrock's Mass illustrates the conflict caused when artistic creativity goes beyond the bounds of church guidelines. A similar dispute arose over a monumental painting of the procession of the Blessed Sacrament in medieval Amsterdam. In 1884 the 25-year-old artist Antoon Derkinderen was commissioned by the rector of the clandestine Catholic church in the Begijnhof in Amsterdam, Bernardus Henricus Klönne, to paint this event, which had been abolished at the Reformation. Klönne was actively campaigning to revive this tradition of pilgrimage. The making of a test piece, a watercolor, revealed a conflict between the two. The rector wanted the medieval procession to be depicted in accordance with the Council of Trent's decrees on decorum in the visual arts. He also wanted to include portraits of co-religionists in his circle. So seventy people from the Catholic world of Amsterdam posed for Derkinderen. "Klönne loved the study of history, whereas Derkinderen wanted to get away from antiquarian accuracy, and this inevitably meant that cooperation between them was an ordeal for both."[50] Before he had finished the painting, Derkinderen traveled to France and Italy, and his artistic views changed as a result.

Influenced by what he had discovered in the work of Giotto and of the modern artist Puvis de Chavannes, and by both monumental art and contemporary impressionism, Derkinderen turned the latest version of the procession into a different painting. He set about covering the work "cold-bloodedly," as Klönne complained, "with a strange misty haze." As a result, the thousand and one historical curiosities that the rector had unearthed so meticulously vanished. The painter was no longer seeking to express personal lyricism. By having the figures move quietly in a single direction, he added devotion and a more pious mood to the procession. "The relaxed turning round, the self-conscious looking about, which made the participants soloists, could not possibly remain. Repentance, blissful peace, was to be evident in everyone's attitude. All the vain jumps in the rhythm, which had earlier made the composition more or less akin to the dance step in Verhulst's theatrical church music, had to merge into a gentle and hence freer gliding or floating."[51] But the rector could not accept this version. Derkinderen had to exhibit it outside the church in 1889. The commission was given to another artist, and Derkinderen's chances of getting work from the church authorities were reduced to nil.[52]

Around the turn of the century a move towards "democratization" of the ritual also found support within the liturgical movement; it was an attempt to bridge the gap between the people and the liturgy and to reduce the distance between the priest and the people. At Keizersberg Abbey near Louvain, in particular, steps were taken to bring about a "participatio activa" of the faithful in worship. Congresses were organized in Western Europe and step by step a change was made that was regarded later in the century as inevitable.[53] After 1903 Pope Pius X issued decrees on how to realize the ideal of active participation, for example through frequent Communion, for children as well. Priests like Klönne and F.C. Beukering tried to promote democratization through their liturgical reforms.

In practice this meant active participation in the ritual by non-ordained believers. After he became priest of the church of St. Antony the Abbot in Delfshaven in 1909, Beukering tried to encourage the congregation to become actively involved. He aimed for soberness and believed that Gregorian chant should be preferred and all other church music, including contemporary compositions, banned. In his newly built church he succeeded in introducing the "celebratio versus populum" – celebrating the Mass while facing the congregation, thus lessening the distance between the ordained and the non-ordained.[54] Rector Klönne sought to enliven popular worship. He tried to mobilize the faithful through a contemporary variant of the procession of the Blessed Sacrament in medieval Amsterdam.

In 1880 one Joseph Lousbergh came across an old text which described the route of the medieval procession around the place where the cult of the Miracle of the Blessed Sacrament had developed. He took the text to his friend, the textile merchant Carel Elsenburg, and together they decided to walk this "holy way" on Saturday night in March during Lent. They gained the support of Rector Klönne. In 1885 there were twelve participants. In 1895 a thousand silent pilgrims walked in the nighttime procession. By 1900 there were 1,500 participants. Particularly after World War I, the number of men taking part increased rapidly. The medieval chapel which had been built at the site of the cult and was known as the Heilige Stede (Holy Place) was pulled down in 1908. The owner, the Reformed Congregation of Amsterdam, faced with the prospect of a revival of the procession of the Sacrament, preferred demolition rather than run the risk that this medieval monument might be reopened at some point.[55] A column was erected on the site of the chapel to commemorate its sacred nature.

Jan Toorop, portrait of Father F.C. Beukering, a pioneer of liturgical reform.

Popular devotion was also revived elsewhere in the Netherlands. It provided an opportunity to mobilize ordinary Catholics and to strengthen the sense of solidarity within what was after all a minority. It was also a way, moreover, of counterbalancing the events staged by the nascent socialist movement. There was a tradition of processions and pilgrimages in places like Uden and Handel, which were in the southern province of Brabant and had once been enclaves outside the sovereignty of the Republic. A significant cult of the Virgin Mary had developed there, and the same was true of Kevelaer, a German town on the Rhine. The purpose of these pilgrimages was a deepening of faith, but other aspects gradually became dominant. Brotherhoods were established as far away as Amsterdam and Zwolle for the organization of an annual pilgrimage. In them the social function of mutual assistance and conviviality was at least as important as the religious dimension. In the eighteenth century pilgrimages had begun on Republican territory as ordinary excursions, but as soon as the border was crossed, out came the attributes of a Catholic procession. "There the Dutch were overwhelmed in a way completely unfamiliar to them by countless proofs of divine grace, baroque luxury and

DOKKUM.   Bonifaciusfontein.   Uitg.J Kamminga,Dokkum.

The new spring (1884) on the site of the devotion to St. Boniface in Dokkum.

impressive ceremonies that left no doubt as to the truth and superiority of the Catholic Church. In Kevelaer, Handel or Uden it was no longer odd and inferior to be a Catholic, but indeed natural and valuable." On their return the pilgrims passed on this sense of solidarity and self-assurance to the Catholics in their circle who had stayed at home.[56]

For the pilgrim of 1900 the train stood ready. The pilgrimage by foot consequently disappeared, together with the influence of the prayer leaders, who were also singers. The liturgical movement took the initiative in collecting, approving and publishing the pilgrims' hymns. Essays on doctrine were included in the guides for pilgrims. The high spirits of the return journey were tempered, at least on paper, as an attempt was made to stick to a fixed repertoire of exercises and hymns. The modern pilgrimage evolved into a character-building journey.[57]

Two trends are evident in the numerous old and new pilgrimages that existed around the turn of the century. The first is the revival of holy places connected to national history. One lies in the town of Dokkum in Friesland. In the Middle Ages it had a memorial church and a freshwater spring to commemorate the murder of Bishop Boniface and fifty-two companions in 754. Boniface was an Anglo-Saxon missionary and a bishop in Germany. This devotion had been officially discontinued at the time of the Reformation, but it was given new life in the nineteenth century. The clandestine church was replaced by a neo-Gothic cruciform basilica designed by Cuypers in 1870. The principal relic of Boniface, part of what was believed to be his skull set in silver, was kept in a separate chapel. The location of the ancient spring was pinpointed at the end of the nineteenth century in a meadow outside the town. It was a "brewers' spring" and was used by Dokkum brewers until 1866. After World War I a chapel and a procession park were built

Pieter Hendrik van Moerkerken, St. John's Procession in Laren, 1898.

on the meadow, creating the kind of "ritual landscape" that is typical both of a place of pilgrimage and of a spa.[58]

Brielle was also accorded a sacred place: the site of the St. Elizabeth convent where nineteen priests had been hung by the Sea Beggars on July 9, 1572. In the nineteenth century, as part of the Catholic presentation of the Dutch Revolt, these martyrs had been upgraded. Around 1840 the priest of Brielle had managed to locate the original convent barn where they were executed. The site was known as the "spring meadow." It was the property of a Protestant orphanage and in 1865 it was bought by a Catholic merchant and presented to the diocese of Haarlem. At the same time the efforts of the Franciscan authorities in Rome to have the martyrs made saints were successful. On June 29, 1867 they were canonized by Pope Pius IX. The Dutch bishops had shown considerable reserve during this process because they wanted to avoid a confrontation in the Netherlands between Catholics and the "Protestant view of history" which might lead to disturbances.[59] The capture of Brielle by the Sea Beggars in 1572 had been an important moment in the history of the Dutch Revolt and marked a turning point in the fortunes of war.

After the canonization there was every reason to provide facilities for a devotion. A pilgrimage complex consisting of a chapel and a procession park was built in 1878. At the center was the burial place, which held the remains of bones excavated from the Martelveld (Martyrs' Field) between 1874 and 1877. Also involved in the devotion was a pond or well that had nothing to do with the story of the martyrs. In 1875 twenty-seven pilgrimages to Brielle involving a total of 9,223 persons were organized; in 1882 there were thirty-one pilgrimages and 11,821 pilgrims. These figures remained stable until World War I. In Brielle too, the pilgrimage was primarily a character-building exercise. Throughout the country, but particularly in the diocese of Haarlem, brotherhoods were established whose task was to promote the veneration of the martyrs and the conversion of the Netherlands.[60]

A second trend in the pilgrimages was brought about by the fathers and brothers of the Congregation of the Most Holy Redeemer, known for short as the Redemptorists. These clergy devoted themselves to spiritual care and preaching among the ordinary people; it was a Catholic version of the Protestant movement for internal missions and evangelical reawakening. The Redemptorists were in charge of the Archbrotherhood of the Holy Family, a religious society that originated in the diocese of Liège in 1844. Around 1900 there were 100,000 members in the Netherlands scattered over 300 branches, most of them from the lower middle classes. The Archbrotherhood was run on strictly hierarchical lines and organized by parish. It was not only an instrument for deepening piety through its own rituals and outward insignia such as banners and medals; it was also a means of idealizing the Christian family. At its high point, around the turn of the century, the brotherhood faced competition from Catholic labor unions and sports clubs, which combined secular aims with supporting religious life.[61] The Redemptorists were in charge of the so-called people's missions, which were internal missions by eloquent priests designed to inspire greater devotion among parishioners through emotional sermons and services. These fathers created a rhetoric of their own and became experts in judging moral standards.

Popular devotions of this type form the reverse, so to speak, of the aristocratization of the liturgy. But both were meant to strengthen the faith of a silent minority of Catholics in the Netherlands and to mobilize them in a social context in which secularization was unmistakably increasing. Judging by the growth in participation, this deliberate revival was fairly successful.

Spiritual leadership

In the Catholic community, which in the Netherlands had a lower level of education, the priest had a natural authority. This was because of his office, the ritual acts he performed and the spiritual care he gave. But he could add to his authority through a combination of erudition and leadership. As a result, the clergy played a predominant role in the social emancipation of Dutch Catholicism that became manifest at the end of the nineteenth century. The priest took part in or was appointed the leader of countless social and cultural organizations.

This made the priesthood attractive to anyone wishing to rise to a respected position in society. To become a priest, one had to complete two periods of training of six years each, first at the preparatory seminary and then at the theological seminary. Both were boarding schools because priests were deliberately educated in seclusion. This alone made it a fairly expensive course of studies. This was not unusual in a society in which access to secondary education cost money. Nonetheless, students could be assisted by financial contributions from parish priests or special funds. Around the turn of the century the threshold was lowered, particularly for the seminaries of recently founded congregations or those which had just come to the Netherlands. Because of their location outside the big cities and because they were boarding schools, these seminaries gave access to an education which would not have been available otherwise.

The picture of the Catholic clergy would not be complete without considering the role of the nuns. Around 1900 their numbers increased sharply. In particular, the so-called active congregations, the women who worked in education or health care, played a more prominent part. The convent became a way in which women could realize ambitions that could not otherwise have been achieved. Devotion to the family, which was seen in Catholicism as a woman's purpose in life, stood in the way of extended education or fulfilling work. Opting for the convent could broaden a woman's existence to take in work in society and the development of management abilities. In return, the individual sister had to take a vow of celibacy and of almost total obedience.

The percentage of Catholics

The percentage of Catholics was virtually the same in 1947 as in 1840. In a graph, however, the line in between looks like a jump rope, with the lowest middle part in the decade between 1899 and 1909. In eighty years (1830-1909) the percentage of Catholics in the Netherlands declined from 38.2 to 35.02, or by 3.8. After 1909 the line curves up in an ever faster increase. From 1930 to 1947 Catholics accounted for 48 percent of the growth in the Dutch population, despite substantial losses due to secularization. If the percentage of Catholics had been the same in 1909 as it had been in 1849, the first year in which they were again counted separately, then there would have been 2,234,895 Catholics; in other words, 181,310 more than the actual number. Taking into account the consequences of population growth over these sixty years, and after eliminating demographic side effects, one is still left with an average loss of 2,300 per year.[62]

In contrast to Protestant ministers, Roman Catholic priests were educated outside the universities. Male candidates went to preparatory seminaries, at the level of high school, and theological seminaries at college level, where they studied philosophy and theology. The organization derived from the Council of Trent, which had laid down that bishops must provide their candidates for the priesthood with four years' education in theology at an institute appointed for the purpose. The Dutch bishops had extended this exclusive education to take in a two-year introduction to philosophy. This decision was influenced not only by a traditional distaste for state intervention in the training of priests, but also by the mentality of the clandestine church, which made people wary of sending their sons to a university dominated by Protestants. Moreover, at that time it seemed inconceivable that the public universities could accommodate a faculty of Catholic theology subject to papal authority.

Training courses for priests were significantly expanded towards the turn of the century: between 1875 and 1905 the number of preparatory seminaries rose from five to seventeen, and the number of theological seminaries from fifteen to thirty-one. This increase was accounted for by the regular clergy (the orders and congregations), and may be explained by two factors. The first was the renewed interest in missionary work, which was a consequence of the imperialism of the European powers and led to active preaching of the faith overseas. The second was that during the *Kulturkampf* in Prussia (1870-1880), and while there was an anticlerical regime in France (1901-1914), the Netherlands became a refuge for emigrating or exiled orders and congregations. These clerical refugees usually settled in religious houses in the border regions and after some time duly opened their doors to indigenous candidates as well.[63] This historical circumstance helped to ensure that the majority of the training courses for priests were located in the country and outside the main cities, particularly in the southern provinces of North Brabant and Limburg.

This expansion led in turn to an increase in the number of ordinations. From the middle of the nineteenth century on average sixty secular and sixty regular priests were ordained each year. From 1895 these figures rose to eighty and one hundred respectively. Between 1891 and 1900 the total number of ordinations was 1,332, of which 663 were secular and 669 regular; between 1901 and 1910 the total rose to 1,807, with 817 secular and 990 regular. Afterwards the number of ordinations stabilized.[64] Such figures show that the increase in the number of priests equaled the increase in the Catholic population and around 1900 even exceeded it.

In the shadow of the male priests stood the nuns, but the increase in their numbers is no less remarkable. Exact figures are not available, but the evidence is clear enough. The commemorative volume *Neerlandia Catholica* presented to Pope Leo XIII in 1853 stated that there were 1,850 nuns; in 1888 there were 9,280.[65] In studies of individual groups, growth seems to be strongest around 1900. From another calculation it can be deduced that from 1800 166 orders and congregations of nuns had established themselves in the Netherlands, as compared with thirty-nine orders and congregations of priests and monks and twenty-three congregations of friars.[66] The curves are highest in the decades around 1900. The rise and growth of congregations for women was a European, not just a Dutch, phenomenon. In England and Wales, for example, around 1900 there were some 600 Catholic convents and between 8,000 and 10,000 nuns. "The nineteenth century was unique in the history of Christian religious life not only because of the number of new foundations that were made, but also because of the number made by and for women."[67]

The nuns – and their Protestant counterparts, the deaconesses – were just what was needed at a time of growing professionalization of health care. Around the turn of the century the old hospices for accommodation and nursing were becoming hospitals for treatment and cure; medical interventions became more important because of scientific advances and because of physicians monopolizing the care of the sick. The qualitative improvement of medicine required nurses who were trained as such and could meet higher standards in practice. This professionalization attracted women from the middle class who could work together with the physicians. The women now going into nursing were often from the same kind of background as the doctors were.[68] Nuns were also welcomed in Catholic schools. The expansion of Catholic elementary schools would have been impossible without recruiting nuns. Obedient as they were, they could be deployed in many parishes, and because of their vow of poverty they were paid relatively little; up to 1889 these schools received no state subsidy.[69] Given the general pattern of norms and values for women, "the congregations offered chances and opportunities that most of them would not have had outside the convent. In Catholic circles certainly, girls' schools and nursing were the almost exclusive preserve of nuns."[70]

A fully robed nun belonging to the order of the Sisters of Charity of Choorstraat in 's-Hertogenbosch.

Seminaries

Who went to the preparatory seminaries? The sons of businessmen, entrepreneurs, farmers, and artisans predominated. The "new" middle class or the professionals and government employees were underrepresented. In the nineteenth century the cost of this type of school was evidently too high: even in 1920 the proportion of boys from the working classes was only five percent. The renowned boarding school at Rolduc in Limburg and the Jesuit colleges at Katwijk aan de Rijn and Nijmegen, which were not only preparatory seminaries, presented a different picture. Both in 1880 and 1920 only about half the pupils they attracted were the sons of businessmen and entrepreneurs.[71] The deliberate exclusivity of the seminaries meant that there was a risk of intellectual inbreeding. In the circumstances this could only be avoided through the international dimension of the Catholic Church. Some orders and congregations had a head start in this respect if they had a tradition of scholarship and close ties with universities elsewhere. This applied to the Franciscans and their Catholic University in Louvain, the Dominicans and their University of Fribourg in Switzerland, the University in Paris and the Angelicum University in Rome, and to the Jesuits and their Gregorian University in Rome. Their institutions had qualified specialist teachers available to them earlier than the theological seminaries in the dioceses, so that they were able to provide the broad education desired

The preparatory seminary in Culemborg.

Students from the theological seminary in Warmond.

at a satisfactory level. The diocesan institutions had fewer staff, and they had to teach several subjects. The teachers at the regular seminaries were more specialized and had more opportunities to study their own subject. Moreover, there are indications that the regular teachers dared to go further intellectually than the seculars, for the superiors were a protective "way station" between the Vatican and the local seminary.

Most of the Dutch bishops were pastors by disposition and were not known for their devotion to theology. Given this interpretation of priestly ideals, a preference for handbooks that set out doctrine in a compact form that could be memorized was only to be expected.[72] All the teachers were waiting for their promotion, they taught with their presbytery in mind, wrote the former seminarian Anton van Duinkerken. "Even the lecturers at the theological seminary thought of teaching as temporary work, which would be crowned by an appointment as a priest. The disadvantage of this enforced impatience is that few devote themselves fully to scholarship, but the much greater advantage is that the young are taught by people who are not yet old and set in their ways."[73]

It had not escaped the notice of the Curia in Rome, the governing body of the Catholic Church, that the scholarly standards of most seminaries in the Netherlands fell short. But the bishops tried to retain as much autonomy as possible in their dioceses and to limit Vatican involvement with their seminaries. "The willingness to adapt the content of education – especially in the fields of moral theology and philosophy – to meet Roman standards was also limited and often went no further than window-dressing."[74] As early as 1877 the internuncio Giovanni Capri had submitted a plan for improving the Dutch clergy's knowledge of theology by establishing an interdiocesan academy on the Roman model, that is "a platform for research and discussion which, of course, would also be highly suitable for introducing Roman viewpoints and models centrally."[75] This plan was never realized. The same applies to a proposal by Capri's successor, Agapito Panici, to found a Dutch college in Rome which could accommodate students for the priesthood. The bishops were against this idea, and it was to be 1930 before the college was actually established.

In 1891 the internuncio Aristide Rinaldini received orders from Rome to evaluate the state of the Dutch seminaries. Had the bishops been able to read his (secret) report, "they would probably not have been dissatisfied. The papal diplomat was full of praise for the material conditions in the seminaries. He was equally positive about the vigorous way in which they were governed and about the religious and spiritual education that the future priests received: discipline, piety and esprit de corps were truly excellent. His judgment as to the content and level of the study program was more cautious. The bishops believed that the training should be primarily directed towards pastoral work in practice and not towards producing 'erudite priests,' which meant that at most seminaries there was a strong emphasis on moral theology. They were also persuaded that piety and impeccable behavior would make more impression on Protestants than profound knowledge of theological doctrine. For this reason, as Rinaldini put it in an elegant paradox, the course was sufficient, but no one would dare say that it also had sufficient depth. He was aware that in the Netherlands moral theology was still very strict and doctrinal, the result of the influence of the 'regrettable poison of the sectarian rigorism' of the Jansenists of the eighteenth century."[76]

Jesuits with former students at St. Ignatius College, Amsterdam, 1912.

By way of an exception, Jan van den Brink, a priest in the diocese of Breda, was sent to Rome to follow a university course of study. The Bishop of Breda was ahead of his colleagues in sending young priests on university courses, preferably in nearby Louvain. In 1893 Van den Brink gained his doctorate for research on predestination in Thomist philosophy. As a curate back in Breda, he became a socialist and was consequently suspended by his bishop. In 1907 he was elected to the Breda city council as a member of the SDAP. But even this did not make the bishop change course. In contrast, Bishop Callier of Haarlem totally rejected any university education for his priests right up to his death in 1928. This was generally thought to be in reaction to the loss of faith of a priest from the Haarlem diocese, Leo Balet, after he had studied at the Catholic University in Fribourg.

Neo-Thomism

Van den Brink had gained his doctorate for work in the field of neo-scholasticism. In August 1879 Pope Leo XIII issued the encyclical *Aeterni Patris*; in it the philosophy of Thomas Aquinas was presented as the core and culmination of everything proposed by the medieval scholastics. Thomism, in a modern framework, was declared to be the authoritative philosophy of the Catholic Church. Scholasticism was to be practiced again, but augmented by new knowledge and not by repeating old theses and methods.

Priests were to orient themselves accordingly. As a consequence of this ruling, the pontifical universities were reorganized on Thomist lines. Important centers developed outside Rome such as the Institut Catholique in Paris and the Catholic University in Louvain, where the priest Désiré Mercier gave his first course in the philosophy of St. Thomas in October 1882. Five years later, thanks to the Pope's efforts and funds, a Higher Institute of Philosophy was founded in Louvain. It was intended to be a center of pure research with a neo-Thomist slant, an attempt to avoid traditional eclecticism in the encounter between positivist science and Catholic philosophy and to formulate a systematic theory. The Institute managed to defend itself against Vatican intrigues and was highly influential, not least in the Netherlands, where around 1900 there was no theological institution that could match the quality of Louvain.[77]

It is clear from the handbooks used in the training of priests in the second half of the nineteenth century that the monastic orders in the Netherlands were guided by neo-scholasticism. This was also true of the theological seminaries, but there the professors supplemented the material with their own treatises. In moral theology at this time, however, neo-scholasticism was less important than the debate on the ethics of Alphonsus Liguori (1696-1787), the founder of the Redemptorists. In the age-old opposition between a strict moral code on one side – the product of a Jansenist tradition from the eighteenth century – and casuistic judgment in practice on the other, he had declared in favor of clear norms but mild practice in the confessional. His "equiprobabilism" had since dominated his order's approach to moral theology.[78] This had a wider importance because the handbook by the Redemptorist Aertnys was a standard component of the teaching of moral philosophy at seminaries; moreover, the Redemptorists were respected and popular as preachers in missions to the working classes. They set the tone in the characteristic distinction in Catholic ethics between the theory of maintaining standards and the practice of the confessional.

Neo-Thomism was not only the guideline for the teaching of philosophy at the theological seminaries, it also opened the way for Catholic philosophers to take up posts in higher education. In 1895 the University of Amsterdam appointed a professor in Thomist philosophy for the first time. Catholic doctrine had not previously been represented at Dutch universities. The man appointed was the Dominican father Joannes Vincentius de Groot, a philosopher at the order's seminary. Like many seminary professors, De Groot was self-taught. He had written about church history and Vondel before specializing in the doctrine of the medieval Dominican Thomas Aquinas. He "presented his hero proudly as a Dominican, without being in the least shy about being a man of the nineteenth century. For the last thing he wanted was to be seen as medieval in the narrow, one-sided sense."[79] But it was the priest and philosopher J.T. Beysens who succeeded in "constructing a complete system of realistic philosophy for our time in the spirit of Thomas Aquinas and according to the principles of the progressive tendency in neo-scholasticism."[80] With no special training, Beysens was appointed professor of philosophy at the theological seminary at Warmond in 1895. At first he was greatly influenced by the Louvain professor Mercier, but after publishing *Ontologie* (Ontology, 1903), he developed his own idiom. He also provided a Dutch-language version of neo-Thomist concepts. He left Warmond in 1909, when he was appointed professor of Thomist philosophy at the University of Utrecht.[81]

The Curia in Rome continued to cherish its project of a higher theological academy. From 1880 Kuyper's Free University in Amsterdam, which was intended for the training of Calvinist ministers, provided the model. But for the time being the bishops rejected this option as well. Mercier was made aware of this when in 1894 he came to the Netherlands to ask for financial support for a new building for his Higher Institute of Philosophy in Louvain. He had a rude awakening. It was clear to him that among Dutch church leaders "respect for higher education is not yet sufficiently deep or widespread to make an effective and well-thought out effort in that field."[82] The bishops thought the idea of a Catholic university was premature (although, according to Mercier, "it would be of great importance for this rich and beautiful country"). For this reason the bishops thought the idea of sending their priests to his institute in Louvain to be trained as "budding professors" was impractical and unnecessary.

The bishops clung to the system of specially appointed professors at the public universities, which they saw as a "corrective" to the education provided by the state. In 1900 a teacher, M.A.P.C. Poelhekke, gave a controversial address in Nijmegen on "The lack of Catholics in scholarship." This sparked off a public debate which provided fertile ground for the idea of a Catholic university.[83] The first step was taken in 1918. In that year a new edition of the code of canon law was published which stated that a Catholic university had to be founded if the public university was not steeped in the doctrine and spirit of the Catholic Church. This was the signal for a new campaign by laity and clergy, and, despite constant opposition from the Archbishop of Utrecht, it led to the founding of a Catholic university in Nijmegen in 1923.

Modernism

The international conflict over new theological ideas in the Catholic Church occurred at a time when in Dutch Catholicism the first fruits of original research were appearing. The purges that resulted from this conflict affected young scholars in the Netherlands who were beginning to test traditional views against modern scientific findings and to reconcile the two. The Vatican policy directed against what was called modernism began in the last years of Pope Leo XIII. His encyclical *Providentissimus* of 1893 warned against some modern developments in Catholic biblical scholarship. In 1899 he openly condemned so-called Americanism, an experience of faith based on activism and ecumenical rapprochement. Under his successor, Pius X, a devout pope concerned with worship, this rejection became still stronger. In 1907 he issued the encyclical *Pascendi* against modernism, and it included a new *Syllabus errorum* (catalogue of errors). Three years later all priests were required to take the anti-modernist oath. This heralded a witch-hunt in the name of so-called "integralism" or "integral Catholicism" which led to the dismissal of numerous theologians, mainly in Europe. This wave of purges did not end until a new pope, Benedict XV, was chosen. His first encyclical *Ad Beatissimi* in 1914 was devoted to the excesses of integralism.

The first – and most important – field of conflict, as said, was Catholic biblical schol-arship, where, as in Protestant theology, there was a confrontation between traditional exegesis and modern science, particularly over the theory of evolution, archeology and textual criticism. This was the field in which the first victim in the Netherlands fell. The young Bible scholar Henricus Andreas Poels was a priest in the Roermond diocese. He had gained his doctorate in Louvain in 1897 with a historical and critical study in French on the sanctuary in the first six books of the Old Testament. In the Netherlands he was told that he was infected with errors from the Protestant theology of Leiden. An investi-gation in Rome, on the initiative of the Bishop of Haarlem, showed that he had done nothing wrong from the point of view of dogma. Poels had the bad luck to be caught between a Haarlem hammer and a Roman anvil. The central authority in Rome accepted that as a scholar he was correct, if indirectly, by appointing him consultor of the papal biblical commission. In the Netherlands the Bishop of Haarlem refused to accept the con-sequences of this rehabilitation for fear of losing face. He kept the matter quiet. The Bishop of Roermond did not keep his publicly given promise of an appointment as a seminary lecturer. As a result, for a long time Poels continued to be associated with unorthodoxy.[84] In 1904 he was appointed a lecturer at the Catholic University of America in Washington D.C. In 1910, however, he was honorably dismissed. The American bishops, who had been forced onto the defensive by the papal condemnation of Americanism, wanted to avoid any suspicion of modernism in their educational institutions.

The Dutch episcopate showed similar caution. A handful of cases are known in which a priest left his office because of modernist beliefs. The best known example is Matthieu Schoenmakers, a priest in the Roermond diocese, who studied at the Gregorian University and then broke with Catholic dogma and developed an esoteric variant of Catholicism. Others were dismissed for holding modernist views. But the strict seminary discipline among the clergy produced a degree of immunity to modernism, which was widely evident elsewhere in Europe, particularly in France, Germany and Italy. Moreover, in the Catholic community in the Netherlands the mentality of the minority prevailed: it was a Catholicism that tended towards ultramontanism, strongly ethical in tenor, little inclined to speculation and generally conservative in political and social mat-ters.[85] This climate of caution strengthened the hand of those advocating purges in the Church. A witch-hunt took place in the Netherlands led by the priest Maria Anthonius Thompson (1861-1938), who branded numerous public figures as heretics, first in the Catholic daily *De Maasbode* from 1898 and later in his own periodical *Rome*. He could count on the tacit support of the Haarlem bishops Caspar Bottemanne and Augustinus Callier, through whose efforts several learned priests and lay persons were placed in a moral dilemma.

Emancipation

The same pattern is repeatedly seen in Dutch Catholicism at the turn of the century: a nervous episcopate urged by active Vatican diplomacy to improve the quality of educa-tion and the presentation of Catholicism in Dutch society. This pattern is again evident in the development of social and political organizations. The reason for this was not only the bishops' decision not to provoke the Protestant and liberal elites by militant action on the part of the Catholic community. They had learnt their lesson in 1853, when the re-establishment of the Catholic hierarchy had produced a fierce Protestant reaction in the so-called "April Movement." Nonetheless, this episcopal reserve increasingly contrasted with the position of the Vatican. In his attempt to retain his sovereignty in the face of the movement for Italian unification, Pope Pius IX adopted a strategy of mobilizing Catholics all over the world.

The battle to preserve the Vatican State led Pius IX and his advisers to abandon the course adopted by his predecessors, which was to be allowed to participate in the Concert of Europe in return for maintaining calm in the Church. After the Roman revolution of 1848 and his exile in Gaeta, the Pope chose to appeal to Catholic public opinion, including the laity, for support in his fight for constitutional independence. In the eighteen-sixties this support was also financial: the introduction of the so-called Peterspence and the floating of loans provided the Vatican with funds from the clergy and the Catholic middle classes in Europe. Another weapon was the mobilization of the Zouaves, a corps of volunteers committed to the armed defense of what was left of the Papal States by this stage. They were recruited mainly in France and the Low Countries. Of a total of 11,000, the Netherlands provided 3,000. Their military effectiveness was very limited; only one percent of the Zouaves died during or after combat. "What counted was not the shots they fired, but the newspaper articles they could inspire, the signatures their example could elicit, the money they helped to raise for the Pope – not the blood but the ink and the gold."[86]

After the (bloodless) capture of Rome by Italian troops on September 20, 1870, the mobilization continued, but now in the form of petitions, "meetings," and calls for a pilgrimage to the Eternal City and the "prisoner of the Vatican." The Dutch variant of the meeting was organized in Amsterdam on the occasion of the silver jubilee of Pius IX. It was "the first large, public and in fact political gathering of Catholics in the Netherlands."[87] This was known as the "Park Meeting," and it was here that the *Pius Cantata* with words by the poet and priest Herman Schaepman and music by Johannes Verhulst was first sung. It included the hymn "Aan U, o Koning der Eeuwen" (To You, O King of Ages), which was sung triumphantly at Catholic events for several decades afterwards. The pilgrimage to Rome could generally be undertaken only by the wealthy and was not a great success in the Netherlands, not least because the bishops did not cooperate enthusiastically in this form of mobilization. In the protocol for papal audiences the bishop present was always placed below the Holy Father.

The Dutch bishops were in two minds. On the one hand, they promoted the mobilization of Catholics for the "prisoner in the Vatican." On the other, they could see that this veneration for the Pope was damaging to their own episcopal policy, which took account of Dutch sensibilities. The Park Meeting, for example, was one of the reasons why there was a majority in the Lower House for a Liberal motion proposing to end the Dutch mission to the Holy See. This left the bishops and the papal representative in the Netherlands in a dispute about areas of responsibility, because the internuncio continued to function in The Hague even after the ending of the Dutch mission in Rome.

The "Roman question" faded away after 1870. In the Netherlands and elsewhere there was a general belief that, now that the Pope had been deprived of his political power, he would be able to concentrate all the better on spiritual leadership. Support for the Supreme Pastor on the other side of the Alps – *ultra montes* – changed in character, especially when Pius IX was succeeded by Leo XIII in 1878. Ultramontanism was no longer nurtured solely by calls to defend the Vatican, but by a rapprochement with the constitutional state as exemplified by the ending of the *Kulturkampf* in Bismarck's Germany and the rallying of French Catholics to the Republic, but above all by new views on labor relations set out in the encyclical *Rerum Novarum* (1891). This was welcomed by the priest Herman Schaepman (1844-1903), who campaigned for a political association of Catholics on the lines of "Zentrum" in Germany, which had defended Catholic interests during the *Kulturkampf*. In 1880 Schaepman became a member of Parliament for the city of Breda.

He had the appearance of an amiable and portly monk, the *prêtre bon enfant*, but appearances can be deceptive. In 1883 he issued a "draft program" through which he hoped to unite his co-religionists in the Lower House. He was the obvious leader among the Catholic members and gradually came to be seen throughout the country as the natural focus of Catholic political unity, but some of his character traits blocked his path. He was quick to take offence. With his deep-rooted penchant for conflict, he easily antagonized others by his often testy and sarcastic remarks.

A reluctant poet.
"Monsignor Bottemanne to Dr. Schaepman: My son, leave the parliamentary proceedings aside and remember that you are a poet." *De Amsterdammer*, August 12, 1894.

De Borromaeus Encycliek.

BIJVOEGSEL van De Amsterdammer, Weekblad voor Nederland, van 12 Juni 1910.

Christiaanzeelen!... De Vaas, de Vaas!

Amst. Boek- en Steendrukkerij, v/h. Ellerman, Harms & Co.

The Borromeo encyclical.
"Good heavens!... The vase, the vase!" *De Amsterdammer,* June 12, 1912.
(On the vase is the word "Coalition.")

Consistency, idiosyncrasy and opportunism alternated in him in an unpredictable fashion.[88] Nevertheless, in Rome Schaepman gained some of the respect denied him by various Catholic members of Parliament. And by some Dutch bishops. For the draft political program, which was steeped in the prevailing ultramontane views, was followed by an approach to the orthodox Protestant Anti-Revolutionary Party of Abraham Kuyper. The political will to form a parliamentary majority opposed to the Liberals finally triumphed over the profound antithesis between Rome and the Reformation. The first coalition government of Christian-Democratic parties took office in 1888.

The bishops had taken a reserved attitude towards the formation of a Catholic political party. In 1891 the Bishop of Haarlem, Caspar Bottemanne, abandoned this reserve in a Lent pastoral letter in which he admonished the faithful to submit to the judgment of the bishops in controversial political matters. This fell on deaf ears. The historian J.A. Bornewasser wrote that the Bishop of Haarlem was "the later prototype of Dutch Catholicism as it had developed in accordance with a long tradition and by making use of the democratic Constitution of 1848."[89] It was inward-looking and content to develop a religious subculture experienced in isolation, and displayed rigid characteristics that were foreign to the national culture. In the absence of a Dutch conservative party, and because of an ineradicable distaste for Protestantism, the bishop actually supported the moderate Liberals. "The avowed loyalty to papal authority functioned more as a protest against the evil, godless world that had eliminated the sovereignty of the Vicar of Christ than as willingness to be open to Leo XIII's plans for ecclesiastical reform and social change."[90]

The other side of this antithesis – Vatican activism versus native caution – could also be seen from time to time. In 1910 Pope Pius X issued the so-called Borromeo encyclical commemorating the tercentenary of the canonization of the Archbishop of Milan, Carlo Borromeo (1538-1584). A Counter-Reformation note was again struck. Reformers like Luther and Calvin had rejected the leadership of the Church and cooperated with the "most degenerate rulers and peoples" to destroy the social order in a tyrannical manner. This pronouncement angered the Protestant rulers, principally the German Kaiser but also Queen Wilhelmina, who could read an implicit condemnation of William of Orange into the encyclical. The idea that as a "Protestant nation" the Netherlands had been insulted by the Pope was not confined to marginal groups but widely accepted by orthodox and liberal Calvinists. It was this majority and this controversy that the spiritual leadership of Dutch Catholicism had always feared; this was what had made them cautious about emancipation.

It was on the basis of Schaepman's views – and of his late conversion to social politics – that the Catholic parliamentary party was able to accept the so-called "Pacification" of 1917: the great compromise by the leading political parties in the Netherlands on universal suffrage and the funding of private schools. This put an end to the schools controversy that had kept the Christian Democrats and the Liberals at loggerheads for decades. This Pacification is a landmark in the development of a pluralist system in the Netherlands. It safeguarded the legal position of the Catholic minority in Dutch society. In 1918 it was followed by the first parliamentary elections based on universal suffrage. Catholics became the largest political minority in the Lower House, a position they were to hold for fifty years.

<h1 style="text-align:center">11</h1>

Utopians and socialists

In 1871 Hendrik Gerhard published a *Sketch of a Communist Society*,[1] in which he set out a clear, comprehensive and attractive picture of society in the future. Money and private property no longer existed, all needs were provided for by a government that took care of the citizen from the cradle to the grave. The sketch begins with the birth of children in one of the many "community maternity wards." Provision for raising and educating children goes on from these maternity wards to children's playschools, free lower and secondary education and, if people wish and are suitable, higher education and advancement. Highly gifted pupils (amongst whom Gerhard included the artistically talented) are given the opportunity to develop into sculptors, architects or writers. Everyone chooses the occupation for which he or she is most suited. There is a six-hour working day. Clothing is provided through "community stores," and is in principle uniform, but people may vary it if they wish. Everyone works; idlers (if there are still such people) are urged to work, on pain of exclusion from the collective provisions. There is virtually no crime, because private property no longer exists. Passion alone may be the cause of an occasional transgression. Should this occur, the miscreant is punished by the "supervisors," who are selected by the workers. If his offence is serious, he appears before a committee of workers from the trade to which he belongs. National government is also organized through this trade union structure; it consists of representatives of all branches of industry. A form of corporative government like this, maintained Gerhard, would inevitably lead to an international federation of peoples.

Gerhard's sketch bears a very strong resemblance to Thomas More's *Utopia* (1516). This work, too, speaks of the abolition of money and private property, of extensive community provisions for child rearing, education, healthcare and housing, with an emphasis on thorough and lengthy education. There, too, the working day lasts six hours, and uniforms are supplied by the government. But religion, held in high esteem in More, has disappeared in Gerhard, and More's powerful state machine has been replaced by a form of workers' self-government that has much in common with the later "council communism." The pressure of the collective on the individual is therefore much less heavy in Gerhard than it is in More. Gerhard's society is orderly, and strict if it has to be, but benevolent in respect of individual peculiarities, and always seeks to promote the welfare of the individual. Does the worker feel like a drink? Then he can have one by spending the voucher issued to him for conscientious work in one of the "refreshment houses." But the most significant difference between Gerhard and More is that More paints a society which does not really exist anywhere nor ever will exist; an a-historical fiction written to be reflected upon, not to be realized; a myth against which the achievements and short-comings of contemporary society can be measured. Gerhard's *Sketch*, in contrast, is located in an existing society and projected into the near future.

Surprisingly, Gerhard nowhere makes any mention of the revolution that must pre-cede the communist society nor even of the conflict between labor and capital. The new society appears to have come about as a result of gradual social change and not through a power struggle culminating in a great crash. Evidently it was his intention to urge social change in the common interest, not to inflame passions and summon people to fight. This is remarkable, because Gerhard was the first Dutchman to join the International (or, to give it its full name, the *Internationale Arbeiterassoziation*, IAA) founded by Marx in 1864, and he intended his essay as a defense and explanation of that same International. His enthusiasm for an international league of workers' movements notwithstanding, Gerhard was not particularly attracted by class struggle and revolu-tion, and he made so bold as to think differently about it than Marx and Engels, just as he made so bold as to produce a utopian sketch of a future society, although this was for-bidden by Marx and Engels.[2] Gerhard's *Sketch* reveals that the first International was still a broad organization in which many conflicting movements were united. Marxist social-ism had not yet been elevated to the status of law. In 1878 Gerhard founded the *Sociaal Democratische Vereniging*, and then, in 1881, the *Sociaal Democratische Bond*, of which he was the first chairman. He endeavored to bring about social change by means of consul-tation and trade union action. His interpretation of international socialism was Dutch in the extreme, as evidenced by his activities in the general workers' union, the *Algemeen Nederlands Werklieden Verbond* (1871). The ANWV reacted skeptically to the International's efforts to politicize and polarize the workers' movement; it was opposed to revolution and class struggle and sought improvement of the workers' social conditions through an institutionalized form of consultation between employers and employees. In comparison with the International, the Dutch workers' movement expressly developed as a consul-tation model. The *Comité ter bespreking der sociale quaestie* (1870) was a shining example of this. In this body set up to discuss the "social question," a number of "gentlemen," among them Johan de Jong van Beek (advocate-general of the Zwolle Court), Professor Pekelharing and Dr. Hubrecht (director of the public trade school in Amsterdam) con-sulted with representatives of workers' organizations, among them Hendrik Gerhard, with the aim of "giving the property-owning classes an opportunity to engage in public debate with the workers, whose dissatisfaction and resentment had been fueled by the dismissive attitude adopted by the upper classes," in order to bring about an improve-ment in class relations and the establishment of "a popular feeling concerning the pend-ing issues." In the Netherlands, the debate about the social question had all the features of a polder model (that is, a consensus-based model) from the outset.[3]

In this chapter we concern ourselves with utopian socialism around the turn of the century. Taking our lead from Karl Mannheim, we define utopia as any design for a hypothetical society. We distance ourselves from the current meaning of utopia as an unachievable scheme for a perfect or ideal state. The thinkers and reformers we describe here as "Utopians" designed schemes with the intention of putting them into practice in the near future. While their sketches or models may not all have been realized, or not in their entirety, the far-reaching political and social changes that took place in the course of the twentieth century and the direction that these changes took were largely determined by them. Mannheim conceived utopia as an impulse for social change. He contrasted the concept with "ideology," which he defined as a rigid social pattern of thought. While outdated standards, values and theories could easily degenerate into ideology and increasingly take on the task of impeding and concealing changes in the social system, according to Mannheim utopian thinking is specifically directed toward inspiring and legitimizing change.[4]

In this sense Gerhard's *Sketch* is a perfect example of utopian thinking. The positive definition of utopia also helps to explain why the nineteenth century was besotted with utopias. The industrial revolution had changed the nature of society (and in part actually dislocated it) to such an extent that existing political and social institutions provided no solution. Reactions to the "social question" came in the form of countless utopias. They offered the indispensable impetus to social change. This is most certainly true in the case of Edward Bellamy's *Looking Backward 2000-1887*. This utopia, an insipid piece of work that is not in the same league as Gerhard's *Sketch*, was published in serial form in *Recht voor allen* (Justice for All) in 1889. A Dutch translation by Frank van der Goes appeared a year later. The book provoked fierce reactions in the circle around the journal *De Nieuwe Gids*. One trivial cause was evidently enough, like a tap on a flask containing a supersaturated solution, to crystallize the slumbering social awareness of Dutch intellectuals. A polemic involving Frank van der Goes, Frederik van Eeden, Lodewijk van Deyssel and Willem Kloos raged from 1890 to 1892.

What was the cause? In his utopia, Bellamy recounted how, under the influence of a "professor of animal magnetism" (in other words, a hypnotist), a young man was put into a trance from which he awoke after more than a century. He was woken by a certain Dr. Leete, who explained to him how the society of Boston was organized in the twenty-first century. Competition between battling corporations had been brought to an end by the introduction of one single, national corporation. The United States was "organized as the one great business corporation in which all other corporations were absorbed," "the epoch of trusts had ended in The Great Trust."[5] Bellamy presented or described a rational and scientifically organized society that had led to close national unity, a reaction to the American Civil War, which had just ended. Division and strife (whether they took place in the form of internecine struggle or competition) were banned for the sake of a rational and tightly organized social life, whose hierarchical relationships and strict discipline betray the model of a military organization. Bellamy had a boundless admiration for the army. It was on that army that he based his *Religion of Solidarity* (1874) and his firm conviction that a stringently disciplined community life had mystical qualities. He believed that humanity was evolving toward a collective consciousness, just as biological life had once evolved from inorganic to organic life. This evolution would be complete at the moment when mankind had returned to its divine origin. In the foreseeable future the "divine secret, hidden in the germ, shall be perfectly unfolded"; the apotheosis of humanity was "lost in light."[6] No wonder that it was primarily theosophists and old soldiers who reacted enthusiastically to *Looking Backward*. They were the nucleus of the "nationalist clubs," which wanted to put into practice the ideals of the "Nationalist Party" described in the novel. In 1890 there were no fewer than five hundred of these "national clubs," with their own journal, *The Nationalist* (later *The New Nation*), of which Bellamy was the editor.

The overwhelming success that the novel enjoyed – in the Netherlands as elsewhere – has to be attributed to its catalytic effect. The novel forced Dutch intellectuals in general and the editors of *De Nieuwe Gids* in particular to show their colors in the social question. Kloos and Van Deyssel reacted negatively. They wanted nothing to do with grayness and with the gray world which, in their view, would be created if society were to become a proletarian one-party state. Frank van der Goes, on the other hand, together with Pieter Lodewijk Tak, later the editor in chief of *De Kroniek*, adopted the socialist standpoint.[7] Van der Goes was particularly attracted by the "progressive thought" embodied in Bellamy's "National Trust." He believed that a form of rational production like this would generate enough material prosperity and leisure time to allow the workers the lifestyle of dandies. It is striking, incidentally, that all those involved unquestioningly regarded the novel as a socialist novel. *Looking Backward* is anything but. Bellamy distrusted socialists. In his novel he refers to the damaging effects of strikes in "the old epoch" and accuses the anarchists of being paid by the large corporations to discredit serious attempts at social reform.[8] Frederik van Eeden took a different position, to the extent that he believed that the emancipation of the people should come about on a spiritual rather than a material level and that this evolution involved everyone, not just the workers. Van Eeden was probably attracted by the same aspects that appealed to the American theosophists. His idea of spiritual evolution was very close to Bellamy's. The polemic heralded the downfall of *De Nieuwe Gids* and the Eighties Movement. The cultural cards were reshuffled and the most striking result was that a number of literary figures came to the conclusion that they were "on the wrong side" and appointed themselves spokesmen for and leaders of socialism. Frederik van Eeden started to make plans for *Rijkshoeven* – state farms – and colonies, Frank van der Goes became a member of the *Sociaal Democratische Bond* (1891) and editor of *De Nieuwe Tijd*. After this journal moved its offices from Sneek to Amsterdam and became the party organ of the Social Democratic Workers' Party (SDAP), founded in 1894, he took Herman Gorter and Henriëtte Roland Holst on as editors. Nothing better illustrates the change in the social and cultural climate of the turn of the century than the move by the former members of the Eighties Movement from the washed-up *Nieuwe Gids* to a journal that, alongside *De Kroniek* and *Het Tweemaandelijksch Tijdschrift*, spread the inspirational fire from the field of culture and literature to the social and political arena.

At the end of the nineteenth century, utopianism and socialism overlapped. The "and" in our title ("Utopians and socialists") consequently has to be understood as an inclusive, not an exclusive "and." The utopian socialists fall roughly into two groups, depending on whether they operated inside or outside the SDAP. On one side there were the colonists: Frederik van Eeden with his *Rijkshoeven* plan, Walden and the *Vereniging Gemeenschappelijk Grondbezit*, Daan de Clerq and Harmannus Groustra's Vrijland movement, and the colony of the International Brotherhood in Blaricum. Their aim was to establish small colonies in which the socialist society would be realized on a small scale and which, when they proved successful, would spawn a great many new colonies, working together, which would presently span the country and the world. The colonists based their views on a long community tradition running from early Christianity through monastic communities (the Brethren of the Common Life) and early nineteenth-century utopians like Fourier, Cabet and Owen, to Tolstoy's peasant community of Yasnaya Polyana.

On the other side stood the utopians of the SDAP: Herman Gorter and Henriëtte Roland Holst. They positioned themselves in a Marxist-revolutionary tradition (the line followed by the SDAP around 1900) and based their arguments on Marx, Kautsky and Luxemburg. Their aims were political. The question they asked themselves was how the workers' movement could acquire sufficient power to decide the battle against capital in its favor in an open confrontation. To them, socialist society was the final step in a historical-materialistic development that would culminate in the great revolution. The utopias that the colonists and revolutionaries developed from their divergent points of view appear irreconcilable.

Land reformers and Vrijland; Frederik van Eeden, Walden and common land ownership

Land reformers

The early socialists believed that social misery was the consequence of private land ownership. They proposed the compulsory acquisition of land, which would then be transferred into communal ownership. The society that the land reformers had in mind was a federation of colonies, in which the land would be worked by proletarians who had escaped the city slums. Leading figures of early socialism – Hendrik Gerhard, Jan Stoffel, Ferdinand Domela Nieuwenhuis, Frederik van Eeden – supported this view of the future. In retrospect, the reduction of the social question to private land ownership seems rather naive. If the proletariat had returned to the countryside en masse, the result would surely have been the collapse of the economy. Why, despite this, did the land reformers fix on land as the key to the problem?

The answer is that they took their cue from early nineteenth-century economists. Their theories were tangled up with romantic ideals, in which land was seen as a natural and regenerative force, as opposed to the degenerative effect of urban civilization. Large-scale land ownership in England had increased significantly at the beginning of the nineteenth century, and in consequence the countryside had been depopulated and the rural population proletarianized. Early economists like Ricardo assumed that the growth of towns and industry would push up the demand for agricultural products and that, with a constant acreage of land, prices would rise enormously. The economist Henry George (1839-1897) drew the conclusion that the ground rent (the income acquired from land) that the large landowners received would rise faster than productivity, resulting in ever falling wages. This was why, according to George, the private ownership of land was "as wrong as owning slaves." The solution, in his view, was to abolish ground rent and replace it with a tax, which he called the "single tax." In 1884 he founded the "Land Restoration League," whose aim was to get workers to go back to the land. The proposition on which he based his *Progress and Poverty* (1879), namely that the large landowners would become ever richer, the poor ever poorer ("progressive poverty through progressive wealth"), is absurd, but this did not stop the book from having a tremendous influence. Leading social reformers like Tolstoy, the British Fabian Society, German theoreticians like Michael Flürscheim, Theodor Hertzka and Franz Oppenheimer, and various Dutch land reformers took their inspiration from this work.[9]

The Deventer lumber merchant Jan Stoffel introduced George in the Netherlands in his brochure *Het sociale vraagstuk opgelost* (1883) (The Social Question Solved). In 1889, with several others, he set up the *Bond voor landnationalisering*, which he modeled on the *Deutsche Bund für Bodenbesitzreform*, which had been founded in 1885 by Michael Flürscheim. Flürscheim was a follower of George, but unlike George he advocated appropriation of the land, not the introduction of the "single tax." The goal of Stoffel's confederation was to have all land compulsorily acquired by central government or municipality, to have the owners recompensed, and to ensure that private land owner-ship could never occur again. These ideas caught on in Friesland, in particular, where there was severe unemployment among peat workers and farm laborers. The establish-ment of the *Comité voor communistische kolonisatie* (Committee for Communistic Colonisation) in Friesland in 1901 was a late consequence of this. Stoffel was an active champion of all sorts of variants of land nationalization. At his request, Flürscheim gave a lecture on land nationalization in Amsterdam in 1888; in 1889 the speaker was Henry George himself. In 1891 there was a breach between the *Bond voor landnationalisering* and Domela Nieuwenhuis's *Sociaal Democratische Bond* (SDB), because the land nationalizers would not speak out plainly in favor of socialism. According to Stoffel, production and consumption would increase as a matter of course if his system of gradual land acquisi-tion were to be adopted. The state would get more money and be in a position to carry out its collective works, such as the draining of the Zuiderzee. Universal prosperity would ultimately render the government superfluous; the communist ideal would have been achieved without a revolution. Stoffel promulgated his ideas in *De Nieuwe Gids* (1888-1889) and in *De Grond aan Allen* (Land for All), the confederation journal that he himself published. Abraham Kuyper and Marie W.F. Treub accused Stoffel of utopi-anism. Treub said in a lecture: "to me, land nationalization and such universal means are like potatoes with watery gravy; they fill the belly, but they don't nourish you" (in *De Grond aan Allen*, 1892).[10]

Ferdinand Domela Nieuwenhuis was another proponent of communal land owner-ship. In his lecture "Grond en bodem in gemeenschappelijk bezit" (1879) he referred, among other things, to the work of Laveleye, Proudhon and Rousseau: "the first person who enclosed a piece of land and said 'that belongs to me!' and found people simple enough to believe him was the actual founder of today's society."[11] The model he had in mind was that of the "Allmenden," the communal land ownership of the Swiss com-munes. The land had to be transferred to the ownership of "communities" like this; the state is nothing but the sum of these "communes." Remarkably, Domela supported the congress of the International of 1869 and Marx, when they declared that land had to be transferred to "state or communal ownership" (Marx). In 1879 Domela had just embraced socialism, resigned as a minister of religion and was full of enthusiasm about Marx. In 1881, with Marx's permission, he translated *Das Kapital* into Dutch under the title *Kapitaal en Arbeid*. It was not until much later – in 1897 – that it came to a split between him and the Marxists on the issue of the power that the Marxist socialists assigned to the state. From then on, Domela rejected any form of state authority and turned to anarchism. In this early phase, however, he was still able to feel comfortable with the existence of a state, because he understood this to mean the "sum of the communes." The title of his lecture, "Gemeenschappelijk Grondbezit," (Common Land Ownership) must therefore be read not as "land owned by the state," but as "land owned by the communities or communes."

The Vrijland movement (1889-1897)

The Vrijland (free land) movement came about in Germany in response to the publication of the novel *Freiland, ein sociales Zukunftsbild* by Theodor Hertzka in 1889. The movement struck an international chord; the Netherlands had the largest and most active association after Germany and Austria. Daan de Clerq, a free-lance engineer and inventor from Haarlem, was the Dutch correspondent, Harmannus Groustra, a schoolteacher from Schildwolde, was the main propagandist. Groustra translated and edited Hertzka's novel under the title: *Vrijland en de Vrijlandbeweging* (1893) and, with Kornelis ter Laan, published the biweekly magazine *Vrijland*, the organ of the *Nederlandsche Vrijland Vereeniging* (1894-1897).

Hertzka's utopia, inspired by Proudhon, is a complex interweaving of fiction and reality. The story of the novel served as a program that was put into effect immediately after its publication; many of the fictitious events corresponded with what actually happened subsequently. The story begins with a notice that appears in the leading journals in Europe and America in 18**. It announces the creation of an international association that has set itself the goal of solving the social question by establishing a colony in a fertile, undiscovered region that is suitable for colonization.[12] The announcement stresses the principle of "common land ownership," a social structure consisting of associations which anyone is free to join or leave, the provision of operating capital from common property, and the express rejection of state authority. The only real difference from similar associations, of course, is that Vrijland envisages foreign colonization and specifically an area in Africa that is still "unruled" ("herrenlos"). In a note, Groustra expressed several reservations about this word "herrenlos," because the indigenous population was totally disregarded. The "domination" of the Dark Continent by a "herrenvolk" or master race certainly sits uncomfortably in the plans of the Vrijland movement. Freedom evidently did not extend to the indigenous people the Vrijlanders expected to find there. Their eyes lit on the high mountains of Kenya. Hertzka based his account on Stanley's reports of his travels in his work *In Darkest Africa*, and used the same source for the detailed description of the equipment of the expedition, composed of two hundred "alert men," among them physicians, engineers and naturalists. Groustra included footnotes in his translation, in which he commented on the expedition that was actually under way.

He got his information from letters that Hertzka wrote to Daan de Clerq. In one of these letters, Hertzka reported that the expedition would set out in 1892. In the same letter, he said that more than ten times the number of people had applied to take part. Several Dutchmen (peat cutters from De Bild) were also to be among the party, but Groustra cast doubt on this in a column printed in December 1892. In the novel the expedition reaches its goal. In a note, Groustra added that at the time of publication (December 1892) the actual expedition had reached this point (in other words, was in Kenya). The subsequent chapters deal with elements of the Kenyan Vrijland society (the novel, in other words).

The novel sold in great numbers. In 1891 dozens of branches of the Vrijland movement were set up in Germany, the Austro-Hungarian Empire, Britain, Switzerland, Sweden, North and South America, and elsewhere. The association was incorporated in the Netherlands in 1896. There were branches in Amsterdam, Haarlem, The Hague, Rotterdam, Bloemendaal and Hilversum. The journal *Freiland, Organ der Freiland-Vereine* had been appearing in Germany and Austria since 1891. The Dutch journal, *Vrijland*, became a weekly as of November 1896. At the end of the first year, it had a circulation of 800. A look at the list of contributors reveals that many of those who were later to become leading lights of the SDAP lent their support and assistance. The driving force behind the magazine, Kornelis ter Laan, was one of these leading lights; there were also articles by B. Bymholt; Henri van Kol sent an enthusiastic endorsement to the first annual general meeting. Most articles were written by Ter Laan; in 1895 the editorial office moved from Schildwolde (Groustra) to Arnhem (Ter Laan). And yet the movement expressly set its face against Marxist socialism. Various articles made much of the differences between the "libertarian socialism" of Vrijland and revolutionary socialism.[13] There were calls for the formation of an "International" which, in contrast to the "despotic" Marxist version, would consist of a federation of free cooperatives. There was a considerable degree of similarity with the ideas of Tolstoy and the Christian anarchists. It is repeatedly stressed that Vrijland promulgates "social Christianity": "The teachings of Christ are the purest and most noble proclamation of social freedom," wrote Groustra in his book. Jesus is actually a "social reformer," "social reform" his joyous message.[14] These goals correspond to a significant degree with those of the later colony of the International Brotherhood.

The movement was focused on action from the outset. On February 28 a group of sixteen scouts (pathfinders) set sail from Hamburg to find land in Kenya. Groustra reported this in the *Vrijland* of July 1896. A certain Dr. Wilhelm had consulted the British Foreign Office (Kenya was a British protectorate), but when the expedition arrived in Zanzibar, it appeared that the British had not been informed. The East Africa Company was hostile and, it subsequently emerged, took the German pioneers for members of the secret service. It was thought that the Vrijland movement was a cover under which the German government was concealing an attempt to establish a German colony in Kenya. The expedition failed. In 1897 there was a second expedition, this time to Venezuela. But the Venezuelan government refused any form of cooperation. A few of the members of the expedition then settled there as ordinary colonists. The movement rapidly crumbled after this debacle, and the last issue of *Vrijland* appeared in 1897.

Frederik van Eeden, Walden and common land ownership

Frederik van Eeden's social awareness was aroused in 1890 by the works of Edward Bellamy. Toward the end of the decade he set himself up as a social reformer, and around the turn of the century he was the guiding force of the land reform movement. Van Eeden followed the line of Proudhon and Henry George, Michael Flürscheim, Theodor Hertzka and the Vrijland movement. Like them, he declared that private land ownership was the cause of all evil. He maintained that injustice had entered the world when people had seized land and made others pay to use it. Every form of private property, argued Van Eeden, came back to land ownership: "...whether you lend your money to railroads, factories, theaters, government securities – it all comes down to land ownership."[15] Money is ultimately the ownership of land: "money is proof of power, conveying the right to land ownership." The solution was that money should be converted back into land and transferred in common ownership to the people who worked it. "There is only one thing that really produces, produces of itself, that is the land, our soil."[16] This is why workers should aspire to have not money, but land. Van Eeden initially conceived the idea of realizing the ideal of common land ownership in the form of cooperative state farms. He launched his *Rijkshoeven* plan in 1897, with references to existing "beggars' colonies" and the *Maatschappij de Veluwe*,[17] where his friend Daan de Clerq worked and which he had visited in February 1897. The state should organize the cooperative farms in the same way as it maintained an army or provided a state water and light supply, with one difference – the farms would be self-sufficient. They would produce for their own needs and give any surplus to groups that were dependent on the state. They were not to make a profit.[18] Van Eeden may have derived his optimism about a state initiative like this from Bellamy; in whose vision the new world was likewise organized like an army; composed of independent corporations that were led and supported by the government.

Later, when he realized that no initiative would be forthcoming from the state, he advocated the formation of small autonomous communities. The best way of achieving a plan like this would probably have been by political means, but Van Eeden had lost all faith in politics and converted to anarchism. He declared that the communities he envisaged would be run on anarchist lines and (referring to Kropotkin) brought together in a loose federal alliance.[19] To widespread surprise and disbelief, Van Eeden outflanked the social democrats on the left. He started to berate Troelstra and his associates for pursuing a reactionary course, for seeking state capitalism and state control of industry and for limiting their political demands to making corrections (working hours, wage increases) to a system whose capitalist basis remained untouched. They "fight for money and work for the bosses. But I say to you; fight for the soil and work for the workers."[20] In Van Eeden's view, the social democrats had corrupted the original socialist Idea, just as the church had corrupted the pure teachings of Jesus. They were a "force for evil, the strongest of all reactions, the most dangerous and pernicious degeneration of that general tendency of mind that socialism is understood to mean."[21]

Van Eeden was not frightened of using machinery when setting up the agricultural cooperatives: "People will continue to use the very latest and most ingenious devices

Frederik van Eeden at Walden.

that have been invented to make the soil fertile. The best farming machinery, selection of seeds, intensive cultivation, and all the improvements must be used as fully as possible without hesitation, without timidity and without fear of monetary sacrifices."[22] By adopting this position, he portrayed himself as a rational entrepreneur and distanced himself from the anti-industrial land-utopians, who had strongly resisted the introduction of machines in order to promote manual work – men like John Ruskin (whom Van Eeden otherwise greatly admired) and, to a lesser extent, William Morris.

Van Eeden took his lead from early nineteenth-century utopians, Saint-Simon, Fourier, Owen and Proudhon, whom he called the founding fathers of socialism.[23] He was also influenced by the economist Henry George and his followers Michael Flürscheim, Theodor Hertzka and Franz Oppenheimer. Their ideas were introduced in the Netherlands and propagated by Jan Stoffel, founder of the *Bond voor landnationalisering* (which brought George and Flürscheim to the Netherlands), Daan de Clerq, Harmannnus Groustra and Kornelis ter Laan, founders of the Dutch branch of the Vrijland movement and disseminators of Hertzka. It was in all probability through them that Van Eeden became acquainted with the thinkers on whose work he based his ideas. Yet he does not acknowledge them anywhere among his sources (something one might reasonably expect, if only to make it easier for the public to have access to these exemplars through translations into Dutch). Van Eeden was probably reluctant to share the honor with other Dutchmen; he considered them to be far below the level of the thinkers with whom he wished to be associated. Another source of inspiration that went unacknowledged by Van Eeden was Tolstoy. Tolstoy proposed the establishment of autonomous farming cooperatives without state authority. He was inspired to a significant degree by the work of Rousseau, Proudhon and Henry George. Van Eeden was familiar with Tolstoy's work and was probably put on the trail of Proudhon and George by it. Be this as it may, Tolstoy had a considerable influence on him. Titles like "What Do We Live On?" and "What Are You Working For?," lectures that Van Eeden gave in 1899, are reminiscent of similar titles by Tolstoy, such as "Where Is The Issue?" and "What Then Must We Do?" Van Eeden, however, played down Tolstoy's influence (we discuss Tolstoy and the Tolstoyans later in this chapter).

To Van Eeden, land was more than an economic and social possession. He contrasted the city, degraded by industry and slums, with the countryside and the earth as regenerating forces. He constantly hammered home the idea that society was sick. As a doctor and social reformer he had seen "how ... in the body of society, things correspond remarkably closely with what I have got to know as disease and deformity in the organic body."[24] What the economist Pierson called the physiology of society was, according to Van Eeden, a pathology. The degeneration was concentrated in the towns and cities: "... those modern, ugly and hideous piles of humanity, those cancerous growths on the beautiful earth, ruined by smoke and stench and degenerate people"; "our cities are truly cancerous growths, constantly spreading their grimy suburbs like diseased cell tissue over the pure earth, exhausting the life force of humanity in a steady fire of luxury and sin."[25] "Degenerate" here has to be understood in the medical sense (Nordau's famous study *Entartung* had not escaped Van Eeden's notice). Van Eeden, a physician, had specialized in neurotic disorders – symptoms of degeneration, according to the views of his time – arising out of a civilization run wild. Van Eeden believed he could see a causal relationship between degeneration (a hereditary symptom of disease) and decadence (a civilization going to ruin).²⁶ This social ill could be cured by returning to the "natural force" of the land²⁷ or, more precisely, to the *Siedlungsgenossenschaft*, (land settlement association) which Oppenheimer advocated in his studies. Oppenheimer, whom he discovered in 1898, confirmed Van Eeden in his view that the most fundamental cause of the disease society was suffering from was private land ownership, an "old injustice" to which the use of violence, extortion and suppression could be traced back.²⁸ In 1893 Oppenheimer had written *Freiland in Deutschland*, in which he advocated domestic colonization and took a clear stance against the foreign colonization promoted by the Vrijland movement. Van Eeden evidently found this an attractive idea. His brochure on domestic colonization, *Binnenlandsche kolonisatie*, which was published in 1901, may well have been inspired by Oppenheimer's work; at all events it supported a similar position, emphasized in the title, against foreign colonizers in the Vrijland movement.

By contrasting the degeneration of the city with the regeneration of rural life, Van Eeden armed himself with an argument against Marx. Whereas Van Eeden believed that industry had to be opposed as the cause of social ills and "morbid growth" of huge proportions, Marx attached great value to industrial development, which he regarded as an essential phase in historical development. According to Van Eeden, the theory of historical materialism led Marx to neglect, indeed even to promote the greatest source of social ills.²⁹ By way of Oppenheimer, Henry George and Rousseau, Van Eeden evoked a paradise myth of unsullied land use, a "Garden of Eeden" one might say, as had existed before mankind succumbed to the sin of private property and money. Socialism, to Van Eeden, was this idyllic *Siedlungsgenossenschaft* and he defended his definition tooth and nail against the social democrats, who tried to make the term their own around the turn of the century. Socialism, insisted Van Eeden, was not the exclusive preserve of the proletariat; it was not a situation in which "the underdog would one day be on top." Socialist thinking was thus anything but thinking in terms of class struggle, the dictatorship of the proletariat and suchlike; it was, on the contrary, a "total purification of all the filth of our sick times."³⁰ From these and other remarks, it appears that Van Eeden made a connection between capitalism, degeneration and sin. His comment in *De blijde wereld*: "I consider the view that degeneration inevitably occurs in urban life to the second or third generation is no exaggeration and well founded" contains a reference to the third commandment, which states that God visits "the iniquity of the fathers upon the children unto the third and fourth generation."³¹ From this perspective, socialism is a community of saints who have progressed to a collective state of grace, redemption, the cleansing of sin, and purification.

After the failure of the *Rijkshoeven* plan, Van Eeden took the reins into his own hands. In the spring of 1898 he purchased part of the Cruysbergen estate on the outskirts of Bussum (a town not far from Amsterdam), including a house, vegetable garden, orchard, meadow and wood.³² He called the colony Walden, for Henry David Thoreau's *Walden or Life in the Woods* (1898), which he had just read. The colony actually started life in June 1898. Willem Bauer designed huts for the colonists, initially a diverse company of artistic young men from well-to-do backgrounds and neurotic patients of Van Eeden's, who

Binding sheaves at Walden, summer 1899.

were being treated with work therapy. But in the course of the first year, the character and objectives of Walden changed as a result of the correspondence Van Eeden was conducting with Franz Oppenheimer. Oppenheimer was critical of the Walden experiment, comparing Walden with the hundreds of failed American colonies. The problem with Walden was its lack of cooperation with other colonies. Because of this criticism, in the fall of 1898 Van Eeden changed his concept of Walden, viewing it not as a retreat for remorseful parasites but as a germ cell of the socialist society.

After an initial period lasting from 1899 to 1900, Walden became a collective cooperative in 1901, with the motto: "give according to ability and take according to need" (a motto that – ironically enough, and probably unconsciously – Van Eeden borrowed from Marx: "from each according to his abilities, to each according to his needs."). This construct was abandoned in turn in 1903 in favor of an alliance of productive associations. They included the various small businesses that had meanwhile established themselves at Walden: the bakery, the candy and chocolate works, the horticultural business, the carpentry workshop and the boarding house (in the Cruysbergen house itself). After the change in 1903, each group made its own decisions about policy questions that affected the group (for instance, the desirability of night work). Business certainly was not bad. From Van Eeden's *De vrije arbeid op Walden* (1905), we learn that the turnover of the bakery rose from 29,000 to 45,000 guilders, that the truck garden generated 9,000 guilders, and that the chocolate and candy works were also making a profit. And all this with only

Group portrait of the colonists at Walden.

fifty-three colonists (including twenty-four children). This success was due to the businesslike approach of Van Eeden, who was convinced of the importance of sound management. It was one of the reasons why he admired Robert Owen (a utopian, certainly, but above all a very energetic and successful entrepreneur), Edward Bellamy and capitalist tycoons like Carnegie and Krupp.[33] It was this businesslike attitude that distinguished Walden from the International Brotherhood, which was established at walking distance from Walden in 1900. During a visit to Walden by the journalist Henriëtte Hendrix in September 1900, Van Eeden summed up the differences between the two colonies as follows: Walden was in society, the International Brotherhood was not; money was not rejected by Walden, it was by the International Brotherhood; Walden had division of labor, they bought what they had to; members of the International Brotherhood worked as they chose and ate what they needed; Walden was happy to make a profit provided it was devoted to the expansion of the colony or to other colonies.[34] Similarly, Walden did not eschew technical gadgets. It was decided, for instance, to purchase an expensive incubator for hatching chicks. Nevertheless the reality fell far short of the ideal. There were numerous scroungers. An epigram coined by the colonists (in which the initial letters spelled out the word WALDEN in the original Dutch) read Where Everyone Is Idle, No One Eats. There was considerable discord between the different sections. The bakers refused to be saddled with the losses made by the other associations. They were also disinclined to submit to the policy set by the administrator, Frederik Emons. Eventually the bakery moved to Bussum; the candy factory to Leusden. In 1907 Walden was declared bankrupt and part of the land was sold.

In 1900 Van Eeden tried to bring about an international federation of colonies. He set out his thoughts on the subject in *Binnenlandsche kolonisatie* (1901) and *Gemeenschappelijk grondbezit* (1903). He made his first attempt to create an International League for Common Land Ownership on May 12, 1900 during a meeting at Walden, to which the International Brotherhood and other supporters of land nationalization were invited. This attempt came to nothing: the land nationalizers clashed with the International Brotherhood on the issue of state and municipal land ownership. A fresh attempt was made early in 1901, in the form of a circular announcing the establishment of a common land ownership association, the *Vereeniging Gemeenschappelijk Grondbezit*. The signatories included Daan de Clerq and Frederik van Eeden. On February 13 a memorandum of association was accepted by Walden and the International Brotherhood; the articles were signed on October 20 of that year. The members of the board included Van Eeden, the minister Anne de Koe and Daan de Clerq. GGB, as the association soon came to be known, was a continuation of Stoffel's *Bond voor Landnationalisering* and the Vrijland movement. During a visit by Stoffel to Walden on April 24, 1900, Frederik van Eeden proposed reorganizing the *Bond voor landnationalisering* into an international federation. In 1901, Stoffel took part in the establishment of GGB.

Growth was impressive in the early years. The number of members rose from 320 in 1902 to 850 in 1903-1904. By the end of two years, twenty branches and thirty productive groups were active throughout the country.[35] Van Eeden was the central figure, alongside Daan de Clerq and Felix Ortt. At the end of 1902 and beginning of 1903 Van Eeden went on a propaganda tour through Friesland, resulting in the establishment of several local branches. The colonies implemented the GGB concept, the branches took care of propaganda through the pages of *De Pionier*, the GGB journal, brochures, courses and suchlike. Lastly, consumer cooperative societies were set up. By 1903 there were already thirteen stores or depots, where the produce of the productive cooperatives was sold. The activities of these stores were again combined. The Zaandam district branch decided to set up a communal purchasing scheme. A "Committee for Central Purchasing" was set up and appointed by the main board of GGB in 1903.

Up to 1902, the Christian-Anarchist *Arbeiders-Weekblad* ran a column devoted to GGB. Van Eeden wanted a journal of his own, and considered merging with the International Brotherhood and using their journal *Vrede* (Peace) as the organ of GGB. But the Christian-Anarchists were suspicious: the other colonies had too much interest in material things for their taste. The first issue of *De Pionier* appeared on June 7, 1902. Felix Ortt was the editor; the journal was printed by the "Vrede" printers. There were continual differences of opinion between the Christian-anarchists and the other GGB members. Felix Ortt stepped down and, commencing in January 1903, Van Eeden took over as editor of *De Pionier*, now upgraded to a weekly. GGB played a significant role during the railroad strike of 1903. After the successful dock and rail strike of January 1903, the Dutch prime minister Abraham Kuyper introduced a bill for legislation to prevent a repetition. These

Felix Ortt reading *De Pionier*.

"draconian" laws prohibited people working for organizations of public importance from striking. Workers' organizations formed a Defense Committee, which called a rail strike after the bill was put before the Lower House of the Dutch Parliament on April 1. Frederik van Eeden urged that GGB should align itself with the Committee. The Amsterdam and Hilversum branches responded to this call. The laws were passed, the strike was broken, the reprisals were severe. The railroads sacked thousands of workers. To aid the victims, Van Eeden set up a cooperative society called *De Eendracht*, which gave savings stamps. When five guilders' worth had been saved, the stamps could be exchanged for goods in *De Eendracht*'s stores. More generally, too, GGB offered an alternative for the sacked railroad workers. Many of those who lost their jobs set up productive groups. These developments meant that GGB's public changed. Whereas the majority of the members had originally been well-intentioned intellectuals and the better off, after 1903 workers gained the upper hand. Jan van Hettinga Tromp wrote in *De Pionier* that although "the interest in colonies, which try to regulate labor on the basis of brotherhood is not necessarily diminished," the "GGB has gradually become convinced that it has to take part in the workers' movement. The primitive colonization idea has been transformed into that of productive association, cooperation, workers allying with the incentive of self-interest, direct improvement of position." In other words, the focus shifted from agricultural colonization to workers' cooperatives. The workers were more interested in setting up their own small businesses than in colony life. Although Van Eeden continued to cling to agricultural colonization as his primary goal, he attributed great importance to the association with the workers' movement.

Meanwhile, the experiment with the cooperative societies came to nothing. They failed because the staff did not really know what they were doing, management was inadequate and inexpert, there was no support from the workers, and there was fraud. By 1905 the Amsterdam store and the Zaandam consumer cooperative were the only two cooperative societies still functioning well.

After 1904, GGB membership fell from 850 to 522 in 1905 and 395 in 1906. The number of branches went down from 23 to 13 in 1905, and 8 in 1906. The Amsterdam and Zaandam district branches were the only two that continued to flourish. Amsterdam had its own branch (founded in January 1902), its own store and its own magazine, and was active in bringing together productive groups: decorators, deliverymen, window cleaners, basket makers, bricklayers, blacksmiths, stonemasons and printers. In 1903-1904 there was a permanent nucleus of associations: the *Résistant* dairy, *De Toekomst* tailors, the *Eureka* furniture makers group, the *Aurora* brush makers group and the *Voorwaarts* printers group. All in all, this meant a move away from the original ideal of common land ownership. The existing colonies (the International Brotherhood, the colony in Nieuwe Niedorp[36] and Walden) were also drifting away from the original ideal. Between 1903 and 1907 the emphasis shifted from collective farming to productive associations.

1904 also saw the overhaul of the internal organization. Until then, there had been a loose grouping of thirty associations and colonies, which received advances from the GGB board. In 1903 it was decided to make a distinction between recognized and non-recognized groups. Economic viability was one of the criteria for recognition. The Christian-anarchists refused to sign up to this. An investigation by the GGB main board led to a proposal to recognize not more than five groups; eventually six were recognized.

Relations between GGB and the social democrats were poor. Van Eeden rejected the idea of class struggle. In his view, the most important social dividing line ran not between workers and the middle class, but between productives and non-productives. This blatantly liberal standpoint provoked fierce criticism from the SDAP. Former friends like Nico van Suchtelen and Frank van der Goes did not spare Van Eeden, calling him a "socialist quack," an "arrogant know-nothing" (Van der Goes in *De Pionier*, 1904) and his social theory "stale, quasi-religious moral tripe" (Van Suchtelen in *De Pionier*, 1903).

GGB, for its part, believed that the SDAP and the trade unions were aiming for too limited material goals. GGB set out this position in a brochure on the trade union movement entitled *De Vakbeweging* (1904-1905), in which it contrasted its own "revolutionary" views with those of the social democrats.

As time went on, Van Eeden became increasingly opposed to the social democrats: "The class struggle is a purely capitalist phenomenon, like the whole trade union business. These things have nothing, nothing, absolutely nothing to do with socialism, with a better social order, with a more just social organization" (*De Pionier*, 1906). Emons, the administrator, followed his lead: "The 'class struggle' has no other basis than that it should satisfy people's material needs" (*De Pionier*, 1906). This polemic also reveals just how open to discussion "socialism" still was around 1900, and how people on various sides tried to appropriate the concept.

However, Van Eeden's views were not shared by the workers in GGB. Resistance continued to grow. Pieter Wink submitted a comment in which he said that if Van Eeden had ever known real poverty, he would not have come down so hard on the trade unions for their "economic actions." The tensions spread into the pages of *De Pionier*. Van Eeden and Emons set the tone of the journal, but the members were increasingly dissatisfied with it. In June 1906, after the umpteenth article in this vein by Van Eeden, the Zaandam branch declared that it no longer recognized *De Pionier* as the official journal. The contrast between worker and intellectual was a major factor. There were letters to the editor asking whether the articles could not be rather simpler. And the final reason why GGB and Van Eeden grew apart (aside from differences of opinion about socialism and editorial policy) was GGB's organizational structure. Van Eeden increasingly saw benefits in a tight organization; he was also in favor of the introduction of a maximum wage. The free socialists wanted none of it. Van Eeden's position hardened. He believed that GGB could only function properly under the "strict, accountable, personal management of a strong, energetic, active manager" (*De Pionier*, September 1906). In August 1907, after a conflict about proposals put forward by the administrator, Frederik Emons, Van Eeden and Emons withdrew from the association. The fact that GGB survived after 1907 and even flourished again for a while was thanks to the efforts of J.C. Methöfer. He was the driving force behind GGB from 1907 to 1912 and from 1921 to 1933. In 1909 he took over as editor of *De Pionier*. He advised the associations on how they could best organize their affairs: "At first, when you want to apply socialism to business, do not depart too far from the existing situation. Without losing sight of your principles, do not charge in, but try to approach what you want to achieve gradually, one step at a time" (*De Pionier*, 1909). "GGB's task is primarily to concentrate on setting up companies that are in the midst of social life; whose organizations do not make all too excessive demands on the workers in terms of community spirit, readiness to sacrifice oneself for a principle, or restriction of liberty." Advice like this reveals just how far GGB had moved away from the original utopian course. Methöfer rejected the idealism of his predecessor, Van Eeden, in no uncertain terms: "People thought that they could form their own society, a closed circle that would provide all the (simple) necessities of life as far as possible through their own labor, a circle that would contrast starkly and favorably with the surrounding capitalist society and would, through gradual expansion, drive back the old, hostile society. Time has taught us that it was always an impractical fantasy."[37]

Tolstoy and the Tolstoyans; the colony of the International Brotherhood

When at the end of September 1900 the Dutch daily *De Telegraaf* assigned the journalist Henriëtte Hendrix to spend a week in the colony of the International Brotherhood in Blaricum, and she asked the leader of the colony, S.C. Kylstra, about his principles, he replied: "We essentially follow the ideas of Tolstoy, we are abolitionists, vegetarians, anti-militarists." The spirit of Tolstoy hovered over the colony. During the recreation period in the evening there were readings from Tolstoy's *Resurrection*; Tolstoy's portrait hung in the library.[38]

Kylstra's words reveal that the Brotherhood did not have a coherent vision of society. Tolstoy had not formulated one. He was first and foremost a novelist, a man who was not really concerned with social theory and provided no descriptions of the ideal society, although his work had a strong ethical bias, particularly after his "conversion" in about 1875. The last chapter of *Anna Karenina* gives an idea of the crisis that Tolstoy went through and the direction in which he sought a way out. After a mental breakdown, Lewin, Tolstoy's alter ego in the novel, retreats to the land he owns. He finds support in the work of the theologian, Chomiakov, who says: "Yes, the one unmistakable, incontestable manifestation of the Divinity is the law of right and wrong, which has come into the world by revelation, and which I feel within myself, and in the recognition of which I not so much make myself but, willy-nilly, am made, one with other men in one body of believers, which is called the Church."[39] One of his peasants shows him that he should live not for his own sake, but for God – not the God of the official church, but the God that lives in popular belief. Lewin retires to his village, Pokrovskoye, and occupies himself henceforth with his land and his livestock. Pokrovskoye is a reflection of Tolstoy's estate, Yasnaya Polyana. The experiments with the village school at Yasnaya, the publication of the journal *Yasnaya Polyana*, the significant area of land that Tolstoy relinquished to his peasants (formerly serfs) when serfdom was abolished in 1861, the beekeeping and the planting of a large apple orchard after his marriage in 1862 – the Dutch utopians must have had all this vaguely in mind when they founded the International Brotherhood. Frederik van Eeden must also have been inspired by this example and particularly by the role of landowner that Tolstoy played in it; an enlightened landowner, of course, but a landowner nonetheless. After *Confession* (1881) Tolstoy wrote a series of essays in which he elaborated on *Confession*: *A Criticism of Dogmatic Theology* (1881) and *The Four Gospels Unified and Translated* (1883). In them he confesses his belief in Christ: "I believe in the doctrine of Christ. I believe that happiness on earth is only possible if all people carry it out." The cornerstone is the Sermon on the Mount, which Tolstoy summarized in five injunctions: Do not become angry. Do not commit adultery. Do not curse or swear. Do not repay evil with evil. Do not act hostilely. And one commandment: Love God and love your neighbor as yourself.[40] Tolstoy's thinking is a singular combination of reason and faith: on the one hand there is his theory, based on land as economic value, on the other his trust in man's spiritual evolution and his following of Christ.

As far as his social ideas were concerned, Tolstoy took his lead from Rousseau, Proudhon and Henry George. He had a lifelong admiration for Rousseau. He read everything he wrote, knew parts of his work by heart, and always wore a medallion bearing a picture of him. Proudhon's influence was particularly important. Pierre-Joseph Proudhon was the father of syndicalism, of workers' self-government, of production and distribution cooperatives and of educational innovations. He introduced the concepts of "éducation permanente" and "révolution permanente." His doctrine cannot simply be dismissed as "utopian." It was Proudhon who coined the term "utopian socialism," and who contrasted it with his own "scientific socialism." His influence was immense, particularly in Russia. Hertzen, Bakunin and Kropotkin were all influenced by him, as, above all, was Tolstoy, who was guided by Proudhon in his ideas, his style and even his conduct. Tolstoy often borrowed passages, subjects and titles from Proudhon word for word. Who, today, knows that titles like *War and Peace* and *What is Art?* are taken directly from Proudhon? And *Kholstomer*, the famous story in which Tolstoy stresses the absurdity of private land ownership, is derived directly from Proudhon's *Qu'est-ce-que la propriété?* In 1882 Tolstoy spent the winter in Moscow in order to take part in a census. The author, who until then had always lived on his country estate, was confronted for the first time with the misery of the city ("until then I had lived my whole life outside the city"). He expressed his malaise in his book *What Then Must We Do?* (1884-1886), in which he described at length the social evils in the capital, and his visits to the poor neighborhoods and the mental institutions. In his view it was the rich with their large-scale waste who were chiefly responsible for this misery, followed by the state and the church. Tolstoy implored the rich to give up their land and their money, but this was not enough. They had to show remorse, obliterate their pride and start working with their hands. "The root of the evil is ownership. Ownership is no more than a means of taking possession of the work of others." The city was rich, but it produced nothing itself. The money that was extorted from the countryside was wasted there or, as a peasant expressed it: "Moscow neither sows nor reaps, but always has its wealth in heaps."[41] The rich used that money to throw up the highest possible barrier between themselves and the poor. This, according to Tolstoy, was also the reason for their immoderate extravagance. Money had to be spent ostentatiously on useless, expensive things: carriages, clothes, exclusive dishes "to surprise and outshine others." This idea accorded with the theory expounded not long afterward by Thorstein Veblen in his *Theory of the Leisure Class* (1899). Among the things on which money was squandered, said Tolstoy, was education: "Education consists in teaching those forms and that knowledge which distinguish one man from others." This specific form of the urge to distinguish oneself through education is very similar to another recent theory – Pierre Bourdieu's *La reproduction* (1970) and *La distinction* (1979). Following exhaustive examples of inhumanly hard and badly paid work, Tolstoy made his diagnosis, "this is modern slavery," and set out the possible solution – the "expropriation of all privately-owned land" suggested by Henry George.[42]

Poster for the Nederlandsche Centraal Spoorweg Maatschappij railroad company.

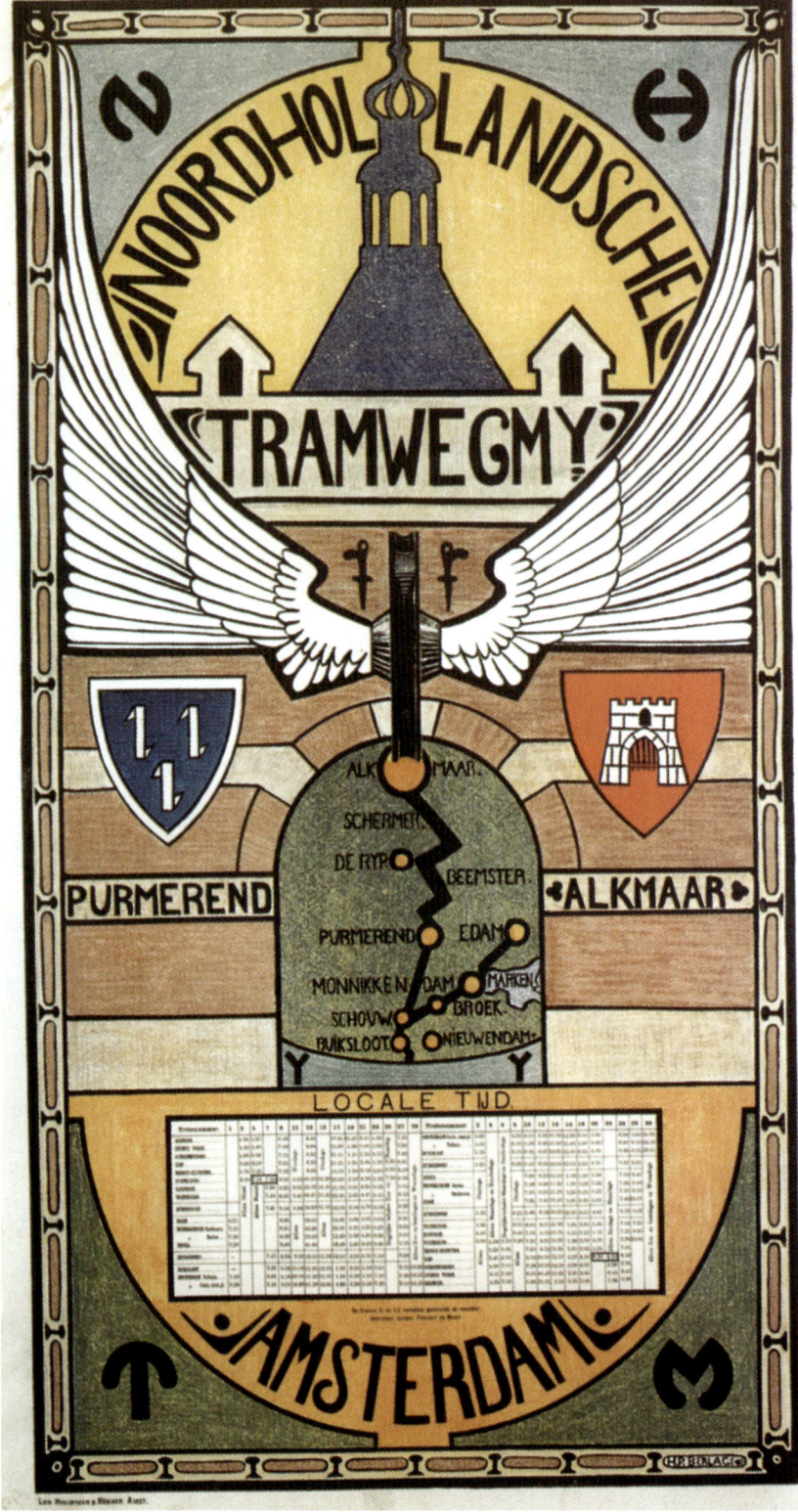

H.P. Berlage, poster for the Noordhollandsche Tramweg Maatschappij streetcar company.

Antoon Molkenboer, poster for the performance of *Lohengrin* by the Wagner Society.

Willy Sluiter, *Carnival Time in Volendam*, 1913.

G. Breitner, *Jacob van Lennepkade.*

Jan Duuselman, *A Dutch Delegation Granted an Audience with Pope Leo XIII, 1885.*

Isaac Israëls, *Café Chantant on Nes, Amsterdam*, 1893.

Amsterdam, Nieuwe Amstelbrug met St. Willibrorduskerk.

Cuypers Senior, St. Willibrord's Church in Amsterdam.

Cuypers Junior, St. Bavo's Cathedral in Haarlem.

Door of the Nieuwe Kerk in Amsterdam. The panel was sawn out by Kuypers and his supporters.

Tolstoï over den Czaar en den oorlog.

BIJVOEGSEL van de Amsterdammer, Weekblad voor Nederland van 3 Juli 1904.

Amst. Boek- en Steendrukkerij, v/h. Ellerman, Harms & Co.

Tolstoï in den Beerenkuil.

"Tolstoy in the Bear Pit." *Tolstoy, the tsar and the Russian-Japanese War. De Amsterdammer,* July 3, 1904.

The title *What Then Must We Do?* may be misleading to modern readers in so far as they are inclined to understand "we" as the whole population collectively. But this was not what Tolstoy meant. By "we", he meant the small elite of noble landowners, to which he himself belonged. The answer to the question of what "they" had to do was hand over their wealth, show remorse, not lie and start working with their own hands.[43]

According to Tolstoy, social reform was inextricably bound up with spiritual reform (moral hygiene). He believed that the use of alcohol and tobacco was fundamentally wrong (they befuddled the mind), cruel pursuits (hunting, waging war, eating meat) equally so.[44] And he was as dismissive of socialism (and other political parties) as he was of the state and the church. "The goal of socialism is to satisfy the basest need of man: his material need." Precisely what sort of future Tolstoy had in mind is not clear: perhaps something along the lines of the Kingdom of the Holy Spirit. According to Tolstoy the seeds of a revolution were germinating, a revolution that would replace corrupted Christianity with "the true Christianity, the basis of unity between people and of the true liberty, for which all reasonable people strive."[45] This revolution would put right the "Great Crime," in other words the monopolizing of the land by a few thousand rich people and the consequent slavery of millions. "The cruelest slavery is to have to do without land. For the slave of a master is the slave of one other, but the man who forfeits his right to land is everyone's slave."[46] Peasants accounted for eighty percent of the Russian population. Hundreds of millions of people died of starvation because of the land ownership of a few. In Tolstoy's view there was no other remedy but to give the land back to the people.

Tolstoy's influence in the Netherlands was broad, but diffuse. Frederik van Eeden must have felt the attraction of his ideas for several reasons. Traces of his influence can be found in the reformist writings Van Eeden published around the turn of the century, whose titles – *What Are You Working For?* (1899) and *What Do We Live On?* (1904) – are very similar to Tolstoy's. Van Eeden's social and ethical ideas were likewise closely related to Tolstoy's. The rejection of socialism as too materialistic, the belief in a spiritual evolution toward a community of saints, the following of Christ with an emphasis on martyrdom and penance – it was all grist to Van Eeden's mill. He, too, was a teetotal, non-smoking vegetarian, and he was extremely suspicious of sexuality (compare Tolstoy's popular novella *The Kreutzer Sonata* about celibacy, even in marriage). In all this he must at least have recognized himself in Tolstoy. Tolstoy's call on the aristocracy to repent, to take pity on the poorest of the poor and to do penance, the power of attraction and influence of Rousseau, Proudhon and Henry George, the experiments with the "colony" of Yasnaya Polyana, must all have appealed very strongly to Van Eeden.

Tolstoy's ideas were generally accepted at Walden. In his novel *Quia Absurdum*, Nico van Suchtelen depicts a prototypical colonist in the character of Odo, a disciple of Thomas à Kempis's *Imitatio Christi*, of Kropotkin's *The Conquest of Bread* and of Tolstoy. Odo "predicted a new religion, of the 'True, Beautiful and Good,' a new society, founded on 'true' liberty and 'true' charity, a society without guns, without alcohol and abattoirs, without lawyers and prisons; where gold and silver are unknown, urinals and phonographs prohibited."[47] There was also a great deal of admiration for Tolstoy in the ranks of the SDAP, but people were unable to express this too effusively because of Tolstoy's

Woning van S. C. Kijlstra.

The colony of the International Brotherhood in Blaricum.

negative remarks about Marx and socialism. Nevertheless Henriëtte and Rik Roland Holst read *What is Art?* (1898) and found in it a confirmation of their ideas that art should lead to a new religious awareness, rooted in a sense of community and Christian charity. In an article in *De Nieuwe Tijd* of 1899, Henriëtte praised him as a representative of the *mir*, the traditional peasant community with common land ownership and self-determination in internal affairs. In this pre-socialist community, according to Henriëtte, the communist principle of "from each according to his abilities, to each according to his needs" was realized; it was a "body, all the members of which felt bound together," where discord was banned. In Henriëtte's view, Tolstoy had not needed to refer to the Bible; charity, as the center of life, was achieved in the *mir*. This *mir* also bore all the characteristics of the medieval community of faith that Henriëtte had passionately described just before this. She pointed out that to Tolstoy "agriculture is still the basis of society, industry an aberration, the class struggle an evil,"[48] and she added that Tolstoy was blind to the essential growth of industry and to the class struggle that would intensify as a result of this growth. But this is something of a token comment. In reality, Henriëtte agreed with Tolstoy. When, much later, she started to distance herself from Marxist dogma and approached the *Religieus Socialistische Bond* (1923), she allowed her admiration for Tolstoy free rein. She gave a lecture in 1928 to mark Tolstoy's birthday, and then worked it up into a biography that was published in *De Gids* in 1929-1930.

Influenced by Tolstoy, all sorts of societies of "abolishers" (as S.C. Kylstra put it) sprung up in the Netherlands: the Dutch Anti-Vivisection Society, founded in 1890,[49] the General Netherlands Teetotalers Society (1893), and the anti-militarist movement. Modernist ministers were the conduit through which Tolstoy's influence flowed into the Netherlands. These progressive and in some respects rebellious theologians regarded Christianity first and foremost as a social doctrine. Louis Bähler was an early adherent.

In 1893 he translated Tolstoy's *Why Do Men Intoxicate Themselves?* The association of Frisian ministers was the most active: S.C Kylstra of Rottevalle, Anne de Koe of Nieuwveen, Louis Bähler of Schiermonnikoog, Sevenster (who was to translate much of Tolstoy's work) and Klein of Beetgum. In Amsterdam there was Jacob van Rees, a professor of histology, who with a number of teachers founded a propaganda club against alcoholism in 1893, which reanimated the "temperance movement." On a propaganda tour in Nieuwveen in 1895 Van Rees met De Koe. They were of the same mind. With De Koe and other supporters, Van Rees founded the teetotalers' organization known as the *Algemene Nederlandsche Geheelonthoudersbond.* Van Rees, following Tolstoy's example, was also a vegetarian non-smoker, and he banned vivisection in his laboratory.[50]

Johannes Koenraad van der Veer was another early Tolstoyan. He edited an anarchist journal in Zeeland. In 1896 he refused to do military service after he had made the acquaintance of some Doukhobors who were traveling through the area.[51] This was the push that led the adherents of Tolstoy to unite: Bähler announced his support for Van der Veer in an open letter; other modernist ministers joined him. They met in December 1896. The group rapidly grew, with Van der Veer as the focal point. Other controversial meetings followed. During one of them – in April 1897 in Amsterdam – the members renewed their support for Van der Veer's initiative. In August of the same year the group met in The Hague. The ministers De Koe, Klein, Bähler and Van der Veer spoke about non-violence, love and passive resistance. A select group among them decided to establish a journal, *Vrede: Orgaan tot bespreking van de praktijk der Liefde.* Van der Veer was joined on the foundation committee by Van Rees, Lodewijk van Mierop (a student of mathematics who later switched to theology) and Felix Ortt (an engineer employed by the government). Van der Veer was in touch with Albert Skarvan, Tolstoy's translator into German. Van der Veer translated Tolstoy from German into Dutch. Through Skarvan he was in contact with Tolstoy, who sometimes sent copy for *Vrede.* In 1897 he wrote *Het einde is nabij* (The Approach of the End) following Van der Veer's refusal to serve in the military.

Felix Ortt was the central figure of a third group, which put Tolstoy's ideas into practice at an early stage. This group, known as the International Brotherhood, came into being in Leiden around 1890. The Brotherhood was against killing animals, against vivisection, alcohol and tobacco, against compulsory vaccination and militarism. It was in favor of free marriage (although against unbridled sexual pleasure). Non-violence was the key principle; "purity" was also very important. This circle of Christian-Anarchists spawned the "Pure Life Movement." Felix Ortt was the most active member. He propagated love in every area and pointed to the "Great Initiates" – Lao-Tze, Buddha and Jesus. From the meeting of the Frisian ministers, the Leiden Brotherhood and the circle around Van der Veer and his journal *Vrede,* there grew the initiative for the establishment of a Christian-Anarchist colony. The colonists had as an example the recently founded Walden (1898), but they also looked at other historical examples, such as the monastic community of the Brethren of the Common Life. There were also striking similarities to the early nineteenth-century *Zwijndrechter Nieuwlichters.*[52] Kylstra and Van Mierop took the initiative (Van der Veer was in England at that moment).[53] The colony of the International Brotherhood was founded on October 10, 1899. Jacob van Rees bought fourteen hectares of land and made money available to get the colony started and keep it going, and the Blaricum colony was opened on June 17, 1900. Initially it resembled a fancy dress party for a pastorale: men with beards wearing corduroy suits or Russian smocks, women without make-up in billowing aprons. They wore sandals or, scandalizing the local people, went barefoot. Atze Spoor, a Frisian, was the only real farmer. The principles were high-minded. Communist principles were strictly observed: there was a communal pot of money, from which everyone took what he or she needed; the diet was vegetarian (nowadays we would call it vegan): even milk and butter were banned. The emphasis was on horticulture (greenhouse crops, asparagus, fruit), but there was also a bakery which was highly successful. One vexed question was whether it was acceptable to make a profit. The answer was no, so initially no products were sold. It was only when people realized that they had to buy clothes, tools and similar goods in the capitalist market that this restriction was eased and Enzlin the baker was able to sell his "colony zwieback" (or "sports zwieback"). There were even orders from Germany.[54] The "Vrede" printing works was moved from The Hague to Blaricum in 1902. The "Vrede" printers also produced *De Pionier*, the GGB journal, an indication of good relations (at the beginning, at least) between Walden and the International Brotherhood. Felix Ortt was the editor of *De Pionier*; Van Rees, the philanthropist, stayed in the background.

Despite all this good will, the colony did not prosper. The colonists found it hard to get along with one another. There was friction. Henriëtte Hendrix reported on the tense atmosphere she found there (at that time – September 1900 – the colony had only been going for a few months): religious believers were suspicious of non-believers. There were few signs of the practice of charity. When Bob (incidentally one of the most colorful colonists: a tall Englishman who ignored the smoking ban and continuously sucked on his pipe, dressed in a Russian laborer's outfit as was customary in the colony in Purleigh, where he came from) – when this Bob fell ill, no one took care of him. They seemed to think it was enough to put a few slices of dry bread beside his bed. Hendrix was surprised to find that everyone was looking out for himself and was concerned only with his own welfare. When the rooms were allocated, the Luitjes family were given the only room where there was never any sunlight because they had not been there right from the start. On a business level, the whole thing was stupidly handled: the land that was purchased was poor, and the price that was paid for it would have bought a piece of first-class land in Friesland.[55] There was also a glaring lack of skill and knowledge: "Everyone imagines himself a farmer. Sticking a spade into the soil isn't such a difficult thing to do. Planting beans, hoeing, weeding – come now, anyone can do it."[56] Another objection was the extent to which the communism was taken. Tjerk Luitjes, who spent the initial period in the colony with his wife, but left, disappointed, at the end of the year (ordered out by Kylstra), later set out in his *Theorie en Praktijk van Binnenlandsche Kolonisatie* (1902) (Theory and Practice of Interior Colonisation) the aspects that, in his view, stood in the way of the colony's success. A lack of privacy was one of them. Luitjes was also unbearably irritated by the improving readings every evening: "The goal is the liberation of labor, the creation of a healthier balance of life. What the deuce does that have to do with catechism?" Luitjes – one of the leaders of the *Sociaal Democratische Bond* – was an important man in the socialist movement.[57] In June 1900 he and his wife had enrolled as members of the International Brotherhood. He was putting into practice the views about the beneficial effects of life on the land that he had expressed elsewhere. Luitjes mytholo-gized the earth in the same way as Frederik van Eeden, contrasting the city as a place of money and decay with the country. The city is Mammon, said Luitjes, it attracts people with its glittering eyes "as the snake attracts its prey." Its characteristics were trade and charging interest. Thus it sucked the countryside dry and was the cause of the poverty that prevailed there. The city was also the center of degeneration: "A sickly and ailing stock is being raised, impotent, to be unsuitable for further procreation." To Luitjes, con-sequently, the return to the land was a way to regenerate the "sickly stock," and the pre-condition for creating genuine socialism: "he who lives by nature, comes to socialism and he who comes to socialism, goes back to nature." Was Luitjes's view a utopian one? Without doubt. Nevertheless it can be argued that the concept he defended in 1890 was less utopian than the same concept in 1900. In 1890 Luitjes's ideas were decisive in deter-mining what, according to the only socialist party at the time, socialism should be under-stood to mean. But after the party conference of 1894, the establishment of the SDAP, the shift in electoral support from the *Socialistenbond* to the SDAP and the winding-up of the Bond in 1897, these same ideas had lost their support base; political developments had left them without a home.[58]

The crisis and the end of the International Brotherhood were heralded by the railroad strike of 1903. The colonists declared their solidarity with the strikers. Out of solidarity, they tore up the rails of the Gooise steam tram that ran past the colony. The fishermen of Huizen and the farmers of Blaricum, who had to rely on the steam tram to transport their products to the market in Hilversum, erupted in fury. During the night of April 13, 1903, there was a savage attack on the "spinach-eaters'" camp. Panic broke out in the colony. Some colonists purchased revolvers. A debacle ensued. Kylstra returned to his parish. The recently formed carpentry group disintegrated; the horticulture group moved else-where. The baker, Enzlin, remained for a while and relaxed the requirements for admis-sion (vegetarianism and total abstinence were no longer compulsory). But eventually the bakery went, too, continuing its operations elsewhere as an independent small business. By September there were only four colonists left. In 1904 Van Rees re-established the colony with free socialists from Friesland, but they did not hit it off with the "phony gar-deners" from Amsterdam. The journal *Vrede* ceased publication in 1909, and was fol-lowed into oblivion in 1910 by *Eenheid*, which was more or less a successor to it, but with a more theosophical slant (articles on Annie Besant and similar). Christian-anarchism became more spiritual and was increasingly absorbed in theosophy. At the same time the affinity with socialism dwindled, for the theosophists had no time for the socialists. The school, originally intended for the colonists, was rescued by Van Rees from the "Blaricum disaster" and, in 1903, extended elsewhere into a "humanitarian school." It was an experiment that attracted international interest. The school was a success, thanks in no small measure to the dedication of teacher and writer Cor Bruijn, an outstanding example of a contemporary alternative educationalist. The children were taught in the spirit of Jan Ligthart, who was influenced in his thinking by Tolstoy. Meanwhile, little of the colony remained. The land was sold, but not until 1911, when the last diehard colonist had to be evicted from the site.[59]

Mystical socialism: Herman Gorter and Henriëtte Roland Holst

Herman Gorter

In the early eighteen-nineties, the poet Herman Gorter was at a spiritual and artistic impasse. His "sensitivist verses" (the *Verzen* of 1890), evocations of emotion and fleeting sensory impressions, mark a high point in Dutch poetry, but in personal terms they reflect the state of deep desperation in which Gorter found himself. Gorter, like Lodewijk van Deyssel in his "sensuous sketches," took impressionism to its ultimate conclusion, thus exposing the point on which the Eighties Movement was vulnerable: its complete lack of any philosophy of life. There was a need for "more style and certainty, more definite direction and faith" (Huizinga). Gorter went in search of a spiritual foundation and initially discovered it in Spinoza.[60] He felt particularly attracted to this philosopher because Spinoza regarded all aspects of what exists as attributes of the Godhead or Substance. Spinoza defined this as the One or Infinite that is beneath and behind things. Substance is identical to God and nature; it has two properties, conception and essence. In this construct, every living being is "Idea" and "Body." Gorter found in this the synthesis of sensuality and inner life that still formed an unresolved contradiction in *Mei* (May) (1889).[61] Above all, Spinoza released him from the individualism into which the aesthetic of the Eighties Movement had maneuvered him. In *The Ethics*, which Gorter translated in 1895, Spinoza discusses ethics as existing for and through the community. Gorter eagerly embraced this view because it led him, while maintaining his own singularity, to a cautious solidarity with mankind. Spinozism made it possible for him to make the transition from the Eighties Movement to socialism.[62] In the summer of 1896, encouraged by his cousin Frank van der Goes, Gorter immersed himself in the writings of Marx and Kautsky. Marxist socialism offered him the certainty and the social engagement that he had lacked until then. He distanced himself from the Eighties Movement in a five-part "Criticism of the literary movement of 1880 in Holland" (in *De Nieuwe Tijd*, 1889-1890) and thenceforth wrote committed poetry in fixed forms. There is a clear division between the sensitivist *Verzen* of 1890 and the socialist poetry that he started to write in 1891.

In the larger works from this later period, *Socialistische Verzen* (Socialist Verses) (collected 1903), *Een klein Heldendicht* (A Small Epic) (1906) and *Pan 1* and *2* (1912, 1916), Gorter paints a high-minded picture of the future socialist society. *Een klein Heldendicht*, dedicated to Marx, is about a young worker and a young working woman called Maria, who achieve socialist awareness, a process that coincides with their growing love for each other. The poem sheds little light on the conditions in which the couple live and work. The reader sees nothing of the factory where they both work, nor of the undoubtedly dismal slum in which they live. Musings about and visions of the golden future set the tone of the poem, and it is these musings that lend the *Heldendicht* a strongly utopian air.

Their future takes place in an Eldorado:

At night he dreamed a golden, golden dream.
It was as if he was come into a golden region
and saw golden people who
passed naked through a gilded light.
Silver streams there were and hills
of gold, and in them he saw the sun people.[63]

Extravagant images of nature give an impression of the young heroes' dawning class consciousness:

As in February and in March
the clouds fly laughing 'cross the sky,
white, blue-flecked, and all of nature,
the mountains, trees and all the animals
feel: it must, it must; so she felt,
when she ran, pure white, to her house.

Just as in the spring the fresh sap
pervades the stem of the lilac iris,
and makes the leaf different and creates the bloom,
so knowledge pervaded this worker.[64]

Such passages are very reminiscent of Gorter's earlier poetry. They could have come from his *Mei*. In terms of form, they are identical to the impressionist poetry of the Eighties Movement. But their function has changed dramatically. No longer do they conjure up a fleeting impression of nature; now they symbolize the inevitability of the dawning of socialist consciousness and the socialist society, which will grow like inexorable natural processes. Gorter derived this conviction from Karl Kautsky, the leader of the German SPD and the most influential theoretician of Marxism around the turn of the century. Gorter first read his work in 1896. Following Kautsky's lead, he looked at history from the perspective of Social Darwinism. According to Kautsky, superior production processes supplanted the older, weaker processes, just as stronger races triumphed over weaker ones. And Gorter repeated after him: "The economy is thus conceived as a special case of general biology, and social and animal organisms are brought in parallel."[65] The images of nature in *Een klein Heldendicht* express this Social Darwinist determinism.

But the images also have another function: they show humankind as part of a nature inspired by God. In Gorter's vision, socialist consciousness acquires the traits of a pantheistic harmony, a process of being absorbed in and carried along by a divine/natural force. Consciousness in the Marxist sense flows over into the belief in a divine force that is present in nature. This does lead to a degree of incongruity. Marx's linear historical process is reflected in cyclical natural processes (spring and fall, dawn and sunset, blossoming and withering). Another incongruity is that whereas Spinoza's pantheism is not teleological, Marx's process of history, in contrast, most definitely is. According to Marx, history moves in the direction of a final goal; according to Spinoza, pantheism is an

A Blue Moon adherent.
How an implacable class warrior fights the class battle.
Albert Hahn, *Herman Gorter in the Eyes of a Social Democrat.*

eternally static state of things. At the moment when Gorter projected the Marxist conception of history onto pantheism, he gave pantheism a historical dimension: a prehistory, a current state of affairs and a final goal. According to this curious, pantheistic/Marxist vision, humans were divorced from nature in the far distant past by the development of markets, capital and property. They had been "alienated" from nature. This separation (symbolized in *Pan* by the separation between the God Pan – nature – and the woman – the spirit of humanity) would, said Gorter, be reversed by the class struggle, the crisis and the subsequent socialist society, as a reuniting of mankind with nature.

In Gorter the inevitable rise of socialism has the characteristics of a spiritual revolution as theosophists imagined it: a gradual abandonment of the material and a refinement in the sense of spiritualization:

The working class climbs up on steps
through the misty sky, on granite mountains.
There through the sky they go, to the clouds.
There they turn a corner, out of sight.

...at the top there stands like a diamond,
like a giant diamond, radiating
on four sides the Ideal, Communism.

...the unconscious clothes itself in the crystal
of the consciousness? Yes, humanity becomes aware
and departs in liberty.

Workers, do you see that gold, that sun,
that pyramid of happiness? Do you see
those riches, do you not feel a breath
of happiness, in which you might lie?
Do you feel the opening atop your head,
Through which your soul might rise?[66]

The reference in the last passage to the crown chakra ("the opening atop your head") through which the soul departs and rises to unite with the Universal Over-Soul, which is depicted as a diamond or as the top of a pyramid, is reminiscent of familiar clichés in theosophy. Hegel and Hegelianism also played a significant role in Gorter's idea of the enlargement of the workers' consciousness into a collective and transcendent Spirit. Gorter gave Marxist consciousness the characteristics of "an upward path, from the material to the light," as Mondrian put it. All the imagery with which Gorter explains the dawning of consciousness: becoming gold (with the alchemistic connotation of transcendence, the "sublimation" of the lower matter), becoming crystal, the images of rising, elevating, levitation ("They strive upward, go into the clouds" "They rise / laboriously but yet become light – upward"[67]) and of enlightenment in the literal sense that people give light and thus rise above their material nature – all this puts Gorter's vision of the socialist consciousness as a spiritual evolution in singular contrast to Marx's materialism.

In this process of becoming aware, the poet is given the role of leader, seer and prophet. The "Idea" in which only the essential is retained, in other words "achieving Unity and Consciousness and the Freedom of the People," is revealed to the Socialist Poet, as the introduction to *Pan* has it.[68] The vision of the "transcendent Idea" is reserved for "only a Few." Gorter was referring here to the idea of a vanguard that went before the masses in the revolution. He had taken the idea from Lenin, who constantly stressed that the working masses needed the leadership of a select, tightly organized advance guard of "professional revolutionaries." Gorter defended the same idea in his work on the principles of Communism, *De Grondslagen van het Communisme*, a revised version of the *Grondslagen der sociaaldemocratie* (1919). He believed, following Lenin, that the party

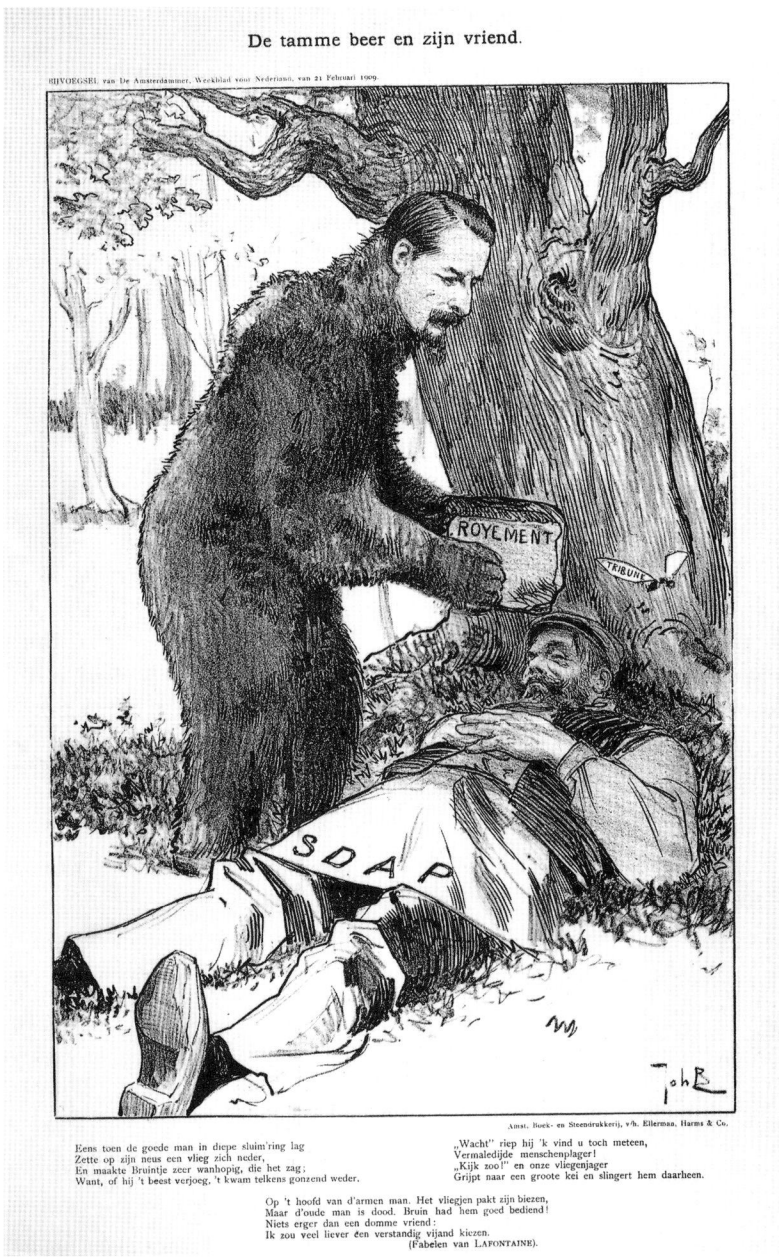

The Tame Bear and his Friend.
Troelstra swats the Tribune wasp with a rock, which strikes the head of the SDAP.
De Amsterdammer, February 21, 1909.

should be a "clear minority," a "rabble" that took no account of existing power relationships and (like the small group around Lenin) preceded the masses in the revolution.[69]
This principle would hardly seem to be consistent with another principle that Gorter
increasingly identified with, namely that of "council communism." Council communism
strove for democratic socialism, embodied in the workers' councils or "soviets," as they

were called in Russia. This form of socialism was decreed by Lenin in the spring of 1917: "all power to the soviets." But in the reality of the war that followed the October Revolution, this form of democracy proved unworkable. Trotsky consequently abolished the soldiers' councils in 1918. The Bolsheviks then won the war, but at the same time lost their democratic freedom embodied in the councils. Anton Pannekoek and Herman Gorter, at this period the party ideologs of the German KPD, refused to accept this shift to a party dictatorship confirmed by Lenin in 1920 (in: *Left-Wing Communism, an Infantile Disorder*). They protested vehemently; the result was a breach between the Leninist Komintern and the KPD. Gorter wrote his famous *Open Letter to Comrade Lenin* in August 1920 as a reaction to Lenin's *Left-Wing Communism* and attached himself to ever smaller factions of council communism that were ever more fanatically committed to the principle. This rigidly maintained democratic principle sat oddly with Gorter's extremely low opinion of the workers as a shortsighted, inert mass, which needed the leadership of a party core "as hard as steel, as clear as crystal."[70] His withdrawal to a select body of crack troops illustrates the increasing isolation to which Gorter's dogmatic attitude brought him. In 1909 he left the SDAP for the small SDP, which remained faithful to its principles; in 1918 he left this party, now redubbed CP Holland, too. The idea of a political party as a "rabble" points up the distance that meanwhile separated Gorter from the SDAP, which aimed to be a broad-based party of the people, and the increasing utopianization of Gorter's ideas.

Henriëtte Roland Holst

Henriëtte Roland Holst came to socialism through Herman Gorter. At the end of 1893, when she first met Gorter and a master-student relationship grew up between the famous poet and his young admirer, Gorter was in his Spinozist phase. Gorter set Henriëtte to reading Plato, Dante and Spinoza. When Gorter started to explore Marxism in 1896, Henriëtte followed him in this, too, and tackled *Das Kapital*. In April 1897 Gorter and Henriëtte (who had meanwhile married Rik Roland Holst) became members of the SDAP. From childhood Henriëtte had a fanatical nature.[71] Her marriage to Rik Roland Holst remained childless; her longing for love unrequited. Various friends said that the Holsts did not have a sexual relationship; their marriage was probably never consummated. Henriëtte focused all her love and desire on the party. She idolized the Idea of socialism. She exhorted fellow party members to "worship" socialism and entered into a marriage with this Idea, as nuns do with God. She wanted to be the "bride of ideas": "Come woman, eternally desiring being, eternally defiled and unfulfilled: let the Ideal make you fertile." She compared Rosa Luxemburg, with whom she identified for a long time, with mystics like Hadewych and Eckhart: "the class struggle became the principal divinity before which she kneeled."[72] A projection that is all the more remarkable, because the real Rosa Luxemburg bore absolutely no resemblance to the picture of the chaste nun of socialism that Henriëtte Roland Holst painted of her. Henriëtte saw herself as the mystic of socialism and, just as medieval mystics were pushed to the periphery or outside the religious community and regarded with not a little suspicion by the church because of their solitary search for salvation, so the party was not always happy with her idealistic endeavors. In a letter dating from 1915 Lenin accused her of being too idealistic; he felt that it was a renewal of ideals, not the revolution, that was her priority. The accusation was justified. Henriëtte imagined the future socialist society as a community of believers. Her image of the future, like that of William Morris, was a projection into the future of an idealized fourteenth-century society.

The Holsts admired William Morris greatly. Richard Roland Holst had met Morris during a visit to England in 1893, shortly before Morris's death. One of the first pieces that Henriëtte wrote after her conversion to socialism was the introduction to a collection of translations of Morris: *John Ball en andere vertalingen* (1898). She herself translated Morris's utopian tale *A Dream of John Ball*, which is set in the fourteenth century, like Morris's earlier work (translated by Frank van der Goes) *News from Nowhere*, which takes place in a future modeled on the fourteenth century.[73] She did not agree with Morris in every respect. The reintroduction of associations of craftsmen (guilds) and the banning of money and trade (according to Morris: "There was no capital in our sense of the word"[74]) seemed to her to go against the flow of the times and not to satisfy the Marxist proposition that capitalism had to come to full fruition and had to lead to revolution first, before the socialist society could be born. She did agree, though, with Morris's image of a fourteenth-century communal mysticism. In that sense it was she who made the fourteenth century absolute and lifted it out of the flow of history as a timeless and unparalleled example of mystical community spirit. According to Henriëtte, the mystical endeavor of the people of the fourteenth century was a musing on, an awareness of, a losing oneself in a reflection of medieval conditions of production: "They believed they could see something supernal, something entirely separate from our world; what they actually saw was the reflection of their own world, their society; it was transparent to them and they knew it well, and therefore this image was clear and bright."[75] The relations which they saw reflected in heaven were feudal relationships, and they were based on the use of the land: "it was not man and not money, at least in the early Middle Ages, but land and soil that was the most productive resource, the most beneficial possession."[76] The most important means of production was thus not people (as in a slave-keeping society), or money (as in capitalism), but land. Respect, power, privileges and justice depended on how much land one owned. Labor relations were determined by "lordship and serfdom, fixed obligations and fixed rights, obedience on the one side, protection on the other."[77] These relations were transposed by the community into the reflection of the social system: their faith. Take note: Henriëtte Roland Holst did not regard these feudal relationships as a class antithesis (nowhere in her essay did she use the loaded word "classes" for lords and serfs); she saw it as a contract with rights and duties on both sides.

This in contrast to William Morris who, in his description of the fourteenth century, placed the emphasis on the class inequality between landowners and peasants: on the abuse of power and the exploitation by the one, and the wretched living conditions of the other. His view was diametrically opposed to Henriëtte Roland Holst's – she saw land ownership as a virtually ideal contractual relationship between vassal and liege lord, a relationship cherished by all and perceived with deep mysticism, because it formed the basis for their conceptual religious universe. This collective spiritual focus of social endeavor was consequently crucial to Henriëtte's vision of socialism "...medieval

with Jesus, both because of his role as a spiritual leader, and because of his desire for suffering. In *Quia absurdum*, Nico van Suchtelen related how Van Eeden reacted to the death of one of the colonists at Walden.[86] Olthoff, called "the prophet" (in other words Van Eeden), "began to tremble, more and more violently, until his whole body shuddered and shook. He spoke loudly, at the last he roared like a hoarsely bellowing beast. 'My Lord God, forgive us our sins! My Lord God; the sin, the sin! Forgive us ... My Lord God!...' Then he collapsed in convulsions." The following day he tells a visitor about the vision that he had had that night: "Jesus Christ has been with me, this very night." Odo, the main character, finds this suspicious, because the vision corresponds down to the smallest details with the notes that Albertus, the suicide, had made before his death and left beside his bed.[87] Dolorism was a common subject among the writers of the Eighties and Nineties Movements: Kloos, Verwey, Swarth, Leopold, Van Eeden, Henriëtte Roland Holst.[88] For some of them (Domela, Van Eeden, Henriëtte Roland Holst), the *imitatio Christi* was the route by which they made the transition from art or faith to socialism.[89]

Conclusion

World War I put a temporary end to idealism and utopianism. Ideas that had until then been interwoven: socialism, utopianism, anarchism, mysticism and religiosity were pulled apart. Some of the elements (the lighter ones) went up in smoke; of the others the only ones to stay in business were those organizations that had built themselves a strong political basis – social democrats and trade unionists. Anarchists, utopians and mystics were blown away during the devastating confrontation between nations.

Frederik van Eeden reacted bitterly to Walden's bankruptcy. The Christian regime of his colony had, he believed, made the people brazen and dishonest. The masses were not capable of self-government; strict, indeed dictatorial leadership was required to bring about future social changes: "Change can only be wrought in this compact mass ... through the influence of strong, not too scrupulous, not too generous, but fairly ambitious persons with a lust for power."[90] Van Eeden was thinking about someone like Bismarck. Despite this, there was a sequel to his colony adventure. In the spring of 1908 and the spring and fall of 1909 he went on speaking tours through America. With the backing of influential businessmen and bankers, he gave lectures on social reform and met President Roosevelt, who, it would seem, was genuinely interested in his colony plans. Together with the enthusiastic banker Hugh MacRea he set up the Cooperative Company of America and founded a colony near Wilmington. In the Netherlands he called upon workers to settle there as colonists. He translated and edited *De blijde wereld* as *Happy Humanity* in 1912, but without success: the book was soon remaindered. In 1926, Van Eeden wondered whether his colony actually still existed. In 1939 the land was purchased to house Jewish refugees from Europe.

Van Eeden's utopianism flared up again just once more. In 1921, under the influence of a medium, Annie Bosch, and partly in her words, he drafted the design for a "City of Light" (*Het Godshuis in de Lichtstad*). In this city, situated on an island somewhere on earth, representatives of all the countries of the world would come together in a sort of

A Dutch family outside their cabin in the Van Eeden Colony in North Carolina, USA.

League of Nations. The city of light would be the radiant center of this league: "like the crystal, around which the human souls will gather in a high, pure Harmony."[91] The architecture, captured in magnificent drawings and engravings by J. London, is concentric: the outskirts (the body) are for businesses, banks and housing residents and visitors; the middle city (the mind) is for knowledge and culture – museums, libraries, concert halls and theaters; the center (the soul), separated from the middle city by a green belt with farms, consists of a ring of temples and churches at the heart of which is an immense cathedral, intended for meditation. The topography is a reversal of the existing relationships in metropolises (where the commercial and business center is in the "city," the residential areas and educational facilities surround it, and the countryside is outside the whole thing) and illustrates Van Eeden's primacy of mind over matter. The architecture is meant to be a stimulus to and pinnacle of a spiritual evolution, which a small elite of visionaries will lead. The aim of the "City of Light," in an obvious reaction to World War I, is to prevent conflicts between peoples in the future by establishing a powerful international federation. Both missions, the spiritual and the political, mark the distance between this utopia and the socialist utopia of around the turn of the century, which was based on the concept of a more just distribution of goods and power.

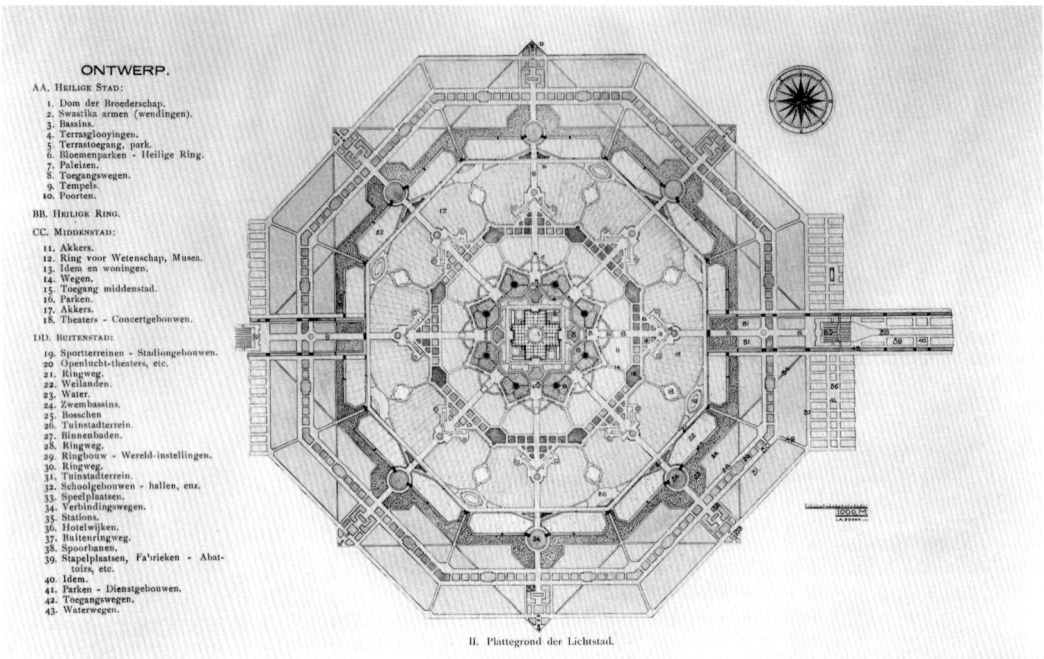

J. London, engraving of *The City of Light*, 1921.

The *Gemeenschappelijk Grondbezit* association, left by Van Eeden as a premature legacy, bounced back surprisingly well after a collapse during and after World War I. The number of affiliated groups rose from seven in 1918 to forty in 1922-25. There was a great influx from the cigar industry, the printing trade and, above all, the construction sector. At the beginning of 1922 there were twenty-one construction associations affiliated to GGB in Amsterdam alone – 2000 workers altogether, united in the "Federation of independent groups in the Amsterdam construction sector." At the start of 1922, working for five housing associations, they were building more than 1000 homes for a contract sum of more than two million guilders. But despite the name of their umbrella organization *(Gemeenschappelijk Grondbezit),* these companies had no connection with the colony life. They were not social experiments, not models for the future, like the original colonies. The fact that the GGB flourished was the result of adapting to the existing political, economic and social system, and thus actually a consequence of a process of de-utopianization.

The only experiment of any note that bucked this trend for a while was the colony known as "De Ploeg" (the Dutch word "ploeg" translates as both "plow" and "team") in Best. It was set up in 1919 as an agricultural colony with the familiar objective of "putting land and means of production into common ownership and use, and achieving a just and effective organization of working community and society." It was the same old story: the men were almost all conscientious objectors; the group was vegetarian and eschewed alcohol; the colonists knew nothing about farming. To make matters even worse, the prices for farm produce plummeted; in short, by the end of 1932 the colony had run itself into the ground. Meanwhile, however, a weavers' association had formed in the colony, and in 1923 this group succeeded in acquiring a splendid building in Best and setting up independently there as "De Ploeg production and consumption association." New, theosophically-minded members joined, people with an outstanding feel for the market, good business sense and artistic talent. Under their guidance, the company flourished. In the war years, compelled by shortages of materials, they turned to all sorts of forms of applied art. The *Spectrum*, the arts and crafts center that grew out of this, experienced a golden age after the war. Eventually the production company really got going, albeit that it was no longer members of a cooperative who worked there, but employees on the payroll. Initially the aim was equal pay for all, but over time this was replaced by wage differentiation and a collective bargaining agreement. In 1957 *De Ploeg* became a limited company and the cooperative was wound up. "We have become more in line with the world," said director Piet Blijenburg.

Utopianism also gradually vanished from the ranks of the SDAP. The main reason for this was that the party focused wholly on improving the living conditions of the workers and abandoned ideas of revolution. This course, doing what was politically feasible, led to the breakaway of the high-principled communist party, led by Gorter, Pannekoek and Saks. In comparison with its sister party in Germany, the Dutch SDAP was much more open-minded about the social reality. The *Sociaal Democratische Studieclub* undertook research without preconceived ideology. This was possible because, among other reasons, prominent theoreticians like Henriëtte Roland Holst, Rudolph Kuyper and Willem Bonger did not have any political responsibility, unlike, say, Rosa Luxemburg. Dutch socialism increasingly plainly chose an undogmatic approach, independent of the International. Doubts about Marxist doctrine were stirred up by Hendrik de Man's *De Psychologie van het socialisme* (1926). In this religious-socialist work, De Man denounced the mechanistic world vision of Marxism ("Scientific socialism is as meaningless as scientific love"). It was not historic materialism that determined the course of history, argued De Man, but a strategy aimed at the future: "it must be determined by the objectives, not by causes."

The rejection of revolutionary Marxism led to a theoretical weakening inside the SDAP, notes Hilda Verweij-Jonker,[92] but the advantage was a more open vision, focused more on improving the present conditions. It is typical that the "Socialistische Rapport," set up as a program for implementation "on the morning after the victory" was used in practice to define more closely the political course of the SDAP. Equally typical was the *Rapport Nieuwe Organen*, (New Bodies Report) in which suggestions were made for an "Economic Council," a consultative body of producers and consumers and a predecessor of the present-day Social and Economic Council. The last step toward adaptation was taken in the "Labor Plan," which described the goals of socialism in a capitalist society. Socialism had grown from a utopian revolutionary movement into a pragmatic party of the people.

This development was the background against which the disappearance of socialist utopianism took place. Utopian socialism disappeared in part because elements of Utopia were actually achieved, and in part because ideas that were far beyond the realms of possibility were marginalized. To the last category, certainly, belong the ideas of Herman Gorter and Henriëtte Roland Holst. Until the end of his life Gorter remained a

Frederik van Eeden (center) receives Henri Borel (left) and Lodewijk van Deyssel (right)
on his seventieth birthday, April 3, 1930.

dogmatic Marxist with high-flown expectations about the enlightened society and the state
of pure consciousness in which the workers would find themselves after the revolution.
Gorter's ideas became increasingly remote from a socialist (and communist) party that was
increasing its grip on the current political and social situation. Gorter continued to strive for
the new crystal age, foreshadowings of which he believed he could discern in successive,
ever smaller, ever more radical splinter movements, but which moved ever further away
from him. By the time of his death in 1927, the world of light, viewed in the political context of the moment, had become utterly utopian in the customary sense of "unworldly."

The modern trends hit Henriëtte Roland Holst even harder. More even than Gorter,
she was tugged back and forth between the SDAP, which became increasingly revisionist
in its operations, and her Marxist principles. She was also torn within herself, because
she could not choose between her party-political engagement and her Marxist ideology
on the one hand and her desire for an ideal community of the faithful on the other.
Eventually she opted for religious socialism. In the same way as Gorter, although it took
a little longer, she was sidelined to the political-ideological margin. In the course of the
nineteen-thirties, the ideal of a socialist community of faith was still kept alive by the
Workers' Youth Central and its leader Koos Vorrink. After World War II it disappeared
soundlessly from the socialist debate.

Once Henriëtte Roland Holst had left the party for good and no longer felt bound to the revolutionary doctrine and the party-political principles, the bottom fell out of the fierce criticism she and Gorter had leveled at Van Eeden and the other colonists. In retrospect, her religious-mystic ideal (and Gorter's crystal world) proved to be surprisingly close to Van Eeden's "City of Light." Henriëtte Roland Holst frankly admitted that her criticism of Van Eeden had been unjustified. On the occasion of Van Eeden's seventieth birthday she wrote in the *Liber Amicorum*: "In your conception of socialism, as far as the heart of the matter is concerned, you were right and we, who were so absolutely convinced that we were right then, were wrong."[93] It must have been cold comfort for the writer whose ideas, just like those of his former opponents, had been consigned to the dustbin of history.

ONDER DE DWANGWETTEN.

The railroad strike suppressed (1903).
Albert Hahn, *Under the Laws of Tyranny. Zondagsblad van het Volk,* March 15, 1903.

12

Flowers in Dutch poetry at the turn of the century

translated by Kist and Killian

The fin-de-siècle in Europe was burdened by an awareness of the decline and imminent downfall of western civilization. The threat of an all-encompassing decadence emerged around the middle of the nineteenth century and crystallized in 1870 with the devastating defeat of the French army and the subsequent collapse of the Second Empire. Various signs appeared to confirm the growing fatalism. The Industrial Revolution had progressed too rapidly and, as was feared, had resulted in regression rather than advancement. This was evidenced by the run-down working-class neighborhoods, where disease, prostitution and alcoholism were rife. Doctors determined that life in the city led to stress and ultimately (dreaded) neurosis, a category which, along with insanity, hysteria, tuberculosis, gout, cancer and forms of paralysis, included alcoholism and moral aberrations such as theft, prostitution and adultery. Once contracted, neurosis was passed on to following generations until, weakened and its strength sapped, the family finally died out.

Famous novels from this period painted a dismal picture of powerful families which met their downfall within a few generations, including Edmond and Jules de Goncourt's *Renée Mauperin* (1864), Emile Zola's twenty-volume *Les Rougon-Macquart* (1871-1893), Thomas Mann's *Buddenbrooks* (1901) and Louis Couperus' *De boeken der kleine zielen* (1902; *The Books of the Small Souls*, 1914-1918). Flowers and plants were an obvious choice for illustrating this degeneration. In *La Curée* (1872), Zola gives a lengthy description of a conservatory with a profusion of tropical plants. The overheated, artificial atmosphere caused their degeneration into repulsive herbage - part animal, part vegetable. They mirror the deterioration of the main characters, a consequence of the neurosis that had taken root in the family in a preceding generation.

At the end of the nineteenth century, the image of the greenhouse or conservatory was the common property of writers, such as Zola, who voiced their criticism of contemporary society (the conservatory in *La Curie* stands for the decadent Second Empire), or who took pleasure in the notion of a decadent society, such as Maurice Maeterlinck in his volume *Serres chaudes* (1889), or as Duke Jean des Esseintes, the main character in Huysmans's *A rebours* (1884), who cultivated flowers associated with disease and decay in the conservatory of his country house. The amorphophallus "reminded one of the mauled limbs of negro slaves," the caladiums "displayed, as though they had almost entirely been eaten away by syphilis or leprosy, deathly pale bits of flesh veined with a red rash and embellished with scales." In 1897 the Belgian poet Ivan Gilkin composed the following variation on the motif of the decadent hothouse plant:

LE MAUVAIS JARDINIER

Dans les jardins d'hiver des fleuristes bizarres
Sèment furtivement des végétaux haineux,
Dont les tiges bientôt grouillent comme des noeuds
Des serpents assoupis aux bords boueux des mares.

Leurs redoutables fleurs, magnifiques et rares,
Où coulent de très lourds parfums vertigineux
Ouvrent avec orgueil leurs vases vénéneux.
La mort s'épanouit dans leurs splendeurs barbares.

Leurs somptueux bouquets détruisent la santé
Et c'est pour en avoir trop aimé la beauté
Qu'on voit dans les palais languir les blanches reines.

Et moi je vous ressemble, ô jardiniers pervers!
Dans les cerveaux hâtifs où j'ai jeté mes graines,
Je regarde fleurir les poisons de mes vers.

THE BAD GARDENER

In the gardens of winter bizarre florists
Furtively sow malignant vegetation,
The branches of which soon become entangled like knots
Of snakes slumbering at the edge of a muddy pool.

Their fearsome flowers, regal and rare,
From which flow vertiginous, heavy scents,
Proudly open their venomous calyxes.
Death blossoms in their barbaric splendor.

Health is destroyed by their sumptuous bouquets
And, having loved their beauty too much
Pale queens languish in palaces.

How much I resemble thee, oh perverse gardeners!
In the precocious minds where I have cast my seeds,
I see the poison of my verse bloom.

An important idea with respect to decadence was the presumed connection between decay and artistic refinement. In his influential *Théorie de la decadence* (1881), Paul Bourget noted that societies fell when their members eschewed the common good in favor of independence. Bourget compared a decaying society with an organism that dies when the autonomous cells begin to fall out of step and grow uncontrollably. But, he added, this sickly autonomy was a necessary condition for artistic genius. Truly important art could only be created by solitary individuals who had withdrawn from the collective. Thus, Bourget validated the image of a fading society which, in a last flicker, spawns sickly geniuses. Various writer/dandies such as Charles Baudelaire, Joris-Karl Huysmans and Oscar Wilde recognized themselves in this image. They saw their fate reflected in flowers of sterile beauty. They abhorred fertility and reproduction. The flowers they identified with had no purpose other than to be pretty and admired. Oscar Wilde said the following about this in a letter:

> Art is useless because its aim is simply to create a mood. It is not meant to instruct, or to influence action in any way. It is superbly sterile, and the note of its pleasure is sterility.... A work of art is useless as a flower is useless. A flower blossoms for its own joy. We gain a moment of joy by looking at it. That is all there is to be said about our relation to flowers.

Lodewijk van Deyssel and Louis Couperus were worthy representatives of dandyism in the Netherlands. In a book on Van Deyssel by Albert Vogel, the writer is characterized as "the man with the orchid." Couperus was always impeccably dressed and wore a white flower in his buttonhole. He surrounded himself with orchids and calla lilies during his lectures. Couperus' original ambition was to become a poet. He made his début in 1884 with *Een lente van vaerzen* (Verses of Spring) which begins with a cycle of "nocturnal flowers" and ends with a "little song." In the last, the poet imagines that he is a rose that his beloved places in her hair. He tries to mollify her, in vain:

> *Gij ruktet mij wreed uit uw lokken*
> *En wierpt mij ter neêr op den grond.*
>
> *Maar onder uw voeten bestrooiden*
> *Mijn blaadjens uw eenzaam pad,*
> *En het wierd u ten minste tot vreugde*
> *Dat ge mij vertreden hadt.*

> You wrested me brutally from your locks,
> And cast me on the ground.
>
> But under your feet my petals
> Were strewn on your lonely path,
> And at least it gave you joy,
> To have trampled on me.

This "little song" is a variation on the theme of the femme fatale whose praises were variously sung during the fin-de-siècle. Couperus may have consulted Algernon Charles Swinburne, who could conceive of nothing more pleasurable than "being the defenceless victim of a beautiful woman's wrath."

In this state I am quite lonely, but my soul
Rests peacefully, like a seed, a rootstock,
From which green sprigs issue
And abide, and tendrils dense with leaves, and abundant
With blossom, fruit ...

He whose will keeps vigil in his heart, his ripe deeds
Fall away from him like fruit from a tree.
The ground preserves, the wind disperses, the stream
Carries the seeds to another, fertile land.

The life cycle, pivotal to which were seeds and dissemination, also determined Verwey's vision of culture and society. For him, the Dutch people had the vital traits of a tree with many branches and shoots; especially a fertile tree, the seeds of which had blown throughout the world and taken root elsewhere. The South African Boers represented such a "kinship" offshoot from the Dutch tree. The wars of independence that raged from 1899 to 1901 between the British, who wanted to colonize South Africa because of the recently discovered gold mines, and the Boers of Dutch origin, were closely followed in the Netherlands. Indignation was great when, after protracted fighting, Britain subjugated the Boers and annexed the territory. Verwey wrote the following poem on the occasion of this defeat:

DE STAM VAN 'T VOLK
De stam van 't volk doet nu zijn loten beven
Omdat een twijg herplant in vreemde streek
Gewond beweegt: geheimnisvol geleek
Eén leven nog door stam en twijg te streven.

Verwantschap trilt in 't bloed en luide spreek'
Ze in eendre taal en dring' de hand tot geven;
Want krachtloos zijn we en ons is niets gebleven
Van hulp die steunde en macht die niemand week.

De stam van 't volk doet nu zijn blaadren ruisen
En vreugd voor 't minst is 't ritselen all' tezaam.
Te lang in stilt hing elk voor zich alleen.

Eén bloed is 't al, hier kronklend, daar aan 't bruisen,
Eén taal is de onze en de onze eenzelfde naam -
Eén is ons voelen, zij 't ook in geween.

THE FAMILY TREE
The shoots of the family tree now tremble
For a twig replanted in foreign regions

Though injured, moves: mysteriously
One life seemed still to struggle through trunk and twig.

Kinship vibrates in the blood and speaks loudly
In the same language and forces the hand to give;
For we are impotent and nothing remains to us
Of help that supported and power that yielded to no one.

Now the family tree lets its leaves rustle
And simple is the joy of the leaves rustling in concert
For all too long each hung alone in silence.

One blood, meandering here, rushing there,
One language is ours, as is a common name –
One are our feelings, also in weeping.

Kinship is a typical turn-of-the-century concept, when one thought in terms of "trees."
Take the many family sagas, in which the degeneration of the family tree is a central concern. The social sciences concentrated on drawing up "family trees" and tracing the "lin-
eage" and "kinship" of all sorts of languages, cultures, and peoples. Examining the use
and the meaning of just the semantic field "stam" (trunk, stem, stock, race, clan, tribe,
phylum) would afford intriguing insight into turn of the century mentality. In 1897,
Maurice Barrès wrote *Les déracinés*, a novel recounting the travails of a group of friends
who migrate from Alsace to Paris where, as a result of having been uprooted, they are
ruined. According to Barrès, peoples and races behaved like trees that are rooted in their
region and in their history, and pass on their life sap to countless leaves that harmoniously rustle in the wind. Did Verwey have this novel in mind when he wrote his poem?
In any case, he clearly sided with the notion of kinship. Verwey was an outspokenly anti-
decadent artist. He made a distinction between his plants bursting with vitality and the
sickly vegetation of Baudelaire, Zola, Bourget, Huysmans and Mallarmé, juxtaposing
their sterile ornamental flowers with the reproductive task of flowers, and he contrasted
the individuality of the dandy with the community of the tree's foliage.

At the beginning of his career, Verwey had joined the Eighties Movement, which also
included Jacques Perk, Willem Kloos and Herman Gorter. At the end of the eighties,
however, he distanced himself from this group, in particular from Willem Kloos, who
had been an intimate friend in the preceding years.

Nature and flowers held a different meaning for the poets of the Eighties Movement
than for those of the Nineties Movement (a breakaway group in the eighteen nineties,
including Verwey, Boutens, Leopold). The members of the Eighties Movement tried to
give expression to their "mood," a subtle combination of an inner feeling and an outer
atmosphere. Moods were fleeting, blessed moments during which the poet (or painter)
felt that his spirit was harmoniously assimilated with the rest of the universe. In this,

nature played an important role as medium. The secret of cosmic unity was revealed to Gorter as musical arrangements sung by nature:

> *Hoor je de boomen wel zingen*
> *eerst daar heel hoog zingen*
> *van de teere bovenste takken*
> *als keelen die braken*
> *in angstig verlangend hoog vreugdeschreien,*
> *hun hoog gierluidende lentelijen,*
> *hoor je den nacht*
> *den eersten lentenacht?*

> Do you hear the trees singing
> high up there singing
> from the tender upper branches
> like voices breaking
> in fearful longing, high-pitched joyous weeping
> their shrill shrieking Spring suffering,
> do you hear the night
> the first Spring night?

It was nature and especially the unspoiled countryside (extensive heaths, woods and beaches) that made Gorter aware of a divinely inspired universe, of a Universal Spirit. Flowers were the closest points of contact with this boundless, ever-expanding spiritual whole, which Gorter passionately wanted to join. There are quite a number of poems in which Gorter describes how, anesthetized by flowers, he lies down on the ground and becomes one with the earth. Gorter was receptive to what nature sang or whispered to him. The mood came from outside and subsequently colored his inner self, as is wonderfully illustrated in his observation of a rose:

> *Een roode roos is in mijn hand,*
> *zie hoe puur*
> *elk blad brandt,*
> *nu is vol vuur*
> *elk mijner oogen, mijn hoofd verbrandt.*

> A red rose is in my hand,
> See how sheer
> Each leaf glows,
> Now is all fire
> Each of my eyes, my head ablaze.[1]

Nature also played a role in Perk's and Kloos's "mood," but they were far less receptive to what nature had to say to them. The starting point of their mood was their inner mental

state which they gave voice to in the form of images drawn from their natural surroundings and sometimes flowers. The path their mood followed (inside out), was the
reverse of Gorter's (outside in). Moreover, their flowers are more stereotypical and
derived from the literary tradition. They are unchanging mourning flowers: *Ik ween om
bloemen in den knop gebroken/ En vóór den ochtend van haar bloei vergaan./Ik ween om liefde die
niet is ontloken/En om mijn harte dat niet werd verstaan* (I weep for flowers broken in the
bud / Ere yet the morning of their bloom had dawned. / I weep for love without love to
respond, / And for my heart that was not understood...);[2] *Rozen, ik vind u droef...* (Roses,
I find you sad...).

This is not to say, however, that Kloos was always in mourning. His downcast state
(which he referred to as his *Welt-schmerz* or ennui) was one sweep of the pendulum, the
other being the realization that he was a god, elevated above the earth and mankind.
Perks's poems on flowers reveal a comparable sweep of the pendulum. For him, too,
flowers were for mourning and associated with the death of Mathilde, to whom he dedicated his only volume of poetry *(Mathilde, een sonnetten-krans* [Mathilde, a Crown of
Sonnets] 1882). Yet, like the flower that symbolizes her, Mathilde returns the following
season and triumphantly leads Perk to his destiny as a poet.

Looking back on the fin-de-siècle, it is noteworthy that all of the poets and thinkers
attested to their faith in a godly power which one called Life, the other the Idea, and
another the Universal Spirit or Total Consciousness. In this context, flowers were readi-
ly assigned the symbolic meaning of a soul striving to attain its divine principle. This is
the case, for example, for Pieter Cornelis Boutens:

> *O ziel, o bloem die tijloos bloeit*
> *In 't zuiver en onwrikbaar licht,*
> *Den weêrglans van Gods aangezicht.*

> Oh soul, oh flower that blooms eternally
> In the pure and steadfast light,
> The reflection of God's countenance.

In *Beatrijs* (1908), Boutens describes a garden, in which the chosen souls bloom as flowers:

> *Maria die woont hoog en stil*
> *Boven der englen prijs en lof,*
> *Die kiest van zielen wie zij wil,*
> *Tot rozen in haren hof -*

> *Die weet hoe schoon karmijnen roos*
> *Verbleeke in 't vuur van felle smart,*
> *Hoe schoon berouw tot purper blooz'*
> *Der blanke rozen hart -*

Mary, who lives high and still
Above the angels' adoration and praise,
Chooses from among souls as she pleases,
To become roses in her garden -

She knows how beautifully the carmine rose
Pales in the fire of fierce sorrow,
How beautifully remorse flushes purple
The white rose heart -

The image of a spiritual flower garden recurs frequently in the fin-de-siècle. In addition to Boutens, Leopold repeatedly mentions the longing for a paradisiacal garden. However, it would be incorrect to ascribe only spiritual value to these gardens. For Boutens, earthly, erotic love also provided access to godly love. The flowers in his poetry – as in that of so many poets –which are simplified to roses, are alternately red and white. They are white when they descend from their heavenly origin to earth; red when they sate themselves with sensual pleasure; and ultimately fade to white again when summoned back to their source.

Finally, scent was also an important element for the symbolist-decadent poets because it gave expression to the – at the time important – concept of refinement. To be sure, mind and matter were opposite forces, so it was believed, but as two ends of a sliding scale. There were intermediate stages of spiritual matter, as was meticulously described by some writers. The Theosophists distinguished ethereal bodies or auras that surround man as fragrance surrounds a flower. This was the background against which Boutens could write:

O ziel, o glans die 't oogeblank gelaat
Omvloeit zooals den eedlen steen zijn schijn,
Ondeelbaar als de geur is om de bloem.

Oh soul, oh glow that suffuses the pale white countenance
As sheen does a precious stone,
Indivisible as the scent surrounding a flower.

Scent is also a component that, together with twilight and music induces nostalgia, reawakening old memories:

Misschien rijst uit de bloem der schemer-volle rozen
Een zachte, lichte geur, die rimpelend deint, omhoog,
Van verre suist, misschien, bij lange vredepozen
Het lover, dat de wind, slechts node ontwaakt, bewoog.

Perhaps the flower of twilight-filled roses exudes
A soft, light scent that bobs, rippling upward,
From afar rustles, perhaps, with long intervals,
The foliage that the wind, arousing only reluctantly, stirred.

In these lines of verse, P.N. van Eyck paraphrases one of Charles Baudelaire's most beautiful poems, *Harmonie du soir*. Van Eyck's admiration for Baudelaire was boundless, and the master's influence is felt in many of his poems. However, upon closer scrutiny, Van Eyck appears to have been interested only in Baudelaire the idealizer, and not Baudelaire the proponent of decadence.

This comment applies in more general terms to all Dutch fin-de-siècle poets. Their flowers are not *Les fleurs du mal,* but a combination of a taedium vitae and a longing for refinement and spiritualization.

While writing *Hilda van Suylenburg* Cecile experienced enough to see that the theme was not just a literary creation devised in the study. Her sister Elisabeth had become engaged to the classical scholar and composer Alphons Diepenbrock and sought Cecile's advice. She encouraged her to marry Diepenbrock rather than Auguste van Lanschot, a scion of a well-known banking family from 's-Hertogenbosch, and cited the example of Lohengrin desiring Elsa's earthly love in Wagner's opera. In turn Elisabeth wrote to her that she thought "Auguste's enormous fortune" would give "added relish" to her triumph over the Catholicism of her lucky fiancé, Diepenbrock.[6] For she refused to give up her Protestant faith for him, and the marriage was not celebrated in church. Meantime Cecile had become involved in the preparations for the *National Exhibition of Women's Work* held in 1898 to mark the inauguration of Queen Wilhelmina. Modeled on the women's exhibition at the World's Fair in Chicago (1893), this event was intended to highlight what women did or could do in the field of work and what the limiting factors were. Cecile eventually became president of the organizing body. A large group of women – the basis for the initiative was formed by a second generation of feminists – did a huge amount of work. But the names De Jong van Beek en Donk and Goekoop in particular were associated with the exhibition. Goekoop was the generous provider of funds. He gave a guarantee when there were financial difficulties and made available free of charge the site in the dunes on his estate, which he had bought three years before from Grand Duchess Sophie van Saxen-Weimar. Elisabeth made herself useful as secretary of the office. The material exhibited in the Historical Section dealing with courageous forerunners of the women's movement was part of the valuable collection of letters, manuscripts, portraits and etchings of Dutch women down the ages made available by their mother.

And then the president herself. The publication of her novel and the fact of "her" exhibition meant that she was even more in the public eye. "The banners of Hilda van Suylenburg fly gaily" above the exhibition, wrote the essayist Carel Vosmaer in an account of the event. Life and literature were interwoven.[7] Moreover, there was something about the actions of the president of the exhibition which charmed even those who were hostile to her book. The Protestant journal *Stemmen voor waarheid en vrede* (Voices for Truth and Peace) reported that she was not the kind of woman that might be expected from her book. On the contrary, "all were impressed by her warm championing of truth and love, all were captivated by the charm of her *genuinely womanly* behavior."[8] At that point she seemed to be the perfect ambassadress for the women's movement.

Cecile Goekoop had not only her "femininity" and her literary initiative in her favor but also her aristocratic background. This enabled her to move in politically influential circles. Within the women's movement, too, she had "a good name" in several respects. She had not been involved in conflicts and had no particular political allegiance, unlike the first woman physician, Aletta Jacobs, who was identified with social liberalism. Nor did she display the character and style of someone who had been active in politics for years with just a little too much personal enjoyment. Her soul aspired to greater and finer things. In a letter to Nellie van Kol, who campaigned for socialism and feminism and whose journal *De Vrouw* (Woman) in her opinion pointed the way to true progress without the old dogmatism, she wrote: "It's all about love, isn't it, not fossilized doctrines?"

The "regulations committee" of the *National Exhibition of Women's Work, 1898*. Third from the left in the front row: Cecile de Jong van Beek en Donk (with the chair's hammer).

Her character made it possible for her to play a coordinating role. As proof of this, during the *National Exhibition* she was made a Companion of the Order of Orange-Nassau.

Cecile's marriage went through a crisis that erupted soon after the end of the exhibition. Goekoop felt that through writing *Hilda* and other feminist activities his wife had become a person in her own right and that he stood in her shadow. He therefore wanted her to give up her activism; "to stay with me in her thoughts, and not distance herself." Cecile in turn felt she was "locked in a dark cage with bars."[9] Hadn't she portrayed her ideal man in Maarten van Hervoren, who was actually pleased when his wife Hilda did useful work and looked outside instead of being completely absorbed in him? By now Goekoop had a mistress. After a short-lived reconciliation husband and wife separated for good in 1899.

Cecile's marriage had proved to be a mistake because it was based on a relation between an extravert and an introvert personality in which, moreover, sexual desire came from one side only. To Cecile's regret, Elisabeth, on being consulted by her sister, took the side of Goekoop and Diepenbrock. The latter, her brother-in-law, believed the cause was "Feminism," in which Cecile had let herself be caught up and swept along because of her emotional nature. The "somewhat overwrought idealism that inspired Feminism at that time in the Netherlands as elsewhere" even provoked an instinctive distaste in her brother-in-law.[10] Cecile let her warm heart be carried away by the things that she thought should govern life and society: love in service, beauty, purity and compassion. On December 17, 1896 she wrote the final sentence of *Hilda*. "Two large, clear tears welled up in her eyes, but she did not notice; there was only one consciousness in her, that in this ecstatic moment of happiness of thanksgiving prayer she wanted to consecrate her child to the highest, so that one day it too could carry a corner of the eternal Banner, which all the greatest and noblest among us have carried, the Banner of high Justice and Love." The sentence was not only long but high-minded too, as befits those campaigning for a better world.

In 1899, a year after the exhibition, Cecile de Jong van Beek en Donk emigrated to France. She settled in Paris and remarried. Her second husband was Michel Frenkel, a Warsaw-born chemist of Jewish origin and Catholic beliefs. By him she had a son, Pierre Michel. In 1907 she published her second novel, *Lilia*. This was a readable and high-minded tale about the true purity of a girl who is abandoned by her lover because she is pregnant. She is hardest hit by the fact that her half-sister leaves her in the lurch. This was an implicit reference to the conflict between Cecile and Elisabeth over her divorce. Her third novel appeared nearly a quarter of a century later, in 1930. In *Bij de waskaarsen* (By the Wax Candles) the now sixty-five-year-old Mrs. Frenkel again told the story of the "initiation" of a young woman, this time into Catholicism. In a footnote she confessed the guilt she felt about the case she had made in *Hilda van Suylenburg* for divorce for the sake of true love.

"The weak cannot feel anything else. They know only a little song, not a great melody." These words are spoken by a character in *Lilia*. The "strong woman" Cecile de Jong van Beek en Donk never held back. She followed her husband in joining the right-wing *Action Française*. She persuaded her sister, with whom she was again reconciled, to become a Catholic. When she died in France in 1944, one obituary noted that the book that had once caused such debate was forgotten, "since the problem it dealt with is now no longer a problem."[11] The disloyalty of the following generation in the women's movement was more tragic. In 1938 a committee of Amsterdam women prepared their own tribute to Queen Wilhelmina on the occasion of her fortieth jubilee. It was a book that "testified to women's work through women's work." The essay on women in literature began as follows: "Which books written by Dutch women could our Queen have read when she acceded to the throne at the age of eighteen?" Four titles were given. There was no mention of *Hilda van Suylenburg* anywhere in the piece.

The struggle

By 1897 the claim that women were suffering injustice but were still asleep had been made for three decades, at first by lone voices but with time increasingly by organizations. From 1884 the *Nederlandse Vrouwenbond ter Verhoging van het Zedelijk Bewustzijn* (Dutch Women's Union for Raising Moral Awareness) drew attention to the double standard inherent in prostitution. The well-known "doctoress" Aletta Jacobs was also active at this time. She demanded access to education and voting rights for women: the first was granted but not the second. A second woman physician, Catharine van Tussenbroek, graduated in 1887. Two years later the *Vrije Vrouwenvereniging* (Free Women's

Association) emerged from social democratic circles. It quickly became entirely independent, because the "class struggle" and the "battle of the sexes" simply did not go hand in hand. Meanwhile another *grande dame* had become known to readers of both sexes. In 1896, two years earlier than Cecile Goekoop, she had been made a Companion of the Order of Orange-Nassau. She was Hélène Mercier, who had written about the social task of women from "the better classes." They were to develop the female virtues that were so indispensable for resolving the social question.[12]

In 1881 Mercier had identified the factors standing in the way of women's "pure character development." They did not prepare themselves for a profession and consequently did not learn to be responsible for their own acts or to rely on their own resources. For work, "the blessing of the curse of Eden", was denied them. Added to this there was the longing – and the "necessity" – to please and to be married. "How many blossoms must she tear from her tree of life for the sake of her womanhood," Mercier exclaimed. "How many wishes must she stifle, how many questions must she suppress, how much strength must she break, how much joy in life must she forego, how much lack of interest must she feign!"[13] Mercier wanted to work together with the other sex to bring about a moral uplifting of society. But when necessary, this liberal champion of social reform would express her sharp condemnation of judgments and laws that reduced woman to "a being who – standing lower than man and dependent on him – need not have equal rights."[14]

Hélène Mercier's influence was evident in the development of the character of Hilda van Suylenburg and of other figures in the novel, but also in the argument that the emancipation of women was a prerequisite for the solution of the social question. Traditional notions about woman and her vocation were accompanied by a lament: "What a huge amount of love and talent must be lost to society as a result!"[15] Aletta Jacobs had shown Mercier the living conditions of the working class in the Jordaan district in Amsterdam. In *Hilda van Suylenburg* this role was played by Corona van Oven, the second most important character. She is a physician and is involved in a relationship with an artist. "Their relationship symbolizes the reforming power that Cecile attributes to the combination of art and science."[16] The character of Van Oven has been linked to Catharine van Tussenbroek, who was well known to the De Jong van Beek en Donk ladies. More interestingly, the female physician was seen as an ideal embodiment of the emancipated woman and her value to the new, just society. Nikolai Chernyshevskii had already portrayed this "new woman" in 1862 in his pro-reform *Tendenzroman* (social-problem novel) *What is to be Done?*, which was popular in Russia.[17]

The profession of physician underlined two aspects: freedom and willingness to serve. This combination was also at the heart of the message of *Hilda van Suylenburg*. Not only did women have a right to the privileges and freedoms enjoyed by men, but society in fact benefited from such equality. This was generally agreed within the women's movement. Whether the first argument or the second received most emphasis was a matter of temperament or political persuasion. Those who resorted more to the first than the second, were judged radical or extreme. Hélène Mercier, who emphasized the aspect of service, was in turn influenced by the British pioneer of social work Octavia Hill, who is mentioned in *Hilda*.

In 1894, while *Hilda van Suylenburg* was taking shape in Sorghvliet, pressure groups were being set up, including the *Comité tot Verbeetering van den Maatschappelijken en den Rechtstoestand der Vrouw* (Committee for Improving the Social and Legal Position of Women) and the *Vereeniging voor Vrouwenkiesrecht* (Society for Votes for Women). Positions were also being taken up in the battle between feminism and socialism. An important trailblazer in this field was Cornélie Huygens, who believed that the doctrine of class conflict made it possible to determine when a sex issue was involved and how it could be resolved. Huygens had written a novel and essays on "the women's question" and had entered into a highly controversial debate with the *Vrije Vrouwenvereniging*. She took the view that the demand by "those calling themselves feminists" for equal rights was premature as long as women had not yet proved themselves the intellectual equals of men.[18] The attitude of Cecile de Jong van Beek en Donk that women from a comfortable background should not waste their time with empty occupations did not go far enough for her. It is quite likely that the author of *Hilda* followed the debate about feminism and socialism with more than ordinary interest, the more so because she valued Cornélie Huygens, though in a different connection, as a sincere defender of her ideals.

The form

Feminism existed, the newspapers were full of it. All Cecile Goekoop had to do was "explain" it in an attractive form. The novel lent itself because it was a popular literary form around 1900. The feminist Wilhelmina Drucker wrote in 1895 that the women's movement needed a didactic novel. A jurist said that what was required was a "well thought-out, substantial book, preferably a novel, in which the issue is viewed from all sides and treated with taste." And why a novel? asked the feminist magazine *Belang en Recht* (Interest and Right). "Because only then did it have a chance of being read by those who ought to read it." The radical Wilhelmina Drucker put it slightly differently: just because it was a novel, the book could reach "circles to which other feminist reading matter is denied access."[19]

Dutch feminists cited George Eliot and George Sand as models and as sources for consciousness raising. In Scandinavia too there was a significant amount of realistic and serious reading matter for women who felt restricted in their freedom and development. In Sweden there was the novelist and pioneer of the women's movement Frederika Bremer. Norway had the playwright Henrik Ibsen, whose *A Doll's House* showed how Nora developed into an independent woman. It was talked about throughout Europe at the end of 1889.

An early source of identification and inspiration was the four hundred pages of *Aurora Leigh*, the melancholy poem of 1856 by Elizabeth Barrett Browning. She is mentioned respectfully in *Hilda van Suylenburg*. Hélène Mercier published a prose translation in 1883 and wrote an essay on the poem.[20] In *Aurora Leigh* the age-old irreconcilability of art and life is interwoven with the same painful irreconcilability of male and female. The story of Hilda closely resembles that of the heroine Aurora. Her mother also died young; the main character grows up with only her father, who treats her not as a little girl but as a fully developed person. The aunt who takes her in after her father's death represents social norms and etiquette. The man in Aurora's life, her cousin Romney Leigh, represents the Fourier socialist from a privileged background. *Aurora Leigh* is a story about nobility of rank versus nobility of character, about the duty to pursue only true love. Aurora twice rejects proposals of marriage, even one from Romney. For in contrast to Van Hervoren and Hilda, who on gender issues were two minds with but a single thought, Aurora has to deal with Romney's "mistaken ideas" about the nature and vocation of woman in the service of man.

In the eighteen-seventies and -eighties several novels dealing with women who rebelled against what others expected of them appeared in the Netherlands. The authors were often well-known advocates of the women's cause, but dissatisfaction with female prospects in life could also be found in impeccably literary quarters. In *Majoor Frans* (Major Frank, 1874) Trui Bosboom-Toussaint, no feminist, turned her rebellious thoughts to the fact that women were expected to wait for a man and then serve and obey him.[21]*Eigen meester blijven* (Remaining Your Own Master, 1878) by Elise van Calcar depicted the lonely sufferings and struggle of a heroine who wants to earn her own living. It ended with the advice that if one wants to change the world one must begin with oneself. Later, in the wake of the feminist mobilization, an emancipation genre developed. One example was *Verwoest leven* (Ruined Life, 1892) by Catharina Alberdingk Thijm, a novel in which a young woman sees all her family's money being spent on the education of her profligate brother (whose character by the way was based on the author's own brother, the writer Lodewijk van Deyssel). There were other resemblances to *Hilda van Suylenburg*. *Verwoest leven* is about an aristocratic young woman from The Hague who wants to marry for love. She founds a journal, *Vrouwenrecht* (Women's Rights), in which she writes about the difficult life of unmarried women. The support she obtains from another deprived woman makes her "ruined life" bearable and gives the book a relatively happy ending. The power of female friendships in which the political and the personal overlapped was also demonstrated in *Hilda van Suylenburg* in sometimes tempestuous ways.[22]

Hilda van Suylenburg was unique in one respect, as a conscientious presentation of just about every case in which women's emancipation provided the answer and as a course for both sexes in the art of living together in small things and in large. However, there were other examples of political art which successfully drew attention to social injustices and called for reform of the law. Of course, Multatuli's indictment of exploitation in colonial society in *Max Havelaar* comes at the head of any list. J.J. Cremer, a writer of village tales, should also be mentioned. He had seen the inside of a textile factory in Leiden and expressed his indignation in *Fabriekskinderen* (Factory Children), whose subtitle was "A plea, but not for money." To strike the right note in this heart-rending, Dickensian story, Cremer outlined the general issues in individual cases without depicting lifeless puppets. Cecile Goekoop had a similar talent. Readers in the United States and beyond had admired *Uncle Tom's Cabin or Life among the Lowly* by Harriet Beecher Stowe in the eighteen-fifties for the same reason. Another novel with a mission that made a deep impression on a wide audience was *Die Waffen nieder* (1889) by the Austrian writer Bertha von Suttner. Again, both authors were respectfully mentioned in *Hilda van Suylenburg*.

Tendenz

Like most examples of the *Tendenzroman* or didactic novel at this time, *Hilda* contains many of the "threadbare conventions of older idealistic prose."[23] However, the reader is not guided by a narrator who can foresee everything. Hilda and the other characters perform this function themselves as obvious embodiments of ideas that can or cannot serve as models. Apart from Hilda, there are fourteen substantial other roles intended to demonstrate in their own stories how the gender question is to be resolved. For the heroine there is a happy outcome. Moreover, the outward and inward natures of the characters correspond reassuringly: those who are bad look unattractive. But this does not apply the other way round. Moisette, a frustrated young preacher, is against feminism not out of laziness or egotism, like other men in the book, but on the grounds that the position of woman is strictly defined and laid down by God. Tragically, he is also shy and secretly in love with Hilda. "His dark, small eyes, the thick, straight black hair, and above the eyes the markedly domed forehead of a fanatic gave him a repellent quality; only the mouth was soft and sad, and lines of goodness curved round the close-shaven chin."

Hilda is the white lily. She "belonged to those rare, completely balanced, pure temperaments which evil glides past like mud spattered on swan's feathers." She also has a natural beauty and charm which make the "empty, banal riches" of her milieu all the more tasteless. An important characteristic of realist authors was dissatisfaction with society: if realism was intended to give greater insight into the reality of phenomena, then *Hilda van Suylenburg* was a realist novel too.[24] One of Hilda's cousins is drawn from the patient described by the physician Catharine van Tussenbroek in an address to the *National Exhibition* when she talked about "the lack of zest for life among our young women and girls" in the upper and middle classes. This was caused by her "education for marriage leading only to lies and economic dependence." Van Tussenbroek may even have been inspired by a character in the novel, Eugenie van Starren, who is finally admitted to an institution with a nervous disease. The description of Eugenie's fate gives the book an uncompromisingly naturalistic element. The implication is, however, that people are not powerless; even under dire social conditions history can still be shaped.[25]

In a sense *Hilda van Suylenburg* belongs to the genre of the utopia, of a new and better world. This required a belief that mankind was fundamentally good and was shaped by circumstances. Faith in progress and public spirit set the tone in *Hilda van Suylenburg*. Yet there were major differences between this novel of emancipation and, for example, the utopian novel *Looking Backward 2000-1887* (1887) by the earlier mentioned Bellamy, which was widely read and reviewed in the Netherlands. Bellamy's new world had been realized and was so perfect that it seemed like a machine that had been programmed in no time at all. Cecile Goekoop's new world still had to be conquered, in a struggle with heart and soul. Bellamy made many things different and better, but man and his work remained the measure of all things. In Cecile's view the new world was also to be liberated from precisely this, in her eyes fundamental, part of the problem with the old one.

Hilda van Suylenburg is full of refutations of arguments against the emancipation of women. But this moralistic novel seemed to have been written principally out of sorrow and indignation at the belief that women were morally inferior, a charge that even deprived them of the possibility of becoming honest and upright persons and citizens. Such unattractive female propensities as "fighting less openly" and "seeking advantages by secret methods" had been socially or historically conditioned. At the point at which Hilda is persuaded of the noble task associated with women's citizenship, she realizes during a sermon by a minister officiating at a marriage of convenience that "love in service" is indeed the essence of woman. "But *not* in the cowardly, stupid, ridiculous sense," that the minister has described. "No, the woman of the future will *not serve man*, her fellow creature, her equal, her brother! But she will serve *with* him, beside him, united in splendid love, the eternal ideals of mercy and truth, beauty and justice."

In this literary encyclopedia of feminism many pages are devoted to the effects of the existing laws on women's lives in practice. The young mother Gladys van Praege is a case in point. Her husband, a worthless character who seeks diversion at the gaming tables every evening, threatens to send their twins to a boarding school if she does not give him the money that is in her name according to the marriage contract. He has the law on his side, because Dutch legislation at this time specifically excluded maternal rights. The father alone had authority over the children. Gladys gives in, but that is not all. While her husband's life is in danger after he falls from his horse, Gladys senses that she will die in giving birth to her third child. She knows that her sister, who offers to take them, cannot be the guardian of her children because only men can do that. In this case, her husband's brother – who is possibly even worse than her husband himself – would become their guardian. On her deathbed – and the bed on which she is to give birth (what symbolism!) – Gladys curses the women who remain apathetic and do not rise up as one against such "shameful laws." After she has given birth to a stillborn child, both parents die. Cecile Goekoop writes, "And for *one* second the world paused in its superficial prattle." The fact that Gladys had been the president of "the society for women's voting rights" is one of the few references to the political dimension of the women's movement. Gladys's rebellious speeches about the marriage laws were not copied out of a feminist manifesto, but personally "struggled through in tears" in the reader's perception.

Women's emancipation was a battle against the outside world, but also against the idle or lazy ego. The second line in the moral politics of *Hilda van Suylenburg* is the task of changing the world by beginning with oneself. Women might be victims, but they were also responsible. The mother of Isabelle Pankaert ought to have supported her daughter in her singing career instead of spoiling her son, a worthless, pleasure-loving student. The intelligent and beautiful Ottilie could have raised herself from her lazy dissatisfaction with the aid of her doctor Corona van Oven.[26] Upper-class ladies receive the sharpest criticism. Although they have the money and the opportunities to do something better, their frivolous and empty entertainments, their appearance of propriety and abominable education of their children make them as guilty as the men who made the laws. The "cowardly comedy" between the sexes must make way for true womanliness, which gives itself heart and soul.

Couperus, Emerson and Wagner

Hilda van Suylenburg was a "physiology" of the world of The Hague. Mrs. Goekoop portrayed her network of "small souls" with the same mildness and fondness that Louis Couperus, that other chronicler of families and coteries in the city, was to show four years later in *De Boeken der Kleine Zielen* (*The Books of the Small Souls*). She had also put in a fair amount of melancholy and suffering. Couperus reveled in the weak and sickly, and in Cecile's novel too the nervous Eugenie, the decadent Ottilie and the nineteen-year-old, already world-weary, "almost foppish" cousin Edward are more colorful characters than the exemplary Maarten van Hervoren.[27] The Hague novel may be considered a genre thanks to Couperus, who is remembered for his masterly depictions of the "refined and enfeebled civilization in aristocratic circles."[28] *Hilda van Suylenburg* was just as closely linked to The Hague as Couperus's *Eline Vere: Een Haagsche roman* (Eline Vere: A Novel of The Hague). Both Hilda and Eline live on Nassauplein. Hilda has also read *Eline Vere*. After all the talk about woman and her vocation, she muses on a long list of very different women: Sarah Bernhardt, Florence Nightingale, St. Teresa and "the Madame Bovarys, the Eline Veres of the whole world, who come to grief in their sensual romantic egotism."

The old and the new world battled away over the heads of Eline and Hilda. The aristocracy was to be defeated by those energetic enough to make something of their lives and overcome fate. This contrast was expressed at the time in concrete world views. The vigorous Lawrence St. Claire, the epitome of will power compared with Eline, comes from North America. Gladys van Praege and her sister were also "imported" from this land of progress. For contemporaries America then had the bloom of youth. Couperus was not alone in having read and digested the essays of Ralph Waldo Emerson, the embodiment of North American idealism.[29] In *Hilda van Suylenburg* there was also a reference to "the land of Emerson." The fact of the emancipation of women having been largely realized on the other side of the ocean to everyone's satisfaction was to serve as a shining example to Europe.

Pursuing this line of thought, Cecile Goekoop introduced feminism as one of the new forces contrasting with "the loss of the inner certainties of the European bourgeoisie." In the liaison between Hilda and the strong and healthy socialist Maarten van Hervoren, who incidentally has been in America (and has seen the belief in progress in England), feminism joined forces with socialism. This was not party political socialism, and the feminism of *Hilda van Suylenburg* equally transcended the everyday reality of politics. This explains why the liaison could be so safe and so reliable. This is why the partners were equal; this is why class did not overshadow gender. Thus this alternative Eline Vere which showed so much affinity with the real *Eline Vere* by Louis Couperus made its own contribution to the new idealism of the eighteen-nineties in the cause of radical reform of society.[30]

On her feminist mission Mrs. Goekoop took with her Richard Wagner, from whom as a child of her time and visitor to Bayreuth she wanted to learn a great deal. As for the reception of Wagner in Dutch literature, her *Hilda van Suylenburg* may be cited as one of the most Wagnerian of novels. Having come to know Wagner's operas at an early age,

Cecile made use of his characters and ideas on five occasions. For the true love without marriage between Corona van Oven and her friend, she made use of Wagner's unfinished text *Jesus of Nazareth*. Hilda compares Ottilie, herself an admirer of Wagner, with the sorceress Kundry, who in *Parsifal* is called to do the "disastrous work" of the woman of fashion, to please. Gladys finds "durch Mitleid wissend," those "beautiful words of Wagner," also from *Parsifal*, so appropriate for the pre-eminently female profession of physician.

When Hilda threatens to consent to the proposal from the man she does not love, she is rescued by the thought that her mother once called her Brünnhilde. Lastly, Maarten van Hervoren says it ("with the tender emotion that can make a strong man so fascinating in the eyes of a woman") with a scene from *Tannhäuser* after he realizes that Hilda wants to become a lawyer for serious, feminist reasons. Elisabeth, says Maarten, is the only woman who does not "decently" flee when *Tannhäuser* confesses his sin. She will be thought unwomanly, for she was the only emancipated one, the only one who followed her conscience and heart instead of traditionally obeying. "But she was also the only one who emanated redemption and purification!"

While in other novels Wagner's music had a fatal effect on young women, in *Hilda van Suylenburg* Wagner gives her heart. Was not Brünnhilde, however tragic, the personification of a "right to rebel" against those you love? Corona van Oven embodies the "pure" power of feminism. As the ultimate sacrifice, she even restrains her sexual desire for her married friend. She believes that as a leader she must set a good example to combat the many misconceptions about women's emancipation. This "high, rich life of study and charity" is a justification of the women's movement and its alarmingly "unwomanly" demands, which are judged so wrongly. As mentioned, motifs from *Parsifal* can also be traced in Hilda's adventures in this exciting tale for girls. Hilda has the innocence of a Parsifal, succeeds like him in resisting the attraction of the opposite sex and has a lofty, responsible task to perform. As a feminist she must help to save humanity. In this case all of humanity must be rescued, not just the male half, so that their partners will automatically be liberated too. Indeed, unless women are emancipated, humanity cannot be saved.

Three ladies and love

In 1897, the year in which *Hilda van Suylenburg* first appeared, two other widely discussed novels by aristocratic women were published. *Het ééne noodige* (The One Thing Needful) was by Anna de Savornin Lohman, who came from an eminent Protestant family. In this book a young woman turns against the hypocrisy and the empty social round in her circle in, yet again, The Hague. She too refuses to go in search of a good match on the marriage market. Here the resemblance to *Hilda van Suylenburg* ends. This girl has only one desire, a marriage for love in which the woman always gives more than the man and becomes completely absorbed in absolute subjection to him. Women who sought emancipation denied the urge in every true woman, that "one thing needful." The heroine cannot get the man she loves and in the end she commits suicide.

Barthold Meryan was by Cornélie Huygens, who has already been mentioned. The book is remembered as a socialist *roman à clef* in which Huygens sets out to explain her conversion to the Social Democratic Workers' Party (SDAP). *Barthold Meryan* is about a young man's initiation into socialism and equally about his initiation into true love. Huygens rejected marriage for money, name or position. Barthold, a child of the small class of "hereditary parasites on society," is putty in the hands of a calculating young woman. The innocent young man has no defense against the acting talent and sexual attraction of this type. After a marriage full of hard and bitter lessons, he eventually finds his true love, an intelligent female comrade who is willing to devote herself with him to the struggle for a socialist society.

Hilda van Suylenburg had more in common with *Barthold Meryan* than with *Het ééne noodige*. Each is a *Tendenzroman* combining a political tract with a girls' book about the ups and downs of an aristocratic family, with its parties, engagements and – described at length – female arts of seduction. *Barthold Meryan* even includes an entire political speech complete with the subsequent debate. In the elevated prose of both novels, which in the case of *Barthold Meryan* verges on the ecstatic, the same advocates of "moral beauty" appear. The key words in the social liberalism of the first and the social democracy of the second are the same. Humanity is going through a "transitional period," a "time of struggle," that will lead to social justice if the oppressed people are helped to liberate themselves.

Hilda van Suylenburg and Barthold Meryan were both born into a class that closed its eyes to the grave social tensions. From that aristocratic circle they moved into a society in ferment to devote themselves completely to the good cause. *Hilda van Suylenburg* has a few lively scenes depicting everyday life among the lower classes, but the author of *Barthold Meryan* did not attempt to follow suit. Much more so than Mrs. Goekoop, Cornélie Huygens had trouble dealing with these "brutalized" human beings. But then her sacrifice was the greater: she had to go entirely out of her milieu, whereas Mrs. Goekoop had joined battle against the injustice done to women in all classes.

Three ladies, three views. Their indictments of marriages not based on love reflected three visions of the female sex in relation to the male. That of *Het ééne noodige* seemed to find the least acceptance. Lohman's absolute surrender was too much even for men. "Her saintly but unhealthy worship of man as a superior being would become healthy love if she dared to admit that the woman giving all this love remains unfulfilled if she receives no love."[31] Cornélie Huygens believed the solution would come from the struggle for socialism. After all, the "women's question" was an offshoot or component of the larger "social question" in which labor and capital confronted each other. Wilhelmina Drucker thought that in her novel Huygens expected the men of the labor movement to do everything. She objected to the fact that in *Barthold Meryan* the prototype of the seductive female contrasted so sharply with the colorlessness of the other women characters on the one hand and with the perfection of the men on the other. The impression given was that women could only be "pupils of man, never the teachers."[32]

Anna de Savornin Lohman thought that women meant nothing without men; man was for ever "superior." Cornélie Huygens believed that women were inferior to men here and now and that they therefore did not deserve the so-called feminist rights (except for working-class women, who did not need them anyway). But that could and must change. Cecile Goekoop, in contrast, did not take man or the male as the measure of things. While she was fiercely critical of women in her own class, she thought that the gender question was also a men's question that made life difficult for women in all classes. Women could read in *Hilda* that they could learn as much from other women as from themselves. There had to be an end to the "foolish silencing of those who are in fact articulate."[33]

This comment comes from the review of *Hilda* by the feminist Frederica van Uildriks, who even compiled an index for it.[34] Her review is typical of the reception of the book by the women's movement. She was critical of the heroine's propaganda speeches, "but since the sympathies of many, and ours too, are with this writer's ideas, we listen gladly, setting aside the criteria of the literary art for the novel as a whole, and gratefully accepting the beautiful images and fragments of which this book has such a wealth." Cecile spoke a language that many real Eugenies, Isabelles and Berthas understood. Or in Aletta Jacobs's martial terms: *Hilda van Suylenburg* had "given many weak followers the strength to march on, the courage to persevere, the help needed to withstand the opposition that might still loom before them."[35] Wilhelmina Drucker saw more in *Hilda* than a feminist *Tendenzroman*. "For the present a means of propaganda, in later years for the historian the work will be a splendid picture of the life of the great figures of the nineteenth century. Written for feminism, this book has become a lively sketch of the extinction of the aristocracy and the rise of democracy."[36]

Then Anna de Savornin Lohman entered the fray with her tract *De liefde in de vrouwen-quaestie* (Love in the Women's Question). She had withdrawn from the preparations for the *National Exhibition* and wanted to make known her personal standpoint on the women's question. Well then, women were disadvantaged. What concerned her, however, was what the executive and in her book the president were claiming, namely that women could find happiness in work of their own, just like men. Together with several male commentators, Lohman cited Laura Marholm, a writer of mixed German and Swedish origin who had tried to prove in six portraits of well-known and successful women that work in society was only a means of making a failed life bearable. A woman's life was a failure if she had to go without the giving love for a man, who "is stronger than she, and whose superiority to her she acknowledges and desires." So this was the view of a real woman: if a woman had not known love she remained "empty." "He possesses in himself. She receives from outside, through him." The independent and emancipated woman was in reality tragic and underprivileged. There were leaders of the women's movement, said Lohman, who had been disillusioned by an unhappy marriage and because of this reviled the entire male sex. She spoke of "a third sex, sadly deviating from the species originally intended by nature," of "men-women," who had killed "the germ of femininity inside them." "What an odd inner aridity and flatness, what a chilliness still characterizes their behavior, making them unsympathetic and their work flawed!"

The author of *Hilda van Suylenburg* had invoked true femininity and true love time and again, but Lohman was not to be fooled. Cecile Goekoop was out to make the difference between the sexes disappear. She denied the true womanly feelings and her dangerous theories about the fulfillment of women's lives could only lead to disillusion among young women. *Hilda van Suylenburg* was "untrue through and through." Others felt called upon not to let this pass. They defended *Hilda* against *De liefde in de vrouwen-quaestie* and *Het ééne noodige*. These publications were dangerous, exaggerated and likely to promote hysteria. *Hilda van Suylenburg* was healthy and life-giving and shook people awake.[37] The gist of the defense was that a woman's love for a man in no way ruled out independence. Cecile Goekoop herself also responded to the "untrue" review of her book. She complained, "Madam, where ever have you met these women of the new movement who would deny the happiness of a loving marriage? *I* have never met them!"[38]

On this occasion Cornélie Huygens joined the camp of the women's movement. It might be that these quarreling middle-class ladies had no greater enemies than themselves, and *Hilda* might be a "painfully superficial" book, but it stood up for truth and justice. Marriage was at least not presented as "a submissive, clinging vine type of love." The author depicted clearly "the fierce revolt of one person against what goes on in one class in society."[39] In a review of this essay her fellow party member the poet Henriëtte Roland Holst cast some badly needed social democratic light on the battle. It was a question of the socialist view of love and the "old-fashioned absolutism" of Anna de Savornin Lohman. Huygens's piece yet again demonstrated "the superiority of our world view to both the hysterical approach that can imagine no happiness for a woman other than being everlastingly in love, and to the feminists' unsympathetic and ridiculous concealment of woman as a sexual being."[40]

In a response Anna de Savornin Lohman did not retract. Feminist criticism of her ideas was "the cackling and crying and babbling of emancipated, unloved and hence embittered women." Those who "aped" men were simply not women. That was an "absurdity" of the third sex, which was "proud of the barrenness of its arid and chilled heart, in which only the *intellect* will grow and *feeling* is stifled."[41] Thus none of the women could be dissuaded from their political philosophies and beliefs regarding love in women's lives and in society.

Criticism by gentlemen

In his overview of fifty years of Dutch literary studies on the occasion of the inauguration of Queen Wilhelmina in 1898, the Amsterdam professor Jan te Winkel described *Hilda van Suylenburg* as a feminist *Tendenzroman*. The book was widely read, although "with the possible exception of the characterization of a few figures, it is not really a work of art, but a good anthology of notes from or on the subject of studies of the women's movement stitched together by a thin story."[42] Most of the male reviewers took a more or less similar view. As a rule *Hilda* was received not favorably but with a remarkable amount of good will. It had the typical faults and irritations of a *Tendenzroman*. One critic said it was poorly written, with characters like "puppets" and "stereotypical expressions of emotions."[43] Another was impressed, however, by the form of this non-literary work. The style was polished and the language pure, "so that the many lengthy speeches are almost a pleasure to read."[44]

"Without entering a debate that lies outside the domain of literary criticism," reviewers were keen to voice an opinion. The points raised were the incorrect use of statistics, the over censorious judgment of the immoral lifestyle of Catherine the Great and the ease with which equal pay for women and men was demanded. Mrs. Goekoop had "wanted to open the eyes of the Dutch ladies." The *"true women's question,"* however, required much more radical, socialist reform. This was a book "that wants only *capitalist* changes in our *ladies* society and does not go a step further."[45]

The men's world of politics and law also took note of this feminist *Tendenzroman*. Cecile Goekoop succeeded in making her feminist evaluation of the law a source of interpretations of the rules in legal debates. Anyone seeking a practical example to illustrate his legal arguments could find one in the fictional world of *Hilda van Suylenburg*. Thus in their discussions of the deficiencies of the law on marriage, a notary at the annual conference of the Brotherhood of Notaries and an – anti-feminist – speaker at that of the Dutch Society of Jurists cited the cases of Gladys and Mistress Zwalve respectively.[46] When supporting the appointment of women notaries, the later member of Parliament Jan Duys demonstrated how right and opportune this reform would be by citing what Hilda van Suylenburg said to Bertha Wendelings.[47]

In the Lower House of Parliament the Protestant leader Alexander de Savornin Lohman was tempted into reacting to *Hilda*. In a debate on legislation to protect children, the question of the right of women to be guardians was raised. De Savornin Lohman referred to the "novelettes" of the day in which one read that the lawmakers had done women an injustice. "We have even been faced recently with the prospect of women shaking their fists at the Parliament building." Lohman said that he therefore thought it "prudent" to support a Liberal amendment in favor of guardianship. Which he duly did.[48]

Writers too read *Hilda van Suylenburg*. In *Langs lijnen van geleidelijkheid* (The Law Inevitable) Louis Couperus dealt with the political reality of feminism. The main character Cornélie de Retz van Loo is modeled on Cecile de Jong van Beek en Donk. The novel contains numerous references to the women's movement and *Hilda*, her marital problems, and to the views of her opponent Anna de Savornin Lohman.[49] The moral is that the protagonist's sexual desire for a man makes a feminist way of life impossible, unlike in *Hilda* and to some extent in agreement with De Savornin Lohman. Thus Hilda van Suylenburg, who also mentions Eline Vere, in turn comes back in a new novel.

Cecile de Jong van Beek en Donk left a book that became an important factor in public opinion and feminism around the turn of the century not because of its literary quality but because of its persuasiveness. She was the driving force behind the *National Exhibition of Women's Work* in 1898. For the following exhibition, on *Women 1813-1913*, she returned from France to speak on French feminism. By then she was a veteran campaigner. During her years in the Netherlands more than any other feminist she represented the cultural dimension of the Dutch women's movement around 1900.

The Concertgebouw Orchestra and Choir, conducted by Willem Mengelberg,
perform Gustav Mahler's Eighth Symphony, 1912.

14

Urban culture

Philharmonic

On the evening of Sunday, October 23, 1904, the Austrian composer Gustav Mahler performed his Fourth Symphony – the most "supernatural" of the series of ten – with the Concertgebouw Orchestra in Amsterdam. It is a work in which the composer succeeded in maintaining his control "in every bar … even where he wantonly has the bells ring out, the trumpet blare, unexpectedly splits the heavens asunder with E major arpeggios and the emphatic triumph of the brass."[1] At the suggestion of Willem Mengelberg, the orchestra's resident conductor, the symphony, a premiere for the Amsterdam audience, was played twice on the same evening: once before and once after the interval. "I think that's exactly what we want with a new composition," Mahler wrote to his wife, Alma ("Almschl"). It meant a second chance for reviewers and the rest of the audience, who had had to hear the work completely unprepared because of the absence of program notes. Mahler was struck by the quality of the Amsterdam performance and the reception accorded it. The audience in a less than full auditorium listened with remarkable concentration and, as movement succeeded movement, with growing warmth. The solo in the fourth movement, a poem about "das himmlische Leben" from the medieval song cycle *Des Knaben Wunderhorn* was sung by the soprano Alida Oldenboom-Lütkemann; a short, fat woman, according to the composer, "but she sings magnificently with a voice as clear as a bell. She performed with simplicity and poignancy, while the orchestra accompanied her as if in a ray of sunlight."[2]

Mahler's impression of warmth and appreciation has to be seen in perspective. Most of the critics were pleasantly surprised by the unaffected simplicity of the symphonic themes, and heard in them echoes of Haydn and Schubert. In contrast, the reviewer for the largest daily newspaper, *De Telegraaf*, who had previously been underwhelmed by performances of Mahler's work, detected uninspired passages in this symphony, too.[3] The weekly music magazine *Weekblad voor Muziek* quoted an "authoritative musician" (probably Bernard Zweers, senior lecturer at the Amsterdam Conservatory), who had left at the interval and could not have imagined "the satisfaction" of an educated audience with this composition. "A large, infernally boring work without a single musical idea, in which how not to use the instruments is demonstrated in an absurd manner and proved beyond question. Mahler is amazingly adept at getting sounds out of instruments that they do not possess." In the next issue, his colleague Alphons Diepenbrock replied to his anonymous fellow artist, asserting that Mahler was a true composer in the line from Orpheus to Beethoven and Wagner; "a composer who conceives of his art as a priesthood, and whom we shall have to thank if posterity is able to discover anything in our woeful era other than the hegemony of the 'educated plebs'." He wrote to Zweers personally, telling him that he was steering his students at the Conservatory in the wrong direction.[4] For to Diepenbrock the Fourth Symphony was "a wonderful dream" or the sensation of a soul freed of all earthly bonds in different dimensions; "be it as childish yet supernatural jollity, be it as the highest ecstasy to which the mystics of the past rose in their contemplation of the divine."[5]

Gustav Mahler had come to Amsterdam for the first time in October 1903 to conduct his Third and First Symphonies. The audience in the Concertgebouw on that occasion had split into two camps; a great many people who walked out, and a body of enthusiasts who applauded loudly at the end. The Concertgebouw Orchestra had faithfully followed his directions, and Mengelberg had repeatedly shown himself to be a fervent champion of his work, because he saw in Mahler a genius, "someone whom I would call the Beethoven of our age." For his part, Mahler welcomed Mengelberg's "sympathetic art of interpretation and his mature understanding of his compositions." In the circles that received and admired him in Amsterdam, to which Diepenbrock also belonged, the Austrian had found a second "Heimat."[6]

But there was not to be wider appreciation until after Mahler's premature death in 1911. The presence of H. de Booy (on behalf of the Concertgebouw) and Diepenbrock (on behalf of the society for the promotion of music, the *Maatschappij tot bevordering der Toonkunst*) at his funeral in Grinzing near Vienna was evidence of the existence of a particular receptiveness to Mahler's music in Amsterdam. Less than a year later, in March 1912, Mengelberg, his orchestra, and hundreds of singers performed Mahler's Eighth Symphony, a monumental piece about the Christian Spirit and about Faust. At the same moment, a wreath was laid on the composer's tomb "as a symbol of the love, respect, and gratitude of his Amsterdam friends." "Although the audience annoyed me by immediately breaking out in cheering and applause," noted the writer Frederik van Eeden in his diary, "I was nonetheless touched by the great general enthusiasm, when everyone stood up and cheered. It was a marvelous moment. One of those rare evenings of high and passionate communal life."[7]

In the two decades since its opening in 1888, the Amsterdam Concertgebouw had become a renowned institution, whose reputation invited imitation and competition in other towns and cities. Two developments are of importance here: a general improvement in concert practice, and the involvement of the urban public in the podium arts (and, for that matter, the visual arts). The new musical culture was expressed in a higher standard of orchestral playing and in greater concentration by audiences in the concert hall. The boom in profits and profit forecasts in the Netherlands around the turn of the century increased the collective interest of businessmen and businessmen's families in cultural development in a number of towns and cities.

Symphony orchestra

The large professional symphony orchestra of the kind that dominated musical life around 1900 developed in the municipal conservatory in Paris, which dated from the time of the Revolution. Within the framework of a musical education there was room for orchestral experiments. Orchestra discipline and the theory of instrumentation were developed in France through the example of a studious Orchestre du Conservatoire de Paris. Hector Berlioz found his platform for new orchestral sounds there, and Richard Wagner and Giuseppe Verdi saw their efforts to upgrade the opera-orchestra come to fruition – an orchestra which, in Wagner's case, assumed monumental proportions because of his demand that the brass and woodwind sections should be doubled in size. In the Netherlands, where in the nineteenth century there had scarcely been any dawning of interest in developments in music and where well-to-do citizens frequently invited foreign musicians and composers, people found out about the higher standard of orchestral playing through a roundabout German route – a concert tour by the Meininger Hofkapelle, the musical ensemble of George II, Duke of Saxe-Meiningen. Just as the Meininger Hoftheater had delighted theatergoers in the Netherlands with the quality of their ensemble work in guest performances in 1880, so the discipline of the members of the court orchestra made an impression in 1885. "The gaze that the players fixed on their conductor or their score was unwavering," wrote the composer Willem Nicolaï. "Their attitude was energetic and alert, and their faces wore an expression in which their love and enthusiasm for what they had to do were clearly reflected."[8]

From then on it had been impossible to conceal the mediocrity of the average orchestral playing in the Netherlands. "People also started to look with new eyes at Dutch conductors, who had been for so long regarded, with chauvinistic short-sightedness, as stars; it was unfair in that many people held them responsible for wrongs that in fact lay in the social and organizational sphere, and of which they were actually the victims."[9] In Amsterdam, both the orchestra of the Paleis voor Volksvlijt (the Amsterdam Crystal Palace) and that of the concert hall in the Plantagebuurt, the Parkzaal, were examples of acceptable ensemble playing and interesting programming. The conductor of the Paleis orchestra, Johan Coenen, was a key figure in the professionalization of orchestras in the Netherlands. The behavior of the public in the Paleis voor Volksvlijt – more of a party venue than a concert hall – was essentially "Dionysian," in other words bent on pleasure. But in what was known as the classical series under Coenen's direction (including programs devoted to Beethoven) and in performances with guest appearances by foreign luminaries like Hans von Bülow, Niels Gade or Franz Liszt efforts were made to rise above the standard of the "beer concerts."[10]

The recognition of a musical deficit created the conditions for a Dutch attempt to make up lost ground. This was in any event the intention of the six founders of the new concert hall – the Concertgebouw – in Nieuwer-Amstel, just outside Amsterdam's city limits. It was to be the replacement for the Parkzaal, which had been demolished in 1882. They collected funds from art-loving citizens for a corporation, a common form of cultural enterprise at this time. Some months after the opening in 1888, they put an orchestra together and appointed Willem Kes (1856-1934) as its conductor. He had studied the viola at the conservatory in Leipzig and then continued his training as a "pensioner" of King William III with the famous violinist Henryk Wieniawski. Willem Kes made great efforts to raise the standard of both his musicians and his audience. In his endeavor to create a homogeneous and principled orchestral culture, he imposed fines on members who missed rehearsals or talked during performances. He was determined to put a stop to prevailing customs among concertgoers, which included smoking and talking during a concert, drinking, or walking about in the auditorium. Starting in 1890, the doors were kept shut during the performance. Kes also wanted to create a symphonic tradition in the Concertgebouw so that audiences could become acquainted with both classical and contemporary compositions. He consequently decided to devote a whole evening's program to a single composer. In the 1893-1894 season all the Beethoven symphonies were played in what was billed as a Beethoven cycle.[11]

Around the turn of the century the Amsterdam example started to have an impact on other orchestras in the Netherlands. In 1918, on the initiative of the violinist Jules Zagwijn, a society of professional musicians, the *Genootschap van beroepsmusici tot onderlinge Kunstbeoefening*, was established in Rotterdam; it was later to become the Rotterdam Philharmonic Orchestra.[12] The Hague, too, certainly felt challenged by the example of Amsterdam. In the nineteenth century, as the residence of the king, the city had enjoyed a certain court culture with a musical dimension. Until 1841 there had been a court ensemble, the first professional orchestra in the Netherlands, which also gave public concerts in the Diligentia concert hall.[13] Throughout the century, a French-speaking company had performed the unofficial function of theater to the court; with royal subsidies it had concentrated on the performance of French operas, and had acquired a certain reputation. The conservatory in The Hague had been founded as the royal school of music, the oldest music academy in the country. Musical court culture in this form had expired by the end of the century, and the initiative was seized by wealthy music-lovers of aristocratic and bourgeois origins. The most remarkable instance of this was to be found in the flourishing seaside resort of Scheveningen. The Berlin Philharmonic Orchestra had played in the Kurhaus there every summer since 1885, enabling an international audience of resort visitors and Hague residents to hear the standard of the professional ensemble and experience first-hand the skill and expertise of conductors like Franz Mannstädt and Arthur Nikisch. The promoter of these Kurhaus concerts, A.J.H. Baron van Zuylen van Nijevelt, gentleman-in-waiting to the king, also set about founding a municipal orchestra in The Hague, to fill the gap left by the former court ensemble. 1903 saw the debut of a Residence Orchestra conducted by Henri Viotta.[14]

Viotta had been the conductor who had opened the Amsterdam Concertgebouw in 1888. Until 1919 he returned to the Dutch capital annually to conduct the performances of the Wagner Society with the Concertgebouw Orchestra, for it was he who had promoted Wagnerian music in the Netherlands in an unparalleled way. In 1896 he had moved to The Hague, where he became the director of the Royal Conservatory. In 1900 he organized the first Dutch Music Festival there. Viotta was able to raise the standard of his Residence Orchestra to great heights, but in the choice of the repertoire he always remained faithful to his old loves, Wagner and Berlioz. In November 1911 a festival in The Hague was devoted to the dramatic work of the young Richard Strauss. The composer came to conduct his operas himself; the modern, sometimes dissonant music of *Salome*, *Feuersnot*, and *Elektra*, as well as the sweet-voiced *Rosenkavalier*. It was The Hague's counter to the sensational performances of Mahler and Wagner in Amsterdam, in what was to prove an ongoing rivalry between the two cities. In the same year, the Residence Orchestra also played all the Beethoven symphonies in a series, which was intended to be an alternative to a commercial concert organization. Willem Hutschenruyter, scion of a family of musicians and administrator of the Concertgebouw, had joined the orchestra in The Hague after a row with Mengelberg. He promoted a campaign for the construction of a Beethoven House, to a design by Berlage, in the dunes at Bloemendaal. A concert hall was to be built there, where people could experience the consecration of art in a combination of Beethoven's music and the ambience of a temple of the arts.

Willem Mengelberg

In Amsterdam, meanwhile, the modern style of conducting and listening had become all the rage. In 1895 Willem Kes had resigned from the Concertgebouw Orchestra, having received a financially irresistible offer to become conductor in Glasgow. The 24-year-old Willem Mengelberg was proposed as his successor by Johan van Riemsdijk, a member of the Utrecht aristocracy and a passionate music-lover, who had supported his young neighbor in Utrecht in his musical education. Mengelberg was a concert pianist and, at this time, director of music in Lucerne. He appeared at the farewell concert for Willem Kes as the soloist in the First Piano Concerto by Franz Liszt and subsequently, on October 27, 1895, as the new conductor of the Concertgebouw Orchestra with Carl Maria von Weber's Jubilee Overture.

Mengelberg established his reputation in a single concert season. Music critics talked about the magic of his "ruler's eyes" and the measured sound of the taps of his baton that he used to focus the orchestra members' attention on him. "We think this 25-year-old Mengelberg is a musical genius," wrote the editor of the Amsterdam daily *Algemeen Handelsblad*.[15] In his programming he adopted Kes's pattern and expanded it to include both an interest in the history of symphonic music and curiosity about contemporary compositions, both German and French. The surprise lay in Mengelberg's singular interpretations, which he could command from an orchestra that was increasingly devoted to him; the introduction of unusual accents, the "improvisando," the unexpected *ralentando* or *accelerando* – "tempo twists," as the composer Daniël de Lange described it. Mengelberg started to invite foreign guest conductors; one of them, the composer Richard Strauss, was so delighted with the Amsterdam concerts that in 1897 he dedicated his symphonic tone poem *Ein Heldenleben* to the Concertgebouw Orchestra. He also started to take the orchestra on tour. The very first of these trips, in 1898, took them to Norway, where they played a concert under the baton of the composer Edvard Grieg.

In 1905, for the first time, Mengelberg was invited to appear as guest conductor by the New York Philharmonic Society. Two years later he received the invitation to appear annually with the orchestra of the Frankfurter Museumgesellschaft. His musical curiosity was equally wide-ranging in the first decades when he was principal conductor. In 1902 he organized a Dutch Music Festival in the Concertgebouw. After welcoming Gustav

Mahler to Amsterdam in the first decade of the new century, in the second he began to take an interest in the composer Arnold Schönberg, the creator of modern music carrying on from Mahler. In 1914 Schönberg came to Amsterdam to conduct his *Five Orchestral Pieces*, famous for having transcended the bounds of tonality. The audience response was at best polite, composers like Diepenbrock and Matthijs Vermeulen were even dismissive, but Mengelberg, with his musical intuition, continued to believe in him.[16]

Mengelberg's commanding personality and the perfection of the orchestra created an atmosphere that could transport audiences. "Music is edification," wrote Rudolf Mengelberg, Willem's nephew and the artistic director of the Concertgebouw Orchestra, in the program for the Mahler festival in 1920. "Music is surrender to the spirit, music knows no class or national boundaries, music is the symbol of a higher fellowship."[17] This was particularly true of Mahler's oeuvre, but it was also experienced to the same extent during the annual performance of Bach's *St. Matthew Passion* on Palm Sunday. The romantic tone of the work had been set by Felix Mendelssohn, who had performed this music again for the first time in more than a century in Berlin in 1829. This rediscovery proved to be a sensation. It eventually reached the Netherlands, where Bach's *Passion* first resounded in Rotterdam in 1870. A tradition of Dutch performances had already been established – in Amsterdam by Johannes Verhulst – before Mengelberg added his interpretation to it in the Concertgebouw on Palm Sunday, April 8, 1899. In his version, characterized by theatrical accents and dramatization, he was an exemplar of the performance practice of the "late romantic espressivo" that was so typical of the post-Wagnerian musical culture. The annual performance of the *St. Matthew Passion* on Palm Sunday in the Concertgebouw gave birth to the tradition of the religious drama – "half worship, half concert" – which, according to the theologian Gerard van der Leeuw, was the offspring "of a singular and, at first sight, even hybrid marriage between Lutheran liturgy and Italian-French baroque music."[18]

In 1920 Mengelberg celebrated his silver jubilee as the conductor of the Concertgebouw Orchestra with performances of all the symphonies of Gustav Mahler. The foundations were laid during this Mahler festival for what was to become, two years later, the International Society for Contemporary Music. Strikingly, the head of state and the state itself were prominently represented in the album of honor for the conductor; Queen Wilhelmina signed it personally, while her husband, Prince Hendrik, was the patron of the festival. Mengelberg not only enjoyed the customary royal patronage of the arts. He was idolized by countless music-lovers and had achieved the status of a national celebrity – and he had precisely the right character to revel in such plaudits.

Opera

In the fall of 1907 the opera *Salome*, based on the play by Oscar Wilde and with music by Richard Strauss, had two premieres in the Netherlands: once in the original German, performed by the *Opera-Vereniging* in Amsterdam, and once in an Italian version by the *Opera Italiana* in The Hague. Interestingly, the composer, Richard Strauss, chose to conduct the second. The orchestra of the *Opera Italiana*, which normally consisted of forty-eight

Jan Toorop, portrait of Gustav Mahler, 1920.

Jan Toorop, portrait of Alphons Diepenbrock, 1911.

musicians, was increased to seventy for the occasion. The performance was excellent, but the premiere had to be postponed "because of the numerous rehearsals Herr Strauss deemed necessary."[19] The soloists of the *Opera Italiana* made a great impression.

The first performance of *Salome* in German took place on September 26, 1907 in the Stadsschouwburg in Amsterdam. This was almost two years after the controversial world premiere in Dresden. Both there and in Amsterdam the opera was regarded as scandalous because of the dissonant, inflammatory music and the erotic dance of the seven veils with which Salome wins the right to claim the head of Jochanaan (John the Baptist), who had spurned her love. The *Opera-Vereniging* had engaged the German Leonore Sengern to play Salome and the Dutch singer Jacques Urlus as Herod. The performance left the audience astounded. "After the last chords, strong and piercing, that are the conclusion of the Wilde-Strauss tragedy, it was as if the people in the auditorium awakened from an anesthetic, from a terrible dream," wrote the reviewer for the *Algemeen Handelsblad*. Nevertheless there was a great deal of criticism of the singing and, even more, of the dancing of the female star.

The Opera Italiana premiered its version in The Hague on November 14, 1907. Whereas the German Salome had taken two curtain calls, at the end of the Italian version there were five. "We have the greatest respect for these singers, who, raised on the comfortable strumming of Bellini or Donizetti, were still able to make so much of their scores and showed so much understanding of style," ran the verdict in the *Nieuwe Rotterdamse Courant*. Salome's dance, which had been regarded as a low point in the first performance, was now seen as a highlight – although it has to be pointed out that it was performed by a dancer, not by the singer. Strauss was surprised at the praise lavished on the production. "Is it that the personal suggestion by my baton was so great that even an expert missed the flaws in the performance, or is the work as a whole not to be disparaged? I actually believe the latter."

The Opera Italiana also performed the work in the Paleis voor Volksvlijt in Amsterdam and in Utrecht. The performance in the Grote Schouwburg in Rotterdam was disrupted by a young man in an inebriated state. This incident prompted the Catholic daily *De Maasbode* to write about the work for the first time. Up to this point, the Catholic press had refrained from expressing any opinion because *Salome* was regarded as a "decadent dance of lewdness" and any encouragement to attend a performance had to be avoided at all costs. In a comment piece, the paper wrote that "the young person" had been no more indecent than the singers, and no coarser nor sunk no lower than the audience. The fact that the audience "sat straight-faced in expensive seats, jewelry sparkling, lapping up the most scandalous lasciviousness, and the young person, on the other hand, without observing the forms, gave full rein to a different passion makes no difference to the essence of the matter." This comment was typical of the objections to the theater in Catholic and orthodox Protestant circles.

The example of this practice of performances in different languages reveals that opera in the Netherlands was parceled out among a handful of companies, which put on performances in the language of the country after which they were called. Around the turn of the century they were the Opera Italiana, the *Théâtre Royal Français* and the *Hoog-Duitsche Opera*, but this tradition goes back to the eighteenth century. There was also a movement in favor of performances in Dutch, and so a *Hollands Opera-gezelschap* and a *Nederlandse Opera* took their place in the motley crowd. Although these companies promoted themselves with repertoire from the country in their name, this by no means ruled out putting on operas from competing nations. The two versions of *Salome* are echoed by the example of *La fille du régiment* by Gaetano Donizetti, which was also produced as *Die Regimentstochter* and *La figlia del reggimento*. *La juive* by Jacques-François Halévy could also be seen as *Die Jüdin*, as *L'ebrea*, and as *De jodin*. The Dutch opera scene was international in outlook and polyglot in approach.[20]

Opera Italiana

The Opera Italiana flourished around the turn of the century as a result of the boldness and the acquisition policy of the Hague violinist and impresario Michel de Hondt. He was the prototype of the cultural entrepreneur, whose business acumen was the indispensable precondition for the continuity and quality of the company. It was in the 1897-1898 season that he first put together an ensemble of Italian singers, which performed in the Gebouw voor Kunsten en Wetenschappen in The Hague, in the Grote Schouwburg in Rotterdam, and in the Paleis voor Volksvlijt in Amsterdam. De Hondt, who later set great store by his Italian decoration of "Cavaliere" (knight), was to bring together a new company no fewer than fourteen times. He introduced operas like *Tosca*, *Madame Butterfly*, and *Turandot* by Giacomo Puccini. Pietro Mascagni came to conduct his own *Cavalleria Rusticana*. Altogether the Opera Italiana kept going for a quarter of a century in the Netherlands – a unique achievement in Dutch opera history, which was characterized by short-lived enterprises.

The Opera Italiana devoted little attention to scenery or direction. The Cavaliere took *bel canto* literally; to him it was first and foremost beautiful singing that mattered. The dramatic narrative of the opera and the portrayal of characters were subordinated to it. If the "maestro d'orchestra," the "prime donne," and the "primi uomini" were good, he saw no need to worry much about the rest of the production. Before the start of the new season, De Hondt went to Italy to look for suitable singers for the proposed repertoire. At first he could only afford musicians who were unknown in the Netherlands, but gradually he was able to engage soloists "di prima cartella," among them Gemma Bellincioni and Rosita Caesaretti. These were evenings of "un-Dutch enthusiasm." After a performance of Verdi's *Il Trovatore*, a reviewer wrote that what had until then been accessible to "our race only as barrel organ music or 'productions' by musical clowns" had now become a "melodious reality" of great originality. "For a Dutch or even a French Troubadour can never compete with an Italian, the *arch*-Troubadour, the *native*, the primogenitor of all those others."

The Opera Italiana traveled around the provinces of Holland and Utrecht but eventually found a second fixed base, in addition to The Hague, in Amsterdam's Paleis voor Volksvlijt. The performances drew mixed audiences. De Hondt succeeded in attracting Catholics by staging a production of Verdi's Requiem conducted by the famous church musician Lorenzo Perosi. Workers and shopkeepers were prominently represented in the audiences for his operas, particularly up in the gods. "This is the home of enthusiasm

and peanuts – of sentimental tears and painful behinds – but above all, of enjoyment!"
A regular section of the audience came from the elite of the working class: the diamond
workers. As soon as a new production was announced, "these people held a family conference. Coins were thrown clinking onto the table, and the next morning the mistress of
the house would go to the Paleis voor Volksvlijt to wait in line for tickets. The people in
the line never lost their good humor or their patience. Melodies were hummed, and there
was no lack of criticism, which was often very shrewd. The prevailing tone was always
enormous admiration for the Southern singers."[21]

Opera in Dutch

Around the turn of the century, there was a move to extend international opera culture
in the Netherlands by adding a Dutch dimension to it; it was a determined attempt to
get foreign operas sung in Dutch and then to create openings for works by Dutch librett-
ists and composers. In 1886 the theater director Johannes George de Groot had founded
the *Hollandse Opera*, a Dutch company that was to give performances in Dutch. On
October 16, a Dutch version of Charles Gounod's opera *Faust* had its premiere in the
Parkschouwburg in Amsterdam. With forty-eight sold-out performances in the first season it was a great success, and it paved the way for works by Dutch composers, among
them an opera about a – supposed – hero of the Dutch Revolt, *Albert Beiling*, by Henri
Brandts Buys, and a musical drama about Count Floris V of Holland by Richard Hol,
who came to conduct the premiere himself in 1892. The press, however, remained stub-
bornly unconvinced about the quality of the translation and of the pronunciation. We
find it hard to imagine, said Carel van Nievelt, the *Nieuwe Rotterdamse Courant*'s reviewer,
the educated Dutchmen who prefer "such unbounded tastelessness in language and
form, made even worse by often excruciating pronunciation" to the "graceful melodi-
ousness" or "poetic beauty" of the original French or German.[22]

The Hollandse Opera eventually went bankrupt in 1895. In 1894, meanwhile, its conductor Cees van der Linden had founded a new company, the *Nederlandse Opera*, and it
was now to put on productions in Dutch. Again the language issue became the subject of
polemics, which flared up in 1900 when this company staged a production of Wagner's
Meistersinger in a Dutch version titled *De Meesterzingers van Neurenberg*. The music critic
Hugo Nolthenius complained about the quality of this Dutchification. "The raw material
is, after all, smuggled in from outside, and the national suit of rags in which it is dressed
makes recognition of the original almost impossible."[23] In the spring of 1916, the daily
Algemeen Handelsblad ran a survey about Dutch-language opera. Among the proponents
of these productions, it emerged, was the writer Louis Couperus, who found the Dutch
more elegant than the German, more human than the French, and richer than the English.
"To laugh because it is sung seems to me a modern form of snobbery."[24] The same year
saw the launch of a new *Nederlandse Opera*, which was to sing in Dutch until 1928.

The Dutch-language opera culture foundered on the international dimension of
music theater and the dominance of foreign opera companies in the Netherlands. The
abiding lack of esteem can also be explained by the taste, if not the snobbism, of the

The Paleis voor Volksvlijt (Amsterdam Crystal Palace), east front viewed from the Amstel Hotel.

national opera audience and by the lack of good operas.[25] The international nature of music theater was the same as that of concert practice. The musicologist Eduard Reeser has lamented that Dutch music in general was so little played around the turn of the century. The festivals of Dutch music in 1902 and 1912 met with virtually no response. The presence of members of the royal family and the awarding of prizes were intended to disguise the indifference to compositions by fellow-countrymen, who had been able to look back with nostalgia to the middle of the nineteenth century, when "they were admittedly considerably fewer in number, but on the other hand could expect more warmth and appreciation from a public filled with national pride."[26]

Wagner Society

The *Wagner-Vereniging* was a society with lofty goals and considerable prestige. It was the Dutch variant in an international network of *Wagner-Vereine*, which were promoted from Bayreuth, the master's last home and final resting place. On January 26, 1884, six months after it was founded, the society organized its first concert in the old Felix Meritis concert hall in Amsterdam. In front of the orchestra podium stood the flower- and wreath-bedecked bust of Richard Wagner, acquired and installed by the men who had initiated the project. They were the banker Jan Wilson, the grain merchant Julius G. Bunge, J. Lublink Weddik, assistant resident of the Indonesian island of Madura on leave in the Netherlands, and Henri Viotta, who conducted that evening. Two soloists, Carl Hill from Schwerin and Marianne Brandt from Berlin, both of whom belonged to the international elite of Wagner singers, sang extracts from his operas.

Twelve years later, Alphons Diepenbrock remembered "the garlanded statue of the Master" and the excitement in the auditorium, "the pressure of the internal and external temperature … Then came the liberator" in the person of Henri Viotta. "With supreme command, his baton summoned up the horn fanfare of the *Flying Dutchman* from the magnificent sound of the strings. There arose the vision of the composer's unstoppable power in the minds of the audience. To many, the triumphal anthems with which the overture of the *Flying Dutchman* ends were sounds of good omen." To Diepenbrock the evening was "evidence of a more ideal musical desire," proof "that music can still be something other than a profane gratification of the senses, than a fatigue for the spirit, or a weakening of the mind. It was the first reaction against the deep decline of music that characterized the period when the school of Mendelssohn reigned."[27]

By the school of Mendelssohn and its influence, Diepenbrock was referring to Johannes J.H. Verhulst, whose prominent place in Dutch musical life had caused the artistic stagnation that blocked the path of a composer like Diepenbrock, a member of the generation of the eighties. Verhulst's retirement in 1886 at the age of seventy was consequently hailed as the dawn of a new era. The reality was that Wagner's music had also been played despite Verhulst. Until well into the eighteen-eighties, the *Hoog-Duitsche Opera* in Rotterdam had been the most important company in the Netherlands for staging his operas in terms both of frequency and of the standard of the performances. This institution had been created in 1860 and is a typical example of Rotterdam's entrepreneurial spirit. In 1887 it had been possible to move into the new municipal theater, the Grote Schouwburg, which was better able to meet the demands of the modern music theater. On March 22, 1890, after unusually intensive rehearsals, *Tristan und Isolde* was given its Dutch premiere in Rotterdam with Alexander Saalborn conducting. Up to the last season of its existence, this company succeeded in putting on seven Wagner operas, including the Dutch premiere of *Das Rheingold*, the prolog to the *Ring des Nibelungen*. In 1891, however, the Hoog-Duitsche Opera in Rotterdam finally lost its lengthy struggle for survival.

In its first decade, the Wagner Society produced nothing but concert performances of acts from Wagner's operas and choral works by Beethoven. It was not until 1893, with a performances of *Siegfried* in the Paleis for Volksvlijt, that it first staged scenic productions, which it then continued to put on with metronomic regularity between 1895 and 1919 at a rate of two music dramas a year. The music and staging of these performances were of a consistently good standard. To anyone who attended the annual performances in Bayreuth, the premiere was a moment of recognition. This was reflected, wrote the *Algemeen Handelsblad*'s reviewer in the 'un-Amsterdam hour at which the performance commenced, the long intervals between the acts, the themes blared out by the brass to

The rebuilt Stadsschouwburg in Amsterdam.

announce the next act, the darkened auditorium, and, first and foremost, the attention of the audience, who sat as quiet as mice so as not to miss a single note." The reviewer for the *Nieuws van den Dag*, Daniël de Lange, added that all the performers were convinced of the great significance of this artistic event."[28]

The acoustics and other facilities at the Paleis for Volksvlijt were far from ideal, so that expectations were all the higher when the new municipal theater, the Stadsschouwburg, opened in Amsterdam in September 1894, four years after the old one had been destroyed by fire. The regular conductor of the Wagner Society, Henri Viotta, had been a member of the building committee and had advocated a good orchestra pit under the stage, a "mystic gulf" like the one in Bayreuth. The Amsterdam fire brigade scotched that idea by insisting on a fire screen in a theater that had burned to the ground in a previous incarnation. Three days after the opening, the Nederlandse Opera performed the Wagner opera *Rienzi*. Not quite three months later the Wagner Society presented the *Ride of the Valkyries*. The director was brought in from Germany, as were the soloists, while the contract for the scenery went to the set designers of the imperial theater in Vienna. This is evidence of the perfectionism that the society aimed for in its performances.

The losses it made were underwritten by wealthy members, amongst whom the grain merchant Julius G. Bunge and his son Julius Carl were particularly prominent. In the nineteen-twenties, when everything that the father and son had purchased for the Wagner Society had to be put into a trust, the inventory listed 8,000 pieces of scenery and

The Ride of the Valkyries in a performance of the opera of the same name by Richard Wagner, staged by the Wagner Society in the Stadsschouwburg in Amsterdam, 1894.

2,500 costumes.[29] Julius Carl was described as assistant director on a few occasions, but in fact he was involved in virtually all the scenic productions. Working with the Stadsschouwburg's technician, he designed the machinery needed for stage effects. From 1901 onwards, Antoon Molkenboer was responsible for the design of the programs. He was the nephew of Antoon Derkinderen, the director of the national art academy, the Rijksacademie voor Beeldende Kunsten. Like his uncle, he felt an affinity with monumental art. "Harking back to old traditions in the decorative arts, he wanted to reflect the abstract idea behind the reality. He believed that Wagner had likewise not tried to render reality directly and realistically."[30] Before long he was designing costumes too. But here Molkenboer came in for criticism – he was accused of excessive pomp on the one hand, and disloyalty to Wagner's directions on the other. In the early years of the Wagner Society, the resemblance to Bayreuth was a constant yardstick.

In June 1905 the Wagner Society took a step that represented a blatant break with the rules of Villa Wahnfried in Bayreuth, the home of the Wagner family, by staging a production of the *Bühnenweihfestspiel Parsifal*, which the composer had reserved for Bayreuth in a letter to the Bavarian king, Ludwig II. The society had two arguments for ignoring the ban on performances outside Bayreuth. Because the organization was a society, its performances were private, not public. Moreover, the Netherlands was not a signatory to the Bern Convention of 1886 governing international copyright rules. In fact the Netherlands did not ratify the convention until 1912. The society consequently did not have to abide by the Bayreuth rules. Willem Mengelberg had already given a concert performance of *Parsifal* with the Concertgebouw Orchestra and a choir in 1902. On that occasion the protest from Villa Wahnfried came after the event. Furthermore, this opera had been performed for the first time outside Bayreuth in 1904 – at the Metropolitan Opera in New York. In 1905, the Wagner Society planned to stage the European premiere.

When the news reached Bayreuth, there ensued a campaign by musicians and friends against what they saw as grave robbery by Amsterdam. The pressure even reached Prince Hendrik, the German consort of Queen Wilhelmina, and Queen Emma, the Queen Mother, who nonetheless attended the premiere. No trouble or expense were spared in the endeavor to put on a flawless performance. Viotta hired the Stadsschouwburg for three weeks so as to get in as many rehearsals as possible. To many the production was a climax. A German reviewer who had been unable to get a ticket wrote regretfully that it had evidently been a success; a colleague who had been luckier thought the second act better than in Bayreuth. "Everything went perfectly, visually and mechanically: the spear stopped at the right moment and the swan fluttered, magnificently shot, across the stage." A critic reported that Viotta had truly succeeded in elevating the Stadsschouwburg to the Temple of the Holy Grail. This production "has destroyed the Jerusalem of the Wagnerians, the Temple of Zion of the worshippers of this Grand Master of art. This is how it must be! It has put an end to the idolatry, to the glorification of personality. Now Wagner can speak to us in all his greatness. Looked at clearly, Viotta, like Parsifal, has returned the holy spear to the Temple of the Holy Grail."[31]

Literature and Wagner

Wagner's art had a great influence – and not just on composers. It also extended to artists like Antoon Derkinderen and the members of the Eighties Movement, and to the generation of the nineties who tried to realize the idea of a *Gesamtkunstwerk* – a total work of art. In 1906 one of them, the architect Hendrik Berlage, was inspired to design a Wagner theater, which in the end was never built. In 1893 Alphons Diepenbrock confessed to the writer Frederik van Eeden – in reference to an article on Wagner by Elisabeth de Jong van Beek en Donk, whom he was later to marry – that he had deliberately not read anything else about the composer for the last ten years. "I was so terribly oppressed by it. My neck is stiff from always looking up at that mountain. I don't think that I'm far enough away from him yet to be able to measure the proportions."[32]

In the Netherlands Wagner's art started to make its presence felt in the eighteen-seventies thanks to the Hoog-Duitsche Opera in Rotterdam. From the outset, artists were fascinated by this phenomenon. In *De boeken der kleine zielen* (*The Books of the Small Souls*), the great novel by Louis Couperus – like Thomas Mann's *Buddenbrooks* the account of the decline and fall of a family – during the final stages, when the fall has become inevitable, Wagner's music can be heard ringing through the house in The Hague. It is played on the grand piano by Paul van Lowe, the bachelor who has escaped from society and speaks, horror-struck, about the ugliness of humanity and the world. Only for Wagner can he still find approval. Van Lowe thought Wagner's music sublime but his libretti mediocre in terms of both their poetic and philosophical qualities. Thus "the proud edifice of Wagner's *Gesamtkunstwerk*" was undermined. This judgment was that of Van Lowe's creator, Louis Couperus, who wrote in an essay on Wagner's *Ring des Nibelungen* that when he was in the theater he tried to forget Wagner the poet, in order to be transported by Wagner the composer.[33] This notwithstanding, in *De boeken der kleine zielen* he wrote passages that were evidently inspired by Wagner's themes and the art of his alliterations.

Frederik van Eeden saw in Wagner's music predominantly its numbing and stupefying character, whereas the artist's ambition had actually been to ennoble and to elevate. During the many performances of Wagner's works that he attended, the composer continued to intrigue him and the enthusiastic audience continued to annoy him. He wrote in his diary, "So we all go there and put on our finest capitalist suits, tails and low-cut gowns. If ever one could speak of bourgeois art, in two senses."[34] But it did not have to be like this. Henri Polak, the first president of the diamond-workers union, provided musical education for his members in which he paid particular attention to Wagner. Again and again he talked about Wagner in a revolutionary socialist interpretation. At the end of a lecture in Antwerp in 1911 "he even had the nerve to compare Siegfried, the hero of *Der Ring des Nibelungen*, with the working class." For this class is like Siegfried, "the revitalizing hero, who himself forged the sword that will bring him victory."[35]

Theater

In their youth, André Jolles, later an art historian, Heinrich Redeke, later a biologist, and Jan Kalf, later the director of the Dutch conservation organization *Monumentenzorg*, formed a symbolist group they called JOREKA. The trio met regularly, swathed in red cloaks; they chanted "Joreka" in Gregorian style, and then recited passages from favorite French authors like Maurice Maeterlinck and Joris-Karl Huysmans, particularly from his novel *A rebours*. "What the hell, one was a symbolist in the nineties or one wasn't," Jolles wrote in a memoir of his youth. The little group was also inspired by the French Rosicrucian Joséphin Péladan – or Sâr Mérodack Joséphin Péladan, to give him his full name – who had visited the art circle known as the *Haagse Kunstkring* in The Hague in November 1892 and been hailed for his esoteric inventions and rituals. They focused their attention chiefly on modernizing Dutch theater.

Maeterlinck was already known as a playwright in the Netherlands and one of his plays had even been staged. But on December 28, 1893, the French company Le Théâtre de l'Oeuvre caused a veritable sensation when it performed his play *Pelléas et Mélisande* at the Koninklijke Schouwburg in The Hague. Maeterlinck himself was present at this performance. Things did not go well in the theater that evening; the seats banged and the curtain kept clattering down. But neither these technical problems nor the shortcomings of the actors could detract from the performance of this avant-garde symbolist work, impressive in the extraordinary manner of speaking the lines and the stylized stage setting by the director Aurélien Lugné-Poë. The set consisted of a hanging tapestry designed by the painter Edouard Vuillard. The stage was empty save for a solitary chair. The actors wore long robes in drab colors and spoke their lines softly and in a singsong tone. The male protagonist, Pelléas, was played by an actress.[36]

Lugné and his Théâtre de l'Oeuvre played works from the French symbolist repertory for six years, but they also produced plays by Henrik Ibsen in a stylized setting with the emphasis on the power of expression and a sparse set. In this approach, Ibsen dramas were directed as symbolic representations of northern chill and silent people. Lugné and his company performed in the Netherlands several times. The three members of JOREKA were in ecstasy. Jan Kalf wrote that the drama had to be seen as the synthesis of all the arts in the "depiction of Life." In the stylized theater, he and Jolles again saw drama's sacred origins, a liturgy of ritualized acts and texts. The trio raised their voices in a plea for the resumption of the medieval miracle play. People turned against the prevailing practice in the Dutch theater of making cuts in plays, and against the rhetorical style of Dutch actors, for instance in their "shouting, quivering, hawking, and exaggerated rolling of their R's."[37] The sound was wrongly subordinated to expressiveness. Actors should stop trying to heighten their powers of expression with empty gestures.

In their critical distance from society as a whole, symbolists like Jolles and his JOREKA brethren were akin to another tendency in the theater in the Netherlands, the naturalism inspired by Emile Zola. But "whereas the naturalists sought a solution in involvement, the symbolists looked for it in distance." For as they perceived it, art was pure freedom and society sheer constraint. "They fled everyday existence and found one another in *chapelles*, closed circles where they read aloud from their own work, softly and liltingly, and shared their solitude. They replaced the grimy outside world of naturalism with the pure Idea, the crude facts with symbols, the moral with a refined, fickle beauty. They embodied the Mind."[38]

In the Dutch theater symbolism manifested itself in stylized drama that flourished around 1900 and expressly distanced itself from illusionist direction. It was also the cradle of original drama in Dutch. Young talents like Willem Royaards and Eduard Verkade sought inspiration in this dramatic school for their productions of the medieval morality play *Elckerlyc* (Everyman) and the medieval drama *Lanseloet van Denemarken*. In June 1907, they organized Summer Plays in Laren, a village in the Gooi district not far from Amsterdam, which had become an artists' colony. During a stay in England, Eduard Verkade, scion of a manufacturing dynasty from Zaandam, had become familiar with the ideas of the avant-gardist Edward Gordon Craig, in which realism was rejected. Craig himself came to the Netherlands in 1906 to oversee an exhibition of his stage sets in the *Rotterdamsche Kunstkring* (and because the famous dancer Isadora Duncan was in Noordwijk aan Zee, expecting his child). The artist Jan Verkade, Eduard's brother, who later became a Benedictine monk, designed the non-illusionist decor. Royaards and Verkade played the leads in *Elckerlyc*. "The harmonic unity in the acting, the anti-illusionist sets, the choice of the plays: it was all perceived as a revelation."[39]

After the Summer Plays, the artists had wanted to set up an *Elckerlyc* trust to enable

Performance of *Elckerlyc* during the summer drama festival in Laren in 1907.

Royaards and Verkade to pursue their quest in "the autonomy of theatrical art work."[40] But each was to go his own way. Royaards concentrated on the dramas of the Renaissance poet Joost van den Vondel, which, as we saw in chapter 1, were performed in a mammoth production. Verkade and his company *Die Hagespelers* (named after the *hageprekers* or field-preachers – Calvinists who preached in the open air to get round a church ban) put on stylized productions of George Bernard Shaw's *Candida* and Shakespeare plays. The *Hagespelers* spawned *Die Haghespelers*, a company based in The Hague that selected part of its repertoire from drawing-room comedies and is therefore regarded as the start of a typically Hague style of under-acting in Dutch theater history, of subtle and distinguished performance.[41]

Bourgeois patronage

Stylized theater, the consequence of a belief in the autonomy of the theatrical work of art, was a specific contribution to the life of the theater in the Netherlands around the turn of the century. It was a new proof of the elevation of art around 1900, which was a broader process and, as well as contemporary artistic ideals, also involved an improvement in the standard of the acting and repertoire, and a different approach on the part of audiences. These changes are typical of the ambitions of the bourgeois patrons of the time.

As the standard of musical life was raised, so, too, was that of the theater. The *Nederlands Toneelverbond* – an organization to promote the theater comparable to the 1829 society for the promotion of music, the *Maatschappij tot bevordering der Toonkunst* – was set up in 1870. It owed its existence to the eleventh Dutch Language and Literature Congress, which was held in the Belgian university city of Louvain in 1869, and where Jacob Nicolaas van Hall, a member of a prominent Amsterdam family, made a plea for better theater in both Belgium and the Netherlands. The Nederlands Toneelverbond, which he subsequently founded with the banker and man of letters Hendrik Schimmel, set itself the goal of gathering together theater-lovers in order to increase the skills of actors, encourage the writing of new plays, and give more attention to theater criticism. It also believed that there should be a decent theater in every town. The Toneelverbond succeeded in its aim of improving the standard of acting: under its auspices, a stage school was established in Amsterdam in 1874. This institution was financed by the Toneelverbond itself and also received a grant from King William III.[42]

Schimmel wanted to go beyond an umbrella organization. In 1876 he had set up a theater society, the *Vereniging "Het Nederlands Toneel,"* with the banker Abraham Wertheim and Gijs van Tienhoven, later a government minister and burgomaster of Amsterdam. This company was to put the ideas about the elevation of the theater into practice. Instead of a theater director, a cultural entrepreneur who was also responsible for earnings from the productions, there was a Board of Governors of well-to-do citizens, who were supposed to guarantee a degree of continuity. The Vereniging started in The Hague and was successful there. The king attended performances, and in 1881 granted the company the right to style itself "Koninklijke" or royal. In the Amsterdam Stadsschouwburg, where it acquired the sole right to put on plays, things went less well at first, but after 1882 the Koninklijke Vereniging started to garner the laurels for which it had been established: a Dutch variant of the great exemplar of national theater, the *Comédie Française*.[43] Eventually Schimmel's society became a burden to him. When he reached the age of seventy he found it difficult to keep pace with modern trends. In the 1889-1890 season, for instance, a contemporary piece, Ibsen's *The Wild Duck*, was put on against his will. When the Stadsschouwburg burned down in 1890 and the Koninklijke Vereniging had to move to a privately owned theater, he resigned.

Another common factor in the raising of the standard of both drama and music was the guest performances by the Meininger Hoftheater in Belgium and the Netherlands in 1880 and 1888. George II, Duke of Saxe-Meiningen, had gone to great lengths to achieve perfection in the performance of traditional and modern plays at his court; Ibsen's *Ghosts* had its German premiere in Meiningen. The theater introduced two reforms: an emphasis on ensemble playing rather than individual brilliance, and historically accurate or realistic sets. The court theater also put on performances outside The Hague and thus set a new standard in European theater. It appeared in Amsterdam in 1880, and in Rotterdam in 1888. The ensemble productions and the technical effects that the Meiningen players demonstrated so tellingly on the stage were swiftly adopted by the Dutch director Louis Crispijn senior.[44] He was to make his name with the *Nederlandse Toneelvereniging* in plays by Hauptmann, Ibsen, and Strindberg, and by the Dutch playwright Herman Heijermans.

The Dutch theater scene was dominated by large companies in "national" theaters, which had to contend with spiraling operating costs and with the desire of wealthy citizens to keep the pleasures of theater-going to themselves, while at the same time claiming that it was primarily good for other people. In the Netherlands' neighbor countries there was a movement in art theory, drama, and acting style that was turning away from the "official" theater culture. This was true of Paris, where alongside the Théâtre de l'Oeuvre we have referred to previously (the center of theatrical symbolism) there was also a Théâtre Libre promulgating new ideas about naturalistic theater. And it was true of a German example in Berlin, where the virtuoso stage director Max Reinhardt got his actors and actresses to rise above themselves to "mimetically gifted personalities."[45]

A focus on the provinces of North and South Holland can be discerned in the organization and spread of the theater in the Netherlands. The large companies had their bases in one of the major cities – Amsterdam, The Hague, or Rotterdam – each of which had a central theater, the center of an urban dramatic culture, as well as smaller theaters that put on the standard repertoire but often also presented the ideal venue for avant-garde drama. The Hague had the Koninklijke Haagse Schouwburg, the former court theater with two royal boxes and the home of the *Koninklijke Vereniging "Het Nederlands Toneel."* In Amsterdam, the Stadsschouwburg, once the leading theater in the Republic, had meanwhile acquired rivals in the Salon des Variétés, and the Van Lier brothers' Grand Théâtre. Since 1887 Rotterdam had had the Grote Schouwburg with a permanent company headed by Antoine Le Gras. He became known in the Netherlands and beyond as an innovator – as the first modern director to promote the individual study of the role rather than the tradition of the ideal-typical style of acting, which prescribed specific gestures and expressions for every sensation and emotion.[46] It gave the director the opportunity to demonstrate his skill and inspiration. In artistic terms, his function was upgraded at the expense of the traditional ascendancy of the management.

The Amsterdam Stadsschouwburg, which had burned to the ground on a freezing cold February night in 1890, reopened on September 1, 1894. The architects, A.E. van Gendt, Jan L. Springer, and J.B. Springer, had designed the new theater as a Renaissance-style building. A number of the twelve hundred or so seats were essentially unusable. The atmosphere of the old theater had been informal, whereas the new one was a "theater of status", where presence and eminence set the tone. For people of standing there were magnificent foyers, marble staircases, and luxurious boxes, but the cheap seats were very poorly served: hard wooden benches, and narrow aisles and stairs. New rules underlined the fact that the days of free and easy behavior in the theater were gone. Ladies were no longer allowed to wear hats in the auditorium, and the "serving of refreshments" during the performance was also outlawed.[47]

The Bouwmeesters, a theatrical dynasty

Around the turn of the century, the existing repertoire was dominated by drawing-room comedies and melodramas. Both had something of a French origin; France was the birthplace of boulevard theater. The import of this style was furthered in 1882, when the famous Parisian actress Sarah Bernhardt came to the Netherlands to play the title role in

Victorien Sardou's *Féodora*. This character was subsequently also played with great success by Theodora Bouwmeester, then known by her married name as Théo Frenkel-Bouwmeester, in a Dutch version in the Grand Théâtre in Amsterdam. "Down to the very lowest classes, everyone knew Doortje Frenkel. The factory girls and shop assistants, in short everyone who wanted to be 'chic,' imitated her hairstyle. 'Féodora hair' was all the rage. *She* was the Van Lier company. *She* was the theater in Amsterdam." Writers and reviewers were passionate in their praise of her.[48] Théo Bouwmeester also shone as Floria Tosca in *La Tosca*, a play by Sardou on which the libretto for Puccini's opera was based. She brought to the Dutch stage the genre with which "the divine Sarah" had earlier gained international recognition: the drawing-room romance of the "grande amoureuse."

Louis Bouwmeester in his starring role as Shylock.

pseudonym Ivan Jelakowitch. This was a resounding success. Heijermans became the writer in residence for the Nederlandse Toneelvereniging, which in 1898 staged his *Ghetto*, a drama about the oppressiveness of the individual stronghold and redemption in the certainty of humanism. He was a successful dramatist. "Of the one hundred and thirty-four plays produced by the Nederlandse Toneelvereniging between 1893 and 1906, thirty-four ran for more than twenty performances; seven of these were by Heijermans."[56] The response to his work can be explained by the attraction of his naturalist drama, which took place in recognizable neighborhoods and settings, was spoken in recognizable colloquial language, and demonstrated a huge talent for dramatic structure.

Heijermans scored his greatest success with his drama about Scheveningen fishermen, *Op hoop van zegen* (*The Good Hope*), which was premiered on Christmas Eve 1900 in the Hollandse Schouwburg in the Amsterdam entertainment district known as the Plantage. The cast had had to learn the piece at breakneck speed. The author delivered three acts on December 5, the fourth just a week before the premiere. The play deals with the confrontation between a callous shipowner and a fisherman's wife, Kniertje, who loses her husband and three sons. Those who saw it long remembered the quiet, touching dramatic intensity of the actress Esther de Boer as Kniertje, in the role of her life.[57] Five months later, the cast gave its hundredth performance. *Op hoop van zegen* not only became the drama of the social misery of the fishermen's existence but also synonymous with a specific image of Holland: it was the theatrical evocation of the picturesque and unspoiled.

Reading and visual culture

In 1901 a book titled *Dutch Life in Town and Country* was published in a British series, *Our Neighbors*. The author, P.M. Hough, talked about the culture of reading in the Netherlands, describing the Dutch as "cosmopolitan readers." The bookseller "is a man of education and judgment, who is well able to give his opinion on books and authors." In many cases he "is the trusted manager and guiding spirit of one or more 'Leesgezelschappen,' or 'Reading Societies'." The British author saw the reading society as the product of a very Dutch characteristic: domesticity.

> Family life is, indeed, the center from which the national virtues emanate, because there the individual members educate each other in the practice of personal virtue. … Club life in Holland is insignificant, and few clubs even attempt to create a substitute for home life; they are merely used for friendly intercourse for an hour or so every day, and as better-class restaurants. A Dutchman prefers to do his reading at home, in the domestic circle, with the members of his family, or in his study if he follows some scientific occupation, and his 'Leesgezelschap' affords him the opportunity of doing this.[58]

Hough wrote about a domestic reading culture which was on the point of changing at the precise moment he made his observations. The essentially closed character of the societies made way for the openness of the library or the café. The appetite for reading could henceforth also be satisfied in reading rooms and bookshops, which were either run commercially or charged a small admission fee without membership requirements. This also meant that literary creativity no longer flourished in the closed circle of the society, but moved to the regular table in the café. In the eighteenth century there had been a highly-developed club life in the Netherlands, but artists had had to manage without the aristocratic salons "à la française" and without the coffee houses that were the home of artistic diversion in England. It was the poets and painters and their followers of the generation of the Eighties Movement who discovered the café, the beer and the *vie bohème*.

Literary life increasingly took place in the public domain. Around 1900, art circles sprang up in the major cities – new institutions that brought together not only the creators and lovers of literature, but also those involved in the other arts (painting, sculpture, theater, and music). The prominent position of the individual societies was undermined by national organizations, which had admittedly been established long before, but now gained in importance at the expense of organizations with a local or regional range because of the increasing mobility of the public. They were primarily national societies of artists and art-loving citizens like the *Maatschappij voor Nederlandse Letterkunde* for literature or the *Maatschappij tot bevordering van de Toonkunst* for music. It was around 1900, moreover, that the first professional associations of publishers and authors were set up. The printers had already organized themselves in unions. This can be seen as a sign that "organized capitalism" in the form of national associations of workers and of employers had also reached the world of the book.

Printing explosion

Around 1900 the reading culture was influenced by a veritable "printing explosion."[59] This was the consequence of innovations in the making of paper and in the printing industry. The introduction of wood pulp and cellulose into paper manufacturing in about 1880 meant that prices fell by more than half and led to a significant increase in sales. In the same period, the manual press was replaced by, in turn, the platen press, the steam press, and the rotary press. The mechanization of typesetting was delayed for a long time by the high cost of new typesetting machines in contrast to the relatively low wages in the printing industry. This, too, changed around 1900. Wages started to rise, and the new typesetting machines became more reliable. From then on, printing technology made it possible to produce all sorts of printed information as mass and relatively cheap consumer items. Whereas in 1892, during the famous book fair in the Paleis for Volksvlijt in Amsterdam, it was the German industry that had led the way, at the Paris Exhibition of 1900, at the foot of the Eiffel Tower, the Grand Prix for printing was awarded to thirty Dutch publishers for the high standard of their products.[60] The modernization of the printing industry brought about a rise in the availability of books. The number of bookshops rose accordingly; in Haarlem, for instance, there were eleven in 1870 – by 1905 there were twenty-seven.[61]

The legacy of the eighteenth century included a reading culture embodied in reading societies and circulating libraries. One form – the literary society also known as the chamber of rhetoric – was entirely in the Enlightenment tradition: the members wanted to generate art through communal exercises. They read their poems or novels aloud to one another, and in due course also declaimed poetry and plays by other people on recitation evenings. They even formed dramatic societies of enthusiasts and amateurs. In the second half of the nineteenth century there must have been around eight hundred literary societies in towns and villages throughout the Netherlands. Amsterdam alone boasted no fewer than thirty-six declamatory societies.[62] Most of the chambers of rhetoric, gradually and not without internal debate, went down the amateur dramatics path.

In the case of the reading societies, the situation was different. These were groups of no more than fifty members, who clubbed together to buy books and then passed them around among themselves. It might sometimes be months before every member had read a book so that it could be discussed by the society. The reading societies did not build up collections. The books were sold to the members at the end of the year, and the money raised went toward purchasing new works. The circulating libraries, finally, did build up collections and had space for a reading table or reading room. To operate effectively they had to have a large number of members. Successful circulating libraries were consequently established in larger towns and cities. The one in Rotterdam was set up in 1859. In the eighteen-eighties it had more than eight hundred members, and it still exists today. The circulating library in Amsterdam was founded in 1800 and continued until 1933. In its peak years it had more than a thousand members.[63] There were even ladies' circulating libraries and reading rooms, spawned in part by the fact that women were excluded from the existing facilities and in part by a desire for education on the part of women from well-to-do circles.

Virtually all the readers who subscribed to the circulating library in Haarlem (1868-1914) read books in Dutch, French, German, and English. Dutch works accounted for fifty percent of the books borrowed, followed by French in second place at twenty percent. Novels and short stories were the most popular categories at the circulating libraries, and more than sixty percent of borrowings were books of this kind. Plays and poetry made up ten percent of the works taken out.[64] The members of the Haarlem reading society almost all came from the upper middle class. Although their levels of prosperity varied considerably, they read the same books and journals. Wealthy merchants and businessmen, and even more noticeably, rich shopkeepers, were underrepresented in the Haarlem society.[65]

New reading conventions

Major changes to the reading culture can be dated to the eighteen-eighties. They reflected the changes that the generation of the Eighties Movement had brought about in Dutch literature. Unlike that of the versifying preachers, their poetry was intended to be read, not recited aloud. In 1895 one of them, Frans Coenen, stated that it was his "firm conviction" that verses should not be spoken because "the sound of the strange voice is an element that is added but does not belong." Anyone who nonetheless wanted to declaim must, above all, "not try to do it beautifully."[66] The poetry written by the creative members was recited less and less frequently in the chambers of rhetoric and reading societies.

Around 1900 their place at the lectern was taken by "elocutionists," who might or might not have been professionally trained, and who traveled the country giving "declamatory soirées" for a fee. Their repertoire consisted of "canonized Dutch texts from Vondel to Potgieter," the work of contemporary Dutch authors, particularly those of the Eighties Movement, and "a goodly number of texts translated from English and French, and also recited in those languages."[67]

The conventions in reading behavior also started to change in the eighteen-eighties. The better booksellers tried to attract customers with a reading circle of Dutch and foreign literature. The publisher Arie Kruseman exploited a collection of more than 12,000 volumes in this way. The Haarlem shop libraries that were associated with a renowned bookstore had a collection that was not so very different from what the Haarlem circulating library or the Haarlem reading society had to offer. There were also store libraries that specialized in horror stories and sensational novels, and in pornography. They were the place to borrow "cheap novelettes" of all kinds.

The best known and also the oldest library in the Netherlands was that of the *Maatschappij tot Nut van 't Algemeen*, a society for the promotion of the public good. "It would not be exaggerating to say that this library taught the Dutch people to read."[68] This society was a pioneer of popular education. Around 1900 it had more than three hundred branches aiming at the lower middle class and the workers because they seemed most susceptible to the pernicious influence of the thriller or the French novel. At first these libraries filled their shelves with instructive works, but in the course of the nineteenth century they also admitted Multatuli's books. However, the Haarlem branch, in any event, drew the line at the novels of Emile Zola and Lodewijk van Deyssel.[69]

Alongside the libraries run by the Society for the Promotion of the Public Good, the second half of the nineteenth century saw the emergence of libraries for the working class. The people behind these initiatives came from orthodox Protestant or Catholic circles. There were also libraries and reading rooms for the working class that were associated with a factory or a trade union. One variant was the "news reading room," a place where readers could get the latest news and stock exchange prices from, for instance, the daily *De Telegraaf*, which had been founded in 1893. The store libraries referred to earlier were run on a purely commercial basis and their stock was dictated solely by demand. Consequently, although these libraries played no role in the education of the working class, they can be seen as an indicator of the popularity of titles.

Around 1900, the private reading societies and circulating libraries found themselves facing competition from the *Openbare Leeszaal & Bibliotheek* – an institution that had the concept of public access in its very name. The first of these public libraries and reading rooms in the Netherlands was established in Dordrecht in 1899, following the example of the Free Public Library in England and the Bücher- und Lesehallen in Germany. It was this institution, too, that was to put an end to the existence of local and more or less notable reading societies. The establishment of a public library had become possible because its promoters believed that a distinction between closed reading societies and libraries for the working class could no longer be justified. The *Openbare Leeszaal & Bibliotheek* spread throughout the country, although to establish one there always had to be a committee of recommendation made up of prominent citizens who were dedicated

The reading desk in a café-restaurant.

to the culture of reading. By 1907 there were public libraries in six cities: Dordrecht had been followed by Groningen, Leeuwarden, The Hague, Rotterdam, and Utrecht. Amsterdam did not get its public library until 1919. The "library movement" was given a boost when it was awarded a one-time government grant in 1907. A year later a central association was set up to promote the spread of libraries nationwide.[70]

The publisher Leo Simons's initiative to create a "world library" of good and affordable reading matter can be seen as another facet of this endeavor to educate the working class. Leo Simons (1862-1932), the son of a prosperous Jewish merchant in Amsterdam, moved in social liberal circles and in the world of the working men's institutes – the earliest form of social work. In 1904 he was the editor at a Haarlem publishing house, which among other things was responsible for the publications of the Society for the Promotion of the Public Good. Simons edited a series of reformist brochures under the title *Studies in Volkskracht*; studies in popular power that could serve as the basis for reforms aimed at activating the physical and intellectual potential of the people.[71] In 1905, with financial backing from the Mees family, who were bankers in Rotterdam, and the Zeeland lumber merchant Floor Wibaut, he set up a society for good and affordable books, the *Maatschappij voor Goede en Goedkoope Lectuur*, better known as the *Wereldbibliotheek*, or world library. Simons had taken the idea from European examples like *Reklams Universal-Bibliothek* in Germany, Dent's Everyman's Library in England and the *Bibliothèque Nationale* in France. He had hoped that the social democrat Wibaut would help him to edit the works they published, but Wibaut preferred to concentrate on local politics. In 1913 Nico van Suchtelen came to assist Simons. He had gained experience in the adult institute in the port of Schiedam and in the colony at Walden. The world library published literary works (with a particular predilection for the Renaissance poet Vondel) and, especially for young people, a "dramatic library," books on geography and ethnology, history, and sociology.

Visual culture

A new medium emerged around 1900. It began in the fairground and then underwent an artistic ascent: it was film. The first forms of "living photographs" were shown in the towns and cities, in the variety theaters and in traveling movie shows. Film was a new visual medium, and the setting in which it was found offered numerous new ways to view it: from stereoscopic (three-dimensional) peepshows to panoramas. The movie was "living photography." Photography itself, meanwhile, had become an accepted part of everyday life.

Photographs taken in 1900 still revealed a certain stagnation. The technique of photography was by now half a century old, but photographers still had to take their time over their shots. Exposure times were still on the long side, even in the studio, although they had been brought down to eight or ten seconds thanks to such technical innovations as electric lights and more sensitive film. Portraiture was a particularly popular genre in photography. This had derived from portrait painting and still bore a great many similarities to it. People still had to pose for the camera, albeit not for so long. The setting could likewise be made to suit. Photographers of this period created romantic woodland scenes, garden backdrops or palace interiors in their studios as required. The portraits could be kept in photograph albums, like photographic exhibitions in miniature, and this caused a veritable craze for fashionable formats, hinges, locks and ornamentations.

Portrait photography was in fact a democratization of self-presentation, which had previously been the province of an aristocratic or bourgeois elite. Now the lower middle classes could also have themselves portrayed in a setting they deemed appropriate. It was not only individuals who had their portraits taken; there were family and group portraits too. Posing for a photograph became an indispensable part of rituals in people's lives, particularly weddings and funerals. Men called up for military service had their photograph taken in uniform. Death was also the subject of photography. The portrait of the deceased could be used on the *in memoriam* card that was sent out.

Another very popular genre around 1900 was the cityscape. A striking feature of this field is the extent to which artists and photographers influenced one another. Like their painted equivalents, the earliest photographs of towns and villages convey a feeling of tranquility. Architecture and space were the main components: moments in time in streets and squares where the figures have been frozen into immobile symbols. But as photography advanced, the static image of the city became a dynamic street scene, and painted cityscapes became more vibrant and lively.

Two pioneers played an important role in that process. One was the Amsterdam carpenter Jacob Olie (1834-1905), who took his camera and tripod all over the city in the last

George Hendrik Breitner, the Gelderse Kade in Amsterdam.

quarter of the nineteenth century. On hundreds of glass plates he systematically recorded Amsterdam's streets, the vitality of its residents and the events that took place in the capital. The other was the painter George Hendrik Breitner, who both photographed and painted city views in Rotterdam and Amsterdam. He was following the example of the author Emile Zola, who was also a keen photographer. Zola took thousands of pictures of Paris, particularly of the boulevards, of servant girls crossing the road, and of rainy weather, when the passers-by and their umbrellas were reflected in the wet sidewalks.[72] This was to be the source of Breitner's inspiration too. But he added images of the construction work going on in Amsterdam: the toiling workhorses and laborers, the pile-drivers and the construction sites.[73] Breitner was not the only one. Another painter who developed into a remarkable photographer was Willem Witsen, who left, among other things, magnificent portraits of the literary figures and artists of the Eighties generation.

A third category was that of art photography. This was a movement that started in Germany and had a major influence on photographers in the Netherlands whose work reflected the values of painting. Johann Georg Hameter and Carl Emil Mögle, both originally from Germany and educated there, led the way for their Dutch colleagues in aesthetic photography. Hameter became known for his striking panoramic photos with huge skies that he took in the port of Rotterdam in the eighteen-eighties. Mögle was an emphatically realistic portrait and landscape photographer, who was also involved in setting up an infrastructure of professional associations in the Netherlands. The English "picturalist" movement also had a visible influence on the work of a new generation of photographers, who started to emerge in the last decade of the nineteenth century. They abandoned the recognizable depiction of objects and people, and concentrated on atmospheric impressions and shades of light. They gathered in clubs and associations, and in 1904 organized the first international salon of art photography in the Pulchri Studio in The Hague.[74]

Another new departure was the portrait photo for police purposes. In Amsterdam this task was officially entrusted around the turn of the century to M.H. Laddé. He is also acknowledged, however, as the producer of the earliest known Dutch movie *De gestoorde Hengelaar* (The Disturbed Angler). It was probably made in the fall of 1896 in the studio set up by M.H. Laddé and his partner Johannes W. Merkelbach. The client was a fairground operator who traveled around with a "kinematograph," a sort of movie projector. The showing of these "Living Photographs" caused a sensation at fairs and as an act in the vaudeville theaters.[75] The greatest surprise provided by this new medium, however, was the film of the inauguration of Queen Wilhelmina in 1898. Watching it gave people the feeling that "for a few moments they had been among the cheering crowds in Dam Square." Until 1902, films in which the Queen played the starring role accounted for a third to a half of the moving pictures in the Netherlands.[76] The rest were current events, films of nature, pictures from distant lands (travelogues), and comedy acts derived from vaudeville.

From 1907 onward, moving pictures were presented in a different way: as a whole evening's show in a theater. The first show took place in the Grand Théâtre in Amsterdam under the French title *Pathé Frères*. The dedicated "Bioscope Theater" soon followed. One thing that these places had in common was their low access threshold – they were much less intimidating than the concert halls and serious theaters. There was no code of conduct in the bioscope, no particular dress was required, and there were no age restrictions. Moreover, there was often no fixed starting time, which also encouraged audiences. Such accessibility also increased the significance of the movie as a democratic instrument of general education. This was recognized during the decade, both in the call for the censorship of the movies that were shown and pessimistic prognostications about the new visual culture, and in approval and endorsement. In September 1913 a socialist movie house, the Rode Bioscoop, opened in Amsterdam after the socialist leader Ferdinand Domela Nieuwenhuis had said, "I tell you that a Bioscope which shows historical events, scenes with a socialist moral, shots of workers' strikes or other events from the workers' movement – and then with an appropriate commentary – has a future."[77]

The Netherlands was open to films from all over the world. Productions from the United States and neighboring countries in Europe dominated movie house programs. Because the movies were silent, language problems could be solved by Dutch titles or by the commentator. Filmmaking got going in the Netherlands itself after 1910. The pioneers Willy and Albert Mullens ("Albert Frères") and Maurits Binger's new movie studio *Hollandia* started work, initially specializing in films about the picturesque aspects of Holland – windmills, dikes, and dramas set in fishing communities.[78]

The Dutch receptiveness to foreign productions did, however, delay the rise of good quality domestic movies until the between-war years. Whereas in countries like

A French film crew shooting a scene from the film *Le Calvaire du Mousse,*
or The Agony of the Ship's Boy, in Volendam, 1912.

Germany, France, Italy, and Russia there was a lively movie culture, in which writers and
artists also took an interest, the Dutch press essentially ignored the merits of the medium.
Stage personalities did not involve themselves in movie production – with the exception
of Louis Bouwmeester, whose appearances in movies and on movie theater stages met
with a mixed reaction. Because it did not have the support of the country's own artists
and intellectuals, Dutch movie culture lagged behind its neighbors, and it was not until
the nineteen-thirties, with the arrival of German directors fleeing Nazi Germany and the
establishment of an artistic film society, the Filmliga, that some of this lost ground was
made up.[79]

"La Bohème"

In the summer of 1883, during the international colonial exhibition in Amsterdam, an
orchestra from Berlin performed in the bandstand which, like the exhibition grounds
themselves, was lit by electric light. Afterwards Lodewijk van Deyssel, who witnessed
the event, wrote that this concert had raised "the series of carnival and Foreign impressions to a constant yet diverse source of delight." He concluded from this "that the best
part of the life of a city-dweller was the Festivity, that the consumption of wine and

strong liquor and the state of mind it engendered was the best part of the Festivity and that, unconcerned by the crowds of people amongst whom one lived outside the Festivity, colorful, loud, extravagant and hence attention-seeking behavior was the supreme attitude to life."[80]

The author Lodewijk van Deyssel is an inexhaustible source of information when it comes to describing the bohemian life in the fin de siècle, particularly in Amsterdam. Cities offered every opportunity. The nightlife, the focus of the bohemian existence, was stimulated by the introduction and spread of electric light. High spirits were stimulated by the proliferation of nightclubs serving the new drink: Bavarian beer.

The bohemian life was already familiar shorthand for an artist's existence in the second half of the nineteenth century before it was immortalized in Giacomo Puccini's opera La Bohème. It had its Dutch premiere in 1897, when the Italian Opera staged it in The Hague. The story of the poor young woman, Mimi, whose lover, the poet Rodolfo, brings her into the loving circle of a poverty-stricken group of artists in Paris, struck a chord with Hans Goedkoop, the biographer of the playwright Herman Heijermans. He placed his hero among the artists and writers who, around the turn of the century, felt drawn by the fate of "la femme perdue," the fallen woman. Heijermans himself had a relationship with Marie Peers, a "chanteuse" who was working in the vaudeville theaters in and around the Nes in Amsterdam when he got to know her. "Multatuli gave advice and assistance to women who were in danger of sinking beneath themselves or helped them to get a job. Vincent van Gogh took care of the pregnant Sien Hoornik, who walked the streets in winter in The Hague to get money ("you know how"), wanted to marry her, and used her as his model. Frederik van Eeden got to know the prostitute and morphine addict, Jeanne Fontaine, was at her side when she died, and wrote about the experience in Johannes Viator. Frans Coenen, a writer of the same generation, had an affair with a waitress, Mientje van Breda, did his utmost to introduce her into better circles, and described his failure in Bezwaarlijke liefde (Troublesome Love)."[81]

The illuminated night

The old oil lamps on posts with which, since the Golden Age, the citizen of a Dutch town "full of self-satisfaction, saw his streets lit at night, made way for the brilliant invention of gas lighting which makes the night an extended day, and in turn is probably threatened by the even more brilliant electricity."[82] The first electrical systems were installed in stores and offices in about 1880, not so much for economic or utilitarian reasons as for advertisement and crowd pulling. Electric light caused a sensation. The "example of the progressive businessman" was rapidly followed, and companies were formed to produce electricity at one central site – the "central station electric generating plant." The earliest customers were chiefly offices, stores, hotels, restaurants, and societies, which used electricity to light the interiors and facades of their buildings. On a modest scale, private individuals also started to install electric light.

A certain Willem B. Smit had founded the first factory designing and producing dynamos in Slikkerveer near Rotterdam. At the end of 1883 one of these was installed in the Grand Hotel Coomans in Rotterdam, where the interior was lit with a hundred and

The Nightly Evacuation of the Clubs (?) in Amsterdam.
"Police (Warmoesstraat side) ordering: Everyone out! Drunks (Damrak side) enticing:
Everyone in!" De Amsterdammer, February 14, 1897.

thirty lamps of thirty-five candle-power and an arc lamp lit up the front of the hotel from dusk until one in the morning. The system worked and the public was fascinated. The factory in Slikkerveer also supplied dynamos for the Central Station in Amsterdam (originally powering twenty-six arc lamps) and the new prisons in Scheveningen, Breda, and Arnhem (each with two hundred and fifty incandescent lamps).[83] The next phase was the scaling-up of the electricity supply. Whole city districts could be supplied with power thanks to the invention of an ex-naval officer from Russia, Achilles de Khotinsky, who in 1884, with the backing of some Rotterdam businessmen, founded an electricity company that bore his name. At first the electricity was used solely to power the lighting in public places, but around 1890 the first experiments were conducted with an electric tram.

City life, both day and night, was also enlivened by the invention of "bottom fermentation beer," which was a definite improvement in terms of quality on the top fermentation beers customarily made in the Netherlands. It was a specialty of the breweries in Bavaria. This light version, lager, quickly became known as "gentleman's beer" to distinguish it from the top fermentation, dark "workman's beer." A change in the levying of excise duty on beer meant that, from the eighteen-sixties on, "Bavarian beer" could also be brewed in the Netherlands. When the difference in price between the two was reduced, there was a rise in the consumption of lager in the Netherlands. "Bavarian" breweries were built in the towns and cities. The first to switch to the production of lager after 1867 was the *Koninklijke Nederlandsche Beijersch Bierbrouwerij*, but the most important was to be the firm run by Gerard Adriaan Heineken, who had owned the brewery known as De Hooiberg in Amsterdam since 1863. In 1870 he switched to the production of "Bavarian beer," which he brewed using a modern cooling technique.[84]

Bavarian beer became the hallmark of the German beer houses that flourished in the Netherlands in the eighteen-eighties. In Amsterdam, many of these establishments were to be found on Warmoesstraat. There "by the will of foreign barbarian beer barons, the last little private dwellings, butcher's shops and shoe stores were swept away so that the full depth of the house could be turned into long, thin beer saloons."[85] The area around the Hotel Krasnapolsky became the capital's beer center and was nicknamed Little Munich. The Bavaria bar was the finest of them all. It was also the center of drinking and conversation for intellectual and artistic Amsterdam. "After a performance by the Wagner Society, one would see Henri Viotta there, dining with famous Wagner singers, and on Friday evenings there would be the gray-haired Verhulst consuming his fish supper." As well as the celebrated artists' tables, there was the "Aldermen's Table," where the burgomaster, Gijs van Tienhoven, sometimes sat, the "Professors' Table," and the students' table.[86]

Non-conformism

As early as the first half of the nineteenth century artists in the major Western European countries had made a habit – alone or in groups – of setting themselves apart by refusing to conform. The movement was fueled by resistance to what they saw as the hidebound views that governed the training at the art academies. They gave the artistic calling a radical image. In the Netherlands this phenomenon among artists did not occur to the same extent, primarily because, thanks to the absence of an official art canon, one major cause for rebellion was lacking. Painters sometimes sported long hair and a beard "because that hair and that beard are a sign proclaiming that this gentleman is a romantic and poetic man." The same had applied to the literary generation of 1840 among the students in Leiden. "Oh black time! Oh, those good old days when we had long hair and were so deeply calamitous," wrote one of them, Johannes Kneppelhout, later.[87]

With the arrival of the literary generation of the Eighties Movement, the image of the artist changed. An eyewitness like Gijsbert Hondius van den Broek, an erudite citizen from the wealthy community of Driebergen, who was a friend of the composer Alphons Diepenbrock, criticized them at a performance of Diepenbrock's music in the Concertgebouw in Amsterdam. "Literature let its hair down! There were people walking around demonstrating their love of beauty by a filthy appearance: uncombed hair, dirty jacket, no collar."[88] Writers later recalled the importance of cafés and beer houses in the political and artistic life of Amsterdam. Frans Erens wrote about "that jawing" in all sorts of rooms in the new district known as De Pijp, in the coffee rooms of the Hotel Krasnapolsky or the Poort van Cleve, or in cafés like the Mille Colonnes on Rembrandtplein. "How we talked and how I talked! What I argued, declared, defended, demolished! This was how the new ideas about literature and other arts were born; they bubbled up on all sides." The painter Isaac Israëls came to the capital from The Hague and the painter and photographer George Hendrik Breitner came from Rotterdam. "And they sat with the literary men in the bars in the evenings and jawed, as it was called, even though it is an ugly word. The birth of the new concepts in art took place in Amsterdam, as it had in Paris, in all sorts of cafés and bars."[89]

This generation of poets, writers, and painters, and their hangers-on was the first to want to try to achieve a special status for the creators of art. Now that art was independent, now that it found its justification in itself, the artist had also become a unique figure – priest or prophet of a self-willed community. The freedoms of an ideal society were possible in a republic of letters, with free love paramount. "The outside world would have to recognize this new status. And, felt some, fund it." This ambition was unprecedented in the Netherlands. Very few people, most of them in the immediate circle of the new elite, proved to be prepared to guarantee the living expenses of some artist or other. Moreover, the heightened sense of life, so typical of the fin de siècle, spawned not only eccentric expressions in their work, but sometimes also eccentric behavior, deliberate or involuntary. "The new spiritual freedom, for which the toll of poverty had to be paid, the isolated position, caused tension – sometimes creative tension – that degenerated into nervous exhaustion."[90]

George Breitner was attracted to Amsterdam by the call of the Bohemians, and by its "grand picturesqueness." As a budding artist in Rotterdam, the city where he was born, he had looked for his subjects in the docks because things were chaotic there, and the place was bustling. This, for him, was where the picturesque lay. In Amsterdam he became fascinated, like his fellow-artist Isaac Israëls, by the reality of urban construction, by the excavations and scaffolding, by the buzz of the city and the horse trams in the squares, by the servant girls and whores along the canals. Breitner wanted to picture city life itself, become the painter of the people. Like so many of his generation, he took his lead from Zola's social novels. He shifted the style and themes of Zola's Parisian examples to Amsterdam, so that the German painter Max Liebermann later remarked that Breitner had "Parisized" Amsterdam.[91] Isaac Israëls chose the same subjects for his images of the city, but in them he never disavowed his past as a Hague-born connoisseur. In time he also became the portrait painter to the "beau monde." Nonetheless, in the words of the art critic Jan Veth, they both depicted "how the turbulent life of the big city burns, flares and then sweeps away time and again before our eyes" and portrayed it "as it can strike the feverish viewer walking through the streets and squares with intense impressions."[92]

Café chantant

France, particularly Paris, was not only the model for painters of city life like Breitner and Israëls, it was also the source of inspiration for new forms of popular theater. In the Second Empire the *café concert* had emerged as amusement both for the urban bourgeoisie and the working class. It blended two traditional forms of dining and music: the combination of drinking and singing in the café and the private entertainment club in the *caveau*, the cellar, where all sorts of topical songs were performed – entertaining rather than satirical, although in times of cultural repression they could be regarded as a threat to public order. In the *café concert* the new form of singing developed into a *tour de chant* but there were also entr'actes of acrobats and dancers. Eventually this circus formula found its home in the music hall, of which the Folies-Bergère (established in 1869) was to become the most famous. The reviews were staged in spectacular fashion, creating a magical impression with the new electric lighting and the clever use of mirrors. The spectacle of the performances was heightened by the "chansons sensuelles" and by the performances of "les girls," an American expression that betrayed Paris's collective love for all things American.[93]

It was in the *café concert* that the singer and lyricist Aristide Bruant began to perform his *chansons réalistes*. He sang about the rise of French colonialism, and about the seamier side of Parisian life. In this setting they were given a hearing, but not taken too seriously.[94] In 1884 he moved to the cabaret Le Chat Noir, which was opened by the businessman Rodolphe Salis in November 1881 at the foot of Montmartre in Paris. At this time, cabaret was entertainment for an artistic elite. Le Chat Noir was decorated in medieval style in line with the prevailing Parisian fashion for "gothic taverns." Authors appeared and gave readings from their works, alongside *chansonniers*, of whom Bruant was to become the most famous. From 1882 on, Le Chat Noir published a satirical weekly of the same name, which rapidly became very popular, even outside Paris, and made a decisive contribution to the creation of the image of the romantic artists' quarter of Montmartre ("a granite breast that fed a generation of poets thirsting after Beauty").[95]

It was not just France that set the tone in the Netherlands; Germany was influential too. Around the turn of the century, on the Montmartre model, cabaret of a high standard developed from the *tingeltangel*, the German variant of the *café chantant*. Three pioneers introduced it almost simultaneously. In Berlin, Ernst, Baron von Wolzogen established a literary salon cabaret, the Bunte Theater, in which actors performed the numbers and

Structure for the *International Hotel and Travel exhibition* on Museum Square in Amsterdam, 1895.

songs like "aristocratic dilettantes." A second pioneer was the young actor Max Reinhardt, whose Schall und Rauch or "hollow words" focused much more on political satire than Von Wolzogen. The third initiative was found in the artists' quarter of Schwabing in Munich, where artists and writers formed a troupe, the Elf Scharfrichter or Eleven Executioners, who presented a cynical cabaret that sometimes verged on the macabre.[96]

In the Netherlands the *café concert* was known as the *café chantant*: these were places where initially only female artistes performed for an audience composed exclusively of men. People smoked, drank, and laughed during the acts of singers and dancers. In the last quarter of the nineteenth century, the *café concert* or music hall developed into full-scale places of entertainment – variety theaters. The difference between café and theater was that in the former it was the buffet that was all-important, while in the latter what was happening on the stage took precedence. The French examples of entertainment were very soon imitated in the Netherlands, in such institutions as the Koninklijk Nederlandsch Circus Oscar Carré by the Amstel river in Amsterdam, which in 1896 was putting on not just circus programs but variety too, or in the reviews of Henri ter Hall, at first in Arnhem, later also in the Circustheater in Rotterdam, which, with the theaters in and around Coolsingel, acquired a reputation as the true city of varieties in the Netherlands. Of the one hundred and ninety-two variety artistes working in 1910, fifty-five lived in Amsterdam, fifty-five elsewhere, but mostly in The Hague, and eighty-two lived in Rotterdam. "International artistes came ashore there and found a specialized little world of agents, transport companies, artistes' boarding houses, ticket printers and artistes' cafés."[97]

Cabaret

The most significant import from the European entertainment scene, though, was the cabaret. Le Chat Noir became known in the Netherlands through Frans Erens's glowing reports and a guest performance, in 1895, by the ensemble led by Rodolphe Salis in the Grand Théâtre in Amsterdam. In August 1902, Von Wolzogen's *Überbrettl* appeared, followed two months later, also under the name *Überbrettl*, by the troupe led by Baron Oskar von Fielitz. He was later arrested in Germany for insulting the German Kaiser, an offence he was alleged to have committed during a performance in Scheveningen. In 1903 an "Original Münchener Überbrettl" came to the Netherlands. It featured Mary Irber, the woman on whom Frank Wedekind based his play *Lulu*. *Überbrettl* became the jargon in the business for this importing of the themes and forms of the new German cabaret.

The Dutch version came into being in 1895. On the occasion of an international exhibition of the hotel and travel industry in Amsterdam, a nightclub was opened in the new district of the city known as De Pijp. Eduard Jacobs, born in 1868 into a family of Jewish musicians, was employed on August 19, 1895 to stand in for the regular pianist. He sang songs as well and, after repeated applause, "in a fit of exuberance, took a tray from the serving table and went round with it, collecting money, as was customary in the café chantant at that time." This event and this date have been immortalized as the birth of Dutch cabaret.[98] The house belonged to Abraham Michael Herzberg, who had fled from Latvia to the Netherlands in 1882 to escape the pogroms. He lived with his family on the second floor; the long, narrow room at street level was turned into a place of entertainment. Attracted by the success of his business, other bars and clubs soon opened in the neighborhood.[99]

Herzberg's club, which went through various incarnations as the *Wapen van Habsburg*, *De Kuil* and *De Sfinx*, became a regular cabaret. The walls were decorated with brightly colored posters, most of them by Jules Chéret. At first, Jacobs sang mainly chansons, but increasingly turned to Dutch songs. He wanted to bear witness in his songs and concentrated on the enunciation of his lyrics. The cabaret in Montmartre was his reference, the singer Bruant his model. "He stood, half-bent, in front of the piano on which he accompanied himself and, half declaiming as it were, snarled his lessons about life at the room."[100] His lyrics were raw and crude because realism was on the rise. "Our singing Zola rapidly became the idol of Amsterdam's artistic and student population." The full-fledged and half-baked intellectuals were joined by the prostitutes from the neighborhood, who came to listen to Jacobs singing about their hardships. "One can say without exaggeration that everyone who aspired to the gilded youth of the Netherlands between 1895 and 1904 sat at least once on the rickety chairs in *De Kuil*, listening to Jacobs."[101]

The singer Koos Speenhoff was the Rotterdam version of this success. He began his career at Circus Pfläging in Rotterdam. The Rotterdam Circus, like the Carré in

Cabaret star Eduard Jacobs in one of his bars in Amsterdam, 1900.

Amsterdam, had abandoned its original purpose and become one of the six leading variety theaters in the Netherlands.[102] Speenhoff discovered his true calling as a cabaret singer at the Tivoli Theater in Rotterdam in December 1902, when he sang songs and accompanied himself on the guitar. A reviewer saw in him "one of those Montmartre singers" with "the charming appeal of the new," while the prominent journalist Marie Joseph Brusse praised this "Montmartre on the Meuse" in the daily *Nieuwe Rotterdamse Courant*.[103] The matinees were continued in 1903 and started to attract ever larger audiences.

Speenhoff was the first person in the Netherlands to specialize in songs about the social and political issues of the day. "There was essentially no competition. The comics and humorists of his early days did occasionally come out with a topical joke, but they anxiously guarded against any risk of offending the 'esteemed ladies and gentlemen' in the audience and skated safely over the surface." Without this topicality Speenhoff would not have been able to come up with the extensive and always new repertoire that his almost continuous returns to the same theaters demanded.

Around the turn of the century, Speenhoff was part of the bohemian scene in Rotterdam, as was the painter Kees van Dongen. "In the Aert van Nesstraat, where Speenhoff lived in poverty in a room next door to a smithy from which the smell of burning hooves emanated, he was all too happy to live the romantic aspects of Puccini's highly

Koos Speenhoff (far left) with his cabaret during a tour of the armed forces, 1914.

popular opera *La Bohème* (1896)." It was here that the Dutch satirical magazine, *De ware Jacob*, was produced in emulation of Le Chat Noir. Speenhoff, Van Dongen and their friends were fascinated by the seamy side of the big city. "The disconsolate horses on the quay; the restless café chantant with its melancholy gaiety and dim light; the sailors, the prostitutes, and not the proletariat." They experienced "that wonderful feeling of being at once familiar with and afraid of the strange, the fascination of the melancholic, which they themselves could remain outside, but in which they could wallow."[104]

15

Retrospect

On August 5, 1914, the day after the German army had invaded Belgium, thus violating its neutrality, Willem Hendrik de Beaufort had to go to The Hague for consultations in Parliament on the statement to be issued by the Dutch government. He left his estate Den Treek at Leusden by car on this occasion, because all his horses but one had been requisitioned by the military authorities as part of a general mobilization. The liberal De Beaufort, former minister for foreign affairs and a member of Parliament, could not be and did not wish to be exempted from this measure. In Utrecht he deposited some shares and other valuables before taking the train to The Hague. At the station the internist Professor S. Talma spoke to him: "I expect you're also entirely confident that we'll be left out of it." De Beaufort recorded his answer in his diary. "I told him that I was not entirely confident, which appeared to amaze him."[1]

The assassination of the heir to the Habsburg monarchy by a Serbian nationalist in Sarajevo, which sparked off World War I, resounds in so many memoirs of the summer of 1914 like a bolt from the blue. With hindsight it was seen as marking the end of the "world of yesterday." It resounded in the Netherlands too. De Beaufort's horses, not only a useful means of transport but a sign of bourgeois affluence, had already been taken away because of the rapid mobilization of the armed forces. But there was a new vehicle in which the journey to the city could be made: the car. De Beaufort was less sure about the outcome than Professor Talma. The latter did not doubt that Dutch neutrality would be respected, while the former, having been minister for foreign affairs, might well have been aware that the military polarization at that time between the various alliances was sweeping away the old European certainties. Both were proved right. The course of World War I was a vindication of the Dutch policy of armed neutrality. But its effects were felt in the Netherlands as well. A flood of hundreds of thousands of refugees from Belgium washed over the southern border in the fall of 1914. And the wave of democratization, the price Europe paid for years of service in the trenches by a whole generation, did not stop at Holland's eastern border in 1918, although it did not take the form of a revolution.

The outbreak of World War I marks a finishing point, an opportunity to look back on the decades around 1900. In this retrospective view we want to answer two questions that arise from what we have written above. Both have a paradoxical element. In what ways does Dutch culture around 1900 reflect the general European sense of decadence and degeneration? How does that sense relate to a climate in the Netherlands that was so marked by renewed self-awareness and belief in progress? And furthermore, how tenable has the thesis of a specific culture of discussion, which was described in the first volume of this series as characteristic of the Republic of 1650, proved to be in an era governed more by intense antitheses: secularization on the one hand and a successful counteroffensive by the orthodox on the other?

Degeneration

The high point of bourgeois culture around 1900 continues to be a fascinating topic a hundred years later. In his 1999 novel *Publieke Werken* (Public Works) Thomas Rosenboom paints a picture of urban expansion and thriving culture shortly before the turn of the century. The central figure, the violin maker Vedder, looks out from his small house on Prins Hendrikkade in Amsterdam on Central Station as it nears completion. The huge building blocks his view of the IJ estuary and the fishing boats that used to moor practically at his front door. But before long the funnels of ocean liners tower over the station; these ships depart again with amazing rapidity because their cargo and passengers are brought and taken away by train. Vedder realizes the importance of new traffic flows: he puts forward proposals for a "West Radial" which will lead traffic westwards out of the city. This will involve clearing a way across the canals by demolishing houses behind the Royal Palace and linking up with a filled-in canal, Rozengracht. Traffic developments mean that his own house is now in a crucial location: isn't the corner of the quay and the new boulevard, Damrak, the perfect spot for a hotel? And the Victoria Hotel is indeed built on the site of the houses of Vedder's neighbors, and his own house would have gone too if he hadn't ruined the negotiations for its sale. The hotel does not wait for him; it goes up in record time, next to, behind and above him. The colossal fin-de-siècle building has clutched Vedder's narrow house in one of its forepaws ever since.

Rosenboom also describes the new temples to the arts in the southern extension to Amsterdam, the Rijksmuseum (1885) and the Concertgebouw (1888), with a large green space between them. "Once past Leidseplein, it quickly became quieter in the street. The city began to unravel at its hem and after the passage beneath the Rijksmuseum – still only four years old and, like Central Station, built by Cuypers with the look yet again of a monastery – appeared the overwhelmingly white, brand-new Concertgebouw, still coming as a surprise, not within the built-up area, surging up like an island, an unapproachable chalk cliff, from the vast empty plain before it, the glacis of the latest bastion of the arts, the proscenium of a higher stage, all framed by the night and the fathomless depths of the country behind it."[2]

Strangely enough, the initial phase of this flourishing had been accompanied by doubt and anxiety. The dream of steel, steam and electricity was undermined by concern that there must be a price to pay for this affluence. Wasn't growth and expansion a form of exploitation that ravaged man and his environment, leaving behind bare land for sickened future generations? These doubts were fueled by the reality of an urban proletariat huddled together in ever greater numbers in filthy quarters. Wretched housing and poor hygiene combined with prostitution and crime ensured that city districts revealed the specter of degeneration that so obsessed contemporaries at the end of the nineteenth century. The self-confident middle class felt threatened by proletarian slums where there were hereditary diseases that could spread to them. Even more serious was the threat that manifested itself in their own ranks. Material prosperity fostered cultural and intellectual development, but this could easily turn, so it was thought, to hysteria, madness, neurasthenia or other variants of "neurosis." The naturalistic novels of the period portray the victims of this neurotic oversensitivity in all their sickly picturesqueness. Hedwig de Fontayne in Frederik van Eeden's *Van de koele meren des doods* (1900; *The Depths of Deliverance*, 1902), Eline Vere in the novel of that name by Louis Couperus, Mathilde in *Een liefde* (A Love) by Lodewijk van Deyssel, and Henri de Graaff in *Martha de Bruin* by August van Groeningen: these are the stereotypical anemic or "highly strung" daughters and sons of large bourgeois families in the fin-de-siècle.

Degeneration, which manifested itself in nervous diseases thought to be inheritable, was all the more threatening because it was viewed as the result of exposure to the unnatural rhythm of industrial society. A civilization that had run amok led, it was believed, to a fatal complex of interrelated diseases that undermined the middle class from within and without. The threat was aimed at the cornerstone of society, the family. The specter of a family that rises to great heights in a few generations, only to be ruined by inner exhaustion, is presented in the outstanding fin-de-siècle novel *Boeken der kleine zielen* by Louis Couperus, which was mentioned in chapter 2 in a colonial context. The drama takes place over three generations, as the family falls from its powerful position in The Hague (one of the Van Lowe brothers is a minister) and dies out in a kind of implosion. The "neurosis" that has established itself in the family finds expression in the minister's nervous breakdown, the mysophobia of one of his brothers and the madness of the other. Addy van der Welcke, the sole scion of the third generation, turns the family estate at Driebergen into a clinic where he (now a psychiatrist) cares for his neurotic relatives.

Degeneration was thought to lead to the decline and eventual downfall of the nation. The specter of decadence haunted European states like France, Germany and Austria, where affluence and the flourishing cultural scene were also viewed as the last flickering of a doomed civilization. The bourgeois elite considered themselves highly cultured, but not equipped to withstand progress, and they feared the barbarians at the gate. Max Nordau's *Entartung* (Degeneration), Thomas Mann's *Buddenbrooks* and Emile Zola's *Rougon-Macquart* mirror these fears. In the Netherlands too it was sometimes claimed that progress was deterioration in disguise, "progrès à rebours," as it was known in France. Everyone had his own view. Henriëtte Roland Holst believed that the signs of decline seen everywhere heralded the collapse of capitalism. The barbarians at the gate were the workers, who would found a healthy society, that is, one rooted in labor and nature, after the revolution. Frederik van Eeden thought that neurosis threatened the whole nation, not just the middle class. The reason, according to him, was the unhealthy industrial city. Salvation lay in a return to the land, where workers transformed into colonists would form natural communes (*Siedlungsgenossenschaften*). Albert Verwey held up to his contemporaries the example of the Dutch Republic in its golden age in the seventeenth century. This was the criterion he also applied, as is apparent from the first quotation in the Introduction, when in 1907 he took stock of the cultural renaissance at that time. Verwey also called for linguistic improvement: balanced sentences would restore the coherence (literally, the syntax) of a language that had been torn to shreds by the poets of the Eighties Movement, including himself.

Artists of the Eighties generation made "community" their rallying cry in the eighteen-nineties and combined painting or sculpture with a quest for the ideal society. They abjured the principle of subjectivism: the expression of individualism, "singularization," the fragmentation of language and the decadence of art and the artist. They sought a new and inspiring form of cooperation in reaction to the supposed social disintegration. The traditional religious links, the Catholic and Protestant Churches, offered no solution because in the prevailing secularization they had lost their intellectual attraction, and because initially they had no proper answer to the all-important "social question." So artists began designing models of a *Gemeinschaft* which, in contrast to the industrial *Gesellschaft*, would safeguard the values of an authentic "community." The "community art" that dominated culture around 1900 was an answer to the apocalyptic notion that society was being torn apart between capital and labor and falling prey to degeneracy and decadence.

The models outlined in works of art but also put into practice in social experiments were utopian; they were blueprints for a future society. Around these utopians gathered supporters who formed colonies or political movements. The nature of the utopias betrayed the fact that they took the place of the Christian idea of salvation. They offered a prospect of the promised land or paradise on earth, where people lived peacefully together, laws and courts were superfluous, and everybody worked according to his ability and was rewarded according to need. The anarchist movements, the colonies and the early socialist groups unwittingly followed the pattern of a religion. They demanded devotion from their adherents, who were guided by the visions of their inspired leaders, people like Domela Nieuwenhuis, Henriëtte Roland Holst, Frederik van Eeden or Herman Gorter. The leaders themselves more than once assumed the role of martyr or redeemer. The Church of 1900 was a community church; community and socialism were often treated as synonyms. This reminds us that the socialism of 1900 aimed not only to improve the workers' conditions, but also to instill the ideal of a new society into a whole generation.

The idealists of 1900 brought a cultural and moral dimension to the struggle for social change and reform. The fact that the society of the future did not turn out as envisaged by Domela Nieuwenhuis, Van Eeden, Roland Holst and Gorter, and also by Diepenbrock and Derkinderen, in their different ways and wordings, does not diminish the significance of this cultural and moral impulse. In this they were pre-eminently Dutch within the European context of community art. But the umbrella term "community" could be so widely interpreted that too many individuals and groups with divergent visions and interests imagined they were talking about the same thing when they used the word. Below that concept stitched in gold one glimpsed a cross, another a lion, a third a distant hammer and sickle, a fourth still further away in the future a swastika. The irreconcilability of these ideals became apparent when World War I broke out.

Culture of discussion

A free culture of discussion is the characteristic that Willem Frijhoff and Marijke Spies found in their study of the Dutch Republic around 1650 – not in itself exceptional in Europe, but different in the Dutch variant because of the remarkable freedom of speech and of disclosure. At that time the public domain could be seen as an "in principle neutral arena" to which nearly everyone had access, where anything could be debated and there was no prevailing view laid down in advance. "Neutrality must be understood here in both senses of the term. The socially privileged or dominant groups in society ... could let their voices be heard but had no advance certainty that they would win the debate. All the evidence indicates however, that this highly cultural shaping of public opinion was also neutral in the sense that it seldom led to consequences of a social nature."[3] Thus tolerance was felt to be of the highest importance.

The question is whether the culture of discussion was still a characteristic feature of Dutch society in 1900. At any rate this culture was then embedded in national legislation, in the provisions dealing with freedom of speech and disclosure. The nation-state as it developed in Europe after the French Revolution resulted in these rights being regulated in the public domain in the Netherlands too, which was thus no longer unique. It lost the lead it had gained in the development of a European charter of human rights when in 1579 it was stated in Article 13 of the Union of Utrecht that each individual should be left free in his religion and that no one could be pursued or examined because of his religious beliefs. In the nineteenth century, moreover, the protection of individual conscience was reinforced by the principle of the separation of church and state, which again placed religion in the private domain. And in an age of secularization freedom of religion had also become freedom of disbelief, although openly professed atheism long continued to be viewed with a measure of disapproval.

The institutional preconditions for the culture of discussion had thus changed. Did that also apply to culture itself around 1900? It was put to the test in the decades before and after the turn of the century because this era was governed by fierce conflicts which can generally be traced back to two sources: a battle within the Church between modernists and the orthodox, and a political battle over how to solve the "social question." So the question of continuity can be answered through a historical analysis of three periods of conflict: the Dutch reactions to the German *Kulturkampf* in the eighteen-seventies and -eighties, the dissenting movement in the Church for and as a result of the so-called *Doleantie* in 1886 and Troelstra's November Revolution in 1918.

The *Kulturkampf* in Germany will serve as an example of the nineteenth-century conflict between liberalism and Catholicism, between the modernization of the state and the mobilization of the faithful for an ultramontane world view. It led to fierce battles not only in Germany after 1870, above all in a controversy about education, but also in Italy and around 1900 in France. The *Kulturkampf* found an echo in the Netherlands, but it was more moderate in two respects. The liberal press, which believed in the principle of separating church and state and continued to show understanding for Bismarck's battle against clericalism, saw the Prussian measures against the monastic orders as "counterproductive"– a practical argument – but also as incompatible with Dutch constitutional law. This argument was derived from a particular view of "the singularity of our national character."[4] A similar moderation was evident in the way in which Westphalian and Rhineland priests and nuns were quietly admitted to the Netherlands in the eighteen-seventies, and French monks and nuns around 1900.

The second example concerns a Dutch variant of the battle within the Church between modernists and orthodox believers. In itself this phenomenon was not exclusively Dutch, but the form it took, the conflict strategy of the orthodox minister Abraham Kuyper, was. This resulted in a schism which, in comparison with similar theological and canonical clashes in the Protestant churches in England and Germany, may be termed unique. Kuyper deliberately sought conflict and wanted to separate the "wholes" from the "halves" in Calvinism. He was able to mobilize his orthodox Reformed followers through the theme of the antithesis, the contrast between belief and unbelief, which was also and above all a political dividing line.

Yet there were limits to this originally religious conflict. Kuyper did not want to divide the state but to secure room for the development of his movement, and push back the alleged "omnipotence" of the state. It is true that in calling for "sovereignty in one's own circle" he laid the basis for his own system of Protestant associations and schools, but that also implied recognition of the right to sovereignty of other religious groups within their own circles. Moreover, when Kuyper came to power in 1901, as premier he tried to bridge this antithesis. In the Lower House he put it like this: "Not to give priority to any group, not to give up the unity of the nation, no privileging or neglecting, but giving an equal chance to both antithetical parts."[5] In this way the basis was laid for a culture of pacification of these religious "antagonists."

The last example is the attempted revolution led by the socialist Troelstra in November 1918. This was the culmination of a revolutionary dimension which Dutch social democracy had always retained, even in its parliamentary form. But after the failure of the idea of a general strike – as in the case of the rail strike of 1903 – the theory of a proletarian uprising was no longer tenable. Troelstra misjudged the readiness of the proletariat to turn their words into deeds. In fact the same mistake was made by the burgomaster of Rotterdam, A.R. Zimmerman, scion of an Amsterdam merchant family and a worthy representative of the Dutch bourgeoisie. Early in the "revolutionary week" in November 1918, he invited the social democrat leaders in his city to discuss an orderly handover of power. He may well have been influenced by a feeling that this really was the end of the old order, an end which others envisaged as degeneration and decadence.

In November 1918 Troelstra was trying to import a German revolution which had led to the flight of the Kaiser and the proclamation of a republic. Other members of his party criticized him for being too preoccupied with Germany and in particular German social democracy, and as a result being out of touch with conditions in the Netherlands.[6] To put it another way, his attempt at revolution overstepped the limits of the Dutch culture of discussion. The sanction for this was the mobilization of large numbers of liberal and church-going citizens in support of the monarchy, a flood of criticism within the party's own ranks, and many years of isolation for social democracy in Parliament in the interwar period.

The forum had changed, because the public domain was governed by new laws. The subject matter of public debate was of a different order and the audience was now more literate. Religion, in the seventeenth century the spiritual mortar binding all manner of social groups together and the central orientation point, again became a significant factor around 1900 through its denial, in secularization. But this dialectic was a source of artistic creativity and a stimulus to science. A highly developed cultural infrastructure was maintained, and amid the fierce conflicts there continued to be a collective awareness of the value of moderation and tolerance. It is in these conventions and this snapshot that cultural identity is revealed.[7]

Notes

Introduction

1 Albert Verwey in: Potgieter, *Het Rijksmuseum*, pp. vi-vii.
2 Albert Verwey in: Potgieter, *Het Rijksmuseum*, p. V; see also Van Sas, "Fin-de-siecle als nieuw begin," p. 609.
3 Romein, "Hendrik Petrus Berlage, bouwmeester der beurs," pp. 850-851.
4 Van Zanden and Van Riel, *Nederland 1780-1814*, pp. 418-419.
5 Aerts in: Kloek and Tilmans, *Burger*, p. 338.
6 Gay, *Schnitzler's Century*, p. 11.
7 Blaas, "Het paradigma van de eeuwwende," pp. 44-47.
8 Blaas, "Het paradigma van de eeuwwende," pp. 44-45.
9 Wesseling, *Oorlog lost nooit iets op*, pp. 303-304.
10 Kossmann, *The Low Countries 1780-1940*, pp. 439-462.
11 Kossmann, "Romeins *Breukvlak* en de Nederlandse geschiedenis," p. 658.
12 Romein, *Op het breukvlak van twee eeuwen*.
13 Romein, "Integrale geschiedschrijving," p. 27.
14 Romein, "Integrale geschiedschrijving," p. 35.
15 Frijhoff and Spies, *1650*, p. 52.
16 Huizinga, *Briefwisseling*, pp. 181-182.
17 Frijhoff and Spies, *1650*, p. 58.

Chapter 1 National celebrations, national images

1 Cannadine, "The Context, Performance and Meaning of Ritual," pp. 120-121.
2 Verburg, *Koningin Emma*, p. 213.
3 Verburg, *Koningin Emma*, p. 192; te Velde, "Het 'roer van staat,'" pp. 169-195.
4 Fasseur, *Wilhelmina*, p. 110.
5 *De Kroniek*, May 31, and June 7, 1896.
6 Brandt Corstius, "Een debat over kunst en leven," pp. 263-275; Reeser, *Verzamelde geschriften van Alphons Diepenbrock*, p. 152.

7 Koch, *De koningsromans van Louis Couperus*, p. 21.
8 Fontijn, *Leven in extase*, pp. 189-192.
9 Simons, *Amsterdam in stukken en brokken*, p. 32.
10 Fasseur, *Wilhelmina*, p. 171.
11 Star Numan, in: P.H. Ritter, *Eene halve eeuw 1848-1898*, p. 44.
12 Quoted in: te Velde, *Gemeenschapszin en Plichtsbesef*, p. 151.
13 Beets, *Dennennaalden*, p. 142.
14 *Officiëel Gedenkboek van de feestelijke ontvangst en de inhuldiging*, vol. 1, p. 103.
15 Quoted in: Couvée, *Leve de Willemien!*, pp. 256-257.
16 Elzenga, *Theater van staat*, p. 5.
17 Jager, *Willem Kromhout*, pp. 22-23.
18 Blaas, "Tussen twee herdenkingen (1884-1933)," p. 149.
19 De Rooy, "De wet verdrukt," pp. 274-275.
20 Boomgaard, *De verloren zoon*, p. 92.
21 De Jong, "Dracht en eendracht," p. 72.
22 Grever and Waaldijk, *Feministische Openbaarheid*, passim.
23 Quoted in: Couvée, *Leve de Willemien!*, pp. 256-257.
24 Van Maarseveen, *Briefwisseling van Nicolaas Gerard Pierson*, pp. 101-102.
25 Kossmann, *The Low Countries 1780-1940*, p. 496.
26 Grapperhaus, *Fiscaal beleid in Nederland*, p. 62.
27 Dudink, *Deugdzaam liberalisme*, p. 253.
28 Rigter, *Tussen sociale wil en werkelijkheid*, p. 18.
29 Stuurman, *Wacht op onze daden*, pp. 222-230 and 294; Van Doorn, "Over liberalisme en sociaal-democratie," pp. 315-316.
30 Stuurman, *Wacht op onze daden*, p. 294.
31 Stuurman, *Wacht op onze daden*, pp. 370-372.
32 Stuurman, *Wacht op onze daden*, pp. 310-314.
33 Van Doorn, "Sporen van nationaal-liberalisme," p. 155.
34 Aerts, *De Letterheren*, pp. 368-374.
35 De Rooy, "Bier, kunst en politiek," pp. 175-187.

36 Van den Berg, *De toegang tot het Binnenhof*, pp. 50-51.

37 Van den Berg, *De toegang tot het Binnenhof*, p. 26.

38 De Haan and te Velde, "Vormen van politiek," p. 171.

39 Kossmann, *Politieke theorie*, p. 379.

40 Bevaart, *De Nederlandse defensie*, p. 473.

41 Te Velde, *Gemeenschapszin en plichtsbesef*, pp. 172-173.

42 Te Velde, *Gemeenschapszin en plichtsbesef*, p. 218.

43 Havard, *La Hollande pittoresque*.

44 Havard, *La Hollande pittoresque*, p. 390.

45 Havard, *La Hollande pittoresque*, p. 45.

46 Amicis, *Hollande*, pp. 296-305.

47 Huussen Jr., "Claude Monet in Nederland," p. 40; Verbeek, "Bezoekers van het Rijksmuseum," p. 64; Kraan, "Nederland en Barbizon," p. 97.

48 Liebermann, *Die Phantasie in der Malerei*, pp. 29 and 77.

49 Wagner, *Max Liebermann*.

50 Koolhaas and de Vries, "Terug naar een roemrijk verleden," pp. 135-137.

51 Bergsma, "Mens en Natuur," pp. 34-35.

52 Dekkers, *Jozef Israëls*, p. 52.

53 Dekkers, *Jozef Israëls*, p. 83.

54 Hoogenboom, *De stand des kunstenaars*, pp. 150-151.

55 Stolwijk, *Uit de schilderswereld*, p. 197.

56 Dekkers, *Jozef Israëls*, p. 117.

57 Stott, *Holland Mania*, pp. 29-30.

58 Stott, *American Painters*, p. 3.

59 Bakker, "'t Was of 'k mijzelven vond," pp. 105-108.

60 Gaehtgens, "Holland als Vorbild," pp. 83 and 90-91.

61 Stott, *American Painters*, p. 45.

62 De Haan, 'Waar Spaarne en Liê tezamen vloeit," p. 36; Broere, "Hans Brinker of De Zilveren Schaatsen," pp. 10-13.

63 Stott, *Holland Mania*, pp. 117-118.

64 Van Rossem, *Het Algemeen Uitbreidingsplan van Amsterdam*, pp. 22-23.

65 Stott, *American Painters*, pp. 257-258.

66 Aerden, "Werken, feesten en flaneren," pp. 50-54.

67 Veurman, *Volendammer Schildersboek*, p. 40.

68 Hecht, *Kunstgeschiedenis in Nederland*, pp. 11-21.

69 Bruin, *De echte Rembrandt*, pp. 42-44.

70 Quack, *Rembrandt's herdenking*, pp. 4, 18-19.

71 Kossmann, *Een tuchteloos probleem*, p. 36.

72 Proceedings of the Lower House 1907-1908; session December 18, 1907, p. 1193.

73 Boomgaard, *De verloren zoon*, p. 73.

74 Boomgaard, "Bronnenstudie en stilistiek," pp. 259-260.

75 Boomgaard, *De verloren zoon*, p. 90.

76 Boomgaard, "Bronnenstudie en stilistiek," p. 256.

77 Boomgaard, "Bronnenstudie en stilistiek," pp. 267-268.

78 Langbehn, *Rembrandt als Erzieher*, pp. 138-139.

79 Stern, *The Politics of Cultural Despair*, p. 132.

80 Kloek, "Naar het land van Rembrandt," p. 139.

81 Smits-Veldt, "De Muiderkring in beeld," pp. 278-288.

82 Spies, "Van mythes en meningen," pp. 179-181; Spies, "Van 'Vaderlandsch Gevoel' tot Europees perspectief," pp. 80-81; Maas, *Pro Patria*, p. 43.

83 Ouwerkerk, "Vondelverehrung in katholischen Kreisen," p. 225.

84 Kemperink, *Nederlands toneel in het fin de siècle*, p. 140.

85 Quoted in: Kemperink, *Nederlands toneel in het fin de siècle*, p. 138.

86 Naeff, *Willem Royaards*, p. 74.

87 De Leeuwe, "Willem Royaards ontvangt een ere-doctoraat," p. 580.

88 Van Miert, *Wars van clubgeest en partijzucht*, p. 63.

89 Beets, *Heiligerlee*, p. 4.

90 Scheffler, *Holland*, p. 26.

91 Fasel, in: I. Schöffer, *Alkmaar ontzet 1573-1973*, pp. 133-134.

92 Fasel, in: I. Schöffer, *Alkmaar ontzet 1573-1973*, p. 150.

93 Hartmann, *Der historische Festzug*, p. 7.

94 Verschaffel, "Het verleden tot weinig herleid," p. 309.

95 Otterspeer, *De wiekslag van hun geest*, pp. 488-490.

96 Banck, in: *De Nederlandsche Spectator*, June 27, 1868, pp. 227, 231.

97 Beets, *Te Alkmaar*, October 8, 1873, pp. 5, 12-13, 15.

98 Vermeulen, "Katholieken en liberalen tegenover de Gentse Pacificatie-feesten," p. 344.

99 Verschaffel, "Het verleden tot weinig herleid," p. 308.

100 Brouwers, *Antwoord aan den heer Groen van Prinsterer*, pp. 31-32.

101 Janssen, "Thijm en Nuyens," p. 246.

102 Janssen, "Thijm en Nuyens," pp. 255-259.

103 Blaas, "De prikkelbaarheid van een kleine natie," p. 279.

104 Blaas, "De prikkelbaarheid van een kleine natie," p. 284.

105 Blaas, "Tussen twee herdenkingsjaren (1884-1933)," pp. 144-145.

106 Blaas, "Tussen twee herdenkingsjaren (1884-1933)," p. 147.

107 Tollebeek, *De toga van Fruin*, p. 72.

108 Tollebeek, *De toga van Fruin*, pp. 84-88.

109 Tollebeek, *De toga van Fruin*, p. 99.

110 Kossmann, "De Nederlandse zeventiende-eeuwse schilderkunst," p. 283.

111 Busken Huet, *Het Land van Rembrand*, p. 628.

112 Kossmann, "De Nederlandse zeventiende-eeuwse schilderkunst," pp. 285-286; Blaas, "De Gouden Eeuw," p. 125.

113 Amicis, *La Hollande*, pp. 567-568; Jensma, *Het rode tasje van Salverda*, p. 184.

114 Illustrated catalogue reprinted in: Livestro-Nieuwenhuis, *Nationale kleederdrachten*.

115 Van Someren Brand, in: *Katalogus van de Tentoonstelling van Nationale Kleederdrachten*; Livestro-Nieuwenhuis, *Nationale kleederdrachten*, pp. 8, 27.

116 De Leeuw, *Kleding in Nederland 1813-1920*, pp. 159-162.

117 De Leeuw, *Kleding in Nederland 1813-1920*, p. 255.

118 De Leeuw, *Kleding in Nederland 1813-1920*, p. 312.

119 *De Amsterdammer*, February 20, 1916.

120 Jensma, *Het rode tasje van Salverda*, p. 254.

121 Jensma, *Het rode tasje van Salverda*, p. 163.

122 Hroch, *Social Preconditions of National Revival*, pp. 132, 136-145.

123 Jensma, *Het rode tasje van Salverda*, p. 167.

124 De Jong, *Dirigenten van de herinnering*, pp.122-124.

125 Van Ginkel, *Op zoek naar eigenheid*, p. 30.

126 Voskuil, "Geschiedenis van de volkskunde in Nederland," pp. 57-58.

127 De Jong, "Dracht en eendracht," pp. 70-74.

128 Wagemakers, "Vaderlandsch Historisch Volksfeest," p. 176.

129 Voskuil, "Het tijdelijke met het eeuwige verwisseld," p. 28 and note 73; Wagemakers, "Het Vaderlandsch Historisch Volksfeest," pp. 171-188.

130 Van der Ven, *Neerlands volksleven*, p. 189.

131 Quoted in: Rooijakkers, "Dragers van traditie?" p. 182.

132 Jong, *Dirigenten van de herinnering*, pp. 367-369.

133 Vos, "Frits Coers (1870-1937)," p. 211.

134 Voskuil, "Geschiedenis van de volkskunde in Nederland," p. 58.

135 Post, "Volkskunde in Nederland," p. 236.

136 Rooijakkers, "Dragers van traditie?" pp. 179-181; Van Ginkel, *Op zoek naar eigenheid*, p. 40.

137 Frijhoff, "Volkskunde en cultuurwetenschap," pp. 119-120; Zeijden, "Wortels van de volkscultuur," p. 339.

138 Huizinga, *Verzamelde Werken*, p. 281.

139 Frijhoff, "Volkskunde en cultuurwetenschap," pp. 116-117.

140 *De Zondagsbode*. Mennonite journal, November 16, 1913.

141 De Jong, "Dracht en eendracht," p. 75.

142 Brugmans and Beets, *1813 – Amsterdam – 1913*, p. 1.

143 Naber, *Om en bij de tentoonstelling*, p. 31.

144 *Propria Cures*. Amsterdam student weekly, November 29, 1913.

145 Huizinga, *Verzamelde Werken*, p. 528.

146 Huizinga, *Verzamelde Werken*, p. 531.

147 Hoek, *Plechtige dankdienst in de Ned.Ev.Kerk*, p. 17.

148 De Ligt, *Profeet en volksfeest*, pp. 38-39, 76.

149 *De Blijde Wereld*. Christian socialist weekly, November 28, 1913 and December 12, 1913.

150 Loeff, *Het Katholiek Nederland 1813-1913*.

151 Eyffinger, *Het Vredespaleis*, pp. 58-61.

152 Van Vollenhoven, "De eendracht van het land," p. 184.

153 Blaas, "De prikkelbaarheid van een kleine natie," p. 292.

154 Te Velde, *Gemeenschapszin en Plichtsbesef*, pp. 234-235.

155 Brugmans, *Nederland oorlogstijd*, pp. 114-115 and 131.

Chapter 2 The Netherlands and the World

1 Grever and Waaldijk, *Feministische Openbaarheid*, pp. 167-175, 196.

2 Bossenbroek, *Holland op zijn breedst*, p. 204.

3 For a summary of the discussion: Bossenbroek, *Holland op zijn breedst*, pp. 15-18.

4 Quoted in: Oostindie and Maduro, *In het land van de overheerser*, p. 21.

5 Oostindie, *Het paradijs overzee*, p. 109.

6 Oostindie, *Het paradijs overzee*, p. 118.

7 Hoetink, *De gespleten samenleving*, p. 71.

8 Oostindie, *Het paradijs overzee*, p. 36.

9 Bossenbroek, *Holland op zijn breedst*, p. 285.

10 Van Doorn, *De laatste eeuw van Indie*, p. 86.

11 Bossenbroek, *Holland op zijn breedst*, p. 58.

12 Bossenbroek, *Holland op zijn breedst*, p. 59.

13 Bossenbroek, *Holland op zijn breedst*, p. 56.

14 Quoted in: Bossenbroek, *Holland op zijn breedst*, p. 142.

15 Bossenbroek, *Holland op zijn breedst*, p. 147.

16 Fasseur, "De puputan," in: Van Oostrom, *Historisch tableau*, pp. 121-124.

17 Wesseling, *Divide and rule*, p. 277

18 Wesseling, *Divide and rule*, p. 276

19 Bossenbroek, *Holland op zijn breedst*, p. 245.

20 Bossenbroek, *Holland op zijn breedst*, p. 346.

21 Bossenbroek, *Holland op zijn breedst*, p. 351.

22 Wesseling, *Divide and rule*, p. 327

23 Bornewasser, *Kerkelijk verleden in een wereldlijke context*, p. 274.

24 De Schryver, *Nieuwe Encyclopedie van de Vlaamse Beweging*, vol. 2, p. 2170.

25 Van Hees and De Schepper, *Tussen cultuur en politiek*; Willemsen, *De Vlaamse Beweging van 1830 tot 1914*, pp. 387-389.

26 Quoted in: Van Hees, "De groot-Nederlandse studentenbeweging," p. 44.

27 Van Hees, "De groot-Nederlandse studentenbeweging," p. 45.

28 Willemsen, *De Vlaamse Beweging van 1830 tot 1914*, p. 389.

29 Te Velde, *Gemeenschapszin en plichtsbesef*, p. 179.

30 Geyl, *Noord en Zuid*, p. 24.

31 De Valk and Van Faassen, *Dagboeken en aantekeningen van Willem Hendrik de Beaufort*, p. 71; Kuitenbrouwer, *Nederland en de opkomst van het moderne imperialisme. Koloniën en buitenlandse politiek 1870-1902* p. 184.

32 Quoted in: Poeze, *In het land van de overheerser* vol. 1, p. 30; Bossenbroek, *Holland op zijn breedst*, p. 147.

33 Quoted in: Poeze, *In het land van de overheerser* vol. 1, pp. 30-31.

34 Poeze, *In het land van de overheerser* vol. 1, p. 24.

35 Fontijn, *Trots verbrijzeld*, p. 316.

36 Poeze, *In het land van de overheerser* vol. 1, p. 151.

37 Quoted in: Poeze, *In het land van de overheerser* vol. 1, p. 33.

38 Poeze, *In het land van de overheerser* vol. 1, p. 53.

39 Quoted in: Oostindie and Maduro, *In het land van de overheerser*, p. 43. Blakely, *Blacks in the Dutch World*, pp. 222-223.

40 Van Amersfoort, "Van William Kegge tot Ruud Gullit," p. 476.

41 Rogier and De Rooy, *In vrijheid herboren*, pp. 299-300.

42 Ellemers, "Migratie van en naar Nederland," p. 326.

43 Miellet, "Immigratie van katholieke Westfalers en de modernisering van de Nederlandse detailhandel." In: *Tijdschrift voor Geschiedenis* 100 (1987): 380.

44 Schrover, "Groepsvorming onder Duitse aardewerkhandelaren," p. 95.

45 Heijs, *Van vreemdeling tot Nederlander. De verlening van het Nederlanderschap aan vreemdelingen (1813-1992)* p. 45

46 Miellet, *Honderd jaar grootwinkelbedrijf*, p. 72.

47 Miellet, "Immigratie van katholieke Westfalers," pp. 374-393.

48 Schrover, *Een kolonie* p. 80.

49 Schrover, *Een kolonie* p. 124.

50 Bruin, *Een herenwereld ontleed*, pp. 50 and 54.

51 De Vries, in: *Nederlands Patriciaat* 72 (1988) xi and xiv.

52 Lucassen en Penninx, *Nieuwkomers*, p. 110.

53 Van Maurik, *Toen ik nog jong was*, pp. 28 and 65.

54 *Woordenboek der Nederlandsche Taal*, p. 991.

55 Lucassen and Penninx, *Nieuwkomers*, p. 110.

56 *Nieuwe Rotterdamse Courant*, September 22, 1875. Quoted in: De Coninck, *Een les uit Pruisen*, p. 296.

57 De Coninck, *Een les uit Pruisen*, p. 297.

58 Rutten, *Limburg*, pp. 196-197.

59 Daalder, "Joden in een verzuilend Nederland," pp. 100-101.

60 Rogier and De Rooy, *In vrijheid herboren*, pp. 299-300.

61 Rogier and De Rooy, *In vrijheid herboren*, p. 300.

62 Rogier and De Rooy, *In vrijheid herboren*, pp. 300-301.

Chapter 3   Urban planning

1 Esquiros, *Nederland en het leven in Nederland*, p. 33.

2 Scheffler, *Holland*, p. 8.

3 Bakker, "De stadsuitleg van 1610", pp. 85-86.

4 De Ruijter, *Voor volkshuisvesting en stedebouw*, pp. 39 and 41.

5 Taverne, *In 't land van belofte*, p. 75.

6 Kromhout in: Berlage, *Arbeiderswoningen in Nederland*, p. xv.

7 Fockema Andreae, *De hedendaagsche stedenbouw*, pp. 39-40.

8 Bosch and Van de Ven, "Rivierverbetering," p. 123.

9 Van Leeuwen, "Waterbouw," p. 238.

10 Van Leeuwen, "Waterbouw," p. 239; Bos, *Sliedrecht*, p. 113.

11 De Vries, *Barges and capitalism*, pp. 211 and 215.

12 Busken Huet, *Van Napels naar Amsterdam*, pp. 247-248.

13 Dijksterhuis, *Spoorwegtracering*, p. 186.

14 Dijksterhuis, *Spoorwegtracering*, p. 58.

15 Dijksterhuis, *Spoorwegtracering*, p. 211.

16 Knippenberg and Nauta, "Naar eenheid van tijd," pp. 325-346.

17 Van Dijk, "Het negentiende-eeuwse stadsbestuur," p. 141.

18 Quoted in: Nieuwenhuis, *Mensen maken een stad*, p. 106.

19 Rogier, *Rotterdam*, p. 85.

20 Van Ravesteyn, *Rotterdam*, pp. 62-63.

21 Quoted in: Nieuwenhuis, *Mensen maken een stad*, p. 160.

22 Van Ravesteyn, *Rotterdam*, pp. 267-268.

23 Oxenaar, *Centraal Station*, p. 13.

24 Oxenaar, *Centraal Station*, pp. 20 and 24.

25 Oxenaar, *Centraal Station*, p. 50.

26 Van Dijk, *Rotterdam 1810-1880*, p. 24; Deurloo and Hoekveld, "The population growth," pp. 257-258.

27 Kooij in: Van Holthoon, *De Nederlandse Samenleving*, p. 97.

28 Kooij in: Van Holthoon, *De Nederlandse Samenleving*, p. 95.

29 Deurloo and Hoekveld, "The population growth," pp. 261-262; Kooij in: Van Holthoon, *De Nederlandse Samenleving*, p. 97.

30 Sommer, "De vlegeljaren van de telefoon," p. 38.

31 De Swaan, *Zorg en de staat*, p. 125.

32 Van Nierop, *De bevolkingsbeweging*, pp. 131 and 169-170.

33 Willemsen, "De volkshuisvesting in Arnhem," p. 8.

34 Fockema Andreae, "De uitbreiding der stad Arnhem," p. 152.

35 Willemsen, "De volkshuisvesting in Arnhem," pp. 14-15; Van Zon in: Lintsen, *Geschiedenis van de techniek*, vol. 3, p. 26.

36 Fockema Andreae, "De uitbreiding der stad Arnhem," p. 164.

37 Willemsen, "De volkshuisvesting in Arnhem," p. 10.

38 Schmal, *Den Haag*, p. 99.

39 De Swaan, *Zorg en de staat*, p. 135.

40 Proceedings of the Lower House of Parliament, 1895-1896 Session, Appendix 25, pp. 2-7.

41 Valkhoff, *Een Eeuw Rechtsontwikkeling*, p. 18.

42 Valkhoff, *Een Eeuw Rechtsontwikkeling*, pp. 20-21.

43 Sitte, *Der Städtebau*.

44 Freijser, *Het veranderend stadsbeeld*, p. 55.

45 Freijser, *Het veranderend stadsbeeld*, p. 62.

46 Summary in: Johanisse, "Nederlandse architectuur 1900-1924."

47 Quoted in: De Ruijter, *Voor volkshuisvesting en stedebouw*, p. 248.

48 Van Rossem, "Een keerpunt," pp. 12-13.

49 Quoted in: Van Rossem, "Een keerpunt," p. 16.

50 Wijdeveld, in: *Wendingen*, 1918. Quoted in: Johannisse, "H.P. Berlage en de Amsterdamse School."

51 Bock, Johanisse and Stissi, *Michel de Klerk*, p. 31.

52 De Ruijter, *Voor volkshuisvesting en stede-bouw*, p. 269.

53 Nieuwenhuis, *Mensen maken een stad*, p. 206.

54 Bosma, *Ruimte voor een nieuwe tijd*, pp. 203-205.

55 Taverne, "Een 'tolerante' steenbouw," pp. 51 and 69.

56 Quoted in: Stott, *American Painters*, p. 61.

57 Peters, *De Nederlandsche Stedenbouw*, Foreword.

58 Hoogenberk, *Het idee van de Hollandse stad*, p. 39.

Chapter 4 Community art

1 Huizinga, *Leven en werk van Jan Veth*, pp. 49-50. Diepenbrock, too, saw *gemeenschap-skunst* as the most important outcome of the eighteen-nineties, *Verzamelde Geschriften*, p. 211.

2 Berlage, "Over architectuur." In: *De Kroniek*, p. 59.

3 See Stuurman, "De produktieve deugd." In: *Wacht op onze daden*, pp. 209-249.

4 See Berlage, "Kunst en Gemeenschap," In: Berlage, *Een drietal lezingen* and Berlage, *Studies over bouwkunst*.

5 In the same article of 1895 he wrote, "For there will again be love for a common ideal, certainly no longer in the old form, that is to say neither a religious nor a polit-ical ideal in the old sense, but a love for the community itself. And is that common ideal not the union of both the highest reli-gious and the highest political ideals? And will the consequence of that not be the highest art of all time?" (Berlage, "Over architectuur," in: *Tweemaandelijksch Tijdschrift*, p. 59 II).

6 Diepenbrock, *Verzamelde Geschriften*, pp. 121, 152.

7 It is telling that in 1895 Berlage wrote an article ("Over architectuur," *Tweemaandelijksch Tijdschrift*), about the architecture of the future, in which he cited not only St. John's Cathedral in 's-Hertogenbosch but also Derkinderen's murals as examples of what he had in mind when he talked about *gemeenschap-skunst*. In the eighteen-nineties the building was often used as an image to explain social cohesion. In Crane's *The Claims of Decorative Art*, London 1892 (translated as *Kunst en samenleving* by Jan Veth and pub-lished in the Netherlands in 1894), commu-nal life is described as the "foundation" of art, the various forms of craft work as the "bricks," and the community as the "cement." The members of the diamond-cutters' union, the Algemene Nederlandsche Diamantbewerkersbond, regarded their muscular union headquarters – built by Berlage and popularly known as "Berlage's bastion" – as emblematic of the strength of their movement. The bricks that Berlage used reflected the insignificant individuals who had been elevated to mass and power by the cement of intellectual solidarity. The memoirs of the ANDB members reveal that they really did perceive the symbolism in this way. "Half in earnest, people pointed to a brick in the wall," said Meyer-Sluizer, "and said, that's my brick." The great interest in freemasonry at the end of the century, particularly among the members of Architectura et Amicitia, the society of architects, goes some way toward explain-ing the popularity of this image. The metaphor of builder, bricks, foundations, masonry etc. is after all a constituent image of freemasonry.

8 Paap, *Alphons Diepenbrock*, p. 200.

9 "Melodie en gedachte," *De Nieuwe Gids*, December 1891. Later Diepenbrock referred to "glorification of form", "indif-ference to the substance," and "unsocial or antisocial anarchist aesthetics," in Diepenbrock, *Verzamelde geschriften*, pp. 310-311, 334.

10 Veth, *De muurschilderingen van Der Kinderen*, p. 9. Other reactions to Derkinderen's wall: Polak, *Het fin-de-siècle*

in de Nederlandse schilderkunst, pp. 148-149.

11 See Thijs, *De Kroniek van P. L. Tak.*

12 According to Diepenbrock this term was coined not by Veth, but by Wagner. Diepenbrock quotes a page reference in "Die Kunst der Zukunft" (*Gesammelte Werke*, Leipzig 1872, vol. 3, p. 58), but the term is not found there, nor anywhere else. See Diepenbrock, *Verzamelde geschriften*, p. 63.

13 Article written in 1843, collected in Alberdingk Thijm, *Over de kompozitie in de kunst*, pp. 19-20.

14 The Mariakerk and the Ridderzaal are moreover examples of vandalism, against which Thijm and De Stuers had fulminated bitterly in the past. Looking after monuments was one of the Rijksmuseum's tasks (see hereafter). The supremacy of architecture was illustrated once more in the design for a painting on the east wall of the entrance hall. The personifications of sculpture and painting sit at the feet of architecture, who is portrayed as a queen.

15 Richard Roland Holst later reiterated this same complaint when he came to discuss museum policy. Museums were the result of a development in art after the Renaissance that was "focused on mobility, movability and marketability." Roland Holst, *Over Kunst en Kunstenaar*, p. 130. He also suggested the image of the medieval cathedral. Just imagine, he said, if Notre-Dame were to be cut up into pieces and exhibited in a museum as mile-long rows of bits and pieces.

16 "Wie sich der Gemeingeist in tausend egoistische Richtungen zersplitterte, löste sich auch das grosse Gesamtkunstwerk in die einzelnen ihn inbegriffenen Kunstbestandteile auf," "Die Art und die Revolution," Richard Wagner, *Gesammelte Werke*, Leipzig 1907, pp. 111-112.

17 Berlage, "Bouwkunst en impressionisme," p. 99.

18 See Bergvelt, *Amsterdamse School*; Lambourne, *Utopian Craftsmen*; Naylor, *The Arts and Crafts Movement*; Martis, *Voor de kunst en voor de nijverheid*; Gans, *Nieuwe Kunst*.

19 Unpublished. Extract in Naylor, *The Arts and Crafts Movement*, p. 9. There is no study of the influence of the Arts and Crafts movement in the Netherlands.

20 Martis, *Voor de kunst en voor de nijverheid*, pp. 31-137; Gans, *Nieuwe Kunst*, p. 15. Nor should we forget the report of 1876 in which J.R. de Kruyff gave a critical analysis of applied arts education in the Netherlands.

21 Bervoets, *Victor de Stuers*, pp. 16-17.

22 Martis, *Voor de kunst en voor de nijverheid*, pp. 186-187. This development from an informally regulated to a legally enshrined structure is comparable to that of Monumentenzorg, see hereafter.

23 For Art Nouveau in the Netherlands see Gans, *Nieuwe Kunst*.

24 *Architectura* 1901, quoted in Gans, *Nieuwe Kunst*, p. 9. The architects Kromhout and Mol made similar remarks. Mol savaged Van de Velde's work as "wood rape" (in *De Kroniek*). According to Berlage, Art Nouveau took "that single step from the sublime to the ridiculous."

25 The same principle also explains Berlage's later resistance to the Amsterdam school. See also: Auke van der Woud, *Waarheid en Karakter*.

26 See the De Kruyff report, 1895, quoted in Martis, *Voor de kunst en voor de nijverheid*, p. 165; see Derkinderen's address upon accepting the directorship of the Rijksacademie in 1908, in which he attacked industry and mass production, which, he said, would crush the crafts to death (in *De twintigste eeuw*, May 1).

27 "As late as," because in Germany the Deutsche Werkbund had been engaged in industrial design since the turn of the century. See Naylor, *The Arts and Crafts Movement*, pp. 184-187, also Lambourne, *Utopian Craftsmen*.

28 This development also encompassed the rise of book illustration and typography. For a detailed discussion of the topic see Braches, *Het book als nieuwe kunst*.

29 Alberdingk Thijm, *De kunst in Nederland*, p. 13. See also Koopmans, "In het voetspoor van Pythagoras." In this otherwise excellent article Koopmans erroneously attributes the term "structural sculpture" to J.E. van der Pek in an article published in 1901 (Koopmans, "In het voetspoor van Pythagoras," p. 25).

30 Oxenaar, *P.J.H. Cuypers. Het Rijksmuseum. Schetsen en tekeningen (1863-1908)*.

31 Bock, *Anfänge einer neuen Architektur*.

32 Lauweriks, "Gemeenschapskunst en individualisme," pp. 241, 270.

33 Pevsner, "Gemeinschaftsideale unter den bildenden Künstlern."

34 In the Netherlands ideas about the "guild" diverged considerably, from a revival of the medieval ideal (Alberdingk Thijm, Derkinderen and Lauweriks), to a sort of contemporary trade union. Holst complained that bourgeois culture had destroyed the remnants of the guild (Roland Holst, *Over Kunst en Kunstenaar*, p. 69). Reading between the lines, it is clear that he, too, essentially longed for a return to the medieval guild and regretted the establishment of trade unions, because they confirmed the conflict between social classes and hence the loss of social unity.

35 Roland Holst, *In en buiten het tij*, p. 134.

36 In "Bouw en Sierkunst," 1898. The articles by De Bazel are virtually unreadable – not, as has sometimes been suggested, because his command of the language was poor, but because, we assume, he wanted to imitate Diepenbrock's style. De Bazel wrote "Diepenbrockish," but even more ethereally, flying off into elevated theosophical spheres.

37 *Tweemaandelijksch Tijdschrift* 1894-1895, quoted in De Vries, "Albert Verwey en de beeldende kunst," p. 13.

38 Bierens de Haan, *De Kroniek*, 1898, p. 337.

39 Alberdink Thijm "De kunst en archaeologie in Holland," in: Thijm, *De kunst in Nederland*. C. Leemans observed that the argument had been blown up out of all proportion (in a response in *De Gids*, 1854, reprinted in Alberdingk Thijm, "Een bouwlootse der XIXe eeuw"). Magnificent works of art had been made for Protestant churches after the Reformation, for instance the windows in St. John's Cathedral in Gouda, superb pulpits, pews and organ screens, see also Tillema, *Schetsen uit de geschiedenis der monumentenzorg*.

40 "... Renaissance ... era that the unity in the mutual bond between the crafts began to crumble; the separation and alienation of architecture and painting dates from this time, too." Roland Holst, "Over de monumentale schilderkunst," p. 297.

41 Art is portable and often speculative property, said Crane in the same book, Crane, *The Claims of Decorative Art*; Roland Holst, "Over de monumentale schilderkunst," pp. 304, 306; Roland Holst, *Over kunst en kunstenaar*, p. 233, gives a list of differences between the art of painting and the making of paintings.

42 Eckermann, *Conversations of Goethe*, p. 126.

43 Richard Roland Holst explicitly used the terms "decadence" and "degeneration" in regard to the members of the Eighties Movement (Roland Holst, *Over kunst en kunstenaar*). In the early eighteen-nineties, Diepenbrock wrote about "the decadence of this age." He suggested that the language had begun to decompose, just as it had in the time of the Church Fathers: "The fifth century saw in heathen literature the decomposition and total rotting of the language, which for centuries had been the idiom of lust for worldly power and sensuality; the fabrics unraveled and the long decayed skeletons of the old rhetorical figures collapsed. That which had not entirely succumbed to decomposition was incorporated in the Christian literature and rejuvenated and ennobled by the new spirit" (Diepenbrock, *Verzamelde Geschriften*, p. 52). Diepenbrock referred explicitly to Huysmans, who described this phenomenon in his novel *A rebours*, 1885, which heralded literary decadence in France. He also referred to the famous article by Paul Bourget, in which he described decadence as a phenomenon of dissolution that would lead society into a state of anarchy, like organs that become autonomous and no longer obey the body, and cells that become autonomous and no longer obey the organs. This social dissolution was directly related to the decay of the language and literature of the age, in which the clauses no longer obeyed the syntax of the sentence, and the words no longer obeyed the syntax of the clauses. Diepenbrock leveled this charge of causing the decay of the language at the members of the Eighties Movement, whom he accused of reducing the language to incoherent impressions. But, just as the dissolute language of the Classics was absorbed and rejuvenated in the language of the Church, so the language of the Eighties Movement could be the "humus" of a new spiritual regeneration.

44 Van Halsema, *Te zoeken in deze angstige eeuw*, in particular pp. 9, 10, 22, 34.

45 See among others Roland Holst, *In en buiten het tij*, pp. 184-192. See also Tibbe, *R.N. Roland Holst*.

46 In the countries neighboring the Netherlands, Gothic was seen as an expression of the "national" character. This also happened in the Netherlands to some extent. Van Lennep made a tentative attempt to demonstrate that Gothic vaults were akin to Dutch beech woods.

47 Quotations in Nikolaus Pevsner, "Ruskin et Viollet-le-Duc."

48 There is no detailed study of the influence of Ruskin and Viollet in the Netherlands, more particularly of Viollet's influence on Cuypers. Reinink, *Amsterdam en de Beurs van Berlage*, is a step in this direction. It is striking, for instance, that in *De heilige linie* Thijm seeks links with kindred spirits like Reichensperger and Didron, but only mentions Viollet in passing. He is rather reserved about the latter's practical approach (see Bekaert, *A la recherche de Viollet-le-Duc*, p. 57). Viollet did collaborate on Thijm's *Dietsche Warande*. Just what did Thijm think of Viollet? He must have given this a great deal of thought and discussed it with Cuypers.

49 Quoted in Van der Plas, *Vader Thijm*, p. 276.

50 See Bock, *Anfänge einer neuen Architektur*, pp. 299-303.

51 In 1895 *Architectura* devoted an issue to Cuypers's 70th birthday. In it, Lauweriks accused him of casting Viollet's principles in a medieval Gothic mold (see Bax,

"Lauweriks en Cuypers," p. 19). Berlage praised Cuypers extensively in "Over architectuur" (1895), but he too felt that Cuypers "has remained too medieval in ideas and deeds." Cuypers remained wedded to a style and Berlage set himself the goal of cutting loose from that style and building "constructively" (Berlage, "Over architectuur." In: *Tweemaandelijksch Tijdschrift*, 2, pp. 219, 223).

52 Quoted in Maas, "Vosmaer en het Rijksmuseum," pp. 202, 203.

53 Quoted in Maas, "Vosmaer en het Rijksmuseum," p. 210.

54 Kiers and Tissink, *Het Rijksmuseum*; Veenland-Heineman and Heijn, *Het nieuwe Rijksmuseum*; Becker, "Ons Rijksmuseum wordt een tempel"; Von der Dunk, "Jhr. Victor de Stuers en het Rijksmuseum," pp. 37-77; Hellenberg Hubar, *Arbeid en Bezieling*.

55 Thijm's article was originally delivered as a lecture in Paris ("L'art et l'archéologie en Hollande") and the French version was printed in Didron's *Annales archéologiques*. The Dutch translation was published in book form in 1855: Alberdingk Thijm, *De kunst in Nederland*, together with a reprint of the reply by C. Leemans (from *De Gids* 1854) and Alberdingk Thijm's response to this in Alberdingk Thijm, *Dietsche Warande*.

56 De Stuers's article was republished in 1975, with a lengthy preface and postscript by a working group from the Kunsthistorisch Instituut at the University of Amsterdam (De Stuers, *Holland op zijn smalst*). We have taken data about the national art collections and the historic buildings principally from this edition and from Tillema, *Schetsen uit de geschiedenis van de monumentenzorg*.

57 Viollet does wrap his statement around in various conditions: 1. the "rétablissement" must be scientifically documented, 2. it may only affect the structure and not the appearance, 3. adaptation to modern use does not have to be rejected out of hand, and (most importantly), 4. all the changes made over the course of time should be respected. As we shall see, Cuypers did not allow this last restriction to cramp his style when he undertook his restoration projects.

58 Other prestige projects carried out by Cuypers include the restoration of St. Servatius in Maastricht and De Haar Castle.

59 In 1879 the minister, Johannes Kappeyne, openly stated that he had no time for old monuments. He even tabled a bill proposing that there should be no further state grants for restoration projects. The new minister, Willem Six, withdrew the bill that same year.

60 For Berlage see: Bock, *Anfänge einer neuen Architektur*; Polano, *Hendrik Petrus Berlage*; Reinink, *Amsterdam en de Beurs van Berlage*; Singelenberg, *H.P. Berlage Idea and Style*; Broekhuis, "Het beeldhouwwerk van Lambertus Zijl," pp. 195-227.

61 See Koopmans, "In het voetspoor van Pythagoras," pp. 23-24.

62 In *De Opmerker* 27 (1892), reproduced in Bock, *Architectura*, p. 20.

63 A good idea of Viollet's importance is to be found in "Zeven voordrachten over bouwkunst," 1907, by Jos Cuypers, Kromhout, Pek, Berlage, et al.

64 Berlage, "Over Architectuur," (1896), pp. 219, 223. Lauweriks (*Architectura*, 1903) accused Berlage of stealing their ideas without understanding what the deeper grounds (relationships) were, see Koopmans, "In het voetspoor van Pythagoras," p. 26. For the relation between Viollet and Vâhâna see also Bock, *Anfänge einer neuen Architektur*, p. 304.

65 Berlage, "Over Architectuur," (1896), p. 232. Elsewhere Berlage said: "Only religious community ideas can be the bearer of such an order." By "order," he meant the unity of social order and architectural form: Berlage, *Een drietal lezingen*, p. 7.

66 Berlage, "Over Architectuur," (1896), p. 232. Berlage's utopia did not materialize. Over time his ideas became increasingly vague; they shifted to an ever more distant, undefined future and became ever more utopian, as they became increasingly impossible to achieve in reality. According to Tak, Berlage's socialism was a "general spiritual movement," "a sort of religion, at worst humanism, not a materialistic philosophy." This is why Berlage's position in the *Kroniek* debate was also unclear. He actually came somewhere between the two schools (socialism and mysticism).

67 See Bock, *Anfänge einer neuen Architektur*, pp. 347-377.

68 Berlage reproached Cuypers for designing the decoration himself instead of leaving it to the painters and sculptors who stood alongside him: Berlage, "Over Architectuur," (1896), p. 221.

69 Verwey, "Bijdragen tot de versiering van de Nieuwe Beurs (1899-1900)," pp. 728-735; Verwey, "Bijdragen tot de versiering van de Nieuwe Beurs," pp. 1-37. He later (*Bouwkundig Weekblad Architectura*, 1934) gave a commentary on the plan. See also Uyldert, *Dichterlijke strijdbaarheid*.

70 See Verwey, "Bijdragen tot de versiering." See also Broekhuis, "Ideologie in steen."

71 See Broekhuis, "Ideologie in steen";

Hammacher, *De levenstijd van Antoon Derkinderen*, pp. 92-93; De Vries, "Albert Verwey en de beeldende kunst," pp. 7-26. There is extensive documentation on Derkinderen in Trappeniers (ed.), *Antoon Derkinderen*.

72   Article by E. Redelé, in Bock, *Anfänge einer neuen Architektur*, p. 347.

73   Reinink, *Amsterdam en de Beurs van Berlage*, p. 33.

74   For documentation we refer to Boterenbrood, *Het scheepvaarthuis*.

75   In Bergvelt and Van Burkom, *Amsterdamse School*, pp. 42-44.

76   It should be pointed out here that buildings were still being constructed in this way at the end of the nineteenth century. The Concertgebouw (1883-1889), for example, is likewise supported by a concrete skeleton designed by A.L. van Gendt (Boterenbrood, *Het scheepvaarthuis*, pp. 83-89). The difference, however, is that the Scheepvaarthuis was "decorated" in modern style and does not, as the Concertgebouw does, attempt to imitate a historical style.

77   See Berlage, "De verhouding van de bouwkunst." The Scheepvaarthuis appears to have influenced German expressionism. Behrens's office lobby for Hoechst in Frankfurt am Main was probably inspired by the foyer of the Scheepvaarthuis (see Bergvelt, *Amsterdamse School*, p. 49). There were many direct contacts between the Amsterdam School and German expressionism.

78   Sigrid Johannisse, "Nederlandse architectuur 1900-1924."

79   Sigrid Johannisse, "Nederlandse architectuur 1900-1924." The Scheepvaarthuis is widely regarded as the first building by the Amsterdam School (see Bergvelt, *Amsterdamse School*; Boterenbrood, *Het scheepvaarthuis*.). Not everyone accepts this. Oud nominates De Klerk's "Hillehuis" of 1911 as the movement's first building; Banham and Cassella agree with him.

80   This direction, which he defended in his oration in 1908, was the rehabilitation of crafts.

81   Jan Engelman, in Bergvelt, *Amsterdamse School*, p. 89.

82   *De Stijl* 1, 1918, see Tibbe, *R.N. Roland Holst*, pp. 235-236.

83   Blotkamp, *Mondriaan*, pp. 138-140, 158.

84   In an article on Thorn Prikker written in 1932, Holst says that the modern artist lacks an ideological guideline, in other words a cohesive idea of social reality, within which he can shape his art (Roland Holst, *In en buiten het tij*, p. 125).

Chapter 5   "In this manner one approaches Spirit" - From symbolism to early abstract painting

1   See among others Lethève, *Impressionnistes et symbolistes*.

2   See also Lövgren, *The Genesis of Modernism*.

3   In fact Emile Bernard painted his *Bretonnes dans la prairie* earlier that year, 1888, which is why he claimed to be the first "synthetist."

4   In subsequent years foreign artists also joined, including the highly interesting Jan Verkade, who later entered the monastery of Beuron but remained close friends with Sérusier. See Boyle-Turner, *Jan Verkade* and Sérusier, *ABC de la peinture*.

5   Aurier, *Le symbolisme en peinture*, p. 13.

6   Vincent van Gogh, *Correspondentie*, Letter 806 (September 19, 1899), lines 237-244, Van Gogh Museum Amsterdam, in preparation. See also Van Buuren, *Vincent van Goghs navolging van Christus*.

7   Baudelaire, *Oeuvres Complètes*, vol.1, p. 11. Translated by Richard Howard, 1982.

8   Baudelaire, "Exposition universelle 1855," in *Oeuvres Complètes*, vol. 2, pp. 575-598. The original reads as follows:
Delacroix, lac de sang, hanté des mauvais anges,
Ombragé par un bois de sapins toujours vert,
Où, sous un ciel chagrin, des fanfares étranges
Passent comme un soupir étouffé de Weber

9   As a poet Baudelaire did not always keep to the aesthetic he outlined in his art criticism and in "Correspondances." For the most part his poems are "symbolic" in the traditional sense that images are developed that stand for the poet and his feelings. Take for example "The albatross" (a symbol of the failed poet) or the chest full of souvenirs and scents (standing for memories stored deep in the poet's mind).

10   Mallarmé, *Oeuvres Complètes*, pp. 57-58. Translation by Keith Bosley in: *Mallarmé: The Poems*, p.139.

11   Sérusier, *ABC de la peinture*, p. 123. On the same lines: "I am now firmly persuaded that all an artist can do is to create a harmony of form and color" (Sérusier, *ABC de la peinture*, p. 122).

12   Denis, *Du symbolisme au classicisme*, p. 73.

13   Quoted in Burhan, *Vision and Visionaries*, p. 20.

14   Henry, "Introduction à une esthétique scientifique," in: *La Revue contemporaine*, 1884. Burhan, *Vision and Visionaries*, p. 37 mentions *L'archéomètre* (1912) by Saint-Yves d'Alveydre, an instrument dating from the late eighteen-nineties that established cor-

respondences between colors, sounds, numbers and letters on a sound scientific basis. There is a painting by Sérusier in which this "compass" is depicted.

15 Denis, *Du symbolisme au classicisme*, p. 96. This deliberate, rational way of working led Denis to call the new art "neo-classicism." Gauguin, Bernard and he himself supposedly composed their canvases like Poussin. "Versailles is the height of fashion, Poussin is praised to the skies. Bach draws full houses, romanticism is scorned," wrote Denis in *Du symbolisme au classicisme*, p. 117. See also Stuart Hughes, *Consciousness and Society*.

16 Aurier, *Albert*, p. 28.

17 Sérusier, *ABC de la peinture*, pp. 87 and 13.

18 Sérusier, *ABC de la peinture*, pp. 16-17 and 24.

19 Denis, *Du symbolisme au classicisme*, p. 70.

20 Denis, *Du symbolisme au classicisme*, p. 33. Similarly Hennequin (1886): "from the most general point of view a painting must indeed be regarded as an ensemble of lines and colors arranged so as to have certain emotional effects," quoted in Burhan, *Vision and Visionaries*, p. 150.

21 Denis, *Du symbolisme au classicisme*, p. 72.

22 Denis, *Du symbolisme au classicisme*, p. 40. The reference to the arabesque seems particularly appropriate. Used in Koran calligraphy and the decoration of mosques, the arabesque is a type of ornament in which the depiction of humans or animals is forbidden and which is generally regarded as expressing the unseen and divine.

23 See Burhan, *Vision and Visionaries*, p. 124; see also the last part of Aurier's definition of symbolism: "5. **decorative**, decorative art in the true sense, as interpreted by the Egyptians and most probably the Greeks and the Primitives," Aurier, *Albert*, p. 26.

24 Gustave Kahn wrote that the symbolist poets were convinced that Seurat's "research into line and color showed exact points of agreement with our theories on the verse and the sentence," in: Signac, *D'Eugène Delacroix*, p. 15. Compare also on similar lines Sutter, "Les phénomènes de la vision," in: *L'Art*, 1880, which was in turn based on Rood, *Modern Chromatics*.

25 Note in February 1881, quoted in: Bronde, *Seurat in Perspective*, p. 14. This remark is entirely in line with Baudelaire's view quoted at the beginning of this chapter. On Seurat see also Homer, *Seurat and the Science of Painting* and Zimmermann, *Seurat and the Art Theory of his Time*.

26 In his extensive study of neo-impressionism, *D'Eugène Delacroix*, Signac explains in detail how neo-impressionism developed in two phases. In the first Delacroix no

longer mixed his colors, but put them next to each other in "hachures." This method was adopted by the impressionists, who extended the dissection of color to the point of "dégradation" (putting shades of the same color side by side). This technique was perfected in neo-impressionist divisionism: unmixed colors applied completely separately.

27 Bronde, *Seurat in perspective* p. 17. Aurier cites Humbert as influencing his ideas: Aurier, *Le symbolisme*, p. 58. Kandinsky's color scheme is based on the same principles and must be derived, directly or indirectly, from Humbert, but Kandinsky does not cite him. Kandinsky, *Uber das Geistige in der Kunst*, pp. 84-105. Mondrian does explicitly mention Humbert: Mondrian, "De nieuwe beelding in de schilderkunst," p. 108, note 14.

28 Most appropriately, since Anquetin and Bernard had studied stained-glass techniques, see Lövgren, *The Genesis of Modernism*, p. 105. Denis points to the anti-representational effect of the heavy cloison lines: "Instead of windows opening on to nature, they are heavily decorative, flat pieces, rich in color and surrounded by a rough line, cloisonned, for it was referred to as cloisonnism or Japonism," Denis, *Du symbolisme au classicisme*, p. 58. Working in stained glass also made it easier for several members of De Stijl to make the transition to abstract art. In 1916 Vilmos Huszár made stained-glass windows with a high level of abstraction. Theo van Doesburg followed his example in the spring of 1917 and used this technique (and the example of Huszár) to achieve the same level of abstraction in a few months that Mondrian and Van der Leck had meantime reached in their paintings. See Blotkamp, *De beginjaren van De Stijl*, p. 25.

29 Aurier, *Le symbolisme*, pp. 28, 23 and 24 respectively. Also written as "signs of ideas."

30 Sérusier, *ABC de la peinture*, p. 44.

31 Aurier, *Le symbolisme*, p. 28.

32 Denis, *Du symbolisme au classicisme*, p. 50; Sérusier, *ABC de la peinture*, p. 9.

33 Interview May 13, 1895 in: *Echo de Paris*, included in: Gauguin, *Oviri*, p. 138.

34 Polak, *Het fin-de-siècle in de Nederlandse schilderkunst*, p. 307.

35 See among others James, "Mondrian and the Dutch Symbolists"; Blotkamp, et al., *Kunstenaren der Idee: Symbolistische tendenzen in Nederland ca 1880-1930*; Steen, "Symbolisme," in: Imanse, *Van Gogh tot Cobra*; Van Uitert and Gerards, *Jan Toorop*.

36 See also the other drawings in the series to which *Les Rôdeurs* belongs: *The Garden of*

Sorrows (1890), *Oh Grave, Where is Thy Victory* (1892) and *The Three Brides* (1893). In *Play of Lines: The Rise, Against Opposition, of Modern Art* (1893) the obstructive art of the past is personified by an aged elephant with worn-down tusks, while the new art is heralded by trumpets.

37 See Van Uitert, "Beeldende kunst en muziek," pp. 67-74.

38 Note by Toorop in the article by De Vries, "Over Toorops Drie Bruiden en Annonciation du Nouveau Mysticisme," in: *Elsevier*, pp. 363-365, occasioned by a passage on sound lines; copy in the Toorop collection of the Koninklijke Bibliotheek, TC C 174,9.

39 Koninklijke Bibliotheek, Toorop collection, TC C 169. With thanks to Tejo Meedendorp, who drew my attention to this source.

40 Plasschaert, *Jan Toorop*, p. 9.

41 Roland Holst, *Over Kunst en Kunstenaar*, pp. 39-47 and 48-54.

42 Roland Holst, *Over Kunst en Kunstenaar*, pp. 143-174.

43 It is likely that Holst derived his theory of the "Sign" from Aurier. See Tibbe, *R.N. Roland Holst 1868-1938*, p. 57. In fact this theory, in which he opposed the art of the image to the art of the sign, dates from quite late. As far as we have been able to establish, he first presented it in 1925 in his article on the death of Derkinderen (Roland Holst, *Over Kunst en Kunstenaar*, pp. 211-215) and later in his inaugural address as director of the State Academy of Art (Roland Holst, "Over vrije en gebonden vormen in de plastische kunst," pp. 227-250).

44 Roland Holst, *In en buiten het tij*, pp. 113-117.

45 See Hammacher, *De levenstijd van Antoon Der Kinderen* and Broekhuis, "Antoon Derkinderen en de Beurs van Berlage," pp. 2 and 4-14.

46 In a review of work that Thorn exhibited at the Rotterdamse Kunstkring (March 19, 1893).

47 Joosten, *De brieven van Johan Thorn Prikker*, p. 127 and letter January 11, 1894, p.162.

48 Joosten, *De brieven van Johan Thorn Prikker*, p. 133.

49 Joosten, *De brieven van Johan Thorn Prikker*, p. 98.

50 Joosten, *De brieven van Johan Thorn Prikker*, p.187, on "Moine Epique."

51 Joosten, *De brieven van Johan Thorn Prikker*, pp. 153, 162.

52 See Bax, "Lauweriks en Cuypers," pp. 8-20, and the same author's highly informative and thorough article "Het 'Sfeeren' systeem 1898-1900," pp. 17-30.

53 Walenkamp, "Voor- Historische Wijsheid,"

in Bock, *Architectura 1893-1918*, p. 63. On similar lines Lauweriks observes, "Is it not the rhythm, the tone, the accent, the secret effect of number, that great master of nature, that eternally brings harmonious rest to the lower man, so that the soul can hear the soul of the poet? Without words." (Lecture for Architectura et Amicitia, 1895 entitled "Art and philosophy," quoted in: Bax, *Mondriaan aan de Amstel 1892-1912*, p. 12.)

54 In *Bouw- en Sierkunst*, 1898, article reprinted in: Bock, *Architectura*, pp. 82-84. Elsewhere in this article De Bazel remarks: "All building elements stand in relationships to each other based on natural laws. This order, which invisibly governs the relationships of forms, must be recognized in man's creations, and all connections opposed to it are arbitrary and ugly."

55 *Architectura*, 1895, quoted in: Bock, *Architectura 1893-1918*, p. 109.

56 According to Seuphor, *Piet Mondrian*, Mondrian first spelt his name with one "a" in the catalogue of the *Moderne Kunstkring* exhibition in October 1912. But *Amaryllis* (1907 according to Seuphor's dating) is already signed "Piet Mondrian." Is the date of *Amaryllis* later? Did Mondrian sign the watercolor at a later date? At all events it seems unlikely that he spelt his name with one "a" prior to 1912.

57 See Blotkamp, *Mondriaan*, p. 59.

58 See Heyting, *De wereld in een dorp*.

59 See various versions of *Pier and Ocean*, 1914; *Composition*, 1915; *Composition in line*, 1916 and above all 1917.

60 On Mondrian's relations with theosophy see among others Blotkamp, *Mondriaan*; Seuphor, *Piet Mondrian*; Bax, "De passies van Piet Mondriaan," pp. 32-42 and Welsh, "Mondrian and Theosophy."

61 See De Jager, *Het beeldende denken*.

62 "I got it all from the Secret Doctrine (Blavatsky), not from Schoenm. Though he says the same," letter from Mondrian to Van Doesburg, quoted in Blotkamp, *Mondriaan*, p. 111.

63 Humbert de Superville, *Essai sur les signes inconditionnels*, pp. 8-9; Kandinsky, *Uber das Geistige in der Kunst*, pp. 84-105.

64 In *De Stijl 1* (1917-1918), p. 30.

65 Mondrian, *Two Mondrian Sketchbooks*, p. 36.

66 Quoted in: Blotkamp, *Meesters van het licht*, p. 80.

67 For example, in: "De nieuwe beelding," *De Stijl 1* (1917), p. 74.

68 Mondrian, "De nieuwe beelding in de schilderkunst," [1917], p.4.

69 Mondrian, *Two Mondrian Sketchbooks*, p, 70. On the same lines: "The surface has little meaning. In the present period there is more penetration. The surface disappears.

One draws near to force" (Mondrian, *Two Mondrian Sketchbooks*, p. 71) and in a letter of 1915 to Augusta de Meester, in which he explains that those who penetrate to the essence approach the spiritual and thus the divine (in Holtzman and James, ed., *The New Art - The New Life. The collected writings of Piet Mondrian*, p. 15). This duality also applies to man: his "cultivated appearance" contrasts with a "deeper, more aware inner self" (Mondrian, "De nieuwe beelding in de schilderkunst," [1917], p. 2).

70 Mondrian, *Two Mondrian Sketchbooks*, p. 67.

71 Mondrian, "De nieuwe beelding in de schilderkunst," (1917), p. 14. Compare also: "balanced relationship depicts most purely the universal, the harmony, the unity characteristic of the spirit," Mondrian, "De nieuwe beelding in de schilderkunst," (1917), p. 4.

72 Mondrian, "De nieuwe beelding in de schilderkunst," (1917), pp. 16-17.

73 In this connection Mondrian talks about the "reductive destruction" (underlined by him) of phenomena for the sake of the "exact" expression of what "shows through" in nature (Mondrian, "De nieuwe beelding in the schilderkunst," [1917], p. 29). Even in its terminology this theory is reminiscent of Edmund Husserl's "eidetic reduction." Mondrian later uses the terms "reduce" or "resolve" quite often.

74 Mondrian, *Two Mondrian Sketchbooks*, p. 47.

75 *De Stijl*, 5 (1922), pp. 24-25.

76 Jaffé, *De Stijl 1917-1931*, p. 125.

77 Mondrian, "Natuurlijke en abstracte realiteit. Trialoog," (1919), p.110; (1920) p. 65.

78 Quoted in Hoek, "Piet Mondriaan, " in: Blotkamp, *De beginjaren van De Stijl*, p. 74.

79 Kandinsky, *Uber das Geistige in der Kunst*, pp. 110 and 120. "Gegensätze und widersprüche - das ist unsere Harmonie" translates as "Opposites and contradictions - this is our harmony" and "zu spalten, in Widersprüche zu tauchen" translates as "breakdown, to bathe in contradictions."

80 Mondrian, *Two Mondrian Sketchbooks*, p. 48.

81 At the end of his life Mondrian began to have doubts about this principle. In a letter to Sweeney in 1943 he wrote that in the past he had paid too little attention to dynamics and that the dynamic should perhaps be preferred to the static. In another letter to Sweeney he drew a distinction between two kinds of balance: the static and the dynamic. A love of static balance was innate to man, he now said, but it was art's task to destroy this balance: "vitality in the continual succession of time always destroys this balance. Abstract art is a concrete expression of this vitality." Sweeney, James Johnson, *Art News*. Quoted in

Seuphor, *Piet Mondrian*, p. 199.

82 Quoted by Hoek in: Blotkamp, *De beginjaren van De Stijl*, p. 81.

83 The mills in question are (according to Joosten and Welsh, *Piet Mondrian: Catalogue raisonné*): A368 "Post Mill at Heeswijk" Rear View, A369 "Post Mill at Heeswijk" Side View, A370 "Post Mill at Veghel," A371 "Post Mill at Uden," A397 "Stammer Mill," A398 "Stammer Mill," A399 "Stammer Mill," A400 "Stammer Mill," A401 "Broekerzijder Mill," A402 "Oostzijdse Mill," A403 "Oostzijdse Mill," A404 "Oostzijdse Mill," A405 "Oostzijdse Mill," A406 "Oostzijdse Mill," A407 "Oostzijdse Mill," A408 Oostzijdse Mill," A409 "Oostzijdse Mill," A410 "Oostzijdse Mill," A411 Oostzijdse Mill"; A412 Oostzijdse Mill," A419 "Oostzijdse Mill," A420 "Oostzijdse Mill."

84 The mills in question are (Joosten and Welsh, *Piet Mondrian: Catalogue raisonné*): A413 "Oostzijdse Mill," A414 "Oostzijdse Mill," A415 "Oostzijdse Mill," A416 "Oostzijdse Mill," A417 "Oostzijdse Mill," A418 "Oostzijdse Mill," A422 "Windmill near Tall Trees," A426 "Mill near Tall Trees," A427 "Wip Mill and Fields," A652 "Study for Winkel Mill," A653 "The Winkel Mill," A654 "The Winkel Mill," A677 "Mill at Domburg," A692 "The Red Mill," C11 two sketches, C12 drawing, C13 "Windmill," C14 "Windmill," C15 charcoal sketch, C16 "Windmill in the Evening."

85 See among others Blotkamp, *Mondriaan*; Welsh, "Mondrian and Theosophy."

86 The Swiss architect Alfred Roth commissioned *Composition with red, yellow and blue* (1930) from Mondrian. He asked Roth how he wanted the painting: "Write to me to say if your preference is for blue and yellow, white and gray, or rather red, a little blue and yellow and white and gray. The latter kind with red are more "real," the others more spiritual, more or less." Quoted by Hoek in: Blotkamp, *De beginjaren van De Stijl*, p. 78; Blotkamp, *Mondriaan*, pp. 204-205.

87 Mondrian "Natuurlijke en abstracte realiteit," (1920), p. 16.

88 Mondrian, "De nieuwe beelding in de schilderkunst," (1917), p. 74.

89 Mondrian, "De nieuwe beelding in de schilderkunst," (1917), p. 6. The whole sentence reads: "Through its exact plastic expression of cosmic relationship it is a direct expression of the universal; through its rhythm, through its material reality, it is an expression of the subjective, of the individual." It is apparent from this that for Mondrian "Rhythm" is an aspect of the material, of nature, of the individual. He states this view elsewhere as well. In his

eyes "Rhythm" is opposed to the universal and abstract. Thus he gives one of the key terms of symbolism a completely different and even opposite meaning compared with the one given by Vermeylen or Holst, for whom "Rhythm" indicates precisely the abstract and universal interrelationship of the cosmos.

90 Mondrian, "De nieuwe beelding in de schilderkunst," (1917), pp. 3 and 128; Mondrian, "Natuurlijke en abstracte realiteit," (1919), p. 88.

91 Mondrian, "Natuurlijke en abstracte realiteit," (1919), p. 99.

92 Mondrian, "Natuurlijke en abstracte realiteit," (1919), p. 110.

93 In 1919 Gino Severini defended this view in De Stijl. He traced De Stijl's approach to art back to symbolism as Mallarmé conceived of it. The present aesthetic "begins with Mallarmé and the symbolists. It is only today that we have art in the same relationship as Mallarmé's work," in De Stijl 2 (1919), p. 25.

I am grateful to Carel Blotkamp and Tejo Meedendorp for their critical comments on this chapter.

Chapter 6   The dawn of mass education

1 Harmsen, Blauwe en rode jeugd, p. 96
2 Harmsen, Blauwe en rode jeugd, pp. 90-91.
3 Harmsen, Blauwe en rode jeugd, pp. 2-3.
4 Turksma, Geschiedenis, passim.
5 Lauret, Per imperatief mandaat, p. 107.
6 Knippenberg, Deelname, p. 69.
7 Harmsen, Blauwe en rode jeugd, p. 71.
8 Knippenberg, Deelname, pp. 69-70.
9 Megens and Rol, "Rijkeluisdochters," pp. 115-117.
10 Boonstra, Waardij, p. 23.
11 Knippenberg, Deelname, pp. 106-107.
12 Karsten, Breukvlak, pp. 58-59.
13 Spies, "De romantische De Ruyter," pp. 264-273.
14 Hroch, Social Preconditions, pp. 145-147.
15 Van den Berg, De toegang, pp.132-133 and 242.
16 Peeters, Excursion pédagogique, passim.
17 De Jong, Jan Ligthart, p. 1.
18 De Jong, Jan Ligthart, p. 250.
19 De Jong, Jan Ligthart, p. 251.
20 Wielinga, "Vernieuwingstendenties," pp. 35-63.
21 Bakker, Kind en karakter, p. 59; Storck, "De eisch van aanschouwelijkheid," pp. 88-89; Doornenbal, "Het kind," pp. 245-249.
22 Gunning, De studie, p. 13.
23 De Vroede, "Onderwijs en pedagogiek," pp. 118-119.

24 Dasberg and Jansing, Meer kennis, p. 83.
25 Doornenbal, "Het kind," p. 249.
26 Imelman and Meijer, De Nieuwe School, p. 30; Noordam, Historische pedagogiek, p. 91; Van der Velde, "Lager onderwijs," pp. 65-91.
27 Mulder, Beginsel en beroep, p. 246.
28 Mulder, Beginsel en beroep, p. 77.
29 Van der Velde, "Lager onderwijs," p. 115.
30 Schwegman, Maria Montessori, p. 214.
31 Quoted in: Grotenhuis, Op zoek, pp. 27-28.
32 Bos, Onze Volksopleiding, passim.
33 Casimir, Nederlandsch Lyceum, p. 31.
34 Mulder, Beginsel en beroep, p. 86.
35 Grotenhuis, Op zoek, p. 94.
36 Pouwelse, Haar verstand, passim.
37 Grotenhuis, Op zoek, pp. 93-100.
38 Quoted in: Bartels, Een eeuw, p. 19.
39 Otterspeer, De wiekslag, p. 292.
40 Willink, Tweede Gouden Eeuw, p. 30.
41 Fortgens, Schola Latina, pp. 221-222.
42 Krul, "Nederlandse gymnasia," pp. 48-51; Boekholt, Klassiek of modern?, pp. 27-28.
43 Mandemakers, Gymnasiaal en middelbaar onderwijs, pp. 91-92.
44 Mandemakers, Gymnasiaal en middelbaar onderwijs, pp. 129-131.
45 Mandemakers, Gymnasiaal en middelbaar onderwijs, pp. 224-228.
46 Mandemakers, Gymnasiaal en middelbaar onderwijs, pp. 235-236.
47 Mandemakers, Gymnasiaal en middelbaar onderwijs, pp. 104-106.
48 Gorter, Mei, p. 93.
"De cirkels draaien en het witte pad Glijdt weg: ze loeren op elkanders wielen En trappen vastberaden, in hun zielen Is nijd en haat, voor 't doel de éne wint, Maar de ander haalt weer in en rijdt verblind. Van wanhoop hem voorbij. De laatste trap. Slaakt los mensengejuich en handenklap."
49 De Liagre Böhl, Met al mijn bloed, p. 90.
50 Gedenkboek HFC, pp. 9-10; Bottenburg, Verborgen competitie, pp. 142-143.
51 Van Dis, Dijkema and Meijer, Ik neem afscheid, p. 35.
52 Ter Gouw, Volksvermaken, p. 586.
53 Ter Gouw, Volksvermaken, p. 331.
54 Stokvis, Strijd over sport, p. 8.
55 Buruma, Voltaire's Coconuts, p. 147.
56 Stokvis, Strijd over sport, pp. 57-58.
57 Bottenburg, Verborgen competitie, pp. 40, 78 and 139.
58 Bottenburg, Verborgen competitie, p. 142.
59 Stokvis, Strijd over sport, pp. 66-67.
60 Stokvis, Strijd over sport, p. 67.
61 Linders-Rooijendijk, Gebaande wegen, pp. 81-84.
62 Linders-Rooijendijk, Gebaande wegen, p. 17.
63 Moll, Jaap Eden, p. 162.
64 Linders-Rooijendijk, Gebaande wegen, pp. 92-93.

65 Te Velde, *Gemeenschapszin*, pp. 216-218.
66 Kramer and Van Reeth, "Schets van de ontwikkeling," p. 26.
67 *Gedenkboek Genootschap van Leeraren*, p. 40.
68 Bottenburg, *Verborgen competitie*, pp. 178-179.
69 Stokvis, *Strijd over sport*, p. 11.
70 Stokvis, "De school en de ontwikkeling," pp. 61 and 63.
71 Stokvis, "De school en de ontwikkeling," p. 66.
72 Stokvis, "Sport en het mediasysteem," pp. 84-86.
73 Dona, *Sport en socialisme*, p. 123.
74 Miermans, *Voetbal in Nederland*, p. 252.

Chapter 7 Higher education and the sciences

1 Otterspeer, "Vereenvoudiging en bezuiniging," p. 253.
2 Groen, *Het wetenschappelijk onderwijs in Nederland*, p.10; Otterspeer, "Vereenvoudiging en bezuiniging," p. 244; Foppen, *Gistend beleid*, p. 44.
3 Boekholt, "De omnibus aliquid, de toto nihil."
4 Otterspeer, "Vereenvoudiging," p. 247.
5 Van Duyvendak, *De motivering van de klassieke vorming*.
6 Matthijssen, *De elite en de mythe*; Matthijssen, *Klasse-onderwijs*.
7 Labrie, *"Bildung" en politiek 1770-1830*; Brookman, *The making of a science policy*; Foppen, *Gistend beleid*.
8 De Vries, "De academicus en het bedrijfsleven," pp. 120-123.
9 De Vries, "De academicus," pp. 118, 123.
10 Westerdijk, "De ontwikkeling van het hoger onderwijs," p. 405.
11 Willink, *De tweede gouden eeuw*, p. 28.
12 Van 't Hoff, *Handelingen van het derde Nederlandse Natuur- en Geneeskundig Congres*, p. 27, quoted in: Willink, *De tweede gouden eeuw*, p. 32.
13 Rupp, *Van oude en nieuwe universiteiten*, p. 62.
14 Bosch, *Het geslacht van de wetenschap*, pp. 198-200.
15 Bosch, *Het geslacht*, p. 197.
16 Groen, *Het wetenschappelijk onderwijs*, p. 45.
17 Willink (1988) tried to define the golden age by counting publications.
18 See among others Kox, in Blom et al. *Een brandpunt van geleerdheid in de hoofdstad*.
19 This is evident from, among other things, the bibliographies published by the Physics and Medicine Congress. In the physics section the topics of heat, light and magnetism/electricity were particularly well represented.
20 For more on the background to these Acts, see Willink, *Burgerlijk sciëntisme*, p. 277ff.
21 A typical feature of professionalization was the systematic publication of research results. The astronomer Kapteyn (Groningen) issued "Publications of the Astronomical Laboratory at Groningen" (in English); Kamerlingh Onnes did something similar in Leiden.
22 Hutter, *Laboratoria in Nederland voor 1940*.
23 Groen, *Het wetenschappelijk onderwijs in Nederland van 1815 tot 1980*, p. 7; Hutter, *Toepassingsgericht onderzoek in de industrie*, p. 8.
24 Brookman, *The making of a science policy*, p. 409.
25 Willink, *De tweede gouden eeuw*, p. 241.
26 Incidentally, the rate of success was quite low. In Leiden thirty-two percent gained their master's degree. It is also noteworthy that most of the still very few women students around 1900 were registered with the math and physics departments (where they mainly studied pharmacy: Bosch, *Het geslacht van de wetenschap*; Kirejczyk, "Vrouwen kozen exact").
27 Wachelder, *Universiteit tussen vorming en opleiding*; see also his contribution in Palm et al., *De toga om de wetenschap*.
28 Willink, *De tweede gouden eeuw*, p. 246ff.
29 Willink, *De tweede gouden eeuw*.
30 Brookman, *The making of a science policy*, p. 107.
31 Van Lunteren, "Van meten tot weten."
32 Van Berkel, *In het voetspoor van Stevin*, pp. 139-143.
33 For biographical information about Van der Waals, see: Kox, "Johannes D. van de Waals"; Kox, "Johannes Diderik van der Waals"; Kipnis, Yavelov and Rowlinson, *Van der Waals and Molecular Science*; Maas, "Over zwoegers en zeloten"; Van Lunteren, "Bosscha's leerboek en Van der Waals' proefschrift"; Rowlinson, *J.D. van der Waals*.
34 For biographical information about Kamerlingh Onnes, see: Van Helden, "Biographies: Heike Kamerlingh Onnes"; Mendelssohn, *De jacht naar het absolute nulpunt*; Lang, "Heike Kamerlingh Onnes"; Van Helden, *De koudste plek op aarde*; Staas, "Cryogenics and low temperature physics"; Maas, *Atomisme en individualisme*.
35 On Kamerlingh Onnes's instrument-maker's school: Van Delft, "De blauwe jongens."
On his inaugural lecture: Laeseke, "Through Measurement to Knowledge."
36 For biographical information about Lorentz, see: Willink, *De Tweede Gouden Eeuw*, pp. 105-110; Van Helden, "Biographies: Hendrik Antoon Lorentz"; Kox, "Hendrik Antoon Lorentz en de 'Tweede Gouden Eeuw'"; De Haas-Lorentz, *H.A. Lorentz*; Kox, "Hendrik A. Lorentz (1853-1928)"; Kuiken, "The centenary of a paper"; Theunissen,

"H.A. Lorentz' visie op wetenschap." See also: Theunissen, *Nut en nog eens nut*, pp. 168-184; Hoorn, "The physics laboratory."

37   For biographical information about Zeeman, see: Van Helden, "Biographies: Pieter Zeeman"; Kox and Troelstra, "Uit het Zeeman-archief"; Kox, "Pieter Zeeman"; Arabatzis, "The discovery of the Zeeman-effect."

38   Servos, *Physical chemistry from Ostwald to Pauling*.

39   For biographical information about Van 't Hoff, see: Van Berkel, "Biographies: Jacobus Henricus van 't Hoff"; Snelders, "The birth of stereochemistry"; Snelders, "J.H. van 't Hoff's research school."

40   A very readable explanation of Van 't Hoff's *Etudes* can be found in Somsen, *Wetenschappelijk onderzoek en algemeen belang*, pp. 13-15. See also: Ramberg and Somsen, "The young J.H. van 't Hoff." To mark the "Nobel Prize Centennial" in 2001 an annotated translation of "L'Équilibre chimique dans les systèmes gazeux ou dissous a l'état dilué" of 1885 was published with the aim of making Van 't Hoff's work accessible to a wider audience. Hornix and Mannaerts, *Van 't Hoff and the emergence of chemical thermodynamics*; Cordfuncke, *Een romantisch geleerde*.

41   Van Berkel, "Biographies: Hendrik Willem Bakhuis Roozeboom"; Snelders, *De geschiedenis van de scheikunde in Nederland*.

42   For biographical information about De Vries: Willink, *De Tweede Gouden Eeuw*, pp. 75-81 provides a brief biography of De Vries and his law of isotonic coefficients. Palm, "Biographies: Hugo Marie de Vries"; Theunissen, *Nut en nog eens nut*, pp. 123-148. In English: Theunissen, "Closing the door on Hugo de Vries' mendelism"; Theunissen, "Knowledge is power." Other English-language publications about De Vries: Meijer, "Hugo de Vries no Mendelian?"; Stamhuis & Meijer, & Zevenhuizen, "Hugo de Vries on heredity"; Zevenhuizen, "Keeping and scrapping"; Stamhuis, "The Reactions on Hugo de Vries's Intracellular Pangenesis"; De Veer, *Leven en werk van Hugo de Vries*; Visser, "Hugo de Vries"; Theunissen, "De beheersing van mutaties"; Coesèl & Zevenhuizen, "Op heterdaad betrapt?" See also: Theunissen, "Ontdekte Mendel de wetten van Mendel?" pp. 113-122.

43   For biographical information about Beijerick, see: Palm, "Biographies Martinus Willem Beijerinck"; Kammen, "Beijerinck's contribution to the virus concept"; Bos & Theunissen, *Beijerinck and the Delft school of microbiology*; Theunissen, "The beginnings of the 'Delft-tradition' revisited."

44   Barron, *The development of the electrocardio-graph*; Snellen, *Selected papers on electrocardiography*; Snellen, *W. Einthoven: father of electrocardiography*.

45   Einthoven, "The string galvanometer and human electrocardiogram."

46   One man who was convinced of the diagnostic value of the electrocardiogram was Thomas Lewis. He published his research results in: Lewis, *Clinical disorders of the heartbeat*.

47   Luyken, *Eijkman's discovery of the vitamins*; Carpenter & Sutherland, "Eijkman's contribution to the discovery of vitamins"; Eijkman & Visser, "Eijkman and the anti-beri-beri vitamin"; Kamminga, "Credit and resistance"; Carpenter, *Beriberi, white rice and vitamin B*.

48   A great deal was written about the beriberi controversy in the press, particularly in the *Algemeen Handelsblad*. For references, see: Bos, "De querulant en zijn prooi."

49   Alberts, Atzema & Van Maanen, "Mathematics in The Netherlands," p. 387.

50   Alberts, Atzema & Van Maanen, "Mathematics in The Netherlands."

51   For biographical information about Korteweg, see: Kox, "Korteweg, de Vries, and Dutch Science"; Kox, "Diederik Johannes Korteweg."

52   Dalen, *L.E.J. Brouwer, 1881-1966*; Dalen, *Mystic, geometer, and intuitionist*.

53   Stigt, *Brouwer's Intuitionism*.

54   For biographical information about Kapteyn, see: Paul, *Seeliger, Kapteyn and the rise of statistical astronomy*; Paul, "The death of a research programme"; Paul, "Kapteyn and the early 20th-century universe"; Willink, *De Tweede Gouden Eeuw*, pp. 88-94; Van Helden, "Biographies: Jacobus Cornelius Kapteyn"; Van der Kruit & Van Berkel, *The legacy of J.C. Kapteyn*. This is a commemorative collection, with all its attendant risks, but it does also provide a glimpse of Kapteyn's personal life, an overview of Kapteyn's correspondence, and an appendix dealing with misleading translations of passages in the only biography of Kapteyn, written by his daughter Henriëtta Hertzsprung-Kapteyn in 1928, and translated into English in 1993 by E.R. Paul as *The Life and Works of J.C. Kapteyn*.

55   An interesting picture of the man behind the scientist can be found in: Krul, "Kapteyn and Groningen."

56   See for example Van Berkel, "The natural sciences in the colonies," pp. 218-219. See also Maat, *Science cultivating practice*.

57   Van Berkel, "The natural sciences in the colonies," pp. 224-225.

58   Van Berkel, "The natural sciences in the colonies," pp. 223-224.

59   Theunissen, *Eugène Dubois en de aapmens van Java*. The English translation: *Eugène*

Dubois and the ape-man from Java; Leackey &
Slikkerveer, *Man-Ape, Ape-Man*; Shipman,
*The man who found the missing link: Eugène
Dubois and his lifelong quest to prove Darwin
right*; Shipman, *The man who found the missing link: the extraordinary life of Eugène
Dubois.*

60   See Snelders's essay on Van 't Hoff, in:
Blom et al., *Een brandpunt van geleerdheid in
de hoofdtad.*

61   Otterspeer, *De wiekslag van hun geest*, p.
290.

62   Lunteren, "Fysica en fin-de-siècle cultuur."

63   Van Berkel, *A History of Science in the
Netherlands.*

64   Daams, "Uit de geschiedenis van het
NNGC."

65   Vermij, introduction to *Balans en perspectief
van de Nederlandse cultuurgeschiedenis.*

66   Crawford, *Nationalism and internationalism
in science.*

67   Stokvis, "Openingsrede."

68   Merz, *A history of European thought in the
nineteenth century*, p. 300.

69   Brookman, *The making of a science policy.*

70   Organized by the Genootschap ter
Bevordering van Natuur-, Genees- en
Heelkunde; Van Berkel et al., *Spiegelbeeld
der wetenschap: Het Genootschap ter bevordering van Natuur-, Genees- en Heelkunde 1790-
1990*, p. 44.

Chapter 8   The future century of psychology

1   Schmidt, *Philosophie*, pp. 1-52. Also
Heymans, *Gesammelte kleinere Schriften*, vol.
1, pp. 1-55.

2   Heymans, *Gesammelte kleinere Schriften*, vol.
1, p. 54.

3   Heymans, *Afscheidscollege*; also as
"Abschiedsvorlesung" in: Heymans,
Gesammelte kleinere Schriften, vol. 3, pp. 621-
630.

4   Heymans, *Gesetze*; Heymans, *Metaphysik*;
Heymans, *Ethik.*

5   Heymans, *Psychologie der Frauen*; Heymans,
Psychologie der vrouwen; Heymans,
Psychologie des Femmes.

6   Heymans, *Toekomstige eeuw*; Heymans,
Künftige Jahrhundert; Heymans, "Siècle
futur"; also in: Heymans, *Gesammelte
kleinere Schriften*, vol. 2, pp. 263-290.

7   Heymans, *Afscheidscollege*, p. 5.

8   Heymans, "Methode."

9   Heymans, *Afscheidscollege*, p. 7.

10   Ibid., p. 9.

11   Ibid., p. 10.

12   Ibid., p. 11.

13   Quoted in: Verwey, *Gerard Heymans*, p. 66.

14   Heymans, *Karakter.*

15   Heymans, *Kritik.*

16   Heymans, "Zurechnung."

17   All in: *Gesammelte kleinere Schriften*, vol. 1,
pp. 59-167.

18   Heymans, *Gesetze*; Heymans, *Schets.*

19   Heymans, *Experiment*; also as Heymans,
"Experiment," *Gesammelte kleinere Schriften*,
vol. 1, pp. 168-186.

20   Heymans, *Experiment*, p. 8.

21   The letter is quoted in its entirety in
Draaisma, *Een laboratorium voor de ziel*,
pp. 12-13.

22   Ibid., p. 12.

23   Ibid., p. 13.

24   Ibid., p. 13.

25   Benschop and Draaisma, "Pursuit of
Precision."

26   Huisman and Draaisma, "Instrumentarium
Psychologisch Laboratorium," p. 96.

27   Danziger, *Constructing the subject.*

28   Danziger, *Constructing the subject*, p. 52.

29   Heymans, "Laboratorium," pp. 90-91.

30   All published in: Heymans, *Gesammelte
kleinere Schriften*, vol. 2, pp. 72-250.

31   Heymans, "Quantitative Untersuchungen,"
also in: Heymans, *Gesammelte kleinere
Schriften*, vol. 2, pp. 1-34.

32   Heymans, "Quantitative Untersuchungen";
also in: Heymans, *Gesammelte kleinere
Schriften*, vol. 2, pp. 35-71.

33   Heymans, *Gesammelte kleinere Schriften*,
vol. 3, p. 42.

34   The articles based on this questionnaire
appeared in the *Zeitschrift für Psychologie*
between 1906 and 1918 and were reprinted
in: Heymans, *Gesammelte kleinere Schriften*,
vol. 3, pp. 41-414.

35   Heymans and Wiersma,
"Geschlechtsanlage," *Gesammelte kleinere
Schriften*, vol. 3, pp. 132-184.

36   Heymans and Wiersma, "Allgemeinen
Erblichkeitsgesetzen," *Gesammelte kleinere
Schriften*, vol. 3, pp. 184-194.

37   Ibid., p. 186.

38   Derksen, *Wij psychologen*, pp. 29-30.

39   Van Strien and Feij, "Heymans," pp. 67-68.

40   Heymans, "Classificatie," p. 5.

41   Van Strien and Feij, "Heymans," p. 68.

42   Gross, *Secundärfunktion.*

43   Heymans, *Inleiding*, vol. 1, p. 30.

44   Van Strien and Feij, "Heymans," p. 70.

45   Heymans, *Inleiding*, vol. 1, p. 21.

46   Van Strien and Feij, "Heymans," p. 70.

47   Heymans, "Uitwassen."

48   Aletrino, *Opstellen.*

49   Heymans, "Uitwassen," p. 51.

50   Ibid., p. 60.

51   Draaisma, "Heymans versus Aletrino."

52   Heymans, "Uitwassen," p. 50.

53   Van Dijck, *Bijdragen.*

54   Pannenborg, *Bijdragen.*

55   De Graaf, *Karakter.*

56   Heymans, *Inleiding.*

57   Van Strien and Feij, "Heymans," p. 70.

58   Bigot, *Leerboek*, p. 232.

59   De Wilde, *Deelgenoten*, p. 186.
60   Quotes translated from the Dutch translation: Heymans, *Vrouwen*, p. 18.
61   Bosch, *Geslacht*, p. 231.
62   Heymans, *Psychologie der vrouwen*, p. 63.
63   Ibid., p. 63.
64   Ibid., p. 82.
65   Jensma and De Vries, *Veranderingen*, pp. 42 and 44.
66   De Wilde, *Deelgenoten*, p. 167.
67   Heymans, *Psychologie der vrouwen*, pp. 135-136.
68   Kirchhoff, *Akademische Frau*.
69   "Coéducation," *La Revue*.
70   Heymans, *Psychologie der vrouwen*, p. 156.
71   Ibid., p. 137.
72   Wisse, "Frage."
73   De Wilde, *Deelgenoten*, p. 189.
74   Heymans, *Psychologie der vrouwen*, p. 133.
75   Ibid., p. 141.
76   Ibid., p. 152.
77   Ibid., p. 157.
78   Ibid., p. 168.
79   Ibid., p. 184.
80   Ibid., p. 100.
81   Ibid., pp. 103-104.
82   Van den Berg van Eijsinga-Elias, "Prof. G. Heymans"; De Wilde, "Gerard Heymans"; De Vries, *Uitvinding*.
83   Wijnaendts Francken-Dyserinck, "Psychologie"; Van der Veen, "Psychologie"; De Wilde, *Deelgenoten*.
84   Heymans, *Psychologie der vrouwen*, p. 193.
85   Bosch, *Geslacht*, pp. 234-236.
86   Ibid., p. 231.
87   De Wilde, *Deelgenoten*, pp. 187-189.
88   Heymans, *Psychologie der vrouwen*, p. 47.
89   Ibid., p. 19.
90   Ibid., p. 286.
91   Ibid., p. 211.
92   Fechner, *Vorschule*, p. 1.
93   Heymans, *Metafysica en aesthetica*.
94   Heymans, *Einführung in die Ethik*.
95   Heymans, *Inleiding in de metaphysica*, p. 7.
96   Heymans, *Inleiding in de metaphysica*, p. 454.
97   Ibid., p. 455.
98   Le Claire, *Letters*, p. 168.
99   Quoted in: Verwey, *Gerard Heymans*, p. 46.
100 Ibid., p. 15.
101 Ibid., p. 47.
102 Heymans, *Inleiding in de metaphysica*, p. 35.
103 Heymans, *Toekomstige eeuw*.
104 Derksen, *Wij psychologen*, p. 50.
105 Heymans, *Toekomstige eeuw*, p. 11.
106 Ibid., p. 12.
107 Ibid., p. 16.
108 Ibid., p. 17.
109 Ibid., p. 23.
110 Ibid., p. 24.
111 Kevles, *In the name of eugenics*.
112 Koster, "Toeneming der krankzinnigheid."
113 Noordman, *Kwaliteit van het nageslacht*.
114 Pannenborg, "Toerekeningsvatbaarheid."
115 Luning Prak, *School, beroep en aanleg*, pp. 145-146.
116 Heymans, *Toekomstige eeuw*, p. 24.
117 Ibid., p. 26.
118 Ibid., p. 26.
119 Derksen, *Wij psychologen*, p. 55.
120 Münsterberg, *Tomorrow*.
121 McDougall, *National welfare*.
122 Morawski, "Assessing psychology's moral heritage."
123 Timmerman, "Prof. G. Heymans," p. 584.
124 Aerts, "De wetenschappelijke burger," p. 28.
125 Heymans, "Presidential address," in: Heymans, *Gesammelte kleinere Schriften*, vol. 2, pp. 360-367.
126 James, *Varieties*.

Chapter 9   Religion: Protestantism

1   *Het Nieuws van den Dag*, Monday, September 15, 1884; *De Amsterdammer*, Saturday, September 13, 1884.
2   *Algemeen Handelsblad*, Friday, September 12, 1884.
3   *De Amsterdammer*, Supplement, Saturday, September 13, 1884.
4   Quoted in: Dongelmans, Van Oostrom and Van Zonneveld, *Dierbaar Magazijn*, p. 95.
5   Pierson, *Oudere Tijdgenooten*, p. 193.
6   *Het Nieuws van den Dag*, Monday, September 15, 1884.
7   Busken Huet quoted in: Anbeek, *Geschiedenis van de Nederlandse literatuur*, pp. 21-22; Brom, *De dominee*, pp. 16-17.
8   Heeroma, "Het probleem-Beets," p. 75.
9   Bos, *In dienst van het koninkrijk*, pp. 206-207.
10   Van Oosterzee, *Uit mijn levensboek*, pp. 154-155.
11   Ibid., p. 38.
12   Van Limburg Brouwer, *Het leesgezelschap*, p. 90.
13   Busken Huet, *Literarische Fantasiën*, vol. 2, p. 47.
14   Bos, *In dienst van het koninkrijk*, p. 127.
15   Huls, *De dienst der vrouw in de kerk*, p. 104.
16   Johannes, *Luthers diakonessenwerk*, pp. 14-15.
17   Quoted in: Brom, *De dominee*, p. 107.
18   McLeod, *Religion and Society*, pp. 13-14.
19   Van den Berg, *De toegang tot het Binnenhof*, pp. 142-143.
20   De Haan and Te Velde, "Vormen van politiek," p. 179.
21   Broeyer, "De predikantsopleiding," pp. 91-92.
22   Scholten quoted in: Otterspeer, *De wiekslag van hun geest*, p. 380.
23   Loman quoted in: Hoekema and Hof, *Illustere Dissenters*, p. 72.

24 Nipperdey, *Deutsche Geschichte*, vol. 1, p. 468.
25 Summary by J. Huizinga in his history of Groningen University, in: Huizinga, *Verzamelde Werken*, vol. 8, pp. 150-151.
26 Rasker, *De Nederlandse Hervormde Kerk*, p. 116.
27 Roessingh, *Moderne theologie*, p. 118.
28 Roessingh, *Moderne theologie*, p. 153.
29 Van Houten, quoted in: Van 't Veer, *Mr C.W. Opzoomer*, p. 147.
30 Roessingh, *Moderne theologie*, pp. 73 and 104.
31 Roessingh, *Het Modernisme in Nederland*, p. 185.
32 Van der Wall, *Het oude en het nieuwe geloof*, pp. 9-10.
33 Ibid., p. 12.
34 Quoted in: Bos, *In dienst van het Koninkrijk*, p. 250.
35 Roessingh, *Het Modernisme in Nederland*, p. 10.
36 Ibid., p. 37.
37 Mönnich, "De ontwikkeling van de vrijzin-nigheid," p. 34.
38 Kuenen quoted in: Otterspeer, *De wiekslag van hun geest*, p. 247.
39 Bavinck, *De theologie van prof. dr Daniel Chantepie de la Saussaye*, pp. 10-11.
40 De Lange, *De verhouding tussen dogmatiek en godsdienstwetenschap*, pp. 153 and 159.
41 De Lange, *J.H. Gunning Jr.*, pp. 9-10.
42 Bruining, "De ethische richting," pp. 131 and 185-187.
43 De Lange, *De verhouding tussen dogmatiek en godsdienstwetenschap*, p. 143; Rasker, *De Nederlandse Hervormde Kerk*, p. 237; Otterspeer, *De wiekslag van hun geest*, pp. 270-271; De Lange, *J.H. Gunning Jr. (1829-1905)*, vol. 1, p. 216.
44 Heering, "Het vrijzinnig-protestantisme," in: Klein Wassink and Van Leeuwen, *Tussen geest en tijdgeest*, pp. 70-75.
45 Otterspeer, *Bolland*, p. 316.
46 Roessingh, *Het modernisme in Nederland*, p. 219; Beversluis, *Een halve eeuw strijd en opbouw*, pp. 32-33.
47 Pierson, "De heerschappij der bour-geoisie," pp. 441-476.
48 Bos, *In dienst van het koninkrijk*, p. 304.
49 Bronsveld quoted in: Herderscheê, *De mo-dern-godsdienstige richting*, p. 163.
50 Knippenberg, *Religieuze kaart*, p. 121.
51 Knippenberg, *Religieuze Kaart*, p. 106.
52 Mönnich, "De ontwikkeling van de vrijzin-nigheid," p. 31.
53 Van Mourik Broekman, *De orthodoxe en moderne geloofsprediking*, pp. 5 and 22-24.
54 Mönnich, "De ontwikkeling van de vrijzin-nigheid," p. 35.
55 De Vrijer, *Gunning Tragicus*, pp. 175-177.
56 Thijssen, *In de ochtend van het leven*, pp. 149-150.

57 Goeman Borgesius in: Sickesz, *Het maatschappelijk vraagstuk*, pp. 40-42.
58 Wilzen and Van Biemen, *Samen op weg*, pp. 17 and 39.
59 Otterspeer, *De wiekslag van hun geest*, pp. 393-394.
60 De Lange, *De verhouding tussen dogmatiek en godsdienstwetenschap*, pp. 11-12.
61 Wilzen and Van Biemen, *Samen op weg*, pp. 17 and 39.
62 Wilzen and Van Biemen, *Samen op weg*, pp. 29-30; Kalma, "F.W.N. Hugenholtz," pp. 95-97.
63 Tromp, *Sociaal-Democratisch programma*, p. 140.
64 Borgeaud, *Pages d'Histoire nationale*, p. 362.
65 Manuscripts "Monument international de la Réformation (Mur des Réformateurs)," Bibliothèque publique et universitaire, Geneva.
66 Kuyper, *Het Calvinisme*, pp. 11 and 62.
67 Kuyper quoted in: Augustijn and Vree, *Abraham Kuyper*, pp. 10 and 14.
68 Augustijn and Vree, *Abraham Kuyper*, p. 11.
69 Kuyper quoted in: Te Velde, "Een aparte techniek," p. 205.
70 Van Lieburg, *De stille luyden*, p. 15.
71 Ibid., p. 17.
72 Zwemer, *In conflict met de cultuur*, pp. 18 and 39.
73 Ibid., pp. 30 and 42.
74 Ibid., p. 30.
75 Kuiper, *De voormannen*, p. 81.
76 Knippenberg, *Religieuze Kaart*, pp. 76-77.
77 Van 't Spijker, "Ik ben een vriend," pp. 76 and 82-83; Van Laarse, *Bevoogding en Bevinding*, pp. 98-99.
78 Kuiper, *De voormannen*, p. 72.
79 Quoted in: Kuiper, *De voormannen*, p. 76.
80 Kuyper, *Souvereiniteit in eigen kring*, p. 23.
81 Augustijn and Vree, *Abraham Kuyper*, pp. 175-176.
82 Ibid., p. 208.
83 De Jong, "Herschikt mozaïek," pp. 216-217.
84 Van der Laarse, *Bevoogding en Bevinding*, p. 158.
85 De Jong, "Herschikt mozaïek," p. 215.
86 Kuiper, "Een antirevolutionair afscheid," pp. 220-243.
87 Nipperdey, *Deutsche Geschichte*, vol. 1, pp. 498-499.
88 Bratt, *Dutch Calvinism*, pp. 42-43.
89 Kuiper, *De voormannen*, pp. 200-201.
90 Kuiper, *De voormannen*, p. 60.
91 Vree in: Augustijn and Vree, *Abraham Kuyper*, pp. 63-64.
92 Vree in: Augustijn and Vree, *Abraham Kuyper*, pp. 63-64.
93 Van den Berg, *De Nederlandse Christen-Studenten Vereniging*, pp. 37-38 and 40.
94 Brouwer, Van Os and Van Swighem, *Een huis voor het Woord*.

95 Steensma and Van Swigchem, *Honderdvijftig jaar gereformeerde kerkbouw.*

96 Scheffler, *Holland*, pp. 27-28.

97 Van der Woud, *Waarheid en karakter*, pp. 251-252.

98 Hoogeveen-Brink, *H.J.Jesse.*

99 De Groot, "De Muiderkerk," p. 17.

100 Bock, *Anfänge einer neuen Architektur*, p. 134; Karstkarel, "De architectonische taal," pp. 135-136.

101 See Chp. 3.

102 Van der Woud, *Waarheid en karakter*, pp. 356 and 359.

103 Telgenhof-Otter, "Kerkgebouwen der dolerenden," pp. 42-43; Kuyt, Middelkoop and Van der Woud, *Bouwmeesters van Amsterdam.*

104 Steensma and Van Swigchem, *Honderdvijftig jaar gereformeerde kerkbouw*, p. 24.

105 Falize in: Steensma and Van Swigchem, *Honderdvijftig jaar gereformeerde kerkbouw*, p. 67.

106 Smilde, "Het protestants-christelijk volksdeel," p. 150.

107 Smelik, *Eén in lied en leven*, p. 191.

108 Smelik, *Eén in lied en leven*, pp. 286-295.

Chapter 10 Religion and emancipation: Judaism and Catholicism

1 Blom, Fuks-Mansfeld and Schöffer, *Geschiedenis van de Joden*, pp. 250-251.

2 Lucassen, "Joodse Nederlanders 1796-1940," pp. 34-38.

3 Van Praag, *Het ghetto*, pp. 14-15.

4 Ibid., pp. 17-18.

5 Meijer, *Hoge hoeden lage standaarden*, p. 28.

6 Leydesdorff in: Verhoeff and Wierema, *Ochenebbisj*, pp. 14-15.

7 Montijn, *Leven op stand*, p. 32.

8 Voorzanger and Polak Jz., *Het Joodsch in Nederland.*

9 Reijnders, *Van 'Joodsche natiën'*, p. 107

10 Blom and Cahen, "Joodse Nederlanders," p. 270.

11 Michman, "The Impact of German-Jewish Modernization," pp. 182 and 187.

12 Meijer, *Rector en raw*, pp. 13-14.

13 Michman, *Het Liberale Jodendom*, pp. 32-34.

14 Rijxman, *A.C.Wertheim 1832-1897*, p. 243.

15 Bregstein, *Gesprekken met Jacques Presser*, pp. 11-12.

16 Heertje, *De diamantbewerkers*, pp. 291-292.

17 Ibid., p. 292.

18 Bloemgarten, *Henri Polak*, p. 645.

19 Leydesdorff, *Bijdrage tot de speciale psychologie*, pp. 32-33, 41 and 43.

20 Hanák, *The Garden and the Workshop*, pp. 176-177.

21 Daalder, *Politiek en historie*, p. 110.

22 Johanisse, *Nederlandse architectuur 1900-1924.*

23 Erftemeijer, Looyenga and Van Roon, *Getooid als een bruid*, p. 94.

24 Ibid., pp. 56-57.

25 Ibid., p. 126.

26 Brom, *Herleving van de kerkelike kunst*, p. 37.

27 De Blaauw, *De Sint Martinuskerk te Sneek*, pp. 14-24.

28 Brom, *Herleving van de kerkelike kunst*, pp. 143 and 144; Van der Woud, *Waarheid en karakter*, pp. 298-314.

29 *Dr Cuypers Gedenkboek*, pp. 67-72.

30 Reeser, *Verzamelde geschriften*, p. 102.

31 Brom, *Herleving van de kerkelike kunst*, p. 148.

32 Cuypers and Kalf, *De katholieke kerken in Nederland*, pp. 7-8.

33 Hoogewoud, Kuyt and Oxenaar, *P.J.H. Cuypers*, pp. 45-51.

34 Brom, *Herleving van de kerkelike kunst*, p. 171.

35 Looijenga, *De Utrechtse school*, pp. 375-391.

36 Ibid., pp. 353-354.

37 De Maeyer, "Katholiek reveil," p. 95.

38 *Sint Nicolaaskerk Amsterdam.*

39 Reith, *Honderd jaar kerkbouw*, passim.

40 Van der Meer in *De Tijd*, May 13, 1953.

41 Van der Meer in *De Tijd*, May 13, 1953.

42 Brom, *Herleving van de kerkelike kunst*, p. 74.

43 Ibid., p. 246.

44 Raedts, "De katholieken en de Middeleeuwen", p. 105.

45 Mähler, *De Sint-Paulusabdij van Oosterhout*, pp. 89-90.

46 Kat, *De geschiedenis der kerkmuziek*, pp. 252-263; Bank, *Geschiedenis der katholieke kerkmuziek*, vol. 1, pp. 147-150.

47 Reeser, *Een eeuw Nederlandse muziek*, p. 147.

48 Alphons Diepenbrock to E.T.Kuiper, November 20, 1890. In: Reeser, *Alphons Diepenbrock*, vol. 1, p. 240; Paap, *Alphons Diepenbrock*, pp. 69-70.

49 Matthijs Vermeulen in *De Telegraaf* (September 30, 1916). In: Reeser, *Alphons Diepenbrock*, vol. 9, pp. 482-483.

50 Brom, "Het treurspel," p. 103.

51 Brom, "Het treurspel," p. 106.

52 Brom, "Het treurspel," pp. 102-120; Rodenburg, "Het verleden opgepoetst," pp. 27-29.

53 Wegman, *Geschiedenis van de christelijke eredienst*, p. 249.

54 Rogier and De Rooy, *In vrijheid herboren*, pp. 599 and 603.

55 Margry in: Margry and Caspers, *Bedevaartplaatsen in Nederland*, vol. 1, pp. 139-142.

56 Wingens, *Over de grens*, pp. 265-266.

57 Evers, "Bedevaart en zang," p. 135.

58 Post in: Margry and Caspers, *Bedevaartplaatsen in Nederland*, vol. 1, pp. 291-293.

59 De Valk, *Roomser dan de paus?*, p. 172.

60 Margry in: Margry and Caspers,

Bedevaartplaatsen in Nederland, vol. 1, pp. 231-241.

61 Reijs and Van Vugt, "Tussen zelfheiliging en belangenbehartiging", pp. 11-40.

62 De Kok, *Nederland op de breuklijn Rome-Reformatie*, pp. 69-70.

63 Dellepoort, *De priesterroepingen in Nederland*, pp. 30-31.

64 Ibid., pp. 45-47.

65 *Neerlandia Catholica. Het Katholieke Nederland.*

66 Van Vugt, "De geschiedenis van zusters," p. 126.

67 O'Brien quoted in: McLeod, *Religion and Society*, p. 166.

68 Eijt, *Religieuze vrouwen*, p. 219.

69 Lauret, *Per imperatief mandaat*, p. 107.

70 Eijt, *Religieuze vrouwen*, pp. 413-415; Lauret, *Per imperatief mandaat*, p. 12.

71 Mandemakers, *Gymnasiaal en middelbaar onderwijs*, p. 244.

72 Winkeler, "Ten dienste der seminaristen," pp. 41-42.

73 Van Duinkerken, *Brabantse herinneringen*, pp. 76-77.

74 De Valk, *Roomser dan de paus?*, p. 274.

75 De Valk, *Roomser dan de paus?*, p. 275.

76 De Valk, *Roomser dan de paus?*, pp. 274-275.

77 Struyker Boudier, *Wijsgerig leven in Nederland*, vol. 5, pp. 93-98.

78 Winkeler, "Ten dienste der seminaristen," p. 24.

79 Molkenboer, quoted in: Struyker Boudier, *Wijsgerig leven in Nederland* , p. 31.

80 Rogier, *Katholieke herleving*, p. 492.

81 Struyker Boudier, *Wijsgerig leven in Nederland*, vol. 7, p. 93; Rogier, *Katholieke herleving*, pp. 493-494.

82 De Valk, *Roomser dan de paus?*, p. 276.

83 Ibid., p. 284.

84 Ibid., p. 191.

85 Rogier, *Katholieke herleving*, p. 434.

86 Viaene, "Roman Question," p. 145.

87 De Valk, *Roomser*, p. 145.

88 Bornewasser, *Katholieke Volkspartij 1945-1980*, vol. 1, p. 24.

89 Bornewasser, *Curiale appreciaties*, p. 231.

90 Bornewasser, *Curiale appreciaties*, pp. 231-232.

Chapter 11   Utopians and socialists

1 The "Sketch" is one part of the *Internationale en hare beoordelaars*, pamphlet 1871, later collected as an extract under this title by Gerhard's widow (Gerhard 1887).

2 See Marx and Engels *Communist Manifesto*, vol. 3, p. 3. See Engels, *Herr Eugen Duehrings Umwälzung, etc*. Engels said that early nineteenth-century utopians could be forgiven for trying "einen neuen Gesellschaft aus dem Kopfe zu konstru-ieren," but that half a century later this was unforgivable, because the socialists of the time could call upon actual historical developments and the scientific conclusions that could be drawn from them (Engels, p. 275).

3 It would be interesting to do further research into the reception of Thomas More in early socialism. Domela Nieuwenhuis translated *Utopia* in 1903. Did his work on the translation cause the about-face that led him to turn his back on socialism and align himself with the anarchists? Did he feel attracted by More's strictly moral (Calvinist) attitude? How did his anarchistic leanings relate to More's strict state structure? 1903 also saw the publication of the translation of Karl Kautsky's *Thomas More und seine Utopia* (the original work had been published in 1887). It was an attempt to reconcile More with revolutionary Marxism. Were Gerhard's endeavors going in the same direction? Henriëtte Roland Holst followed Kautsky in her play *Thomas More* (1913), but she primarily projected her own desire for suffering onto the English author.

4 Mannheim, *Ideologie und Utopia* (1929); in his footsteps Ricoeur, *Lectures on Ideology and Utopia* (1986) and Cioran: "Mécanisme de l'Utopie," in: *Histoire et Utopie* (1960): "mankind only acts under the fascination of the impossible; a society that is not capable of bringing forth Utopias and dedicating itself to them is in danger of degeneration and decay."

5 Edward Bellamy, *Looking Backward*, p. 127.

6 Bellamy, *Looking Backward*, p. 69.

7 For a discussion see Ruiter and Smulders, *Literatuur en moderniteit in Nederland*, pp. 134-153.

8 Bellamy, *Looking Backward*, p. 259; it is true that Bellamy points to the harmful effects of the capitalist system, but taken as a whole his sketch is a "piece of social conservatism, fashioned to reinforce accepted American values and traditions" (John L. Thomas in Bellamy, p. 87).

9 See among others Hofmann, *Ideengeschichte der sozialen Bewegung* (1974).

10 See Vrankrijker, *Anarchisten* (1972); Becker and Frieswijk, *Bedrijven in eigen beheer* (1976). The Bond spawned all sorts of splinter groups, including the Grondpartij (land party), which was founded in 1918. The renowned *Gemeenschappelijk Grondbezit* foundation, set up by Frederik van Eeden and Daan de Clerq in 1901, can also be regarded as a continuation of the *Bond voor landnationalisering*. The abolition of private land ownership had been advocated in the Netherlands before this by Hendrik Gerhard. In his articles for *De Werkman* in the early 1880s he was already writing

about the abolition of private ownership, particularly in regard to land.

11 Rousseau quoted in: Nieuwenhuis, *Grond en Bodem* (1879), p. 6.

12 Groustra, *Vrijland en de vrijlandbeweging* (1893), p. 8; see also Vliegen, *Die onze kracht* (1926), pp. 275-79; Vrankrijker, *Anarchisten*, pp. 30-47.

13 For example in 1895, number 28; see particularly the two engravings in annex 22 (1895), in which the differences are illustrated.

14 *Vrijland* (1895), numbers 30 and 31; Groustra, *Vrijland en de vrijlandbeweging*, p. 85.

15 Van Eeden, "Waarvan leven wij?" (1904), p. 133.

16 Van Eeden, "Waarvoor werkt gij?" (1899), p. 169.

17 The Maatschappij de Veluwe was an industrial commune established by paint manufacturer F.A. Molyn. Daan de Clerq was employed there as a chemist. There was a community house and communal facilities. Van Eeden was very impressed when he visited in 1897.

18 Van Eeden, "Werk en brood" (1897).

19 Van Eeden, *Binnenlandsche kolonisatie*, (1901).

20 Van Eeden, "Waarvoor werkt gij?" (1899), p. 180.

21 Van Eeden, *De blijde wereld* (1903), p.11. Van Eeden does have a point. The term "socialism" was used for the first time by Robert Owen and other early nineteenth-century "utopian socialists." Marx later annexed the term, but because he gave "socialism" a political meaning, the term was divorced from the original idea of a "community." Van Eeden was thus essentially right when he claimed that his endeavors accorded with authentic socialism.

22 Van Eeden, "Werk en brood" p. 229.

23 Van Eeden, *Binnenlandsche kolonisatie*, p. 16; *Blijde wereld*, p. 259.

24 Van Eeden, "Recht of Macht" (1898), p. 198.

25 Van Eeden, "Waarvan leven wij," p. 147; Van Eeden, *Het godshuis in de lichtstad* (1921), p. 2.

26 See Van Buuren, "Hystérie et littérature" (1994); "De anatomische les" (1993).

27 Van Eeden, "De cooperatie in Kettering" (1901), p. 243.

28 Van Eeden, "Recht of Macht," p. 229, *De blijde wereld*, p. 183.

29 Van Eeden, "Recht of Macht," p. 221, *De blijde wereld*, p. 285.

30 Van Eeden, "Recht of Macht," p. 207, p. 217.

31 Van Eeden, *De blijde wereld*, p. 154; *Exodus* 20:5; see also Van Buuren "De anatomische les"(1993), p. 44.

32 See Fontijn, *Tweespalt* and *Trots verbrijzeld*; Ley and Luger, *Walden in droom en daad*; Mooyweer, *De Amerikaanse droom van Frederik van Eeden*; Vrankrijker, *Anarchisten*; Becker and Frieswijk, *Bedrijven in eigen beheer*.

33 In *De blijde wereld* Van Eeden holds these two businessmen up as examples to the colonists. They would have to run their associations as efficiently as, no, even better than, these captains of industry, otherwise they could not count on success, *De blijde wereld*, p. 325.

34 Hendrix, *Een week in de kolonie* (1901), p. 48.

35 For these and subsequent data: Becker and Frieswijk, *Bedrijven in eigen beheer*, pp. 148-179.

36 Nieuwe Niedorp, in the Province of North Holland, was a small but effective commune consisting of two men and one woman. It was founded in 1902 and in 1904 entered into a federation with "Vrede" (the printers group of the International Brotherhood). The GGB foundation made repeated efforts to ally the colony to GGB because of its financial success, but to no avail. In 1907 the colony abandoned its communist principles and the workers were paid wages. Its success continued. The colony remained a flourishing enterprise until well into World War II.

37 Methöfer, in: *Verbonden Schakels: Verzamelde opstellen uit het maandblad der Vereeniging "Gemeenschappelijk Grondbezit,"* pp. 88, 56/7, 55/6.

38 Hendrix, *Een week in de kolonie*, pp. 4, 28, 56.

39 Tolstoy, *Anna Karenina*, Part 8, Chapter 19.

40 Tolstoy, quoted in Rolland, p. 87.

41 Tolstoy, *What Then Must We Do?*, p. 71.

42 Tolstoy, *What Then Must We Do?*, p. 166; Tolstoy, *Moderne slavernij*; (The Hague: Vrede, 1900), p. 38. In both publications (the latter title is a sequel to the former) Tolstoy describes Henry George's initiative as the expropriation of privately owned land. That is actually not correct. George proposed levying a tax on land ownership: the "single tax." It was George's followers, Tolstoy, Flürscheim, Oppenheimer, Van Eeden, who replaced this suggestion with the idea of expropriation, of "land nationalization."

43 Tolstoy, *What Then Must We Do?*, pp. 174, 295.

44 See Tolstoy, *Plaisirs vicieux* (1892); *The Kingdom of God is Within You* (1894).

45 Tolstoy, letter of 1904, quoted in: Rolland, *Vie de Tolstoï* p. 163.

46 Tolstoy, *Het einde is nabij* (1898).

47 Van Suchtelen, *Quia absurdum*, p. 79.

48 Roland Holst, "Maatschappelijke oorzaken," vol. 4, pp. 6-26.

49 Kluveld, "Anti-vivisectionisme en feminisme," in: *Gezond en wel*, pp. 141-155.

50 For these and subsequent data: Rudolf Jans, *Tolstoj in Nederland* (1952).

51 The Doukhobors were a Russian Christian sect that had practiced the principles of defenselessness and anarchism for centuries. Many Doukhobors emigrated to Canada. Tolstoy supported them. Loosjes discussed them as early as 1838. Felix Ortt mentioned them in his publications and harked back to them.

52 In 1816, barge skipper Stoffel Muller, bailiff Dirk Valk and Maria Leer set up a commune in Puttershoek on the lines of the first Christian community. The commune had communist features and despised social conventions but was made up of hard workers, and in consequence it was gradually accepted. The group grew steadily, and moved to Zwijndrecht in 1829, where it continued to exist until 1843.

53 Jans, *Tolstoj in Nederland*, see also Kylstra, "De betekenis van onze kolonie," (The Hague: Vrede, 1900), and his book *Geestelijk en maatschappelijk leven* (1909), previously published as an article in 1908.

54 See Becker and Frieswijk, *Bedrijven* pp. 100-111; Hendrix, *Een week in de kolonie*, Jans, *Tolstoj in Nederland*.

55 Luitjes, *Theorie en praktijk van binnenlandsche kolonisatie* (1902), p. 98.

56 Luitjes, *Theorie en praktijk*, p. 95.

57 Luitjes, *Theorie en praktijk*, pp. 108-109. From the outset Luitjes worked for the abolition of private land ownership. The majority of the early socialists, united in the Sociaal Democratische Bond, shared this view. In 1893, during a party conference in Groningen, there was a clash between a faction that wanted state power through elections and parliament (proposed in the Maastricht motion by Troelstra and Van Kol) and the Hoogezand-Sappemeer motion, which advocated revolution as the means of putting an end to private property. This motion, drawn up by Tjerk Luitjes and supported by Domela Nieuwenhuis, won a majority. In 1894, with the establishment of the SDAP (Van der Goes, Van Kol, Vliegen etc.) there was an outright break with the Sociaal Democratische Bond, but the latter remained the larger party (in 1895 the SDAP had 700 members, the Bond 3500). These proportions were reversed over the next few years. In 1897 Luitjes suggested that the Socialistenbond should be merged into a free federation of local groups. Domela supported this proposal. The central board and the central treasury were wound up. In practice this meant the disappearance of the Bond.

58 Luitjes, *Theorie en praktijk*, pp. 11, 18, 167. Luitjes opposed the SDAP for the same reasons as Van Eeden did: the party wrongly sought state power, it accustomed workers to capitalist models, it supported industry – all issues to which Luitjes was vehemently opposed. After his expulsion from the colony of the International Brotherhood, Luitjes set up a boarding house in huts in Blaricum, described by the local people as a "nudist camp"; see Lien Heyting, *De wereld in een dorp*, pp. 138-141.

59 See Heyting, *De wereld in een Dorp*, pp. 73-74; Jans, *Tolstoj in Nederland* p. 110; Becker and Frieswijk, *Bedrijven*, pp. 100-111; for the humanitarian school and other educational experiments, see the chapter on education elsewhere in this book.

60 According to Anton Constandse, he *re*discovered Spinoza, with whose work he had already become familiar in his youth. Constandse in: Stuiveling, *Acht over Gorter*, p. 213.

61 See Herman de Liagre Böhl, *Met al mijn bloed*.

62 Cf. Brandt Cortius, *Herman Gorter* (1934), p. 55.

63 Herman Gorter, *Een klein heldendicht* (1906), p. 18.

64 Gorter, *Heldendicht*, pp. 18, 29.

65 Gorter, quoted in: Liagre Böhl, *Met al mijn bloed*, p. 249.

66 Gorter, *Socialistische verzen* (1903), pp. 427, 429, 435, 438.

67 Gorter, *Socialistische verzen*, p. 445.

68 Gorter, *Pan*, p. 16.

69 See De Liagre Böhl, "Herman Gorter en Lenin," in: Stuiveling, *Acht over Gorter*, pp. 335-369.

70 Gorter, *Open brief*, quoted in: Liagre, "Herman Gorter en Lenin," (1978), p. 366.

71 For details of the life of Roland Holst, see Elsbeth Etty, *Liefde is heel het leven niet* (1996). Etty even suggests hysteria.

72 Roland Holst, quoted in: Etty, *Liefde is heel het leven niet*, pp. 310, 115.

73 The ideas of the "Arts and Crafts" movement and the Fabians (the British socialist movement) were very popular with the Holsts and with the early socialists in general. Morris's *News from Nowhere* appeared in a translation by Frank van der Goes as *Nieuws uit nergensoord* (1897); other stories were translated by Gorter and Holst as *John Ball and andere vertalingen* (1898); there was also a collection of essays, *Kunst en Maatschappij*, with a foreword by Henri Polak (1903). Walter Crane, *Kunst en samenleving* was translated by Jan Veth (1894), the translation of John Ruskin's *Man and Society*, *Mensch en Maatschappij* (1901) appeared with a foreword by Frederik van Eeden. Henri Polak translated Robert

Blatchford's *Merrie England* as *Het Heden en de Toekomst*, (1895), Wibaut translated the *Fabian Essays* (1891). Henriëtte Roland Holst wrote a biography of D.G. Rossetti (1898); she admired the work of Sidney (leader of the Fabians) and Beatrice Webb, and shared this admiration with her husband, Wibaut, Troelstra and Henri Polak.

74 Morris, "Art and Industry" (1890), p. 388.
75 Roland Holst, "Maatschappelijke oorzaken," p. 330.
76 Ibid., p. 327.
77 Ibid., p. 330.
78 Ibid., p. 329.
79 Nature is also an important factor in Henriëtte Roland Holst's utopian vision. *Het Feest der Gedachtenis* (1915) is set in an idyllic life in harmony with nature. The city and industry are portrayed as the breeding grounds of disease and illness. The lass who speaks in *Het Feest* says that she was born in an alley where the sun never reached. She suggests that her wickedness is the result of her urban origins. Here Henriëtte Roland Holst makes the connection with the land mythology that she derived from Morris, from the other land utopians, and ultimately from Rousseau.
80 Henriëtte Roland Holst, *De opstandelingen*, p.107.
81 Ibid., p. 97.
82 See Meyers, *Domela,* p. 128.
83 Van Zinderen Bakker, quoted in: Meyers, *Domela,* p. 205.
84 Cf. Fontijn, *Tweespalt,* pp. 191-198.
85 Van Eeden, "Het hypnotisme en de wonderen," in: *De blijde wereld;* Jan Fontijn, *Trots verbrijzeld,* pp. 37-8.
86 In December 1899; this was the death of Simon van der Vijgh, who was visiting his friend, the colonist Dirk van der Woude, Cf. De Ley and Luger, *Walden in droom en daad,* p. 93.
87 Van Suchtelen, *Quia absurdum,* pp. 86-89.
88 Cf. Van Halsema, "Christusvoorstellingen."
89 An aspect that is strongly represented in Henriëtte Roland Holst's work is one that is present to some extent in the work of all the utopian socialists and has left its mark on the iconology of socialism. This is the description of the ideal state in inchoate terms – linguistic forms and, above all, images that depict the arrival of a new situation, such as awakening, dawn, crowing cocks etc…: "yearning eyes as if it already dawned, the Day / gold-edged, … and now the / glory-sun was risen / triumphant music rang out from the city" (*Het Feest der Gedachtenis,* pp. 168-169); "… morning-bright hours / swelling on shafts of rose red, / then illuminated the great heroic deeds, / and spilled their golden rays /

over the far future focused knowledge!" (*De Opstandelingen,* p. 8). Henriëtte Roland Holst, Herman Gorter and other socialists gave form to what Ernst Bloch somewhere referred to as "advent consciousness." They derived imagery from the medieval genre of the *aubades* and saw themselves in the role of the sentinel who announces the new day.

90 Van Eeden, "Mijne ervaringen," 1954 (1907), p. 26.
91 Van Eeden, *Het godshuis in de lichtstad,* p. 16.
92 Verweij-Jonker, "Vijfentwintig jaar" (1938).
93 Quoted in: Van Hettinga Tromp, "Van Eeden en Walden," in: Van Tricht, *Onzekerheid is leven,* p. 74.

Thanks to Piet de Rooy and Frans Ruiter for their critical reading of this chapter and their suggestions for additions and corrections.

Chapter 12   Flowers in Dutch poetry at the turn of the century

1 Translation by Theodoor Weevers, in: *Poetry of the Netherlands in Its European context 1170-1930,* p. 303.
2 Translation by Adriaan J. Barnouw, *Coming After: An Anthology of Poetry from the Low Countries,* p. 168.

Chapter 13   The life of women

1 This chapter is a revised and expanded version of an essay by Dr. Marianne Braun on *Hilda van Suylenburg* which was written for the NWO program on Dutch culture in a European perspective and published in part in: *Tijdschrift voor Sociale Geschiedenis* 24 (1998) 209-234.
2 Prick, *Briefwisseling van Deyssel – Verwey,* p. 292.
3 Meyboom, "De vrouwenbeweging in Nederland," pp. 475-485, 477 and 483.
4 Bel, *Nederlandse literatuur,* p. 149.
5 Jonckbloet, *Jonkvrouwe Anna de Savornin Lohman,* p. 97.
6 Dieteren, "Twee levens, twee geloven," p. 41.
7 *Nederlandsche Spectator,* July 30, 1898, p. 249.
8 Snoeck Henkemans, "Het congres voor weezen-opvoeding," p. 804.
9 Diepenbrock, *Brieven,* vol. 3, pp. 97 and 94.
10 Diepenbrock, *Brieven,* vol. 2, p. 508.
11 *Het Vaderland,* July 11, 1944.
12 Dudink, *Deugdzaam liberalisme,* pp. 181-219.

13 Mercier, "Karaktervorming der vrouw," pp. 50 and 54.

14 Mercier, *De vrouw tegenover de vrouwenarbeid*, p. 140.

15 Bervoets, *Opvoeden tot sociale verantwoordelijkheid*, pp. 44-45.

16 Dieteren, *Twee levens, twee geloven*, p. 46.

17 De Maegd-Soëp, *De progressieve vrouw*, pp. 269-332; Bosch, "Honderd jaar Hilda," p. 101.

18 Huygens, *Een woord aan de Nederlandsche vrouwen*; Huygens, "Karl Pearson," pp. 374-376.

19 *Evolutie* 5 (1897-1898) 165

20 Mercier, "Aurora Leigh"; Dudink, *Deugdzaam liberalisme*, pp. 201-204.

21 Braun, *De prijs*, pp. 50-57.

22 Alberdingk Thijm, *Verwoest leven*, p. 69; Prick, "Alberdingk Thijm," pp. 179-203; Jansz, "Het luchtkasteel," pp. 30-45.

23 Bel, *Nederlandse literatuur*, pp. 315, 316-318.

24 Schenkeveld, "Vormen van realisme," p. 227.

25 Bosch, "Honderd jaar Hilda," pp. 100-103, 128-131 and 113-116.

26 Dudink, *Deugdzaam liberalisme*, pp. 208-212.

27 Bosch, "Honderd jaar Hilda," p. 103; Anbeek, *De naturalistische roman*, p. 104.

28 De Vooys, *Historische Schets*, p. 114

29 Fontijn, *Leven in extase*, pp. 138-152; Klein, *Over Eline Vere*, pp. 36-37.

30 Braun, "Drie sprookjes van Wilhelmina Drucker," pp. 11-29; Anbeek, *De naturalistische roman*, p. 79.

31 Maas, *Letterkundige tijdsidealen*, p. 18.

32 Huygens, "Barthold Meryan," in: *Evolutie* 5 (1897-1898) 132.

33 Uildriks, "Van vrouwenlevens," pp. 57-86, 67-68.

34 Uildriks, "Van vrouwenlevens," pp. 68-69.

35 Jacobs, "Het doel der vrouwenbeweging," pp. 503-522, 504.

36 *Evolutie* 5 (1897-1898) 162.

37 Clant van der Myll-Piepers, *Een woord*; Meyboom, "Open brief aan freule Anna de Savornin Lohman," p. 176; "De liefde in de Vrouwenbeweging," pp. 177-179; Wijnaendts Francken-Dyserinck, "De Liefde in de Vrouwenkwestie," pp. 64-47.

38 Goekoop-De Jong van Beek en Donk, "Ingezonden," in: *Belang*, p. 65.

39 Huygens, *De liefde in het vrouwenleven*, p. 16.

40 Roland Holst, "Boekbeoordeeling," pp. 460-461.

41 De Savornin Lohman, "Naschrift op De liefde," pp. 5, 15 and 16.

42 Winkel, "Letteren en taal," p. 295.

43 Netscher, "Het boek van de maand," pp. 504-513.

44 Jaeger, "Oorspronkelijke romans," pp. 412-415.

45 Netscher, "Het boek van de maand," p. 513.

46 *Verslag jaarvergadering Broederschap van Notarissen*, pp. 371-373; *Handelingen der Nederlandsche Juristen-vereeniging*, 34 (1904) 227.

47 Duys, *Feminisme*, pp. 19-21.

48 De Vries and Van Tricht, *Geschiedenis der Wet*, p. 130.

49 Geest-Jacobs and Klein, "Couperus en de Vrouwenquestie," pp. 127-136; Dudink, *Deugdzaam liberalisme*, pp. 213-219; Bosch, "Honderd jaar Hilda," pp. 106-110.

Chapter 14   Urban culture

1 Vestdijk, *Gustav Mahler*, pp. 51-52.

2 Gustav Mahler to Alma Mahler, October 20 and 24, 1904, quoted in: Reeser, *Alphons Diepenbrock*, pp. 288 and 292.

3 Reeser, "Die Mahler-Rezeption," pp. 86-87.

4 Quoted in: Reeser, *Alphons Diepenbrock*, vol. 4, pp. 296 and 465.

5 Alphons Diepenbrock in: Reeser, *Verzamelde Geschriften*, pp. 246 and 250.

6 Zwart, *Willem Mengelberg*, pp. 197-199.

7 Giskes, *Mahler in Amsterdam*, pp. 39-40.

8 Van Dokkum, *Honderd jaar muziekleven*, p. 264; Reeser, *Een eeuw Nederlandse muziek*, p. 135.

9 Reeser, *Een eeuw Nederlandse muziek*, p. 137.

10 Wennekes, *Het Paleis voor Volksvlijt*, p. 170.

11 Zwart, *Willem Mengelberg*, pp. 52-53.

12 Kosten, *Kroniek van vijfenzeventig jaar*, pp. 13-19.

13 Van Dokkum, *Honderd jaar muziekleven*, p. 9.

14 Van Dokkum, *Honderd jaar muziekleven*, pp. 284-285.

15 Zwart, *Willem Mengelberg*, p. 62.

16 Zwart, *Willem Mengelberg*, p. 235.

17 Quoted in: Schuijer, "In het teeken van Mahler," p. 114.

18 Quoted in: Schmidt et al., *De Matthäus-Passion*, p. 59.

19 Op de Coul, "Een Italiaanse *Salome*," pp. 236-251.

20 Wennekes, *Het Paleis voor Volksvlijt*, p. 203.

21 Wennekes, *Het Paleis voor Volksvlijt*, pp. 212-213.

22 Bottenheim, *De opera in Nederland*, pp. 196-200; Streevelaar, "Eigen taal is eigen kunst," pp. 193-194.

23 Streevelaar, "Eigen taal is eigen kunst," p. 196.

24 Quoted in: Streevelaar, "Eigen taal is eigen kunst," p. 198.

25 Streevelaar, "Eigen taal is eigen kunst," p. 196.

26 Reeser, *Een eeuw Nederlandse muziek*, p. 143.

27 Reeser, *Verzamelde geschriften*, p. 91.
28 Quoted in: Suèr and Meurs, *Geheel in de geest van Wagner*, pp. 37-38.
29 Suèr and Meurs, *Geheel in de geest van Wagner*, p. 47.
30 Suèr and Meurs, *Geheel in de geest van Wagner*, p. 57.
31 Meurs, *Wagner*, p. 311.
32 Reeser, *Alphons Diepenbrock*, vol. 1, pp. 440-441.
33 Meurs, *Wagner*, p. 278.
34 Meurs, *Wagner*, p. 285.
35 Bloemgarten, *Henri Polak*, p. 500.
36 Kemperink, *Nederlands toneel in het fin de siècle*, pp. 100-101.
37 Kemperink, *Nederlands toneel in het fin de siècle*, p. 125.
38 Goedkoop, *Geluk*, p. 78.
39 Erenstein, "Zomerspelen in Laren," p. 559.
40 Erenstein, *Een eeuw Nederlands toneel*, p. 8.
41 Groeneboer, "De première van Shaws *Candida*," p. 565.
42 Post, "Oprichtingsvergadering," pp. 445-449.
43 Post, "Koning Willem III," pp. 480-483.
44 De Feyter, "De Meiningers treden op," pp. 511-512.
45 Hunningher, *Een eeuw Nederlands toneel*, p. 109.
46 Achten, "Opening van de Tivoli-Schouwburg," p. 521.
47 Suèr and Meurs, *Geheel in de geest van Wagner*, p. 39.
48 Herman Schwab quoted in: Koster, *De Bouwmeesters*, p. 247.
49 Kemperink, *Nederlands toneel in het fin de siècle*, pp. 33-44.
50 Koster, *De Bouwmeesters*, p. 142.
51 Note from Dr. Henk Gras for the NWO priority program *Dutch Culture in a European Perspective* - 1800.
52 Leek, "Burgersdijk voltooit de vertaling," pp. 496-497.
53 Leek, "Burgersdijk voltooit de vertaling," p. 499.
54 Goedkoop, *Geluk*, p. 66.
55 Ibid., p. 78.
56 Hunningher, *Een eeuw Nederlands toneel*, p. 91.
57 Ibid., p. 92.
58 Hough, *Dutch Life*, pp. 179-180.
59 Blokker, *De wond'ren werden woord en dreven verder*, p. 4.
60 Van Lente and De Wit, *Geschiedenis van de grafische techniek*, pp. 199-220; Visser, "De grote sprong voorwaarts," p. 84.
61 De Vries, "De roman *Lidewijde*," p. 152.
62 Van den Berg, *Een bedachtzame beeldenstorm*, p. 95.
63 De Vries, "De roman *Lidewijde*," p. 138.
64 Ibid., pp. 148-149.
65 Ibid., pp. 145-146.
66 Coenen quoted in: Van den Berg, *Een bedachtzame beeldenstorm*, p. 89.
67 Van den Berg, *Een bedachtzame beeldenstorm*, p. 106.
68 Schneiders, *Lezen voor iedereen*, p. 27.
69 De Vries, "De roman *Lidewijde*," pp. 151-152.
70 Van Riemsdijk, *Geschiedenis van de Openbare Bibliotheek*, vol. 1, p. 50.
71 De Glas, *Nieuwe lezers*, p. 67.
72 Van Veen, *G.H. Breitner*, p. 22.
73 Goedkoop, *Geluk*, p. 51.
74 Leijerzapf, "Hetgeen ik zoek met stift of lens," pp. 42-43.
75 Donaldson, *Of Joy and Sorrow*, p. 51.
76 Van der Maden, *Mobiele filmexploitatie*, p. 38; Van Beusekom, *Film als kunst*, p. 31.
77 Quoted in: Van Beusekom, *Film als kunst*, p. 70.
78 Van Beusekom, *Film als kunst*, pp. 50 and 58.
79 Ibid., p. 85.
80 Lodewijk van Deyssel quoted in: Prick, *In de zekerheid van eigen heerlijkheid*, pp. 415 and 417.
81 Goedkoop, *Geluk*, p. 131.
82 Blok in: Ritter, *Eene halve eeuw 1848-1898*, vol. 1, p. 13.
83 *De ontwikkeling onzer electriciteitsvoorziening*, p. 12.
84 Schippers, *Het nieuwe bier*, passim.
85 Wierdels, "Klein München in Amsterdam," pp. 97-98.
86 Van Harpen in the *Algemeen Handelsblad*, November 28, 1922.
87 Hoogenboom, *De stand der kunstenaars*, pp. 196-197.
88 Hondius van den Broek to F.C. Coenen Jr., May 31, 1894. In: Reeser, *Alphons Diepenbrock*, vol. 2, p. 186.
89 Erens, *Vervlogen Jaren*, p. 178.
90 Endt, *Het festijn van tachtig*, p. 36.
91 Quoted in: Bakker, "'t Was of 'k mijzelven vond."
92 Quoted in: Bakker, "'t Was of 'k mijzelven vond."
93 Whiting, *Satie the Bohemian*, p. 24.
94 Ibid., p. 20.
95 Ibid., p. 42.
96 Klöters, *100 Jaar amusement*, pp. 124-125.
97 Ibid., p. 66.
98 De Haas, *De minstreel van de mesthoop*, pp. 57-58.
99 Kuiper, *Een wijze ging voorbij*, pp. 31-33.
100 De Haas, *De minstreel van de mesthoop*, p. 61.
101 Ibid., p. 62.
102 De Haas, *'t Was anders*, pp. 18-19.
103 Quoted by De Haas, *'t Was anders*, p. 60.
104 De Groot, *De dichter-zanger J.H. Speenhoff*, pp. 16-17.

Chapter 15   Retrospect

1   Beaufort, *Dagboeken en aantekeningen*,
     pp. 617-618.
2   Rosenboom, *Publieke Werken.*
3   Frijhoff and Spies, *1650*, p. 225.
4   Coninck, *Les uit Pruisen*, p. 188.
5   Quoted in: Augustijn and Vree, *Abraham
     Kuyper*, p. 174.
6   Scheffer, *November 1918*, p. 245.
7   Fokkema, *Culturele identiteit*, p. 13.

Works cited

Achten, Wim. *4 oktober 1890: Opening van de Tivoli-Schouwburg in Rotterdam: Toneel en realisme in Rotterdam.* In: R.L. Erenstein et al. (eds.), *Een theatergeschiedenis der Nederlanden: Tien eeuwen drama en theater in Nederland en Vlaanderen.* Amsterdam 1996, pp. 520-525.

Aerden, Monica. "Werken, feesten en flaneren." In: Moniek Peters, and Peter Marijnissen, *Willy Sluiter 1873-1949: Gentleman-kunstenaar.* Dordrecht and Ghent 1999.

Aerts, R.A.M. "De wetenschappelijke burger: Gerard Heymans en de thema's van het fin de siècle." In: D. Draaisma, *Een laboratorium voor de ziel: Gerard Heymans en het begin van de experimentele psychologie.* Groningen 1992, pp. 27-39.

Aerts, Remieg. *De Letterheren: Liberale cultuur in de negentiende eeuw: Het tijdschrift De Gids.* Amsterdam 1997.

Aerts, Remieg. "Burgerlijk sciëntisme? Over wetenschap en burgerlijke cultuur 1840-1880." In: R. Aerts, et al. (eds.), *Geleerden en leken: De wereld van de Hollandsche Maatschappij der Wetenschappen 1840-1880.* Haarlem and Rotterdam 2002, pp.17-31.

Aerts, Remieg, et al. (eds.). *Geleerden en leken: De wereld van de Hollandsche Maatschappij der Wetenschappen 1840-1880.* Haarlem and Rotterdam 2002.

Al, J. *Research als overheidstaak.* The Hague 1952.

Alberdingk Thijm, C. *Verwoest leven: Ware geschiedenis uit onze dagen.* Utrecht 1892.

Alberdingk Thijm, J.A. *De kunst in Nederland.* Nijmegen 1855.

Alberdingk Thijm, J.A. "Een bouwlootse der XIXe eeuw." *De Dietsche Warande* 1 (1855): 276-282.

Alberdingk Thijm, J.A. *Over de kompozitie in de kunst.* Amsterdam 1857.

Alberts, G., E. Atzema, and J. van Maanen. "Mathematics in The Netherlands: A brief survey with an emphasis on the relation to physics, 1560-1960." In: K. van Berkel, A. van Helden, and L. Palm (eds.), *A history of science in The Netherlands: Survey, themes and reference.* Leiden 1999, pp. 367-404.

Aletrino, A. *Twee opstellen over crimineele anthropologie.* Amsterdam 1898.

Algemeen Handelsblad. September 12, 1884.

Algemeen Handelsblad. November 28, 1922.

Alkemade, A.J.M. *Vrouwen XIX: Geschiedenis van negentien religieuze congregaties 1800-1850.* Den Bosch 1966.

Allart, Barbara. *"De wetenschap heeft 't uitgemaakt": Wetenschapsbeelden in Nederlandse publiekstijdschriften 1840-1900.* Utrecht 2003.

Amersfoort, J.M.M. van. "Van William Kegge tot Ruud Gullit: De Surinaamse migratie naar Nederland: Realiteit, beeldvorming en beleid." *Tijdschrift voor Geschiedenis* 100 (1987): 475-490.

Amicis, Edmondo de. *La Hollande.* Trans. Frédéric Bernard. Paris 1878.

De Amsterdammer. February 20, 1916.

De Amsterdammer. September 13, 1884.

Anbeek, T. *De naturalistische roman in Nederland.* Amsterdam 1982.

Anbeek, Ton. *Geschiedenis van de Nederlandse literatuur tussen 1885 en 1985.* Amsterdam 1990.

Arabatzis, T. "The discovery of the Zeeman-effect: a casestudy of the interplay between theory and experiment." *Studies in History and Philosophy of Science* 23 (1992): 365-388.

Arondéus, W. *Figuren en problemen der monumentale schilderkunst in Nederland.* Amsterdam 1941.

Augustijn, C. et al. *Abraham Kuyper: Zijn volksdeel, zijn invloed.* Delft 1987.

Augustijn, C., and J. Vree. *Abraham Kuyper: Vast en veranderlijk: De ontwikkeling van zijn denken.* Zoetermeer 1998.

Aurier, G. Albert. *Le symbolisme en peinture.* Paris 1991.

Baggen, P. *Vorming door wetenschap: Universitair onderwijs in Nederland, 1815-1960.* Delft 1998.

Bakker, B. "De stadsuitleg van 1610 en het ideaal van de 'volcomen stadt': Meesterplan of mythe?" In: *Jaarboek Amstelodamum* 87 (1995): 71-96.

Bakker, Boudewijn. "'t Was of 'k mijzelven vond': Het stadsgezicht als spiegel van de tijd." In: Martha Bakker (ed.), *Amsterdam in de Tweede Gouden Eeuw.* Bussum 2000, pp. 100-135 and 408-411.

Bakker, Nelleke. *Kind en karakter: Nederlandse pedagogen over opvoeding in het gezin 1845-1925.* Amsterdam 1995.

Bakker, W. et al. *De Doleantie van 1886 en haar geschiedenis.* Kampen 1986.

Baljet, B. "Dutch anatomy at the turn of the century [1900]." *Scientiarium Historia* 26 (2000): 83-96.

Bank, J.A. *Geschiedenis der katholieke kerkmuziek.* Vol. 1: *De liturgische muziek, het Gregoriaans.* Amsterdam 1947.

Barnouw, Adriaan J. *Coming after: An anthology of poetry from the Low Countries.* Trans. Adriaan J. Barnouw. New Brunswick 1948.

Barron, S.L. *The development of the electrocardiograph:*

Boeren, C.J.C.M. *N.G. Tsjernysjevski, strijder voor de nieuwe mens in de nieuwe wereld*. Unpublished PhD diss. University of Nijmegen 1968.

Boersen, M. *De Kolonie van de Internationale Broederschap te Blaricum*. Blaricum 1987.

Boersma, K. "De ontwikkeling van röntgentechnologie in de beginjaren van het Philips' Natuurkundig Laboratorium." *NEHA-jaarboek* 62 (1999): 291-318.

Bolland, G.J.P.J. *Nieuwe kennis, oude wijsheid: Eene poging tot voorlichting*. Leiden 1910.

Boomgaard, Jeroen. "Bronnenstudie en stilistiek: Van de kunst der werkelijkheid tot de werkelijkheid der kunst." In: Frans Grijzenhout, and Henk van Veen (eds.), *De Gouden Eeuw in perspectief: Het beeld van de Nederlandse zeventiende-eeuwse schilderkunst in later tijd*. Nijmegen and Heerlen 1992, pp. 255-279.

Boomgaard, Jeroen. *De verloren zoon: Rembrandt en de Nederlandse kunstgeschiedschrijving*. Amsterdam 1995.

Boonstra, O.W.A. *De waardij van eene vroege opleiding: Een onderzoek naar de implicaties van het alfabetisme op het leven van inwoners van Eindhoven en omliggende gemeenten, 1800-1920*. In: *AAG Bijdragen* 34. Wageningen 1993.

Borgeaud, Charles. *Pages d'Histoire nationale*. Geneva 1934.

Bornewasser, J.A. *Curiale appreciaties van de priesterpoliticus Schaepman*. In: *Mededelingen der Koninklijke Nederlandse Akademie van Wetenschappen, afdeling letterkunde* 49-7. Amsterdam, Oxford, and New York 1986.

Bornewasser, J.A. *Kerkelijk verleden in een wereldlijke context: Historische opstellen, gebundeld en aangeboden aan de schrijver bij zijn aftreden als hoogleraar aan de Theologische Faculteit Tilburg*. Amsterdam 1989.

Bornewasser, J.A. *Katholieke Volkspartij 1945-1980*. Vol. 1: *Herkomst en groei (tot 1963)*. Nijmegen 1995.

Bos, D. *Onze Volksopleiding*. Groningen 1898.

Bos, David. *In dienst van het koninkrijk: Beroepsontwikkeling van hervormde predikanten in negentiende-eeuws Nederland*. Amsterdam 1999.

Bos, J. "De querulant en zijn prooi: Evert van Dieren versus Christiaan Eijkman en de beri-beri controverse (1897-1898)." *Gewina* 26 (2003): 127-147.

Bos, P., and B. Theunissen (eds.). *Beijerinck and the Delft school of microbiology*. Delft 1995.

Bos, W.Jzn. *Sliedrecht, dorp van wereldvermaardheid*. Zaltbommel 1969.

Bosch, A., and G.P.van de Ven. "Rivierverbetering." In: H.W. Lintsen et al., *Geschiedenis van de techniek in Nederland: De wording van een moderne samenleving 1800-1890*. Vol. 2. Zutphen 1993, pp. 103-128.

Bosch, M. *Het geslacht van de wetenschap: Vrouwen en hoger onderwijs in Nederland 1878-1948*. Amsterdam 1994.

Bosch, M. "Honderd jaar Hilda van Suylenburg: Een tendentieuze geschiedenis." *Armada* 3 (1997): p. 101.

Bosma, J.E. *Ruimte voor een nieuwe tijd: Vormgeving van de Nederlandse regio 1900-1945*. Rotterdam 1993.

Bosscha, J. *Leerboek de Natuurkunde en van hare voornaamste toepassingen*. Leiden 1875.

Bossenbroek, Martin. *Holland op zijn breedst: Indië en Zuid-Afrika in de Nederlandse cultuur omstreeks 1900*. Amsterdam 1996.

Boterenbrood, H. and J. Prang, *Van der Mey en het Scheepvaarthuis*. The Hague 1989.

Bottenburg, Maarten. *Verborgen competitie: Over de uiteenlopende populariteit van sporten*. Amsterdam 1994.

Bottenheim, S.A.M. *De opera in Nederland*. Amsterdam 1946.

Bouman, P.J., and W.H. Bouman. *De Groei van de grote Werkstad: Een studie over de bevolking van Rotterdam*. Assen 1952.

Bourget, Paul. "Théorie de la décadence." In: Paul Bourget, *Oeuvres Complètes*. Paris 1899, pp.14-20.

Boyle-Turner, Caroline. *Jan Verkade: Hollandse volgeling van Gauguin*. Zwolle 1989.

Braches, Ernst. *Het boek als nieuwe kunst 1892-1903*. Utrecht 1973.

Brandt Corstius, J.C. *Herman Gorter, de mens en dichter*. Amsterdam 1934.

Brandt Corstius, J.C. "Een debat over kunst en leven in 1896." *Apollo* 2 (1947): 263-275.

Bratt, James D. *Dutch Calvinism in modern America: A History of conservative Subculture*. Grand Rapids, MI, n.d.

Braun, M. *De prijs van de liefde: De eerste feministische golf, het huwelijksrecht en de vaderlandse geschiedenis*. Amsterdam 1992.

Braun, M. "Drie sprookjes van Wilhelmina Drucker: Een bijdrage aan de cultuurgeschiedenis van het fin de siècle." *Jaarboek voor vrouwengeschiedenis* 14 (1994): 10-29.

Braun, Marianne. "'Het recht even goed te leven als een man': Hilda van Suylenburg: tekst en context van een emancipatieroman." *Tijdschrift voor sociale geschiedenis* 24 (1998): 209-234.

Bregstein, Philo. *Gesprekken met Jacques Presser*. Baarn 1999.

Brinkman, H. *Honderd jaar experimenteel-natuurkundig onderzoek in Groningen*. Amsterdam 1980.

Broekhuis, Madelon. "Ideologie in steen: Het beeldhouwwerk van Lambertus Zijl aan het Beursgebouw te Amsterdam." *Nederlands Kunsthistorisch Jaarboek* 34 (1983): 195-227.

Broekhuis, Madelon. "Antoon Derkinderen en de Beurs van Berlage." *Jong Holland* 2 (1988): 4-14.

Broere, Anrie. "Hans Brinker of De Zilveren Schaatsen: De geschiedenis van een kinderboek." *Boekenpost* 5 (1997): 10-13.

Broeyer, F.G.M. "De predikantsopleiding in de negentiende eeuw." *Jaarboek voor de geschiedenis van het Nederlands Protestantisme na 1800* 5 (1997): 91-92.

Brom, Gerard. "Het treurspel van Der Kinderen's processie." *Studia Catholica* 7 (1930-1931): 102-120.

Brom, Gerard. *Herleving van de kerkelijke kunst in Katholiek Nederland*. Leiden 1933.

Brom, Gerard. *De dominee in onze literatuur*. Nijmegen and Utrecht, n.d.

Bronde, N. *Seurat in Perspective*. Englewood Cliffs 1878.

Brookman, F.H. *The making of a science policy: A histori-cal study of the institutional and conceptual back-ground to Dutch science policy in a West-European perspective.* Amsterdam 1979.

Brouwer, T., W. van Os, and C.A. van Swighem. *Een huis voor het Woord: Het protestantse kerkinterieur in Nederland tot 1900.* The Hague and Zeist 1984.

Brouwers, J.W. *Antwoord aan den heer Groen van Prinsterer op zijn "Heiligerlee en Ultramontaansche Kritiek."* Amsterdam 1868.

Browning, E. Barrett. *Aurora Leigh.* Haarlem 1883.

Brugmans, H. (ed.). *Nederland in den oorlogstijd: de geschiedenis van Nederland en van Nederlandsch-Indië tijdens den oorlog van 1914 tot 1919, voor zoover zij met dien oorlog verband houdt.* Amsterdam 1920.

Brugmans, H., and N. Beets. *1813 - Amsterdam - 1913.* Amsterdam 1913.

Bruin, Kees. *Een herenwereld ontleed: Over Amsterdamse oude en nieuwe elites in de tweede helft van de negen-tiende eeuw.* Amsterdam 1980.

Bruin, Kees. *De echte Rembrandt: Verering van een genie in de twintigste eeuw.* Amsterdam 1995.

Bruining, A. "De ethische richting en de godsdienst." *Theologisch Tijdschrift* 11 (1977): 131, 172-173, 185-187.

Brunetière, F. "Après une visite au Vatican." *Revue des Deux Mondes* 65 (1895): 97-118.

Burhan, Filiz Eda. *Vision and Visionaries: Nineteenth Century Psychological Theory: The Occult Sciences and the Formation of the Symbolist Aesthetic in France.* Michigan 1983.

Burkom, Frans van, and Hans Mulder. *Erich Wichmann 1890-1929: Tussen idealisme en rancune.* Utrecht 1983.

Buruma, Ian. *Voltaire's Coconuts or Anglomania in Europe.* London 1999.

Busken Huet, C.D. *Van Napels naar Amsterdam: Italiaansche reis-aanteekeningen.* Amsterdam 1877.

Busken Huet, C.D. *Het Land van Rembrand: Studiën over de Noordnederlandsche beschaving in de zeven-tiende eeuw.* Haarlem 1941.

Busken Huet, Conrad. *Litterarische Fantasiën en Kritieken.* Vol 2. Haarlem, n.d.

Buuren, Maarten van. "De anatomische les." *Feit en fictie* 1 (1993): 39-53.

Buuren, Maarten van. "Hystérie et littérature." *Poétique* 100 (1994): 387-411.

Buuren, Maarten van. "Een schip voor het volk." In: Etty Mulder, and Hans Ester, *De schone leugen en de steen der dwazen.* Baarn 1998, pp. 142-151.

Buuren, Maarten van. *Vincent van Goghs navolging van Christus.* Utrecht 2001.

Cannadine, David. "The Context, Performance en Meaning of Ritual: The British Monarchy and the 'Invention of Tradition', 1820-1977." In: Eric Hobsbawm en Terence Ranger, *The Invention of Tradition.* Cambridge 1984.

Carpenter, K. *Beriberi, white rice and vitamin B: A dis-ease, a cause and a cure.* Berkeley 2000.

Carpenter, K.J., and B. Sutherland. "Eijkman's contri-bution to the discovery of vitamins." *Journal of Nutrition* 125 (1995): 155-163.

Casimir, R. "Heymans: De toekomstige eeuw der psy-chologie." In: R. Casimir, *Opbouw: een bundel verza-melde opstellen.* Groningen 1927, pp. 292-306. (Original *Ploeg*, 2, 1910.)

Casimir, R. *Het Nederlandsch Lyceum van 1909 tot 1934.* Groningen, The Hague, and Batavia 1934.

Chantepie de la Saussaye, P.D. "Eene halve eeuw, 1848-1898." *Historisch Gedenkboek* 19 (1898): 1-35.

Charité, J. (ed.). *Biografisch Woordenboek van Nederland.* Vol. 1. The Hague 1979.

Cioran, E.M. "Mécanisme de l'utopie." In: E.M. Cioran, *Histoire et Utopie.* Paris 1960, pp. 103-125.

Claire, R.C. le (ed.). *The letters of William James and Théodore Flournoy.* Madison and London 1966.

Clant van der Myll-Piepers, A.J.F. *Een woord naar aan-leiding van Anna de Savornin Lohman's: "De liefde in de vrouwenquaestie."* Amsterdam 1999.

"La coéducation des sexes et leurs résultats pour la femme." *La Revue* (1903): 545-570.

Coesèl, M., and Zevenhuizen, E. "Op heterdaad betrapt? Hugo de Vries en zijn houding tegenover vrouwen in de wetenschap." *Gewina* 23 (2000): 266-284.

Coninck, P.J.M. de. *Een les uit Pruisen: Nederland en de Kulturkampf, 1870-1880.* Leiden 1998.

Constandse, A.L. "Herman Gorter en Spinoza." In: G. Stuiveling (ed.), *Acht over Gorter.* Amsterdam 1978, pp. 213-253.

Cordfuncke, E.H.P. *Een romantisch geleerde: Jacobus Henricus van 't Hoff.* Amsterdam 2001.

Cornets de Groot, R. *De dichter-zanger J.H. Speenhoff of zelfportret met liedjes.* Leiden 1990.

Couvée, D.H. *Leve de Willemien! Het jaar 1898 van Wilhelmina's inhuldiging opnieuw beleefd.* The Hague 1958.

Crane, Walter. *The claims of decorative art.* Boston, MA and Cambridge, MA 1892.

Crane, Walter. *Kunst en samenleving.* Amsterdam 1894.

Crawford, E. *Nationalism and internationalism in science, 1880-1939: Four studies of the Nobel population.* Cambridge 1992.

Cuypers, P.J.H., and Jan Kalf. *De katholieke kerken in Nederland: Dat is de tegenwoordige staat dier kerken met hunne meubilering en versiering beschreven en afgebeeld.* Amsterdam 1906.

Dr. Cuypers Gedenkboek, 1827-1927. Sittard 1927.

Daalder, H. "Joden in een verzuilend Nederland." *Hollands Maandblad* 17 (1975): 3-12.

Daalder, H. *Politiek en historie: Opstellen over Nederlandse politiek en vergelijkende politieke weten-schap.* Amsterdam 1990.

Daams, J.H. "Uit de geschiedenis van het NNGC." In: *Van vonk tot vlam: 100 jaar natuurwetenschap in Nederland: Het Nederlands Natuur- en Geneeskundig Congres 1887-1987.* Amsterdam 1989.

Daels, van P. *Sint Nicolaaskerk Amsterdam.* Amstelveen 1987.

Dalen, D. van. *Mystic, geometer, and intuitionist: The life of L. E. J. Brouwer.* Vol. 1: *The Dawning Revolution.* Oxford 1999.

Dalen, D. van. *L.E.J. Brouwer, 1881-1966: Een biografie: Het heldere licht van de wiskunde.* Amsterdam 2001.

Danziger, Kurt. *Constructing the subject: Historical origins of psychological research*. Cambridge 1990.

Dasberg, Lea. "De visie van de negentiende-eeuwse onderwijzer op zijn taak als maatschappelijk en cultureel werker." *Bijdragen en Mededelingen betreffende de Geschiedenis der Nederlanden* 92 (1977): 266-267.

Dasberg, L., and J.W.G. Jansing. *Meer kennis, meer kans: Het Nederlandse onderwijs 1843-1914*. Haarlem 1978.

Dekkers, Dieuwertje. *Jozef Israels, een succesvol schilder van het vissersgenre*. The Hague 1994.

Dellepoort, J.J. *De priesterroepingen in Nederland: Proeve van een statistisch-sociografische analyse*. The Hague 1955.

Delft, D. van. "De blauwe jongens: de opleiding tot instrumentmaker in het natuurkundig laboratorium van Heike Kamerlingh Onnes." *Gewina* 25 (2002): 137-153.

Denis, Maurice. *Du symbolisme au classicisme: Théories*. Paris 1964.

Derksen, M. *Wij psychologen: Retorica en demarcatie in de geschiedenis van de Nederlandse psychologie*. Groningen 1997.

Deurloo, M.C., and G.A. Hoekveld. "The population growth of the urban municipalities in the Netherlands between 1849 and 1970, with particular reference to the period 1899-1930." In: H. Schmal (ed.), *Patterns of European Urbanisation since 1500*. London 1981.

Diepenbrock, Alphons. "Melodie en gedachte." *De Nieuwe Gids* 7, no. 2 (1891): 291-297; 7, no. 3 (1892): 455-463; 8, no. 6 (1892): 434-443.

Diepenbrock, Alphons. *Verzamelde Geschriften*. Utrecht 1950.

Diepenbrock, Alphons. *Brieven en Documenten*. Edited by Eduard Reeser. 10 vols. and register. The Hague and Amsterdam 1962-1998.

Dieteren, Fia. "Twee levens, twee geloven: Feminisme en katholicisme in de levens van Elisabeth en Cécile de Jong van Beek en Donk." *Jaarboek voor Vrouwengeschiedenis* 18 (1998): p. 41.

Dijck, J.V. van. *Bijdrage tot de psychologie van den misdadiger*. Groningen 1905.

Dijk, Henk van. *Rotterdam 1810-1880: Aspecten van een stedelijke samenleving*. Schiedam 1976.

Dijk, H. van. "Het negentiende-eeuwse stadsbestuur: Continuïteit of verandering?" In: P.B.M. Blaas, and J. van Herwaarden (ed.), *Stedelijke naijver: De betekenis van interstedelijke conflicten in de geschiedenis: Enige beschijvingen en case-studies*. The Hague 1986, pp. 128-149.

Dijksterhuis, Roelof. *Spoorwegtracering en stedebouw in Nederland: Historische analyse van een wisselwerking in de eerste eeuw: 1840-1940*. Delft 1984.

Dis, L.M. van, P.A. Dijkema, and J. Meijer (eds.). *Ik neem afscheid van U: In memoriam dr C. Spoelder (1885-1958)*. Haarlem 1959.

Dokkum, J.D.C. van. *Honderd jaar muziekleven in Nederland: Een geschiedenis van de Maatschappij tot bevordering der Toonkunst bij haar eeuwfeest 1829-1929*. Amsterdam 1929.

Dona, J.C. *Sport en socialisme: De geschiedenis van de Nederlandse Arbeiderssportbond 1926-1941*. Amsterdam 1981.

Donaldson, Geoffrey. *Of Joy and Sorrow: A Filmography of Dutch Silent Fiction*. Amsterdam 1997.

Dongelmans, B., F. van Oostrom, and P. van Zonneveld (eds.). *Dierbaar Magazijn: De bibliotheek van de Maatschappij der Nederlandse Letterkunde*. Amsterdam 1995.

Doorn, J.A.A. van. "Over liberalisme en sociaal-democratie: Kanttekeningen bij Siep Stuurman: Wacht op onze daden." *Beleid & Maatschappij* 19 (1992): 315-316.

Doorn, J.A.A. van. "Sporen van nationaal-liberalisme: Opmerkingen over Henk te Velde: Gemeenschapszin en plichtsbesef." *Beleid & Maatschappij* 20 (1993): 155.

Doorn, J.A.A. van. *De laatste eeuw van Indië: Ontwikkeling en ondergang van een koloniaal project*. Amsterdam 1994.

Doornenbal, Jeannette. "Het kind en de rode schoolmeester: Een analyse van de ideeën van de Bond van Nederlandse Onderwijzers ten aanzien van de kindgerichte pedagogiek in het begin van de 20e eeuw." *Comenius: Wetenschappelijk tijdschrift voor democratisering van opvoeding, onderwijs, vorming en hulpverlening* 3 (1983): 245-249.

Draaisma, D. et al. *Gerard Heymans: Objectiviteit in filosofie en psychologie*. Weesp 1983.

Draaisma, D. "Heymans versus Aletrino." *De Psycholoog* 27, no. 1 (1992): 16-19.

Draaisma, D. (ed.). *Een laboratorium voor de ziel: Gerard Heymans en het begin van de experimentele psychologie*. Groningen 1992.

Draaisma, D., B. Lalbahadoersing, and E. Haas. "Een laboratorium voor de ziel: Heymans' Laboratorium voor Experimentele Psychologie 1892-1927." In: D. Draaisma (ed.), *Een laboratorium voor de ziel: Gerard Heymans en het begin van de experimentele psychologie*. Groningen 1992, pp. 12-26.

Dudink, Stefan P. *Deugdzaam liberalisme: Sociaal-liberalisme in Nederland 1870-1901*. Amsterdam 1997.

Duinkerken, Anton van. *Brabantse herinneringen*. Utrecht and Antwerp 1964.

Dunk, Th.H. von der. "Jhr. Victor de Stuers en het Rijksmuseum." *Bulletin van het Rijksmuseum*. 42, no. 1 (1994): 37-77.

Duys, J.E.W. *Feminisme en staats-notariaat*. Breukelen 1899.

Duyvendak, Arie Jan van. *De motivering van de klassieke vorming: Een historisch-paedagogische studie over twee eeuwen*. Groningen 1955.

Eckerman, Johann Peter. *Conversations with Goethe*. Trans. J.K. Moorhead. London, n.d. [1951].

Eeden, F. van. "Het hypnotisme en de wonderen." In: F. van Eeden, *Studies: Eerste reeks*. Amsterdam 1890, pp. 139-167.

Eeden, F. van. "Over de toekomst." In: F. van Eeden, *Studies: Tweede reeks*. Amsterdam 1894, pp. 64-81.

Eeden, F. van. "Artiest en socialist." In: F. van Eeden, *Studies: Derde reeks*. Amsterdam 1897, pp. 240-268.

Eeden, F. van. "Coöperatieve rijkshoeven." In: F. van Eeden, *Studies: Derde reeks*. Amsterdam 1897, pp. 268-330.

Eeden, F. van. "Werk en brood." In: F. van Eeden, *Studies: Derde reeks*. Amsterdam 1897, pp. 203-239.

Eeden, F. van. *Binnenlandsche kolonisatie*. Amsterdam 1901.

Eeden, F. van. *De blijde wereld: Rede over mensch en maatschappij*. Amsterdam 1903.

Eeden, F. van. "De coöperatie in Kettering." In: F. van Eeden, *Studies: Vierde reeks*. Amsterdam 1904, pp. 236-248.

Eeden, F. van. "Recht of macht." In: F. van Eeden, *Studies: Vierde reeks*. Amsterdam 1904, pp. 193-236.

Eeden, F. van. "Waarvan leven wij." In: F. van Eeden, *Studies: Vierde reeks*. Amsterdam 1904, pp. 115-153.

Eeden, F. van. "Waarvoor werkt gij?" In: F. van Eeden, *Studies: Vierde reeks*. Amsterdam 1904, pp. 153-193.

Eeden, F. van. *Mijne ervaringen op sociologisch gebied*. Amsterdam 1954. 1st ed. 1907.

Eeden, F. van. *De idealisten of Het beloofde land*. Amsterdam 1909.

Eeden, F. van. *Het godshuis in de lichtstad*. With drawings by J. London. Amsterdam 1921.

Eerenbeemt, H.F.J.M. van den (ed.). *Geschiedenis van Noord-Brabant*. Vol. 2: *Emancipatie en industrialisering 1890-1945*. Amsterdam and Meppel 1996.

Eichner, Johannes. *Kandinsky und Gabriele Münter: Von Ursprüngen moderner Kunst*. Munich, n.d.

Eijkman, C. & Visser, H.K.A. "Eijkman and the anti-beri-beri vitamin." *Proceedings of the Koninklijke Nederlandse Akademie van Wetenschappen: biological, chemical, geological, physical and medical sciences* 100 (1997): 101-112.

Eijt, J.M.A. *Religieuze vrouwen: bruid, moeder, zuster: Geschiedenis van twee Nederlandse zustercongregaties, 1820-1940*. Hilversum and Nijmegen 1995.

Einthoven, W. "The string galvanometer and human electrocardiogram." *Koninklijke Akademie van Wetenschappen te Amsterdam: Proceedings of the section of sciences* 6 (1903): 107-115.

Ellemers, J.E. "Migratie van en naar Nederland in historisch perspectief: een beknopt overzicht." *Tijdschrift voor Geschiedenis* 100 (1987): 326.

Elzenga, Eelco. *Theater van staat: Oude tradities rond een jong koningschap*. Apeldoorn 1990.

Endt, Enno. *Het festijn van tachtig: De vervulling van heel groote dingen scheen nabij*. Amsterdam 1990.

Engels, F. *Herrn Eugen Duehrings Umwälzung der Wissenschaft*. Glashütten im Taunus 1970.

Erens, Frans. *Vervlogen Jaren*. With comments of Harry G.M. Prick. Amsterdam 1989.

Erenstein, R.L. et al. (eds.). *Een theatergeschiedenis der Nederlanden: Tien eeuwen drama en theater in Nederland en Vlaanderen*. Amsterdam 1996.

Erenstein, R.L. "25 en 26 juni 1907: Zomerspelen in Laren onder leiding van Royaards en Verkade: Het begin van het moderne theater." In: R.L. Erenstein et al. (eds.), *Een theatergeschiedenis der Nederlanden: Tien eeuwen drama en theater in Nederland en Vlaanderen*. Amsterdam 1996, 552-559.

Erenstein, R.L. *Een eeuw Nederlands toneel: Tussen traditie en vernieuwing*. Hunningher Lecture 1999. Amsterdam 1999.

Erftemeijer, Antoon, Arjen Looyenga, and Marike van Roon. *Getooid als een bruid: De nieuwe Sint-Bavokathedraal te Haarlem*. Haarlem 1997.

Esquiros, Alphonse. *Nederland en het leven in Nederland*. Amsterdam 1858.

Etty, Elsbeth. *Liefde is heel het leven niet: Henriëtte Roland-Holst 1869-1952*. Amsterdam 1996.

Evers, H. *Pastoraat en bedevaart: Een onderzoek naar het pastorale aanbod in het kader van de devotie tot Sint Gerardus Majella en de bedevaart naar Wittem, met bijzondere aandacht voor het zangrepertoire*. Etten-Leur 1993.

Evers, H., and P. Post. *Historisch repertorium met betrekking tot Wittem als bedevaartoord*. In: *HTP-Katernen* 2. Heerlen 1986.

Evers, J.H.M. "Bedevaart en zang: Een analyse van het liedgoed van twee bedevaartoorden." In: M. van Uden, and P. Post (eds.), *Christelijke bedevaarten: Op weg naar heil en heling*. Nijmegen 1988.

Evolutie 5 (1897-1898): 162.

Eyffinger, Arthur. *Het Vredespaleis*. Amsterdam 1988.

Fasel, W.A. "De ontzetviering te Alkmaar in de loop der eeuwen." In: I. Schöffer, *Alkmaar ontzet 1573-1973*. Alkmaar 1973, pp. 85-196.

Fasseur, Cees. *Wilhelmina: De jonge koningin*. Amsterdam 1998.

Fasseur, Cees. "De puptan." In: Frits van Oostrom (ed.), *Historisch tableau: Geschiedenis opnieuw verbeeld in schoolplaten en essays*. Amsterdam 1998, pp. 121-124.

Fechner, G.T. *Nanna, oder das Seelenleben der Pflanzen*. Leipzig 1848.

Fechner, G.T. *Zend-Avesta, über die Dinge des Himmels und des Jenseits*. Leipzig 1851.

Fechner, G.T. *Vorschule der Aesthetik*. Leipzig 1876.

Fechner, G.T. *Die Tagesansicht gegenüber der Nachtansicht*. Leipzig 1879.

Feyter, Johan de. "De Meiningers treden op in Brussels en Antwerpen." In: R.L. Erenstein (ed.), *Een theatergeschiedenis der Nederlanden: Tien eeuwen drama en theater in Nederland en Vlaanderen*. Amsterdam 1996, pp. 511-512.

Fockema Andreae, J.P. *De hedendaagsche stedenbouw*. Utrecht 1912.

Fockema Andreae, S.J. "De uitbreiding der stad Arnhem tusschen 1815 en 1878." *Gelre: Bijdragen en Mededeelingen* 28 (1925): 152.

Fokkema, D.W. *Culturele identiteit en literaire innovatie*. Utrecht 1996.

Folkertsma, E.W. "Hildo Krop en de gemeente Amsterdam." *Nederlands Kunsthistorisch Jaarboek* 34 (1983): 227-278.

Fontijn, J. *Leven in extase: Opstellen over mystiek en muziek, literatuur en decadentie rond 1900*. Amsterdam 1983.

Fontijn, Jan. *Tweespalt: Het leven van Frederik van Eeden tot 1901*. Amsterdam 1990.

Fontijn, Jan. *Trots verbrijzeld: Het leven van Frederik van Eeden vanaf 1901*. Amsterdam 1996.

Foppen, J.W. *Gistend beleid: Veertig jaar universitaire*

onderwijspolitiek. The Hague 1989.

Forman, P., J.C. Heilbron, and S. Weart. "Physics circa 1900: Personnel, funding, and productivity of the academic establishments." *Historical studies in the physical sciences* 5 (1975): 1-185.

Fortgens, H.W. *Schola Latina: Uit het verleden van ons voorbereidend hoger onderwijs*. Zwolle 1958.

Freijser, Victor (ed.). *Het veranderend stadsbeeld van Den Haag: Plannen en processen in de Haagse stedebouw 1890-1990*. Published on the occasion of the 100th anniversary of the Geschiedkundige Vereniging Die Haghe. Zwolle, n.d.

Frijhoff, W.Th.M. *Volkskunde en cultuurwetenschap: de ups en downs van een dialoog. Mededelingen der Koninklijke Nederlandse Akademie van Wetenschappen* 60 (1997) 89-143.

Frijhoff, Willem, and Marijke Spies. *1650: Hard-Won Unity*. With the collaboration of Wiep van Bunge and Natascha Veldhorst. Trans. Myra Heerspink Scholz. Vol. 1 of *Dutch Culture in a European Perspective*. Assen and Basingstoke / New York 2004.

Fuerstein, Carol (ed.), *Piet Mondrian, 1872-1944: Centennial exhibition*. New York 1971

Gaehtgens, Barbara. "Holland als Vorbild." In: Angelika Wesenberg (ed.), *Max Liebermann: Jahrhundertwende*. Berlin 1997.

Galton, F. *Hereditary genius*. London 1869.

Galton, F. *English men of science*. London 1874.

Gans, Louis. *Nieuwe Kunst: De Nederlandse bijdrage tot de Art Nouveau: Dekoratieve kunst, kunstnijverheid en architektuur omstreeks 1900*. Utrecht 1960.

Gathorne-Hardy, Jonathan. *The public school phenomenon*. Hamondsworth 1977.

Gauguin, Paul. *Oviri: Ecrits d'un sauvage*. Paris 1974.

Gay, Peter. *Schnitzler's Century: The Making of Middle-Class Culture 1815-1914*. New York and London 2002.

Gedenkboek MCMI-MCMXI. Tenth annual report 1911-1912 of the Katholieke Kunstkring "De Violier". Amsterdam 1912.

Gedenkboek ter gelegenheid van het honderdjarig bestaan van het Genootschap van Leeraren aan Nederlandsche gymnasiën, 1830-1930. Amersfoort 1930.

Gedenkboek ter gelegenheid van het 40-jarig bestaan van de Haarlemsche Football Club, 1879-1919. Haarlem 1919.

Geertz, Clifford. *The Interpretation of Culture*. New York 1993.

Geest-Jacobs, I. van, and M. Klein. "Couperus en de Vrouwenquestie." *De nieuwe taalgids* 78 (1885): 127-136.

Genestet, P.A. de. *Leekedichtjens: Rijmen en dichten, zoo oude als nieuwe*. The Hague 1978.

Gerhard, Hendrik. "Schets van een Communistische Maatschappij." In: Hendrik Gerhard, *Verzamelde en nagelaten opstellen*. N.p. 1887, pp.43-67.

Gerrits, G.C. *Grote Nederlanders bij de opbouw der natuurwetenschappen*. Leiden 1948.

Gerstel, J.J., and L.J. Rogier. *Gedenkboek der Eerste H.B.S. 5-J.C. met gewijzigd leerplan (Eerste Handelsschool) te Rotterdam, uitgegeven ter gelegen-*

heid van het vijftigjarig bestaan. Rotterdam 1925.

Gevers, Ine. *Janus de Winter: De schilder mysticus*. Amsterdam 1985.

Geyl, P. *Noord en Zuid: Eenheid en tweeheid in de Lage Landen*. Utrecht 1960.

Ginkel, Rob van. *Op zoek naar eigenheid: Denkbeelden en discussies over cultuur en identiteit in Nederland*. The Hague 1999.

Giskes, Johan (ed.). *Mahler in Amsterdam: Van Mengelberg tot Chailly*. Bussum 1995.

Glas, Frank de. *Nieuwe lezers voor het goede boek: De Wereldbibliotheek en Ontwikkeling / De Arbeiderspers voor 1940*. Amsterdam 1989.

Goedkoop, Hans. *Geluk: Het leven van Herman Heijermans*. Amsterdam and Antwerp 1996.

Goekoop-de Jong van Beek en Donk, C., and J. Snellen. "Ingezonden." *Androcles, maandschrift aan de belangen der dieren gewijd*, 26 (1892): 27-31.

Goekoop-De Jong van Beek en Donk, C. "Ingezonden." *Belang en recht* 3 (1898-1899): 65.

Gorter, Herman. *Verzen*. Amsterdam 1903.

Gorter, H. *Een klein heldendicht*. Vol. 4. of *Verzamelde Werken*. Bussum and Amsterdam 1950.

Gorter, H. *Pan*. Vol. 5. of *Verzamelde Werken*. Bussum and Amsterdam 1951.

Gorter, Herman. *Mei: Een gedicht*. With an introduction by Garmt Stuiveling. Bussum 1956.

Gouw, J. ter. *De Volksvermaken*. N.p., n.d.

Graaf, A. de. "Gemeenschapskunst, de wandschildering van Derkinderen." *De Nieuwe Gids* 7 (1892): 325-330.

Graaf, H.T. de. *Karakter en behandeling van veroordeelden wegens landlooperij en bedelarij*. Groningen 1914.

Grapperhaus, Ferdinand H.M. *Fiscaal beleid in Nederland van 1800 tot na 2000*. Deventer 1997.

Grever, Maria, and Berteke Waaldijk. *Feministische Openbaarheid: De Nationale Tentoonstelling van Vrouwenarbeid in 1898*. Amsterdam 1998.

Grever, Maria, and Berteke Waaldijk. *Transforming the Public Sphere: The Dutch National Exhibition of Women's Labor in 1898*. Durham 2004.

Grijp, Louis Peter (ed.), *Zingen in een kleine taal: De positie van het Nederlands in de muziek*. Amsterdam 1995.

Groen, M. *Het wetenschappelijk onderwijs in Nederland van 1815 tot 1980: Een onderwijskundig overzicht*. Vol. 2: *Wis- en natuurkunde, technische wetenschappen, landbouwwetenschappen*. Eindhoven 1987-1989.

Groeneboer, Joost. "De première van Shaws *Candida* door De Hagespelers onder leiding van Eduard Verkade: Society drama en Haagse stijl." In: R.L. Erenstein (ed.), *Een theatergeschiedenis der Nederlanden: Tien eeuwen drama en theater in Nederland en Vlaanderen*. Amsterdam 1996, p. 565.

Groot, A. de. "De Muiderkerk: protestantse kerkbouw in Amsterdam aan het eind van de 19e eeuw." *De Sluitsteen: Bulletin van het Cuypers Genootschap* 6 (1990): 17.

Gross, O. *Die cerebrale Sekundärfunktion*. Leipzig 1902.

Grotenhuis, F.C.M. *Op zoek naar middelbaar onderwijs: Het VHMO in discussie tussen 1900 en 1970*. Amsterdam 1997.

Groustra, H. *"Vrijland" en de vrijlandbeweging*. Amsterdam 1893.

Gunning, J.H. Wzn. *De studie der paedagogiek in Nederland gedurende de jaren 1898-1938: Een schets*. Amsterdam, n.d.

Haan, Ido de en Henk te Velde. "Vormen van politiek: Veranderingen van de openbaarheid in Nederland 1848-1900." *Bijdragen en Mededelingen betreffende de Geschiedenis der Nederlanden* 111 (1996): 171.

Haan, Jacob Israël de. "Een Joodsche Tentoonstelling." In: Maurits Verhoeff en Thijs Wierema (eds.), *Ochenebbisj: Verhalen en geintjes over het Amsterdamse getto (1870-1925)*. Amsterdam 1999, pp. 382-383.

Haan, Tj.W.R. de. "Waar Spaarne en Liê tezamen vloeit: Het een-en-ander over geschiedenis en volksleven van Spaarndam en naaste omgeving." *Neerlands Volksleven*. 8 , no. 1 (1958): 36.

Haar Romeny, R.B. ter, and Joh.Tromp (eds.). *Quisque suis viribus 1841-1991: 150 Jaar theologie in dertien portretten*. Leiden 1991.

Haas, Alex de. *De minstreel van de mesthoop: Liedjes, leven en achtergronden van Eduard Jacobs, pionier van het Nederlands cabaret 1867-1914*. Amsterdam 1958.

Haas, Alex de. *'t Was anders: Leven en levenskring van de heer J.H. Speenhoff, dichter-zanger (1869-1945)*. Rotterdam and The Hague 1971.

Haas-Lorentz, G.L. de. *H.A. Lorentz: Impressions of his Life and Work*. Amsterdam 1957.

Hakfoort, C. "Geschiedschrijving van de Nederlandse natuurwetenschap: de verruimende beperking." *Theoretische Geschiedenis* 10 (1983): 436-452.

Halsema, J.D.F. van. *Te zoeken in deze angstige eeuw: Sporen van décadence-voorstellingen in de Nederlandse letterkunde aan het einde van de negentiende eeuw*. Groningen 1994.

Hammacher, A.M. *De levenstijd van Antoon Derkinderen*. Amsterdam 1932.

Hanák, Péter. *The Garden and the Workshop: Essays on the cultural history of Vienna and Budapest*. Princeton, NJ 1998.

Handelingen der Nederlandsche Juristen-vereeniging 34 (1904): 227.

Harmsen, Ger. *Blauwe en rode jeugd: Ontstaan, ontwikkeling en teruggang van de Nederlandse jeugdbeweging tussen 1853 en 1940*. Assen 1961.

Hartmann, Wolfgang. *Der historische Festzug: Seine Entstehung und Entwicklung im 19. und 20. Jahrhundert*. Munich 1976.

Havard, Henry. *La Hollande pittoresque: Voyage aux villes mortes du Zuiderzée*. Paris 1874.

Hecht, Peter, Annemieke Hoogenboom, and Chris Stolwijk (eds.). *Kunstgeschiedenis in Nederland: Negen opstellen*. Amsterdam 1998.

Heering. "Het vrijzinnig-protestantisme." In: B. Klein Wassink and Th. M. van Leeuwen (eds.). *Tussen geest en tijdgeest: Denken en doen van vrijzinnig protestanten in de afgelopen honderd jaar*. Utrecht 1989, pp. 70-75

Heeroma, K.H. "Het probleem-Beets." *Jaarboek van de Maatschappij der Nederlandse Letterkunde te Leiden, 1947-1949*. Leiden 1950, p. 75.

Heertje, Henri. *De diamantbewerkers van Amsterdam*. Amsterdam 1936.

Hees, Pieter van, and Hugo de Schepper (eds.). *Tussen cultuur en politiek: Het Algemeen-Nederlands Verbond 1895-1995*. Hilversum and The Hague 1995.

Hees, Pieter van. "De groot-Nederlandse studentenbeweging." *Utrechtse Historische Cahiers*. 19 (1998): 44.

Heijbroek, J.F., and Margaret F. MacDonald. *Whistler en Holland*. Amsterdam and Zwolle 1997.

Heijden, Marien van der. *De Burcht van Berlage*. Amsterdam 1991.

Heijs, E.J.M. *Van vreemdeling tot Nederlander: De verlening van het Nederlanderschap aan vreemdelingen (1813-1992)*. Amsterdam 1995.

Heilbron, J.C. *A history of the problem of atomic structure from the discovery of the electron to the beginning of quantum mechanics*. Berkeley 1964.

Helden, A. van. "Biographies: Heike Kamerlingh Onnes 1853-1926." In: K. van Berkel, A. van Helden, and L. Palm (eds.), *A history of science in The Netherlands: Survey, themes and reference*. Leiden 1999, pp. 491-494.

Helden, A. van. "Biographies: Hendrik Antoon Lorentz 1853-1928." In: K. van Berkel, A. van Helden, and L. Palm (eds.), *A history of science in The Netherlands: Survey, themes and reference*. Leiden 1999, pp. 514-518.

Helden, A. van. "Biographies: Jacobus Cornelius Kapteyn 1851-1922." In: K. van Berkel, A. van Helden, and L. Palm (eds.), *A history of science in The Netherlands: Survey, themes and reference*. Leiden 1999, pp. 495-497.

Helden, A. van. "Biographies: Pieter Zeeman 1865-1943." In: K. van Berkel, A. van Helden, and L. Palm (eds.), *A history of science in The Netherlands: Survey, themes and reference*. Leiden 1999, pp. 606-608.

Helden, A.C. van. *De koudste plek op aarde: Kamerlingh Onnes en het lage-temperaturenonderzoek 1882-1923*. Leiden 1989.

Hellenberg Hubar, B.C.M. *Arbeid en Bezieling*. Nijmegen 1997.

Hendrix. H. *Een week in de kolonie der Internationale Broederschap te Blaricum*. Amsterdam 1901.

Herderscheê, J. *De modern-godsdienstige richting in Nederland*. Amsterdam 1904.

Herk, G. van et al. *De Leidse Sterrewacht: Vier eeuwen wacht bij dag en nacht*. Zwolle 1983.

Hertzsprung-Kapteyn, Henrietta. *The life and works of J.C. Kapteyn*. Trans. E. Robert Paul. Dordrecht 1993.

Heymans, G. *Karakter en methode der staathuishoudkunde*. Leiden 1880.

Heymans, G. "De methode der moraal." *De Gids* 45 (1881): 193-223 and 414-448.

Heymans, G. "Die Methode der Ethik." *Vierteljahrschrift für Wissenschaftliche Philosophie* 6 (1882): 74-86,162-188 and 434-473.

Heymans, G. *Zur Kritik des Utilismus*. Altenburg 1882.

Heymans, G. "Eene nieuwe oplossing der sociale quaestie." *De Gids* 2 (1883): 107-140.

Heymans, G. "Zurechnung und Vergeltung: Eine psychologisch-ethische Untersuchung." *Vierteljahrschrift für wissenschaftliche Philosophie* 7 (1883): 439-462; 8 (1884): 95-111, 193-220, 341-369, 438-455.

Heymans, G. "Erkenntnistheorie und Psychologie." *Philosophische Monatshafte* 25 (1889): 1-28.

Heymans, G. *Het experiment in de philosophie.* Leiden 1890.

Heymans, G. *Schets eener kritische geschiedenis van het causaliteitsbegrip in de nieuwere wijsbegeerte.* Leiden 1890.

Heymans, G. *Die Gesetze und Elemente des wissenschaftliches Denkens.* 2 vols. Leipzig 1890-1894.

Heymans, G. "Quantitative Untersuchungen über das 'optische Paradoxon'." *Zeitschrift für Psychologie* 9 (1895): 221-255.

Heymans, G. "Een laboratorium voor experimentele psychologie." *De Gids* 60 (1896): 73-100.

Heymans, G. "Quantitative Untersuchungen über die Zöllnersche und Loebsche Täuschung." *Zeitschrift für Psychologie* 14 (1896): 101-139.

Heymans, G. "Uitwassen der crimineele anthropologie." *De Gids* 1 (1901): 50-91.

Heymans, G. *Einführung in die Metaphysik auf Grundlage der Erfahrung.* Leipzig 1905.

Heymans, G. *De classificatie der karakters.* Lecture Vereeniging Secties voor Wetenschappelijke Arbeid, no. 8, 1907.

Heymans, G. *De toekomstige eeuw der psychologie.* Groningen 1909.

Heymans, G. *De kritiek van den heer Bolland.* Groningen 1910.

Heymans, G. *Die Psychologie der Frauen.* Heidelberg 1910.

Heymans, G. *Psychologie der vrouwen.* Amsterdam 1911.

Heymans, G. *Das künftige Jahrhundert der Psychologie.* Leipzig 1912.

Heymans, G. "Le Siècle futur de la psychologie." *Revue du mois.* 7, no. 14 (1912): 581-603.

Heymans, G. *Einführung in die Ethik auf Grundlage der Erfahrung.* Leipzig 1914.

Heymans, G. *Psychologie des Femmes.* Paris 1925.

Heymans, G. *Afscheidscollege.* Groningen 1927.

Heymans, G. *Gesammelte kleinere Schriften zur Philosophie und Psychologie.* 3 vols. The Hague 1927.

Heymans, G. *Inleiding tot de speciale psychologie.* Haarlem 1929.

Heymans, G. *Inleiding in de metaphysica op grondslag van de ervaring.* Amsterdam 1933.

Heymans, G. *Metafysica en esthetica.* Edited by H. Hubbeling. Baarn 1987.

Heymans, H.G. *Wetenschap tussen universiteit en industrie: De experimentele natuurkunde in Utrecht onder W.H. Julius en L.S Ornstein 1896-1940.* Rotterdam 1994.

Heyting, Lien. *De wereld in een dorp: Schilders, schrijvers en wereldverbeteraars in Laren en Blaricum 1880-1920.* Amsterdam 1994.

Hoek, W. *Plechtige dankdienst in de Ned. Ev. Kerk te Brussel.* N.p., n.d.

Hoekema, Alle, and Sonny Hof (eds.). *Illustere Dissenters: Aspecten van de positie der Nederlandse Lutheranen en Doopsgezinden.* Zoetermeer and Woerden 1996.

Hoetink, H. *De gespleten samenleving in het Caribisch gebied: Bijdrage tot de sociologie der rasrelaties in gesegmenteerde maatschappijen.* Assen 1962.

Hofmann, Werner. *Ideengeschichte der sozialen Bewegung.* Berlin 1974.

Holthoon, F.L. van (ed.). *De Nederlandse Samenleving sinds 1815: Wording en Samenhang.* Assen and Maastricht 1985.

Holtzman, H., and M. James (eds.). *The New Art - The New Life: The collected writings of Piet Mondrian.* London 1987.

Homburg, E. Rip, A., and Small, J. "Chemici, hun kennis en de industrie." In: J.W. Schot, H.W. Lintsen et al. (eds.), *Techniek in Nederland in de twintigste eeuw.* Vol. 2: *Delfstoffen, energie, chemie.* Zutphen 2000, pp. 299-315.

Homer, W.J. *Seurat and the Science of Painting.* Cambridge MA 1964.

Hoogenberk, Egbert J. *Het idee van de Hollandse stad: Stedebouw in Nederland 1900-1930, met de internationale voorgeschiedenis.* Delft 1980.

Hoogenboom, A.M.E.L. *De stand des kunstenaars: De positie van kunstschilders in Nederland in de eerste helft van de negentiende eeuw.* Utrecht 1991.

Hoogeveen-Brink, J. *H.J. Jesse, architect 1860-1943.* Rotterdam 1997.

Hoogewoud, Guido, Janjaap Kuyt, and Aart Oxenaar. *P.J.H. Cuypers en Amsterdam: Gebouwen en ontwerpen 1860-1898.* The Hague 1985.

Hoogewoud, Guido. "Een protestantse kerk van P.J.H. Cuypers: Kerken als herkenningsteken van een nationaal verleden." In: Wim Denslagen et al. (eds.), *Bouwkunst: Studies in vriendschap voor Kees Peeters.* Amsterdam 1993, pp. 278 and 282.

Hoondert, M., and Paul Post. "De dynamiek van het Gregoriaans." *Jaarboek voor liturgie-onderzoek* 15 (1999): 7-26.

Hoorn, M. van. "The physics laboratory of the Teyler Foundation (Haarlem) under professor H.A. Lorentz, 1909-1928." *Bulletin of the Scientific Instruments Society* 59 (1998):14-21.

Hornix, W.J., and S.H.W.M. Mannaerts. *Van 't Hoff and the emergence of chemical thermodynamics: Centennial of the first Nobel Prize for Chemistry, 1901-2001.* Delft 2001.

Hough, P.H. *Dutch life in town and country.* London 1901.

Houtman, C. "Een episode uit het leven van een oriëntalist en oudtestamenticus aan de Vrije Universiteit: Prof. dr C. van Gelderen in conflict met deputaten tot oefening van het verband." In: C. Augustijn et al., *In rapport met de tijd: 100 Jaar theologie aan de Vrije Universiteit.* Kampen 1980, p. 86.

Hroch, Miroslav. *Social Preconditions of National Revival in Europe: A Comparative Analysis of the Social Composition of Patriotic Groups among the Smaller European Nations.* Cambridge 1965.

Huisman, J.W. en D. Draaisma. "Instrumentarium Psychologisch Laboratorium." In: D. Draaisma (ed.), *Een laboratorium voor de ziel: Gerard Heymans en het begin van de experimentele psychologie*. Groningen 1992, pp. 96-145.

Huizinga, J. *Leven en werk van Jan Veth*. Haarlem 1927.

Huizinga, J. *Verzamelde Werken*. Vol. 2: *Nederland*. Haarlem 1948.

Huizinga, J. *Verzamelde Werken*. Vol. 8: *Universiteit, wetenschap en kunst*. Haarlem 1951.

Huizinga, J. "De geschiedenis der [Groningse] universiteit gedurende de derde eeuw van haar bestaan, 1814-1914." In: J. Huizinga, *Verzamelde werken*. Vol. 8: *Universiteit, wetenschap en kunst*. Haarlem 1951, pp. 36-339.

Huizinga, J. *Briefwisseling*. Vol 2: *1925-1933*. Utrecht and Antwerp 1990.

Huls, Gerard. *De dienst der vrouw in de kerk: Een onderzoek naar de plaats der vrouw in een presbyteriale kerkorde*. Wageningen 1951.

Humbert de Superville, David P.G. *Essai sur les signes inconditionnels de l'art*. Leiden 1827.

Hunningher, B. *Een eeuw Nederlands toneel*. Amsterdam 1949.

Hutter, J.J. *Laboratoria in Nederland voor 1940*. Eindhoven 1986.

Hutter, J.J. *Toepassingsgericht onderzoek in de industrie: de ontwikkeling van kwikdamplampen bij Philips, 1900-1940*. Eindhoven 1988.

Huussen, A.H. jr. "Claude Monet in Nederland." In: *Monet in Holland*. Catalogue Rijksmuseum Vincent van Gogh, Amsterdam. Zwolle and Amsterdam 1986.

Huygens, C. "Karl Pearson over de vrouw." *Sociaal weekblad* 8 (1894): 374-376.

Huygens, Cornelie. *Een woord aan de Nederlandsche vrouwen: Rede, uitgesproken den 3den Maart 1896 in een openbare vergadering van de Vrije Vrouwenvereeniging*. Amsterdam 1896.

Huygens, Cornelie. *Barthold Meryan*. Amsterdam 1897.

Huygens, C. *De liefde in het vrouwenleven voorheen en thans: Naar aanleiding van "De liefde in de vrouwenkwestie" van Anna de Savornin Lohman*. Amsterdam, n.d. [1899].

Huygens, C.W. *De Nederlandse auteur en zijn publiek, een sociologisch-litteraire studie over de ontwikkeling van het letterkundig leven in Nederland sedert de 18e eeuw*. Amsterdam 1946.

Imanse, G. et al. *Van Gogh tot Cobra: Nederlandse schilderkunst 1880-1950*. Utrecht 1981.

Imelman, J.D., and W.A.J. Meijer. *De Nieuwe School, gisteren en vandaag*. Amsterdam and Brussels 1986.

Jacob, M.C., and W.W. Mijnhardt (eds.). *The Dutch Republic in the eighteenth century*. Ithaca 1992.

Jacobs, A.H. "Het doel der vrouwenbeweging." *De Gids* 1 (1899): 503-522.

Jaeger, F.M. "Oorspronkelijke romans." *De tijdspiegel* 3 (1897): 412-415.

Jaffé, Hans Ludwig. *De Stijl 1917-1931: The Dutch Contribution to Modern Art*. Amsterdam 1956.

Jager, H. de et al. *Het beeldende denken: Leven en werk van Mathieu Schoenmakers*. Baarn 1992.

Jager, Ida. *Willem Kromhout Czn.: 1864-1940*. Rotterdam 1992.

James, Martin S. "Mondrian and the Dutch Symbolists." *Art Journal* 23, no.2 (1963): 104-110.

James, W. *The varieties of religious experience*. New York 1902.

James, W. *Varianten van religieuze beleving*. Zeist 1963.

Jans, Rudolf. *Tolstoj in Nederland*. Bussum 1952.

Janssen, A.E.M. "Thijm en Nuyens: over een esthetisch en moreel beproefde vriendschap." In: P.A.M. Geurts et al. (eds.), *J.A. Alberdingk Thijm 1820-1889: Erflater van de negentiende eeuw*. Baarn 1992, pp. 233-263.

Jansz, Ulla. *Denken over sekse in de eerste feministische golf*. Amsterdam 1990.

Jansz, Ulla. "Het luchtkasteel van Catharina Alberdingk Thym." *Jaarboek voor Vrouwengeschiedenis* 14 (1994), pp. 30-45.

Jensma, Goffe. *Het rode tasje van Salverda: Burgerlijk bewustzijn en Friese identiteit in de negentiende eeuw*. Ljouwert and Leeuwarden 1998.

Jensma, G., and H. de Vries. *Veranderingen in het hoger onderwijs in Nederland tussen 1815 en 1940*. Hilversum 1997.

Johannes, Ant. *Luthers diakonessenwerk: geschiedenis van 100 jaar Lutherse Diakonessen Inrichting te Amsterdam*. Zutphen 1986.

Johannisse, S.C.M.I. "Nederlandse architectuur 1900-1924." Manuscript PhD diss. for the NWO priority program *Nederlandse cultuur in Europese context. Vantage point 1900*. Chapter 1.

Johannisse, Sigrid. "H.P. Berlage en de Amsterdamse School." Manuscript PhD diss. for the NWO priority program *Nederlandse cultuur in Europese context. Vantage point 1900*. Chapter 2.

Jonckbloet, G. *Jonkvrouwe Anna de Savornin Lohman in en uit hare werken*. Leiden 1912.

Jong, Ad de. "Volkskunde in de open lucht: Musealisering en nationalisering van het platteland 1850-1920." *Volkskundig Bulletin* 20 (1994): 292-294.

Jong, Ad de. "Dracht en eendracht: De politieke dimensie van klederdrachten, 1850-1920." In: Dolly Verhoeven (ed.), *Klederdracht en kleedgedrag: Het Kostuum Harer Majesteits onderdanen 1898-1998*. Nijmegen 1998, pp. 67-82.

Jong, Ad de. *De dirigenten van de herinnering: Musealisering en nationalisering van de volkscultuur in Nederland 1815-1940*. Nijmegen 2001.

Jong, Barbara C. de. *Jan Ligthart (1859-1916): Een schoolmeester-pedagoog uit de Schilderswijk*. Groningen 1996.

Jong, O.J. de. "Herschikt mozaïek: Enkele hervormde ontwikkelingen na de Doleantie." In: L.J. Wolthuis et al., *De Vereniging van 1892 en haar geschiedenis*. Kampen 1992, pp. 215-217.

Jong van Beek en Donk, C. de. *Hilda van Suylenburg*. Amsterdam, n.d. [1897].

Jong van Beek en Donk, C. de. *Lilia*. Amsterdam, n.d. [1907].

Jong van Beek en Donk, C. de. *De Tentoonstelling van Vrouwenarbeid 1898: De vrouw, de vrouwenbeweging*

en het vrouwenvraagstuk: Encuclopaedisch handboek.
Vol. 2. Amsterdam 1918.

Joosten, J.M. *De brieven van Johan Thorn Prikker aan Henri Borel en anderen 1892-1904.* Nieuwkoop 1980.

Joosten, J.M., and Robert P. Welsh. *Piet Mondrian: Catalogue raisonné.* Blaricum 1998.

Kalma, J. "F.W.N. Hugenholtz." In: *Biografisch Woordenboek van het socialisme en de arbeidersbeweging in Nederland.* Vol. 4. Amsterdam 1990, pp. 95-97.

Kalmthout, A.B.G.M. van. *Muzentempels: Multidisciplinaire kunstkringen in Nederland tussen 1880 en 1914.* Hilversum 1998.

Kammen, A. van. "Beijerinck's contribution to the virus concept: an introduction." *Archives of Virology* suppl. 15 (1999): 1-8.

Kamminga, H. "Credit and resistance: Eijkman and the transformation of beri-beri into a vitamine deficiency disease." In: K. Bayertz, and R.Porter (eds.), *From physico-theology to bio-technology: Essays in the social and cultural history of biosciences: A festschrift for Mikulas Teich.* Amsterdam and Atlanta 1997, pp. 232-254.

Kandinsky, W. *Uber das Geistige in der Kunst.* Bern 1952.

Karsten, Sjoerd. *Op het breukvlak van opvoeding en politiek: Een studie naar socialistische volksonderwijzers rond de eeuwwisseling.* Amsterdam 1986.

Karstkarel, G.P. "De architectonische taal van de verzuiling: De neo-stijlen in de kerkbouw." In: J. de Bruijn (ed.), *Bepaald gebied: Aspecten van het protestants-christelijk leven in Nederland in de jaren 1880-1940.* Baarn 1989, pp. 135-136.

Kat, A.I.M. *De geschiedenis der kerkmuziek in de Nederlanden sedert de Hervorming.* Hilversum 1939.

Kautsky, K. *Thomas More en zijne utopie.* Rotterdam 1903.

Kemperink, M.G. *Nederlands toneel in het fin de siècle 1890-1900.* Amsterdam 1995.

Kevles, D.J. *In the name of eugenics: Genetics and the uses of human heredity.* New York 1985.

Kiers, Judikje, and Fieke Tissink. *Het Rijksmuseum van Schets tot Schatkamer.* Amsterdam 1992.

Kipnis, A.Ya., B.E. Yavelov, and J.S. Rowlinson. *Van der Waals and Molecular Science.* Oxford 1996. 1st ed. in Russian 1985.

Kirchhoff, A. *Die academische Frau.* Berlin 1897.

Kirejczyk, M. "Vrouwen kozen exact: studie en beroepsuitoefening rond de eeuwwisseling." *Gewina* 16 (1993): 234-247.

Klein, M., and H. Ruys. *Over Eline Vere van Louis Couperus.* Amsterdam 1981.

Klein Wassink, B., and Th. M. van Leeuwen (eds.). *Tussen geest en tijdgeest: Denken en doen van vrijzinnig protestanten in de afgelopen honderd jaar.* Utrecht 1989.

Kloek, J.J. "Naar het land van Rembrandt: De literaire beeldvorming rond de zeventiende-eeuwse schilderkunst in de negentiende eeuw." In: Frans Grijzenhout, and Henk van Veen (eds.), *De Gouden Eeuw in perspectief: Het beeld van de Nederlandse zeventiende-eeuwse schilderkunst in later tijd.*

Nijmegen and Heerlen 1992, pp. 139-160.

Kloek, Joost, and Karin Tilmans (eds.). *Nederlandse begripsgeschiedenis.* Vol. 4: *Burger.* Amsterdam 2002.

Klöters, Jacques. *100 Jaar amusement in Nederland.* The Hague 1987.

Kluveld, Amanda. "Anti-vivisectionisme en feminisme: De strijd van Maria Jungius tegen 'Een kwaad dat uit de samenleving moet verdwijnen'." In: Rineke van Daalen, and Marijke Gijswijt-Hofstra (eds.), *Gezond en Wel: Vrouwen en de zorg voor gezondheid in de twintigste eeuw.* Amsterdam 1999, pp. 141-155.

Kluveld, Amanda. *Reis door de hel der onschuldigen: De expressieve politiek van de Nederlandse anti-vivisectionisten, 1890-1940.* Amsterdam 2000.

Knippenberg, Hans. *Deelname aan het lager onderwijs in Nederland gedurende de negentiende eeuw: Een analyse van de landelijke ontwikkeling en van de regionale verschillen.* In: *Nederlandse Geografische Studies* 9. Amsterdam 1986.

Knippenberg, Hans. *De Religieuze Kaart van Nederland: Omvang en geografische spreiding van de godsdienstige gezindten vanaf de Reformatie tot heden.* Assen and Maastricht 1992.

Knippenberg, Hans, and Bart Nauta. "Naar eenheid van tijd in Nederland 1835-1909." *Tijdschrift voor Sociale Geschiedenis* 15 (1989): 325-346.

Koch, Jeannette E. *De koningsromans van Louis Couperus: Achtergronden.* Naples 1989.

Kok, J.A. de. *Nederland op de breuklijn Rome-Reformatie: Numerieke aspecten van protestantisering en katholieke herleving in de Noordelijke Nederlanden.* Assen 1964.

Konijnenburg, W.A. *Karakter en eenheid in de schilderkunst.* The Hague 1910.

Koolhaas, Eveline, and Sandra de Vries. "Terug naar een roemrijk verleden: De zeventiende-eeuwse schilderkunst als voorbeeld voor de negentiende eeuw." In: Frans Grijzenhout, and Henk van Veen, *De Gouden Eeuw in perspectief: Het beeld van de Nederlandse zeventiende-eeuwse schilderkunst in later tijd.* Nijmegen and Heerlen 1992, pp. 107-138.

Koopmans, Ype. "De rehabilitatie van de steenhouwer." *Jong Holland* 2 (1989): 18-27; 3 (1989): 24-35.

Koopmans, Ype. "In het voetspoor van Pythagoras: Kosmische symboliek in de Nederlandse architectuur tussen 1900 en 1940." *Jong Holland* 5 (1989): 23-34.

Koopmans, Ype. *Muurvast en gebeiteld: Beeldhouwkunst in de bouw 1840-1940.* Rotterdam 1994.

Kosten, Jan. *Kroniek van vijfenzeventig jaar Rotterdams Philharmonisch Orkest.* Vol. 1. Rotterdam 1994.

Koster, Simon. *De Bouwmeesters: Kroniek van een theaterfamilie.* Assen 1973.

Koster, W. "De toeneming der krankzinnigheid." *Nederlandsch tijdschrift voor geneeskunde* 8, no. 2 (1893): 293-311.

Kossmann, E.H. *The Low Countries 1780-1940.* Oxford 1978.

Kossmann, E.H. *De Lage Landen 1780-1980: Twee eeuwen Nederland en België* Vol. 1: *1780-1914.* Amsterdam and Brussels 1986.

Kossmann, E.H. *Politieke theorie en geschiedenis:*

Verspreide opstellen en voordrachten. Amsterdam 1987.

Kossmann, E.H. "Romeins *Breukvlak* en de Nederlandse geschiedenis." *Bijdragen en Mededelingen betreffende de Geschiedenis der Nederlanden* 56 (1991): 658.

Kossmann, E.H. "De Nederlandse zeventiende-eeuwse schilderkunst bij de historici." In: Frans Grijzenhout, and Henk Th. van Veen (eds.), *De Gouden Eeuw in perspectief: Het beeld van de Nederlandse zeventiende-eeuwse schilderkunst in later tijd.* Nijmegen and Heerlen 1992, pp. 280-298.

Kossmann, Ernst H. *Een tuchteloos probleem: De natie in de Nederlanden.* Leuven 1994.

Kosten, Jan. *Kroniek van vijfenzeventig jaar Rotterdams Philharmonisch Orkest.* Rotterdam 1994.

Koster, Simon. *De Bouwmeesters: Kroniek van een theaterfamilie.* Assen 1973.

Koster, W. *De wetten der erfelijkheid en het toenemen der krankzinnigheid: Een medisch-sociale studie.* Haarlem 1900.

Kox, A.J. "Hendrik A. Lorentz (1853-1928): Grootmeester van den wereld-aether." In: A.J. Kox, and M. Chamalaun, *Van Stevin tot Lorentz: Portretten van Nederlandse natuurwetenschappers.* Amsterdam 1980, pp. 220-235.

Kox, A.J. "Johannes D. van der Waals (1837-1923): De realiteit van atomen." In A.J. Kox, and M. Chamalaun, *Van Stevin tot Lorentz: Portretten van Nederlandse natuurwetenschappers.* Amsterdam 1980, pp. 149-161.

Kox, A.J. *Physics in Amsterdam: A brief history.* Amsterdam 1990.

Kox, A.J. "Johannes Diderik van der Waals (1837-1923): Theoreticus van de Amsterdamse natuurkunde." In: J.C.H. Blom et al. (eds.), *Een brandpunt van geleerdheid in de hoofdstad: De universiteit van Amsterdam rond 1900 in vijftien portretten.* Hilversum 1992, pp. 201-212.

Kox, A.J. "Pieter Zeeman (1865-1943): Meester van het experiment." In: J.C.H. Blom et al. (eds.), *Een brandpunt van geleerdheid in de hoofdstad: De Universiteit van Amsterdam rond 1900 in vijftien portretten.* Hilversum 1992, pp. 213-228.

Kox, A.J. "Korteweg, de Vries, and Dutch Science at the Turn of the Century." *Acta applicandae mathematicae: An international journal on applying mathematics and mathematical applications* 39 (1995): 91-92.

Kox, A.J. "Hendrik Antoon Lorentz en de 'Tweede Gouden Eeuw'." In: H.M. Beliën, and M.P. Bossenbroek, *In de vaart der volken: Nederlanders rond 1900.* Amsterdam 1998, pp. 197-213.

Kox, A.J. "Diederik Johannes Korteweg: schakel tussen de Amsterdamse wiskunde en natuurkunde. In: P.J. Knegtmans, and A.J. Kox, *Tot nut en eer van de stad: Wetenschappelijk onderzoek aan de Universiteit van Amsterdam.* Amsterdam 2000, pp. 67-78.

Kox, A.J., and M. Chamalaun (eds.). *Van Stevin tot Lorentz: Portretten van Nederlandse natuurwetenschappers.* Amsterdam 1980.

Kox, A.J., and W.P. Troelstra. "Uit het Zeeman-archief: de ontdekking van het Zeeman-effect." *Gewina* 19 (1996): 153-166.

Kraan, Hans. "Nederland en Barbizon: kunstenaars gaan en komen.' In: John Sillevis en Hans Kraan (eds.), *De School van Barbizon: Franse meesters van de 19de eeuw.* The Hague 1985, pp. 84-104.

Kramer, J., and C. van Reeth. "Schets van de ontwikkeling van de lichamelijke opvoeding in Nederland." In: Mark D'Hoker en Jan Tolleneer (eds.), *Het vergeten lichaam: Geschiedenis van de lichamelijke opvoeding in België en Nederland.* Leuven and Apeldoorn 1995, p. 26.

Kramers, H.A., and H. Holst. *De bouw der atomen.* Amsterdam , n.d. [1927].

De Kroniek, May 31 and June 7, 1896.

Kruit, P.C. van der, and K. van Berkel (eds.). *The legacy of J.C. Kapteyn: Studies on Kapteyn and the development of modern astronomy.* Dordrecht 2000.

Krul, W.E. "De Nederlandse gymnasia in de negentiende eeuw." In: M.A. Wes (ed.), *Van Parthenon tot Maagdenhuis: Moet het gymnasium blijven?* Amsterdam 1985, pp. 48-51.

Krul, W.E. "Kapteyn and Groningen: a portrait." In: P.C. van der Kruit, and K. van Berkel (eds.), *The legacy of J.C. Kapteyn: Studies on Kapteyn and the development of modern astronomy.* Dordrecht 2000, pp. 53-78.

Kuiken, H.K. "The centenary of a paper on slow viscous flow by the physicist H.A. Lorentz." *Journal of engineering mathematics* 30 (1996): 1-2.

Kuiper, Arie. *Een wijze ging voorbij: Het leven van Abel J. Herzberg.* Amsterdam 1997.

Kuiper, D.Th. *De voormannen: Een sociaal-wetenschappelijke studie over ideologie, konflikt en kerngroepvorming binnen de gereformeerde wereld in Nederland tussen 1820 en 1930.* Kampen 1972.

Kuiper, R. "Een antirevolutionair afscheid van Duitsland: Abraham Kuyper (1837-1920) en Adolf Stöcker (1835-1909)." *Tijdschrift voor Geschiedenis* 111 (1998): 220-243.

Kuitenbrouwer, M. *Nederland en de opkomst van het moderne imperialisme: Koloniën en buitenlandse politiek 1870-1902.* Amsterdam and Dieren 1985.

Kuyper, A. *Het Calvinisme, oorsprong en waarborg onzer constitutioneele vrijheden: Een Nederlandsche gedachte.* Amsterdam 1874.

Kuyper, A. *Souvereiniteit in eigen kring: Rede ter inwijding van de Vrije Universiteit.* Amsterdam 1880.

Kuyt, Janjaap, Norbert Middelkoop, and Auke van der Woud. *Bouwmeesters van Amsterdam: G.B. Salm & A. Salm Gbzn.* Amsterdam 1997.

Kylstra, S.C. *De beteeknis van onze kolonie.* The Hague 1900.

Laarse, Rob van. *Bevoogding en Bevinding: Heren en kerkvolk in een Hollandse provinciestad, Woerden 1780-1930.* The Hague 1989.

Labrie, Arnold. "'*Bildung*' en politiek 1770-1830: De '*Bildungsphilosophie*' van Wilhelm von Humboldt bezien in haar politieke en sociale context.* Amsterdam 1986.

Laeseke, A. "Through Measurement to Knowledge:

The Inaugural Lecture of Heike Kamerlingh Onnes (1882)." *Journal of Research of the National Institute of Standards and Technology* 107 (2002): 261-278.

Lamberty, M. et al. (eds.). *Twintig Eeuwen Vlaanderen.* 15 vols. Hasselt 1972-1979.

Lambourne, Lionel. *Utopian Craftsmen: The Arts and Crafts Movement from the Cotswolds to Chicago.* London 1980.

Land, J.P.N. 'De oude en de nieuwe universiteit.' Redevoering uitgesproken door den Rector Magnificus op den 311den verjaardag der Universiteit te Leiden, 8 februari 1886." In: *Jaarboek der Rijks-Universiteit te Leiden, 1885-1886.* Leiden, n.d., pp. 4-37.

Lang, H.N. de. "Heike Kamerlingh Onnes (1853-1926): De wetenschappelijke noodzaak van lage temperaturen." In: A.J. Kox, and M. Chamalaun, *Van Stevin tot Lorentz.* Amsterdam 1980, pp. 220-235.

Langbehn, Julius. *Rembrandt als Erzieher.* Leipzig 1890.

Lange, Albert de. *J.H. Gunning Jr. en het Spinoza-standbeeld.* Leiden 1982.

Lange, A. de. *De verhouding tussen dogmatiek en godsdienstwetenschap binnen de theologie. Een onderzoek naar de ontwikkeling van het theologiebegrip van J.H. Gunning Jr. (1829-1905).* Kampen 1987.

Lange, A. de. *J.H. Gunning Jr. (1829-1905): Een leven in zelfverloochening.* Vol. 1: *1829-1861.* Kampen 1995.

Lauret, A.M. *Per imperatief mandaat: Bijdrage tot de geschiedenis van onderwijs en opvoeding door de katholieken in Nederland, in het bijzonder door de Tilburgse Zusters van Liefde.* Tilburg 1967.

Lauweriks, J.L.M. "De kathedraalbouwers." *Architectura* 12 (1904): 177-178, 194-197, 204-206, 211-212, 219-220, 241-242, 269-270.

Lauweriks, J.L.M. "Gemeenschapskunst en individualisme." *Wendingen* 1 (1918): 5-10.

Leackey, R.E., and L.J. Slikkerveer. *Man-Ape, Ape-Man: The quest for human's place in Nature and Dubois' 'missing link'.* Leiden 1993.

Leek, Robert H. "Burgersdijk voltooit de vertaling van Shakespeares verzameld werk." In: R.L. Erenstein (ed.), *Een theatergeschiedenis der Nederlanden: Tien eeuwen drama en theater in Nederland en Vlaanderen.* Amsterdam 1996, pp.496-490.

Leeuw, K.P.C. de. *Kleding in Nederland 1813-1920: Van een traditioneel bepaald kleedpatroon naar een begin van modern kleedgedrag.* Tilburg 1991.

Leeuwe, H.J.J. de. "Willem Royaards ontvangt een ere-doctoraat van de Rijksuniversiteit van Utrecht: Royaards' bijdrage aan de bloei van het Nederlands theater begin twintigste eeuw." In: R.L. Erenstein (ed.), *Een theatergeschiedenis der Nederlanden: Tien eeuwen drama en theater in Nederland en Vlaanderen.* Amsterdam 1996, pp. 580-585.

Leeuwen, W.R.F. van. "Waterbouw." In: H.W. Lintsen et al. (eds.), *Geschiedenis van de techniek in Nederland: De wording van een moderne samenleving 1800-1890.* Vol. 3. Zutphen 1993, pp. 233-249.

Leijerzapf, Ingeborg. "*Hetgeen ik zoek met stift of lens.*" Henri Berssenbrugge en het picturalisme in de Nederlandse fotografie. Leiden 1996.

Leijnse, Elisabeth. *Symbolisme en nieuwe mystiek in Nederland voor 1900: Een onderzoek naar de Nederlandse receptie van Maurice Maeterlinck.* Liège 1995.

Lemoine, Serge. *Mondrian et De Stijl*, Paris 1987.

Lenoir, T. "Instituting science: The cultural production of scientific disciplines." Berkeley 1997.

Lente, D. van, and O. de Wit. *Geschiedenis van de grafische techniek in Nederland in de 19e eeuw.* Amstelveen 1993.

Lethève, J. *Impressionnistes et symbolistes devant la presse.* Paris 1959.

Leuker, Maria-Theresia. "De mythe van het hoge paar: Joost van den Vondel en Maria Tesselschade Roemers in de historische verhalen van J.A. Alberdingk Thijm." *Tijdschrift voor Geschiedenis* 112 (1999): 522-542.

Levelt Sengers, J. "How fluids unmix: Discoveries bij the school of Van der Waals en Kamerlingh Onnes." Amsterdam 2002.

Lewis. Th. *Clinical disorders of the heartbeat: A handbook for practitioners and students.* London 1912.

Ley, J.S. de, and B. Luger. *Walden in droom en daad: Walden-dagboek en notulen van Frederik van Eeden e.a. 1898-1903.* Amsterdam 1980.

Leydesdorff, J. *Bijdrage tot de speciale psychologie van het Joodsche volk.* Groningen 1919.

Liagre Böhl, Herman de. "Herman Gorter en Lenin." In: G. Stuiveling, *Acht over Gorter.* Amsterdam 1978, pp.335-369.

Liagre Böhl, Herman de. *Met al mijn bloed heb ik voor U geleefd: Herman Gorter 1864-1927.* Amsterdam 1996.

Liebermann, Max. *Die Phantasie in der Malerei: Schriften und Reden.* Frankfurt am Main 1978.

Lieburg, F.A. van (ed.). *De stille luyden: Bevindelijk gereformeerden in de negentiende eeuw.* Kampen 1994.

Lieburg, M.J. van, and H.A.M. Snelders. "*De bevordering en volmaking der proefondervindelijke wijsbegeerte": De rol van het Bataafsch Genootschap te Rotterdam in de geschiedenis van de natuurwetenschappen, geneeskunde en techniek (1769-1988).* Amsterdam 1989.

Ligt, B. de. *Profeet en volksfeest: Rede naar aanleiding van het verzoek van de Algemeene Synode der Nederlandsche Hervormde Kerk om den 16en Nov. 1913 het onafhankelijkheidsfeest godsdienstig te vieren.* Amsterdam 1913.

Limburg Brouwer, P. van. *Het leesgezelschap van Diepenbeek.* In: *Bibliotheek der Nederlandse Letteren.* Amsterdam 1939.

Lindeboom, G.A. *Geschiedenis van de medische wetenschap in Nederland.* Bussum 1972.

Linders-Rooijendijk, M.F.A. *Gebaande wegen voor mobiliteit en vrijetijdsbesteding: De ANWB als vrijwillige associatie.* Heeswijk 1989.

Lintsen, H.W. (ed.). *Geschiedenis van de techniek in Nederland: De wording van een moderne samenleving 1900-1890.* 5 vols. Zutphen 1994.

Livestro-Nieuwenhuis, Fea. *Nationale klederdrachten.* Zutphen 1987.

Loeff, J.A. et al. (eds.). *Het Katholiek Nederland 1813-*

1913: Ter blijde herinnering aan het eerste eeuwfeest onzer nationale onafhankelijkheid. 2 vols. Nijmegen 1913.

Looijenga, A.J. *De Utrechtse school in de neogotiek: De voorgeschiedenis en het Sint Bernulphusgilde.* Amsterdam 1991.

Loosjes-Terpstra, A.B. *Moderne Kunst in Nederland 1900-1914.* Utrecht 1959.

Lövgren, Sven. *The Genesis of Modernism: Seurat, Gauguin, Van Gogh and French Symbolism in the 1880's.* Uppsala 1959.

Lucassen, Jan. *Naar de kusten van de Noordzee: Trekarbeid in Europees perspektief, 1600-1900.* Gouda 1984.

Lucassen, Jan, and Rinus Penninx. *Nieuwkomers: Immigranten en hun nakomelingen in Nederland 1550-1985.* Amsterdam 1985.

Lucassen, Jan. "Joodse Nederlanders 1796-1940: Een proces van omgekeerde minderheidsvorming." In: Hetty Berg et al. (eds.), *Venter, fabriqueur, fabrikant. Joodse ondernemers en ondernemingen in Nederland 1796-1940.* Amsterdam 1994, pp. 34-38.

Luitjes, Tjerk. *Theorie en praktijk van binnenlandsche kolonisatie.* Bussum 1902.

Luning Prak, J. *School, beroep en aanleg.* Groningen 1932.

Lunteren, F.H. van. "Fysica en fin-de-siècle cultuur." In: J.J. Kloek, and W.W. Mijnhardt (eds.), *Balans en perspectief van de Nederlandse cultuurgeschiedenis.* Vol. 3. Amsterdam 1990.

Lunteren, F. van. "'Van meten tot weten': De opkomst der experimentele fysica aan de Nederlandse universiteiten in de negentiende eeuw." *Gewina* 18 (1995): 102-138.

Lunteren, F.H. van. "Bosscha's leerboek en Van der Waals' proefschrift: Aantrekkende krachten in Den Haag." *Gewina* 23 (2000): 247-265.

Luyken, R. *Eijkman's discovery of the vitamins and some history of nutrition research in Indonesia.* Leiden 1992.

Maarseveen, J.G.S.J. van (ed.). *Briefwisseling van Nicolaas Gerard Pierson 1839-1909.* Vol. 3: *1898-1909.* Amsterdam 1993.

Maas, A. "Over zwoegers en zeloten. J.D. Van der Waals en veranderingen in het studentenleven, 1877-1900." *Gewina* 22 (1999) 65-82.

Maas, A.J.P. *Atomisme en individualisme: De Amsterdamse natuurkunde tussen 1877 en 1940.* Hilversum 2001.

Maas, A.J.P. "Tachtigers in de wetenschap:een nieuwe kijk op het ontstaan van de 'Tweede Gouden Eeuw' in de Nederlandse natuurwetenschap." *Tijdschrift voor Geschiedenis* 114 (2001): 354-376 and 583-586.

Maas, L.H. *Pro Patria: Werken, leven en streven van Gerrit Kalff 1856-1923.* Hilversum 1998.

Maas, Nop. "Carel Vosmaer en het Rijksmuseum." *Nederlands Kunsthistorisch Jaarboek* 35 (1984): 195-225.

Maas, Nop. *Letterkundige tijdsidealen van Marcellus Emants, W.G. van Nouhuys en A.W. Stellwagen.* Nijmegen 1985.

Maat, H. *Science cultivating practice: A history of agricultural science in the Netherlands and its colonies, 1863-1986.* Dordrecht 2001.

MacLeod, R. "The 'bancruptcy of science' debate: the creed of science and its critics, 1885-1900." *Science, Technology and Human Values* 7 (1982): 2-15.

Maden, Frank van der. *Mobiele filmexpoitatie in Nederland 1895-1913, voor zover het mogelijk is deze te beschrijven en te analyseren aan de hand van de ontwikkeling te Nijmegen.* Nijmegen 1981.

Maegd-Soëp, C. de. *De progressieve vrouw in de Russische literatuur: Een bijdrage tot de kennis van de Russische samenleving in de jaren 1855-1866.* Brussels 1970.

Maeyer, Jan de. "Katholiek reveil, kerk en kunst." In: P.A.M. Geurts et al., *J.A. Alberdingk Thijm 1820-1889: Erflater van de negentiende eeuw.* Baarn 1992, p. 95.

Mähler, M. *De Sint-Paulusabdij van Oosterhout onder het bestuur van haar eerste abt dom Jean de Puniet, 1907-1941.* Tilburg 1991.

Mallarmé, Stéphane. *Mallarmé: The Poems.* Trans. Keith Bosley. Harmondsworth 1977.

Mallarmé, Stéphane. *Oeuvres Complètes.* Paris 1998.

Mandemakers, C.A. *Gymnasiaal en middelbaar onderwijs: Structuur, sociale achtergrond en schoolprestaties: Nederland, ca 1800-1968.* Almere 1996.

Mannheim, K. *Ideologie und Utopie.* Frankfurt 1952.

Manuel, Frank E. "Toward a Psychological History of Utopia's." *Daedalus* 94 (1965): 293-322.

Margry, Peter Jan, and Charles Caspers (eds.). *Bedevaartplaatsen in Nederland.* Vol. 1: *Noord- en Midden-Nederland.* Amsterdam and Hilversum 1997.

Marholm, Laura. *Das Buch der Frauen en Mevrouw Goekoop: Hilda van Suylenburg.* Amsterdam, n.d. [1898].

Martis, Adi. *Voor de kunst en voor de nijverheid: Het ontstaan van het kunstnijverheidsonderwijs in Nederland.* Amsterdam 1990.

Marx, Karl, and Friedrich Engels. *Het communistisch manifest.* Amsterdam 1972.

Mathews, Patricia Townley. *Aurier's Symbolist Art: Criticism and Theory.* Michigan 1986.

Matthieu, Pierre-Louis. *The Symbolist Generation 1870-1910.* New York 1990.

Mathijssen, Marita. *De gemaskerde eeuw.* Amsterdam 2002.

Matthijssen, M.A.J.M. *De elite en de mythe: Een sociologische analyse van strijd om onderwijsverandering.* Deventer 1982.

Matthijssen, M.A.J.M. *Klasse-onderwijs: Sociologie van het onderwijs.* Deventer 1985.

Maurik, Justus van. *Toen ik nog jong was.* Amsterdam 1901.

McDougall, W. *National Welfare and National Decay.* London 1921.

McLeod, Hugh. *Religion and Society in England, 1850-1914.* London 1996.

Megens, Inge, and Pieternel Rol. "Rijkeluisdochters en arbeiderszonen: Sociale afkomst, opleiding en organisatie van onderwijzers en onderwijzeressen rond 1900." *Jaarboek voor de geschiedenis van socialisme en arbeidersbeweging in Nederland.* (1979): 91-92.

Meijer, J. *Zij lieten hun sporen achter: Joodse bijdragen tot de Nederlandse beschaving.* Utrecht 1964.

Meijer, Jaap. *Hoge hoeden lage standaarden: De Nederlandse joden tussen 1933 en 1940.* Baarn 1969.

Meijer, Jaap. *Rector en raw: De levensgeschiedenis van dr J.H. Dünner (1833-1911).* Vol. 1: *1833-1874.* Heemstede 1984.

Meijer, O.G. "Hugo de Vries no Mendelian?" *Annals of Science* 42 (1986): 189-232.

Mendelssohn, K. *De jacht naar het absolute nulpunt.* Hilversum 1966.

Mercier, H. "Aurora Leigh." In: *Verbonden schakels.* N.p. 1881.

Mercier, H. "Karaktervorming der vrouw." In: *Verbonden schakels.* N.p. 1881.

Mercier, H. *De vrouw tegenover de vrouwenarbeid: Sociale Schetsen.* Haarlem 1897.

Merz, J.Th. *A history of European thought in the nineteenth century.* Vol. 1. Edinburgh 1907.

Methöfer, J.C. *Verbonden Schakels: Verzamelde opstellen uit het maandblad der Vereeniging Gemeenschappelijk Grondbezit.* N.p. 1932.

Meurs, Josine. *Wagner in Nederland 1843-1914.* Zutphen 2002.

Mey, J. van der. "Bouwkunst en maatschappij." *Wendingen.* 1 (1918): 3-4.

Meyboom, M. "De vrouwenbeweging in Nederland en 'Hilda van Suylenburg'." *De Gids* 62 (1898): 475-485.

Meyboom, M. "Open brief aan freule Anna de Savornin Lohman, naar aanleiding van haar brochure 'De liefde in de vrouwenkwestie'." *Evolutie* 6 (1898-1899).

Meyers, Jan. *Domela, een hemel op aarde: Leven en streven van Ferdinand Domela Nieuwenhuis.* Amsterdam 1993.

Michaël, Hubert, Dorine Raaff, and Aart Hoekman, *Nederlandse literaire prijzen 1880-1985.* The Hague 1986.

Michman, Dan. *Het Liberale Jodendom in Nederland 1929-1943.* Amsterdam 1988.

Michman, Joseph. "The Impact of German-Jewish Modernization on Dutch Jewry." In: Jacob Katz (ed.), *Toward Modernity: The European Jewish Model.* New York 1987, pp. 182 and 187.

Miellet, R.L. "Immigratie van katholieke Westfalers en de modernisering van de Nederlandse detailhandel." *Tijdschrift voor Geschiedenis* 100 (1987): 380.

Miellet, Roger. *Honderd jaar grootwinkelbedrijf in Nederland.* Zwolle, n.d.

Miermans, C. *Voetbal in Nederland.* Assen 1955.

Miert, Jan van. *Wars van clubgeest en partijzucht: Liberalen, natie en verzuiling: Tiel en Winschoten 1850-1920.* Amsterdam 1994.

Moll, Maarten. *Jaap Eden: Wereldkampioen op de schaats, wereldkampioen op de fiets.* Amsterdam 1996.

Mondrian, Piet. "De nieuwe beelding in de schilderkunst." *De Stijl* 1 (1917-1918): 2-6, 13-18, 29-31, 41-45, 49-54, 73-77, 88-91, 102-108, 121-124, 125-134, 140-147; 2 (1918-1919): 14-19.

Mondrian, Piet. "Natuurlijke en abstracte realiteit: Trialoog (gedurende een wandeling van buiten naar de stad)." In: *De Stijl* 3 (1919): 85-89, 97-99, 109-113, 121-125, 133-137; 3 (1920):15-19, 27-31, 41-44, 54-56, 58-60, 65-69, 73-76, 81-84.

Mondrian, Piet, Robert P. Welsh, and J.M. Joosten (eds.). *Two Mondrian Sketchbooks 1912-1914.* Amsterdam 1969.

Mondrian, Piet, H. Holzman, and M. James (eds.). *The New Art - The New Life. The Collected Writings of Piet Mondrian.* London 1987.

Mönnich, C.W. "De ontwikkeling van de vrijzinnigheid in Nederland van de negentiende eeuw af." In: B. Klein Wassink, and Th.M. van Leeuwen, *Tussen geest en tijdgeest: Denken en doen van vrijzinnig protestanten in de afgelopen honderd jaar.* Utrecht 1989, p. 34.

Montijn, Ileen. *Leven op stand 1890-1940.* Amsterdam 1998.

Mooijweer, Marianne L. *De Amerikaanse droom van Frederik van Eeden.* Amsterdam 1996.

Morawski, J.G. "Assessing psychology's moral heritage through our neglected utopias." *American Psychologist* 37 (1982): 1082-1095.

Morris, William. *John Ball en andere vertalingen.* Trans. Henriette Roland Holst-Van der Schalk. Amsterdam 1898.

Morris, William. "Art and Industry in the fourteenth Century." In: William Morris, *Collected Works.* Vol. 12. London 1914, pp. 375-390.

Morris, William. "A Dream of John Ball." In: William Morris, *Stories in Prose, Stories in Verse, Shorter Poems, Lectures and Essays.* London 1944, pp. 198-266.

Morris, Willam. "How we live and How we might live." In: William Morris, *Stories in Prose, Stories in Verse, Shorter Poems, Lectures and Essays.* London 1944, pp. 565-587.

Morris, William. "News from Nowhere." In: William Morris, *Stories in Prose, Stories in Verse, Shorter Poems, Lectures and Essays.* London 1944, pp. 3-197.

Morris, William, *Stories in Prose, Stories in Verse, Shorter Poems, Lectures and Essays.* London 1944.

Mourik Broekman, M.C. van. *De orthodoxe en moderne geloofsprediking uit psychologisch oogpunt vergeleken.* Zaltbommel 1915.

Mulder, Ernst. *Beginsel en beroep: Pedagogiek aan de universiteit in Nederland 1900-1940.* Amsterdam 1989.

Münsterberg, H. *Tomorrow: Letters to a friend in Germany.* New York 1916.

Naber, Johanna W.A. *Om en bij de tentoonstelling "De Vrouw 1813-1913."* Groningen 1913.

Naeff, Top. *Willem Royaards: De toneelkunstenaar in zijn tijd.* The Hague 1947.

Nagel, W.H. "De Groningse School." *Nederlands tijdschrift voor criminologie* 8 (1966): 81-93, 122-134.

Het Natuurkundig Laboratorium der Rijks-Universiteit te Leiden in de jaren 1882-1904: Gedenkboek aangeboden aan den hoogleraar H. Kamerlingh Onnes. Leiden 1904.

Naylor, G. *The Arts and Crafts Movement: A Study of its Sources, Ideals and Influence on Design Theory.* London 1971.

De Nederlandsche Spectator, June 27, 1868.

De Nederlandsche Spectator, July 30, 1898.

"De Nederlandse Vereeniging tot bescherming van vogels." *Androcles, maandschrift aan de belangen der dieren gewijd* 31 (1899): 17.

Neerlandia Catholica: Het Katholieke Nederland. Utrecht 1888.

Nes, H.M. van. *De nieuwe mystiek*. Rotterdam 1900.

Netscher, Frans. "Het boek van de maand: Hilda van Suylenburg door mevrouw Goekoop-de Jong van Beek en Donk." *De Hollandsche Revue* 3 (1898): 504-513.

Nierop, Leonie van. *De bevolkingsbeweging der Nederlandsche stad*. Amsterdam 1905.

Nieuwenhuis, Ferdinand Domela. *Grond en bodem in gemeenschappelijk bezit*. N.p., n.d. [1879].

Nieuwenhuis, Jan. *Mensen maken een stad: Uit de geschiedenis van de Dienst van Gemeentewerken te Rotterdam, 1855-1955*. N.p., n.d. [1955].

Het Nieuws van de dag. September 15, 1884.

Nipperdey, Thomas. *Deutsche Geschichte 1866-1918*. Vol. 1: *Arbeitswelt und Bürgergeist*. Munich 1991.

Nissen, Peter. "Het esoterisch katholicisme van Mathieu Schoenmaekers (1875-1944)." In: Judith de Raat, Gian Ackermans, and Peter Nissen (eds.), *De verleiding van het vreemde: Katholieke eigenzinnigheid in de twintigste eeuw*. Hilversum 2002, pp. 92-109.

Noordam, N.F. *Historische pedagogiek van Nederland: Een inleiding*. Groningen 1981.

Noordman, J. *Om de kwaliteit van het nageslacht: Eugenetica in Nederland, 1900-1950*. Nijmegen 1989.

Obbema, Pieter F.J. *Boeken in Nederland: Vijfhonderd jaar schrijven, drukken en uitgeven*. N.p. 1979.

Officiëel gedenkboek van de feestelijke ontvangst en de inhuldiging van Hare Majesteit Koningin Wilhelmina Helena Pauline Maria binnen Amsterdam in 1898. Vol. 1 and 2. Amsterdam 1898.

De ontwikkeling onzer electriciteitsvoorziening 1880-1938. Published on the occasion of the 25th anniversary of the Vereeniging van Directeuren van Electriciteitsbedrijven in Nederland. Arnhem 1948.

Oosterhoff, J.L. "De opkomst van een 'vaderlandsche natuurkunde' aan de Leidse universiteit in de tweede helft van de negentiende eeuw." In: W. Otterspeer (ed.), *Een universiteit herleeft: Wetenschapsbeoefening aan de Leidse universiteit vanaf de tweede helft van de negentiende eeuw*. Leiden 1984, pp. 103-124.

Oosterzee, J.J.van. *Uit mijn levensboek: Voor mijne vrienden*. Utrecht 1883.

Oostindie, Gert. *Het paradijs overzee: De "Nederlandse" Caraïben en Nederland*. Amsterdam 1998.

Oostindie, Gert, and Emy Maduro. *In het land van de overheerser*. Vol. 2: *Antillianen en Surinamers in Nederland, 1634/1667-1954*. Dordrecht and Cinnaminson 1986.

Oostrom, Frits van (ed.). *Historisch Tableau: Geschiedenis opnieuw verbeeld in schoolplaten en essays*. Amsterdam 1998.

Op de Coul, Paul. "Een Italiaanse *Salome* in Nederland." In: A. Annegarn, L.P. Grijp, and P. Op de Coul (eds.), *Harmonie en perspectief: Zevenendertig bijdragen van Utrechtse musicologen voor Eduard Reeser*. Deventer 1988, pp. 236-251.

Op de Coul, Paul. *De droom van het alomvattende kunstwerk*. Utrecht 1992.

Opzoomer, C.W. *De hervorming onzer hoogescholen: Rapport, wetsontwerp en memorie van toelichting*. Leiden and Amsterdam 1849.

Otterspeer, W. "Vereenvoudiging en bezuiniging: Een 19[e]-eeuwse discussie over taakverdeling en concentratie." In: Fr. v.d. Meer (ed.), *Universiteit in beweging: Een aantal beschouwingen bij gelegenheid van het 410-jarig bestaan van de Rijksuniversiteit te Leiden*. Leiden 1985, pp. 239-261.

Otterspeer, W. *De wiekslag van hun geest: De Leidse universiteit in de negentiende eeuw*. The Hague 1992.

Otterspeer, W. *Bolland: Een biografie*. Amsterdam 1995.

Ouwerkerk, A. "Vondelverehrung in katholischen Kreisen zu Köln und Amsterdam." In: Herman Vekeman, and Herbert Van Uffelen (eds.), *"Jetzt kehr ich an den Rhein": Een opstellenbundel bij Vondels 400ste verjaardag*. Keulen 1987, pp. 209-229.

Oxenaar, Aart. *Centraal Station Amsterdam: Het paleis voor de reiziger*. The Hague 1989.

Oxenaar, Aart. *P.J.H. Cuypers: Het Rijksmuseum: Schetsen en tekeningen (1863-1908)*. Rotterdam, n.d.

Ozinga, M.D. *De Protestantsche Kerkenbouw in Nederland van hervorming tot Franschen tijd*. Amsterdam 1929.

Paap, Wouter. *Alphons Diepenbrock: Een componist in de cultuur van zijn tijd*. Haarlem 1980.

Pais, A. *Inward bound*. Oxford and New York 1986.

Pais, A. *Niels Bohr's times*. Oxford 1991.

Palm, L.C., G. Vanpaemel, and F.H. van Lunteren (eds.). *De toga om de wetenschap: Ontwikkelingen in het hoger onderwijs in de geneeskunde, natuurwetenschappen en techniek in Belgie en Nederland (1850-1940)*. Gewina 16 (1993): 119-122.

Palm, L.C. "Biographies: Hugo Marie de Vries 1848-1935." In: K. van Berkel, A. van Helden, and L. Palm (eds.), *A history of science in The Netherlands: Survey, themes and reference*. Leiden 1999, pp. 592-595.

Palm, L.C. "Biographies: Martinus Willem Beijerinck 1851-1931." In: K. van Berkel, A. van Helden, and L. Palm (eds.), *A history of science in The Netherlands: Survey, themes and reference*. Leiden 1999, pp. 414-416.

Pannenborg, W.A. *Bijdragen tot de psychologie van den misdadiger, in het bijzonder van den brandstichter*. Groningen 1912.

Pannenborg, W.A. "Over de toerekeningsvatbaarheid van eenige misdadigersgroepen en de criminele politiek der toekomst." *Tijdschrift voor strafrecht* (1913): 477-488.

Paul, E.R. *Seeliger, Kapteyn and the rise of statistical astronomy*. Unpublished PhD diss. Indiana University 1976.

Paul, E.R. "The death of a research programme: Kapteyn and the Dutch astronomical community." In: *Journal for the history of Astronomy* 112 (1981): 77-94.

Paul, E.R. "Kapteyn and the early 20th-century universe." *Journal for the history of Astronomy* 117 (1986): 155-182.

Pax, "Onze Eeuw." *Dompertje*, 21, no. 17 (1889): 134-135.

Peeters, C. "Het schemerlicht van de neogotiek: wisselend oordeel over een stroming in de negentiende-eeuwse kunst." In: P.A.M. Geurts et al., *J.A. Alberdingk Thijm 1820-1889: Erflater van de negentiende eeuw*. Baarn 1992, pp. 103-123.

Peeters, Edward. *Excursion pédagogique en Hollande: Notes & Impressions*. 3 vols. Oostende 1907.

Pek. J.E. van der, W. Kromhout Czn., J.H. Leliman et al. *Zeven voordrachten over bouwkunst*. Amsterdam, n.d. [1930].

Peters, C.H. *De Nederlandsche Stedenbouw: De stad als veste, woon- en handelsplaats*. Leiden, n.d.

Pevsner, Nikolaus. "Gemeinschaftsideale unter den bildenden Künstlern des 19. Jahrhunderts." *Deutsche Vierteljahrschrift für Literaturwissenschaft und Geistesgeschichte* 1 (1931): 125-155.

Pevsner, Nikolaus. "Ruskin et Viollet-le-Duc: l'élément anglais et l'élément français dans l'appréciation de l'architecture gothique." In: G. Bekaert, *A la recherche de Viollet-le-Duc*. Brussels 1980, pp. 173-206.

Pierson, Allard. *Oudere Tijdgenooten*. 2nd ed. Amsterdam 1904.

Pierson, H. "De heerschappij der bourgeoisie in de Nederlandsch Hervormde Kerk." In: *De Gids*. 33, no. 1 (1869): 441-476.

Plas, Michel v.d. *Vader Thijm: Biografie van een koopman-schrijver*. Baarn 1995.

Plasschaert, Albert. *Jan Toorop*. Amsterdam 1925.

Poeze, Harry. *In het land van de overheerser*. Vol. 1: *Indonesiërs in Nederland 1600-1950*. Dordrecht and Cinnaminson 1986.

Polak, Bettine. *Het fin-de-siècle in de Nederlandse schilderkunst: De symbolistische beweging 1890-1900*. The Hague 1955.

Polano, Sergio. *Hendrik Petrus Berlage: Het complete werk*. Alphen aan den Rijn 1989.

Poldervaart, Saskia. *Tegen conventioneel fatsoen en zekerheid: Het uitdagende feminisme van de utopisch socialisten*. Amsterdam 1993.

Poorter, Laurent de. *Opstand en pacificatie in de Lage Landen: Bijdrage tot de studie van de Pacificatie van Gent*. Ghent 1976.

Post, Paul. "Volkskunde in Nederland: Notities over disciplinaire eigenheid." *Volkskundig Bulletin: Tijdschrift voor Nederlandse cultuurwetenschap* 20 (1994): 229-244.

Post, Paul. "Koning Willem III verleent de Vereeniging 'Het Nederlandsch Tooneel' het predikaat 'Koninklijk'." In: R.L. Erenstein (ed.), *Een theatergeschiedenis der Nederlanden: Tien eeuwen drama en theater in Nederland en Vlaanderen*. Amsterdam 1996, pp. 480-483.

Post, Paul. "Oprichtingsvergadering van het Nederlandsch Tooneelverbond." In: R.L. Erenstein (ed.), *Een theatergeschiedenis der Nederlanden: Tien eeuwen drama en theater in Nederland en Vlaanderen*. Amsterdam 1996, pp. 445-449.

Potgieter, E.J. *Het Rijksmuseum*. Haarlem 1907.

Pouwelse, W.J. *Haar verstand dienstbaar aan het hart: Middelbaar onderwijs voor meisjes: debatten, acties en beleid, 1860-1917*. Tilburg 1993.

Praag, Siegfried van. *Het ghetto: Een beschouwing en bloemlezing van West- en Oost-Joodsche ghettoschetsen*. Zutphen 1930.

Prick, H.G.M. (ed.). *Briefwisseling Lodewijk van Deyssel - Albert Verwey II*. The Hague 1985.

Prick, H. "Catharina Alberdingk Thym (1849-1908)." *De negentiende eeuw* 2 (1978): 179-203.

Prick, Harry G.M. *In de zekerheid van eigen heerlijkheid: Het leven van Lodewijk van Deyssel tot 1890*. Amsterdam 1997.

Proceedings of the Lower House 1907-1908.

Proceedings of the Lower House 1895-1896.

Propria Cures: Amsterdamsch Studentenweekblad. November 29, 1913.

Quack, H.P.G. *Rembrandt's herdenking: Toespraak in de Westerkerk, 16 Juli 1906*. Amsterdam 1906.

Querido, Isaac. *Letterkundig leven*. Vol. 2. Amsterdam 1916.

Raedts, P.G.J.M. "De katholieken en de Middeleeuwen: Prosper Guéranger OSB (1805-1875) en de eenheid van de liturgie." In: R.E.V. Stuip, and C. Vellekoop, *De Middeleeuwen in de negentiende eeuw*. Hilversum 1996, p. 105.

Ragghianti, Carlo L. *Mondrian e l'arte del XX secolo*. Milan 1962.

Ramberg, P.J., and G.J. Somsen, "The young J.H. van 't Hoff: the background to the publication of his 1874 pamphlet on the tetrahedral carbon atom, together with a new English translation." *Annals of Science* 58 (2001): 51-74.

Rasker, A.J. *De Nederlandse hervormde Kerk vanaf 1795: Geschiedenis, theologische ontwikkelingen en de verhouding tot haar zusterkerken in de negentiende en twintigste eeuw*. Kampen 1981.

Ravesteyn, L.J.C.J. van. *Rotterdam in de achttiende en negentiende eeuw*. Schiedam 1974.

Reeser, Eduard (ed.). *Verzamelde geschriften van Alphons Diepenbrock*. Utrecht and Brussels 1950.

Reeser, Eduard. "Die Mahler-Rezeption in Holland 1903-1911.' In: Rudolf Stephan (ed.), *Mahler-Interpretation: Aspekte zum Werk und Wirken von Gustav Mahler*. Mainz 1985, pp. 86-87.

Reeser, Eduard. *Een eeuw Nederlandse muziek 1815-1915*. Amsterdam 1986.

Reinink, A.W. *Amsterdam en de Beurs van Berlage: Reacties van tijdgenoten*. The Hague 1975.

Reith, B. *Honderd jaar kerkbouw in Nederland*. Haarlem 1953.

Reijnders, C. *Van 'Joodsche natiën' tot Joodse Nederlanders: Een onderzoek naar getto- en assimilatieverschijnselen tussen 1600 en 1942*. Amsterdam 1969.

Reijs, Wil, and Joos van Vugt. "Tussen zelfheiliging en belangenbehartiging: De Aartsbroederschap van de Heilige Familie in Nederland, 1850-1969." *Jaarboek van het Katholiek Documentatie Centrum* 21 (1991): 11-40.

Ricoeur, Paul. *Lectures on Ideology and Utopia*. New York 1986.

Riemsdijk, G.A. van. *Geschiedenis van de Openbare Bibliotheek in Nederland*. Vol. 1: *Van de beginjaren tot mei 1940*. The Hague 1978.

Righart, J.A. *De katholieke zuil in Europa: een vergelijkend onderzoek naar het ontstaan van verzuiling onder katholieken in Oostenrijk, Zwitserland, België en Nederland*. Amsterdam 1986.

Rigter, D.P. et al. *Tussen sociale wil en werkelijkheid: Een geschiedenis van het beleid van het ministerie van Sociale Zaken*. The Hague 1995.

Rijxman, A.S. *A.C. Wertheim 1832-1897: Een bijdrage tot zijn levensgeschiedenis*. Amsterdam 1961.

Ringbom, Sixten. *The Sounding Cosmos: A Study in the Spiritualism of Kandinsky and the Genesis of Abstract Painting*. Abo 1970.

Ritter, P.H. (ed.). *Eene halve eeuw 1848-1898: Nederland onder de regeering van Koning Willem den Derde en het Regentschap van Koningin Emma, door Nederlanders beschreven*. Vol. 1. Amsterdam 1898.

Rodenburg, Herman. "Het verleden opgepoetst: Pastoor Klönne, het 'folkore' en de zestiende-eeuwse sacramentsprocessies." In: Peter Jan Margry (ed.), *Goede en slechte tijden: Het Amsterdamse Mirakel van Sacrament in historisch perspectief*. Aerdenhout 1995, pp. 27-29.

Roessingh, K.H. *De moderne theologie in Nederland: Hare voorbereiding en eerste periode*. Groningen 1914.

Roessingh, K.H. *Het Modernisme in Nederland*. Haarlem 1922.

Rogier, L.J., and N.de Rooy. *In vrijheid herboren: Katholiek Nederland 1853-1953*. The Hague 1953.

Rogier, L.J. *Rotterdam in het derde kwart van de negentiende eeuw*. Historisch Genootschap Roterodamum. Rotterdam 1953.

Rogier, L.J. *Katholieke herleving: Geschiedenis van Katholiek Nederland sinds 1853*. The Hague 1956.

Roland Holst, H. "Maatschappelijke oorzaken van midden-eeuwsche en moderne mystiek." In: *De nieuwe tijd* 2 (1897-98): 324-337; 3 (1898-99): 120-131, 353-375; 4 (1899-1900): 6-26; 5 (1905): 647-665.

Roland Holst, H. "William Morris als letterkundige." In: William Morris, *John Ball en andere vertalingen*. Trans. H. Roland Holst. Amsterdam 1898, pp. i-x.

Roland Holst, H. "Boekbeoordeeling." *De nieuwe tijd* 3 (1898-1899): 460-461.

Roland Holst, H. *Het feest der gedachtenis*. Rotterdam 1917. 1st ed. 1915.

Roland Holst, H. *De opstandelingen*. Amsterdam, n.d.

Roland Holst, Richard N. "Derkinderens nieuwe muurschildering in de kunst-zaal van het panorama." *De Amsterdammer* 15, no. 760 (1892): 3.

Roland Holst, Richard N. "Over Derkinderen." *De Nieuwe Gids* 7 (1892): 321-325.

Roland Holst, Richard N. "Over beeldende kunst in verband met de maatschappij." *Het jonge leven* (1910): 3-4, 13, 23, 31-32, 53-54.

Roland Holst, Richard N. "Over de monumentale schilderkunst en hare beïnvloeding door de maatschappij." *De Nieuwe Tijd* 15 (1910): 297-306, 391-398.

Roland Holst, Richard N. *Over Kunst en Kunstenaar*. Amsterdam 1923.

Roland Holst, Richard N. "Over vrije en gebonden vormen in de plastische kunst." *De Gids* (1927): 227-250.

Roland Holst, Richard N. *Over Kunst en Kunstenaar*. Amsterdam 1928.

Roland Holst, Richard N. *In en buiten het tij*. Amsterdam 1940.

Roland Holst-v.d. Schalk, Henriëtte. *De kinderjaren en jeugd van R.N. Roland Holst*. Zeist 1940.

Rolland, Romain. *Vie de Tolstoï*. Paris 1919.

Romein, Annie. "Hendrik Petrus Berlage, bouwmeester der beurs." In: Jan and Annie Romein, *Erflaters van onze beschaving: Nederlandse gestalten uit zes eeuwen*. 11th ed. Amsterdam 1976, pp. 841-864.

Romein, Jan. "Integrale geschiedschrijving." In: Jan Romein, *Eender en anders: Twaalf nagelaten essays*. Amsterdam 1964, pp. 25-42.

Romein, Jan. *Op het breukvlak van twee eeuwen*. 2 vols. Leiden and Amsterdam 1967. Translated as *The Watershed of Two Eras: Europe in 1900*, 1978.

Rood, O.N. *Modern Chromatics*. French trans. 1881. New York 1879.

Rooden, Peter van. "Van geestelijke stand naar beroepsgroep: De professionalisering van de Nederlandse predikant, 1625-1874." *Tijdschrift voor Sociale Geschiedenis* 17 (1991): 369-370.

Rooden, Peter van. *Religieuze regimes: Over godsdienst en maatschappij in Nederland, 1570-1990*. Amsterdam 1996.

Rooijakkers, Gerard. "Dragers van traditie? Klederdracht als culturele constructie." In: Dolly Verhoeven et al. (eds.), *Klederdracht en kleedgedrag: Het Kostuum Harer Majesteits onderdanen 1898-1998*. Nijmegen 1998, pp. 173-188.

Rooy, P. de. "Bier, kunst en politiek: De Nieuwe Gids in Amsterdam." *Jaarboek van het Genootschap Amstelodamum* 81 (1989): 175-187.

Rooy, Piet de. "Een hevig gewarrel: Humanitair idealisme en socialisme in Nederland rond de eeuwwisseling." *Bijdragen en Mededelingen betreffende de geschiedenis der Nederlanden* 106 (1991): 625-641.

Rooy, Piet de. "De staat verdrukt, de wet is logen." In: N.C.F. van Sas, and H. te Velde (eds.), *De eeuw van de Grondwet: Grondwet en politiek in Nederland, 1798-1917*. Deventer 1998, pp. 266-294.

Rooy, Piet de, and Frits Boterman. *Op de grens van twee culturen: Nederland en Duitsland in het Fin de Siècle*. Amsterdam 1999.

Rosenberg, H.P.R. *De 19de-eeuwse kerkelijke bouwkunst in Nederland*. The Hague 1972.

Rosenboom, Thomas. *Publieke werken*. Amsterdam 1999.

Rossem, Vincent van. "Een keerpunt in de Nederlandse stedebouw: plan Zuid." In: Karin Gaillard, and Betsy Dokter, *Berlage en Amsterdam Zuid*. Amsterdam and Rotterdam 1992.

Rossem, Vincent van. *Het Algemeen Uitbreidingsplan van Amsterdam: Geschiedenis en ontwerp*. Rotterdam 1993.

Rowlinson, J.S. *J.D. van der Waals: On the continuity of the gaseous and the liquid states*. Amsterdam 1988.

Roy, J.J. le. "De vacantie-cursus te Groningen." *Album der natuur* 45 (1898): 244.

Ruiter, Frans, and Wilbert Smulders. *Literatuur en moderniteit in Nederland 1840-1990*. Amsterdam 1996.

Ruijter, Peter de. *Voor volkshuisvesting en stedebouw: Over woninghervormers en de beweging voor een goede stedebouw 1890-1920*. Amsterdam 1986.

Rupp, J.C.C. *Van oude en nieuwe universiteite: De verdringing van Duitse door Amerikaanse invloeden op de wetenschapsbeoefening en het hoger onderwijs in Nederland, 1945-1995*. The Hague 1997.

Rutten, Felix. *Ons mooie Nederland: Limburg*. Amsterdam 1918.

Sas, N.C.F. van. "Fin-de-siecle als nieuw begin: Nationalisme in Nederland rond 1900." *Bijdragen en Mededelingen betreffende de Geschiedenis der Nederlanden* 56 (1991): 609.

Savornin Lohman, A. de. *Het ééne noodige*. Amsterdam 1897.

Savornin Lohman, A. de. *De liefde in de vrouwenkwestie*. N.p., n.d.

Savornin Lohman, A. de. *Naschrift op De liefde in de vrouwenquaestie*. Amsterdam, n.d.

Scheffer, H.J. *November 1918: Journaal van een revolutie die niet doorging*. Amsterdam 1968.

Scheffler, Karl. *Holland*. Leipzig 1930.

Schenkeveld, M.H. "Vormen van realisme." In: W. van der Berg, and P. Zonneveld, *Nederlandse literatuur van de negentiende eeuw*. Utrecht, n.d., pp. 226-244.

Schippers, Hans. *Het nieuwe bier: Technische innovaties in de Nederlandse biernijverheid in de tweede helft van de negentiende eeuw*. Zutphen 1992.

Schmal, Hendrik. *Den Haag of 's-Gravenhage? De 19de-eeuwse gordel, een zone gemodelleerd door zand en veen*. Utrecht 1995.

Schmidt, Christian et al. *De Matthäus-Passion: 100 Jaar passietraditie van het Koninklijk Concertgebouworkest*. Bussum and Amsterdam 1999.

Schmidt, R. (ed.). *Die Philosophie der Gegenwart in Selbstdarstellungen*. Vol. 3. Leipzig 1922.

Schneiders, Paul. *Lezen voor iedereen: Geschiedenis van de openbare bibliotheken in Nederland*. The Hague 1990.

Schöffer, Ivo et al. *Alkmaar ontzet 1573-1973*. Alkmaar 1973.

Schöffer, Ivo. *Veelvormig verleden: Zeventien studies in de vaderlandse geschiedenis* Amsterdam 1987.

Schorske, Carl E. *Fin-de-siècle Vienna: Politics and culture*. New York 1981.

Schrijvers, P.H. *Rome, Athene, Jeruzalem: Aspecten van leven en werk van prof. dr David Cohen (1882-1967), classicus, zionist, hoogleraar Oude Geschiedenis, voorzitter Joodse Raad (1941-1943)*. Amsterdam 1999.

Schrover, Marlou. *Een kolonie van Duitsers: Groepsvorming onder Duitse migranten in Utrecht in de negentiende eeuw*. Amsterdam 2002.

Schryver, Reginald de et al. (eds.). *Nieuwe Encyclopedie van de Vlaamse Beweging*. Vol. 2. Tielt 1998.

Schuijer, Michiel. "In het teeken van Mahler: Religieuze achtergronden van de Mahlerverering in Nederland." In: Johan Giskes (ed.), *Mahler in Amsterdam: Van Mengelberg tot Chailly*. Bussum and Amsterdam 1995, p. 114

Schwegman, Marjan. *Maria Montessori 1870-1952: Kind van haar tijd, vrouw van de wereld*. Amsterdam 1999.

Sérusier, Paul. *ABC de la peinture*. Paris 1950.

Servos, J.W. *Physical chemistry from Ostwald to Pauling: The making of a science in America*. Princeton 1990.

Seuphor, Michel. *Piet Mondrian: life and Works*. Amsterdam 1956.

Sevensma, T.P. (ed.). *Nederlandsche helden der wetenschap: Levensschetsen van negen Nobelprijswinnaars: Hoogtepunten van wetenschappelijken arbeid in Nederland*. Amsterdam 1946.

Shipman, P. *The man who found the missing link: Eugène Dubois and his lifelong quest to prove Darwin right*. Cambridge, MA 2002.

Shipman, P. *The man who found the missing link: The extraordinary life of Eugène Dubois*. London 2002.

Sickesz, C.J. et al. *Het maatschappelijk vraagstuk beschouwd uit het oogpunt van het godsdienstig-zedelijk leven*. Amsterdam 1887.

Signac, Paul. *D'Eugène Delacroix au néo-impressionisme*. Paris 1964. 1st ed. 1897.

Simons, L. *Amsterdam in stukken en brokken: Uitgegeven vanwege de Vereeniging tot Bevordering van het Vreemdelingenvertier*. Haarlem 1891.

Singelenberg, P. *H.P. Berlage: Idea and Style*. Utrecht 1971.

Sitte, Camillo. *Der Städtebau nach seinen künstlerischen Grundsätzen*. Vienna 1889.

Smelik, Jan. *Eén in lied en leven: Het stichtelijk lied bij Nederlandse protestanten tussen 1866 en 1938*. The Hague 1997.

Smilde, Bernard. "Het protestants-christelijk volksdeel en de muziekcultuur." In: J. de Bruijn (ed.), *Bepaald gebied: Aspecten van het protestants-christelijk leven in Nederland in de jaren 1880-1940*. Baarn 1989, p. 150.

Smit, J.W. *Fruin en de partijen tijdens de Republiek*. Groningen 1958.

Smits-Veldt, Mieke B. "De Muiderkring in beeld: Een vaderlands gezelschap in negentiende-eeuwse schilderijen." *Literatuur* 15 (1998): 278-288.

Snelders, H.A.M. "The birth of stereochemistry: An analysis of the 1874-papers of J.H. van 't Hoff and J.A. le Bel." *Janus* 60 (1973): 261-278.

Snelders, H.A.M. "De beoefeningvan de natuurkunde in het negentiende-eeuwse Utrecht." *N.G. 200. Natuurkundig Gezelschap te Utrecht* (1977): 83-98.

Snelders, H.A.M. "De schei- en natuurkunde aan de Utrechtse universiteit in de negentiende eeuw." *Gewina* 7 (1984): 32-48.

Snelders, H.A.M. "J.H. van 't Hoff's research school in Amsterdam (1877-1895)." *Janus* 71 (1984) 1-30.

Snelders, H.A.M. "Professors, amateurs and learned societies: The organization of the natural sciences. In: M.C. Jacob, and W.W. Mijnhardt (eds.), *The Dutch Republic in the eighteenth century*. Ithaca 1992. pp. 308-323.

Snelders, H.A.M. *De geschiedenis van de scheikunde in Nederland: Van alchemie tot chemie en chemische industrie rond 1900*. Delft 1993.

Snellen, H.A. *Selected papers on electrocardiography of Willem Einthoven: With a bibliography, biographical notes and comments*. Leiden 1977.

Snellen, H.A. *W. Einthoven: Father of electrocardiography: Life and work, ancestors and contemporaries*. Dordrecht 1995.

Snethlage, R.A.I. "Opleiding en positie der Civiel-Ingenieurs," In: *De Ingenieur*, 6, no. 18 (1891): 159-162; 6, no. 19 (1891): 168-170; 6, no. 20 (1891): 175-179.

Snethlage, R.A.I. "Het standpunt der commissie in zake het technisch onderwijs en een beginsel voor de wettelijke regeling van het onderwijs aan de Polytechnische School." *De Ingenieur*, 8, no. 1 (1893): 11-14.

Snoeck Henkemans, J.R. "Het congres voor weezen-opvoeding op 25 en 26 juli 1898 in het gebouw der tentoonstelling van vrouwen-arbeid." *Stemmen voor waarheid en vrede* 35 (1898): 804.

Someren Brand, J.E. van. *Katalogus van de Tentoonstelling van Nationale Kleederdrachten, bijeengebracht ter gelegenheid van de inhuldiging van Hare Majesteit Koningin Wilhelmina 1898*. Amsterdam 1898.

Sommer, Martin. "De vlegeljaren van de telefoon." In: Paul Brill (ed.), *Opmaat van een nieuwe eeuw: Hoofdstukken uit het Nederlandse fin de siècle*. Amsterdam 1995, pp. 27-49.

Somsen, G.J. *Wetenschappelijk onderzoek en algemeen belang: De chemie van H.R. Kruyt (1882-1959)*. Delft 1998.

Spaander, Ineke, and Paul van der Velde (eds.). *Reunie op 't duin: Mondriaan en tijdgenoten in Zeeland*. Middelburg and Zwolle 1994.

Spies, Marijke. "Van mythes en meningen: Over de geschiedenis van de literatuurgeschiedenis." In: Marijke Spies (ed.), *Historische letterkunde: Facetten van vakbeoefening*. Groningen 1984, pp. 171-193.

Spies, Marijke. "Van 'Vaderlandsch Gevoel' tot Europees perspectief: De studie van de 17e en 18e-eeuwse literatuur in de 19e en 20e eeuw: En hoe verder?" In: Jan W. de Vries, "*Eene bedenkelijke nieuwigheid*": Twee eeuwen neerlandistiek. Hilversum 1997, pp. 69-83.

Spies, Marijke. "De romantische De Ruyter: 'Vlissinger' Michiel in de negentiende-eeuwse jeugdliteratuur." In: K.D. Beekman et al. (eds.), *De as van de Romantiek: Opstellen aangeboden aan prof. dr W. van den Berg bij zijn afscheid als hoogleraar Moderne Nederlandse Letterkunde aan de Universiteit van Amsterdam*. Amsterdam 1999, pp. 264-273.

Spijker, W. van 't. "Ik ben een vriend en metgezel." In: F.A. van Lieburg, *De stille luyden: Bevindelijk gereformeerden in de negentiende eeuw*. Kampen 1994, pp. 67-84.

Staas, F.A. "Cryogenics and low temperature physics in The Netherlands." In: R.G. Scurlock (ed.), *History and origins of cryogenics*. Oxford 1992.

Stamhuis, I.H. "The Reactions on Hugo de Vries's Intracellular Pangenesis: The Discussion with August Weismann." *Journal of the History of Biology* 36 (2003): 119-152.

Stamhuis, I.H., O.G. Meijer, and E.J.A. Zevenhuizen. "Hugo de Vries on heredity, 1889-1903: statistics, mendelian laws, pangenes, mutations." *Isis* 90 (1999): 238-267.

Star Numan, O.W. "Nederland en Oranje." In: P.H. Ritter, *Eene halve eeuw 1848-1898: Nederland onder de regeering van Koning Willem den Derde en het regentschap van Koningin Emma*. Vol. 1. Amsterdam 1898, pp. 17-50.

Steensma, R., and C.A.van Swigchem (eds.). *Honderdvijftig jaar gereformeerde kerkbouw*. Kampen 1986.

Stellingwerff, J. *Dr Abraham Kuyper en de Vrije Universiteit*. Kampen 1987.

Stern, Fritz. *The Politics of Cultural Despair: A Study in the Rise of the German Ideology*. New York 1965.

Stigt, W.P. van. *Brouwer's Intuitionism*. Amsterdam 1990.

Stokvis, B.J. "Openingsrede." In: *Handelingen van het Eerste Nederlandsche Natuur- en Geneeskundig Congres*. Haarlem 1888, pp. 15-30.

Stokvis, Ruud. *Strijd over sport: Organisatorische en ideologische ontwikkelingen*. Deventer 1979.

Stokvis, R. "De school en de ontwikkeling van de sport- en spelbeweging in Nederland." In: Mark D'Hoker, and Jan Tolleneer (eds.), *Het vergeten lichaam: Geschiedenis van de lichamelijke opvoeding in België en Nederland*. Leuven and Apeldoorn 1995, pp. 59-79.

Stokvis, Ruud. "Sport en het mediasysteem." In: Wilfred van Buuren, and Theo Stevens (eds.), *Sportgeschiedenis in Nederland*. Amsterdam 1998, p. 94.

Stolwijk, Chris. *Uit de schilderswereld: Nederlandse kunstschilders in de tweede helft van de negentiende eeuw*. Utrecht 1997.

Storck, Elise. "'De eisch van aanschouwelijkheid': schoolplaten en didaktiek van het geschiedenis-onderwijs 1880-1920." In: D.P. Snoep (ed.), *De geschiedenis gekleurd: Historie-schoolplaten van J.H. Isings*. Assen and Utrecht 1982, pp. 88-89.

Stott, Annette. *American Painters who worked in the Netherlands, 1880-1914*. Unpublished PhD diss. Boston University 1986.

Stott, Annette. *Holland Mania: The Unknown Dutch Period in American Art & Culture*. New York 1998.

Streevelaar, Marjolein. "Eigen taal is eigen kunst: Het vergeten verleden van de Nederlandstalige opera." In: Louis Peter Grijp (ed.), *Zingen in een kleine taal: De positie van het Nederlands in de muziek*. Amsterdam 1995, pp. 193-194.

Strien, P.J. van, and J. Feij. "Heymans over temperament en karakter." In: D. Draaisma (ed.), *Een laboratorium voor de ziel: Gerard Heymans en het begin van de experimentele psychologie*. Groningen 1992, pp. 66-79.

Struyker Boudier, C.E.M. *Wijsgerig leven in Nederland en België 1880-1980*. Vol. 2: *De dominicanen*. Nijmegen and Baarn 1986.

Struyker Boudier, C.E.M. *Wijsgerig leven in Nederland en België 1880-1980*. Vol. 5: *De filosofie van Leuven*. Leuven and Baarn 1989.

Struyker Boudier, C.E.M. *Wijsgerig leven in Nederland, België en Luxemburg 1880-1980* Vol. 7: *Op zoek naar zijn en zin.* Nijmegen and Baarn 1992.

Stuart Hughes, H. *Consciousness and Society: The Reorientation of European Thought 1890-1930.* New York 1977. 1st ed. 1950.

Stuers, Victor de. *Holland op zijn smalst.* Bussum 1975.

Stuiveling, G. (ed.). *Acht over Gorter.* Amsterdam 1978.

Stuurman, Siep. *Wacht op onze daden: Het liberalisme en de vernieuwing van de Nederlandse staat.* Amsterdam 1992.

Stuurman, Siep. "De produktieve deugd." In: Siep Stuurman, *Wacht op onze daden: Het liberalisme en de vernieuwing van de Nederlandse staat.* Amsterdam 1992, pp. 209-249.

Suchtelen, Nico van. *Quia absurdum.* Amsterdam 1925. 1st ed. 1906.

Suèr, Henk, and Josine Meurs. *Geheel in de geest van Wagner: De Wagnervereeniging in Nederland 1883-1959.* Amsterdam 1997.

Sutter, D. "Les phénomènes de la vision." In: *L'Art.* N.p. 1880.

Swaan, Abram de. *Zorg en de staat: Welzijn, onderwijs en gezondheidszorg in Europa en de Verenigde Staten in de nieuwe tijd.* Amsterdam 1989.

Swaan, Abram de. *In care of the state: Healthcare, education and welfare in Europe and the USA in the modern era.* Cambridge 1988.

Taylor, Keith. *The Political Ideas of the Utopian Socialists.* London 1982.

Taverne, Ed. *In 't land van belofte: in de nieue stadt: Ideaal en werkelijkheid van de stadsuitleg in de Republiek, 1580-1680.* Maarssen 1978.

Taverne, Ed. "Een 'tolerante' stedenbouw: De esthetiek van de Raadhuisstraat in Amsterdam (1895-1899)." *Leidschrift* 15 (2000): 49-71.

Telgenhof-Otter, Margriet. "Kerkgebouwen der dolerenden: eene genadige voorziening." In: C. Augustijn (ed.), *Gereformeerd Amsterdam: sedert 1835.* Kampen 1989, pp. 42-43.

Theunissen, B. *Eugène Dubois en de aapmens van Java: Een bijdrage tot de geschiedenis van de paleoantropologie.* Amsterdam 1985.

Theunissen, B. *Eugène Dubois and the ape-man from Java: The history of the first "missing link" and its discoverer.* Dordrecht 1989.

Theunissen, B. "De beheersing van mutaties, Hugo de Vries' werdegang van fysioloog tot geneticus." *Gewina* 15 (1992): 97-115.

Theunissen, B. "Closing the door on Hugo de Vries' mendelism." *Annals of Science* 51 (1994): 225-248.

Theunissen, B. "Knowledge is power: Hugo de Vries on science, heredity and social progress." *British Journal for the History of Science* 27 (1994): 291-311.

Theunissen, B. "The beginnings of the 'Delft-tradition' revisited: Martinus W. Beijerinck and the genetics of micro-organisms." *Journal of the History of Biology* 29, no. 2 (1996): 197-218.

Theunissen, B. "Ontdekte Mendel de wetten van Mendel?' In: B. Theunissen, and C. Hakfoort (eds.), *Newtons God en Mendels bastaarden: Nieuwe*

visies op de 'Helden van de wetenschap'." Amsterdam 1997, pp. 99-122.

Theunissen, B. "H.A. Lorentz' visie op wetenschap." *Gewina* 21 (1998): 1-14.

Theunissen, B. "Kennis is macht: De Vries' biotechnologie avant la lettre' In: B. Theunissen, *Nut en nog eens nut: Wetenschapsbeelden van Nederlandse natuuronderzoekers, 1800-1900.* Hilversum 2000, pp. 123-148.

Theunissen, B. *Nut en nog eens nut: Wetenschapsbeelden van Nederlandse natuuronderzoekers, 1800-1900.* Hilversum 2000.

Theunissen, B., and C. Hakfoort (eds.). *Newtons God en Mendels bastaarden: Nieuwe visies op 'helden van de wetenschap'."* Amsterdam 1997.

Thijs, Walter. *De Kroniek van P.L. Tak: Brandpunt van Nederlandse cultuur in de jaren negentig van de vorige eeuw.* Antwerp 1956.

Thijssen, Theo. *In de ochtend van het leven: Jeugdherinneringen bezorgd en van een nawoord voorzien door Peter-Paul de Baar en Rob Grootendorst.* Amsterdam and Antwerp 1994.

Thorn Prikker, Johan. *De brieven van Johan Thorn Prikker aan Henri Borel en anderen, 1892-1904: Met ter inleiding fragmenten uit het dagboek van Henri Borel, 1890-1892.* Edited by Joop M. Joosten. Nieuwkoop 1980.

Tibbe, Lieske. *R.N. Roland Holst 1868-1938: Arbeid en schoonheid vereend: opvattingen over gemeenschapskunst.* Amsterdam 1994.

Tigchelaar, Joh. "Meer uitgebreid lager onderwijs." In: J.W. van Hulst, I. van der Velde, and G.Th.M. Verhaak (eds.), *Vernieuwingsstreven binnen het Nederlandse onderwijs in de periode 1900-1940.* Groningen 1970.

De Tijd, May 13, 1953.

Tillema, J.A.C. *Schetsen uit de geschiedenis van de monumentenzorg.* The Hague 1975.

Timmerman, Æ.W. "Prof. G. Heymans' De toekomstige eeuw der psychologie." *De Nieuwe Gids*, 24, no. 2 (1909): 584-595.

Tod, Ian, and Michael Wheeler. *Utopia.* New York 1978.

Tollebeek, Jo. *De toga van Fruin: Denken over geschiedenis in Nederland sinds 1860.* Amsterdam 1990.

Tolstoj, L.N. *What then must we do?* Oxford 1925. 1st ed. 1886.

Tolstoj, L.N. *Het einde is nabij.* Delft n.d. [1898].

Tolstoj, L.N. *Moderne slavernij.* The Hague 1900.

Tolstoj, L.N. *Anna Karenina.* In: L.N. Tolstoj, *Verzamelde Werken.* Vol. 5. Amsterdam 1965.

Tolstoj, L.N. "Cholstomjer." In: L.N. Tolstoj, *Verzamelde Werken.* Vol. 2. Amsterdam 1970.

Tolstoj, L.N. *Mijn biecht.* Utrecht 1998.

Trappeniers, Maureen (ed.). *Antoon Derkinderen.* 's-Hertogenbosch 1980.

Treub, H. en C. Winkler. *De vrouw en de studie.* Haarlem 1898.

Tricht, H.W. van (ed.). *Onzekerheid is leven: Beschouwingen over Frederik van Eeden.* Leiden 1983.

Tromp, Bart. *Het sociaal-democratisch programma: De*

beginselprogramma's van SDB, SDAP en PvdA, 1878-1977. Amsterdam 2002.

Turksma, Roelf. *De geschiedenis van de opleiding tot onderwijzer in Nederland aan de openbare, protestants-christelijke en bijzonder-neutrale instellingen.* Groningen 1961.

Tussenbroek, C. van. *Over de aequivalentie van man en vrouw.* Amsterdam 1898.

Tussenbroek, C. van. *Over het tekort aan levensenergie bij onze jonge vrouwen en meisjes: Rede uitgesproken op de Nationale Tentoonstelling van Vrouwenarbeid.* N.p. 1898.

"De tyrannie der wetenschap." *Dompertje,* 28, no. 22 (1896): 337-340.

Uildriks, F.J. van. "Barthold Meryan." *Belang en recht* 2, Jan. 1, 1898: 46-47.

Uildriks, F.J. van. "Van vrouwenlevens." In: *Nederland.* Vol. 1. N.p. 1898.

Uitert, E. van et al. "Het nieuwe wereldbeeld: Het begin van de abstracte kunst in Nederland 1910-1925." *Museumjournaal* 6 (1972): 241-308.

Uitert, E. van. "Beeldende kunst en muziek." In: Carel Blotkamp et al., *Kunstenaren der Idee: Symbolistische tendenzen in Nederland ca 1880-1930.* The Hague 1978, pp. 67-74.

Uitert, E. van, and Inemie Gerards. *Jan Toorop: Symbolisme in de kunst.* The Hague 1994.

Uyldert, Maurits. *Dichterlijke strijdbaarheid: Uit het leven van Albert Verwey.* Amsterdam 1955.

Het Vaderland. July 11, 1944.

Valk, Gerrit. "Het verblijf van Picasso in Nederland in 1905." *Holland* 27, no. 2 (1995): 94-111.

Valk, J.P. de, and M. van Faassen (eds.). *Dagboeken en aantekeningen van Willem Hendrik de Beaufort 1874-1918.* Vol. 1: *1874-1910.* The Hague 1993.

Valk, J.P.de. *Roomser dan de paus? Studies over de betrekkingen tussen de Heilige Stoel en het Nederlandse katholicisme 1815-1940.* Nijmegen 1998.

Valkhoff, J. *Een Eeuw Rechtsontwikkeling: De ver-maatschappelijking van het Nederlandse Privaatrecht sinds de codificatie (1838-1938).* Amsterdam 1938.

Veen, Anneke van (ed.). *G.H. Breitner: Fotograaf van het Amsterdamse stadsgezicht.* Amsterdam 1997.

Veen, H.G. van der. "Psychologie der vrouwen." In: D. Draaisma et al, *Gerard Heymans: Objectiviteit in filosofie en psychologie.* Weesp 1983, pp. 122-144.

Veenland-Heineman, K.M., and A.A.E. Vels Heijn. *Het nieuwe Rijksmuseum: Ontwerpen en bouwen 1863-1885.* Amsterdam 1985.

Veer, H. van 't. *Mr C.W. Opzoomer als wijsgeer.* Assen 1961.

Veer, P.H.W.A.M. de. *Leven en werk van Hugo de Vries.* Groningen 1969.

Velde, H. te. "Het 'roer van staat' in 'zwakke vrouwenhanden': Emma en het imago van Oranje." In: C.A. Tamse (ed.), *Koningin Emma: Opstellen over haar regentschap en voogdij.* Baarn 1990, pp. 169-195.

Velde, H. te. *Gemeenschapszin en Plichtsbesef: Liberalisme en Nationalisme in Nederland, 1870-1918.* Groningen 1992.

Velde, Henk te. "Een aparte techniek: Nederlandse

politieke acteurs en de massa na 1870." *Tijdschrift voor geschiedenis* 110 (1997): 198-212.

Velde, Henk te. *Stijlen van leiderschap: Persoon en politiek van Thorbecke tot Den Uyl.* Amsterdam 2002.

Velde, Henk te, and Hans Verhage (eds.). *De eenheid en de delen: Zuilvorming, onderwijs en natievorming in Nederland 1850-1900.* Amsterdam 1996.

Velde, I. van der. "Lager onderwijs." In: J.W. van Hulst, I. van der Velde, and G.Th.M. Verhaak, *Vernieuwingsstreven binnen het onderwijs in de periode 1900-1940.* Groningen 1970, pp. 65-91.

Ven, D.J.van der. *Neerlands volksleven.* Zaltbommel 1920.

Verbeek, J. "Bezoekers van het Rijksmuseum in het Trippenhuis 1844-1885." *Bulletin Rijksmuseum* 6 (1958): 64.

Verberne, L.G.J. *De Nederlandsche arbeidersbeweging in de negentiende eeuw.* Amsterdam 1940.

Verbong, G.P.J., and E. Homburg. "Chemische kennis en de chemische industrie." In: H.W. Lintsen, *Geschiedenis van de techniek in Nederland: Wording van een moderne samenleving 1900-1890.* Vol. 5. Zutphen 1994, pp. 243-269.

Verburg, Marcel E. *Koningin Emma, Regentes van het Koninkrijk.* Baarn 1989.

Verhoeff, Maurits, and Thijs Wierema (eds.). *Ochenebbisj: Verhalen en geintjes over het Amsterdamse getto (1870-1925).* Amsterdam 1999.

Vermeulen, U. "Katholieken en liberalen tegenover de Gentse Pacificatie-feesten van 1876." In: Poorter, Laurent de, *Opstand en pacificatie in de Lage Landen: Bijdrage tot de studie van de Pacificatie van Gent.* Ghent 1976, pp. 332-350.

Vermij, R. "Inleiding." In: J.J. Kloek, and W.W. Mijnhardt (eds.), *Balans en perspectief van de Nederlandse cultuurgeschiedenis.* Vol. 3. Amsterdam 1990.

Vernooij, Anton. *Het rooms-katholieke devotielied in Nederland vanaf 1800.* Nederlands Instituut voor Kerkmuziek. Voorburg 1990.

Verschaffel, Tom. "Het verleden tot weinig herleid: De historische optocht als vorm van de romantische verbeelding." In: Jo Tollebeek, Frank Ankersmit, andWessel Krul (eds.), *Romantiek en historische cultuur.* Groningen 1996, pp. 297-320.

"Verslag jaarvergadering Broederschap van Notarissen 2 aug. 1900." *Weekblad voor privaatrecht, notarisambt en registratie* 31, no. 1598 (1900): 371-373.

Versluis, W.G. *Geschiedenis van de emancipatie der katholieken in Nederland van 1795 - heden.* Utrecht and Nijmegen 1948.

Verwey, Albert. "Bijdragen tot de versiering van de Nieuwe Beurs." In: Albert Verwey, *Proza.* Vol. 7. Amsterdam 1922, pp. 1-37.

Verwey, Albert. "Bijdragen tot de versiering van de Nieuwe Beurs (1899-1900)." In: Albert Verwey, *Oorspronkelijk Dichtwerk.* Vol. 2. Amsterdam 1938, pp. 728-735.

Verwey, G. *Gerard Heymans (1857-1930) en het equilibri-ummodel.* N.p. 1998.

Verwey-Jonker, Hilda. "Vijfentwintig jaar socialistische theorie." In: E. Boekman, *Ir. J.W. Albarda: Een kwarteeuw parlementaire werkzaamheid*. Amsterdam 1938, pp. 330-348.

Vestijk, Simon. *Gustav Mahler: Over de structuur van zijn symfonisch oeuvre*. The Hague 1960.

Veth, Jan. *Derkinderens Wandschildering in het Bossche Stadhuis*. Amsterdam 1892.

Veth, Jan. *De muurschilderingen van Der Kinderen in het trappenhuis van het gebouw der algemeene maatschappij van levensverzekering en lijfrente te Amsterdam*. Amsterdam 1900.

Veurman, B.W.E. *Volendammer Schildersboek*. The Hague 1979.

Viaene, Vincent. "The Roman Question: Catholic Mobilisation and Papal Diplomacy during the Pontificate of Pius IX (1846-1878).' In: Emile Lamberts (ed.), *The Black International 1870-1878: The Holy See and Militant Catholicism in Europe*. Brussels 2002, pp. 135-177.

Visser, Rienk. "De grote sprong voorwaarts: De twintigste eeuw." In: Pieter F.J. Obbema, *Boeken in Nederland: Vijfhonderd jaar schrijven, drukken en uitgeven*. N.p. 1979, p. 84.

Visser, R.P.W., and C. Hakfoort (eds.). *Werkplaatsen van wetenschap en techniek: Industriële en academische laboratoria in Nederland 1860-1940*. Special edition of *Gewina*. Amsterdam 1987.

Visser, R.P.W. "Hugo de Vries (1848-1935): het begin van de experimentele botanie in Nederland." In: J.C.H. Blom et al. (eds.), *Een brandpunt van geleerdheid in de hoofdstad: De Universiteit van Amsterdam rond 1900 in vijftien portretten*. Hilversum 1992, pp. 159-178.

Vledder, I., E. Houwaart, and E. Homburg, "Particuliere laboratoria in Nederland: deel 1: opkomst en bloei, 1865-1914." *NEHA-jaarboek* 62 (1999): 249-290.

Vliegen, W.H. *De dageraad der volksbevrijding*. Amsterdam 1905.

Vliegen, W.H. *Die onze kracht ontwaken deed*. Vol. 1. Amsterdam 1926.

Vollenhoven, C. van. "De eendracht van het land." In: C. van Vollenhoven, *Mr. C. van Vollenhoven's Verspreide Geschriften*. 2 vols. Haarlem and The Hague 1934, pp. 173-209.

Voorzanger, J.L., and J.E. Polak Jz. *Het Joodsch in Nederland*. Amsterdam 1915.

Vooys, C.G.N de. *Historische Schets van de Nederlandse Letterkunde*. Groningen and Batavia 1949.

Vos, Jozef. "Frits Coers (1870-1937) en het Nederlandse lied." In: Louis Peter Grijp (ed.), *Zingen in een kleine taal: De positie van het Nederlands in de muziek*. Amsterdam 1995, p. 211.

Voskuil, J.J. "Het tijdelijke met het eeuwige verwisseld, of: op de klank van de midwinterhoorn de eeuwigheid in." *Volkskundig Bulletin* 7 (1981): 28.

Voskuil, J.J. "Geschiedenis van de volkskunde in Nederland: portret van een discipline." *Volkskundig Bulletin* 10 (1984): 57-58.

Vrankrijker, A.J.C. de. *Onze Anarchisten en Utopisten rond 1900*. Bussum 1972.

Vrede: orgaan ter bespreking van de praktijk der liefde. The Hague 1897-1909.

Vries, A.D.W. de, and F.J.G. van Tricht. *Geschiedenis der Wet op de Ouderlijke macht en de Voogdij (6 februari 1901, Staatsblad no. 62)*. Vol. 2. Groningen 1905.

Vries, Boudien de. "De roman *Lidewijde* en de burgerlijke leescultuur: lezers en leesgezelschappen in de negentiende eeuw.' *Tijdschrift voor Sociale Geschiedenis* 25 (1999): 152.

Vries, J. de. "Albert Verwey en de beeldende kunst." *Jong Holland* 1 (1985): pp. 7-26.

Vries, Jan de. *Barges and capitalism: Passenger transportation in the Dutch economy, 1632-1839*. Utrecht 1981.

Vries, Joh. de. "De academicus en het bedrijfsleven: historische perspectief." In: A.L. Mok (ed.), *Jonge academici en het bedrijfsleven*. Rotterdam 1972, pp. 111-130.

Vries, Johan de. In: *Nederlands Patriciaat* 72 (1988) xi en xiv.

Vries, P. de (ed.). *De uitvinding van de "psychologie der vrouw"*. Amsterdam 1990.

Vries, R.W.P. "Over Toorops Drie Bruiden en Annonciation du Nouveau Mysticisme," *Elsevier* 11 (1925): 363-365.

Vrijer, M.J.A. de. *Gunning Tragicus: Prof. Dr J.H. Gunning Jr. in den kring zijner broeders*. The Hague 1946.

Vrijland: Tijdschrift van de "Nederlandsche Vrijland-Vereeniging." 1894-1897.

Vroede, M. de. "Onderwijs en pedagogiek: Karaktertrekken van de ontwikkeling in Nederland en België tijdens de 19de en 20ste eeuw." In: J.J.H. Dekkeer, M. D'Hoker et al. (eds.), *Pedagogisch werk in de samenleving: De ontwikkeling van professionele opvoeding in Nederland en België in de 19de en 20ste eeuw*. Leuven and Amersfoort 1987, pp. 118-119.

Vrouwenarbeid: orgaan van de Nationale Tentoonstelling van Vrouwenarbeid, July 28, 1898, p. 80.

Vugt, Joos van. "De geschiedenis van zusters, paters en broeders: Geschiedschrijving over het religieuze leven in Nederland in de laatste twee eeuwen: Resultaten tot nu toe en wensen voor de toekomst." *Jaarboek Katholiek Documentatie Centrum*. 26 (1996): 126.

Wachelder, J. *Universiteit tussen vorming en opleiding: De modernisering van de Nederlandse universiteiten in de negentiende eeuw*. Hilversum 1992.

Wagemakers, Ton. "Het Vaderlandsch Historisch Volksfeest: Over D.J. van der Ven, massatoerisme en de moderne folklore." *Jaarboek Nederlands Openluchtmuseum* 2 (1996): 171-188.

Wagner, Anna. *Max Liebermann in Holland*. Bonn, n.d.

Wagner, Richard. *Gesammelte Werke*. Leipzig 1907.

Wall, E.G.E. van der. *Het oude en het nieuwe geloof: Discussie rond 1900*. Leiden 1999.

Weevers, Theodoor. *Poetry of the Netherlands in its European context, 1170-1930*. London 1960.

Wegman, H.A.J. *Geschiedenis van de christelijke eredienst in het Westen en in het Oosten: Een wegwijzer*. Hilversum 1983.

Welcker, J.M. *Heren en arbeiders in de vroege Nederlandse arbeidersbeweging 1870-1914*. Amsterdam 1978.

Welsh, Robert P. "Mondrian and Theosophy." In: Fuerstein, Carol (ed.), *Piet Mondrian, 1872-1944: Centennial exhibition.* New York 1971, pp. 35-51.

Welsh, Robert P. "Sacred Geometry: French Symbolism and Early Abstraction." In: Maurice Tuchman (ed.), *The Spiritual in Art: Abstract painting 1890-1985.* Los Angeles and The Hague 1986, pp. 63-87.

Welsh, Robert P. "Mondriaan in Amsterdam." In: Boudewijn Bakker et al. *Mondriaan aan de Amstel 1892-1912.* Amsterdam 1994, pp. 55-68.

Wennekes, Emile. *Het Paleis voor Volksvlijt (1864-1929): "Edeler uiting eener stoute gedachte!"* The Hague 1999.

Wesseling, H.L. *Verdeel en heers: De deling van Afrika 1880-1914.* Amsterdam 1991.

Wesseling, H.L. *Oorlog lost nooit iets op: Opstellen over Europese geschiedenis.* Amsterdam 1993.

Wesseling, H.L. *Divide and rule: The partition of Africa 1880-1914.* Westport, CT 1996.

Westerdijk, Johanna. "De ontwikkeling van het Hooger Onderwijs." In: W.G. de Bas (ed.), *Gedenkboek 1898-1923: Uitgegeven ter gelegenheid van het zilveren regeeringsfeest van hare majesteit Koningin Wilhelmina der Nederlanden, op 6 september 1923.* Voorschoten 1923, pp. 401-413.

Whiting, Steven Moore. *Satie the Bohemian: From Cabaret to Concert Hall.* Oxford 1999.

Wielinga, G. "Vernieuwingstendenties in het buitenland." In: J.W. van Hulst, I. van der Velde, and G.Th.M. Verhaak, *Vernieuwingsstreven binnen het onderwijs in de periode 1900-1940.* Groningen 1970, pp. 35-63.

Wierdels, Ferd. "Klein München in Amsterdam." *Amsterdamsch Jaarboekje* (1890): 97-98.

Wiessing, H.D. *Bewegend portret: Levensherinneringen.* Amsterdam 1960.

Wijck, B.H.C.K. van der. *Zielkunde.* Groningen 1872.

Wijdeveldt, H. Th. *Wendingen 1918-1931: Gemeentelijk museum Het Princessehof, 2 oktober-1 december 1982.* Leeuwarden 1982.

Wijnaendts Francken-Dyserinck, W. "De Liefde in de Vrouwenkwestie." *Belang en recht* 3 (1898-1899): 64-47.

Wijnaendts Francken-Dyserinck, W. "De psychologie der vrouwen." *De Ploeger* 5 (1911): 6-7.

Wilde, I. de. "Psychologie der vrouwen: Gerard Heymans over vrouwelijke studenten." *Intermediair* 6, no. 46 (1980): 13-23.

Wilde, I. de. *Nieuwe deelgenoten in de wetenschap: Vrouwelijke studenten en docenten aan de Rijksuniversiteit Groningen 1871-1919.* Assen 1998.

Wilkeshuis, C. *Meester, welbedankt! De school van 1900 tot nu.* Leiden 1968.

Willemsen, A.W. *De Vlaamse Beweging van 1830 tot 1914.* Vol. 4 of M. Lamberty et al. (eds.), *Twintig Eeuwen Vlaanderen.* Hasselt 1974.

Willemsen, J.Th.W. "De volkshuisvesting in Arnhem 1829-1925." Vol. 3 of *Bijdragen tot de Geschiedenis van Arnhem.* Arnhem 1969.

Willen wij alleen de gothiek? Propaganda voor de gotiek in de negentiende eeuw, Duitsland, Frankrijk, Nederland. Groningen 1979.

Willink, B. *Burgerlijk sciëntisme en wetenschappelijk onderzoek: Sociale grondslagen van nationale bloeiperioden in de negentiende eeuwse bètawetenschappen.* Amsterdam 1988.

Willink, B. *De Tweede Gouden Eeuw: Nederland en de Nobelprijzen voor natuurwetenschappen 1870-1940.* Amsterdam 1998.

Wilzen, H.J., and A. van Biemen. *Samen op weg: Vijftig jaar ontmoeting tussen Christendom en Socialisme in De Blijde Wereld en Tijd en Taak.* Amsterdam 1953.

Wingens, M.F.M. *Over de grens: De bedevaart van katholieke Nederlanders in de zeventiende en achttiende eeuw.* Nijmegen 1994.

Winkel, J. te. "Letteren en taal." In: P.H. Ritter (ed.), *Eene halve eeuw 1848-1898: Nederland onder de regeering van koning Willem den derde en het regentschap van koningin Emma door Nederlanders beschreven.* Vol. 2. Amsterdam 1898.

Winkeler, Lodewijk. "Ten dienste der seminaristen: Handboeken op de Nederlandse priesteropleidingen, 1800-1967." *Jaarboek van het Katholiek Documentatie Centrum.* 17 (1987): 41-42.

Wisse, A. "Zur Frage nach den Geschlechtsdifferenzen im Akademischen Studium: Ergebnisse einer Studentenenquête." *Zeitschrift für angewandte Psychologie* (1916): 341-385.

Wolfgang van der Mey, H. "Een nieuw werk over 'de vrouw'." *De Nederlandsche spectator*, December 4, 1897: 391-392.

Wolfgang van der Mey, H. "De vrouwenquestie en de liefde." *De Nederlandsche Spectator*, February 11, 1899.

Woordenboek der Nederlandsche Taal. Vol. 9. The Hague and Leiden 1913.

Woud, Auke van der. *De Bataafse hut: Verschuivingen in het beeld van de geschiedenis (1750-1850).* Amsterdam 1990.

Woud, A. van der. *Waarheid en Karakter: Het debat over de bouwkunst 1840-1900.* Rotterdam 1997.

Zanden, Jan Luiten van, and Riel, Arthur van. *Nederland 1780-1914: Staat, instituties en economische ontwikkeling.* Amsterdam 2000.

Zeijden, Albert van der. "De 'wortels' van de volkscultuur: Retorische elementen in het werk van Jos. Schrijnen (1869-1938)." *Volkskundig Bulletin: Tijdschrift voor Nederlandse cultuurwetenschap* 21(1995): 331-350.

Zevenhuizen, E. "Keeping and scrapping: The story of a Mendelian lecture plate of Hugo de Vries." *Annals of Science* 17 (2000): 329-353.

Zimmermann, Michael F. *Seurat and the Art Theory of his Time.* Antwerp 1991.

De Zondagsbode. November 16, 1913.

Zwart, F.W. *Willem Mengelberg (1871-1951): Een biografie 1871-1920.* Amsterdam 1999.

Zwemer, J.P. *In conflict met de cultuur: De bevindelijk gereformeerden en de Nederlandse samenleving in het midden van de twintigste eeuw.* Kampen 1992.

Chronological table
1848-1919

Cultural	Political

1848	Marx and Engels, *Communist Manifesto*	1848	February Revolution in Paris, revolutionary movements elsewhere in Europe
1848	John Stuart Mill, *Principles of Political Economy*		
		1848	revision of the Dutch Constitution
		1848 - 1852	Second French Republic
		1848 - 1916	Francis Joseph, emperor of Austria
1849	*Maatschappij tot Nut der Israëlieten in Nederland* (Society for the Promotion of the Israelites in the Netherlands)	1849	end of Navigation Act, England
		1849 - 1853	first liberal Cabinet Thorbecke I, the Netherlands
1849	founding of the Park Orchestra, Amsterdam	1849 - 1890	King William III of the Netherlands
		1850	Provinces Act (the Netherlands)
1851	J. de Bosch Kemper, *Geschiedkundig onderzoek* (Historical Investigation)	1851	Municipalities Act (the Netherlands)
1851	First World Exhibition, Crystal Palace, London		
1851	*Koninklijke Nederlandse Akademie van Wetenschappen* - KNAW (Royal Netherlands Academy of Arts and Sciences)	1852 - 1870	Napoleon III: Second French Empire
1853	restoration of the Roman Catholic Church hierarchy in the Netherlands		
1853 - 1890	Vincent van Gogh		
1854	*Koninklijk Nederlands Meteorologisch Instituut* - KNMI (Royal Dutch Meteorological Institute)	1854 - 1856	Crimean War
1858	*Koninklijke Natuurkundige Vereeniging* (Royal Society of Physics)	1855 - 1881	Alexander II, tsar of Russia (assassinated)
1859	Charles Darwin, *On the Origin of Species*	1859	Austrian-Italian War
		1859 - 1870	unification of Italy (Risorgimento)
1860	Multatuli, pseudonym of Eduard Douwes Dekker, publishes his novel *Max Havelaar*, an indictment of Dutch colonial rule; first English translation in 1868		
1860 - 1890s	*Haagse School*, impressionist painters living in The Hague; Jozef Israëls is a central figure	1862 - 1866	liberal Cabinet Thorbecke II, the Netherlands
1863	introduction of the *Hogere Burger School* (HBS, Higher Public School) in the Secondary Education Act	1862 - 1871	Bismarck, prime minister of Prussia
		1863	abolition of slavery in Dutch colonies
1865	founding of the Palace Orchestra, Amsterdam		
1865	Mary Mapes Dodge, American author, publishes *Hans Brinker, or the Silver Skates*, a children's book with the now world-famous story of a boy who stuck his finger in the dike		

Index of names

Subject index

List of the illustrations